JAPAN EXPERIENCES
FIFTY YEARS, ONE HUNDRED VIEWS

T0346618

JAPAN EXPERIENCES: FIFTY YEARS, ONE HUNDRED VIEWS

Post-War Japan through British Eyes
1945-2000

Compiled and Edited

by

HUGH CORTAZZI

Routledge
Taylor & Francis Group

LONDON AND NEW YORK

Compiled and Edited by Hugh Cortazzi

First published 2001 by Japan Library

2 Park Square, Milton Park, Abingdon, Oxon OX14 4RN
711 Third Avenue, New York, NY 10017, USA

Routledge is an imprint of the Taylor & Francis Group, an informa business

First issued in paperback 2016

Copyright © 2001 Taylor & Francis

All rights reserved. No part of this book may be reprinted or reproduced or utilised in any form or by any electronic, mechanical, or other means, now known or hereafter invented, including photocopying and recording, or in any information storage or retrieval system, without permission in writing from the publishers.

Notice:
Product or corporate names may be trademarks or registered trademarks, and are used only for identification and explanation without intent to infringe.

ISBN 978-1-903350-04-1 (hbk)
ISBN 978-1-138-99278-8 (pbk)

British Library Cataloguing in Publication Data
A CIP entry for this book is available
from the British Library

SPECIAL THANKS

The Japan Society and publishers wish to thank the Daiwa Anglo-Japanese Foundation, the Great Britain-Sasakawa Foundation and the UK-Japan Joint Research Project for their generous support.
   This book is published as part of 'Japan 2001', which celebrates, in the UK, the culture and lifestyle of Japan. Its purpose is to deepen existing UK-Japan relationships and to foster new ones.

Set in Garamond 11 on 11.5 pt by Bookman, Hayes, Middlesex

This volume is dedicated to
Haruku Fukuda and Lew Radbourne
Joint Chairmen of the Japan Society, 1995-2000

William Adams, who was the navigator of the Dutch ship 'Liefde' which foundered off the coast of Kyushu in 1600, was the first Englishman to arrive in Japan. After the English 'factory' at Hirado had closed in 1623, contact between the two nationalities was at best intermittent until the reopening of Japan to the West in 1853. The British subsequently played a significant role in the development of modern Japan in the Meiji period (1868 - 1912) and the relationship blossomed into the conclusion of the first Anglo-Japanese Alliance of 1902.

The British role in post-war Japan has inevitably been secondary to that of the United States, but it should not be underestimated. After the occupation, in which British Commonwealth Forces played a part, the British were suspicious of Japan, initially fearing a military revival and then the impact of Japanese exports on sections of British industry. But, as many of the contributions in this book show, the relationship gradually improved and by the end of the twentieth century Britain and Japan had developed warm and friendly relations, which covered the whole spectrum of activities - cultural, economic and political and which are based on a great mutual respect, synergies of circumstances and a deep mutual liking.

The second half of the twentieth century has demonstrated that the skills of the Japanese in design, business and manufacture, combined with a strong sense of social discipline has created structures and institutions envied by many countries as they survey the 21st Century.

My brother William served in the British Embassy in Tokyo in the 1960s when Hugh Cortazzi, the Editor and Compiler of this volume, was Commercial Counsellor. I was fortunate enough to be able to visit him at that time and to see how traditional Japanese Architectural values were adapted to modern conditions and become a major contributor to the International style of building.

I am delighted that this Japan Society Publication is to be one of the Society's contributions to 'Japan 2001': the year will also mark the 110th anniversary of the founding of the Society, of which I am Patron. I believe that readers will find in this book not only much of interest but also some surprises and an overall sense of a growth of mutual regard and understanding.

Patron

Table of Contents

[Plate Section opposite page 294]

Preface

This book does not pretend to be a history of Anglo-Japanese relations since the Second World War. It aims rather to provide some of the raw material for aspects of such a history and to cast some light on the life of British people in Japan in the post-war era. The main focus is on the first thirty to forty years following the end of the war in 1945. This is because Japan today has changed so much – especially since the era of poverty which followed Japan's defeat. Moreover, if impressions of those years are not recorded now they may never be as people pass on and memories fade. In recent years, in sharp contrast to the position two to three decades ago, there have been so many British people living in or visiting Japan that for many living in Japan has become like living anywhere abroad.

In 1987 I produced a book *Victorians in Japan*, published by Athlone Press, in which I tried to depict the life in Japan of British people in the latter part of the nineteenth century. I was fortunate that a number of diplomats, residents and 'globe-trotters' had put down their impressions of Japan either in published works or in letters. Unfortunately, today few people write letters in the way that their ancestors did. A small number still write memoirs and a few write travelogues about Japan, but the latter often seem to pick on the exotic aspects of Japan in order to attract readers or authors concentrate more on themselves rather than on Japan.

For Volumes II and III of *Biographical Portraits* (of personalities in Anglo-Japanese relations) published by Japan Library for The Japan Society in 1997 and 1999 I produced portraits of three post-war personalities who played important roles in the British Embassy in Tokyo and in British relations with Japan. These were the late Sir Vere Redman, Sir John Pilcher and Sir John Figgess. In preparing these I was able to draw not only on my own memory of them but also on the memories of some of their friends and relations still living, but I wished that they had written their own memoirs or that there were collections of letters on which I could draw.

The problems I encountered in writing these portraits helped to induce me to write my own memoir, *Japan and Back and Places Elsewhere*, published by Global Oriental in late 1998, although I had originally decided that one thing I was not going to do was to write another boring diplomatic memoir! While I doubted whether my life as such would be of more than marginal interest to anyone except my family, I thought that how I saw Japan and events in Anglo-Japanese relations might, at least, be of some interest to diplomatic historians at some future date.

Having produced my own memoir I suggested to my colleagues in the Japan Society that instead of producing at this stage a fourth volume of *Biographical Portraits* the Society should focus on post-war Japan. The Council of the Society agreed and I undertook to put together a collection of sketches, vignettes and reminiscences by British people of post-war Japan. The Council thought that such a volume might be a fitting contribution to Japan 2001 and could mark the 110th anniversary of the founding of the Japan Society. Our hundredth anniversary had been marked by the publication of *Britain and Japan 1859-1991: Themes and Personalities*, edited by Gordon Daniels and myself.

I considered whether the proposed book might be based on a series of interviews and be a sort of oral history. But I decided against this, because it seemed to me that many of those approached would probably prefer to write their own pieces after they had had time to reflect. Initially, I thought of some twenty to thirty contributions of up to 5000 words each, but I soon realized that some shorter pieces could be just as interesting as longer ones. I also realized that I could not possibly cover the whole spectrum at all adequately with so few contributors. Unfortunately (or fortunately?), as with many projects in which I become involved, it 'grew like Topsy'. I thought of more and more people to approach and many of those approached suggested others. In addition, I realized that there was a good deal of interesting and relevant material in lectures to the Japan Society and in already published books. In the end, over sixty British people offered me written contributions and I have drawn on over forty published pieces.

The result is inevitably unbalanced. Some periods and some aspects of life in Japan are covered in much greater depth than others. It might have been more balanced if I had been a tougher editor, if I had managed to persuade more people to contribute and if I had quoted from a wider selection of published material. But the book is already too long.

Japan Experiences does not attempt to throw new insights into Japanese character. Nor is it in any way intended as an assessment of modern Japan. It is anecdotal and essentially personal. For these reasons I have refrained from including analyses by British observers, however good their insights. I have also concentrated on British people currently living away from Japan on the grounds that they may find it easier to remember more clearly specific periods of their time in Japan than long term British residents who understandably focus more on the present. But I have made exceptions as every editor has the right to do!

I thought hard about quoting from books by authors such as Pico Iyer, Ian Buruma and Peter Tasker, but decided that their books did not lend themseleves to selective quotation and I suspected that these authors would prefer that their books should be read as a whole. I also decided that travelogues if only for reasons of space had to be omitted. I concluded that I would not attempt to draw on any of the many novels which have been written by British authors about post-war Japan. There have been some good novels but also quite a few which are probably best forgotten. The literature is in any case too vast for the purposes of this book which concentrates on what actually happened rather than imaginary events and characters and how British people saw Japan at the time when they worked there,

In presenting these pieces I have generally tried to avoid anything more than light editing. In a book of this kind styles will inevitably vary and some pieces will be more interesting to some readers than to others. Some duplication has also been unavoidable e.g. about the problems of teaching English or learning Japanese, but the duplication amounts to a form of underlining of the issue discussed. In any case, this is an anthology of memories which few if any are likely to read from cover to cover, certainly not at one sitting!

I have limited my requests for contributions to British people. This is not for nationalist reasons, but simply because this volume is intended primarily for an Anglo-Japanese readership and any attempt to include Americans or other nationalities would have made it even more unwieldy than it is.

It was not easy to know how to present the various pieces. I had at first thought of trying to do this chronologically, but as many contributors were in Japan over different periods this would have meant splitting up contributions requiring additional explanatory notes. Instead, I decided that after the Occupation years which represented a clearly defined period. I would divide the remaining material into categories depending on the principal occupations of the contributors. This, too, involved some arbitrary decisions; I hope contributors will not be offended by being placed in one category rather than another or being grouped together with others.

I have started with cultural relations because these underlie the rest of our relationship with Japan. I have then grouped together a few events in Japan such as Expo '70 in which Britain had a part, if only a minor one, to play. This is followed by comments by journalists and politicians under the broad heading 'Some observers'. Then I have included a major section on business and finance. The last part has been devoted to contributions from officials including members of the diplomatic service.

The final chapter has been devoted to 'The Ambassadors' on the basis that the first shall be last and the last shall be first!

I am most grateful to all those who responded positively to my importunate requests for contributions. Some, for understandable reasons including fading memories, felt unable to write anything. This is sad but emphasises the need to catch memories while they are still fresh. I am also grateful for the permissions granted by authors and publishers to quote from published works (see Acknowledgements). I wish to thank various members of the Society who have encouraged me in this task not least Haruko Fukuda, Lew Radbourne, Ian Nish, Carmen Blacker and Ben Thorne. Robert Guy as well as Jill Brooks have given me unstinted administrative help. Dugald Barr has been a major help in ensuring consistency and felicity in the presentation of contributions. Any errors, of course, remain my responsibility.

HUGH CORTAZZI
Heathfield, Summer 2000

NOTE: Modern Japanese names follow the English order i.e. given name followed by surname. Historical names are given in the Japanese order with family names given first.

INTRODUCTION

Anglo-Japanese Relations Since the War: The Framework

HUGH CORTAZZI

This book is not a survey of Anglo-Japanese relations since the end of the Second World War, but it may be helpful to set out the general framework of Britain's relations with Japan since 1945.

British relations since 1945 have been very different from what they were before the war. British influence in Japan in the second half of the nineteenth century had been significant and more British nationals were employed by the Meiji government than nationals of any other country. At the beginning of the twentieth century a shared interest in countering the perceived Russian expansion in East Asia led to the first Anglo-Japanese Alliance in 1902 and British opinion supported the Japanese in the Russo-Japanese War of 1904-5. Japan was an ally in the First World War, but when the Japanese took advantage of the allied preoccupations in Europe to further their demands on China relations cooled. Economic friction developed as the recession deepened in the 1920s/30s. British opinion was alienated by the Japanese decision to set up the puppet state of Manchukuo and by Japanese aggression in China. British trade with Japan before the war was limited and there were few exchanges of visits if only because of the time taken to travel to Japan (mainly by sea, although a few made use of the Trans-Siberian Railway). Japanese behaviour in China and American and Australian discriminatory immigration policies incited ethnic feelings against the yellow races. Before the war Japanese studies hardly existed in Britain and the only Japanese linguists, apart from a few missionaries, were a small number of members of the Japan Consular Service and some officers in the three services who had been language students in Japan.

The war brought about radical changes. A major effort was made to train young men as Japanese linguists (largely at the School of Oriental and African Studies (SOAS)) and the need for a deeper understanding of Japan was recognized in the report of the Scarbrough Commission.

During the Occupation years (1945-52) British relations with Japan were dominated by the Anglo-American relationship and direct British interests in Japan were strictly limited. The British Commonwealth role in the Occupation was marginal to the Occupation as a whole and its implication for Anglo-Japanese relations was minimal. Britain did attempt to influence the Peace Treaty negotiations but British concerns over, for example, claims and commercial issues tended to be negative rather than positive factors in relations with Japan. British proposals on, for example, China were sensible although they were overruled by John Foster Dulles who played the key role in negotiating the Treaty.

When the Peace Treaty came into force in 1952 the official British attitude towards Japan can be summed up in the words 'cold and suspicious'. The memories of Britain's defeat at Singapore in 1942 and of the inhumane treatment of British prisoners of war in Japanese hands were bitter. Although the bitterness lessened with time the failure of the Japanese authorities to provide adequate compensation to those who had suffered at the hands of Japan's imperial forces remained a sore in our relations up to the end of the twentieth century.

British manufacturers, especially in the 1950s and 60s, accused their Japanese competitors with some justification of copying designs and with less justification of flooding markets with cheap Japanese goods 'made by sweated labour'. These issues dominated and bedevilled economic relations until the late 1960s.

The pattern of economic friction gradually changed in the 1960s as the Japanese economy took off. By the late 1960s it was becoming apparent that Japan – from having possibly a permanent balance of trade deficit as a result of its lack of raw materials and energy resources – was moving into a position where it would have a huge and enduring balance of trade surplus. Britain, on the other hand, was facing a serious balance of trade deficit and sterling was under pressure. It became vital for Britain to increase its exports to Japan and a massive effort was put into export promotion.

Economic frictions, however, continued to grow. British exporters complained loudly about Japanese tariffs but above all about non-tariff barriers which hindered efforts to expand exports to Japan. Increasing complaints were heard about Japanese 'torrential' exports in certain sectors, especially electronic goods and motor cars. The Japanese were accused of adopting 'laser beam tactics' in targeting their exports. Intergovernmental discussions designed to reduce Japanese barriers were tough and difficult. At the same time, negotiations on an inter-industry basis, but with governments holding a watching brief, were conducted with a view to establishing so-called 'voluntary restraint arrangements' (VRAs). By the 1990s the Japanese market was seen to be increasingly open although complaints were still heard about the attitude of the Japanese bureaucracy towards newcomers. The VRAs were by then becoming increasingly anachronistic and were generally seen as anti-competitive. Moreover, in many areas Japanese manufacturers were themselves facing increasing competition, for example, from Korea, while Japanese-branded products were being produced in other Asian countries where labour was more plentiful and cheaper than in Japan.

Britain, in the late 1970s but especially in the 80s and early 90s, launched a major campaign to attract Japanese productive investment into Britain. This was largely successful and contributed significantly to a lessening of economic friction.

Financial services also caused problems especially in the 80s and 90s. There was talk of an over-presence in London in the 80s of Japanese banks able to provide cheap capital and undercut margins. At the same time the Japanese financial services sector was seen to be not only over-regulated but also to a considerable extent closed to British financial services institutions. By the mid 1990s many of these problems had been mitigated, if not solved, partly as a result of the bursting of the Japanese economic bubble which had forced moves to introduce a Japanese 'big bang' in financial services.

It would be an exaggeration to say that by the end of the century economic frictions were all history. There were still problems but with the arrival of the single market in Europe frictions had become more multilateral than bilateral.

*   *   *

The first Japanese prime minister to visit Britain after the war was Shigeru Yoshida in 1954. He encountered some hostile questioning although he and Winston Churchill had a reasonable dialogue. In the 1960s and 70s more Japanese Ministers visited Britain than British Ministers visited Japan, but the Japanese mainly came in the course of trips to Europe or in the context of UN meetings.

British politicians were slow to recognize the growing importance of Japan in the world and it was not until Edward Heath visited Japan in 1972 that a Brtish Prime Minister in office had ever visited Japan. A political dialogue had, however, begun in the early 1960s although it had been maintained in a rather desultory fashion. From Mrs Thatcher's first visit to Japan as Prime Minister in 1982 political contacts intensified and by the 1990s British and Japanese ministers began to talk of a 'special relationship'.

Royal visits, especially those of the Showa Emperor to Britain in 1971, of the Queen to Japan in 1975 and of the Emperor (Akihito) and the Empress (Michiko) to Britain in 1998, were significant signs of the improvement in Anglo-Japanese relations.

Cultural relations resumed fairly quickly after the end of the war. Japanese wanted to improve their English and British culture and top British universities were admired by many educated Japanese. The British Council played a valuable role in promoting British culture and Anglo-Japanese exchanges and significant manifestations of British culture have been organized in Japan. The most important were 'UK 90' and 'Britain in Japan' in 1998. At first, British interest in Japan was limited but writers, performers and artists of all kinds, initially perhaps attracted to Japan because it was thought to be exotic, came and recognized that Japanese culture was a world class phenomenon. As more and more concert halls, museums and art galleries were built Japan became part of the world cultural circuit.

Major efforts were made in Britain with the help of the Japanese government, the Japan Foundation and Japanese companies to promote interest in Japanese culture. 'The Great Japan Exhibition' at the Royal Academy in 1981/2 was followed by 'The Japan Festival in the United Kingdom' in 1991. This marked the centenary of the Japan Society and was on an unprecedented scale. It is to be followed by 'Japan 2001'.

A valuable contribution to better understanding of Japan in Britain has been made in the last fifteen years or so by the Japan English Teachers (JET) scheme which brought many young British men and women to teach and work in Japan. The Daiwa Anglo-Japanese Foundation and the Great Britain Sasakawa Foundation have also played a significant role in promoting exchanges.

British studies of Japan and the Japanese language had been given a fillip by the war because of the need of the British services for Japanese linguists. The war-time generation of teachers sadly found that commerce and banking were generally not interested in recruiting linguists and by the early 1980s it looked, for instance, as if Japanese studies at Cambridge would cease as staff retired. However, the Parker Report 'Speaking for the Future' (1985) focused attention on the problems facing studies of hard languages and additional resources became available for Japanese studies. A new generation of scholars had grown up while investments in Japan and by Japanese companies in Britain increased the demand for young people competent in Japanese, and young British men and women responded to the new opportunities that had been created.

The 'cold and suspicious' attitude of the British towards Japan in the early 1950s had by the end of the century become much warmer and there was a greater depth of understanding between the two countries and peoples. The heated exchanges of the middle years were largely past history. But complacency was not justified. The average educated Britisher still knew little about Japan and not all his prejudices had been modified. At the political level Japan, as a result of the bursting of the bubble and recession, as well as of the perceived growing importance of China, was no longer quite the top priority it had been. Japanese politicians were not seen as 'buddies' in the way that American or European politicians were. There were thus some question marks over the future development of Anglo-Japanese relations.

British interest in the Far East has inevitably been divided between those who looked first to Japan and others, especially in the trading and banking community whose prime focus was China, but at least until the latter part of the twentieth century the Far East came after Europe and the USA in most British people's priorities. For the Japanese Britain was important, not least because of the English language and British parliamentary system; but it was only one of a number of leading European countries in which Japan had major interests (especially France and Germany). At the end of the century the Japanese were increasingly focusing on relations with the European Union and bilateral relations were beginning to take second place. The British position as a permanent member of the UN Security Council and as a member of the G8, however, meant that the Japanese still needed to take account of the British position on world issues.

There will inevitably be ups and downs in our relations with Japan in the twenty-first century, but in an increasingly globalized world economy Japan now plays such an important economic, political, social and cultural role that it is essential for both the British and the Japanese to continue to strive for better mutual understanding.

Alphabetical List of Contributors

Abraham, Captain A. J. RN. Service Attaché.
Baker-Bates, Merrick, CMG. Diplomat and businessman.
Baker, Kenneth (Lord Baker of Dorking), CH. Politician.
Barr, Dugald. Stockbroker.
Barrington, Sir Nicholas, KCMG, CVO. Diplomat.
Barrett, Mike, OBE. British Council.
Bates, Paul. Businessman.
Beasley, (W.G.) Professor Bill CBE. Scholar.
Boyd, Sir John, KCMG. Diplomat.
Boyd, Julia, (Lady Boyd). Author.
Bownas, Professor Geoffrey. Scholar.
Bradley, Dr Clive. Scientist/Attaché.
Britton, Dorothy (Lady Bouchier). Author.
Buckley, Professor Roger. Scholar and teacher.
Bull, George, OBE. Author.
Campbell White, Martin. Businessman.
Connors, Leslie. Scholar.
Cortazzi, Sir Hugh, GCMG. Diplomat.
Dore, Professor Ronald, CBE. Scholar.
Ellingworth, Dick (R.H.). Diplomat.
Elstob, Eric. Investment manager.
Elston, Chris. Bank of England.
Emery, Fred. Journalist.
Emmott, W.G. Journalist.
Fakes, Neville, CBE. Businessman.
Forrest, Gail.
Forrest, Captain Mike, RN. Service Attaché.
Fraser, Duncan, CBE. Businessman.
Giffard, Sir Sydney, KCMG. Diplomat.
Gomersall, Lydia (Lady Gomersall).
Guest, Harry. Author.
Hand, Peter, OBE. Banker.
Haylock, John. Author.
Hitch, Brian, CMG. Diplomat.
Horsley, William. Journalist.
Hudson, Sue. Teacher.
Hunter, Dr Janet. Scholar.
Jenkin, Patrick (Lord Jenkin of Roding). Politician.

Kaneko, Anne.
Kornicki, Dr Peter. Scholar.
Large, Dick (Richard). Businessman.
McCallum, Graham, CBE. Businessman.
Martin, Peter, MBE. British Council.
Naish, John. Merchant banker.
Naylor, Martyn, MBE. Businessman.
Nish, Professor Ian, CBE. Scholar.
Parker, Sir Peter, KBE, LVO. Businessman.
Perry, Sir Michael, CBE. Businessman.
Pinnell, Alan. Diplomat.
Powers, David. Journalist.
Purvis, Christopher. Merchant banker.
Purvis, Phillida. Diplomat, mother, scholar.
Radbourne, Lew, OBE. Businessman.
Ridsdale, Sir Julian, CBE. Politician.
Ripley, Eddie, OBE. Diplomat.
Robinson, Professor Peter. Author.
Scott-Stokes, Henry. Journalist.
de Stains, Ian, OBE. Journalist and businessman.
Thorne, Ben, CMG, MBE. Diplomat.
Thwaite, Anthony, CBE. Author.
Trenchard, Hugh (Viscount Trenchard). Merchant banker.
Warner, Simone (Lady Warner).
Whitehead, Carolyn (Lady Whitehead).
Whitehead, Sir John, GCMG, CVO. Diplomat.
Wilford, Sir Michael, GCMG. Diplomat.
Wilkinson, Ann.
Wilkinson, David, OBE. Businessman.
Williamson, Bill. Atomic energy attaché,
Wright, Sir David, KCMG, LVO. Diplomat.

Alphabetical List of Authors/ Lecturers quoted

Allen, Louis. Scholar (1922-91).
Ashton-Gwatkin, Frank. CMG. Diplomat (1899-1976).
Bates, Peter. Author.
Blacker, Dr Carmen FBA. Scholar.
Blunden, Edmund, CBE, MC. Author (1896-1974).
Bottrall, Ronald, OBE. British Council (1906-89).
Bramall, Edwin (Lord), Field Marshal, KG, GCB, OBE. Soldier.
Britten, Lord Benjamin, OM, CH. Composer (1913-76).
Bush, Lewis. Writer (deceased).
Casson, Sir Hugh, CH, KCVO. Architect/Artist (1910-99).
Ceadel, Dr Eric. Scholar (1921-75).
Clark, Kenneth (Lord Clark), OM, CH. Author/Art Critic (1903-83).
Close, Reginald, CBE. British Council (1906-96).
Dean, Colonel Peter. Service Attaché.
Enright, Dennis, CBE. Author.
Everest, Philip. Teacher.
Figgess, Sir John, KBE, CMG. Service Attaché/Diplomat (1909-97).
Fraser, George. Author (1915-80).
Gardner, Kenneth. Scholar/Librarian (1924-95).
Healey, Denis (Lord Healey of Riddlesden), CH. Politician.
Hendry, Dr Joy. Scholar.
Hockney, David, CH. Artist.
Johnson, Sarah. Teacher.
King, Francis,CBE. Author.
Koestler, Arthur, OBE. Author (1905-83).
Littler, Sir Geoffrey, KCB. Official, HM Treasury.
Mayall, Sir Lees, KCVO, CMG. Diplomat (1915-92).
McGreevey, Adrian. Teacher.
Morland, Sir Oscar, GBE, KCMG. Diplomat (1904-80).
Morris, John. Author (died 1980).
Okada, Sumie. Author.
Pfeiffer, Susan. Teacher.
Piggott, Major General F.S.G, CB, DSO. Service Attaché. (1883-1966).
Powell, Anthony, CH. Author (1905-2000).
de Rothschild, Edmund. Merchant banker.
Rundall, Sir Francis (Tony), GCMG, OBE. Diplomat (1908-87).

Spender, Sir Stephen, CBE. Author (1897-1988).
Storry, Professor Richard. Scholar (1913-82).
Swan, Peter. Art Curator.
Tiltman, Hessell. Journalist (deceased).
Tomlin, Frederick, CBE. British Council (1913-88).
Tracy, Honor. Author (died 1989).
van der Post, Sir Laurens, CBE. (1906-96).
Wedderburn, Gren. Doctor/Surgeon (1916-98).
Wingate, Michael. Businessman.
Wood, Christopher (deceased).
Young, David (Lord Young of Graffham). Businessman and politician.

Acknowledgements

The editor and the publishers acknowledge with many thanks the following permissions to reproduce quotations from the works listed:

Peter Bates: *Japan and the British Commonwealth Occupation Forces, 1946-52*, Brassey's, 1993.

Sir Hugh Casson Ltd: *Japan Observed* by Sir Hugh Casson, Bellew, 1991.

Mervyn Cooke and Boydell and Brewer Ltd, publishers: *Britten and the Far East*, Boydell Press, 1998.

Denis Enright: *The World of Dew*, Secker and Warburg, 1955.

The Last Country by E.W.F.Tomlin, Faber and Faber,1974.

Journals 1939-1983 by the late Sir Stephen Spender, Faber and Faber, 1985.

Mrs George Fraser and Asahi Shimbunsha: *Impressions of Japan and other Essays.* by George Fraser, Tokyo, 1952.

Robert Hale: *The Road to Inamura* by the late Lewis Bush, 1960.

Lord Healey of Riddlesden: *The Time of My Life*, Michael Joseph, 1989 and Penguin Books, 1990.

Joy Hendry: *An Anthropologist in Japan*, Routledge, 1999.

David Hockney and Thames and Hudson: *David Hockney by David Hockney*, Thames and Hudson, 1976.

Francis King: *Yesterday Came Suddenly*, Constable, 1993.

John Murray; *The Other Half* by Kenneth Clark, John Murray, 1977.

Sumie Okada: *Western Writers in Japan*, Macmillan, 1999.

A.D.Peters and Co, Literary Agents and Asahi Shimbunsha, Edmund Blunden, *A Wanderer in Japan*, Tokyo, 1950.

Peters, Fraser and Dunlop: *The Lotus and the Robot* by the late Arthur Koestler, Hutchinson, 1960.

Anthony Powell and David Higham Associates: *To Keep the Ball Rolling.*

Edmund de Rothschild and John Murray: *A Gilt Edged Life* John Murray, 1998.

Random House Archive and Library: *A Portrait of Japan* by the late Sir Laurens van der Post, Hogarth Press, 1968.

Mrs C. Stowell for permission to quote from *No Lotus Garden: A Scottish Surgeon in China and Japan*, by Gren Wedderburn.

Lord Young of Graffham: *The Enterprise Years*, 1990.

Every effort has been made without success to trace the copyright holders of;

Lees Mayall: *Fireflies in Amber*, Michael Russell (Publishing) Ltd, 1989.

John Morris: *The Phoenix Cup*, Cresset Press, 1947.

Honor Tracy: *Kakemono*, Methuens, 1950.

1

Aftermath of War:
Occupation and Poverty

PETER DEAN ● LEWIS BUSH ● JOHN FIGGESS ● BILL BEASLEY
PETER PARKER ● PETER BATES ● EDWIN BRAMHALL ● IAN NISH
LEW RADBOURNE ● PAUL BATES ● CHRISTOPHER WOOD
JOHN MORRIS ● EDMUND BLUNDEN ● HONOR TRACY

IT IS HARD for someone who has not seen a country defeated and devastated
by war to imagine what Japan was like in August 1945. Most Japanese cities had
been destroyed by high explosive and fire bombs. Hiroshima and Nagasaki
had suffered horrific attacks by atomic bombs. The Japanese infrastructure
was in ruins and basic necessities were in very short supply. It should have been
obvious to Japanese leaders at the very latest by March of 1945 that not only had
they no chance of winning the war, they would have to accept whatever terms
the Allied Powers were prepared to offer them. The only alternative was to see
the whole of Japan totally destroyed as Okinawa had been in early 1945 in the
merciless fighting for control of the island. But the Japanese leadership dallied
and quarrelled while the casualties and the damage mounted.

The first British people to experience Japan after the surrender had been
announced by the Emperor's enigmatic broadcast on 15 August 1945 were the
British prisoners of war who had been brought to Japan, largely from South
East Asia and forced to work in mines and in other forms of slave labour.
PETER DEAN (later Colonel and Military Attaché in Tokyo – see his article
in the Japan Society's *Proceedings* No. 120, Autumn 1992, entitled 'A Guest of
Japan – Uninvited and Invited') was one of these. He had been a subaltern in
an infantry battalion which had reached Singapore on 13 January 1942. After
the British surrender in Singapore, Peter Dean, with other British and Commonwealth POWs, was forced to work for the Japanese on the Burma-Siam
railway and suffered much at the hands of prison guards and as a result of the
failure of the Japanese to observe the Geneva Conventions.

On completion of work on the railway he and others were sent to Japan. The
conditions on board ship were horrendous and when in September 1944 his
ship was sunk off the Philippines Peter was fortunate in managing to escape
from the battened-down hatches. He, along with other survivors, was picked
up by a Japanese gun-boat whose commander treated them kindly and was

taken to Manila from where they were transported to Japan.

On arrival at Moji Peter was sent to a lead mine where he was one of thirty British POWs, the rest being American. Conditions were appalling especially for the sick. They expected that if the Allies invaded Japan all POWs would be executed. They were forced to dig a tunnel into which they were herded by their surly guards.

On 20 August 1945 the Camp Commandant informed them 'in somewhat grandiose terms' that the war was over, but they did not leave for repatriation until mid-September. 'We passed train loads of fully-armed Japanese troops whose discipline in defeat was admirable.'

Another former POW who had lived in Japan before the war and had married a Japanese lady was LEWIS BUSH. He has left an account of his life in Japan in his book *The Road to Inamura* (published by Robert Hale Ltd in 1946). Lewis Bush described in Chapter Thirty-one how he met his wife at Kobe in late 1946 when she was allowed back to Japan from Britain and how they travelled to her home town. Lewis Bush had not yet been demobilized from the Royal Navy and had been helping with war crimes investigations.

The following extracts from *The Road to Inamura* describe his experiences and feelings:-

●

As we slid to a stop at Okayama a train was moving away from the opposite platform crammed with ill-clad, miserable people, who even perched on the carriage roofs, on the steps, and as the last coach sped by there were two men sitting on the buffers.

'God! Makes you feel a bit of a heel to ride in comfort like this,' expressed an American.

'Yeah, but wonder how we'd have been riding if the Nips had won?' retorted a companion.

A wretched Japanese ex-soldier, clad in what had once been a white hospital jacket, on his head a military cap from which the yellow star had been removed, stumbled along the platform on steel legs supporting himself with two sticks.

An American handed him two packets of cigarettes and some chocolate, a New Zealander gave him a packet of biscuits, and then an American MP started dressing them down for their charity.

Kaneko was watching, and I saw a tear. 'No one cares now,' she said. 'When I went to look for you last August [i.e. 1945] the people stopped the soldiers boarding the trains; jeered at them, called them cowards, said they'd brought on the war. It was shameful. They'd given the soldiers send-off parties, cheered them, praised their victories, and few of those men wanted to go to war.'

'Can't understand it,' remarked an American major. 'I find them as nice folk as you'd meet anywhere. Don't seem possible they treated our boys so bad and raped and murdered in the Philippines and wherever else they went.'

Understand! I preferred to hope it was simply a case of the small percentage who'd always been criminally minded and took advantage of the lack of discipline, of the licence given them by war? Or was it merely because any evil perpetrated against the enemies of the Emperor became worthy of merit? Tokyo's Sugamo Prison was filled with those charged with war crimes, and the majority were nonplussed, bewildered at being there for what they apparently considered had only been committed in line of duty.

In that prison, I had interviewed Hiroshi Fuji, the excellent cadet doctor at Omori who was there through the deposition of someone who accused him of refusing medical treatment to B-29 aircrew. The fact was he'd treated patients at night in direct contravention of his colonel's orders and had, I knew, always done his best to uphold the medical code. I was thankful that I was able to assist in delivering him.

*   *   *

Day after day I ran into old students, some legless, some without an arm, and learned of those who perished.

Pheips Phelps, a kindly American captain I assisted in his investigations of Omori Camp, was an outstanding character who asked me to take him to the families of those in prison to see if they were in want and seemed to spend his military pay on such charity.

'I don't know if those fellows are guilty,' he'd say, 'that's for the courts to decide. But the women and children must not suffer.'

I prayed they'd get through with the war crimes trials with justice and without delay. A Japanese had told me: 'A long drawn out demonstration will back-fire, people will start to wonder if they are really guilty if it takes too long to prove them so.'

An old man said: 'Why pick on them? We are all guilty for having permitted our affairs to be handled by such men'; and a housewife speaking over the radio in connection with the general foreign admiration for Japanese women had remarked: 'I do not find this complimentary; to me it implies that we are a lot of docile dolls, and this is true otherwise we could never have permitted our men to commit such evils.'

But were we entirely blameless? I thought of the brash RAF Regiment officer who boasted at a naval party of how he'd received the swords of three Japanese officers, shot them and then handed over their men to the Chinese who bayoneted all to death! There were the news pictures of hundreds of men being incinerated in caves with flame-throwers. The Occupation was probably the most benevolent in history, but shocking crimes were reported, chiefly rape and robbery with violence by the mor-

ons one finds in any army, but whereas crimes seemed to have been condoned by the Japanese Army, when the Occupation authorities caught the
culprits in most cases justice was swift and relentless.

*   *   *

A charcoal-burning taxi bore us across the familiar countryside to Naga-
hama. Little had changed, more barley and potatoes were being cultivated, there was little for sale in the wayside shops and in the villages.
The same shrine of the Fox God, the same grey-roofed temples, the bamboo groves, the pines and cryptomeria and below majestic Mount Ibuki,
and near the lake the imposing image of Kwannon whose expression reminded me of great-aunt Esther.

We might have been royalty for the reception accorded us. There was
no doubt about the sincerity of the family and relatives, but Kaneko remarked, 'They are so kind aren't they, but not so long ago many here
heaped scorn upon me and my family and certain shopkeepers even refused to serve us.'

'Oh, well, that is war . . . now they probably feel ashamed.'

It was a joyous family gathering, but I wished so much that bull-necked
old father-in-law could have been with us, even the crotchety old aunt
from Formosa, and Kimi with the Fox in her stomach, and One-armed
Cho.

*   *   *

In the middle of our party a policeman arrived to tell me that I should
telephone Military Government at Otsu, who'd told him that I'd no right
[to be] in the area. 'Well, tell them to come here and see me about it,' I
replied.

At the bath-house an ancient woman in the ticket-box was vastly
startled to see me in blue naval battledress. An old man hastened to introduce us, and chuckled, 'They used to call him Honourable Mr Nose-
Paper!'

I sat in the bath recalling old Ogawa, and Yano, and Ishii, the jolly
policeman, and other friends. Mount Fuji was a little more steamed and
faded, and the mirror with the geisha at top and bottom unrecognizable
as such. My presence appeared to cause a sudden rush on the establishment, heads peeked over from the women's department and I listened to
a perfect chorus of reminiscences concerning my idiosyncrasies in other
days. On my way back to the small hotel I noticed that all the houses in
Cat Street bore the sign OFF LIMITS.

In one of the better quarters of Tokyo I had noticed many private
houses with the sign, VD KEEP OUT, on their gateposts and was astounded
when I found a similar sign outside the home of an old friend. He

laughed when I expressed surprise, and said, 'Well, sometimes drunken soldiers come around looking for girls and so people think this is one way to keep them out.'

The very handsome and dignified wife of a former ambassador and court official had been surprised one evening by half a dozen GIs seeking entrance to her home and, in her impeccable English, inquired what they wanted.

'Just dames, ma'am, girls, broads!' one cried. 'All were young enough to be my grandsons,' she told me, 'and I stifled a smile and pointed to the house opposite and said, 'Well, if I were you I'd go over and ask your general, for his house is always filled with very pretty women!'

* * *

We paid our respects at the family graves, trudged across the fields past the water-wheel of 'blood churning' fame and the lightning-riven tree beside the stone Jizo, saviour of little children, to visit Hidesaburo and his family; renewed so many other old friendships, and then left that town where I'd received so many of my first impressions of this land I had come to love, and from which not even war and prison camps could tear me away, eager for demobilization and to pick up the old threads.

JOHN FIGGESS (Sir John Figgess, KBE, CMG, later Military Attaché and subsequently Information Counsellor in the British Embassy and British Commissioner General for Expo '70 in Osaka) was among the first of the British contingent to arrive in Tokyo in 1945. John Figgess, who had been in Japan before the war as a businessman and had learnt to speak fluent Japanese, had been working in Intelligence in India. At the end of the war he had no more work to do in Delhi and was sent to Japan. He described his arrival in Japan and his work there in his article in the Japan Society's *Proceedings* entitled 'Japan under Occupation: A Personal Reminiscence':-

●

The party set off for Japan from Calcutta airport on 21 September. . . We flew 'over the hump' to Kunming and thence to Manila where we spent a couple of nights. On 26 September in a US Army transport plane, we landed at Atsugi and disembarked. The US Army, apprised of the party's arrival, cheerfully organized transport for ourselves and our small amount of baggage and, in convoy, we headed towards Yokohama and Tokyo.

I shall never forget that ride. The landscape on all sides was flattened and black. Where buildings still stood they were half-destroyed. Nothing but ruins as far as the eye could see and amidst the ruins a few pathetic shacks roofed with rusting corrugated iron. The road was badly potholed and, as we bumped our way through the unending scene of devastation that had been the city of Yokohama, the only traffic encountered, apart from US Army vehicles, was in the form of an occasional charcoal-engined three-wheeled truck belching smoke.

As we approached Omori we were greeted by a huge sign strung across the highway, 'WELCOME TO TOKYO – COURTESY OF THE 1ST CAVALRY DIVISION'. The Americans were in evident control. We were to become aware in the next few weeks of the ubiquitous presence in Tokyo of this organization commanded by a colourful character in the person of Major-General Bill Chase of the US Army.

On the outskirts of Tokyo we picked up a guide provided by the Royal Navy which had ships anchored in Tokyo Bay, and our convoy made its way through the ruins to the site of the British Embassy – no longer an embassy of course but now a naval shore-station which had been re-named HMS *Return*. A Commander Stokes RN was in charge with an office in the main (No. 1) house, while naval ratings were billeted in the smaller houses of the compound. It turned out that a Foreign Office representative, Mr Dermot MacDermot, was already installed in No. 2 House. I don't think I ever discovered how he reached Tokyo. Dermot was a man of few words. Although the grounds had been 'singed' by the fires following air raids and some of the trees and shrubs had suffered there was little or no damage to the fabric of the buildings, all of which had been well cared for by the Swiss custodians under the watchful and no doubt (having regard to their view of the likely outcome of the war) prudent eye of the Gaimusho. At any rate, everything in the residences was in excellent order including carpets, curtains, tableware and, if I remember correctly, even the central heating was working. Our party, that is the General's party, was allotted No. 4 house where we were soon suitably settled. At first we were looked after by a cook provided by the Royal Navy who did his best with the American army rations that were our sole means of sustenance, but in short order the Swiss custodian conjured up a Japanese staff including a real pre-war chef, who took over and made life comfortable, not to say luxurious, – luxurious that is for me after the somewhat spartan conditions of Burma and wartime India.

The immediate task was to make contact with the headquarters of the Supreme Commander for the Allied Powers, located in the fortress-like Dai Ichi Sogo building in Hibiya which, miraculously (or perhaps even by design), had escaped serious damage in the widespread bombing. In fact several buildings in the Marunouchi district had survived more or less intact, including the NYK building which housed the important Allied Translation and Interpreter Service (ATIS) and the Counter-Intelligence Section (CIS) under a Lieutenant-General Thorpe, with which I was to become involved almost on a daily basis. My principal contact there was a Colonel Hoover, younger brother of the fearsome J. Edgar

Hoover, head of the FBI, but there were a number of other helpful people including Australian officers, some of whom I had known as language students before the war. The headquarters staffs were in general very forthcoming and cooperative, providing available information about the Occupation freely and without restriction other than the appropriate security classification. I think that this was largely because of the excellent relations established by General Gairdner with the senior officers of the US forces with whom he was very popular. Not only was he a fine sportsman – he had played hockey and polo for Ireland in spite of a bad leg wound sustained in the First World War – but he was a spellbinding after-dinner speaker. I have never known anyone tell a tale better, and the American officers liked that. General MacArthur himself of course remained aloof. Any meeting with him had to be sought through his protective screen of personal staff and was strictly formal. But even there, General Gairdner and any of us who accompanied him to such meetings were cordially received.

*   *   *

In the very early days, contact with the Japanese population while not forbidden by SCAP was not exactly encouraged but no obstacles were placed in the way of normal association and so, before many days had passed, I was able to get in touch with some of my old friends. All had suffered privation in the last months of the war and most were hungry. There was little food to be had in the towns, money was all but worthless; people survived by journeying to the countryside in search of almost anything edible which usually meant *satsumaimo* (sweet potatoes) for which clothes or other chattels were bartered. Above all, one felt, this was a society shattered by its defeat in the war and torn from its roots.

One of the saddest sights in Tokyo was the large number of pathetic young children orphaned by the bombing or abandoned who were to be found huddled in the passages around Ueno station where they could beg for food from travellers to the countryside. Because anything in the nature of community care had broken down, their numbers continued to increase and it was several weeks or even months before they could all be collected and provided with some kind of shelter.

On a fine Saturday in mid-October I remember organizing a weekend visit to the Izu peninsula. We travelled in three cars with our designated American army drivers, jolting along the dusty pot-holed Tokaido through the dilapidated villages to Odawara, Atami and Ito. We stayed at a hot-spring inn in Izu Nagaoka, where we were well looked after as we had taken the precaution of carrying with us a substantial quantity of army rations which were rapturously received in exchange for the simple Japanese fare the locals were able to offer. This was, strictly speaking, out

of order as the SCAP regulations prohibited any call on domestic resources by the Occupation forces, but in those unusual conditions a
two-pound tin of plum jam and a good-sized pack of processed pork
represented unattainable delicacies and were regarded by the recipients
as more than a fair exchange for the fresh fish and vegetables which my
companions and I in our turn were delighted to have.

Most of the details of that first visit escape me now but I do remember
vividly that, as we came into Hiratsuka on our outward journey, a large
banner stretched across the road above our heads read 'WELCOME ALLIED
FORCES – SOUVENIRS FOR SALE', a remarkable testament to the pragmatism of
the ordinary Japanese people and perhaps for those with vision to see it, a
sign of the future course of Japan. Certainly, the Japanese wasted little
time on regrets and recrimination.

At the beginning of October General Gairdner had left for the UK
taking Brigadier Daley with him, and we did not see him again until
mid-November when he returned with Brigadier Jack Profumo who replaced Daley. They brought the news that the CIGS, Field Marshal Alan
Brooke (later Viscount Alanbrooke), was to come to Tokyo shortly to visit
General MacArthur and get a first-hand view of Japan under occupation.
This news was swiftly followed by a signal from London saying that the
Field Marshal particularly wished during his visit to meet a Prince Takat-
sukasa with whom he shared an interest in ornithology. The text of the
signal was corrupt, I remember, but when the message was sorted out it
sent me scurrying round to locate the prince who, I discovered, was a
senior member of the Imperial family, currently the Keeper of the Meiji
Shrine but also a distinguished ornithologist of world repute with numerous published works to his credit. With the help of friends in the Imperial Household office I made contact with the prince who received me
graciously and, after I had explained what it was all about, said he would
be delighted to meet the CIGS but was nervous about it because he had
all but forgotten his English which had not been very good in the first
place. Rashly, how very rashly as it turned out, I said that I thought that
wouldn't be a problem as I would be happy to interpret.

We fixed on a time for a meeting in the early evening after the CIGS
should have returned from a day visit to Nikko. When the time came, I
think it must have been at about 5.30 pm, I went with him in a staff car to
the Meiji Shrine office where we found the prince surrounded by books
and a mass or ornithological paraphernalia. After introduction they fell
to and I quickly discovered that my presence was quite unnecessary and
even unhelpful as I knew nothing of the subject and they seemed to be
communicating perfectly well, mostly in Latin. Soon they were both on
the floor engrossed in discussion and as I was clearly of no help but only
an impediment I asked for permission to withdraw and arranged to send
the staff car back for the CIGS to return to the Embassy at his conveni-

ence. As it happened, there was to be a dinner party at our house that evening to which Admiral Brind, whose flagship was still in Tokyo bay, was invited, but by 8.00 pm there was no sign of the Field Marshal and General Gairdner was beginning to get restive and to look menacingly at me. Happily, at about 8.15 pm he appeared, having spent more than two hours with the prince, which was about twice as long as he stayed with General MacArthur.

One of the tasks that fell to me in Tokyo in the absence then of a British consular representative was to keep an eye on the resident Indian community. The job was slightly complicated by the fact that during the war the Indians, to a man, though technically subjects of the King Emperor, had escaped internment by adopting an anti-British stance, partly pressured, no doubt, by the presence among them of a sinister relative of Subhas Chandra Bose, the seditious Bengali leader responsible for raising the Indian National Army from British-Indian army prisoners of war in Burma. (S.C. Bose, who tried to run away to Japan, had reportedly died recently in an air crash in Taipei.) Now, not surprisingly, the Indian community sought the favourable status of Allied National which would give them the right to better rations, travel facilities and medical care.

The leader of the community, as it happened a very decent man named Ramamurthi, understood the dilemma this posed for all concerned and was anxious to be cooperative. At our first meeting he told me that he was sheltering in his home a Major Habibullah Rahman, an officer of the Indian National Army who had accompanied Bose on his ill-fated flight from Singapore, and invited me to meet him and hear what he had to say. This was useful because the Government of India was anxious to receive independent confirmation that Bose was dead, since troublesome rumours were circulating in India that he had survived. Rahman, whose left arm was heavily bandaged, told me that after the Japanese army plane in which they were travelling crashed on take-off at Taipei airport and burst into flames, he and the Japanese officers with them had great difficulty in getting Bose out of the wreckage because he was so corpulent. His clothes were on fire, he was badly burnt and died of his injuries in a military hospital in Taipei a day or two later. The pilot of the aircraft also died. I could see no reason to doubt this story (which was later confirmed by GHQ SCAP after detailed interrogation of the surviving Japanese officers concerned) and I signalled HQ SACSEA accordingly. Incidentally, the rumour of Bose's survival seems to have continued to circulate among his followers in India, and even after Independence in 1947 the Government of India was still seeking proof of his death.

Some time early in 1946 I was told by Ramamurthi that an Indian journalist named Lahiri wished to speak to me on 'a highly confidential subject', could I see him urgently? I arranged for them both to come to my office where Lahiri revealed that Ba Maw, the puppet Prime Minister of

Burma under the Japanese, had been brought secretly (and illegally) to Japan by the Japanese Army at the time of the surrender. He had been in hiding in a remote mountain village in Nagano prefecture called Echigo Yuzawa and now wished to give himself up. But he was anxious to surrender to the British and not to the American army who, he feared, would not appreciate his particular circumstances. I explained to Lahiri that what he asked was not possible. The British had no independent status in Japan under the Occupation. I could receive Ba Maw but would have no option but to hand him over to the Americans who, I felt sure, would immediately put him into Sugamo prison where suspected war criminals and others were held.

Lahiri undertook to convey this to Ba Maw, who a day or two later found himself in Sugamo. He said he wished to make a statement to be passed to the British authorities so I visited him there and took down his statement. He proved to be an interesting and cultivated person who spoke several languages. I believe he was partly European, perhaps Roumanian, by birth and had been educated at the Sorbonne among other institutions. If I remember rightly, the main burden of Ba Maw's statement was that he was in no sense anti-British, and his single purpose had been to use his position to protect the Burmese people from the worst ravages of the Japanese occupiers. This statement was duly passed to the authorities in Singapore and in due course, that is after some weeks, Sir Alvary Gascoigne was instructed to arrange for his return there after first giving him a severe dressing down, a somewhat embarrassing procedure which took place in His Excellency's office with several of us present, presumably to add majesty. On his eventual return to Rangoon, Ba Maw was placed under house arrest by the Burmese Government where he remained, I believe, for the rest of his life.

I don't remember exactly when we ceased to be HMS *Return* but it must have been early in 1946 when the Royal Navy went away and Sir Alvary Gascoigne arrived from London with the personal rank of Ambassador to take over the Mission which from then on became the United Kingdom Liaison Mission, UKLM for short. General Gairdner stayed on as the Prime Minister's personal representative notwithstanding that the Prime Minister had changed and was now Mr Clement Attlee.

One local problem that soon engaged Sir Alvary's attention was brought about by the critical line adopted by *The Times* towards General MacArthur's policies in Japan. The General was sensitive to any criticism and it was perhaps somewhat unfortunate that *The Times'* correspondent in Japan, Frank Hawley, a Japanologist of some repute, made no secret of his view that the Americans were blundering around in Japan and lacked understanding of the right way to go about things. This view was reflected in articles in the newspaper, the editors of which were no doubt influenced by the fact that at this time public opinion in Britain (as also in Australia) was bitterly hostile to Japan. The main charge seemed to be that SCAP was being unduly lenient. Of course, Sir Alvary made the point in reply to the General's complaint that a free press meant that one had to put up with this sort of thing, but MacArthur was not happy, and to some degree the row did disturb our relations with GHQ for a while.

*   *   *

By the middle of 1947 SCAP was under pressure from Washington and London (and no doubt other centres indirectly) to open up the country to foreign trade. General MacArthur had made no secret of his determination to 'preserve Japan from carpet-baggers' but in August of that year limited foreign trade was authorized and, shortly afterwards, foreign commercial representatives began to arrive in Japan. Gradually, with the presence of a growing number of American, British and other 'traders' all of whom were permitted to operate under the strict guidelines laid down by the Occupation authorities, Tokyo began to assume a more normal, that is to say less exclusively military aspect. The changed situation was highlighted by a notable addition to a sign placed by the Military Police on the outer wall of a well-know hostelry on the road to Yokosuka which for many months had read 'OFF LIMITS – VD'. Now someone had added in equally large letters 'FOREIGN TRADERS WELCOME'.

The UKLM, a steadily expanding organization, eventually with commercial, consular and political departments, remained in being until April 1952 with the entry into force of the Peace Treaty which had been signed at San Francisco on 8 September 1951 whereby Japan regained her sovereignty. Diplomatic relations were resumed and the Embassy became once more an Embassy with a fully fledged Ambassador in the person of Sir Esler Dening.

A BRITISH OFFICER who arrived with the Americans in 1945 was BILL BEASLEY (Professor W.G. Beasley CBE, former Professor of History at SOAS, University of London, and British specialist on Japanese history). He described his experiences in a lecture at a seminar organized at the London School of Economics under the auspices of the Suntory Toyota Centre in July 1991 (STICERD booklet 1991/1 I). Beasley entitled his talk 'Personal reminiscences of the early months of the Occupation: Yokosuka and Tokyo, September 1945 – March 1946'. The following extracts describe some of his experiences during this period:-

●

In the last weeks of the war I had been in the Pacific islands, interrogating Japanese naval prisoners (who were very rare and never seemed to possess important information). Late in July 1945 I was ordered to join the flagship of the British Pacific Fleet, HMS *King George V*, so as to be available for duty in Japan, if needed. Presumably, my superiors had some knowledge of the coming atomic bomb, though, if so, they did not confide the information to me. At all, events, by the time I reached the fleet the first atomic bomb had been dropped. I was therefore just in time to be present in Tokyo Bay during the surrender ceremony.

I did not attend the ceremony aboard USS *Missouri*. Instead, like most members of the task force, I listened to the radio commentary provided for ships in the anchorage. Soon afterwards, I landed at Yokohama as one of a group of British representatives from all three services, who set up offices in the British consulate general. An immediate task was helping to evacuate civilian internees and prisoners of war, but in other respects activity was chiefly directed towards bringing more men and equipment into the allied beachhead. It is often forgotten how different the situation in Japan was from that in Germany. When Germany surrendered there were already large allied land forces in the country, complete with supply lines, communications, interpreters. In Japan there was nothing of the kind.

The Japanese surrender had been sudden. Few forces, other than the fleet, were immediately available to be sent there. There had been discussion about surrender terms in Washington and London, but in other respects most of the planning had been for invasion, not occupation, that is, invasion of both the Japanese home islands and Japanese-held areas in Southeast Asia. As a result, there was an air of makeshift about almost everything that was done in the immediate aftermath of surrender. An American airborne division moved into Tokyo, presumably briefed and certainly competent. By contrast, the shores of Tokyo Bay were taken over by men landed from the fleet: American and British marines, who had some training for what they were doing; a large number of sailors, who had not. Transport consisted of a handful of jeeps, requisitioned from reluctant aircraft carriers, plus vehicles commandeered from the Japanese.

In these circumstances it was thought to be a matter of urgency to consolidate the military position, since there was great uncertainty about possible Japanese reactions. And putting the occupation on a more organised footing took time. Some parts of Japan were to remain unoccupied for several weeks for simple logistical reasons. I remember going with American colleagues to inspect a radar station in the Izu peninsula, only to find ourselves outside the occupied zone, somewhere between the Eighth and Sixth Armies. The mayor of the town offered to surrender the district to us.

There was another aspect of lack of preparedness. The allied forces had come ready for fighting, if there were resistance, but not in the full sense for civil administration. Throughout Southeast Asia there were Japanese forces, whose surrender had to be secured, and territories where government had to be established. This put an enormous strain on administrative resources throughout the region. In Japan, for example, there were few allied personnel who could speak and read the language. Military government officers, when they began to put in an appearance, proved in large part to be men with a background in American politics, who had been given only a sketchy knowledge of things Japanese. Even typists were at a premium. One result was that from the beginning there had to be a considerable dependence on Japanese staff. Those who rightly believe that the political aspects of occupation made a slow and uneven start should bear all this in mind.

For my own part, once the first flurry of activity was over, I moved to the newly-created US naval headquarters at Yokosuka as the self-styled British Naval Intelligence Liaison Officer (one had to have a title of some kind in order to be acknowledged to exist). There was a certain amount of interpreting to be done; there were post-box duties, forwarding American queries to appropriate British authorities; and for a week or two there was the task of correcting our highly inaccurate information about the facilities of the dockyard. Otherwise I joined in the work of my American colleagues, with one or two of whom I had trained in the United States. A summary of some of our activities might serve to illustrate what this phase of the occupation entailed for those who were outside the main stream of military government

One major undertaking was demilitarization. The Japanese army and navy were promptly demobilized after the surrender, but in a large establishment like Yokosuka dockyard there remained quantities of weapons, ranging from swords and rifles to torpedoes, midget submarines and fast attack boats. There was also ammunition of many kinds (some of it British naval ammunition from Hong Kong and Singapore, apparently removed to Japan after the capture of those bases in the winter of 1941-2). Arms and ammunition had to be destroyed, usually by being dumped at sea, or rendered safe, or removed for technical study. In addition, there were many tunnels in the cliffs which ringed the dockyard, used for stores and equipment. All these had to be examined. They contained a number of machine shops, installed there to enable work to continue on building midget submarines, or effecting urgent repairs to ships, despite the frequent air raids in the closing stages of the war.

There was an operations room from which the naval sector of the air defences of Tokyo had been controlled. On its wall was a large chart on which the positions of aircraft were marked by lights (used, so one of the former Japanese air controllers told me when I expressed doubts about its value, chiefly to impress politicians). Exploring these tunnels was not a welcome duty, since they were infested with fleas. It was also handicapped at first by the absence of people who could remember where things were: instant demobilization had removed the relevant Japanese staff. There were no usable lists or inventories.

The contents of the tunnels included, as one would expect on a naval base, a good deal of food, clothing, and bedding. In view of the desperate shortage of such things among the Japanese population, it was GHQ policy that they were to be turned over to the civil authorities. Properly this was a function of army military government, which soon found itself facing evidence of local corruption in the matter, apparently involving both the mayor and the chief of police. The navy became involved because the corruption extended also to the provision of Japanese labour for the dockyard. A related problem was the black market. Yokosuka was a main port of arrival for American supplies. It transpired that large-scale thefts were taking place from ships in the harbour of tobacco, chocolate, soap and other goods for which there was a ready, if illegal, sale in Tokyo and Yokohama. This time many of those responsible turned out to be foreigners resident in Japan, or members of the American forces.

Security was also a matter of concern in the early months. Many members of the Occupation forces, especially those with combat experience, were suspicious of the apparent quiescence of the Japanese people. Their fears were fuelled by regular reports from the Counter Intelligence Corps of the discovery of secret arms dumps, or resistance groups, or even on one occasion a supposed plot for a Japanese rising. Since many of America's seasoned troops were melting away, qualified to go home by reason of long service, there was an element of doubt about whether those who remained could react effectively to a crisis. All the same, by Christmas these alarms were almost all forgotten: nothing had happened, after all; and the young men who came to replace those going home lacked the memories of Guadalcanal and Okinawa. In fact, the occupation was settling down to what was to be normality, the age of the pan-pan girl and candy.

As individuals we seem to have had greater freedom at Yokosuka in meeting local Japanese residents than did those who were stationed in the British Commonwealth zone round Kure. It was possible, for example, to get advice from people living in the city and nearby about aspects of Japanese life and culture which interested us. I began to learn something about Japanese prints and painting at this time. Sometimes we in turn were approached for help by Japanese groups who saw the surrender as an opportunity for 'democratic' political activity – they were not always sure of the meaning of the word – or who wanted to improve their English, believing it was the language of the future in Japan. On some occasions the two motives came together: there was a society calling itself the Pupils' League which met to discuss political questions in the English language. It turned out that the title was meant to be People's

League. As this misunderstanding illustrates, several years of official disapproval had done much to lower standards of English, especially among
the young. Resuming the teaching of it in schools clearly posed problems. In the autumn of 1945 one was occasionally greeted in English
by enthusiastic groups of tiny children, who appeared to be in some confusion about the difference between 'hello' and 'goodbye'.

When not on duty it was possible to move about the area – as far as
Kamakura and Hakone, at least – by Japanese public transport. The chief
difficulty about doing this, in fact, was what might be called the feudal
separatism of military bureaucracy. In Yokosuka one needed passes from
the US Navy (for the headquarters area), the US Marine Corps (for the
dockyard), and Eighth Army (for nearby districts not under naval control). To travel farther afield required travel orders, though we found that
it was possible to write them for each other. By comparison, we encountered few obstacles about staying in Japanese hotels or *ryokan*, provided
we took our own food.

From these comments it is probably evident that life in Yokosuka had
as much in common with what was described in *Teahouse of the August Moon*
as with what is to be found in SCAP summations of non-military activities. In December, when I moved to Tokyo, I found myself in a very
different world. I joined the staff of the United Kingdom mission. It
was housed in the British Embassy, which had been commissioned as
HMS *Return*, flying the white ensign and mounting a marine guard: a
step officially described as being necessary for logistic reasons, unofficially held to have been taken in order to ensure supplies of duty-free
alcohol.

*   *   *

My own duties were nominally concerned with naval intelligence, but for
all practical purposes there was none, so I spent most of my time collecting political and economic information for the regular reports to London. A little came from American colleagues at GHQ, but far and away
the most useful portion was taken from Japanese newspapers. Trying to
resolve their contradictions and discrepancies proved in later years to
have been a valuable training for a potential historian.

*   *   *

I spent quite a lot of time trying to secure information about the Japanese
economy, but achieved no results that would now be worth stating. In
that first winter after the war the most obvious economic facts were that
very little was being produced by industry, that farmers were making
large black-market profits from food, and that many people in the cities
were nearly or actually starving. It was inconvenient to me personally

that no two sets of statistics ever seemed to agree, but the Japanese people were suffering much more than inconvenience. It is possible to argue that bringing some order into this situation justified the gradual strengthening of authority in the year or two which followed, whatever the loss in terms of democracy, but I cannot claim to have seen the force of this at the time. My chief reaction was a certain impatience with countries which were calling for reparations from Japan, when all that seemed available to provide them was disused weapons and battered factories. Clearly, I acquired no insight into Japan's industrial future.

I did not much enjoy that winter in Tokyo. There was a sense of inadequacy: if I counted as an expert, we were singularly ill-equipped to decide the fate of a country. In addition, I was disturbed by the relative comfort of the embassy and the stark hardship outside it: the shanties springing up in the heavily bombed areas; the crowds of people on trains going into the countryside, carrying possessions which they hoped to barter for food; the drabness of a city in which nearly everyone was wearing khaki, or something close to it; above all, the human evidence of defeat, seen in bowed heads and dragging feet. I left in March 1946 with no regret and no intention of ever going back again.

Of course he did go back! See below [Ed].

ANOTHER BRITISH officer who reached Japan in October 1945 was PETER PARKER (Sir Peter Parker, KBE, LVO). He described his experiences as follows:-

•

There were no prophetic signs to be found in the rubble of defeat when I first saw Japan. I reached Atsugi Airfield outside Tokyo in October 1945, and the bleakness of the scene was soul-boggling. How had their war effort on that shattered island survived so long? Daylight bombing, at will, by the American B29s, cruising up and down Hirohito Alley from the Mariana Islands, had taken an awful toll, and that was before the two atomic bombs ended it all. One raid on 10 March 1945 is said to have cost 100,000 lives. By the time I arrived, Tokyo was autumnal with rust and ruin.

The small American unit to which I was attached as a British officer was a mission from Washington. We were held up at the airport, for no good reason but, so we were told later, by MacArthur's express order: we had to be thoroughly checked out; in the General's eyes anything that hailed from Washington was always suspect, and, worse still, this unit included a British element, and that doubled his suspicions. He was ruling Japan and he revelled in it: he had pushed the Emperor off his white horse and climbed on it himself. There is little doubt that history will have to admit his reign was glorious – and I write this through my gritted teeth.

It is hard to praise people one does not like at all. MacArthur's arrogance and vanity were blatant. My frank admiration of what he did is not warmed by any liking for the American Caesar at all. I agree with Truman: 'This pompous popinjay, this courageous outrageous ego, this clever bastard – he set up Japan. On the foundations he laid, the old virtues of Japan rebuilt the nation.'

The MacArthur reign, or the 'Macasa Period' as the Japanese called it, endowed Japan with democratic elections; a vote for women; agricultural reform; and radical economic plans for recovery. All these initiatives were inspired by the Supreme Commander of the Allied Forces, the broad title that he relished as it helped him to elude some of the specific pressures from Washington – was he not responsible to all the Allies, not only to America? His balance of military and civil achievements are probably unmatched even by the two other great Western commanders of the time who were converted from military to political roles. Eisenhower's presidency was unmarked by any originality, and the glories of the great de Gaulle were civil rather than military, although he did have a moment to prove his military brilliance in the field during the disastrous defeat of 1940.

We had found beds in the NYK building in Marunouchi; actually, bunks, four in a room which had once been a small office. A cliché-picture of Fuji-san was still on the wall – that sticks in my mind because one dawn I experienced my first earthquake, very minor but it slid me out of the bunk and the room swung eerily yet symbolically while the picture of Fuji-san hung steady. . . The mood of the Japanese seemed to revert to that of the Meiji Revolution, arguably the only successful revolution anywhere in 150 years. In the Meiji times, the slogan had been 'Catch up with the West', and that is what post-war Japan set out to do again. Then, a feudal society had been inspired by its controlled outrage at the forced opening of their country by the *kurofune*, the black ships of Commodore Perry in 1853. In 1945 it was the controlled outrage at their own humiliating failure militarily and politically that galvanized the country.

Since then their sun has risen in economic triumph and the world has wondered at the Japanese miracle. Studies of it are published galore. Behind all the sophisticated analysis of Japanese success, I simply keep remembering the evidence of their startling energy and discipline – in the midst of stark adversity. We drove daily by jeep from the NYK building to the warehouse which we had made our base, in what was left of Tokyo Arsenal No. 1. That was a cruel winter. The people, mostly in rags and many starving, some reduced to eating weeds and frogs – desperate but disciplined. We drove through the smashed city streets full of busy people, bustling on the pavements, scavenging, hammering flat twisted scraps of metal salvaged from the devastation, putting pieces together to make shelters. And they had been ready to die in what they had expected to be the inevitable invasion: they had been told 'to kill at least one American'. The Intelligence Unit I had been called from in Burma to join Camp Mitchie, Maryland, had been grimly studying what had been gleaned about the formidable coastal fortifications of Japan. Any invasion would have been a bloody business – Okinawa-style resistance on a national scale. In the event, the Occupation itself has no record of a shot being fired in anger.

My intelligence unit had made contact with a professor [Professor Azuma] from Tokyo Imperial University who helped us with some specialist translations and through him I and my friend, Otto, an American officer, came to be friends of his family. These friendships made in that bitter season lasted the century. Miraculously, their family house had come through the bombing to tell the story of much more cordial confident times at the turn of the century. The family had been well off and had travelled the world: the design of the house reconciled the meeting of East and West: one wing was Western-style, the other *Nihonshiki* (Japanese-style).

Otto and I were frequent overnight guests on the Japan side, arriving with pockets loaded with whatever basic goodies we could lay hands on. Over bean soup at breakfast, we would try to teach the young boys some English. Over dinner, or rather the evening carve-up of goodies into six, we amazed ourselves with our war-stories. Otto and I came to realize the shock we had given the family: they had expected the occupation to be savage. The sweetly smiling mother (Mutsuko Azuma) told us of the family planning regarding suicide. This would be signalled by the conqueror's knock on the door. 'I would have to do the shooting,' she said cheerfully, without bravado. 'The children to be shot first. Then I would shoot my husband – he is a professor and you know how forgetful they are.' Finally she would fling open the door, shoot the invader and then herself. . . 'kill at least one American'. . .

On a beautiful spring day in 1946, Otto and I were heading back to Washington and the family, the professor, his enchanting wife and two boys escorted us to a bus stop. We parted from the little family, looking bereft, smiling and in tears at a crossroads. None of us could imagine the direction that Japan was to take. The old order was unravelled. The scene seemed still totally confusing: politics were in disarray; lorry-loads of shouting workers waving red flags were hooting around the city; the Russians were still in the west-wing of the house; consumer prices had risen ten times in just six months of Occupation and kept spiralling with shortages and strikes. Who was it said that in terms of political, economic, social, intellectual and moral change the Occupation was the equivalent to the French Revolution, the Russian Revolution, the Reformation, the Industrial Revolution and the Renaissance, all happening at once? But Japan, fundamentally lucky in the wise leadership of Prime Minister Yoshida, slowly recovered itself. And the Occupation which had begun, as Yoshida himself put it, in 'happy ignorance' of the people it had come to govern, ended with Japan, in the early 1950s, well set on the way to its phenomenal resurgence.

THE BRITISH COMMONWEALTH element of the Allied Occupation force did not arrive until early in 1946. The area allocated to BCOF (British Commonwealth Occupation Forces) was the Chugoku part of western Honshu (i.e., the Sanyo prefectures of Okayama, Hiroshima, and Yamaguchi, and the Sanin prefectures of Tottori and Shimane) and the island of Shikoku (consisting of the four prefectures of Tokushima, Kagawa, Ehime and Kochi). The background to the British part in the occupation and the history of the force have been ably described in *Japan and the British Commonwealth Occupation Forces 1946-52* by Peter Bates (published by Brassey's of London and New York in 1993).

In his Foreword Field Marshal LORD BRAMALL who was a senior officer in the British element concluded: 'Although the Force had no direct responsibility for the military government of Japan in the early days, and later on for the putting in place of the democratic institutions which were to benefit Japan so much, its mere presence and the way it carried out its task made a significant contribution to the Japanese attitude to the occupation generally.

'Nor was its task – our task – all that easy. When we started to arrive from India, Australia and New Zealand, and I, being on the advance party, was able to appreciate some of the problems more than most, we had no idea about what sort of reception we were going to receive, particularly after the atomic bombing of Hiroshima, which was in our designated area, and of Nagasaki. Conditions for the reception of such a force, in a Japan which was still very backward in many respects, were often primitive and amenities few and far between.'

PETER BATES sums up the feelings of the arriving British troops and their impressions in the following extracts from his book which anyone interested in this period of British relations with Japan should read in full:-

•

As their ships slowly wound their way through the wintry waters of the Inland Sea towards Kure, the troops huddled deeper into their newly-issued greatcoats and wondered what the future held for them in this mysterious and defeated country. At the same time there was a feeling of great relief that the need for a final invasion had been averted: most shared the emotions of a sergeant in the Dorsets who said '. . . as the numerous small islands slid past I could only . . . think how grateful I was that the dropping of the atom bomb had saved the lives of thousands of

Allied troops who would have had to storm these island bastions of Japan'. The view of the intensive cultivation and the steeply terraced hillsides provided another unexpected insight. 'It's no wonder', men said, 'that they wanted more room.'

The sea was always busy with a cloud of small fishing boats, but the first Japanese sighted at close quarters was usually the pilot, whose little boat would appear suddenly out of the mist to run alongside, and his busy upholstered figure would clamber up the ladder to the deck and then to the bridge. It seemed odd that the invaders were still dependent on the invaded to find their way ashore.

In contrast to the scenic beauty of the Inland Sea and the coast itself, Kure, the port designated as the port of entry and base port for BCOF, was a dispiriting sight. High explosive and incendiary bombing raids had destroyed the naval base, the largest in Japan, together with much of the town. Along the waterfront, in the words of a newly-arrived Australian, '. . . the battered remains of half a dozen warships, including two battleships, stood out against the foreshore, itself a tangled mass of churned-up earth and masonry, festooned with twisted steel . . . Kure is defunct'. The winter snow accentuated the desolation of the scene. The docks, however, were coming back to life and work was already in hand on the disarming and refitting of Japanese naval vessels to render them capable of taking part in the repatriation of Japanese surrendered personnel from the different theatres of war.

Hiroshima, the capital of the prefecture and twenty miles from Kure, was a vastly more depressing sight of complete demolition. The only buildings still standing were those of reinforced concrete and even they were badly cracked and damaged by the blast. Otherwise the remainder of what had been the city was a wilderness of broken glass, tiles, furniture, pillars, graves and shrines. Trees were charred stumps and steel electric lamp poles heeled over at crazy angles. Sightseers were particularly struck by the vast number of rusted fire-scorched bicycle frames and melted masses of bottles. The rubble of the devastated city had been neatly piled on the blocks between the roads to allow clear passage for traffic; trams were running, crowded to overflowing; and an active shanty town was springing up on the ruined blocks, especially around the railway station.

*   *   *

The troops' strongest impression at the outset was of the vast numbers of Japanese and their apparent imperviousness to the occupation. Men, women and children wandered everywhere, some in kimonos, others in drab Western-style dress, most clip-clopping on wooden *geta* sandals. Women carried infants on their backs or else a huge pack or basket, as if they were beasts of burden. Battered and unpainted buses and trams, running on stinking gas-producing engines, with broken or boarded windows, were so crowded with passengers that it seemed impossible either to get on or get off.

Although the inhabitants of what was left of Hiroshima were noticeably and understandably more stolid and sullen, the city-dwellers generally were cooperative, and those who entered the service of the occupation, which was a boon in the conditions of poverty then prevailing, were naturally enough industrious and reliable. For their part, the country-dwellers were generally speaking better off than the townspeople, whose access to food over and above the official ration of rice and wheat or barley was restricted and often depended on the black market.

In country areas, when troops passed, the older men would frequently smile, bow and raise their hats, although younger men would sometimes stand and leer and take delight in minor embarrassments such as a stalled engine. However, the general acceptance of the occupation and the passivity of the people was reassuring, although an occasional wave of emotion could not be suppressed. A British officer wrote:

> '.. the Japanese men I dislike intensely... I felt a little out of place sitting [in a train] surrounded by these slit-eyed cunning-looking men who stared at me all the time, peering through their specs with an expression that read curiosity and dislike! I should loathe to have been a prisoner in Japanese hands as I can see the bestiality in their faces. However, when I asked the way or name of the station they were very polite and after a curt bow and indrawing of the breath through the teeth, told me...'

An understandable lack of understanding of Japanese ways and memories of the war often produced an extreme reaction and it was difficult to bridge the gap of understanding between East and West. 'I made it my business in my rare off-duty time to try to delve into the Japanese mind', said a Dorsets sergeant, 'but I soon realized that I could devote a lifetime to this subject and still get nowhere!'

Japanese officialdom presented yet another face. It had been decreed from the beginning of the occupation that, in order to accomplish the occupation with the least possible expenditure of Allied manpower and resources, SCAP would conduct government through the existing Japanese administrative machinery, and so the local government structure remained in being. Although they were denied any involvement in the actual military government, BCOF units had continuous contact with local authorities, mainly the mayors and the chiefs of police, in the implementation of their occupation activities, especially the gathering of intelligence information and the prevention of illegal immigration.

There were occasional links of common experience. The Mayor of

Okayama, for example, turned out to have been a senior officer in the Japanese invasion of Burma from Indo-China in 1942, and to have commanded the very troops to have defeated the British at the battle of the Sittang Bend. The Gurkhas in Okayama had been part of that defeated British army, and the battle was refought at an extraordinary ceremonial dinner arranged between some of the officers and the Mayor. The fact that he had lost his wife and family in the fire-bombing of Okayama strangely did not affect the cordiality of the occasion.

BCOF personnel continued to be amazed by the diligence with which the Japanese carried out to the extreme the Emperor's directive to cooperate with the occupation forces. On one occasion two small boys were reported to the Director of Education in Matsue for having thrown stones at a passing jeep with soldiers aboard. The stones missed their target and the soldiers were quite unaware of the incident. But the parents and the Director of Education presented themselves to the local headquarters to make a formal and ceremonial apology, and strict instructions were issued by the Education Department to all schools on the need for proper respect for the occupation forces.

The police were all-powerful: 'the people were far more frightened of the police than they were of the occupation forces', said a British NCO. The officials were excessively helpful and embarrassingly polite. One British officer reported: '. . . the Japanese here have been most cooperative, almost overdoing it. The Chief of Police is the "big" man of the town: a monkey-like little man in his black and gold uniform and sword. He does and arranges practically everything for us. The Mayor and town officials are also most helpful. All the same I could never conjure up any love for these little men – I am sure they are completely double-faced – so scrupulously polite with their bowing and scraping.' The failure to appreciate the Japanese way of doing things is reflected in another account of this kind of contact: '. . . they are polite to the extent of sitting and fanning you if it happens to be hot! . . . talking to these Japanese officials is a long and tedious business. Whereas we can usually answer a question in a short sentence or even one word, the Japanese has to go round and round the point first, eventually giving the answer . . . it tries one's patience somewhat. . .' It was, of course, good policy for the local officials to keep on the right side of the occupation: they could safeguard their own positions and use BCOF to help them get things done. There were even cases where the local authorities played the local BCOF unit off against the local US military government in situations where they could see some advantage.

I HAVE DESCRIBED my experiences in Iwakuni and Yonago as an RAF Flight Lieutenant working on provost and security duties between June 1946 and August 1947 in both my lecture to the STICERD seminar mentioned above and in my memoir *Japan and Back and Places Elsewhere* (Global Oriental, Folkestone 1998) and it would be otiose to repeat them here, but some other personal reminiscences of BCOF are of general interest.

IAN NISH (Professor Ian Nish CBE) gave an account of his work with the Combined Services Detailed Interrogation Centre (CSDIC) in an interesting lecture to the Japan Society in 1996 (*Proceedings*, No. 128, Winter 1996) under the title 'Early Experiences in the British Commonwealth Occupation Force in Japan':-

•

I first arrived at Kure in October 1946. So I was by no means the first to arrive: Sir Peter Parker had been in Japan from October 1945 to March 1946 and Professor W.G. Beasley from September 1945 to March 1946. In that sense I was a latecomer. I might also have been an early goer. Although I did not know it at the time, the Labour government decided in October 1946 to withdraw British troops from the occupation of Japan on the grounds that it could not afford to keep them there. It complained of its needs for campaigns elsewhere in Asia and difficulties over shipping and finance. This might have been awkward for me, having to disembark and then re-embark on the same ship. Fortunately, six months' notice of withdrawal had to be given; and the Australian government on 6 January 1947 sought the agreement of the United States to the withdrawal of the British brigade. Two weeks later, Washington agreed. Soon the orderly withdrawal took place, followed in August by that of the Indian troops.

Despite all this, I was able to spend two years in Japan, of which the first six months were at Kure. Kure Bay was a staggeringly beautiful sight for which we had been prepared by the trip through the Inland Sea. Kure was like a horseshoe with mountains all around and reclaimed land in the middle. The reclaimed land in the middle of the horseshoe had been totally destroyed by the B29 attacks in the first week of May and the fire-bombings of 1-2 July and was a sad and desolate place. The shipyards and dock had been destroyed also but their cranes and the dockside sheds remained as did the concrete buildings in the city itself. The houses which survived were around the rim of the horseshoe on elevated land or to the west of the river Nikogawa. Kure was, therefore, rather different from Hiroshima and Tokyo where the ground was much flatter.

I was on my way to the Combined Services Detailed Interrogation Centre (CSDIC) commanded by Squadron Leader Cheeseman but otherwise administered by the Australian army. The CSDIC building was on the western periphery of the city on the main road running to Yoshiura and ultimately to Hiroshima. It had been used by the Imperial Japanese Navy and resembled a prewar elementary school made wholly of wood.

Its shape was that of an aircraft with its wings along the roadside and its tail being the ablution block, open to the air in summer and winter. The ground rose steeply behind us and the hillside was made into terraced rice fields. In the evening the farmer would walk up the slope with buckets of night-soil on his shoulders.

In retrospect, I have to say that CSDIC was a bizarre place. All other BCOF installations were protected with barriers and barbed wire and were heavily guarded on a 24 hour basis by armed soldiers. CSDIC was by contrast unguarded. There may have been patrols because it stood right on a major road but there was no guard and we did not have to perform any guard duty. The assumption must have been that it was a rather low-level intelligence organization.

The first difficult decision which I had to make was which bedroom to choose. The rooms on the front were right on the main road. They commanded the marvellous views of the bay and caught the sun. The road was not particularly busy but the occasional army truck and the local bus passed by. There was the rub. The bus was powered by a charcoal burner at the rear which was barely adequate to take the bus up the fairly steep gradient. It was often necessary for the passengers from the overcrowded buses to alight and walk up the hill and join the bus at the top. By contrast, the rooms at the back of CSDIC had an unenviable view of the toilet block and never got the sun. They were dominated by the hillside. That was where I spent six winter months without any heating.

I had been posted to Japan as an interpreter/translator and spent most of my time at HQ CSDIC in the Translation Section. Since we lived above the shop, we tended to work six days a week because there was nothing else to do, except to go travelling, which was of course free with a railway warrant. I was sometimes required to spend two days a week on interpreting duty.

Our prime task was to translate relevant newspapers. The problem at CSDIC was not that the work was difficult but that the language was in the process of change. The kind of translations on which I had been engaged at SEATIC (South East Asian Translation and Interrogation Centre) in Singapore was that of handwritten diaries of Japanese officers on the Burma front, notably the diary of Colonel Tadahiko Hayashi. The problem there had been the handwriting but Hayashi was around and could be consulted.

On arrival at CSDIC I was presented with two documents dealing with *toyo kanji*. One was a small dictionary of the *toyo kanji* (everyday use characters) issued by the Japanese whose pages have since turned rather brown; the other was the equivalent list published by SCAP on rather superior paper. The Japanese government had issued a list introducing the 1,850 *toyo kanji* which was distributed to all government departments and newspapers for use by 1 December 1946. So far as I can establish this was not mandatory; but many in Japan wanted to simplify the language and get rid of the complex older characters. In practice, the newspapers had already adopted this limited range. This coincided with the scheme for character simplification. You may say – what a boon! But in fact I realized that I had learnt the prehistoric *kanji* and it was not easy to throw off the old conventions in writing and reading. Naturally, I grudged the time I had spent learning pre-war Japanese.

The prime task at CSDIC was to translate the headlines of newspapers. These were supplied to HQ Britcombase which was located in the old naval college at Etajima. They would ask for a full translation of the articles or the reports that interested them. We were concerned with local city newspapers throughout the BCOF area which were very often hand-set and, of course, the main regional newspaper *Chugoku Shimbun*. The subjects that we were interested in were anything to do with the British occupation forces; crime, especially involving BCOF; black market; criticism of American Military Government (AMC) or BCOF in speeches etc.

Everyone who has worked on Japanese newspapers knows how difficult it is to judge the contents of an article from its headlines. One really has to read the whole article. We were engaged in rather a hit-and-miss operation. SCAP itself was responsible for translating the national press and its translations were widely circulated. It is sometimes said nowadays that the Japanese press is concentrated in the major cities and that the provincial press is inconsequential. Whatever the truth of that in general, it was not true in the immediate postwar period when I suppose they tried to revive prewar newspaper practices. There was therefore a good case for translating local newspapers which were less subject to central Government censorship, if indeed they were censored at all.

A second range of material was connected with wartime publications. SCAP had published an order forbidding the dissemination of wartime publications (for obvious and legitimate reasons). In practice many booksellers or newspaper shops did try to sell wartime material, journals or books, presumably either because they did not know of the SCAP order or because they needed the sale desperately in order to make ends meet. These items were often confiscated and brought to us for translation. We were – and still are – very ignorant about Japanese thinking during the war; and these materials were a gold mine for understanding wartime attitudes. The American organization with the rather unacademic title, the Strategic Bombing Survey, had by 1946 already done much work on this front. BCOF did hardly any.

Another group of materials were the unsolicited letters from Japanese to the occupation authorities. These were few and probably a bit unrepresentative. There was nothing to prevent Japanese from writing to the BCOF authorities or individual units with complaints, suggestions or declarations of affection. More often it was philosophical reflections on the war and I give a translation from one later.

I should like to dwell in more detail on these sets of materials, starting with newspapers. There was a remarkable coverage in the Chugoku newspapers about China and Korea where savage civil wars had been going on since the surrender and the intervention of Russians in the area. In Manchuria there was a battle between the Nationalists and Communists to take over the former Japanese towns, ports and industries. As of January 1947 the Chinese Nationalists (KMT) had the ascendancy in most of south and central Manchuria. From the start of 1947, however, the Communists began to wage a series of minor offensives, probes to test the strength and loyalty of the KMT forces. These proved successful and the offensive became wider and stronger. But there was still no thought during my time in Japan of Chinese Communists being ultimately successful. In Korea where Japan had had a stake since 1910 the position was even more worrying with the involvement of the Soviet Union in Pyongyang. Similar disruption was taking place in Vietnam, Indochina and the Philippines.

My first comment would be how difficult it was to translate this stuff. It was confusing that the characters for Chugoku were the same as for China (Chukoku [literally Middle Kingdom]). It was inconvenient that Kanto (the rival of Kansai) meant a geographical area quite different in Manchuria, sometimes known as 'Kuantung'. I made not a few errors in my translations on that score. Then there was the problem of Chinese place names and the rather strange way in which Japanese pronounced them.

To me as a historian the significant thing is that the Chugoku newspapers were saying in effect 'what we did in China, Korea and Southeast Asia has brought ruin to these countries'. So far from Japan saying we have liberated Asia, they were saying 'what we did has destroyed Asia'. The notion was that Japan's actions had dragged down her neighbours. Japan herself was impoverished and humiliated; but the fate which she had inflicted on China, Korea and the countries of Southeast Asia was arguably worse. These are judgments of mine, based on recollections from 50 years ago. What the Japanese were writing and thinking on this point in the 1940s is something that needs to be researched. Nowadays, some Japanese are putting a new gloss on the subject which seems to many of us to be at odds with the way Japanese saw matters at the time.

I have always felt that the people of the Chugoku region had a special interest in, and understanding of, the Asian continent which the people of Tokyo did not share to the same extent and which was rivalled only by the people of Kyushu. I cannot entirely explain why but can only guess at the reason. Historically they had to a great extent supplied the garrisons and bases which provided the soldiers which fought in Japan's three continental wars. They had continental links insofar as these were permitted. Japan was at that time left wing but anti-Communist because of the Soviet entry to the war at the last minute and the large number of Japanese prisoners of war held in their labour camps. The *hikeagesha* [repatriated people] were therefore very carefully interrogated as they landed at Ujina.

Another of our duties was to translate wartime material though this was not done systematically. One item I translated was about Subhas Chandra Bose whose name was already familiar to me as the leader of the Indian National Army. Bose himself had died in an aircrash off Taiwan in August 1945. I had been in India at the time of the INA trials in Delhi which had come to a head in December 1945. Many issues about Bose's life and death have interested historians: did he try to persuade Japan to let him go there? or had Japan for some time been trying to persuade him to visit Japan?

The article I translated was written in 1943 after Subhas Chandra had just arrived in Tokyo by submarine from Germany and was just about to go to Singapore in order to launch the Indian National Army among disaffected prisoners of war there. It was published by Yuji Satsuma MP.

Iron Leader of India; Subhas Chandra Bose
At the start of the 82nd Extraordinary Diet before Prime Minister Tojo was due to make his speech on the Great East Asia declaration, there was a rumour circulating in the corridors of the Diet that Subhas Chandra Bose would attend the session in person. The members all asked me when he had come and by what route. It was being kept totally secret. He did indeed sit through the Diet proceedings in the Strangers' Gallery.

Satsuma goes on to tell that he had met Bose first in Calcutta in 1938 when Bose was the twenty-eight-year-old mayor of the city and that in 1941 while he was staying in Berlin he had met him in the Tiergarten. What went on in their conversations he does not say.

'Our third meeting was when Bose came to Tokyo recently and we sat together on chairs in the garden of the Imperial Hotel and talked. Bose-kun has now flown on to Singapore Island... I pray for the achievement of his desires and have every confidence in his success.'

Although dates in this article are unspecific, certain facts shine through: Bose as the anti-British leader of one of the factions in the Indian Congress party had been in contact with the Japanese; and these contacts continued during his days in Berlin when he often broadcast to Japan and India.

The third group of material that I mentioned was unsolicited letters. One of the pieces of translation that I did was a letter from an anonymous Japanese of no certain date and to no one in particular. Perhaps one might describe it as an extended essay which was (so far as I know) never published. It was evidently an attempt by the author to unburden himself about the state of Japan around New Year 1947.

Why is Patriotism Wrong?

We believe that the Japanese nation has displayed its loyal and patriotic spirit to the utmost in the Greater East Asia war. Throughout the history of Japan we can find no period when the whole nation showed its patriotism to such an extent as in the last war, not even in the Kemmu or Meiji eras. Patriotism reached a high-point with the Death without Honour squads or the Suicide squads which were unprecedented in world history as much as in our own and which struck the whole world with admiration. The world was frightened of the Japanese as the incarnation of patriotism itself. In fact Japan's strong point lies in her spiritual power derived from patriotism. This power was the essential factor which was expected to give us victory and would make up for our shortage of equipment, resources and mechanization.

As the last war unfortunately ended in our unexpected defeat and surrender, the people have become absent-minded and demoralized. This cannot be helped and must be overlooked for the time being. It is our regret, however, that some men have begun to lose confidence as well as courage, to become servile, to curse the Holy War, to disapprove of everything in the past and to have doubts as to the merits of patriotism. They curse the war-leaders, call the last war absurd, grumble that they were deceived by their leaders, try to pass the responsibility on to others and regard patriotism as dangerous thinking or as an antique and bigoted idea.

Taking advantage of the fact that the enemy countries have accused the war leaders of war crimes and purged from public office those who ardently cooperated in the war effort, these men who were idle during the war have tried to fix war-guilt on these accused and purged men. Shamelessly and proudly they have tried to take over the latter's positions and to lay the blame on their compatriots by blindly following the enemy. For thoughtful persons this is a most deplorable fact. We feel indignant not so much at our defeat as at those Japanese who were indifferent to the war in which their brothers sacrificed their lives and homes and who have sought personal profit by preying upon such sacrifices.

Whereas it is a natural thing that a man who loves his fatherland and his own race should exert himself to fight to the last gasp, we believe that thoughtless people have been dazzled by defeat into forgetting patriotism, into professing that patriotism reflects an obstinate and obsolete mentality and even into refraining from talking of patriotism at all. Prince Konoe has said 'The victors are oppressive while the defeated are servile'. He is right: once defeated, they have become as shameless and mean as we have described.

A Japanese yesterday is the same Japanese today. No change of race could have resulted from defeat. Blood, tradition, history and culture are not subject to alteration as easily as you might think. Perhaps such people have been dazzled by defeat and possessed by an evil spirit.

This is a very small part of a much longer document which I should like to publish in full some day. It is an important translation which gives an interesting – I shall not say representative – insight into Japanese thinking. It reminds me that, different from the view usually taken, the Japanese were often quite critical of the Occupation.

It was of course a right-wing appreciation stressing that, since August 1945, patriotism, faith in things Japanese, had collapsed and that the Japanese had switched their allegiance to things American. Presumably the author, who (one suspects) was anti-American, sent these thoughts to BCOF as a sort of neutral readership. It would be interesting to know what BCOF did with the CSDIC translation. The article is also critical of the new Japanese leadership which had been lying low during the war. He does not specify names but his criticisms would probably cover Shigeru Yoshida.

Translations such as this supply a partial answer to one of the questions that people often ask: 'what did the Japanese say to you during the occupation years?' The proper answer should be nothing at all because BCOF imposed a non-fraternization order on all its troops. This was contained in a Personal Instruction of 20 February 1946 from General (Sir) John Northcott, the first commander-in-chief, to all ranks of BCOF which stated:

> You must be formal and correct; you must not enter their homes or take part in their family life; you must strictly obey all instructions regarding establishments or areas which are placed out of bounds. . .

In itself this was not unreasonable. The fact is that the full terms of this order were not widely known; and it was assumed that the policy was a blanket of non-fraternization. That was rather different from the American approach which permitted conditional fraternization. It probably came from the animosity towards Japan on the part of Australia and Britain being much greater than in the case of the Americans. The Japanese history of BCOF in Kure states:

> The Kure citizens' initial bewildered impression of the rather unresponsive BCOF troops was not exactly inaccurate, because there was a difference between the generous and merry-making American approach in relating to [the Japanese] and that of BCOF.

The Japanese experienced culture-shock when the happy-go-lucky Americans who won the hearts of Japanese children were replaced by taciturn Australians and British. The mind boggles.

The problem with the BCOF approach was that it lacked flexibility. In spite of the fact that the nature of the occupation changed over the years, the non-fraternization policy changed very little. The military objectives with which the occupation had been planned disappeared relatively

quickly without a new approach being introduced. It is doubtful, therefore, whether the occupationaires understood what the Japanese were
thinking and their governments correspondingly.

We as linguists naturally came under a different dispensation. We made
contact with maids, Japanese translators, shopkeepers in order to practise our Japanese. But these conversations were non-political and rarely (I
imagine) touched upon the war. As interpreters it was in the nature of our
duty to have contact with the Japanese and speak to the Japanese in Japanese, which was likely to be more productive than speaking through an
interpreter.

Our translations also served the purpose of overcoming the lack of
knowledge and communication which came from the non-fraternization
policy. How the Japanese were reacting to the occupation could not be
understood without some provision for reading what the Japanese were
writing about themselves. Because this problem was only partially
solved, I fear that the occupation passed without friendship being established between the British Commonwealth and Japan.

AFTER SIX or seven months in Kure Ian Nish was sent to work 'in the field'.
One of his first tasks was to take part in one of eleven BCOF mobile sections to
observe the first post-war general election in April 1947 to ensure that the elections were 'conducted in a manner completely in keeping with the tradition of
freedom and democracy'. The main duty of the mobile sections was to visit the
polling stations on the day of the election to ensure the secrecy of the ballot
and to prevent soliciting and buying of votes and police interference. In an
article entitled 'Britain and the Occupation of Japan – Some Personal Recollections' IAN NISH described the results of this operation:-

●

A number of 'violations' of electoral law were reported to the observation teams; but the election was on the whole conducted in exemplary fashion.

Certainly that was my own experience since I was responsible for in-
specting polling stations in Joge-gun in upper Hiroshima prefecture.
This was a picturesque and primitive agricultural area where there were
no 'municipal' buildings to serve as polling stations. Instead schools and
improvized huts were brought into service. On the whole, it was an impressive, if slightly ritualized, performance.

As a result of the election, the Socialist party secured a majority in the
lower house and its leader, Tetsu Katayama, formed a coalition cabinet
with the Democratic party and the People's Cooperative party. Though
Katayama's tenure as prime minister was short-lived, the impression
which he made on me was much stronger than that of the conservative

political leaders of the day. Was it because he was a Christian? Was it because BCON (the British Commonwealth occupation newspaper), my main reading in English, portrayed him sympathetically? Was it that opinion in Britain and Australia, which were both then under Labour governments, welcomed the Katayama administration? It may, however, be that Katayama succeeded in projecting himself more effectively in the Chugoku region than others.

IN THE LATTER PART of 1947 Ian Nish was posted to Shikoku island which was by that time largely unoccupied territory following the withdrawal of the British 5th Infantry Division. This meant that Shikoku became the responsibility of the Australian 34th Infantry Brigade with its headquarters near Kure, but as the Australians were short of manpower they decided to arrange surveillance by sending regular patrols. As part of such 'patrols' Ian Nish stayed in Shikoku for almost a year.

Apart from some small units at Takamatsu the only permanent allied presence consisted of American Military Government (AMG) teams in the prefectural capitals and a few individuals like Ian Nish who could be at times over 130 miles from the nearest occupation unit. As he noted the Japanese telephone system could not be relied on and security largely depended on the willingness of Japanese citizens generally to accept the occupation as a matter of routine.

IAN NISH described the scene and his duties as follows:-

•

S hikoku in 1947 was a place of attractive landscapes and rural delights. Parts of it were relatively primitive. Most roads, even the arterial ones, were unmetalled, because the natives of Shikoku depended on railways for transport. The roads deteriorated badly in wet weather and became unbelievably dusty in the dry season. Buses, trucks and cars – few as they were – threw up vast clouds of dust and small stones behind them. This was a great hazard for those who followed.

The main problem for the occupation in Shikoku was the black market in rice. I had to take part in many anti-black market operations in support of the Japanese police. This involved searching warehouses and other centres of hoarding and setting up checkpoints on major roads.

The black market (*yami ichiba*) can be described in simple terms. Food was scarce in Japanese towns and cities – indeed, it was scarce throughout Asia until 1948. Similarly, clothing and other necessities of life were not readily available in rural communities. There developed a traffic in food surpluses from the countryside in exchange for products of the town. This was often the function of the *katsugiya*, the middleman who carried the wares of one to the other. This had to be done by public transport and was therefore a fairly blatant operation which could not have been unknown to the police.

The central government was drawn in through its programmes for rice requisition. Each agricultural cooperative had to collect a certain percentage of a farmer's output of rice, store it and make it available to the government or its agencies. This depended of course on fixing a quota for each farmer, on fixing a national price for the rice and on punishing defaulters. There was evasiveness on the part of the farmers who wanted to hold on to as much rice as possible, since its value was a great deal more stable than yen currency. The farmers claimed to be aggrieved; most claimed that they had been over-assessed; most claimed to be in difficulties over the making of saké. The officials of cooperatives (*nogyo kumiai*) were dealing with a scarce and highly valued commodity. Scarcity breeds corruption; and farmers, *nogyo kumiai* leaders and police were all under severe temptation. It became a way of life.

I took part in searches of farmers' godowns, of *nogyo kumiai* godowns and in checks at ferry terminals. In this case, BCOF was acting in cooperation with the local police in support of central government policies of which SCAP and AMG fully approved. To the unfortunate individual on the ground, things were less easy. One bale of rice looked very much like another; and it was far from easy to calculate the numbers of bales which had been stacked. Moreover, it was an unpleasant job to intercept 'black marketeers' at ferry terminals for carrying *'yami'* materials such as war surplus clothing. The newspapers of the time reported discoveries of black market materials on a large scale; but perhaps these were carried in the press *pour encourager les autres*. There must have been widespread evasion and concealment.

It might be thought that this sort of activity would have made occupation personnel unpopular or led to them being ostracized. But in general this did not happen. We continued to receive complaints in a manner reminiscent of a district officer in a colonial territory. These complaints might come in the form of anonymous or signed letters, or of personal callers seeking interviews or of tales by middlemen. There might be complaints about Japanese officials; complaints about left-wing activities such as the actions of *hiki-agesha* (repatriated people) and complaints about right-wing activities which very often included reported activities against the occupation. In other words, the complaints were sufficiently broad-based to suggest that the Japanese did not assume that the occupation was necessarily either right- or left-wing in its political complexion. Of course, some of the complaints were ventilations of private grudges; and some were, I dare say, bogus. But they suggested a strange measure of confidence in occupation personnel.

And some of that confidence was misplaced. They were made presumably on the assumption that the powers of SCAP, or AMG or even of

BCOF were supreme. But this was an illusion. Certainly, these complaints were a great embarrassment because they were extremely difficult to investigate without seeking the cooperation of the Japanese police. And to contact police regarding these complaints meant violating the trust of the complainants.

This role of receiving complaints was not one which we sought. Indeed, I blush to think how little we could do, individually or collectively, to resolve the complaints we received. But, looking back, I think that these complaints were a valuable safety-valve in Japanese society which at the time was full of personal tension and communal stress. It provided members of the occupation, whose sources of information were pitifully limited, with some inkling of what lay beneath the surface of local politics or local commerce. Possibly it also had a negative benefit in that the Japanese knew we were in receipt of such complaints, but never knew their precise nature.

In conclusion, one may contradict the view that the occupation of Japan was totally American. Such is a not uncommon view in Japan and is based upon a Tokyo-centred view of events. The truth of the matter is that a distinction has to be made between occupation and military government. Occupation was joint and allied, while military government was exclusively American. Even in the British occupation zone, military government was American military government. BCOF acted to help AMG and generally in the role of policeman.

The British perception of the occupation was a detached one. We were rather more objective and less committed to the aims of the reforms than were the Americans. This partly reflected a generation gap on the part of the 'occupationaires'. The American army of occupation was a new force whose members had not in the main fought the Japanese during the war; those who had been involved in the fighting had, by and large, qualified for early repatriation. Repatriation policies within BCOF seem to have worked differently. Because of shortage of transport, the uncertainties of the home economy and the slower rate of repatriation, the forces in BCOF were not 'a new force'. They may, therefore, have carried forward to the occupation period some of their wartime thinking. Generalizations of this kind are hard to make; but the American attitudes towards the Japanese were probably more favourable and generous than these of BCOF, both administratively and personally.

*   *   *

Thinking of Western Japan in these two years, it is possible to describe it as 'idyllic'. At a superficial level it was possible to walk along roads which had no pavements without fear of being run over by mighty lorries; it was possible to cycle on the road rather than on the pavement; there was a lack of

pollution for Japan was in an intermediate phase between the industrialization of the 1930s and the re-industrialization of the 1950s. But this picture of
a rural paradise would be the grossest distortion. For most Japanese families
in the Chugoku region conditions were harrowing. For us in the occupation
also they were basic and spartan. The fairest thing to say is that Japan between 1946 and 1948 was a sad but beautiful country.

LEW RADBOURNE (Lew Radbourne, OBE) in a lecture to the Japan
Society on 11 March 1997 (*Proceedings*, No. 129, Summer 1997) described how,
after studying Japanese at SOAS, in the army he was sent to Japan in 1947:-

●

At the end of the course, after being commissioned about two-thirds
of the way through, we eventually sailed for Japan on a troop ship,
the *Dunera*, to join the British Commonwealth Occupation Force
(BCOF). We travelled in fair comfort in comparison with early post-
war English standards of living. En route in Singapore we picked up a
contingent of Japanese troops for repatriation to Japan – their *esprit de
corps*, discipline and teamwork in the very basic quarters they occupied
below decks stirred my first faint thoughts that this was a race that had
something that would see them through. After six weeks, we arrived in
Kure following a never-to-be-forgotten journey through the Inland Sea
whose beauty has always superseded in my mind subsequent visions of
Japan in industrial and highly urbanized belts. The first thing one had to
do was to start unlearning some of the SOAS Japanese so politely
learned, and instead of requesting baggage porters to be 'so kind as to
do one the honour of graciously unloading one's trunks', this had to be
transformed into the local idiom equivalent to 'Unload these mate'
('*Hayaku oroshite kure*').

We were attached to the Combined Services Detailed Interrogation
Centre (CSDIC) in Kure which was a pool of Commonwealth Services
linguists who worked in CSDIC and were also attached to various units as
Japanese Interpreters throughout BCOF territory.

After some months, I was posted as the Language Officer to the Australian 34th Brigade and subsequently to Headquarters on Etajima. One
of the tasks of my unit during the Occupation was to report monthly to
BCOF headquarters under a series of headings one of which was 'overt
acts against the Occupation'. In the whole of the eighteen months there,
never once was there a report other than 'nil'.

I still recall clearly the poverty of Japan at that time. BCOF employed
thousands of local workers right across the board, and alongside us in the
Translation Bureau were highly educated Japanese translators. One of
these later became Managing Director of a major shipping organization

in Tokyo, but in those early days he used to appear for work wearing a very thread-bare pair of blue plimsolls – the best he could muster at that time.

Much has been talked about fraternization by occupationaires with Japanese nationals; the most striking feature of this was the difference in attitudes by the Americans and the Commonwealth troops. Both the British, in the form of Mountbatten who suggested to MacArthur that a very tough line should be taken with Japanese, and the Australians who had after all suffered in the North from Japanese air-raids, considered that a severe line should be taken with Japan. From the beginning the Americans did nothing to discourage fraternization by the GIs with the local population, whereas a personal instruction was issued to Commonwealth troops prohibiting any contact that was not official, visits to Japanese homes and procurement of food from local sources. Hunger, however, worked against this in that troops were often asked for sweets and snacks and those disinclined to 'donate' these found easy outlets for their spare rations on the black market. With over 20,000 Japanese workers employed by BCOF at its peak, informal daily contact was inevitable and, towards the end, marriages between BCOF personnel and Japanese women started to take place, but only with the written authority of Commanding Officers, and no Australian marrying a Japanese could expect permission for his wife to take up permanent residence in Australia upon return.

ANOTHER FORMER student of Japanese at SOAS who spent some time with the British Commonwealth Occupation Force in Kure and Shikoku was PAUL BATES (who returned later to work for Shell in Japan). He summed up his time in the Occupation in the following way:-

•

Having sweated through eighteen months at SOAS, the graduates of the last Service Japanese course arrived in Japan to join CSDIC, just at the time when the last of the British and Indian elements in BCOF were returning home and the management became predominately Australian. Having survived to finish in London, I certainly thought my Japanese was pretty good and it was a bit of a shock to find oneself hardly able to make oneself understood, let alone understand what was being said back to you. The fact that our Japanese teachers had, for the most part, lived in England longer than we had, continued to make me feel over the years to come that I was a product of the Meiji period so far as vocabulary, knowledge of characters etc, were concerned. Our Japanese was the pre-MacArthur version and did not conform to the 'simplified' language then being taught in schools.

It was the ambition of most of us to get out into the field as soon as

possible. My first experience was to join an expedition from Kure to Kochi to help supervise the first democratic election of the prefectural governor. As even in the BCOF area the military government was carried out
by the American Army, this supervision exercise was under their direction. The teams, consisting of an interpreter, Australian NCO/driver, a
Jeep and a trailer of provisions, were sent off to all points of the prefecture. Our good fortune was to be sent to the east along the coast to a small
town where our supervisors assured us we would find a comfortable hotel with all the required amenities. While nobody had ever heard of a
hotel, on our arrival we were directed to a room over a liquor store run
by a couple of elderly geisha which became a very comfortable base for the
ten days or so that we spent there. While we had taken our own supply of
rations, the local worthies made us very welcome and steadily supplied us
with deliveries of beer from the establishment below.

Our days were spent travelling around the polling booths in our area, a
glorious area of mountain and sea, endeavouring to ensure that there
were no undue fiddles being carried out. How successful we were was
not easy to determine, but when the results of the election came in even
we were found to have received a number of votes, as well as General
MacArthur, and 'the candidate who would be most sympathetic towards
the black market'.

Returning to Kure, I was very fortunate to find myself sent back to
Shikoku, this time to Takamatsu, to join the Military Government of
Kagawa Prefecture as interpreter to an Australian Captain. The assignment was to try and improve the control of the black market in fish and
vegetables in the prefecture. This was very widespread at the time and
the main weapon of control was to supply the inputs to the industries at
low prices in exchange for the sale of their products in the legal markets.
Together with that was the role of the police in seeking out and dealing
with offenders. Before long, my Australian superior was recalled to his
unit without replacement and I took his place acquiring my own Japanese interpreter. This was very satisfactory from my point of view and
this assignment occupied the remainder of my time in BCOF.

One amusing incident I often recall from this period was going, I
think it was to Sakaide, to see the police chief to demand better cooperation. For anyone who has only known Japan since the phoenix rose it
would be difficult to imagine the low standard of living and lack of most
amenities which was the norm in the early post-war days. One minor
aspect was that the stuffing on all chairs in government offices had lost
their strength and sagged into a deep well. It was in the summer and
either the summer uniform I was wearing had been tailored on the tight
side or I had put on weight, but in the middle of haranguing the police
chief for his excessive sympathy with the blackmarketeers, I sat down on
the chair in front of his desk and felt my trousers parting at the back

seam. I had to beat a hasty retreat and I never knew whether the police-man was unaware of what had happened or whether he was too polite to show any sign of mirth!

I cannot have been too hard on the police because the last memory of that period is being tossed in the air by a bunch of them at the farewell party they gave me when they also presented me with a very nice *meito* (a fine sword) from their collected stock.

CHRISTOPHER WOOD in an article in the Japan Society's *Proceedings*, No. 109, Spring 1993, described what life was like for the British soldier in Shikoku in 1946. He was enchanted and wanted to return. In 1991 he was instrumental in getting the Kyoto Garden in Holland Park completed in time to mark the Society's centenary and I hope was equally enchanted by the garden:-

•

If you were in the army in India at the end of 1945, you had a 'demob' number. Long Service, a wife, children, age, all brought the number down to, say, seven or five or even two, and demobilization that much nearer. My number was sixty-three, a life sentence, and so I volunteered to go to Japan. The rat-ridden troopship, *Rajula*, sailed via Calcutta, Singapore and Hong Kong, while we drafts for the Dorsets, Royal Welsh Fusiliers, Camerons and Gurkhas lolled in squalid idleness, and awaited the future in that peace of mind induced by total ignorance.

Hiroshima was difficult to see through the mist from the troopship. I saw one tall chimney standing on the outskirts of the city, but for the rest it looked like a large municipal refuse-dump: formless and grey. Much nearer, the islands in the bay gave a more immediate indication of the scale of the catastrophe. They had been wooded, but on the landward side of each island, not a tree remained. All, all had been sheared off and swept clean, and it was then that, among the new-arriving members of the Commonwealth Occupation Force, a certain silence fell. Here was the site of the event which, for us who had been serving in India and Burma, had ended the war, and almost certainly saved our lives. Kobe was a more familiar sight. Coventry, Hamburg and Dresden were known to us from newsreels, and here were displayed the last, best achievements of the old technology: a submarine hurled into the main street, remains of sunken ships lying everywhere in the great harbour. ruins as far as the eye could see, but with an occasional human figure at least and even some dock workers on the quayside.

The First Battalion of the Queen's Own Cameron Highlanders was based in Asakura, near Kochi on the island of Shikoku. Our draft arrived in the early dawn, to be challenged by the guard who had blackened faces, wore fatigues and boots, and carried pick-axe handles. Our beds were wire stretchers set on packing cases but we had been travelling for ever and were past caring.

The Camerons were passionately regimental. When 'Retreat' was played at six o'clock every evening, everyone in earshot (and the skirl of bagpipes carries a long way) stood to attention; soldiers of course, but all civilians too: all the villagers for miles. This ceremony offered the first hint I received of the particular flexibility and absorptive capacity of the Japanese. Originally, standing to attention for Retreat had been imposed on the populace to rub in the fact that they had lost, and we had won the war. Finding that it made a pleasant enough moment at the end of every day, they adopted the ceremony! Once, when I fidgeted during the performance, an old granny frowned at me reprovingly. She was playing by the rules (her rules!): I should be too. What was the world coming to? Imperceptibly, we were adopted. No other town in Japan could boast of kilted soldiers. No other town had such a high proportion with red hair. Small boys danced ecstatically about our flanks (*Banzai! Banzai!*) when we marched abroad. Slowly, some individuals among us became adopted by the locals, and Jocks could be seen expounding to their adoptive families the strip cartoons in their own local papers sent from home.

Insensibly, we learned the few words necessary to get along in these new surroundings. In India, these had been '*Hidderao*', come here: '*Jao*', get out: '*Munkta*', I want: '*Chup*, shut up: '*Kitna*', how much?: '*Jildi*', quick. Hence a typical sentence might be '*Hidderao, jildi*, Johnny. *Munkta pukka do annas cha*', if one wanted a good two-annas-worth of tea quickly. In Japan the words and phrases we needed were: '*Ohayo gozaimas*', good morning, how are you: '*Dozo*', please: '*Arigato*', thank you: '*Wakarimasen*', I don't understand: '*Sayonara*', goodbye: even '*Do itashimashite*', not at all, don't mention it. Bear in mind that these were the same soldiers, but how else – in this society – would we be able to make our wishes known?

Once, on night-guard, I disturbed a village woman scavenging among the dustbins behind the cookhouse, and she scurried away with a clatter. The kilted guard on the main gate opened it for her, and she recovered her poise. 'Good night.' 'Good night, ma'am.' 'Thank you.' 'Not at all.' I shouldn't have frightened her, he said. Had I no tact?

The father of my particular family was a sorting-clerk in the Post Office. He had a lifetime's hobby of collecting bank notes. He had specimens from Tsarist Russia, from the Third Reich, from Mussolini's Italy, from already-forgotten warlords in China, from every country in the Far East. I remember the (doubtless illegal) trouble I went to in letters home to get some current English banknotes to add to his collection. One of my friends even contributed a Bank of Scotland one-pound note! Later, in another country, he said to me: 'For why did we no' steal his albums, Jock? Ah'll never ken.'

The wife and daughter of my adoptive family would preside with poise over our small soirées. It is indeed, extremely restful to be a man and live in Japan. If you think that something is so, why, it's true. If you want something, it's important (though you may not necessarily get it!). If you say something, it was 'ne'er so well expressed'. Admire with me the way the Japanese women wear their kimonos. Imagine one in, say, apple-green embroidered with white flowers. To say 'No', she makes some small, restrained gesture, but see how emphatic is the flash of scarlet from the inside of her sleeve, how entrancing her demure look when she sees that her point has been taken.

It was winter in 1946 when the earthquake and *tsunami* (tidal wave) struck Kochi. The wooden houses buckled under the weight of their tiled roofs which fell down onto the open hearths in the living rooms causing fires to break out in all parts of the town simultaneously. Then the sea came in over the coastal dunes and took what the fires had left. My friend, Joe Boyle, and I were bicycling about in the outskirts of the town in the snow laying telephone lines. Up to our pedals in water we were, when he cycled into an open ditch about five feet deep. Every roof in the road (all at ground level on top of the ruins of the houses) had its poor little remnant family camping out on the tiles, and I shall never forget the kindly malice of their laughter. 'Now you really have joined us in misery', it said. 'Come on in: the water's fine.' With heavy bombers able to make three trips a day from Okinawa, there has never been any doubt in my mind that, had Japan tried to fight the war to the bitter end, there would have been very few Japanese survivors. How wise those decisions were that saw Joe Boyle and me laughing heartily with the villagers in the sleet rather than killing them.

And the incomparable countryside! I remember a path cantilevered out from the mountainside. Wherever a small stream tumbled down, the path had semi-circular 'bites' out of it. Round about the streams grew flowers: on the flowers fed butterflies: on the butterflies fed birds, circling endlessly, hurtling up through the gaps between the road and the mountainside. We went through clouds of whirling birds and butterflies amid near-vertical meadows starred with flowers hanging over deep gorges.

The hot springs in Matsuyama were used as public baths which admitted all ages and both sexes. Never have I seen a party of soldiers less brutal and licentious than we: hauling ourselves ashore to escape the almost unbearable heat, and being chivvied back in under pailfuls of ice-cold water wielded by the amused and motherly municipal matrons of the establishment. On another wooded hillside, I found all the air full of musical tinklings, '... sounds and sweet airs, which give delight and hurt not'. The water supply for the village below was led through the woods from one section of propped bamboo to another, falling down an inch or two from each one to the next as it went. Where the path crossed this rural pipeline, there was a carved wooden ladle hung from a post so that the traveller, having removed a section of bamboo in order to pass through, should be rewarded for putting it back by so considerate a concern for his thirst. Another memory: my platoon billeted in a public library where all the 'books' were scrolls in racks. Above each rack was a sign asking the reader to re-roll his scroll to the beginning before he put it back. So beguiling and confiding was the society in which we found ourselves.

I remember the Inland Sea between Shikoku and Honshu jewelled with islands floating in the water like clouds, but clouds with trees and reflections, and little sails like birds flying – a sort of rural Venice.

Oh, to return to Japan!

ONLY A FEW British individuals without any services connections reached Japan in the early days of the occupation. One of these was JOHN MORRIS who had been in Japan before the war and had written during the war a popular book about his experiences, *Traveller from Tokyo*. He managed to make a return visit to Japan in 1946 which he described in his book *The Phoenix Cup* (Cresset Press, London, 1947.) (See also Chapter on John Morris and George Orwell in *Biographical Portraits III*, Japan Library for the Japan Society, 1999.)

The air journey from London to Tokyo these days is simple compared to what it was in January 1946. Here are excerpts from John Morris's account of how he set off from India:-

•

In January 1946 the British Overseas Airways did not extend beyond Calcutta; for the rest of the journey I was to travel in one of the planes of the American Army Transport Command, for which orders had already been given me before leaving London. . . We were told to report to Barrackpore Airport, twenty-five miles outside Calcutta, at half-past two in the morning, and it appeared that we should have to make our own arrangements to get there. It is not easy to find transport at such an hour. But eventually we found the place and an American sentry, after looking at our papers, let us in through the barbed wire and told us to report at a building of which the outlines were faintly visible in the distance.

There was nobody there and the building was locked. It was obviously the wrong place. . . There was the usual perfunctory medical examination and we had then to make a customs declaration. . .

Now followed the briefing, presided over by a captain. We were huddled into a small room, without ventilation or fans, and given a lecture on the perils of the onward journey. It went, something like this. 'Now see here, you bastards! The C54 ("Skymaster") is a mighty good aircraft, but even the best aircraft in the world sometimes have to ditch, and the journey you're going on is mostly over the sea. I've never heard of a C54 ditching, but if she does this is what you bastards do. . .' and so on for about half an hour about how to operate a floating wireless set and mend a puncture in a 'Mae West'. Being an unpractical sort of person, I find it difficult to follow this kind of thing even when I am feeling mentally alert. But now I was dog-tired and the room was very hot, so that I could barely keep my eyes open. I could remember only one phrase, which the captain kept repeating: 'Don't forget – everything yellow floats.' This was in reference to the fact that some of the life-saving gear was painted in that colour. . .

JOHN MORRIS described his arrival in Tokyo and his first impressions as follows:-

●

I found that I was to be billeted in the Correspondents' Club, a former restaurant and only a stone's throw away, so I set off on foot, dragging my kit through the slush as best I could.

It was now getting on for ten o'clock, and my first impression of the club was that it was a cross between a waterfront sailors' bar and a brothel. . .

Drunken brawls were frequent and there were occasions when firearms were discharged in the lounge. But at this time conditions were quite abnormal. There was absolutely nothing to do in Tokyo after dark, and drink was plentiful and cheap. Besides, many of the correspondents, of whom there were about seventy in the club, would not normally be considered to have the necessary qualifications for the work they were now doing. Some of them had been knocking about in the Pacific for years and had lost what civilized standards they ever had. But it was a little disconcerting, at first, to be considered stand-offish just because one neither over-drank nor kept a woman. . .

I shared a room with four others, and such is the American passion for heating that in spite of the intense cold outside I could only sleep at all with the thinnest of cotton sheets over me. Moreover, it was not conducive to a good night's rest when one or other of one's companions would come up in the early hours of the morning, switch on the lights, and try to start a conversation. And sometimes he would bring his girl. . . I think myself that another man's private life is entirely his own concern, but I do feel very strongly that the sexual act is something which should only be performed in private.

* * *

I had left Japan eight months after Pearl Harbor, in July 1942. There had
been one raid, led by General Doolittle, but it was little more than a
demonstration, and when I rode through Tokyo for the last time (it was
in a prison bus on my way to the exchange ship) the city, although shabby,
still was a city, a place where some seven million people lived, worked
and played.

During the war and until I left London to come back I was closely
concerned with Japanese affairs. I had studied hundreds of reports and
documents and had built up in my mind a fairly clear picture of what to
expect. It bore no resemblance whatever to the Tokyo I saw on the first
morning of my return. . .

The middle part of the city, which centres around the Imperial Palace,
is battered, but remains more or less as it was before the war. A building
here and there has been gutted, and the general effect is similar to the less
badly bombed parts of London. It is an area of modern steel and concrete
buildings, and was occupied mostly by the banks and other big business
houses. Today it is used almost entirely as offices and barracks for the
army of occupation. . .

The number of people inhabiting Marunouchi now is probably considerably more than 40,000, and of this number possibly some 400 are Japanese, and they seem strangely out of place. It might now be described as a
small American island surrounded by a Japanese sea of ashes, rubble and
rusted cans. Walking around the blocks, discordant music, from the Armed
Forces Radio Station, batters on the eardrums, and ruminating GIs off
duty stand propped against the nearest convenient wall. One might be in
Denver or any other of the smaller American cities.

. . . On this winter morning smoke was belching from every chimney,
and the temperature inside most of the buildings seemed not very different from the normal temperature of Tokyo in August. . . I noticed that
most of the present occupants, in spite of the bitter cold outside, were in
their shirt sleeves. It was in strange contrast to the conditions I was later
to find in Japanese offices where, owing to the complete lack of any kind
of heating, the clerks sat wearing every article of clothing they could lay
their hands on.

As soon as you leave this small westernized area the picture changes
completely. It should be realized that the average Japanese city has a
hard core of solid modern buildings, but 90 per cent of the houses
and even the factories are made of wood. In Tokyo, practically everything except the solid core has gone, and all you see for miles around is
nothing but a vast sea of ashes; no bits of walls, no cellars even; just
ashes. There were, of course, a few solid buildings, schools, municipal
offices, hospitals, and so on, outside the centre. Many of them have
been badly damaged but most of them still exist, and they are the only
remaining landmarks. With the one exception of Kyoto, which was

never bombed, these are the conditions I found in every major city in Japan.

It was curious to find the streets, although sadly in need of repair, practically undamaged. There were no taxis, but the trams were still rumbling along in a rather inefficient way.

To board a tram necessitates waiting in a queue for anything up to one hour. You have to fight your way on and every car carries about double its capacity; even the running boards are covered by passengers. Breakdowns, of course, are frequent because the rolling-stock is old and worn out; it is only with great difficulty that the average tram can climb even the gentlest slope. Conditions are the same on the district railway and the underground, which before the war were clean and efficient. Nowadays, the stations are dirty, ill-lighted, and smell like a sewer. You just travel from one ash heap to another, and although the names of the districts are, of course, unchanged, there is little else by which to recognize them.

The Japanese claimed before the war that Tokyo was the third biggest city in the world. The population was somewhere around seven millions, but it has now been reduced by more than half, of whom only a small proportion are able to live in the city itself. Most of the people live out on the fringes, in the more or less undamaged suburbs. Four or five families are now occupying a tiny house intended originally for just two people.

The daily journeys to and from the city take anything up to six or seven hours, and in the present conditions of overcrowding it is inevitable that most people arrive at their offices already tired and with nerves frayed. Few restaurants are open, and the prices they charge are far beyond the means of the average city-worker, whose usual midday meal is a small portion of cold boiled rice brought from home. Words like democracy and liberty can have little meaning for a people whose whole energies must at present inevitably be devoted to solving the difficulties of mere existence.

*   *   *

On my first afternoon I went out by the underground to where I used to live. It is a district called Shibuya, about twenty minutes away from the centre of Tokyo. Before the war it was a busy shopping district, its main streets filled with people at all hours of the day and night. When I came out of the station I could hardly believe my eyes. The skeleton of the place, the streets and alleys, were still there, just as I used to know them, but the flesh, the life and blood had gone. It was no longer snowing, but the roads were deep in slush and filth. Because I used to know my way about here so well I had no difficulty in finding the exact spot where once my own house stood. I was able to trace the remains of the stone steps and the charred stump of a tree under which I had often sat reading on warm spring evenings. For some time I just stood staring at this awful desolation. Memories of the times I had spent in the house came crowding into my mind. I remembered particularly the last time I was here, when my old housekeeper stood bowing at the gate as the policeman took me away. I wondered what had happened to her, and whether she had been persecuted for her loyalty to an enemy alien. There was no one to ask where she was; no trace of any of my neighbours. I did not see even a cat or a dog. Standing there in the cold and wintry silence I felt a strange inaction, as though I, too, belonged to the general desolation.

Digging about in the ashes I turned up a little saké cup, one of a set out of which, lolling in front of the fire on winter nights, we would lie sipping the warmed amber spirit. It is a plain little cup, the size of a liqueur-glass, and slightly cracked. Round its base is a simple conventional pattern, glazed in blue, and I have thought often of the fingers that once grasped it.

This was the only material link with what, in spite of many difficulties had been a happy time of my life. It is of no intrinsic value, this cheap little cup, but there is about it something essentially Japanese. It is for me a symbol of the phoenix, a reminder that underneath the present chaos and destruction there are civilized virtues in the Japanese which, if we desire peace for that country, we must help to revive.

*   *   *

It is very difficult to get in touch with people. I still have the addresses of most of my friends, but as yet I have been able to trace hardly anybody. The post office still functions, but there is a strict censorship, and even in Tokyo it sometimes takes several weeks for a letter to be delivered. In any case it is useless to write to an address when it is almost certain that the house no longer exists. . .

It was not until many weeks later, after I had given an interview to one of the big Tokyo newspapers, that I was able to begin picking up the threads. Most of my friends, I now discovered, were no longer living in the city, but at least they knew where I was, and as time went on and I travelled about the country I was able to meet many of them.

*   *   *

For days I just wandered disconsolately about the ruins of the city. It was all so very different from what I had known before. One of the attractions of the old Tokyo had been the hundreds of little tea-shops and cafés into which one could drop and spend an hour chatting with a friend, or sit listening to the gramophone. Now they had gone; and even if one did by chance run into an old acquaintance (and this was now beginning to happen) there was nowhere to take him.

Most of these places were about the Ginza, which used to be the main shopping district. Before the war it was ablaze with neon lights until the early hours of the morning; now it is ghostly and deserted as soon as darkness falls. But during the day, despite the crumbling pavements and the litter it still has a trace of its former tawdry gaiety; some magnet-like attraction seems to draw the crowds from long-formed habit. And how shabby they look! Most of the women wear *mompei*, rather ugly baggy trousers normally worn only when working in the fields. They are doubtless very practical, but nothing could more accentuate the aesthetic deficiencies of the Japanese woman's figure, which only the traditional kimono can decently conceal. Many of the men, since they have nothing else, are still in uniform, stripped, of course, of its badges; otherwise they wear the drab suits of olive-khaki shoddy which the military tried to make obligatory during the war.

It is an almost daily experience to be stopped in the street by some complete stranger and asked if one has anything to sell. One day I was followed all the way home by a man who pestered me to sell him the shoes I was wearing. He offered me an absurdly high price but when I refused he immediately raised it and continued to do so until finally I shook him off on the doorstep. . .

Although the main Ginza street was badly damaged and disappeared, many of the shops have disappeared, many things could still be bought. There is a great deal of tawdry junk on display which seems to have been manufactured specially to appeal to the unsophisticated GI's taste. It is very expensive, quite worthless, and, for the most part, in execrable taste. Yet there is so much of it on sale that I wonder whether it has all been manufactured since the war ended.

A sort of black market is carried on quite openly on both sides of the Ginza, on the pavements in front of the bombed-out stores. Most of the stuff is food and household utensils, but there are also shoes and a good deal of second-hand clothing. The prices are exorbitant, but there seems no dearth of buyers. Except for the basic food ration (which, by itself, is barely sufficient to sustain life) there appears to be no sort of price control, and the black market is the normal means of shopping. The occupation (which is, of course, a charge on the Japanese Government) is being paid for by the simple expedient of printing more and more paper money. This tends to drive the price of commodities ever upwards and to encourage a perfect orgy of spending. Meanwhile, a large proportion of the people does no work; it is not worthwhile when money has so little value. . .

A very few of the Ginza shops are still intact, and in the window of one, which used to be Tokyo's most fashionable hatter, I noticed an English silk hat, together with a bowler. Later on in the afternoon I saw both hats on the heads of two American sailors, much to the astonishment of the strolling Japanese. Towards the evening I saw both these hats again; they had been crushed in and lay discarded in the gutter.

*   *   *

Coming home late one night after visiting some friends, I had to wait some time on a distant Underground station. I was alone, and the station was deserted. After I had been there for perhaps fifteen minutes a solitary Japanese came slowly and unsteadily down the stairs. He was not exactly drunk but had reached that stage when the legs are slightly out of control.

The average Japanese does not distinguish between the various allied uniforms, so although I was wearing British battle-dress it was no surprise when he mistook me. 'Come here, you American soldier,' he said in a threatening voice. 'You "hairy ones" may think you have won the war, but we Japanese are not so easily defeated.'

I did not, of course, reply, and started to walk away; but thinking that perhaps I did not understand Japanese he did what many of us do in talking to a 'stupid' foreigner; he repeated the sentence slowly and at the top of his voice. While I was wondering what to do he stood there glaring through his spectacles which, I noticed, had slipped forward on his nose, giving him a somewhat clownish appearance. And then he made a sudden rush and gripped me. He was a good deal smaller than I, and I was not afraid that he could knock me down. But every Japanese has a certain skill at *judo*, of which I knew nothing; and as we stood there locked together it occurred to me that he was manoeuvring to throw me on to the live electric line. I knew very well that my greater physical strength would give me no advantage.

While we were locked in this ridiculous embrace. I became aware that another passenger, also slightly inebriated, had joined us. 'I Korean; American's friend,' he shouted, and pulled the Japanese away. Just at this moment the train came in and the young Korean (I afterwards learned that he had been a soldier) made one, wild rush at the Japanese and knocked him completely out. As the train started to move out of the station I noticed that he still lay unconscious on the platform.

This incident is in itself of no importance; it is only worth relating because during the time of my stay in Japan it was the only sign of resenting defeat that I came across. I have since often wondered whether, behind the Japanese smile of politeness, there is not a great deal of smouldering resentment. If there is not (and certainly I could find no evidence) then the Japanese are in this respect even more odd than the rest of the world imagines.

On the journey out to Japan I worried a good deal about the sort of reception I should get. I had felt that my more intimate friends might at first feel slightly embarrassed to meet me, but that this would quickly pass, and we could then take up where we had left off in 1942. It turned out to be exactly as I had hoped and imagined; defeat had had the effect of separating the goats from the sheep. My real friends behaved with a truly civilized diffidence, waiting for me to intimate that the war had made no difference to our friendship; the others, the superficial acquaintances, crowded round for recommendations for employment, and explained volubly that food and cigarettes were in very short supply. They usually called upon me at meal-times.

It is very strange, this entire lack of resentment; and also very disarming, because already there is a feeling that the country is occupied not by a victorious army but by a horde of honoured tourists. It was not so in the first few months of the occupation. The present army consists mostly of very young men, few of whom saw any combat service. It is the first time that the majority of them have been away from home; and the ties and restrictions of family life, which in normal conditions are loosened gradually, have been cast aside with thoughtless speed. Only the man of exceptional character can remain unaffected by these conditions. Japanese friends have told me that the troops who first came in, at the time of the surrender, were far more dignified; they had all seen service in the Pacific, and although they were not particularly friendly, there was behind their attitude of frigid toughness a feeling of fair-play and human kindness which, to the Japanese, was truly impressive. If these men had stayed, fraternization might have developed along very different lines.

I believe in fraternization, provided it is properly controlled and not construed merely as an opportunity for sexual promiscuity. In Japan it could help greatly in the introduction of democratic ideas, which can never be taught by the mere issue of formal directives.

It is unfortunate that in Japan fraternization has developed in such a way that the ordinary American soldier has little chance of being received in decent middle-class families. It is not that the soldier does not wish it; but the behaviour of the more conspicuous minority has been such that no decent Japanese is willing, to put the matter bluntly, to risk having his daughter seduced. Yet one must in fairness state that in many ways the Japanese are themselves to blame.

*   *   *

The Tokyo Symphony Orchestra was kept going all through the war. It was never at any time a first-class orchestra. Nevertheless, it did a useful job in familiarizing the Japanese with the classical repertoire. Like everything else, however, it came under the control of the militarists and was forced to confine its wartime concerts to programmes consisting entirely of military marches by Japanese composers.

Mr Josef Rosenstock, who did so much to improve the standard of playing until, as an anti-Nazi German, the Japanese interned him, is once again the permanent conductor, but he is struggling against every kind of difficulty. Even in the months before the war it had almost become impossible to obtain spare strings and reeds for the instruments, which were already beginning to deteriorate. Moreover, many of the best players have now resigned. It was difficult for them to resist the much higher salaries which they could earn by playing in one or other of the numerous dance bands attached to the various American officers' clubs.

The orchestra is now partly sponsored by the Occupation authorities and gives concerts to the troops every Sunday afternoon and occasionally during the week. The programmes are all selected in accordance with the troops' requests. Rosenstock told me that he felt very depressed when this arrangement was first suggested; he foresaw himself conducting an almost unending series of Strauss waltzes and the like. The hall is packed at every performance with men listening with complete absorption to the most unlikely programmes. There was not a single request for the lighter items, and the Brahms' symphonies were in the greatest demand. . .

At one of these concerts I heard a performance of Verdi's *Requiem*. The orchestra played exceptionally well, and the singing, by a vast choir of Japanese schoolboys who had rehearsed for several weeks, was so youthfully fresh and sincere that the performance was extremely moving. On another occasion I heard Elgar's *Enigma Variations* played for the first time in Japan. This, I now recollect, had been banned when its performance was proposed just before the war.

JOHN MORRIS, despite his status as a foreign correspondent, was treated in very surly fashion by an Australian officer when he first visited BCOF. He found conditions in the British zone 'extremely uncomfortable'. He did not think that the Americans were responsible for this situation. The fact was that the troops were brought in before any base facilities had been provided. 'The landing of the Australians was treated as if it were a combat operation, and it was so badly organized that for some time the arrival of supply ships was irregular . . . There seemed also to be a feeling, which was sometimes vaguely expressed by Australian officers, that in order to be efficient it is necessary also to be uncomfortable'.

One port in the British Commonwealth zone which he visited was Otake in Yamaguchi prefecture. Here he saw the arrival of Japanese forces returning from overseas:-

•

When I was there the *Yuki Kaze*, a battered and rusty old cruiser, had just come in from Bangkok. She was lying offshore and we went out in a launch to board her. Most of the prisoners looked ill and dejected and very definitely less well-fed than people in Japan. It was an incredibly lovely day and all around us were pine-clad islands which seemed to float in the opal-coloured bay. Across the bay was Miyajima... Some of these prisoners, I thought, must in the past have been here on a pilgrimage, but now they just stood on the decks like cattle, waiting for someone to give them orders. Their eyes had a peculiarly dead expression; it was as though they could no longer see into the distance. Although they answered my questions willingly enough, all seemed strangely apathetic. Not one expressed joy at coming home.

In the wardroom we were given Japanese tea and cigarettes, and the few formalities were soon completed. Meanwhile, a fleet of barges had come alongside and into these the prisoners were herded without regard to rank. We passed them in our quicker launch. Even then, as they were about to set foot on their homeland after so long an absence, there was not the slightest sign of emotion; they just sat there quiet and tense, as though this were a combat landing on some enemy island. Perhaps that is what, in their minds, Japan had now become.

Each prisoner had been allowed to bring back two hundred and fifty pounds of personal belongings, and they now formed up for their kits to be inspected. Most of the stuff was the remnants of military uniform, but nearly every man had also a bottle of quinine. One or two had even an English book and some had brought pathetic little souvenirs to give their relatives...

The proceedings ended with a final inspection by the New Zealand officer in charge. A few of the men had somehow managed to retain their badges of rank. These were now taken from them and destroyed in their presence. The prisoners had now been officially repatriated. They were no longer soldiers, but civilians, and were now quite free to order their own lives. When this was explained to them and they were told to dismiss, most of them seemed bewildered and just stood on the vast parade ground, not quite knowing what to do. They reminded me of a pack of stray dogs that had been rounded up and then let go. They still did not speak to one another, expecting some further order, and it was only when we started to walk away that they began to drift off, dragging their kits across the sandy ground. Most them went singly; they seemed suspicious of each other. The herd instinct, which had kept them together for so many years, seemed suddenly to have been destroyed. It had been replaced by something else, and something peculiarly Japanese; the fear of not behaving correctly in a situation which had been unforeseen.

There was also another secret fear, one which had been hidden in the minds of these men for months. It, too, had now to be faced... all were faced with the same problem, that of whether or not families would receive them back. The Japanese, underneath their veneer of formal etiquette, are highly emotional, and it would be absurd to suppose that the relatives of these men would not welcome them with love and affection. . . So many other prisoners had already been returned that the conception of captivity as the ultimate disgrace had largely disappeared. But as I watched these men shamble off to their billets their weary and expressionless faces seemed to express these lurking fears.

ANOTHER CIVILIAN who returned to Japan as cultural adviser to the United Kingdom Liaison Mission in Japan was the author and poet EDMUND BLUNDEN who had made many friends in Japan before the war. In his book *A Wanderer in Japan* (Asahi Shimbunsha, 1950) he described the Japanese rural scene as he viewed it from the train. He was struck by the large numbers of Japanese working in the fields without at that stage any machinery to help them, but it was the ruins of Tokyo that left the most indelible impression on him:-

•

The Tokyo which I formerly knew was in ruins, after the earthquake and the fire, though some districts had been spared; and now I was coming again to a desolated and incinerated city. I cannot say, in the light of the memories I now brought, that I was surprised at the destruction which I found. If surprise arose, it was rather at discovering that there were some parts of the city which had not been battered down and burned. Among these, the group of buildings in which I was to have my home was standing, like a cluster of rocks at the edge of a discoloured sea.

The wilderness near our door, with all its broken stones, its shattered pavings, meaningless gateways, and other symbols of life extinguished by the forces of ruin, spoke with accents of grief and mourning. It was impossible to walk fifty yards without some sense that, here and there, something intolerable had befallen a household, and that the innocent and kind hearted had suffered pains not easy to tell.

When I had the infinite comfort of seeing once more one of my oldest and ever most understanding friends, – I had not dared to tell myself that he still lived, – I heard by degrees of one of these calamities. *He* still lived, and nobly lives; but *she*, most selfless and sweet of all human natures, had not come through that fatal hour. Nor was that the entire tale of the miseries which the demons of ruin had so swiftly inflicted on my friend's house and home.

Hundreds of thousands of people totally unknown to me seemed to be telling me quietly and simply, while the evening airs rustled among the dry and reeds in the dead gardens, of hateful tragedies. I was made acquainted with the plans and wishes of many years of care and self-denial, all gone to nothing. . .

A SARDONIC AND generally anti-American view of Japan in the latter days of the Occupation was given by HONOR TRACY in her book *Kakemono: A Sketch Book of Post-War Japan* (Methuen, 1950). She began by describing Tokyo in the following way:-

●

Tokyo is two cities, two conceptions, unreconciled and even hostile. . . Merely by standing before the Palace and looking first in one direction and then in another, you may get a vivid sense of this split in the Japanese mind; but the Ginza is the place to study it, in all its horrid confusion. Amplifiers placed at intervals along the street indiscriminately bawl out a Beethoven symphony, an American dance hit, a *geisha* song or a chant from a *Noh* play. Often you may see two girls walking together, one in native, one in Western, dress. The first is a graceful little creature dressed in colours that, however bright, are always harmonious, who trips along on her clogs as lightly as a young deer. The second wears a short dress, giving full value to each awkward lump in her figure, and shapeless shoes a size or two too large, to which the eye is guided by a pair of bright green or pink bobby socks. They seem to belong to different races but, very likely, they are sisters. Business men drive up and down, honking fiercely at the pedestrians, while the rickshaw men pad silently along in bare feet. Here and there are old-style Japanese shops selling books and colour prints, or works of art and craftsmanship, quiet pleasant places, with dwarf trees planted in beautiful or curious pots outside the door, and silk cushions strewn about on the rush matting inside, where the customer may rest and consider a purchase in the leisurely style of old days. The stalls jostling each other on the kerb outside, each only a few feet wide, are crammed with all the ignoble knick-knacks and gewgaws that the ingenuity of Japanese manufacturers can devise. There are tiny booths and imposing department stores. Dance-halls advertise 'Avec-time To-Nite'. Avec-time is a great new attraction, where the lights in the hall are lowered and the young men, with their stickily pomaded hair, and the girls, with their garish make-up, press their cheeks tightly together and circle the floor, an expression of near imbecility on their faces.

*   *   *

The *pompom* girls are another depressing feature of contemporary life in the capital. *Pompom* is a word from the southern regions meaning stomach, and the name is applied to girls who go with foreign soldiers for the sake of food, cigarettes and sweets. They are a squalid tribe of harpies, loud of voice, vulgar and without manners of any kind and, while there seems to be nothing Japanese left in them, they somehow contrive to be

more degraded than any European whore. In the daytime, they stroll
about in cheap, smart dresses from the PX, noisily talking and laughing,
almost invariably chewing gum, or enraging hungry citizens in trains and
buses by a display of their ill-gotten gains; and at night they lead a furtive
little existence, plying their trade in dark corners and doorways, pursued
by foreign and Japanese police alike, but sure of their clientele. Walking
late in the evening through those parts of Tokyo frequented by the
troops, you will come on some very remarkable sights indeed. No over-
fed and idle men stationed as conquerors in a foreign country can be
expected to behave as they would at home, but for the brutality of their
ways they surpassed anything I have seen, and added to it a kind of nau-
seating exhibitionism which is apparently special to themselves.

*   *   *

Life in Tokyo follows the pattern of life in any defeated or occupied capital. People who counted before, are today ruined and forgotten. Affairs
are in the hands of men too obscure or too ambitious to be afraid of
collaborating. The former ruling class lives from the sale of such valu-
ables as remain to it, heirlooms, household treasures and, finally, their
wardrobes; they call it the onion life because every time they peel off a
coat, they cry a little more. . . Wealth and power, if not prestige, have
passed into the hands of a set known as the 'new-yen' people, who have
risen to the top in the economic chaos following the collapse and who are
now in control of the hugely ramified black market. There is the usual
flood of sensational and pornographic literature, and a crop of earnest,
short-lived political magazines that veer uncertainly from one extremist
point of view to another. For the great majority of the people, the only
concern is to get food enough to keep body and soul together. The women go regularly out to the countryside around and buy surreptitiously
from the farmers, who, after the manner of their kind everywhere, make
a good thing out of the city's distress. These forays are a hazardous undertaking because, on the way home, the traffickers are liable to be pounced
on by the railway police and to have their booty taken from them.

2

Nostalgia for Pre-war Japan

MAJOR GENERAL F.S.G. PIGGOTT • FRANK ASHTON-GWATKIN

THE BRITISH who came to Japan in the immediate post-war years had few illusions about Japan's militarists. They hoped that Japan's new democracy would succeed, but many were doubtful. They were generally concerned by the poverty and destruction they found and many of them sought to establish friendships with individual Japanese.

There remained in Britain a small number of Japanophiles who had a nostalgia for the Japan they had known in the early years of the twentieth century. They recalled in particular the period of the Anglo-Japanese Alliance as a golden age of Anglo-Japanese friendship when Britain and Japan cooperated closely, or so they thought. They preferred to overlook the worst excesses of Japan's pre-war leaders and viewed the life they had led in pre-war Japan through rose-tinted spectacles.

The leading nostalgic Japanophile was Major General F.S.G. PIGGOTT, known to most of us young war-time students of Japanese at the School of Oriental and African Studies (SOAS) as simply 'the General'. General Piggott (1883-1966) was the son of Sir Francis Piggott (1852-1925) who had been legal adviser to the Japanese government. An account of their lives has been given by Dr Carmen Blacker in *Britain and Japan: 1859-1991: Themes and Personalities* edited by Sir Hugh Cortazzi and Dr Gordon Daniels, published by Routledge in 1991.

General Piggott's affection for Japan was undoubtedly genuine. He had worked hard at learning the Japanese language, spoken and written, and his knowledge of it was outstanding for his time. He was an upright soldier and a gentleman in the best sense of the term, but he was, it has to be said, a bit of a snob especially in relation to the Japanese pre-war aristocracy. His judgement regarding Japanese politics was at best shallow and often blind. I recall being told by the late Sir Arthur de la Mare, who served in Tokyo before the war, that relations between the Embassies in Japan and China became acrimonious over the different way in which Japanese behaviour in Shanghai was reported to London. General Piggott simply would not believe that the Japanese military were behaving atrociously. So, eventually, it was suggested that General Piggott, who was then Military Attaché in Tokyo, should visit Shanghai to see for himself. According to Arthur de la Mare Piggott is reported to have declared sadly: 'How the Japanese Army have let me down!'

In the difficult years after the war General Piggott was indefatigable in his efforts on behalf of his Japanese friends. He particularly deplored the conviction and execution of General Homma for war crimes in the Philippines. He declared (see Carmen Blacker's piece cited above) that Homma '. . . loved England more than any Japanese officer'. He was also incensed by the conviction by the International War Crimes Tribunal in Tokyo and subsequent imprisonment of Mamoru Shigemitsu who had been Japanese Ambassador in London at the outbreak of the Pacific War. General Piggott worked hard to revive the Japan Society in which in pre-war days he had been an advocate of Japanese policies in China.

The Japanese authorities greatly appreciated General Piggott's efforts at a time when they had few friends left in Britain. Accordingly, in 1955 Mamoru Shigemitsu, then Foreign Minister, invited him and his daughter to visit Japan as his guests. In a lecture to the Japan Society in June that year he gave a detailed account of his visit. The following excerpts underline the warm welcome he received and the depth of his affection for the old Japan he had known.

PIGGOTT began by writing: '. . . the physical and mental strain, and still more the emotional and psychological strain of this Great Adventure (as it may fairly be called) was quite exceptional but he was helped by '. . . the unceasing solicitude and consideration of the innumerable Japanese friends who surrounded and overwhelmed me with their affection and hospitality.' Then:-

●

A foretaste of what was to come occurred on Friday night, 6 May, two days after leaving London, when our SAS plane landed at Haneda Airport. Just before this, with the lights of Tokyo stretching out below, Juliet said 'Daddy, do you suppose that the Foreign Minister will be here to meet us?'; 'Of course not,' I replied – knowing full well that he would! However, as we touched down and the doors opened, I warned her to be prepared; and there he was, faithful and dear friend, great Statesman and great Gentleman. It was one of those rare moments in one's life when all the past seems to be concentrated in the present: neither of us could speak as we grasped hands – the cameramen had an unusually favourable opportunity for their work – and thoughts of what had happened to us both since our last meeting fifteen years ago passed through our minds. Mr Shigemitsu was accompanied by his daughter, Hanako, who acts as his official hostess owing to her mother's frail health; she and Juliet made friends instantaneously.

In a reserved enclosure a group of about twenty friends clustered round us: recent members of the Japanese Embassy in London and visitors to England; Tokyo friends from before the War; older ones from the years after the First War, and of times still more remote. From the reserved enclosure we passed to a larger group outside the barrier, a cross-section of those who were once part of our lives. There were two features of this warm welcome: one, that among the ladies present, none wore bright colours – a delicate note of sympathy [Mrs Piggott had recently died]; and another, that many friends of days now long past were represented by the second and even third generations of their families.

It was nearly midnight when we arrived at the Imperial Hotel, unchanged from of yore, and with a dignity and aloofness all its own.

* * *

It was nearly three in the morning before I had unpacked and turned out my light, with several matters still unsettled. I think it was at this precise moment that my brain registered clearly the fact that the Japanese language had returned to me in fuller measure than I could have conceived possible; and this was just as well, as within forty-eight hours I was broadcasting to the nation.

* * *

I feel it necessary to answer the question that may be in the minds of many of you: 'WHY?' Why, in fact, was I, a retired General of no particular eminence, in Tokyo at all; and here let me emphasize that I had no official instructions or position whatever – I was a private individual. Why therefore was I about to receive a welcome from all classes, from the Emperor downwards, that was almost unprecedented? Part of the answer to the question is to be found in the brief account of the reception at the Airport, and the reference to the second and third generations. My wife's friendships in Japan began forty-five years ago, and my own from childhood. That was the main reason why not only Mr Shigemitsu and the Government, but the late Prime Minister, Mr Yoshida, were anxious that I should come. To put it succinctly, if Mr Yoshida had been in power he would have invited me; there was no secret about this, it was common knowledge.

* * *

Many Japanese whom I knew well, and many whom I did not know at all, insisted in letters and verbally that our name was known so well that the frequent references to our doings in the press and on the radio interested 'everyone'. I heard many echoes of my broadcasts, and of an appearance on Television with the Foreign Minister; while press interviews were of daily occurrence in Tokyo, and also during our brief stays at Nikko, Osaka, Kyoto and Gifu.

* * *

Among our engagements, three stand out in a very special category: an intimate private tea-party in their own apartments given by Their Majesties themselves, a full-dress dinner-party by the Crown Prince, and a small select luncheon-party by Princess Chichibu, at which Prince Mikasa, the Emperor's youngest brother, was present.

It is, perhaps, permissible to refer briefly to the occasion when Juliet and I took tea with the Emperor and Empress. Once again, after many years, I talked freely in his own language to His Majesty: in appearance and manner he was little changed, and all the old charm was there. And I seemed to detect something more: for as the minutes passed the expressions that he used, and the turns of phrase, became more and more intimate and easy – there was clear indication of pleasure and even happiness. I am proud indeed to have had this rare privilege of over an hour's conversation with the Ruler of the Japanese Nation, whom adversity and his own strength of character has moulded into one of the Great Figures of History.

GENERAL PIGGOTT also enjoyed dinner with the Crown Prince when Princess Chichibu acted as hostess. 'The Princess and many others made no secret of their admiration and respect for our own Royal Family, and of their wish to emulate them and follow their example, especially as regards public duties, social customs and Palace administration.'

An early engagement was an official dinner in his honour given by the Foreign Minister. Another was a dinner given by the Japan-British Society. He was also entertained to dinner by ex-Prime Minister Shigeru Yoshida at his 'country house' at Oiso. 'The late Prime Minister was the picture of health, and good spirits, much engrossed with his big dogs and his little dogs, and also with his strawberries- "I intend to become a millionaire by skilful cultivation of these," he informed his guests with gusto.'

At the Tokyo Club where some 100 members collected one afternoon to greet him: 'Just before I left there was a poignant moment when a retired Admiral led the company in "For he's a jolly good fellow"; could it be true, I thought, that this was 1955 and not forty years ago, when such an occurrence would have been quite normal? The war seemed far away, or as if it had never been.'

GENERAL PIGGOTT gave two tea parties, one primarily for officers of the Japanese army: 'I invited, with official cognizance, Marshal Hata and General Baron Araki, who both came from Sugamo [where they were serving sentences for war crimes] on parole':-

●

There was no awkwardness or constraint, indeed their mutual pleasure and satisfaction was unconcealed.

So also was the happiness at their reunion of many friends who met again at one or other of these parties; the confusion and destruction in Tokyo, and breakdown of communications had caused the permanent disappearance of numerous friends from one another's lives. Many gaps were filled and breaks repaired on those two afternoons; it will always be a source of pride to me that in a minor way I played some part in the happy ending of many inevitable separations and estrangements.

* * *

You will want to hear something about the changes that have taken place in Tokyo. These are less marked than I had expected. Certainly there are more people in the streets (and in the shops, the trains, the trams, and the stations), and there are more motor-cars with their accompanying noise. But by and large the great city seemed to have developed rather than changed its character. The little side-streets and alleys, with their many shops, were as I remembered them, and I had little difficulty in finding familiar landmarks. Even the neighbourhood of Prince Ito's Tomb at the suburb of Omori (where I placed a wreath in the presence of the present Prince) was as it used to be. One change I am constrained to refer to with regret: the bronze statues of three great soldiers of the Russo-Japanese War – Yamagata, Oyama and Terauchi – had been removed from their plinths near the Diet. More than this, where Terauchi stood are now three unclothed young women; it was not clear to me, nor, indeed, to many Japanese whom I questioned, whom exactly they represented; but perhaps they will have disappeared before long and the famous soldier be replaced.

The former common sight of parties of school-children under their teachers paying their respects to the Emperor before one of the entrances to the Palace, disciplined and decorous, was as of yore – except, indeed, that the parties seemed larger, and more numerous.

This increase was even more noticeable at Nikko, where we spent two days, walking once again round the immemorial Temples. The station-master, successor to several others I had known, said that 'thousands' of students and schoolchildren passed through on sightseeing expeditions every day, during eight or nine months of the year. The Kanaya Hotel still stands, as popular now as before, during, and immediately after the War. Mr Kanaya himself, with his gentle and devoted wife, is frail in body but alert in mind; we talked of many things, which perhaps may one day be published. Of course Juliet and I went up to Chuzenji; with the widow of our old boatman, we stood by our old house on the shores of the Lake Beautiful . . . I saw, as in a dream, yacht races of the past, with Sir Claude MacDonald at the tiller of *The Ark*; I saw my three children as they grew up; and I saw my dear wife too. Juliet and I did not stay very long. . .

Let me sum up: as regards the people themselves there was no doubt left in my mind that the old virtues of courtesy, cheerfulness, and industry are even more pronounced than before. The War is over and seldom mentioned; the Japanese nation faces the unknown future with confidence. There is intense vitality, seen on the ground and felt in the air; everyone, from the Imperial Family down to the maids and page-boys in the hotels, the porters on the railways, and the men and women in the fields, is alert, determined and getting on with their job.

Another important fact struck me: three weeks may not be a long. time in which to form an opinion, but nevertheless, by applying previous knowledge to the innumerable personal contacts I am fortunate enough to possess in a complete cross-section of the nation of all generations and classes, I am convinced that there is a powerful though latent, repeat 'latent,' feeling of respect, admiration, and even affection, for Great Britain. This only requires encouragement to become an active and potent element in restoring Anglo-Japanese relations to a point not far from the pinnacle they attained in the early years of the century, and which some of us still remember. The evidence for this opinion is absolute and conclusive; but we should not wait too long before taking steps to turn this latent feeling into something more. Of course there are various ways, as obvious to you as to me; so let us pursue them together. Need I add that this subject, Anglo-Japanese relations, was the principal topic which my host and I discussed at great length and with the utmost freedom – as befits personal friends – during the many, many hours of intimate conversation that we had alone together.

FRANK ASHTON-GWATKIN, better known, perhaps, as John Paris, the name he adopted when writing novels in a Japanese setting, such as *Kimono*, joined the Japan Consular Service in 1913 (see 'In One Day I Have Lived Many Lives: Frank Ashton-Gwatkin, Novelist and Diplomat, (1889-1976)' by Ian Nish in *Biographical Portraits* (vol I), edited by Ian Nish and published by Japan Library 1994). He revisited Japan for the first time after the war in 1974. He spoke to the Japan Society about this visit in April 1975 (Bulletin No 76). As Sir John Pilcher, a former British Ambassador to Japan, said in introducing Ashton-Gwatkin to his audience: 'His successful and brilliant novels have revealed a love for Japan which continues until the present day.'

After quoting a Japanese poem ASHTON-GWATKIN explained that Japan first came into his life when he was five years old at the time of the Sino-Japanese war of 1894 when Japan '. . . became visible as a power, a minor power, in the then modern world'. He felt that 'the great fundamental problem of the Far East' lay in '. . . the difficulties and contradictions between the two great Eastern protagonists' which must ultimately be solved.

He explained his earliest memories of Japan:-

•

E ighty-one years ago, I was given a Japanese doll to whom I was much attached – the only doll in my life. My father called him Marshal Yamagata. I did not know why. Twenty years later I was escorting the authentic Prince Yamagata to his box at the Imperial Theatre in Tokyo. He was old and lean and unsmiling, about the same age as I am today. Yes: I have seen or been presented to two of the original *genrō* (elder statesmen), Yamagata and Matsukata. Itō and Inouye were dead before I arrived in Japan but I met Count Okuma and Prince Saionji, who were, as it were, junior *genrō*. I have been presented at an Imperial Garden Party to Admiral Tōgō, the victor of the Tsushima battle which was Japan's Trafalgar. I attended the funeral of Prince Tokugawa Keiki, the last *shōgun* of the Tokugawa line actually to rule from Yedo, which is now Tokyo, over feudal Japan.

* * *

And in England I have visited and taken tea with another very old man, Sir Ernest Satow, as old as I am now – in a green tweed tail coat and attended by Saburo, his Japanese butler, living in retirement at Ottery St Mary. He had seen the processions of the *daimyō*, the *norimono*, the two-sworded samurai. He had seen the last act in the Tokugawa drama, and the first act in the Meiji Restoration. He had been Minister in Tokyo and in Peking. He was a notable scholar in the Japanese language.

* * *

In 1905 I was given the first book which told me about the home-life of the Japanese people. Here it is – the very book: *Kokoro* by Lafcadio Hearn. And in 1910 I visited the Japanese Exhibition at Shepherd's Bush [White City] and was thrilled by the exquisite beauty of Japanese artistic fabrics of all kinds.

When I went to Oxford in 1908, I met a Japanese for the first time. He was Keimin Matsudaira, afterwards Chamberlain to the Emperor, then an undergraduate at Balliol College. I did not know him well, but I liked what I knew. Four years later, I met him again in Japan.

I had not chosen Japan. Japan had chosen me. In the period of a young man's despair – everything going wrong – I had taken (for the second time) the Foreign Office Entrance examination. I failed; but I had done fairly well, and the Foreign Office offered me a Student Interpretership in the specialized Japan Consular Service. It meant a lifetime to be spent very far from England and I was delighted. To me it meant independence and security and a new world.

And that is what I owe to Japan – my career in diplomacy, my marriage (at Christ Church, Yokohama April, 1915 – just sixty years ago) and, but this was a by-blow, my success as a novelist.

I was in Tokyo for two years, attached as student interpreter to the British Embassy; three years at Yokohama as Consular Assistant; and one year in Singapore as Japanese adviser to the General Officer Commanding. Then, after six years' absence, I returned to England – a very different person to a very different England. I was taken over by the Foreign Office and I worked at the Japanese desk for ten years.

In 1929 I was appointed Acting Counsellor to our first Embassy to Soviet Russia. I had had sixteen years of Japanese experience in Japan and in England. And in 1929 came the Wall Street crash, and the bottom fell out of the artificial world which had existed since the end of the First World War.

But to return to the beginning of my life in Japan, to the year 1913, the year before the deluge. Japan was very, very far away. It had taken me six weeks by slow boat from Tilbury to Kobe, touching at Gibraltar, Port Said, Aden, Colombo, Penang, Singapore, Hongkong, Shanghai – all of them then, in fact, British ports. In 1974, except for Gibraltar and Hongkong, there were no more British ports on the way to Japan. In 1974, I flew from London to Tokyo in about twenty-four hours, almost all the way across the desolate vastness of Siberia.

In 1913, I had found Japan at the end of its stage of emergence from a feudal state of the Middle Ages – mainly agricultural. Tokyo, Osaka, Yokohama, Nagoya, Kobe and Moji were the only modern industrial towns, and even they were more like clusters of native villages than like modern cities. Japan's principal exports were of textiles, of cotton and silk fabrics and of raw silk. The idea of Japan becoming one of the world's principal manufacturers of ships, motor cars, machinery and machine tools, chemicals, electronics of all kinds was quite fantastic. Why? Japan could scarcely manage to make a bicycle. The quality of Japanese goods was notoriously cheap and shoddy. Only in cotton textiles Japan was already in competition with Lancashire; a sore point in Anglo-Japanese relations.

Apart from that, the two nations appeared to be friendly; and in foreign affairs Japan took her lead from England – everywhere except as regards China. Just two months after my arrival in Tokyo, a Mr Abe, head of the China Section of the Foreign Office, was assassinated on leaving his office by a 'patriot' in protest against the tameness of the Government's policy in China. This came as a shock and a surprise to me, for such things did not happen in Downing Street.

*   *   *

Since the Great Surrender of 1945, Japan has been on her best behaviour and has been richly rewarded. It is a rule, I believe, of *ju-jutsu* to yield where pressure comes; and for the last thirty years (almost), as far as foreign policy is concerned, Japan has obediently followed the lead of the conqueror, the USA. With a whole country to rebuild and to equip with the latest machinery, with military expenditure forbidden, with American military occupation enlarged and increased with the advent of the Korean War, with unlimited credit from American sources, and with immense drive and energy in her working classes of all degrees, Japan has raised herself up from ruin to the position of the second or third greatest industrial and commercial country in the world.

This is a miracle which I wanted very much to see. I was enabled to see something of it through the kindness and courtesy of Japan Airlines, the *Yomiuri Shimbun* and The Japan Travel Bureau for the occasion of the Golden Wedding of The Emperor and Empress.

I saw Tokyo (population now ten million compared with one million in my day) where the geographical configuration is still the same – like an enormous spider's web spun round the central mystery of the Emperor's moated palace. All the rest of the city had been refashioned on quasi-American lines (the Coca-Cola period of Japanese architecture) with roadways and subways interwoven in tier over tier, impressive in its way and redeemed by the beauty of the Japanese script. A city teeming like an anthill; and buzzing with taxis and private cars and lorries and omnibuses (the rickshas and the clanking trams of my day have vanished). Very few men wear kimono now although they put them on with relief when they get home; but the women (of whom far more are now in circulation) have not entirely discarded their gracious national dress.

I was most tenderly looked after by my hosts. They even supplied a personal attendant, the charming Miss Jill Bull, to guide my tottering steps and to record my appointments. My old friends were dead; but their children remember me and welcomed and entertained me.

I was not expected (thank goodness) to attend geisha dinners, which are the regulation entertainment, paid for from expense accounts, for eminent businessmen visiting Japan.

I went by train to Yokohama, which was quite unrecognizable; and to Kamakura, where Daibutsu, the Great Buddha, still reigns untroubled and aloof in his wood-enshrouded valley. At my special request, I spent three days in Kyoto, one of the world's loveliest cities, still prevalently Japanese and comparatively unviolated. In its temples and temple gardens, remote from coca-coladom, the spirit of traditional Japan still breathes and broods. All is not lost. [Ashton-Gwatkin had been out of touch with Japan for over forty years.]

And then the Emperor and Empress came to England on their state visit in 1971. And I was disinterred. Someone had discovered that I was still alive, the last British survivor from the Emperor's last visit as Crown

Prince in 1921. I like to think that this second journey was his own choosing, because he had liked our country then and wanted to see it once more and to show it to his Empress – a treat well-deserved after the appalling strains and stresses of his reign. In a very special sense, Japan's emergence is due to the Emperor's survival.

*   *   *

The Emperor of Japan, by nature a modest and retiring Professor of Marine Biology, has never been a war-lord; but in spite of his own rescript he is still a God; and he is the Foundation Stone of their great and growing prosperity.

THE LATE Sir John Pilcher told me that General Piggott was the only person he knew who believed in the divinity of the Japanese Emperor. Ashton-Gwatkin apparently shared this mistaken belief. [Ed.]

3

'Return of a Native'

DOROTHY BRITTON

DOROTHY BRITTON was born in Japan before the war and returned there during the Occupation. She became a writer, translator, composer and musician. Over many decades she has been a bridge between Japanese and English cultures. Her account of how this happened makes fascinating reading and connects pre-war times, the Occupation and modern Japan:-

•

I was born in Japan – a BIJ as they used to call them then – the result of my parents' fortuitous romantic encounter. Alice Hiller, from San Francisco, had always felt the 'call of the East', and when a friend left her some money she decided to spend it travelling to China to further her study of Chinese art – disregarding the advice of her eldest brother, who urged her to invest the money 'toward her old age', being quite sure he foresaw almost certain old maidhood for his thirty-nine-year-old sister.

Passenger liners en route to Shanghai usually made a three-day call in Yokohama, and on her first afternoon there, Alice met Frank Britton, a bachelor two years her senior, who had arrived in Japan from England about fifteen years earlier as a very young chief engineer on a Japanese cargo ship, and had remained in the country, founding a thriving engineering company. He fell in love with Alice – an amateur musician like himself, with whom he had much in common – and followed her to Shanghai on the very next steamer, where they were married, in spite of a cable from Alice's hidebound brother enquiring whether she was out of her mind, 'marrying a foreigner in a heathen land'.

Frank and Alice chose to live among the Japanese, in a suburb of Yokohama, rather than on 'The Bluff' where the Americans and Europeans congregated with little or no contact with the indigenous population except for their servants. Frank, fluent in the language, had many Japanese friends, and Alice was agog to learn more of the land, its culture and its people. They summered in the almost exclusively Japanese seaside resort of Hayama, whereas most other Westerners flocked to the mountain resorts of Karuizawa and Nojiri.

Naturally, Frank and Alice saw to it that I, their only child, learned to speak Japanese. The local vernacular school they chose would not accept foreigners, so in addition to private lessons in music and French, I had a Japanese tutor is well. But since retired school teacher Mrs Iwamoto's husband worked for my father, she was loth to make the boss's daughter work as hard as she should have.

By the time my father died suddenly when I was twelve, and I left Japan with my mother to go to boarding school in England, I had only mastered *katakana*. But I took my primary school textbooks with me, and whenever I had a spare moment I would systematically work my way through them. How I loved those stolen periods. They took me back to my beloved Japan, for which I was dreadfully homesick. I had memorized my *hiragana* and quite a lot of *kanji* before one of the mistresses came over and asked me what on earth I was doing.

'I'm studying Japanese', I said.

She frowned. 'That's not on the curriculum of this school', she said disapprovingly. She went on: 'If you have any time left over you should be doing your Latin prep.' But I was far from discouraged.

World War II found my mother and me on holiday in Bermuda. I was recruited by the Censorship Department when it set up headquarters there, to censor letters in French, as well as the odd missive in Japanese that trickled through. It sometimes took me almost a week to struggle through one of those, with my small Rose-Innes dictionary, but it gave me valuable reading practice.

In 1941 I went to California, to study composition with the famous French composer Darius Milhaud, a refugee from the Nazis who was teaching at Mills College, and thence, just as the war ended, to London where I joined the BBC Japanese Service.

My mother was anxious to return to Japan as soon as possible, to see what had become of our beach house in Hayama. We had rented it to British Ambassador Sir Robert and Lady Clive when we left in 1935. They enjoyed it as a quiet hideaway closer to Tokyo than the Embassy's mountain villa on Lake Chuzenji, near Nikko. Clive's successor, Sir Robert Craigie, however, preferred a larger house further up the road, where they could entertain more lavishly. His memoirs, *Behind the Japanese Mask*, contain a photograph of themselves in the garden there, with Prince and Princess Chichibu, whose villa was in the vicinity.

Various members of the Embassy took over our house after the Craigies moved. The last pre-war tenant was Vere Redman, and when he went back to the Embassy after the war as Information Counsellor, he commandeered the house for the use of senior embassy staff. On leave in

London in 1947, he called on us, and said: 'Dorothy, why not come back to Japan with me? I can offer you the job of librarian in the Information Section.' But since I would not have been able to take my mother with me, I decided to wait until we could both go back to Japan together.

It was not until 1949 that my mother and I were finally able to return to Japan, having at long last obtained permission from SCAP in the curious category of 'commercial representatives to inspect property!'

We crossed America and travelled on the *President Cleveland*, chaperoning an elderly American general's widow whom my mother had known at the US army post in the Philippines when visiting cousins there as a young girl, and whose family had refused to let her make the trip alone, 'Miz TQ', a still scintillating former 'southern belle', was determined to visit Japan now that her old friend Douglas MacArthur was there, who, as it happened, had taken over from her husband, General T.Q. Donaldson, as C in C, Philippines. With a trunk full of new clothes for the round of parties she envisaged, she was met in Yokohama by a colonel who had been her husband's aide, and who kindly offered to put us up, too, on our arrival on 20 August.

The Colonel and his wife lived in one of the prefabricated officers' quarters that filled Yamashita Park during the Occupation. Vere Redman came down from Tokyo to see us the very next day, and offered me the job of publications officer in the Information Section. I accepted with alacrity.

Mrs TQ also lost no time in making her call on the Supreme Commander. 'Dressed to kill', she drove up to Tokyo with the Colonel's wife, But she returned in the depths of dejection. She had expected at least to be asked to stay for lunch, but Mrs MacArthur merely received her briefly at eleven o'clock, without so much as a glass of fruit juice for refreshment. No invitations of any sort were forthcoming, and the General made no appearance.

'Where's Doug?' Mrs TQ had asked. 'Can't I see Doug?'

'The General never sees anyone socially', Mrs MacArthur had replied coldly. 'The General works very, very hard.'

'But I'm *sure* he'll see *me*', Mrs TQ had persisted, but to no avail.

The dear lady simply could not believe it. On the verge of tears, back in Yokohama, she told us in her southern drawl: 'Why, I once danced all the way across the Pacific with Doug.' She had never expected an overly warm reception from the second Mrs MacArthur, whom she hardly knew, but Doug, if only she could have seen Doug, she was certain all would have been quite different.

At least she was certain the colonel and his wife would throw a party or two for her. But very soon the colonel's wife took to her bed with DTs. It appeared they were both alcoholics, and had few friends. My mother and I were Mrs Donaldson's last hope. But when our house, that she knew we had rented to the British ambassador when we left before the war, turned out to be not a grand house in the British Embassy compound in Tokyo – as she had apparently fondly imagined – but merely a little summer cottage in the country, poor Mrs TQ was utterly devastated. In fact she suffered a nervous breakdown and had to be hospitalized, and as soon as she recovered sufficiently, we had to arrange for her return to the United States.

Sorry as I was for poor, dear Mrs TQ, my regard for the Supreme Commander Allied Powers rose sky-high. It was certainly not a time for parties. General MacArthur's dedication to his job was awe-inspiring. He did indeed work very, very hard. The lights in his office were on until all hours. Crowds gathered at the entrance to his headquarters to see him arrive and depart each day as if he were royalty. Whether a kind of hero-worship or mere curiosity, I am sure the Japanese were impressed by his sincerity – a highly regarded trait in Japan – and they lined the roads for miles sadly watching him go when he was 'sacked' by President Truman part way through the Korean War.

My future husband, Air Vice Marshal Cecil Bouchier, had a tremendous regard for General MacArthur, conferring with him as he did for almost an hour each day during the Korean war, and told me of the General's eloquent command of the English language.

One of the first things my mother and I did on returning to Japan was to find Kin-san, my old nanny. She was living with her nephew and his family in a thatch-roofed farmhouse among the rice fields in Totsuka, about eight miles from Yokohama. It was fourteen years since we had left, and all those years – many of them wartime ones – of helping in the paddy fields had left her bent double with rheumatism and hardly able to walk,

The hospital we put her in for treatment was depressing. Although it had been recommended by an eminent Japanese doctor, it was grubby and bleak. No food was provided, and nursing was only what was strictly clinical. Patients were required to bring their own helper, who not only cooked their meals, right beside their bed, but attended to all the patient's non-clinical needs as well. It provided constant companionship, of course, and twenty-four-hour care of a sort, so I suppose there was something to be said for the system. But it is hard to believe nowadays, when more and more hospitals in Japan are so spick and span and 'state of the art'.

I started work at the British Embassy as soon as possible, and was billeted at the Marunouchi Hotel. A stone's throw from Tokyo Station, it was once said to be the sort of hotel where men stayed when they told their wives they were off to Osaka on business. Souvenirs from all over Japan are still conveniently sold in a centre nearby, although the refurbished hotel is now on the international circuit, catering especially to

Australians, who are still assured there of a good strong cup of tea.

During the Occupation, the hotel was run by the Australian Army, and served mainly as a Tokyo billet for the Commonwealth Forces of Occupation based down in Kure and Iwakuni in southwest Japan.

My room at the Marunouchi faced the railway line, and trains went by constantly, jam-packed with 'salarymen', all in black trousers and white, short-sleeved shirts, with fans tucked into their belts against the stifling humid heat. There was no air-conditioning.

Four years had passed since the end of the war, and everyone was working terribly hard. I was not the only one impressed by the 'let's get on with the reconstruction of our country' attitude. An American uncle of mine, inventor and aviation pioneer Stanley Hiller, came to Japan in 1950 to talk to General MacArthur about the use of helicopters in the Korean war. While in Tokyo, he was immensely intrigued by the charcoal-powered taxis, which had some sort of burner in the boot. I remember how nice and warm they used to keep one's back in the winter! My uncle came back again the following year to try and buy one of those cleverly devised contraptions, but by then there was not a single one to be found anywhere – not even lying discarded in the corner of a garage. My uncle was astounded by the industry and speed with which they had not only been made redundant, but had already been recycled.

The Japanese were indeed working very hard. I was particularly amazed by the way nobody talked about the war. That was all people were talking about in England in 1945 when I arrived there from America just after VE Day, and I expected it would be the same in Japan. In fact I was interested in hearing what they would have to say about the war. But everyone seemed far too busy looking towards the future to dwell on what was past. Perhaps the Japanese were so used to earthquakes, typhoons, and similar disasters that traditionally they avoided wasting time talking about such things. You just picked yourself up and got on with whatever had to be done. What our friends did say was that it was worth losing the war to get rid of the militarists. And a taxi driver told me what an immense relief it was to be able to call a monkey-wrench a *monkii* again. He said that during the war English words were taboo, and it was so difficult to remember the obligatory Japanese equivalents. One of the few that has remained, of course, is *yakyu* – literally 'field ball', and so much more euphonious than *'besuboru'*.

One thing I hated during the Occupation was the way crowds getting on and off trains were funnelled along very narrow roped-off passages hugging the walls of both stairways and concourses, hustled along by whistle-blowing US military policemen, while we – the conquerors – could stroll in a leisurely fashion in the uncluttered centre portion. It was worse on the trains. I found it embarrassing sitting in the almost empty coaches reserved for us while you could see the indigenous personnel – as the Occupation designated them – stuffed into the next coach so tightly their faces were pushed up against the glass of the doors. My inclination was to join them in their discomfort, but it would obviously have only compounded their lack of space.

Commodities were still scarce, inflation was rife, and a black market flourished. I wondered why a store in Hayama whose sign read: *hanaya* (Flower Shop) contained only American packaged goods at inflated prices, and I realized post-war austerities were well and truly over when the shop started selling plants and flowers again as befitted its name. Our Japanese friends lived a 'bamboo shoot existence', peeling off and selling layer after layer of family heirlooms to make ends meet. Many invested in knitting machinery and sold sweaters they made, and even former princesses who had once done carving as an elegant pastime, carved objects for sale. And they all made the best of things, and not a soul complained.

I met 'Boy' Bouchier during my very first week at the Marunouchi Hotel. After commanding the British Commonwealth Air Forces of Occupation at war's end until 1946, as well as acting as Commander-in-Chief for part of that time, he had taken early retirement to represent the Confederation of British Industry (CBI) and was staying at the hotel. We fell in love – but since he had a wife and mentally-handicapped son in England, we determined to 'skate on the surface' and not become too deeply involved. It was not until fourteen years later that we finally married – four years after his first wife had died.

Boy was called back into the Royal Air Force in 1950 and returned to Tokyo to represent the British Chiefs of Staff at MacArthur's headquarters during the Korean War, with a suite at the famous old Imperial Hotel, designed by Frank Lloyd Wright – the Occupation billet for colonels and above.

I bought an Austin from a departing Embassy typist, and Boy taught me how to drive it on the almost empty Tokyo streets – so empty that one evening, while taking a stroll, we even kissed once standing right in the middle of the now busy boulevard that passes the Imperial Plaza!

Driving in Tokyo was a cinch using the Occupation map – a *tour de force* produced by the US 64th Engineer Base Topographic Battalion, who took a map of Tokyo, printed it faintly, and superimposed lettered avenues and numbered streets in red. Appropriate street signs were of course erected. I still think of Aoyama-dori as F Avenue. The Japanese for the most part ignored the splendid Occupation system, and when Saburo Matsukata and his Commission in the early sixties tried hard to reorganize the chaos of Japanese addresses, they got no further than making numbers more consecutive and naming only a few principal roads – names still ignored by the post office.

One American Occupation signpost was misleading. It read 'Siamese Connection' and was on the wall of a building in the business district. A man I knew was invited to a party by the Ambassador of Siam (now Thailand), and since the American Embassy was called a 'Section' during the Occupation, and there were others called 'Liaison Missions' he assumed there must be some called 'Connections'. Anything was possible in these topsy-turvy days. Anticipating a nice drink and something to eat, he drove to where he remembered having seen the sign, but all he found when he got there was a shining brass double-headed fire hydrant! Then there was the sign near the moat, with an arrow, that read: 'Bond Street, W1'.

My work at the embassy as publications officer included book rights negotiations. Japanese wishing to translate a British work had to go through me. Currency regulations were in force, and I remember once an English publisher had asked how royalties would be paid, and the Japanese publisher had cabled: 'Harston of Bond Street, W1 will arrange.' The English publisher replied that they had gone up and down Bond Street, but could find no such person or establishment. Mr Harston, it transpired, was simply a British expatriate entrepreneur in Tokyo who had opened a shop of that name.

As a child I often heard my parents talk about Kei Kurosawa's Madrigal Society, as well as the Amateur Dramatic Club, in which their friend Mrs de Havilland (mother of the film stars Olivia de Haviland and Joan Fontaine) used to shine. I was delighted to find both groups in full postwar swing, and joined them. At Mills College I had 'minored' in drama in addition to 'majoring' in music. The ADC had changed its name to the TIP – Tokyo International Players.

I also joined the poetry reading group that met in the Redmans' house and had been started by Edmund Blunden. Mrs Vining, Crown Prince Akihito's tutor, was a member and we became good friends. She invited me to her house one afternoon, with my guitar, to sing folk-songs for her English Club girls. The occasion is mentioned in her autobiography, *Quiet Pilgrimage*.

One day I had a phone call from a lady called Eloise Cunningham, who had somehow heard I was a musician, inviting me to tea at the Union Club – the Occupation guise of the Tokyo Kaikan. She told me how she had been born in Japan of missionary parents, and of her training as a musicologist, and I looked forward to a cosy chat, but arrived to find sixteen other people there – from American Occupation headquarters, various embassies, and a Japanese newspaper man. To our surprise, we were informed that we were the Planning Committee of the Young People's Symphony Concert Association, and would we each speak for five minutes giving our suggestions for raising money!

An enterprising Japanese confidence man raised some money for himself by approaching each of the group in turn after seeing a photograph of us all next day in the *Nippon Times*. The man used various names and various hard luck stories, and always said he had been sent by one of the others in the picture, who had assured him that the current victim was a kind person.

Eloise, at nearly 100, still manages to raise funds with great determination, imagination and flair for her splendid Music for Youth.

Being a bookworm I enjoyed facilitating the dissemination of English literature and was continually amazed at the industry and speed with which new British books were being translated into Japanese. British publishers arrived from time to time to collect the advance royalties I banked on their behalf, and I would interpret at their meetings with Japanese publishers. That is when I first became aware of the importance in Japan of sometimes saying nothing. I had read Maurois' *Les Silences du Colonel Bramble*, but Colonel Bramble had nothing on the Japanese. At those Anglo-Japanese meetings, the Britisher would say something like, 'What do you think about modern English poetry?' and an interminably long silence would ensue while the Japanese gentleman contemplated his shoes. Invariably the silence would become so intolerable that our man would say something like, 'Well, I imagine that from your *haiku* point of view most English poetry these days must seem wordy and incomprehensible' whereupon the Japanese would gratefully agree, saying, 'Yes, yes. Quite so.' And the upshot was that the Britisher learned nothing whatsoever. If he had but waited, he might well have obtained the profound insight he was hoping for.

As nature abhors a vacuum, so we Europeans seem to abhor silences. It took me a long time after coming back to Japan to learn not to feel uncomfortable at Japanese receptions if I was not holding a lively conversation with someone, and to realize it is perfectly all right to drink your beer and eat your smoked salmon canapé by yourself in silence, like most of the other guests.

At the Embassy, besides book transactions, I looked after most of the cultural requests, such as those for articles and talks about things like British music. So when the British Council set up premises in Tokyo in 1952, I transferred to them as a matter of course, and became the librarian. The following year, 1953, Kei Kurosawa and I relayed to radio listeners in Japanese the commentary on Queen Elizabeth's coronation as it was happening. Like air-conditioning, television was yet to come.

During the Occupation, some people I knew who spoke Japanese chose to conduct their business in English, saying, 'Well, after all they lost the war', but I always made a point of speaking in Japanese. It was far more practical if you wanted to be properly understood. It also put visitors more at ease.

Two of the first visitors to the British Council Library certainly had no need to be greeted in Japanese. One was Prince Mikasa, the youngest brother of the Emperor (Hirohito). His Imperial Highness, an eminent scholar of Hebrew history, and a university professor, wanted to learn about the Dewey system of library classification for use with his own books. Another visitor, the American-educated granddaughter of a famous Japanese elder statesman, and sister-in-law of historian Edwin Reischauer, came to consult our books on British education, going on to found the prestigious Nishimachi International school.

Many were the articles I wrote on Britain in English that appeared in translation in Japanese books and magazines, but for a long time I lacked the confidence to write in Japanese. However, when I was asked to provide a weekly essay for a short daily column in the *Asahi Shimbun* called *sutendogurasu* (Stained Glass), I was determined to try. There was to be a panel of seven contributors – one for each day of the week – made up of both foreigners and Japanese, and they told me that like the other Western authors, I could write my essays in English and they would happily translate them. But I persisted, and learned so much from the way the talented editor transformed my pieces and gave them style, that thanks to him, I have become reasonably at home in the Japanese essay medium.

The daily *'Stained Glass'* piece had to be based on a single everyday phrase in English. One of the Japanese contributors was the celebrated writer, and translator of *Lady Chatterley* fame, Kenichi Yoshida, the Oxford-educated son of the prime minister. Fond of his booze, he had agreed to contribute provided he could choose phrases connected with drink – things like 'One for the road' or 'Hair of the dog'. After a while, the newspaper asked him to write about something more wholesome, because the column was becoming popular with young people. When Yoshida bowed out, his contribution that week just happened to be on 'Mud in Your Eye'!

Up to the time I left for school in England before the war, my summers in Hayama were idyllic times of fun, playing on the beach with the children of our Japanese neighbours who had villas there – mostly members of royalty and the aristocracy. I introduced an English variation of hide-and-seek called 'sardines', and one day noticed a new little boy, a year or two younger then me, as we all crowded into a closet in the elegant, rambling villa across the road that belonged to Baron Takuma Dan, who was assassinated in 1932. It was his grandson Ikuma.

After the war, in Hayama we met again, and were amazed to discover we had both become composers, and a close collaboration ensued. I translated his beautiful opera *Yuzuru* ('The Twilight Heron') and introduced him to Boosey & Hawkes in London, who published it, as well as his second opera, *Kikimimi-zukin* ('The Listening Cap'), which I also translated. Ikuma Dan in turn introduced me to the inner circles of music in Tokyo, which led to many opportunities, including being commissioned to write music for the traditional Japanese dance – possibly the

first Westerner ever to be asked to do so. I also composed music for films.
Ikuma often conducted the instrumental ensembles for me. Most of the
musicians were from the leading orchestras, needing the extra money in
those straitened times.

I remember once, during a break, Ikuma introduced me to the violinist who was playing the solo in my suite *Tokyo Impressions* for a Capitol Records LP album. Mr Kuroyanagi was the leader of the NHK Symphony,
after having recently returned from the Soviet Union. Captured in Manchuria at the end of the war, he had been held prisoner in Siberia under
gruelling conditions with hard labour. He looked as though he had endured much, but was still remarkably handsome, and his violin playing
was superb. Years later, I was to translate the autobiographical record-
breaking best-seller by his daughter Tetsuko – *Totto-chan: the little girl at the
window.*

Being bilingual as well as a musician, I had since childhood been
acutely aware of the rhythm in language and its relation to a nation's
thought and culture. I felt like Alice in *Through the Looking Glass* as I freely
moved back and forth at will, blending into my two vastly different
worlds, and wished so much that everyone could share the same delight.
I have found time and again that not only speaking a language, but entering into its rhythm seems to wipe out perceived differences – truly
making all people one.

I called a volume of essays I wrote in Japanese *warutsu to hayashi* –
roughly 'In Two-step and Waltz time' – explaining that I felt rather like
someone dancing the Awa Odori in the middle of London Bridge. In my
suite *Tokyo Impressions* I tried to capture the feeling of the *hayashi* festival
rhythms with Western instruments, and was thrilled when the American
Record Guide praised what they called my 'translation of the koto-sami-
sen aesthetic into Occidental terms'.

Having all my life tried hard to explain Japan to my American and
British friends, one of the things that pleased me most, coming back to
Japan during the Occupation, was to find that the ill wind of war had
blown Japan a public relations windfall of inestimable value. It had produced a host of British and American Japanophiles – not only scholars,
busy promoting its culture, but scores of ordinary families who were living all over Japan and learning to like the country and its people.

4

Cultural Relations Resumed

EDMUND BLUNDEN • GEORGE FRASER • D.J. ENRIGHT
REG CLOSE • RONALD BOTTRALL • E.W.F. TOMLIN • FRANCIS KING

A NUMBER OF British poets and writers were invited to Japan before the war to give lectures and teach at Japanese universities. Among these were poets such as Ralph Hodgson and William Empson. Other writers who found their way to Japan in the inter-war years included William Plomer and Laurens van der Post. Celebrities such as Bernard Shaw and Aldous Huxley also visited Japan during these years. Plomer never returned to Japan after the war although he had been deeply attached to individual Japanese. Van der Post was one who bridged the pre- and post-war periods, but in Japanese eyes, at least, the English writer who had won the hearts of young Japanese before the war and who returned to Japan after the war was the poet Edmund Blunden.

In about 1947 Vere Redman, then Counsellor for information work in the United Kingdom Liaison Mission to SCAP in Tokyo, discussed with a group of Japanese professors of English the possibility of getting a teacher of English attached to the mission 'so that his services might be placed at the disposal of Japanese universities'. The unanimous request was: 'Bring back Blunden'. (See my biographical portrait of Sir Vere Redman in *Biographical Portraits* Vol. II, page 297.)

EDMUND BLUNDEN returned and cultural relations were revived, at first inevitably in a limited way. I have quoted some of Blunden's impressions in the chapter on the Occupation, but as an introduction to this chapter I should like to quote from his article 'A Party at the Palace' published in *A Wanderer in Japan* by Asahi Shimbunsha in 1950. It covers the annual imperial poetry competitions in the New Year when large numbers of *tanka* are submitted and a small number are selected '. . . to be read aloud and judged, in the presence of the Emperor and before an audience of authors and others'. Blunden describes the scene as follows:-

•

It was on a bright morning at the end of January that we found ourselves on the way round the ever enchanting Moat, making for the Palace as guests on this annual occasion. It seemed wrong, on such an occasion of fancy and sentiment, that we should be arriving in a *car* (however beautiful and gentle-voiced) at the tall towered gate, whence one half expected several knights and one or two henchmen with silver trumpets to appear in stately challenge. However, the mild policeman waiting there collected the pass and admitted the car; the age of chivalry faded out; and we were at the modern steps rising to the door of the Palace.

*   *   *

Before long we were guided into the long room in which the great business of the day was to be transacted. At one end, a long screen and several tables; before them, a table ... for the judges and readers of the poetry; alongside, the rows of chairs for the poets who had got so far in the competition; at the other end, the chairs for the rest of the company...

The Emperor entered, together with the Empress Dowager and Princess Takamatsu; they occupied their several places, and with no more than simple decorum the party began. The characteristics of the ceremony were silence (apart from the readings), stillness and slow motion. The director whose function it was to deliver the manuscripts in turn to the 'lecturer' and the little court of judges, or chorus of chanters – for the poems were not only read but chanted – handled each paper with reverent nicety. Such matters as poetry, the style seemed to say, are eternal; there can be no hurrying over them. It was a long time before I saw on any face the relaxation of a slight smile, and that I think was when one of the poets forgot that he should rise to his feet during the recitation of his own composition. How much I sympathized with his absent-mindedness!

The Emperor in his dark morning coat, the Empress Dowager in her purple velvet gown sat movelessly, impartially, as guardians of the treasure of poetry, while the readers intoned poem after poem. The voices and the tones, as I felt, had a resemblance to the choral responses in which I was trained in a shadowy old church as a child.

*   *   *

... I reflected that of all the solemnities and traditional observances which I had been enabled to attend here in Japan, this undecorated and straightforward commemoration of poetry in the Palace itself brought me nearest to the particular quality of the Japanese mind. It was not an archaic occasion, and the lacquered chairs with the golden chrysanthemums dappling their black frames were looking at me from a modernized Japan – but here was the antiquity, here was the dignity, here the contemplation and intuition of Japan's earlier ages.

BLUNDEN was such a popular figure in Japan that he was invited back. He visited Kyoto while FRANCIS KING was in charge of the British Council's office there in the 1950s. King commented in his autobiography *Yesterday Came Suddenly* (Constable 1993) that Blunden received

•

... immeasurably more attention than he would have done on a visit to any English city. The reason for this was that, during his previous stays in Japan, first before and then in the immediate aftermath of the war, he had made a profound impression with his courteousness, his humility and his devotion to his students. Even his lectures, which stuck me as singularly devoid of any substance, aroused enthusiasm among the Japanese.

Blunden had one enviable gift: he could write verses, impeccable in scansion and rhyme on any subject, at any time of the day or night, within literally minutes. When a foreign writer visits a famous temple or garden or even a school or university, his Japanese hosts have a way of producing a book and asking him to 'compose' something. On such occasions I used to be totally nonplussed. Should I write, as tourists do in visitors' books in England, 'A truly memorable experience' or 'It was worth coming all this way to see this'? James Kirkup would always resort to an English haiku. But, perhaps unduly fastidious, I shrank from producing something like:

> In the Moss Temple a crane cries
> Evening falls and my home is far.

Asked by the Mayor of Kyoto, at a reception in his honour, to 'compose' something 'about our beautiful city', Blunden at once sat down in a corner and, to my amazement, produced a Shakespearian sonnet, of which he later presented me with a copy in his elegant Italic script. In it he referred to 'Kyoto, with all her tinted leaves' (it was then autumn). When the English language *Japan News* published this poem, the leaves had somehow become 'tainted'. Blunden was vexed; but in view of the pollution that was, even then, affecting the city, I approved of the emendation.

WHEN BLUNDEN returned home the poet GEORGE FRASER was invited to take his place. George Fraser's stay in Japan was sadly cut short after his attempted suicide. Sumie Okada in her book *Western Writers in Japan* notes that the Frasers (he was accompanied by his wife and daughter) enjoyed their stay in Japan. George Fraser mainly lectured on twentieth-century English writers and Sumie Okada states that Japanese intellectuals 'found his lectures ... refreshingly attractive' partly, perhaps, because they were 'different from those concerning the Romantic poets specialized in by Edmund Blunden'. She adds that: 'Unlike Blunden, who had willingly accepted the norms of Japanese conformity, G.S.Fraser tried to challenge the passive attitude of the Japanese students of English.'

Edmund Blunden in his Foreword to Fraser's *Impressions of Japan and other Essays* published by *Asahi-shimbunsha* in 1952 asserted that: 'Mr Fraser was at once and constantly supported with enthusiasm, affection and insight by Japanese well-wishers everywhere.'

In his opening essay GEORGE FRASER began with these words:-

One reason, I think, why it is difficult for anybody from Great Britain to give a quick and vivid impression of Japan is a certain affinity which there is between the Japanese and the British temperament; so that somebody from England or Scotland soon begins to feel very much at home in Japan, to feel about his Japanese friends just as he does about his British friends, and to lose the sense of strangeness and foreignness, and the vivid awareness of "local colour".'

Later in the same essay Fraser wrote:

We were aware, in a word, as we would have been at home, of *persons*, not of a race. One realized, almost at once, that the idea of the 'inscrutable Oriental' was, as far as the Japanese people were concerned, a myth . . . And when I meet a new Japanese acquaintance I do not ask myself to-day, 'What sort of Japanese is this'. I ask myself as I would at home in England, 'What sort of *man* is this?'

George Fraser, like so many who have followed in his footsteps, urged his students to ask him questions about anything that puzzled them in his lectures. He wanted to ask his students to prepare a number of questions for him to answer. It is improbable that he had much success in this endeavour.

Unlike some other British visitors and residents he was attracted by the Noh and declared in another essay:

'It is impossible, I think, to leave a Noh play performance without feeling that one has been in some sense purified. Japan is lucky in having both this tradition, and the other more lively and earthy, more secular tradition, of the Kabuki play. I would think it a most unfortunate thing if this tradition were to be sacrificed for, say, the realism of Ibsen and Shaw.'

GEORGE FRASER'S feeling for nature in Japan is shown by the following passage written while resting in the middle of a busy lecture tour on the island of Miyajima:-

●

I am not really much in a mood for writing: for all around me are beauties which I want to explore. Yesterday, . . . I watched a great yellow gingko tree gradually shedding its leaves. A mild wind was blowing and the beautiful leaves, with their shape broadening out from the stem rather like a fan, fluttered gently and softly, almost rhythmically, down to the ground, and I thought that this did not look like a real tree, but like a tree on the stage, part of the setting of a ballet representing the spirit of autumn. The golden colour and the thick velvety texture of the gingko leaves, so thick and juicy, when I picked some up from the ground, contrasted strangely with the silky, texture of the delicate star shape, and the vivid crimson colour of the maple leaves, which I had also been collecting. The maple, when it turns really bright red, seems to me always like the pure yellow of these gingko leaves, to belong not so much to nature, as to art. In the *Momiji* park, I noticed that the Japanese seem to have the same feeling about these maple leaves, as something exquisite and ornamental. A little party was sitting on a low wooden platform, drinking tea, and admiring the leaves. There were three elderly ladies in kimonos of a subdued colour and a young girl in a very bright, rich, and beautiful kimono: she had stuck these maple leaves, like so many crimson stars, all over her dark hair. . .

GEORGE FRASER'S successor in 1953 was another poet, D. J. ENRIGHT who was accompanied by his wife and daughter. Sumie Okada notes that '. . . his poems on Japan reveal many humanitarian concerns, depicting with sharp pathos the differences of culture and sensibility'.

Enright set out his impressions and reactions to Japan in *The World of Dew: Aspects of Living Japan*, published in 1955 by Secker and Warburg. Enright's view of Japan was less sentimental than that of Blunden and Fraser and some of his observations had a sharper tone than that of his predecessors but he was a sensitive observer and had a sympathetic understanding of aspects of post-war Japan.

ENRIGHT differed from Fraser in his attitude towards the Japanese as a race. He wrote:-

●

It really appears that the Japanese have always had some kind of grudge against the 'merely human'. For the sake of its very existence every race has built up a more or less complicated system of behaviour; however fanciful that system at the heart of it is a piece of sound common sense – the recognition that we are all human. The Japanese may be unique in that their unusually complicated system of behaviour is based not on a recognition of humanity but on a proud and yet pathetic denial of it. It may strike the outsider that they adopted precisely those ideals which by nature they were least fitted to fulfil. Unless the race has changed physically since feudal times, and changed for the worse, the ideal of the samurai seems a peculiarly inappropriate one to set up. How could a

country continually visited by natural disasters on a huge scale – typhoons, floods, landslides and earthquakes – ever conceive itself to be
the land of the gods? Rather a land accursed by the gods. Why should
such a country set out to be master of the East when it cannot catch up on
the damage caused by one typhoon or one rainy season before the next is
upon it?

*   *   *

All my sympathies are with the young Japanese of today, whether a young
writer, the young man in the street or the young woman who manages to
keep off the streets. They have had a raw deal from history – from both
their own ancient history and contemporary world history too. The rest
of the world has praised their country for the wrong things and failed to
praise them for the right; it has condemned them for their violence without proposing any remedy for the disease which lies at the heart of that
violence. In a number of ways, indeed, the rest of the world has encouraged that violence, sometimes romantically and sometimes cynically. The
young Japanese is bewildered and unsure – how could he be otherwise?
– but he is chastened and only too eager to be sensible, to find some way
of living and letting live. And now the world will not let him.

ENRIGHT shared Fraser's frustration at the lack of questioning by his students.
His colleagues told him that 'Discussion in class is not a Japanese tradition.' 'The
student is told; he does not ask and he is not asked.' Enright supposed that in
some subjects it did not matter that the student believed the teacher all the time.
'But in literature, where the important part depends upon personal judgements,
the teacher can hardly contemplate with equanimity his every word pass into his
students' note-books with all the authority of Holy Writ.'

Enright found Japanese academics 'the most academic in the world'. 'It is
distressing, in the extreme to see a man wearing out his eyes on collecting
footnotes to *Beowulf*, to all intents already blind to the world around him –
especially when everything worth saying about the poem has already been said
several times.'

Enright was scathing about the Japanese attitude towards Lafcadio Hearn.
He found it difficult to comprehend that '. . . university professors of eminence
have throughout taught their students to believe that Lafcadio Hearn is a classic of English (American?) literature. . . The Hearn myth strikes me as dangerous because it is the classic, the most powerful, instance of the foreign devotee
praising a past in which he would never have had to live and complaining bitterly of those inevitably crude efforts which people are at last making to loosen
the traditional social chains.'

Enright began a chapter entitled 'Having one's cake and eating it' with these
words:

Repression has its own peculiar beauties. So much good is mixed with so much that is indefensibly callous in traditional Japanese behaviour that today, when the unaesthetic concomitants of their transplanted democracy flourish so openly, it is understandable that many Japanese (and especially perhaps the more cultured) should look back to their past with nostalgia. Freedom they welcome sincerely, and yet they remember the glory that was feudal Japan. Whatever our nationality, few of us can avoid sentimentalising the past.

In his final chapter Enright gave this advice to his Japanese friends:

It would be a great advance if the Japanese could rid themselves of that persistently self-conscious attitude towards their own past. I am forever being told that some Japanese tradition or other is in danger . . . What a ridiculous situation it is! Are the Japanese such a feeble race that they will collapse at the loss of a few ambiguous traditions? . . . The Japanese have had Shinto, the Way of the Gods; and Bushido, the Way of the Warrior; and Kodo, the Way of the Emperor. What they might try now is the Way of the Human. All the circumstances are against them. Yes. But circumstances will not change until there has been a change of heart. If the Japanese can finally liberate themselves from the past and survive the present, they should do great things. There is an unused fund of virtue in them.

One of Enright's tasks in Japan had been to oversee the British Council library in Kyoto while at the same time lecturing at the private university of Kohnan. FRANCIS KING, who was appointed the first Regional Director Kansai for the British Council, took over from Enright his responsibilities in the area. In his autobiography *Yesterday Came Suddenly* Francis King commented on Enright in the following terms:-

. . . A dear man, benign, perceptive and humorous, Enright would often justifiably complain that, whereas his Council career had been beset with usually undeserved disasters, I (as he put it) 'got away with murder time after time'. He had already left Japan when I arrived there; but a number of people, English and Japanese, were only too eager to tell me of the latest disaster which had precipitated yet another move for him. At a club for the foreign community in Kobe, some drunken American had suggested, totally erroneously, that Enright – whose manner might indeed be thought slightly camp – was a 'faggot'. There had followed an altercation, after which Enright, who had been asked to leave the club, returned to smash the glass panel of its front door. Although, because of this incident, Enright spent only a year in Japan, he wrote one of the best books about the country that I have ever read (*The Year of the Monkey*).

The British Council had set up a small library in Tokyo in 1940, but this had to be closed on the outbreak of war in 1941 and the British Council did not again open an office in Tokyo until 1952. REG CLOSE was appointed the first representative of the Council in Japan.

In a lecture to the Japan Society on 5 March 1957 Close gave some account of his work in Japan. An immediate problem had been to find an appropriate Japanese name for the British Council and after various suggestions had been made and rejected he decided to call their office the *Buritishu Council* although this led at first to his receiving communications intended for the British Consul.

Before he left London for Japan a colleague asked him '"Where on earth will you begin?" and that question came back to my mind very forcibly when I found myself, a total and bewildered stranger, in a city that is well on its way to being the most crowded in the world and was already by far the noisiest.' But '. . . there were many threads, broken and still unbroken, that I could pick up'. Sir George Sansom had been the first British scholar to become an honorary member of the Japan Academy. The memory of dozens of British teachers who had taught in Japanese universities and schools from one end of the country to another was indestructible. Close was greatly helped by famous scholars of English and by the Presidents of Japanese universities. He '. . . found immense enthusiasm for the development of Anglo-Japanese cultural interchanges'. Sadly, the Council's funds '. . . were almost, but not quite, hopelessly inadequate'. He began with one assistant but eventually had two assistants from London and an office and library staff of eight, '. . . all of whom were very loyal and keen and immensely overworked'.

One of Close's first tasks had been to find an office. Initially, he had to work from a small house in Denenchofu, twelve miles from the centre of Tokyo. But he then succeeded in acquiring space in Maruzen's new building on the Ginza. This was opened in May 1953 by Sir Esler Dening, the British Ambassador in Tokyo, in the presence of various representatives of the Imperial Family.

Close explained that among their many activities the Council had played the decisive role in the tours arranged for Sir Malcolm Sargent in 1954, and of Benjamin Britten and Peter Pears in 1956 (see Chapter 5). He and his deputy W.R.McAlpine were in constant demand to give lectures around Japan. Close remembered '. . . having to give five different lectures within thirty six hours in Kyushu; having to speak on six subjects in one two-hour lecture to an audience of 700 in Sapporo, my interpreter being a French woman, so that I had to speak out loud and clear in English and then make rapid asides to my interpreter in French; and having to talk for four hours, with two brief intermissions, in Hiroshima'.

Close put considerable emphasis on arranging for Japanese scholars and officials to study in Britain. The vast majority became good friends of Britain.

Close concluded his lecture with the following words:-

I knew something about Japan in the not so happy days twenty years ago. In the four years I spent in Japan from 1952-56 I made more friends than I have made in any of the countries I have been in. My Japanese friends kept me pretty busy; but I could not have been treated with greater courtesy, nor with more genuine kindness.

Reg Close's successor as British Council representative was LESLIE PHILLIPS described by Francis King in his autobiography as '. . . a man who, devoid of any outstanding qualities of mind, managed to get surprisingly far in the Council on a combination of kindliness and craftiness'.

Phillips' successor was another poet, RONALD BOTTRALL, who died in 1989 aged 82. When Sumie Okada asked him for an interview shortly before he died he replied: 'I am 81 and my memory has diminished, but I am certainly a better poet than Edmund Blunden.' He also enclosed a collection of mostly one-line appreciations of his poetry by various reviewers.' FRANCIS KING wrote of Bottrall:-

•

B ottrall was so unsuited to Japan, both physically and temperamentally, that it is unlikely that any organization other than the British Council would have ever thought of dispatching him there . . . When we were invited to a Japanese tea-house, restaurant or home, I would invariably hear a crack, followed by 'Ouch!' or even 'Fuck!' Yet again he had managed to bang his head on a low beam. Whether the increasingly slurred speech which followed was caused by this injury or by the enthusiasm with which he threw back cup after cup of saké, I could never be certain . . . Having lowered himself to the floor, with a succession of groans and grunts, and as often as not, an aside to me of 'Why the hell can't they provide a proper table and chairs?', he would then stretch out his immensely long legs and so inadvertently kick the shins of whoever was seated opposite to him. On one occasion, making an extravagant gesture, chopsticks in hand, he managed to put an elbow through a fragile paper screen.

Just as the Japanese physical world was too narrow and delicate to accommodate him, so was the whole Japanese code of behaviour. The candour, directness and domineering vigour which had served him so well in Italy and Greece were here appalling handicaps . . . If one is given a present in Japan, etiquette demands that one should not immediately open it in front of the giver. Ronald, however, would at once tear off the wrapping paper and then make it abundantly clear whether he approved of the gift or not. 'Splendid, splendid, very decent of you!' he would exclaim; or 'Well, well, well! What on earth is the purpose of *this*?'

The fact that the Japanese were so submissive brought out the worst in him ... He would storm about the Tokyo office ... like one of those Japanese typhoons which, in a few moments, can create so much havoc. Then he would disappear into his office, leaving behind him a number of men ashen-faced over their ledgers and a number of women sobbing into their typewriters. Half an hour later, he would re-emerge, a benevolent sun shining over his little empire. He had totally forgotten his rage and the reason for it. The Japanese, however, never forgot.

The most memorable clash between Ronald and the Japanese way of life took place when ... he gave a lecture at Kobe University, where the Dean of the Faculty of English, Professor Kozu, was an old and valued friend of mine ... Ronald's subject was 'Twentieth Century English Poetry'. His was a masterly essay but a poor lecture, since he read it out – such was his custom – in a monotonous voice, head lowered over text. The students, like all Japanese students in such tedious circumstances, sat absolutely still, their eyes fixed on him. At the close, he looked up and demanded, 'Well, now, how about some questions?'

There was a silence, which prolonged itself. I was just about to intervene, when Professor Kozu rose to his feet:

'Er – Mr – Professor Bottrall, sir – I have a, er, question.'

'Yes.'

'Whom do you consider the greatest poet – Yeats, Eliot or Auden?'

'Oh, my God!' Ronald slapped what little forehead he had with the palm of a hand. (Roger Hinks, asked by a Greek woman whether Ronald was handsome, replied: 'Well, that all depends on whether you are attracted by men with eyes on the tops of their heads.') 'What a stupid question! What an incredibly stupid question! It's *unbelievable*! No, I absolutely refuse to answer that!' Professor Kozu at once sat down; his students all began to giggle in embarrassment, hands over mouths.'

WHEN BOTTRALL had departed Professor Kozu who had bowed him away turned to Francis King and said in a quiet steely voice: 'Mr Bottrall will never again lecture at Kobe University.'

Nevertheless, Francis King remained on good terms with Bottrall and when Bottrall was prematurely retired King who had been asked to act as a reference lavished praise on Bottrall's abilities; but the Council rejected Bottrall's appeal.

On his last visit to Kyoto Francis King recorded that

> ... Ronald was drinking even more than usual. After one particularly bibulous luncheon, I staggered into my sitting-room, where a conversation class of beginners was awaiting me, Ronald had said that he was going to 'have a snooze'. The Council insisted that all teaching of English must be by the direct method; and so – much

though I hated it – this is what I now used. I held up a bottle of gin. 'This is a bottle.' I said. I shook it. 'This is a full bottle.' I retrieved from the waste-paper basket a gin bottle, its contents drunk chiefly by Ronald, which I had thrown there. 'This is an empty bottle.' I repeated, 'This is a full bottle . . . This is an empty bottle.' Suddenly a flushed face appeared round the door. 'This is a Bottrall,' Ronald announced. He hiccoughed. 'This is a full Bottrall.' He then disappeared. The students were astounded. To distract them, I again held up one of the bottles on the table before me. 'What is this?' I asked. 'That is a Bottrall,' the dimmest student, a girl, replied. 'That is a full Bottrall,' she added.

Bottrall was succeeded by E.W.F. TOMLIN as head of the British Council in Tokyo. His book *The Last Country, My Years in Japan* was published by Faber and Faber in 1974. According to Francis King, Tomlin was '. . . a most effective lecturer. During the course of a lecture by him on some extremely abstruse philosophical subject, I used to think with amazement, "But I *understand* all this!" Sadly, the following day I would have absolutely no idea of what the lecture had been about.'

Freddie Tomlin clearly enjoyed his time in Japan. He was attracted by the traditional aspects of Japan. In the 'Prelude' to his book Tomlin wrote:

In Japan, you still feel, though dimly, that you are living in a community which obeys the rules not merely of politics and economics but of the cosmic order. You feel nearer to the essence of things and the beginning of things. You feel that there *is* a natural life and a natural order, which, perpetually renewed and sanctioned, are the fount and condition of human happiness. No other land that I have known retains precisely this quality, though I think that ours did until recently. That is why I have called Japan the Last Country.'

Further on he wrote: 'What in particular distinguishes the Japanese mentality from that of the West is, it would seem, *a refusal to draw a distinction between the sacred and the secular*. All life is sacred, or all life is secular. It makes no difference. Life is one.' In a chapter headed 'Feeling at home' he reverted to this theme: 'The deeper I familiarized myself with Japanese life, the more I found that behind the common activities, as well as behind, the more specialized ones, the sense of the sacred was present.'

It is clear from his account of his life in Japan that his enjoyment of Japan was, however, often on a more mundane level. He was an accomplished amateur conjuror and his housekeeper Teiko-san was his 'ideal confederate' in more than conjuring performances.

Tomlin recorded that at the beginning of his stay in Tokyo he spent much time in cafes and bars. He rejected the view that '. . . the majority of bar girls were disguised prostitutes . . . Yet I heard that most bar-girls would agree, if the subject were raised with discretion, to sell their favours . . . Some of my most pleasant hours were spent practising Japanese with bar-girls, though I had to fit in these visits at week-ends, and in my last years I was so busy that such moments were very rare. Once or twice in my first year, when my circle of friends was limited, the cost of living reasonable, and my energy abundant, I would make a night of it.'

Tomlin also said that '. . . some of his most enjoyable evenings I spent in Tokyo were at a hall called the *Shichi-go-san* (literally "seven-five-three"). Here was true *"family* entertainment" with solo-singing, acrobatics or juggling.'

He was also introduced to the *geisha* world by a Japanese friend and greatly enjoyed the experience.

He was once strolling through Shimbashi when he passed what 'seemed to be an ordinary chemist's shop':

> An elderly man behind the counter beckoned to me with a look compounded of furtiveness and amusement. Curiosity overcoming me, I stepped in. From a drawer beneath the counter, he produced a variety of rubber contraptions the like of which I had neither seen, nor, in most cases, heard of. What the vendor chiefly pressed on my attention were aids specially designed for men of failing powers, in which Japanese ingenuity had reached a high degree of perfection. That he should have thought me to belong to this category somewhat abashed me; but this he took for foreign prudery and tried all the more to persuade me to make a purchase. I had difficulty in retiring with dignity, especially as he kept producing even more ingenious gadgets for my inspection, complete with detailed explanations as to their use.
>
> A man on his own in a large city is an obvious target for the tout, the pimp, and the con-man. I was sometimes invited to visit establishments which, judging from the lurid descriptions given, were obviously the resort of hard-drug addicts; but it was a trifle sad to be offered girl students, though this happened to me more than once.

FRANCIS KING wrote as follows about his relationship with TOMLIN:-

●

Perhaps because of his own lack of small talk and a similar lack in most of his Japanese guests, Tomlin would play music throughout his dinner-parties. As the noisy gulping of soup (to slurp is not bad manners in Japan) vied with the strains of the Elgar cello concerto, for which Tomlin had an inordinate affection, I often used to find myself wishing that I were somewhere else.

Divorced, Tomlin, like at least one Representative who succeeded him, started an affair with a girl in the office. When he finally decided to terminate the affair, the girl stole the manuscript, the only one in existence, of a novel on which he had been working, and refused to return it. Since Tomlin's talent for fiction certainly did not equal his talent for lecturing on philosophy, perhaps one should be grateful to her. . .

Tomlin came to the beautiful resort of Amano-Hashidate to attend the closing ceremony of a summer school which I had directed. The students all gone, he and I found ourselves having dinner alone together in a now totally deserted Japanese inn. Tomlin began talking about the women students. Although he had only been in their company for a day I was amazed by how much he had noticed about them. 'That was a pretty little girl with the cast in her left eye . . . That Miss Ishiyama is really very attractive, even though she must be well over forty . . . I was awfully taken by that teacher from Okayama – do you know the one that I mean?'

After dinner, a long evening stretched ahead of us. How was I to entertain him

'Would you like to go to a strip-show?' I asked.

'A strip-show? *Here*?'

Even the smallest and most remote towns in Japan can usually provide at least one strip-show.

'Yes, it's not far from the hotel. Five minutes' walk.'

'I've never been to a strip-show.' He pondered. 'Well, why not?'

For a while he stared intently at the girl in no more than black G-string and a rosette covering each nipple. He shifted uneasily in his seat. He coughed. Eventually, she pulled off one rosette and then the other. She grinned around the half-empty auditorium and advanced to the footlights, peering out at the audience. She ripped off the G-string and whirled it round and round over her head, while opening her legs wide. Then she threw the G-string towards Tomlin. To a guffaw from the audience it landed in his lap.

He jumped up, pushing the G-string away as though it were a dead bat which had fallen on him. 'Come along! Come!'

He stormed out of the hall. I followed. There was a lot of giggling from the all-male audience.

'How could you have inflicted an exhibition like that on me? *How could* you?'

Things were never quite the same between us after that.

FRANCIS KING was the first British Council representative in Kyoto. He was officially 'Regional Director Kansai'. Among his responsibilities was supervision of the British Council Library, previously supervised by D.J. Enright.

As King explains in his autobiography *Yesterday Came Suddenly*, the British Council Library

> ... was sited in a quarter largely inhabited by *hinin* or outcasts. These were originally people involved in such 'unclean' pursuits as the slaughter of animals, the curing of leather and the removal of night-soil. The British Council officials who had chosen the building had thought merely of its cheapness and its convenience, so near to the four major universities. They had never thought that the presence of a *hinin* community would act as a deterrent to visitors. Why should they have done so? Not merely had the distinction between *hinin* and the rest of Japanese society been legally abolished, but it was forbidden even to refer to it.
>
> Unfortunately, many things can exist in Japan even if they have been 'abolished' and even if no one ever refers to them except in private conversation. Even today, a shadow line sets the *hinin* apart from the rest of the population, so that only recently my Japanese translator asked if he could remove a reference to them in one of my short stories since, as he put it, 'it might embarrass some of your Japanese readers.'

One day each week King used to travel over to Kohnan University, in a suburb of Kobe

> ... to give two lectures. Before I acquired a car, I used to go there by train; later I drove there. I had already been told that one of my two classes would consist of graduate students who would require a course on Shakespeare and the other of beginners who would re-quire a course in 'conversation'. On my first day, the professor in charge of me said that the beginners' class would come first, the Shakespeare class second. I went into the first class. 'Good morn-ing,' I enunciated very clearly. I turned to a student in the front row: 'How are you?' 'I am very well, thank you,' he answered. I turned to another student: 'And how are you?' 'Very well, thank you.' 'And how old are you?' I asked another student. So it went on. I was pleased that beginners should prove so responsive.
>
> To the second class I gave a lecture on Shakespearian tragedy, which owed a lot to a lecture which I had once heard David Cecil deliver in Oxford. The students were admirably attentive. They kept their eyes on me. No one spoke. No one even stirred.
>
> As I left the lecture hall I ran into a Canadian who was also teach-ing at Kohnan.
>
> 'How did you get on with those beginners?' he asked.
>
> 'Oh, I had the beginners for my first period. Those are the grad-uate students.'

'No, they're not! They certainly are not!'

He was right. It amazed me that not one of those graduates had protested, 'But, Mr King, you are supposed to be lecturing to us on Shakespeare,' and that all those beginners had given such whole-hearted attention to a lecture that must have been totally incomprehensible to them.

At Kohnan King became a friend of David Kidd, a kindred spirit. David did some desultory teaching; he also began to deal with increasing success in oriental ceramics. King wrote:

While I was in Japan, he moved from his Western-style house on the fringe of Kohnan campus to a Japanese farmhouse of extraordinary beauty but scant comfort and convenience, not all that far from it. On my weekly visits to Kohnan I would bring a picnic luncheon with me and eat it with David. What was luncheon for me was breakfast for him. Terrified of the dark, he would sit up most of the night and then sleep on until noon. In consequence, he would greet me in silk pyjamas, the bottoms of the trousers abnormally wide, over which he would wear a flowered kimono. On first seeing this kimono, a student friend who was acting as my driver, could not control his giggles. 'What are you laughing at?' David demanded. 'Kidd-sensei – forgive me for saying this . . .' Again the boy began to giggle. He pointed: 'That kimono . . . It is woman's kimono, Kidd-sensei.' 'Of course it's a woman's kimono,' David retorted. 'That's why I'm wearing it.' To my embarrassment, David would be wearing this kimono on those occasions when he decided to walk with me back to the university for what he called 'a breath of stale air'. Like my driver, students would stare and giggle at this tall, sinuous American in a garishly flowered kimono, one hand agitating a fan before his extraordinarily pale face.

But David's appearance was wholly deceptive. He was both physically and mentally strong; as brilliant a businessman as linguist, connoisseur and writer.

At first, Francis King was

. . . totally foxed by Japan; I could not understand it. This puzzlement produced in me irritation, exasperation, even anger. It also produced in me the urge to write a novel about the place, since I knew, from previous experience, that the act of writing about something which baffled me usually brought an end to the bafflement. So it was that I started on one of the three best of my novels, *The Custom House*. Like my *The Woman Who Was God* and *Act of Darkness*, and unlike any other of my novels, it was a book which seemed to be written by someone other than myself, a disembodied entity

for whom I was no more than willing amanuensis, so that, reread-
ing a page just completed, I would find myself asking myself,
'Where on earth did this come from?' I am now amazed by the
frenzy with which, despite a long day of work for the Council, I
raced through chapter after chapter. I managed to do this by getting up at five o'clock each morning and working for two or three
hours before dressing, having breakfast and setting off for the office. The manuscript – in those days I wrote by hand – was an extraordinarily clean one.

But

... Two things changed my hatred of Japan into a love which has
now lasted for almost thirty years. The first of these was that, having
drifted for so long at sea, I suddenly felt firm land under my feet.
'I've got it, I've got it!' I could almost have cried out. I had found the
key, deciphered the code. I was now able to understand precisely
why, in a certain situation, the Japanese behaved in a certain way,
and I could myself behave in a similar way in a similar situation. In a
society in which there is so little spontaneity and in which people
tend to behave according to rigid rules, it is only necessary to learn
the rules to find that life becomes extraordinarily easy. One small
example will suffice. In the West, when I was young, I was always in
an agony of indecision about when I should leave a dinner or
luncheon party. In Japan, at a certain hour, the host himself rises
from the table and thanks his guests for their attendance. They then
all leave together.

The second reason for my hatred of Japan all at once changing
into love was the arrival into my life of a young man whom I shall
call Noboru. Ebullient, impetuous, constantly laughing, constantly teasing, constantly speaking his mind, he was totally unty-
pical of his race.

Francis King felt that the Japanese were

... no more concerned with one's sexual orientation than with
whether one has tea or coffee for breakfast, or whether one enjoys
Noh or Kabuki the more. Their interest in sex is the same as a gour-
met's interest in food, whereas the interest of the English in sex is
all too often that of a sufferer from bulimia – now indiscriminately
overeating and now vomiting in remorse. Sexual gossip, of the
kind so common in England, is extraordinarily rare in Japan. I
was always careful to be discreet about my sexual tastes; but if anyone guessed at them, they aroused little interest, and absolutely no
disapproval.

After four-and-a-half years in Kyoto King was told by the Council that they planned to move him. He was very reluctant to go: he wondered how he could bear to quit a country in which, even more than in England, he felt so much that he belonged. He told many Japanese friends of his reluctance and received many offers of jobs at universities. But he decided in the end against taking up residence in Japan. For him the hardest part was parting from Noboru.

5

Some Interesting Visitors

**BENJAMIN BRITTEN ● THE ROYAL BALLET ● KENNETH CLARK
SACHEVERELL SITWELL ● LEES MAYALL ● STEPHEN SPENDER
SOMERSET MAUGHAM ● ARTHUR KOESTLER ● ANTHONY POWELL
LAURENS VAN DER POST ● DAVID HOCKNEY ● HUGH CASSON**

AS AIR SERVICES developed and Japan became much more accessible the number of visitors from Britain increased. Among these were writers, performers, composers and artists, some of whom recorded their impressions, or there are impressions of their visits to be found in the writings of others.

One of these early (and important) visitors was the composer BENJAMIN BRITTEN who arrived in Tokyo with Peter Pears on 8 February 1956. Mervyn Cooke in his book *Britten and the Far East: Asian Influences in the Music of Benjamin Britten* (Boydell Press, 1998) gives an interesting account of this visit. According to Cooke, Britten wrote to Roger Duncan on the flight from Hong Kong to Tokyo that he did not really want to go to Japan: 'I don't like what I know about the country or the people . . . and judging by the difficulty Peter and I had in getting our visas, they don't like me any more than I like them . . . But I mustn't be silly and must try to like them.' Later, Britten wrote to Roger Duncan: 'It is far the *strangest* country we have yet been to, like, in a way, going to a country which is inhabited by a very intelligent kind of insect. Very industrious, very clever, but very different from us, very odd. They have very good manners, they bow and scrape all the time: they have most beautiful small things, all their houses, their flowers, the things they eat drink out of, are wonderfully pretty, but their big things, their cities, their way of thinking, and behaving, have all got something wrong. . .'

Britten's visit had been arranged by NHK. His party was greeted on arrival by Kei Kurosawa and his son Hiroshi (but generally known as Peter). Kei who died in 1976 had been at Trinity College, Cambridge, from 1925-28 and was the founder of the Tokyo Madrigal Singers. Britten had a full programme during his brief visit. At the British Embassy he played Bach and Mozart on two pianos with Sir Esler Dening, the British Ambassador, who was an accomplished amateur pianist. Perhaps his most important early engagement was a visit to the Noh theatre at the suggestion of William Plomer who was to write the libretto for Britten's 'Curlew River', based on the play Britten saw on 11 February 1956. This was *Sumidagawa* given by the Umetani group of the Kanze school of Noh. His interest was aroused and he saw the play a second time before leaving Japan.

Cooke notes that Britten's initial reaction to the Noh convention was apparently '. . . one of humour rather than aesthetic profundity. . . Something of this humour is reflected in an amusing photograph taken by the Kurosawas which shows Pears indulging in mimicry of Noh drumming techniques with the aid of a wastepaper basket. Noh vocal chanting sounds uncannily like the comic character Eccles created by Spike Milligan in the 1950s radio hit *The Goon Show*: possibly this irreverent identification appealed to Britten's almost schoolboyish sense of fun.'

Britten wrote to Roger Duncan: 'One thing that I unreservedly loved in Japan was the theatre . . . The Noh is very severe classical – very traditional, without any scenery to speak of, or lighting, and there are very few characters . . . At first it all seemed too silly, and we giggled a lot. But soon we began to catch on a bit, at the end it was very exciting.'

By now Britten was finding Japan much more interesting and he 'had wonderful experiences' but 'he was not sure he wanted ever to go back', although he greatly enjoyed a visit to Kyoto. On return to Tokyo Britten and Pears joined the Tokyo Madrigal Singers at a rehearsal conducted by Kei Kurosawa at the British Council Library on 16 February. He also visited the Music Department of the Imperial Household Agency and heard '. . . the haunting sonorities of the *gagaku* orchestra which were to leave their mark on the musical textures of the Church Parables'. On his return to England Britten wrote to Humphrey Searle: 'Japanese music is the oddest I've ever heard, but very impressive and beautiful.'

Cooke describes in detail Britten's composition of the music for *Curlew River* and the influence of *Sumidagawa* and the Japanese Noh tradition in it.

THE ROYAL BALLET and top ballet dancers from Britain have been frequent visitors to Japan from the late 1950s. LEES MAYALL, then Counsellor and Head of Chancery in the British Embassy in his autobiography *Fireflies in Amber* (Michael Russell (Publishing) Ltd, 1989) recorded:-

Margot Fonteyn came in 1959 with Michael Soames to dance *Swan Lake* and *The Sleeping Beauty* with a Japanese ballet company. Her week's visit became a sort of gala in Tokyo and she was fêted wherever she went in Japan. We saw a lot of her, the more so because Yaki Morris had been her pupil in London. Ivan [Morris] and Yaki gave a dinner party for her at which we ate *fugu* (blow fish) which can only be eaten at certain times of the year and even then is very poisonous and has to be prepared by specially licensed chefs. It is delicious. In her autobiography Margot complained that eating sea slugs may have upset her stomach during her Tokyo visit but she probably did not know the potential danger of eating *fugu*. There are several deaths every year in Japan caused by people eating *fugu* which has not been properly prepared.

FRANCIS KING in *Yesterday Came Suddenly* wrote that:

... a small contingent of the Royal Ballet, led by Margot Fonteyn and Rudolf Nureyev and with Robert Helpmann in charge, arrived in the area. Travelling with them, I was present in Nagoya at one of the frequent arguments between Nureyev and Helpmann.
   'Tonight I dance *Corsair*!' Nureyev announced.
   'No, I'm sorry. Tonight is the night for *Swan Lake*.'
   'No, no! Tonight – *Corsair*!'
   Eventually, his patience exhausted, Helpmann hissed, 'Dance what you like, ducky! The orchestra will be playing *Swan Lake*.'
   It was on this visit that Helpmann asked me if I could find for him a theme, from myth or folk-tale, for a 'Japanese' ballet which he wanted to choreograph. I suggested *Sumidagawa*, later to provide the basis of William Plomer's libretto for Britten's *Curlew River*. Helpmann expressed delight at the suggestion; but, as so often in the world of show business, nothing further happened.

Francis King on another occasion gave a cocktail party in Kyoto

... for the Royal Ballet, then on an exhausting and highly successful tour of the country. So large was the company that the Japanese impresario hired a bus to bring them from Osaka to Kyoto. Each time that this bus bounced over a rut in the unmade road up to my house, many of the male dancers emitted shrill squeals and squawks. John Field, in charge, eventually jumped to his feet. 'Oh, for God's sake. Pull yourselves together. What will Mr King think if you camp it up like this?' The incident was relayed to me by two of the offenders in a gay bar after the party.

STEPHEN SPENDER, the poet, as he described in his journal for 1954-8 (*Journals 1939-1983*, published by Faber and Faber, 1985) was in Japan in 1958.
   Spender was bored by the slowness of Noh plays but got '. . . a lot out of them retrospectively, remembering, for instance, the slow-motion walking on to the stage of a woman (really a man) wearing a brocade coat and with a mask superimposing on her features a gracious downward or upward smile'. He thought that the Japanese, especially the young, 'were to be admired for going at all'. 'It is difficult to see how a form, divorced from the ritualistic attitudes and the mythology which could make it a focus of belief and aesthetics, can survive.'
   Spender travelled and lectured widely. He did not care for Kyushu which he found 'an ugly place filled with people of almost unrelieved ugliness':-

The hotel where we stayed was womanned by a staff of frightful sluts who would not leave me alone for a moment. After tea two professors called to take us to an exhibition of pottery in a department store. One of the professors was fat and coarse-looking, the other thin and tormented. We had lunch at a Western-style restaurant. The fat professor ate macaroni by the vacuumatic method, forcing his mouth into an O and drawing in his breath with a loud hissing noise. . . . After the lecture an extraordinary creature called Sivo, wearing a sky-blue beret, and sweating in large clear drops from every pore of his nose, came up to me and said excitedly, 'You remember me from the PEN Club Conference, Mr Spender. I translate your poems and want to publish them in my magazine *Apollon*. I admire you greatly. I want to be your introducer to Japanese people. Here is a girl who would also admire you if she knew English' – and he suddenly dragged forward a girl who was by his side. 'I want to see you tonight – tomorrow – every time', etc. He pushed himself into the car and sat beside me, talking absurdly. We managed to get away from him but he appeared half an hour later at the dinner the professors gave. This time he was with another maiden – a very attractive one – and said, 'Beautiful art-student admirer of your poems brought this big bunch of flowers.' With a kneeling bow she gave me a huge bunch of enormous flowers. . . As soon as the meal was finished he got up and recited 'The Funeral' in Japanese. I protested that this was my worst poem and mentioned that I had written as much in the Introduction to my *Collected Poems*.

Hokkaido did not prove any better. The journey (train and ferry) had been a long and tiring one. At Sapporo station he was met 'by a lot of photographers and pressmen'. One of the interviewers asked: 'Evidently you are deeply in love with Japan, please will you tell us why?'

A professor took him to Jozankei hot spring:

He is by far the most boring professor I have met so far, and in the car his conversation literally sent me to sleep, while Shozo tried to explain to him that I was tired after the journey. When we got to the hotel, I hoped he would say goodbye and take advantage of having the car to go back to the university with it. But no. He said, 'It is my duty to look after you. Let us go to your room.' We went upstairs and then he said, 'We shall now take a multitudinous bath, after which you will feel greatly refreshed.' The idea of having a bath with this professor really infuriated me. But there was nothing to do except have a bath as quickly as possible. . . After bathing, we went back to our room. The professor said, 'And now we shall have some beer. Let us order three bottles.' So we each drank an inter-

minable bottle of beer while he said, 'I am not a great lover of poetry. In fact, I do not like literature at all. Literature I consider to be
specialization. I let the other professors specialize. What I am interested in is just ordinary English. I am exactly your age, Mr Spender,
and I'm getting very old. At my age I can no longer interest myself
in what is new. . .' He spoke in a way that seemed to me slightly
malicious. as bores do sometimes when they find out they are boring you and decide to take pleasure in it. He told us he was giving a
course of radio programmes in English on Tennyson's 'The Brook'.
'Now it is very difficult for me to do this. I do not understand what
the brook symbolizes and I do not even know how it should sound
when I come to read it aloud.' 'It is about a brook and sounds like a
brook,' I said. . .

There were two watches with faces down on the table. . . Professor T. suddenly turned one of the watches over. It was six twenty.
'I'll have to be going very soon now,' he said, and settled back comfortably again. However, at about six forty he suddenly jumped to
his feet, was changed from his kimono to his clothes in a moment
and rang for the bill. We had quite a job preventing him from paying. He did not want to impose on us by letting us pay, and I did not
want to impose on him. We won.

SOMERSET MAUGHAM was very popular among Japanese students of English literature. (Once, when I was Ambassador in Tokyo, I had to think twice
before responding to Prince Hitachi, the Emperor's brother, at a dinner party
when he said how much he enjoyed what sounded like 'Mum'!)

Maugham visited Japan in 1959 with his secretary Alan Searle. LEES
MAYALL in *Fireflies in Amber* recorded that he and his wife

> . . . met him at lunch at the Embassy; he was then eighty-five but
> still fairly spry though he forgot names. He said that in one of the
> sacks of fan mail, which followed him across the world, he had
> found that morning a letter which ran roughly as follows: 'Dear
> Mr Maugham, I have read all your books and as you seem to know
> about life, I should be grateful for your advice. I am eighteen years
> old and very pretty. I am in love with a man. What should I do to
> win him and keep him?' His secretary, Alan Searle, wanted to put
> the letter in the waste paper basket but Maugham insisted on writ-
> ing back in his own hand: 'Dear Miss –, To achieve the first you
> must be very sexually attractive and to achieve the second sexually
> satisfying. Yours truly, Somerset Maugham.' He seemed inordi-
> nately pleased with this not very witty reply and hugged himself
> as he chuckled over it. He told us that he did not intend to publish

any more but was now only writing for pleasure. Alan Searle said that he was writing his real opinion of people he knew for posthumous publication.

FRANCIS KING who, having won the Somerset Maugham award, had from time to time exchanged letters with Maugham met him for the first time in Kyoto. King wrote of this visit:

> He was in Kyoto for more than a week and, during that week, I saw him every day, often for hours on end. Such continuous proximity is an excellent test of character. He was then extremely old and frail and tired easily; but never once did he show any anger or even irritability towards me, Alan Searle or anyone else.
>
> Maugham's reputation at that period was far higher in Japan than in England – a fact on which he commented to me, with the sardonic ruefulness of so much of his conversation. 'University professors queue up each morning in my hotel to get me to sign copies of my books. But when I stay in London, no one cares a damn that I'm there.'
>
> Maugham put up some pretence of wishing to be free of the crowds, many of them students, who gathered around him in any temple, garden or museum which we visited; but it was easy to see that all this clamorous attention, as to some pop star, secretly delighted him. On one occasion, he told me how he had taken Johnny Ray then at the height of his fame as a singer, from Cap Ferrat into Toulon. The American fleet was in. 'Not one sailor recognized m-m-e of course. But they all recognized J-J-Johnny. "J-J-Johnny, J-J-Johnny, J-J-Johnny!" they kept c-c-rying out, as they b-b-brandished bits of p-p-paper for him to s-s-sign!'
>
> 'How ghastly!'
>
> 'G-g-ghastly? Not at all! Things will really b-b-become g-g-ghastly when sailors stop shouting "J-J-Johnny, J-J-Johnny, J-J-Johnny!"'
>
> Similarly, things would really have become ghastly for Maugham, if with their identifying cries of 'Mom! Mom! Mom!', excited students had ceased to throng round him.
>
> It was I who took Maugham to the Noh Theatre for the first time. Later he told me that it had been one of the most remarkable experiences of his whole life. Wrinkled and bowed, the great writer had sat watching while the great actor had prepared himself for his role: being sewn into his robes; applying wet white with infinite care; then taking a hand-mirror and staring into it for minutes on end, as though by doing so he could leave his own body and enter an alien one. Although we had to sit on the floor during the long performance, Maugham betrayed no sign of weariness or discomfort.

ANOTHER EMINENT writer to visit Japan was SACHEVERELL
SITWELL whose book *Bridge of the Brocade Sash* (i.e. the famous Kintaibashi at
Iwakuni) was published by Weidenfeld in 1959. This is essentially a travelogue.

Sitwell noted in his Introduction how rapidly Japan was changing. He
hoped that this would be 'for the better of its teeming population. That much
is being lost in the process is undeniable. All the more reason, therefore, for
going to Japan before it is too late. For the sake of the old, though in the end it
is possible that the new Japan may not be less sensational.

Much of this book is devoted to a eulogy of Kyoto where he stayed for four
weeks and which to him 'seemed little less beautiful than Rome or Venice'.

ARTHUR KOESTLER who visited India and Japan published his impressions in *The Lotus and the Robot* (Hutchinson, 1960). He wrote:-

> During my stay in Japan I went through three emotional phases.
> The first few days I lived in a colourful haze of euphoria. This
> was followed by a period of mounting exasperation, occasionally
> verging on hatred. In the third phase, some bits of the puzzle began
> to fall into their places with a succession of almost audible clicks,
> and progress in understanding led to the acceptance of what Zen-
> inclined Japanese call 'the such-ness of things'
>
> The three phases were not neatly separated in time; towards the
> end of my stay they would alternate in quick succession within a
> single day or hour – a rather unsettling experience. The old hands
> whom I met, seemed to live permanently in this unstable equili-
> brium and were showing the strain, regardless of how many years
> they had spent on the islands. Life in Japan may be compared to a
> scented bath which gives you electric shocks at unexpected mo-
> ments. At least, I think that is as good a metaphor as any – for it
> is a country that compels one to think in images and to write with a
> brush.

In his first phase he was happy enough.

> Strolling through the Ginza in the spring sunshine was like being
> taken to a toyshop in one's childhood: huge, gaudy balloons, hung
> with streamers, were floating in the sky; helicopters, were hum-
> ming like dragonflies; uniformed chauffeurs were dancing around
> their parked shiny cars with feather-dusters, like chambermaids in
> the first scene of a French comedy; girl guides, waving yellow flags,
> were leading an Indian-file of cow-eyed rustics through the roaring
> traffic of their capital; two elderly gentlemen in black morning
> coats were bowing and bowing and bowing each other through

the revolving doors of a bank; earnest infants with running noses, strapped to their mothers' backs, were riding through the world as if in kangaroo pouches put on the wrong side; everybody seemed to be taking snapshots of everybody else, and buying little bunches of scented violets from dignified urchins, and giggling at their narrow escapes from taxi-drivers with music streaming from their transistor radios.

Koestler thought in his third phase that he understood Zen but he did not, as the following quotation shows.

Taken at face value and considered in itself, Zen is at best an existentialist hoax, at worst a web of solemn absurdities. But within the framework of Japanese society, this cult of the absurd, of ritual leg-pulls and nose-tweaks, made beautiful sense. It was, and to a limited extent still is, a form of psychotherapy for a self-conscious, shame-ridden society, a technique of undoing the strings which tied it into knots; in a word, Zen was the tranki of feudal Japan.

KENNETH CLARK (Lord Clark) the art historian and critic visited Japan in September 1963 as he described in *The Other Half*, published by John Murray in 1977. Japanese art had been his first love and at school he had collected Japanese prints. He was accordingly delighted to be invited by the Japanese government to visit Japan for a month in the autumn of 1963.

Kenneth Clark found the language barrier in Japan insurmountable. Except for his old friend Yukio Yashiro he '. . . did not meet a single Japanese who could speak more than a few necessary words. The Foreign Office [Gaimusho] supplied me with a guide-companion called Mr Maeda, who had spent seven years in Bombay and nine in Washington, but spoke and understood less English than an air hostess or taxi driver.' Mr Maeda's only interest appeared to be baseball.

Clark's 'first disillusion' with Japan was the drive from Tokyo airport to the centre of the city. It took him over two hours and he could not discover 'a single building with any character, let alone style'. He was not impressed by the New Imperial Hotel which he found 'a large, impersonal, American-type hotel'.

His first visit outside Tokyo was to Nara, but he found 'a great deal of Buddhist sculpture monotonous'. He admired Japanese temples in Kyoto and their gardens, but when he visited Ryoanji in Kyoto with its Zen garden of stones and sand he found himself thinking nostalgically of Europe, '. . . and wondering how people who are dedicated to these sand gardens could swallow Bernini. Surely he would make them feel sick.' He decided, somewhat surprisingly, that the Japanese were 'supreme portraitists'.

He preferred Kabuki which he described as 'a grandiose riot' to Noh, although he watched Noh 'with a kind of solemn reverence and it produced '. . . a feeling of long-drawn out expectancy, so that when at last something happens (and terrible things happen) it strikes one with irresistible force. Also it is full of ghosts, which gain from this severely formalised treatment. But four hours!'

In Kyoto he stayed first in a Japanese inn where he was attended by 'an extremely plain young woman'. He thought most Japanese girls very attractive, but saw that it was prudent of the landlady to entrust this duty [waiting on Clark and putting out his bedding] to a plain one.'

When he was asked by a Japanese lady about the state of calligraphy in Britain he realized in a flash '. . . what deserts of incomprehension exist between our two cultures. I sometimes believe that I can distinguish between good and bad calligraphy; but I expect I could easily be taken in by a showy or an archaising piece. I remember seeing over the door of a temple in a very remote part of the country what looked like a magnificent piece of calligraphy and asked my companion what it said. He replied "Coca-Cola".'

He regarded the Inland Sea as 'a dream'. He was lucky enough to see Mount Fuji almost every day. He '. . . watched it turn every colour and can guarantee that Hokusai's prints are correct'.

Although he found a heavy balance for Japan on the credit side, on the debit side he found the Japanese character wanting. 'They seem to be almost entirely dependent on instructions, preferably written instructions, and a formalised code of behaviour. They cannot perform a spontaneous act of kindness or compassion; it would not be "in the book".' He noted also the 'terrible streak of violence'. 'Everything related to old Japan, . . . is beautiful and moving. Almost everything developed in modern Japan, except in architecture, is heartless, inhuman and unsympathetic. It is a triumph of efficiency and obedience.'

ANTHONY POWELL, the famous novelist, visited Japan in 1964. He gave a brief account of his visit in *The Strangers are all gone/To keep the ball rolling.*

1964 was the four-hundredth anniversary of Shakespeare's birth and the British Council arranged a book exhibition and 'three writers were chosen as anthropological specimens of that trade'. The other two were Alan Pryce Jones, formerly editor of the *Times Literary Supplement*, and Muriel Bradbrook, a Cambridge Professor who was an authority on Shakespeare.

Before going to Japan, Anthony Powell '. . . had not taken in what could be implied by belonging to the male sex. In Japan – anyway at that period – it was impossible to have a dish set in front of one by a waitress, ascend in a lift worked by a lift-girl, without being made aware of male status as such. At the same time, if apparently submissive (no doubt extremely tough beneath the surface), Japanese women seemed unselfconsciously at ease with men. One had the sense far more than in the West, submission not implying the least sense of inferiority, if anything awareness of power. At several academic functions attended it was literally impossible – short of picking them up and putting them through the door – to persuade distinguished female professors to pass over the threshold first. Among such learned ladies one could not help feeling moved that some of them had been persecuted during the war years by their devotion to Jane Austen. At one of the university 'quizzes' during which I was on the platform replying to questions a Japanese professor asked: 'What do you think of Shakespeare?' Off the cuff that was a tall order, not least in front of a quite a large assemblage of people.

Fortunately, before leaving he had put a three-volume pocket edition of Shakespeare in his luggage and '. . . had cast my eye over a page or two of *Richard III* the previous evening before going to sleep. "Well as a matter of fact I was reading *Richard III* last night and it struck me that particular play was etc, etc".'

The agent of his English publishers wanted Powell to try a bottle of Japanese red wine. 'I can unhesitatingly confirm that Japanese red wine is better than Guatemalan (to be sampled on a visit to Central America some years later).' On his final day before leaving for Manila he split a final flask of saké with Frederick Tomlin, head of the British Council (see Chapter 3).

LAURENS VAN DER POST who had been in Japan before the war and had been a Japanese prisoner of war in Java, was commissioned to write the text of a book *A Portrait of Japan*, published in 1968 by the Hogarth Press. He wrote a number of other books relating to his experiences in Japan, but it seems appropriate here to quote from this work. In the opening section van der Post recalled how he had managed to escape death on being captured by calling on his attackers in polite Japanese to wait a moment. They had been so surprised to hear him speaking Japanese that they had paused.

On his return to Japan twenty -five years after this encounter van der Post wrote: 'Tokyo was an enigma. It surely must be one of the most afflicted cities in the world.' He found to his surprise that the '. . . customs, medical and immigration inspectors, who had once examined foreigners as if they were notorious enemy agents, dealt with me with despatch and the utmost courtesy'. [He was lucky!] He had found it impossible to arrange hotel accommodation 'by cable' but he was soon fixed up in a hotel, which had only been opened a month earlier, with a tiny single room. 'There was a flower vase on my table. It was not full of flowers; there was a single rose in it. The "Eminent professor of Flower Arrangement," who came each day to do the flowers in the hotel and whom I was to meet, had fixed the rose in a vase at a subtle angle as if it were bowing politely to the wind of change blowing in the mind of Japan.'

The following morning he walked along the Ginza. 'At first I had no eyes for the city because of the people. I thought that such a density and concentration of human beings was purely local and due to some abnormal attraction in the vicinity. I expected at any moment to break out of the swarms of people and find some less congested quarter. But before long I discovered that the apparently abnormal was the normal. . . As bewildering as the numbers was the outward appearance of the crowd. I looked in vain for some master fashion in their dress. Outwardly all was mixture and confusion. The kimono, except for a few elderly ladies and a few little girls, seems to have vanished.'

Van der Post was struck by the Japanese concentration on work:

> It is not hard to detect — behind the almost desperate ingenuity, invention and sustained energy with which Tokyo's millions set about their tasks — the silent, stifling pressure of the expanding millions which makes production a matter of life and death. [The problem of an ageing and declining population was not yet on the horizon]. The skill and inventiveness of the Japanese manufacturer, judging by what I saw in shops, factories and shipyards, was truly stupendous.
>
> In my hotel American, Australian, English, Swiss and Italian businessmen tried to persuade me that the whole of Japanese industry is nothing but a swindle and a gigantic cribbing of others' inventions and industrial designs. It is an old story and one that no doubt was largely true in the modern beginnings.

But he felt that 'all in all' the Japanese 'were potentially the most skilled and original industrial nation of our time'.

He was greatly impressed by Japan's department stores:

> I mingled with the Japanese crowds in many of them all over the country and was convinced that the people went not merely to buy but to satisfy their innate all important *Gemuetlichkeit* and all together, to sample visually the character and nature of a feverishly changing modern world.
>
> Finally, there is Tokyo at night . . . One could not believe there were so many young women in the world free to give themselves over to this sort of life. In every bar behind the counter there is not only a barman to serve the customers, but shoulder to bare shoulder a line of young bar hostesses talk to each customer as he is drinking.

Then there were the night clubs and the strip shows.

JAPAN BECAME ever more accessible as air travel became faster and cheaper. By the 1970s and 1980s Tokyo was becoming just another capital which performers and 'cultural' figures visited as part of their normal day-to-day business. Visits were often brief and the impact of Japan on the visitors lessened. But two artists who have left some account of their reactions to Japan should be mentioned.

The first is DAVID HOCKNEY. In his book *David Hockney* by David Hockney, published by Thames and Hudson in 1976, Hockney wrote of his visit in 1971:

> In November 1971 I went to Japan with Mark Lancaster. I thought it would help me to forget things. We went to America first and spent a few days in California with Christopher Isherwood. Then we stopped in Honolulu for two days. Mark had a shirt exactly like one Peter had been wearing once when I'd drawn him; I didn't know this until one morning I woke up and the shirt was lying on a chair, and I drew it, early in the morning. I made a painting of it later, called *Chair and Shirt*. During the trip I used to get up early and make drawings. Mark complained he was always woken up either by the scratching of my pen writing a long letter to someone, or by the pencil sharpener whizzing because I was drawing. I made a lot of drawings of Mark and various places.
>
> Basically I was disappointed by Japan. I'd expected it to be much more beautiful than it is. At the time I thought most of it extremely ugly. I had expected factories carefully and precisely placed against mountains or lakes and instead I found that any spare, flat bit of land had the most uninteresting factories. We spent just two weeks there; it's not very long, I know. In retrospect it becomes more beautiful. I'm sure it's just a case of remembering what interested me and forgetting what didn't, but it certainly kindled an interest in Japanese art. The temples and gardens of Kyoto are well-known and I wasn't disappointed, but I found something just as exciting because it was unexpected: in the municipal art gallery there was an exhibition called 'Japanese Painters in the Traditional Style'. They were contemporary paintings done from about 1925 to the present, using traditional Japanese techniques (painting in silk and screens), but occasionally treating modern Japan as subject. One picture in particular, called *Osaka in the Rain*, I thought exceedingly beautiful. The misty clouds over the river and street were suggested only by the thin bars of rain, and the little cars and people walking about all had just the slightest suggestion of reflection under them, making the whole thing look extremely wet. I thought perhaps the nearest thing in European art to the painting of the figures and cars was Dufy, an artist I have never been greatly interested in; yet the whole effect was quite magical. I loved the idea of these old men (most of the artists were born about 1900) probably ignoring European painting and yet producing something highly sophisticated and modern.

David Hockney returned to Japan from time to time and seems to have developed more of a feeling for Japan. Japanese themes have featured in a number of his paintings.

When I was British Ambassador in Tokyo in the early 1980s and I heard that he was in the city I invited him to lunch. He accepted and asked if he could take some photographs during the lunch. I agreed. I was astonished by the way in which he used a tiny Japanese camera to take reel after reel of photographs of the guests and the table. The result was his photo-montage 'Lunch at the British Embassy', a copy of which was bought by the British Government and loaned to the British Embassy in Tokyo.

Another artist who came to Japan while I was British Ambassador was the late HUGH CASSON who was accompanied by his wife Rita, who was herself an artist and photographer. Sir Hugh Casson had been President of the Royal Academy in 1981 when the 'Great Japan Exhibition' of Edo period art was held at the Academy. With his habitual enthusiasm and verve Hugh Casson had supported the project. With my encouragement the Japan Foundation invited the Cassons to visit Japan. They stayed with us at the Embassy and I worked out with the Foundation a suitable programme for them. This included a visit to Kyoto accompanied by my wife and myself.

Hugh Casson always carried a pencil and paper and enjoyed himself sketching with a few brief and speedy strokes scenes which interested him. I hoped that he would bring these together one day and publish them. I finally persuaded him to do so on the understanding that I would help with the text.

Hugh Casson's *Japan Observed: A Sketch Book* was published in 1991 by Bellew Publishing in time for the 1991 Japan Festival in Britain. The slim volume was sponsored by the Japan Society.

In his Introduction Hugh Casson wrote as follows:-

To visit Japan is to pass through a looking-glass into a country and culture of paradox. Despite the post-war industrial miracle, the Japanese traditional strengths and attitudes maintain their steady grip. There are still shrines on suburban rooftops, but the explosion of post-war development has left a tide of uncontrolled building. It has also left some of the most exciting new architecture to be seen anywhere in the world. The obligation to conform means emotional pressures must increasingly seek release in fantasies sometimes artificially staged. The wildest 'jungles' are found in the cities, not in the tidily farmed countryside. But through it all still runs a highly developed national sense of beauty. In Japan all senses are engaged, responding to the faint tinkle of water, the scent of waxed wood, the soft tattoo of slippered feet on cotton mats, the light that penetrates the paper screens. That is why the content of this travel diary consists largely of tiny 'eyeshots' caught on the spot by the pen or camera, rather than portraits of famous buildings or beauty spots.

6

Four English Writers in Japan

ANTHONY THWAITE • HARRY GUEST • JOHN HAYLOCK
PETER ROBINSON

THE TRADITION of inviting English writers to lecture and teach in Japanese universities has continued. Many of these, in addition to those mentioned in Chapter 4, have had distinguished careers as poets and novelists.

ANTHONY THWAITE who worked in Japan from 1953 to 1957 writes in 1999 about his experiences in Tokyo at this period:

•

1955 was a momentous year for me. In June I took my final examinations at Oxford. Early in August, I married: Ann, my wife, had been an undergraduate at St Hilda's, I at Christ Church. And in September we sailed for Japan, where I had been appointed as a so-called 'Visiting Professor' at Tokyo University. I was 25.

This job, now I look back, seems to have come about without any very clear intention. During my final year at Oxford, I suppose I had the vague notion that I had better try to find a job, since I was engaged. I knew very little about Japan. Somewhere, perhaps in the *TLS* or *New Statesman*, I noticed an advertisement placed by the British Council, announcing teaching posts in Tokyo, Kyoto, and Jogjakarta in Indonesia. At the same time, or pretty nearly, I was encouraged by some BBC 'talent-spotters' (though I doubt the term existed at that time) to apply for one of the newly-founded General Traineeships. And from what was then known as the *Manchester Guardian* came an invitation to be interviewed.

As things turned out, after interviews in London for both the British Council appointments and the BBC ones and in Manchester for the newspapers it was Tokyo University (Tokyo Daigaku or Todai) that made the first decision: I was wanted there, for two years

Again, looking back, I think I can begin to see how this came about. Some time in 1954, when I was Secretary of the university Poetry Society, I had had an urgent message from the local British Council office, telling me that a very distinguished Japanese Professor of English Literature was in Oxford and eager to meet poets. I agreed to meet this man and offered to take him to the next meeting of the society, at which our invited guests were Laurie Lee and Anne Ridler. Lee and Mrs Ridler were due to join me in a pub, the Eagle and Child (or 'Bird and Baby'), opposite St John's. And that was where I first met Takeshi Saito.

Being then totally ignorant of Japan, I did not know that Saito was the doyen of English literary studies in his country, Edmund Blunden's trusty friend. Nor did I know that he was a devout Christian and a total abstainer. I think I remember that this tiny, delicate, gentle, fastidiously polite man accepted a tomato juice. Whether the subsequent events of the evening followed the usual pattern or Oxford University Poetry Society meetings – gently drunken chaos – I don't remember. If Saito had a great deal to do, subsequently, with my Todai appointment, which I think must have been the case, I reckon that at any rate he must have enjoyed his evening.

Almost as soon as my appointment had been confirmed in that summer tern, of 1955, I was paid a visit in Christ Church by Jiro Ozu, then in his early thirties and a lecturer in English Literature at Todai, a devoted Shakespearian. I now see that Ozu, in typically thoughtful Japanese fashion, had been appointed as my 'minder', someone who had been delegated as Ann's and my mentor and, in a very broad sense, *nakodo* or go-between.

Ann and I sailed from England in September 1955, on the long sea voyage to Hong Kong, where we spent a week before boarding a French liner bound for Yokohama. One fact that has always struck me as significant is that the British P & O liner had a free library but one paid for one's drinks, whereas Messageries Maritimes gave free wine, but one paid for the library.

We arrived in Yokohama on a stormy wet day, and were met by not only Jiro Ozu but also Toru Ueda, head of the English Department at Komaba. After a few days in the Shiba Palace Hotel in Tokyo, we were taken to what was to be our home for the next two years: a small house rented for us by Todai, in Shinmachi, Setagaya-ku. It was simple, comfortable, and almost entirely equipped in what was then traditional Japanese fashion, with a few exceptions: the sitting-room had a wooden floor, our bed was raised on planks above the tatami, and heating was provided by a fearsome gas contraption about which I was handed notes of instruction written in highly ambiguous English by a Todai administrative official.

Tokyo resembled, and was, a city that was still recovering from a terrible war. At Shibuya, our nearest important junction, mutilated service veterans, clad in shining white uniforms, stood silently with their begging boxes. Very few private cars were on the streets, and my journey to the Komaba campus of Todai, via Shibuya, was taken on the slow-moving, jerking, heavily-laden Tamagawa-*den* tram, before I changed to what was then the easily negotiable subway. The complex and efficient horrors of present-day Shibuya and Shinjuku were far off.

In October, the new term began. First, I was ushered into Komaba by Toru Ueda – a vast shabby wooden hall, with a huge wood-burning stove at the far end, away from the lecture platform. 'This is your new professor from England', announced Ueda. 'He is a poet. Please be kind to him, because he is only a little older than you are.' (This was true. Two students who became my closest friends there, Hisaaki Yamanouchi and Hiroshi Izubuchi, were perhaps 20 to my 25.)

Then there was my second Todai campus, Hongo, at which I soon made equally close friendships – mainly because it was suggested, by a young assistant Minoru Hashiguchi, that perhaps I might take some voluntary classes, small discussion groups, with post-graduate students. These weekly seminars, on poetry, drew in some extraordinary talents: chief among them, perhaps, Yasunari Takahashi, who went on to become an almost bewilderingly diverse scholar and critic – translator of Lewis Carroll and Samuel Beckett, re-creator of Falstaff in Noh style, tele-don and radio commentator on music, theatres fantasy and nonsense. But there was also Hidé Ishiguro, voluntarily coming to these classes from her studies in French and in philosophy, who quickly convinced me – in the nicest possible way – that there was little I could teach her.

It is probably invidious of me to mention these names: I was educated by so many Todai students and colleagues. Foreign teachers, at that time, were comparatively rare. Probably we were over-valued. Certainly I feel that I was – young, intellectually arrogant, self-assured in a way I have never felt since. But I hope I had some sense of humility too. Years later, in 1986 on a return visit, I talked with the novelist Kenzaburo Oe. He told me that, when he had last seen me, I looked sad. I asked him why. He told me that it was during an exam in 1956, on the poetry of John Donne: he had attended some of my lectures on Donne, though he was actually from the French department, and thought he should know about this poet. Apparently I had stood by Oe's desk and had asked why he had written nothing. 'I have written nothing', said Oe, 'because I understand nothing.'

It was a time of politics, too. though nothing as fervent or fierce, perhaps, as a little later. There was a day when Zengakuren, the all-Japan students' union, had ordered a one-day strike in protest against the British nuclear tests on Christmas Island. It was on a Friday. Knowing nothing of the strike, I went as usual to Komaba to give my weekly lecture on Shakespeare. All the students seemed to be there. The following Monday, having heard about the strike, I asked one student why everyone had turned up to my class. He replied, 'Sir, Shakespeare did not drop an atomic bomb.'

My wife and I were very happy in Japan during those two years, and all my subsequent visits (1962, 1980, 1982, 1985-86, 1989, most recently 1996) have confirmed my feeling that this is my second country. Our first child was born there, in April 1957, just ten weeks before we left – and her eldest son, now aged thirteen, is happily studying Japanese in his secondary school in Gloucestershire. It seems that what began as a random application for a job almost fifty years ago has become a vital part of three generations of our family. Though I am now almost seventy, I trust that I have not made my last visit.

□

Two poems by Anthony Thwaite recall the Japan he knew:-

Joshidaimae

That thin, sweet, pure cry
Like a hymn to the lost gods
Echoing over the traffic

At last comes into view:
A battered track, its back
A banged-together oven,

Jerking between the gleaming
Nissans and Toyotas,
On this cold, brilliant day,

Crisp leaves falling like money,
The smell of roast sweet potatoes
Wafts from the glowing embers.

No one seems to want them.
Over the fortunate city
The January sun

Hands down magnificence
To the traffic-jams and the truck
And that thin, sweet, pure cry.

Shock

An easing of walls,
A shuddering through soles:
A petal loosens, falls.

In the room, alone:
It begins, then it has gone.
Ripples outlast stone.

Rain-smell stirs the heart;
Nostrils flare. A breath. We wait
For something to start.

The flavour of fear,
Something fragile in the air,
Gone, it remains here.

ANOTHER POET who worked in Japan from 1966 to 1972 was HARRY
GUEST who writes:

•

In 1966 it took twenty-nine hours from London to Tokyo flying via
Beirut thronged with white-robed sheikhs, Delhi where a lone cyclist
crossed the tarmac under an umbrella and Rangoon with a tantalizing
silhouette of pagodas beyond palm-trees. At Haneda, the entire English
department of Yokohama National University greeted me, a welcome
foreshadowing all their friendliness over the next six years.

My wife followed me after five weeks, introducing me to our first child
at the same airport. Our daughter, blonde in those days, was of course a
great hit – indeed, the JAL pilot insisted on carrying her through customs. *'Kawaii aka-chan desu nē.'*

Our tiny wooden house had orange-trees darkening the terrace. A
spindly tree dangled gold persimmons over the path. Geoffrey Bownas,
the previous incumbent, had kindly provided much essential information about the district. In those days, Kugahara's 'Ginza' had no pavements. April lamp-posts became decked with pink plastic blossom.
Tinny speakers spewed *Jinguru beruzu* before Christmas. Only a few shops
(the chemist's, a fancy grocer's proudly selling Oxford Seville marma-
lade) sported plate glass. The others, open to the street, displayed fish,
bright fruit, bulging rice-sacks, crates of Kirin beer. Some traders,
hoarse by evening, encouraged customers with fortissimo praise of their
wares. When nine-months pregnant with our son, my wife's progress was
marked by tender enquiries from shopkeepers too polite to observe the
obvious. *'Mada desu ka?'*

One fishmonger, a strict disciplinarian with a twinkle in his eye, refused to understand what was required until he heard the correct counter
for *ebi* or *hirame*. He would ignore a pointing finger and never allowed the
cop-out *hitotsu futatsu*.

As we were practically the only *gaijin* in the suburb, the postman used
us as a drop for any envelopes in *rōmaji*. It seemed that even he, short of
consulting the map fixed outside the *kōban*, could not easily work out the
eccentric numbering of the building-plots. Originally 780, ours was effi-

ciently re-addressed *Kugahara 4 Chome 23 no 9 ban*. Modernizing did not please everyone. Our landlord had the unusual given name of Atau and waged an ultimately unsuccessful battle to retain its one *kanji* in the new telephone directory.

There was a superb sushi-shop. Once, waiting to collect our order, an earthquake struck. Rushing home, I found our landlord's son worriedly berating Lynn because she had not gone out into the garden. She explained it took time for a heavily pregnant woman to scoop up a child and get down narrow stairs. A doctor now, Hideo has three children of his own. The Mugishima family were wonderful landlords. On rainy afternoons Mrs M. practised her *samisen*. Her husband, a keen golfer, putted round the carp-pond under a banana-tree with those long, ragged leaves which Bashō compared to 'the injured tail of a phoenix'.

I walked each day to Chidori-cho on the Ikegami Line to catch the first of three trains (always on time) transporting me to the campus, then at Minami-ota where the uphill road was frothed with (genuine) cherry-blossom in season. Sometimes a policeman (always the same one) would pounce, demanding a passport – chagrined each time by the checkmate when one produced one's alien certificate. All *gaijin* look alike.

We did have one brush with the law. My wife is American and she was apprehensive in case the Vietnam War would still be raging when our son (born in 1968) became of military age. So Nichol was not registered. Summoned to the police station we watched in fascination the skilful way criminals used *hashi* to down soba despite being handcuffed. During our legitimate dressing-down, the children, apparently on cue, started to cry. Everyone (officers, offenders) burst out laughing. We were all four released with a caution.

Tasha at four was enrolled at the local *yochien*. Children walked two-by-two in crocodile fashion holding hands for safety. On the first day, Mizuno-kun, weeping, refused to take her hand. Within a day she had been accepted and merged with the others, the fair hair escaping from compulsory headgear alone separating her from her classmates. Her lunch-box contained hard-boiled quail's eggs, a *mikan* or two, a rice-ball belted with a strip of seaweed. In 1972, Yorkshire television allowed some journalist who had spent five minutes there to make a 'documentary' on Japan. With typically slick obtuseness, he used a shot of children responsibly supervized on their way to school along a busy street in order to sneer at what he dubbed Japanese conformity.

My students loved *Three Men In A Boat*. The English department, 95% female, moved in their fourth year to Yeats and Virginia Woolf. However, the Economics department seemed, rather sadly, to attract the most gifted linguists, all male and dressed in black uniforms with brass buttons. Perhaps as a relief from being moulded into future cogwheels for the GNP, they relished their exposure to fiction. Although I found it strange that they showed no interest in their own heritage – never, for instance, wishing to experience the richnesses of Noh, Kabuki or *bunraku* – their keenness to acquire all aspects of 'Western' culture was most attractive. Even during the dark days of 1968-9 when Maoist lackeys screamed abuse through loudspeakers and eventually closed the university, students eager to learn came to our house for lessons. Girls, well trained in etiquette, would be sure to leave two inches of fruit-juice in their glass however long they stayed.

The university became the focus for much appalling violence. A small minority of dedicated fanatics killed a girl for wearing ear-rings in defiance of 'revolutionary' ethics. Each day, the *Asahi Shimbun* carried reports of fearful atrocities. One hesitated to glance at the headlines in dread of seeing yet again the *kanji* for *Yokohama Koku Dai*. I remember wondering what logic transformed certain words like 'gas' into *katakana* whereas 'Molotov cocktail', surely a gift for linguistic mangling, became tamely *kabin*, 'fire-bottle'.

It all blew over eventually like typhoons in September. I suppose each of the ringleaders has mutated into a *sararī*-man. It must however be conceded that the protests did have some justification. The buildings, thrown up soon after the war, were makeshift and soulless. The only aesthetic concession had been to plant purple cabbages in the grubby quadrangles. Undergraduates had nowhere to go in their free time except the grim lecture-rooms. Some good resulted from the bloody upheaval: the campus is now set in spacious grounds at Hodogaya.

As I had been appointed by the British Council, I taught evening classes for the Cambridge Proficiency Exam in a ramshackle building at Yotsuya 3 chome. I took an afternoon course at the Tokyo Nihongo Gakko (language school) in Shibuya on the same days each week so as to be on the receiving as well as the giving end. The class, mostly middle-aged teachers, were very gifted and immensely enthusiastic. We studied *Adam Bede* and *Othello*. Seeing the play in translation, it was fascinating to watch Shima Iwashita as Desdemona, but Shoroku Onoe (wonderful as Tomomori in *Yoshitsune Sembonzakura* winding the fatal anchor round his waist before flinging himself overboard) seemed oddly hesitant as Othello. We saw a fine production of *Julius Caesar* with Kusaka intensely moving as Brutus, although the audience, gorily used to the tradition of *seppuku*, found his need to have someone else hold his sword rather bizarre. It is parenthetically interesting to note how Japanese actors prefer to drop on their knees as often as possible. 'Body language' must of course differ nation by nation. A Japanese will indicate himself by pointing to his nose not his heart, and I've often thought how that deft way of calculating up to ten by bending and then unbending the same five fingers is a Zen-like instance of the sight of one hand counting.

We did a fair amount of work on radio and television. It was immodestly gratifying to be recognized furtively in department-stores. NHK tended to reward one genteelly with a vase whereas the commercial stations paid lavishly. I received $100 for translating the Fujitsu company song (Chorus: *'A-ah Fujitsu-u'*) but whether it is still (or was ever) sung in Surrey I cannot say. There is a 45rpm record. . .

In 1968 William I. Elliott and Kazuo Kawamura founded the Kanto Poetry Center. At that first session in Kanazawa-Hakkei (sadly changed from the ravishingly tranquil scene depicted by Hiroshige) James Kirkup, Gary Snyder and I gave readings and lectures in alternation with Shuntaro Tanikawa and Taro Kitamura. Schoolteachers and academics, local and foreign students all signed up for a stimulating interchange of traditions and ideas. It was a joy to see many of my former students turning up when I was invited back in 1987, this time to perform with Makoto Ooka and Seamus Heaney.

Nikos Stangos, then with Penguin, commissioned me to produce an anthology of contemporary Japanese poetry. Fortunately, my colleague Shozo Kajima, renowned not only as a poet and the translator of Faulkner but also as a painter, cooperated with my wife and myself in the scheme. He had been an active member of the 'Arechi' group. *Post-War Japanese Poetry* appeared in 1972.

Seiichi Niikuni died in 1979. I still miss that most scrupulously inventive of poets who in 1964 had founded the ASA group to focus internationally on concrete and phonetic poetry. We spent hours in his house at Yukigaya-Ōtsuka, two stops up the line from Kugahara, testing sounds and signs on tape-recorder and paper. His beautiful visual poem *Ame* hangs now on the wall, a lucid reduction of the ideograph to its component parts to show drops trickling down the page.

Seeds often unconsciously planted during those six rich years have borne fruit. My wife would not perhaps otherwise have found the theme for her prizewinning novel *Children Of Hachiman* nor its brilliant successor *Yedo*. It is hard (and probably undesirable) to seek influences in one's own work, but, although my own novels are set securely in Europe, Japan is present in many poems – in *Matsushima*, in *Zeami In Exile* (for the rain falling among drifting petals in *Yuya*) and in *The August Notebooks* tracing a journey to the Noto peninsula.

Tasha and Nichol spoke Japanese so well that on a visit to Korea they embarrassed their parents not only by raising their arms and shouting *'Banzai!'* when about to choke (a trick learned from Kimura-san, our trusty baby-sitter) but by accusingly (and vulgarly) interrogating waiters: *'Dōshite Nihongo o shaberanai ka?'* (Why don't you speak Japanese?) Alas now their conversation retains only *chūsha* (parking), *abunai* (dangerous) – and *mikan* for they would never lapse into using *satsuma*.

Three decades on one's own memories lose detail. Or sift so that the sharper ones stand out like those rocks above raked sand in a Kyoto garden. How is it possible not to be grateful for the privilege of having lived in a land of so many fruitful contradictions? A hectic land with pockets of serenity, a land of skyscrapers and brocade, tradition and technology – a changing land which nevertheless abandons neither a taste for comedy nor a shrewd ability to duck behind enigma, the glimpse maybe of a scarlet *torii* perched on the cement roof of an office-building.

JOHN HAYLOCK is a novelist who first went to Japan in 1956. He is a friend of Francis King who first met him in Florence. Francis King would stay frequently with John Haylock in the latter's flat in Tokyo. King describes Haylock as 'Always jolly, always resourceful, always stoical . . . an ideal travelling companion . . . He is naturally kind without being in the least sentimental. He has an eighteenth-century horror of excess. . . Haylock has called his contribution 'Remembering Japan':-

•

Altogether I lived in Japan for fourteen years, apart from regular sojourns of several months, which still continue. As I have aged, Japan has changed.

My first visit to Japan was a tourist one. I arrived at Haneda Airport on 11 July 1956 and was the only passenger in the BOAC bus, which took me to the Ambassador Hotel, near Iidabashi Station.

The Ambassador was excellent. A single room cost 2000 yen, which in those days was £2; but unlike today, in 1956 £2 was a respectable sum.

I was at once enchanted with Japan. It was so different. Ceylon, Singapore and Hong Kong, which I had visited on my way, were not a bit like England, but there existed in those places remnants of the Empire that mitigated their strangeness. In Hong Kong the Union Jack was ubiquitous, in Singapore British troops were in evidence, and at the Galle Face Hotel in Colombo one was warned that dinner jackets were *de rigueur* on dance nights. But Tokyo, in spite of the American presence still visible here and there, although the Occupation was over and 'Emperor' MacArthur had departed, seemed wonderfully alien.

The Ambassador Hotel, a white and not very tall building, towered above the wooden shops outside which hung paper lanterns; pink and blue streamers criss-crossed the narrow curling street; the clip-clop of *geta* was the predominant noise. The hotel no longer exists and the wooden shops have been demolished to make room for giant blocks. But in the summer of 1956 the atmosphere was distinctly Japanese and to me attractively foreign.

I took up an introduction to an English businessman who had an office in one of the brick buildings (now no more) in Marunouchi. He arranged for me to go on a trip with Geoffrey, a colleague of his, who wanted to have a short break.

We flew to Fukuoka and stayed in a Japanese inn. I was grateful to Geoffrey for teaching me the rules of conduct in a *ryokan*. I got muddled with the etiquette of putting on and taking off slippers, and horrified the maid, who discovered me in the *tatami* bedroom wearing the lavatory slippers. Geoffrey instructed me how to tie the *obi* round the *yukata* and how to hold chopsticks when we sat on the floor in the bedroom to have a Japanese meal. The maid was in attendance and I was told to hold up my *saké* cup when she refilled it.

We took a train to Beppu. In those days trains were not air-conditioned and Japanese male passengers stripped down to their underwear without a qualm. It was the accepted convention so to disrobe when travelling in the summer. Geoffrey carried a fan which he used constantly. 'It saves you,' he explained, 'from breaking out into a muck sweat. You must get one.' I did. Today fans are out of fashion and they to longer stick out of the back pockets of trousers.

We sailed to Kobe calling in at Miyajima. I was amused by the playing of *Auld Lang Syne* and the severing of the streamers joining passengers to their well-wishers as the ship left Beppu. The farewell was like that given to a transatlantic liner in the Thirties.

'They love saying sayonara,' remarked Geoffrey.

'The bitter joy of parting,' I suggested.

'That's it. And they're probably only going away for a few days.'

From Kobe Geoffrey returned to Tokyo and I took a train to Kyoto, where I put up at the Kyoto Hotel, then still in its pre-war state: comfortable and friendly. I was unable to see many of the main temples as they were on strike in protest against a tax which the municipality wished to impose on entrance fees. This was a disappointment, but I was able to watch the Gion Festival procession. I stood among a crowd in a side street off Kawara-machi and was fascinated to see the passing *hoko* and *yama*, both pulled or carried by young men in *happi* coats and *fundoshi*. The procession, dating from the ninth century, indicated the Japanese respect for tradition.

I went to the usual places a tourist visits from Tokyo: Nikko and Lake Chuzenji, Kamakura and Hakone, and I saw two performances at the Kabuki-za. I contacted Professor Fukuda, to whom I had an introduction, and he gave me lunch at a restaurant near my hotel. We sat on the floor in a private room and were served with eels which, the professor explained, were supposed to be good for one in the summer.

I was impressed by Fukuda's wide knowledge of English and French literature and by his acquaintance with not a few European and American authors. I did not realize at that first meeting that we were to become fast friends or that he was to be my invaluable mentor.

When I left Tokyo at the end of August 1956, I longed to return. There was so much more I wanted to see in Japan, to know about, to understand. I was struck by the politeness of people, the general kindness, the desire to do a job well, however lowly, and by the determination of everyone to succeed. In 1956 only eleven years had passed since the end of World War II, and there was still evidence that the nation was smarting under the sting of defeat, but the hurt acted as a spur.

At Liverpool, in the middle of February 1958, I embarked on the *Atreus*, a Blue Funnel cargo ship, bound for Japan. I had been living and teaching in Baghdad, but my contract had come to an end because of a book (*New Babylon*) I wrote about Iraq with the distinguished Arabist the late Desmond Stewart. Professor Fukuda had fixed me up with a job teaching English conversation in the Law Department of Waseda University. How on earth was I going to teach English conversation to a class? I dismissed the problem from my mind. I was going where I wanted to go: Japan.

The infinitely kind Professor Fukuda took me to Waseda University, where he introduced me to Professor I. of the Law Department. Professor I., whom I was to get to know well, took me to see the President, who said to me: 'We Japanese are very weak in English conversation. You must realize that we Japanese are shy people. You have to make us speak.' Professor I., though, was not in the least shy; on the contrary, he could be quite aggressive; his hesitant, faulty English did not deter him from speaking his mind.

Professor Fukuda found me an apartment in Ichigaya, a short tram-ride away from Waseda. The apartment consisted of the upper floor of a wooden hut in the back garden of a two-storey house owned by a Mr Oya, a pharmacist. The little abode had two rooms furnished with no more than the bare essentials, and they, the bed, the chest of drawers, the sofa and the dining-table were shoddily made. There was a minute bathroom off the sitting-room and the kitchen was in the small space at the top of the ladder-like stairs.

My rent came to half my salary (£30 a month), but Professor Fukuda found two side jobs for me at two women's universities. I was able to keep my head above water, but only just; due to currency restrictions I could not draw on my income in England.

As the beginning of the term drew near, I went hot and cold at the thought of my conversation lessons.

No one would advise me. I did not then realize that the Japanese do not like shouldering the responsibility of giving advice in case they might be wrong. It is this Asian dislike of committing oneself that is ingrained in the Japanese character and causes them to evade a definite answer and agree with you when in truth they do not.

When I asked a female teacher at one of my women's universities what I should teach, she replied, like the President of Waseda, 'We are very weak in English conversation', as if confessing to some congenital ailment.

'What can be done about it?'

'We must try harder.'

I went to Kanda, where I had heard there were a number of bookshops with English departments. In Sanseido, I discovered some books on teaching the impossible subject of conversation. The contents, however, provided no succour at all. How could I spend two hours (I had learnt to my horror that lessons lasted this inordinate time) repeating such banalities as: 'Hi, how are you?' 'I'm fine, thanks, just fine, and you?' 'I'm fine too, thanks.' 'Good, that's good. I'm glad to hear it. How's your old man?' 'He's fine, thanks, just fine. How's yours?' 'Fine, thanks, fine.'

In the same shop I fell upon some annotated versions of English and American plays and chose a few of them for my lessons.

So anonymous did the crowded campus of Waseda University seem (the buildings were mostly uninspiring blocks) that I felt I had parachuted from the skies into Room 308 of Building 21. I found thirty blank faces, three of which belonged to women, and wondered how to begin *The Importance of Being Earnest*. The cliché that the Japanese look alike is true to a tyro in Japan, especially when everyone is dressed identically in black uniforms done up at the neck with a celluloid collar peeping over the top. Today, uniforms have disappeared from the universities and students wear casual clothes. But in 1958 the affluence that was to come to Japan had not yet arrived; the country was still struggling out of the devastation of the war. The uniforms were practical. They saved the wearing of a shirt, and, being made of strong serge, were durable; they were often handed down from elder brother to younger. The hair, sleek with camellia oil, was the same hue as the uniforms and added to the similarity of appearance – now hair is worn any-old-how and is ungreased. The faces between the black oiled grass and the black jackets glowed like the moon. . . What was I to say to this group of unflickering lamps? There the thirty sat, their dark eyes upon me.

Only two students (both women in Western dress) had bought the paperback edition of the Wilde play. I held forth about the play, the author, British society in the 1890s, speaking slowly and articulating with exaggerated precision, but the dark eyes gave no indication of comprehension. At the end of my performance I asked a question and instead of thirty faces I was confronted with thirty glistening black heads; each student had put his chin on his chest; it was like regarding thirty full stops. I wrote on the blackboard the first two lines of the play.

Algernon: Did you hear what I was playing, Lane?

Lane: I didn't think it polite to listen, sir.

I tried to explain the humour in this, but the smiles I managed to extract were polite rather then appreciative.

With trepidation I alighted from a bus at the gates of one of my women's universities. Girls in navy blue costumes and white blouses busily populated the campus of plain wood and plaster buildings. It was the lunch break. Each time a student passed by she doubled up in a sort of walking bow. Mrs Asano, who met me outside the main block, doubled up too; also she put a hand over her mouth when she spoke, which made it difficult to hear her quiet, apologetic voice. The hand-over-mouth gesture, born out of modesty, was a favourite one for Japanese women and some men to adopt. It was often placed over protruding teeth when one's interlocutor laughed or giggled nervously. However, behind Mrs Asano's screen of shy courtesy was an admirable practicality and helpfulness. I was provided with a neat list of my students' names in Roman letters, and when I got to my class of fifty-eight girls there was not one without a copy of the play I had chosen: Eugene O'Neill's *Beyond the Horizon*. As at Waseda lessons lasted two hours, and two long hours they turned out to be.

I was lucky enough to meet a young Japanese, who, like me, was interested in Kabuki. Every Saturday we would go to the *Kabuki-za* or to one of the other theatres which was doing Kabuki plays; there were about three in those days. With the help of my friend (the English programmes at that time were incomprehensible) I learned a lot about Kabuki and about Japan too.

One day, Professor I. of Waseda took me to a performance of *Chushingura* at the *Kabuki-za*. To see Parts I and II together is called *toshi* (right through) and the two parts last from eleven in the morning to ten at night, and this is what the professor and I did. He arranged for us to go backstage just before the spectacular Ichiriki tea-house scene. The stage manager showed us the gorgeous set and the mechanics of the revolving stage. It was a memorable outing.

When my two-year contract was up I wanted to stay on, but nevertheless I left; however, I returned after two years and, was again employed by Waseda University.

The late Meredith Weatherby invited me to be a lodger in his house in Roppongi. The house was a traditional Japanese one which he had had dismantled and re-erected in Roppongi. Meredith had just started his own publishing firm after being Tuttle's chief designer for some years. The new company was called Weatherhill. Meredith had impeccable taste as was shown in his book designs and in the way he grafted Western comforts on to his Japanese house without spoiling its character. He translated *Confessions of a Mask* and therefore was responsible for introducing Yukio Mishima to the West. Mishima, whom I met occasionally at the house, had a lively and incisive mind, but he always seemed tense and ill at ease. I shall not forget his staccato laugh, devoid of any ring of humour. A man who left an indelible impression (I can see his dark, soulful eyes and his pale face topped by a crew cut as I write) but one who lacked warmth and was inordinately vain; he was, though, a writer of great distinction. The less said about his miserable and despicable end the better. I was living in Cyprus when it occurred. In a letter Meredith wrote. 'You must not think he was mad.' Professor I., who came to stay, said about Mishima 'Unbalanced'.

My teaching passed off more easily than before. I even enjoyed some of my classes. I have kept up with a group of students and see them every year when I visit Japan. I have known them for thirty-seven years. Now fathers, if not grandfathers on the point of retirement, they have all had good jobs.

I was sorry to leave Japan in March 1965. I could possibly have had my contract renewed, but with the beginning of the era of prosperity prices had risen and I was finding it difficult to manage on my salary; also, Europe and its attractions were beckoning.

During the next ten years I wandered, living in Morocco, Egypt and Cyprus. I visited Japan in 1971 and was amazed at the rise in the standard of living. Salaries were higher and the Japanese had begun to travel to all parts of the world. European capitals were full of groups of neatly dressed Japanese with their cameras and their eagerness to see as much as possible during their lightning visits. In Tokyo there was a general air of affluence. I took Professor I. out to dinner in the restaurant of a well-known hotel and he remarked disparagingly, and, one might say, prophetically, 'Too much luxury. It is danger. It will not last.'

In 1974 Turkey invaded Cyprus, where I was living. I left the island. The ever helpful Professor Fukuda came to the rescue and I was appointed a Professor of English Literature at Rikkyo University. Thus began the happiest years of my life – 1975-1984: a good job (I could even save part of my salary), reasonable accommodation and a wonderful Japanese friend made them so.

The students had become more self-confident and were proud of their country's economic success. They thought, as did I, that the golden days would go on forever. My old Waseda students felt secure. They were doing well. They had joined golf clubs, bought houses in the suburbs, owned cars, travelled abroad. I retired from teaching in 1984 and took up residence in Brighton, where I had a house. Every year since I have visited Japan in the autumn.

In autumn 1998, in spite of the much-spoken-of recession, Tokyo outwardly looked the same: trains were full, so were popular restaurants and the streets were as crammed with traffic as ever. I asked a Japanese friend about the recession and he said, 'It's only on television'. But there were signs if one looked under the surface: construction had slowed down, some small restaurants had had to close or were struggling, department stores seemed bereft of customers and a friend's company had gone bankrupt and he was out of work. One of my ex-Waseda students, who once held a senior position in an import-export firm had lost his job owing to the folding of the company; he had taken a job selling electric pianos. At the annual dinner party I felt that behind the brave faces of my old students were worries, but of course they did not mention them. The Japanese are adept at hiding their troubles. They are also blessed with a remarkable resilience that enables them to overcome adversity.

In 1956 when I paid that short tourist visit to Japan, it was obvious that life was hard for most Japanese. As the years passed, slowly did conditions improve until by the 1980s Japan was a rich country, thanks to the determination and hard work of the people. Now the affluence is threatened, but the Japanese have not forgotten their favourite word of encouragement: *gambatte* (endure); and endure they will and succeed again.

PETER ROBINSON, who was Professor of English at Sendai University, sent me the following moving piece (which he entitled 'Lost and Found') about aspects of working in Japan:

•

Japanese hospitals do not exactly have an appointments' system. If you think there's something wrong with you, you try to get there as early as the admission opens, enter your name on a list and then just wait for as long as it takes. It can take the best part of a day. During 1992, living in Sendai, I began to hear a faint tinnitus in my right ear and thought I was becoming slightly deafer in that one than in the other. There is a poem made of four fragments about this from *Lost and Found* (1997) called 'Hearing Difficulties'. It begins:

> About the shell of my right ear
> it's true there's something ominous.
> Added to the chorus
> of voices I can hear
> is a thin continuous
> rushing noise like the sound of the sea
> or like an old valve record player
> left on through the night.

That autumn, while taking tablets for a supposed inner ear infection, I started to feel stabbing pains across my right cheek, and, unconvinced by the private clinic's diagnosis, booked myself in to have some more extensive checks at the City Hospital – well, not booked myself in, because I am afraid my Japanese was not that good; I had been in the country for just over three years, and the English department assistant had volunteered to act as a guide.

Visiting professors in Japan are often treated royally by students and colleagues, and the social attitudes towards academics are far more respectful than in England. Such things can go to your head, and on one occasion, waiting and waiting, I complained to our assistant about the lack of a more personal treatment. He quietly rebuked me. 'When it comes to sickness, we're all of us equal,' is more or less what he said.

My first two years in the country had been spent in Kyoto, living in traditional-style houses, being taken to famous temples and beauty spots, suffering acute loneliness: my marriage was disintegrating, the time I spent alone being interrupted by brief and difficult visits from a wife whom I had known for over twenty years, but whom I was beginning not to recognize. The feeling may well have been mutual. This, however, is not the occasion to go into that story.

Japan being a place to learn patience, it must have been the third or fourth time we went through the hospital process that the specialist in the ENTdepartment tentatively uttered the one word 'diagnosis' in English – and handed me a piece of paper with the words 'acoustic neuroma' on it. When I asked the assistant to ask him what it meant, the doctor again reached into his English vocabulary and found the words: 'brain tumour'. Out in the waiting area, among all the other people and their illnesses, I felt as if I been punched in the stomach:

> In a hearing clinic's waiting-room
> someone's worse off than yourself
> putting up the CT scan
> he shows what lies beneath the skin
> and bad news after hours of patience
> arrives in the shape
> of a paler shape about the size of a coin.

That half-line, 'what lies beneath the skin', remembers T. S. Eliot's phrase about Webster, who 'saw the skull beneath the skin' and 'was much possessed by death' – as indeed was I, sitting there among the other patients and digesting the simple words 'brain tumour': a diagnosis that (not knowing any better) I took to be tantamount to a death sentence.

In the head of department's office with the junior professor and assistant one day later, I found myself with a choice of having the tumour removed at the University Hospital in Sendai, or going back to England and undergoing the operation there. My decision to return home, where I could have family and friends nearby, was accepted with equanimity. So, at the ENTdepartment in Addenbrookes, Cambridge, that early December, it was explained to me that mine was a benign tumour, and that, not being a cancer secondary, there was little chance of death (they had only lost one patient in some 80 operations) – though the side effects and the convalescence would be serious: partial deafness, some facial paralysis, headaches, chronic tiredness... Since my tumour had been there for seven or eight years already, and was growing at a very slow rate, there was no danger in simply adding my name to the waiting list. They would let me know some time in January when the operation could be performed:

'God help you' comes from overseas.
It means *the very best of luck*
in the English of a Japanese,
and it's true you need it when

a consultant pats you on the knee
offering some courage,
lays his hands on you and says,
'You'll be wondering soon: why me?'

No sooner had I arrived in England than I began to receive 'Get Well' cards (and a tiny origami crane) from Japan – from, for instance, the Kyoto professor who had first arranged for me to take up a one-year post there as a visiting lecturer. His knowledge of idiom is not perfect; but his phrase 'God help you' was evidently meant to be taken literally, which is how I took it.

However, it was not until some time in February that the hospital finally informed me that my operation was booked for 12 May 1993. Long before being told this, I reported the basic situation back to my department in Sendai by fax. Early in the new year, a reply came from Japan which said that since I could not say when the operation was going to be, and could not fulfil my duties, my contract would be terminated at the end of March. This seemed the final blow: I was facing major surgery, my wife was divorcing me, and now my job was lost as well. As the poem says, '... why me?'

But I was thinking: Well, why not?
What would they mean, the hours of boredom
and jokes about a poet going deaf,
all things being equal in sickness and in death,
if not that here's just another of those people?

So when you tell him we're getting a divorce
(letting him know as a matter of course)
he replies, 'It never rains but it pours.'

That's how 'Hearing Difficulties' ends, with no mention of the threatened job loss. Among the many reasons for its absence from this autobiographical collage is that only a day or two after getting the message terminating my contract, I received another which said something like: 'disregard previous fax'. What had happened?

*   *   *

From what I later gathered, it seems the head of department (a year or two away from retirement age) had gone to the dean and described my health predicament. Together, with the best interests of their faculty in mind, they had decided to replace me, so as to make sure that the visiting professorship post was not lost through falling vacant should I be unable to return by 31 March 1993 to re-sign the annual contract. The Ministry of Education had been making noises about abolishing such positions and its loss would mean a reduction in the faculty's standing in the Japanese academic world. It would also mean the end of a tradition: the post has been occupied by, among others, Ralph Hodgson, George Barker and James Kirkup.

When he heard of this decision, the junior professor had telephoned the older Kyoto academic – in tears, as I was later told. During my first year in Japan, he had listened to a paper I gave on *The Rape of Lucrece* at a Shakespeare conference in Shikoku, and when, the following year, a vacancy in Sendai had arisen, he contacted me about the possibility that I might take up the position. He would also become the head of department in just a year or two and had expected that I would be his colleague during the interval when there might well be only himself and the foreign professor to run the English teaching. With or without the encouragement of my Kyoto sponsor, the junior professor confronted his senior and protested that terminating the contract in absentia was not the right course of action.

Such behaviour is (I understand) rather unusual in Japan; after all, a junior member of a hierarchy had opposed his direct senior and, what's more, he had done it at least partly in the interests of a foreigner – someone categorically outside the hierarchy. At this point, the head of department also did an unusual thing: he suggested that, since there was a conflict between what he had done and what his junior felt should have been done, they would resolve the dilemma by asking the opinion of the only other member of the department on a salary from the Ministry of Education: the assistant who had accompanied me on my hospital visits. He supported the younger man's point of view against his professor, the professor whose sponsorship would assist him in finding a post of his own while I was away. It was then that I received the second fax.

Once the decision had been reversed, the senior man put himself out to make sure that the new line of action would succeed. There followed complex bureaucratic processes for arranging that the post should be kept open over the course of one semester. A special intensive course was arranged with a visit by the foreign professor at the University of Tokyo, so half my credits could be granted to the students, the other half being covered by the department head's extra classes on Natsume Soseki [the renowned Japanese novelist]. I would go off salary, but continue to rent my flat, and had to promise to be back in Japan again by 14 September 1993.

You do not just get up and walk away from brain surgery. The removal of the tumour required an eight-hour operation and a twenty-four-hour anaesthetic. Modern hospital practice, however, puts the emphasis on rapid recovery by pushing patients to become autonomous again as soon as possible. I have a clear memory within a surrounding blur of coming to consciousness in the intensive care unit, finding myself attached to various machines with wires and tubes. The team, when they realized this, made a bold attempt to get me back on my feet. But the removal of the right inner ear had destroyed my ability to balance, and I immediately collapsed to the floor. The result of this total failure at the first hurdle was that I was moved out of intensive care, but into a separate room where, among other things, I would not scare the patients awaiting similar operations.

Just ten days after, having relearnt how to walk and other basic bodily skills, I was released into the community for convalescence – a process that was interrupted a month later when I suffered an infection of the right ear which produced newly unbearable headaches and was thought to be meningitis. Being back in hospital for two weeks of intravenous penicillin, and with the prospect of a second investigative operation to find out and put right whatever might be wrong, made me begin to doubt whether I would make that September deadline. However, by the end of August, and without need of a second operation, the ENT specialist at Addenbrookes felt confident enough of my improvement to allow me to take the twelve-hour flight to Japan. That autumn I was just about able to get through my classes, and kindly encouraged to cancel anything I felt unable to manage. Fortunately, the occasion did not arise.

When I later spoke on the telephone to my Kyoto sponsor, who mentioned the junior professor's tears, he gave me a piece of advice.'Don't,' he said,'hold it against your head of department that he'd agreed to terminating your contract; it was nothing personal: he would have done the same with anyone in that situation.' Here was another lesson to learn.

However, reflecting over the years on what happened, I suspect the lessons may be more various and complex. After all, the junior professor and the assistant had not done the expected thing. If the older man, born in 1930, had behaved in what he thought were the best interests of the institution (regardless of the individual concerned), the younger, born in 1954, had done what he thought best (by following his own judgement and considering the individual). Nor, by trying not to take it personally, did I feel inclined to discount the kindness that had been shown me by the junior professor and the assistant, born in 1963 – a kindness which meant that within a year of returning to Japan I was able to become a father for the first time, and, within 18 months (the no-fault divorce came through), was free to marry my first daughter's Italian mother. Being an unemployed semi-invalid would have made both of those events much less likely.

With such thoughts in mind, a few years later I wrote a poem for my forthcoming book entitled 'Back to Work'. Towards the close, it includes a chance meeting and exchange of words between myself and the same junior professor, by then head of department, who is the poem's dedicatee:

> For a moment between obligations
> and feeding where it can, my time
> is mine to alight on what you will:
> ancestral tombs in a pine-tree shroud,
> castle remains on the opposite hill;
> but then once, at that rising parapet,
> a colleague appeared as if from the world –
> 'Have you finished your work?' he called,
> and me, awoken from my daydream,
> 'No, I'm just going back to it.'
>
> Only a moment between obligations
> unremembered for months, I admit;
> yet it's on just such a piece of land
> scattered with weeds, leaves lying around,
> between the new bridge approach's mound
> and dirt patch of a baseball ground,
> that, passing, I would make my stand.

When I first came to Japan it was to take up a job. I did not come to develop a prior interest in the country, its language or arts. That I still live in Japan is only because over the years I have come to admire and enjoy qualities in the culture, qualities which have helped me grow in unexpected ways, it is because at a crucial moment a few individuals particularly wanted me to be here. I am, and shall be, eternally grateful to them.

7

The British Council Follows Through

PETER & JOAN MARTIN • MIKE BARRETT

THE BRITISH COUNCIL recognized the importance of Japan for their work and generally appointed able representatives. One of these was PETER MARTIN who took over from Francis King in Kyoto and later returned to head the Council in Tokyo. While in Kyoto he and his first wife Joan produced one of the first books in English entitled *Japanese Cooking*. It was published by André Deutsch in 1970 with a Foreword by Sir John Pilcher, then British Ambassador in Tokyo, who declared:- 'To write about Japanese cooking is to discourse about Japanese aesthetics, philosophy and way of living. . . All Japanese cooking needs its setting. A Japanese meal is unthinkable without a quiet, withdrawn room looking on to the garden, which must be a picture to be seen from inside, beautiful at all seasons . . . Freshness and a certain astringency are the qualities most prized . . . The feast is for the eye and the mind. . . It is vulgar to show hunger, which can so easily be assuaged. A Japanese banquet, like a tea ceremony, is food for the spirit. Mere eating can be done elsewhere. . .' [I remember that Sir John Pilcher would often say that the greatest pride of a Japanese chef lay in making a salmon look like Nagoya Castle! Ed.]

In their introduction Peter and Joan Martin commented:-

The Japanese cuisine has been much maligned, though probably unintentionally. The reasons are not hard to seek, and consist principally in the virtual insurmountability of the language barrier so far as the overwhelming majority of visitors are concerned, and the preference on the part of the Japanese for entertaining out, at restaurants, rather than in their own homes. Japanese generosity in hospitality is proverbial, and has the paradoxical disadvantage that foreigners are almost always taken by their Japanese hosts to expensive restaurants which restrict their offerings to a limited range of dishes thought to be elegant. This is apt to induce in the guest a feeling of simultaneous surfeit and disappointment, much as though one were to dine off canapés for a week.

The lucky few who speak Japanese or live in Japan long enough to explore the small eating houses favoured by the man in the street know better than to suppose that the tid-bits served in ceremonial style to honoured guests, even supplemented by the heartier meals of *sukiyaki* and *tempura* which are thought to be more amenable to the foreign palate, are typical of what most people eat.

Peter Martin while in Japan began to write detective stories in Japanese settings which have been very popular with readers of this genre of fiction. He acquired his feel for the Japanese criminal scene by careful observation as he revealed in a lecture to the Japan Society on 11 December 1984 (Bulletin No. 103) on the subject of 'Crime and Punishment in Japan'. He said that he owed his '. . . present happy way of life . . . to the fact that from my very earliest day in Japan I was fascinated by Japanese attitudes to authority in general and the law in particular, and by those two remarkable species of Japanese fauna, policemen and gangsters'.

After giving a flattering account of the life of the average Japanese policeman (the *o-mawari-san*) he described the more frightening image of the riot police. This was followed by a pen portrait of a 'grandee gangster' (*yakuza*) whom he saw in Hiroshima:-

After a few minutes a huge Cadillac with rear windows of tinted glass drew up outside [the Grand Hotel in Hiroshima]. From the front leapt two tough-looking men in dark suits who glanced around warily before one of them opened the rear passenger door and bowed. Then out from the gloomy interior came an impressive figure indeed. He was a man in his early middle age, dressed in a *yukata*, with *zori* or sandals of fine straw on his otherwise bare feet. The hair of the head was cut cruelly short, almost shaved, and he wore dark glasses and smoked a cigarette. He had about him an air of immense authority, and acknowledged the profound bows of the hotel staff with an easy, off-hand grace as his lieutenants led him to a lift whose doors were held open for him.

Westerners, Peter noted, were usually treated by Japanese police with helpful courtesy:-

. . . and nowadays find it hard to understand the reasons for the hateful reputation they had before the Second World War. One everyday experience drives the average Westerner to distraction, though. This is when they are discovered to be guilty of some minor technical offence, such as failure to carry an Alien Registration Card on the person, or tardiness in renewing it.

In such cases most of us expect to be fined, would grumble a bit but then pay up without much in the way of protest or fuss. But things are not so simple and straightforward in Japan. No indeed. On the contrary, the offending foreigner is summoned to the police station and bombarded with the most extraordinary questions, most of them sublimely irrelevant to the offence. He is asked about his educational, family and occupational background and a host of other personal matters, and those who have been through the experience – and there are a great many of them – are agreed that the policemen who conduct the inquisition seem to approach their task with leisurely relish.

Even the ordeal by questioning is not the whole of the matter, though. When it eventually comes to an end, the offender is usually made to compose a grovelling letter of apology, expressing contrition and the determination never to sin again, after which he will probably be allowed to go about his business. This kind of treatment drives the average Westerner to mild hysteria, especially the requirement that he should sincerely apologize. This is of course because he is conscious not of a sense of guilt but merely of extreme annoyance at having been found out; and expects to pay the penalty and have done with the matter. He would much prefer to pay a fine of five or even fifty thousand yen than be treated like a naughty child, and cannot understand why the police seem to be ready to waste hours of his and their own time in dealing with his transgression in such a fashion.

BUT JAPANESE cooking and writing detective stories had inevitably to take second and third place after doing the various tasks which fell to PETER MARTIN as a representative of the British Council in Japan. One of these chores was to look after VIP visitors, as he described in the following amusing account (entitled 'Eminent Tourists') of his Kyoto years:-

●

'Right, Martin!' said the General briskly in his clipped senior officer's voice. 'They tell me that while I'm here I should see a temple, a shrine and a garden. Take me to one of each, would you, there's a good chap.'

Back in the early 1960s Britain still maintained a military presence in Singapore, and the C-in-C Far East Command was based there. The incumbents were by turns an Admiral, a General and an Air Marshal, who invariably made a courtesy visit to Japan during their year of office. They always fitted in a day or two's sight-seeing in Kyoto and Nara, and it fell to me, as the only official Briton resident in the area, to act as their guide, as I did for VIP visitors from a variety of other walks of life.

The Service chiefs – in mufti, of course – were surprisingly tractable, and as a former RAF National Serviceman who stuck at the rank of acting sergeant, I rather enjoyed telling them what was what. General Sir Michael Carver, who went on to even grander things, seemed to

find Kiyomizudera, the Yasaka Shrine and the moss garden at Saiho-ji
to be entirely satisfactory, and he was affability itself throughout our
tour.

When Admiral Sir Peter Hill-Norton came a year or two later I decided
to give him a watery experience, and we shot the Hozu River rapids together. It is definitely a white-knuckle ride between the rocks down to
Arashiyama, and I think that I was not the only one holding on tight.
Next came Air Marshal Sir Hector MacGregor, who brought Lady Mac-
Gregor with him. We dined out together, and afterwards they expressed a
wish to go to a typical bar. Playing safe, I took them to one in Gion which
I knew was frequented by eminent scholars from Kyoto University, rea-
soning that the hostesses there, however disconcerted they might be by
the apparition of a dignified foreign lady, would behave with appropriate
decorum. And so they did, until they relaxed. 'MacGregor' is a good
name to render in katakana, and Sir Hector happily answered to '*Maku-
guregaa-San*. I had been in Japan long enough to be quite accustomed to
having my thighs squeezed by bar hostesses, and Sir Hector took to the
experience with every sign of nonchalance. Lady MacGregor, however,
was obviously taken aback when the kimono-clad vision beside her extended the same friendly courtesy to her, and, as they say in the tabloid
press, after a while we made our excuses and left.

*   *   *

The politicians who came to Kyoto were very different and tended to be
heavy going, though I have good reason to be grateful to Anthony Wedg-
wood Benn, as he was then known; still in his thirties and Postmaster
General. As the guest of the Japanese government he arrived with something of a retinue, including the Consul General from Osaka. I was asked
to join the party in the capacity of local expert to answer any informal
questions he might have, and turned up having not yet recovered completely from a bout of gastric flu. After visiting Ginkaku-ji, we all proceeded to a magnificent multi-course Western-style luncheon at one of
the grander hotels. Sadly for me, I was unable to enjoy the lobster, the
Kobe beef or the fine wines; and indeed as the meal progressed faced the
literally sickening prospect of disgracing myself. There were ten or a doz-
en of us seated facing each other at a long table in the private dining
room, and fortunately my lowly status meant that I was placed near the
exit. The moment of truth arrived and I left the table as unobtrusively as
possible and crept out. Once outside the door I fled to the nearby men's
room, reaching it in the nick of time. A few minutes later, pale and trembling, I slunk back to my place at the table, to be greeted with a glare from
the Consul-General and a sweet smile from Mr Benn 'Been chucking up,
old man?' he enquired in a warmly sympathetic manner. Then he ad-

dressed everybody else at the table.'You know, I thought he was looking a bit green this morning.'

The late, publicity-hungry Ernest Marples, sometime Minister of Transport, took possessive pride in the Chiswick flyover in London. He spoke of this as though its construction had been an achievement comparable to the building of the Pyramids (but the film star Jayne Mansfield, when formally opening it, memorably described it as 'this cute little bridge'). He was still boasting about it when he came to Kyoto alone in 1968, at the height of the university unrest, having worn out his welcome in Tokyo. I had been instructed by a weary diplomat there to '. . . meet him at Kyoto Station, amuse him and give him lunch. Then send him back, I suppose.' So I took him to the Kyoto Hotel grill room, where we were shown to a table near the huge plate-glass windows which overlooked Kawaramachi, the main shopping thoroughfare in the centre of the city. Mr Marples waved the menu away and lunched off three, or it may have been four dry martinis, talking mainly about the Chiswick flyover and himself while I tucked into a large steak. He paused when a column of student demonstrators flanked by riot police snake-danced past the hotel, headed by Zengakuren members wearing masks and headbands, shouting and waving large banners on which were written various slogans. My guest regarded them through the window, nodding his head in complacent satisfaction. 'I assume they are objecting to my being here. What do the banners say, Martin? "Marples Go Home" or something similar?'

As a British Council officer, strictly speaking I had no business to be hobnobbing with politicians and military bigwigs. My job was concerned with education and culture, and many of the VIP visitors I escorted in the legitimate line of duty were actors, artists, writers, or musicians. It was a great privilege to meet them informally, and to make their acquaintance as private persons. All were interesting, some nicer than others, and some engagingly eccentric. Notable among the last group was the late Iris Murdoch who came with her devoted husband John Bayley. She gave a philosophical lecture at the British Council Centre on 'Is Moral Action Like A Work Of Art?', which was adjudged a huge success, mainly, I inferred, because it was so abstruse as to be incomprehensible even to native speakers of English. During her stay Miss Murdoch was lionized by her Japanese publishers, who laid on an exquisite *kaiseki* luncheon in her honour, with geisha in attendance, at one of the most expensive traditional restaurants in Kyoto. I was invited too, and will never forget the occasion.

The food was beautiful to the eye, and the dishes on which it was served were no doubt priceless, but in fact there was not a great deal to eat: that was hardly the point of the exercise. Miss Murdoch did enjoy the Fushimi saké, however, and thanked her hosts most gracefully. The slightly gauche, jolly hockeysticks side to her character came to the fore as we were leaving the restaurant, when she paused in the perfect garden beside one of the freshly watered stone lanterns, slapped me on the back and boomed 'You know, Peter, I really enjoyed that! Super grub!' And when I said goodbye to the Bayleys at Osaka Airport I was enchanted when they each planted kisses simultaneously on my cheeks.

*　　*　　*

Donald Sinden was a delightful visitor: every inch the actor, he arrived wearing a huge camel-hair topcoat and never failed to address me as Dear Boy. In contrast Emlyn Williams, who came to give his one-man performance as Charles Dickens, was throughout the several days he spent in Kyoto squabbling with his dresser. 'All I require from you,' he said to me with a baleful scowl when I welcomed him on arrival, 'is a bottle of gin and to be left alone'. In the event he and his dresser used my services as a kind of interpreter, addressing each other only through me. His magnificent performances were triumphantly successful, and both Mr Williams and his dresser turned out to be quite human after the final show was over.

Angus Wilson, Anthony Powell (who had an endless fund of entertaining gossip but seemed to be oblivious to his physical surroundings) and Alan Pryce-Jones the critic were amusing and amiable companions. So was David Blair the dancer, except when he was briefly outraged, when I took him by arrangement to a private ballet school for little girls, which was run by a stern Japanese lady. When he entered the room, she commanded the assembled moppets in their tutus to rise and wobble on their points with arms outstretched in honour of the distinguished British dancer, and was justly ticked off by him for recklessly risking damage to their vulnerable young ankles.

Bridget Riley amazed me by sitting through a long afternoon of performances of Noh and Kyogen, transfixed and scarcely moving a muscle, and many other visitors wanted to explore the more arcane – to Westerners – aspects of traditional Japanese culture. Looking back, though, it was the musicians whose company I most treasured, and of these among the most charming and appreciative was Dame Janet Baker. She, her husband and Felix Aprahamian the critic were my guests for the whole of a sunny summer's day in Kyoto in 1970, which in retrospect I regard as the grand finale of my seven-year career as a part-time tourist guide.

MICHAEL BARRETT who spent much of his career in Japan between 1970 and 1999, and whose last job was that of Director of the British Council in Japan, writes under the general heading of 'Mutual Impact – British Culture in Japan 1970-2000'. His contribution begins with a depressing description of the problems of teaching English in Japan and ends with a full and enthusiastic account of the major British promotion which went under the title of UK98:-

•

There is no country in the world where more time, effort and money has been spent on teaching English to so little effect as Japan. A massive industry pumps out courses, publications, media, but somehow – in spite of some outstanding exceptions among diplomats, businessmen and academics (scientists rather than professors of English Literature!) – it just does not produce practical results.

In the late 1960s The British Council thought that English by Television would conquer the world. Robin Duke, the Council's representative in Japan at the time, arranged for two educational TV specialists to work with NHK's Channel 3 to produce an innovative weekly programme for adults, and at the same time drive a small cultural wedge into the predominantly American English influence. I arrived in 1970 to work with Don Gillate, who was already discovering that innovation was the last thing NHK wanted. After the initial impression on the way in from Haneda airport of a grey, polluted, ugly concrete world, the cool technological atmosphere of the NHK TV centre at Yoyogi was a pleasant relief. But behind the lights and cameras was a traditional culture.

Our first programme Director, Ohno-san, fancied himself as a junior Kurosawa, and wanted dramatic low angle shots through the legs of chairs for a scene illustrating a simple grammatical point. Don and I had been trained as TV scriptwriters and knew what shots would unobtrusively help viewers to understand the English content. Mr Ohno made it clear that 'in the studio, the Director is like a *kami*', although it was the inflexible central computer system which really dominated the use of studio time and equipment. The way Ohno treated cameramen and technicians would have had a British crew out on strike in five minutes, but we were prepared to bow diplomatically to his technical authority. What could not be compromised was the educational value of the programmes. We were producing the only programme entirely in colloquial English, instead of the usual ponderous grammatical explanations by screen professors who merely perpetuated everything that was wrong with the teaching of English in Japan.

We wanted to know more about the needs and interests of our audiences. Such information was not available, we were told. What? One of the world's leading public service broadcasting organizations did not carry out audience research? Well, there was of course some research, but the findings were confidential. Really? Were all NHK's educational programmes produced by people who did not know who they were teaching or why? We got our audience survey eventually, but at the cost of a steep learning curve in relation to Japanese organizational culture. By this time, we were coming under pressure from the NHK authorities, who had decided that we were far too subversive. Over dinner, a senior producer explained patiently: 'We want all our language programmes to look the same.' They did. They still do.

Things improved greatly when Mr Ohno was replaced by Hidekazu Yoshimatsu, a sophisticated, intelligent and sympathetic man who is now a senior NHK executive. The weekly audience figures allegedly reached 250,000 in spite of the fact that 'How English Works' was at a fairly advanced level and did not look at all like the rest of NHK's language programmes. We had real live Brits on the screen too, including some of the long-term pillars of the community in Japan such as Alan Turney, Ken MacDonald, Alan Booth and Geoff Hamilton. The fun only lasted until 1972, but in that time we were able to incorporate a wide range of short films about the UK into the language material and produce some general programmes about British culture and society into the bargain.

Ultimately, however, we were defeated by the innate conservatism of the Japanese approach to language teaching. There is now no British English on the screen in Japan. Even when offered excellent BBC material in the 1990s which other countries such as China leapt at, NHK rejected it on the grounds that it would not suit the format of their programmes, which are still heavily dominated by grammatical explanation in Japanese. Like my colleagues, including Jean-Jacques Dunn, who for nine years worked to introduce professional English teaching to Japan, I was frequently asked advice on points of English by Japanese examination boards, then told that what I had said was unacceptable had been passed by Professor X of Todai, so it must be correct. The ultimate was when a police officer came to get my view as evidence in the case of a candidate bringing a suit against a major university as a result of being rejected by one contested point in his English exam. If I had confirmed that the answer he gave was in fact acceptable, the Professor of English who set and marked the test would have lost much more than face.

*   *   *

One place where serious attention is paid to the meticulous use of English – and British English at that – is the Imperial Palace. The honour of being asked in 1971 to help develop the already good English of the Crown Prince (Akihito) (now The Emperor) turned into a personal pleasure. Firstly, there was the chance of an occasional game of arena polo with mainly Gakushuin graduates on lumbering police horses in the grounds of the Togu Gosho (The Crown Prince's palace). In spite of the encouragement of the only professional-class player there to improve our follow-through by imagining 'you are cutting off heads with a sword', these games were fairly light-hearted. They could hardly be too aggressive when riding off your opponent or hooking his stick could bring the heir to the Chrysanthemum Throne crashing off his horse, a risk which eventually had to be taken seriously.

But the lasting satisfaction from the privilege of contact over the years has been the insight into the character of the Japanese Imperial family and the personalities of the Emperor and Empress (Michiko). I have been savaged by English people on occasion for what they take to be unfair comparisons of the educational and cultural attributes of the British and Japanese monarchies. But how could one not admire a family whose activities include accomplished musical performance, creative writing and publishing in two languages and serious scientific research. The Empress's encyclopaedic knowledge of English (and other) literature is well known. The Emperor's memory and concern for exactitude is also extraordinary, and not only in ichthyology. At a private visit to the 1998 exhibition of British art from the Tate Gallery, HIM left the museum director visibly shaken by correcting him gently over William Adams's dates.

In spite of the restrictions placed on them by their responsibilities and by the conservative Imperial Household Agency (Kunaicho), these very modern representatives of an ancient state also manage to take a well-informed, active and caring interest in ordinary people and in socio-economic issues at both the local and global levels. It is hard for those used to a British-style monarchy with its independent wealth and constant publicity, to understand also that the Japanese Imperial family owns virtually nothing of its own and demonstrates its symbolic values by living in comparative simplicity.

*   *   *

In spite of the frustrations of the NHK episode, the UK variety of English has had a boost in Japan from various sources over the past twenty years. One is the JET scheme, originally the Wolfers scheme, which has been a great PR success for Japan but has also introduced Japanese schoolchildren and people throughout Japan to thousands of native speakers of English with a real, live modern culture. Another is the British Council's own language schools. These started in Tokyo and Kyoto in 1986 under the guardianship of the then Representative, Jo Barnett, and were made possible through funding from UCLES (the University of Cambridge Language Examinations Syndicate).

With the opening of schools in Osaka, Nagoya and Fukuoka in the late 1990s, there are now five schools teaching over 7,000 students as well as contract classes for clients such as All Nippon Airways. Well-established private sector schools such as ILC, and British teachers in commercial language schools, universities and colleges add to the subterranean influence. But the establishment of the English Speaking Union of Japan in 1998 recognizes the international nature of the language. Any internecine war between British and American English would be pointless, anyway, not just because it is a lost cause, but because it is Japanese English that is now becoming the acceptable compromise. Professor X of Todai was obviously right, after all!

*   *   *

While the teaching of English in Japan has not changed that much in 30 years, and perhaps not since Lafcadio Hearn's day in the universities, the cultural scene has been transformed out of all recognition. In 1970, there were few professional impresarios and the British Council was still having to subsidise exhibitions and the small number of visiting performers from the UK. Ballet connections were particularly strong, with British choreographers and directors like Jack Carter working with Japanese companies and trying to get the best out of dancers with short, bandy legs. The physical transformation of the Japanese in one generation by the change in lifestyle and diet is vividly illustrated by the young Japanese dancers who are now stars in international companies, as well as by Japan's rugby players. The other transformation is from a sea of undifferentiated dark suits and slick black haircuts on the subway in 1970, to today's trendy youth with multi-coloured hairdos and international fashion wear. It would be good to think that we had something to do with this.

The first deliberate attempt to present a view of Britain beyond Shakespeare, Turner and Beatrix Potter was in 1982. 'Aspects of British Art Today', sponsored by the *Asahi Shimbun*, had an immediate and electrifying impact on the Japanese art world. Artists such as David Nash, Richard Deacon and Tony Cragg demonstrated variety, individualism, seriousness and wit along with a small group of works by established artists such as Philip King (elected President of the Royal Academy in 1999). The British Council Representative, Peter Martin, survived one of his more embarrassing moments when HIH Princess Chichibu decided to halt in front of a sprawling female nude by Lucian Freud past which he had been trying to hustle her. Peering through her lorgnette, she showed extremely close interest in the picture and the artist, testing Peter's artistic knowledge and blood pressure to the limits. He was rewarded as HIH left the exhibition with the charming comment: 'I enjoyed that much more than I expected to.'

'Gilbert & George' provided the 'embarrassment' factor in later exhibitions, as did Tracy Emin in 1998, but these things are always far more likely to worry Ambassadors than the public, even in Japan, where customs officials take on the role of moral guardians (I once had an art ex-

hibition catalogue confiscated from my baggage). The 1982 group of contemporary events included a gritty British film week at the National Film
Centre, full of Bill Douglas-type docudramas with UK regional accents
which challenged the comprehension of even the Brits in the audience.

The biggest risk was the participation of the performance group 'Welfare State International' at theatre director Tadashi Suzuki's experimental
Toga Mura festival. They insisted on performing on a ski slope some way
from the theatre centre up in the hills of Toyama Prefecture. For each
performance, they would not accept more than 100 people, who had to
follow the action up and down the hillside. And they wanted to use giant
fireworks, which meant that I had to perjure myself, signing a certificate
to say that the man with the matches was licensed to the UK equivalent of
Japanese Grade 1 pyrotechnics standards. They went grossly over-budget;
two of the male members of the company were thrown naked out of the
women's bath by a ferocious Japanese actress into the corridor of the
dormitory area; and on the first night it poured with rain. But the audience loved the magic of the production with its giant puppets, shadow
play and barn dance; NHK TV covered it; and *Pia* magazine later voted it
the most significant new cultural event of the year.

*   *   *

The next major UK cultural landmark was in 1990. By this time, Japan
was at its economic height and funding flowed in for UK90, 'A
Celebration of British Arts' as a backdrop to the UK's growing economic
and political ties with Japan. Japan had also become an important cultural market-place and this was the first high-volume programme of UK arts
product, with 120 events taking place all over Japan. Jenny White, who
would in due course go on to contribute her experience to UK98 as well,
cut her teeth on UK90. Welsh National Opera showcased the high quality
of the UK's regional and national cultural scene, building on the strong
links forged by inward investment. These would be strengthened even
further by the appointment of conductor Tadaaki Otaka to the National
Orchestra of Wales in the late 1990s.

Once again, the *Asahi Shimbun* presented a major showing of British
contemporary art, with work by the rising women artists Lisa Milroy
and Helen Chadwick, ageing *enfant terrible* Ian Hamilton Findlay, and
Anthony Gormley's enigmatic human figures alongside the Scottish fig-
urative painters such as Steven Campbell. British film was more upmar-
ket this time, with Nicholas Roeg visiting Tokyo for a season of his finely
wrought teasers. The Michael Clark dance company introduced another
controversial but extraordinarily talented and creative figure from Britain. Parco department store, given its young clientele, saw the potential
in so much lively new activity and hosted its own mini-festival 'Alterna-

tive UK'. After UK90, the flow of creative work from Britain to Japan became a major export.

It was almost with a sense of inevitability that the British Council in Tokyo began to think in the summer of 1994 about planning another large-scale British event in Japan as a successor to UK90. By chance, the Japanese-British Parliamentary group, pushed by the politician Ichiro Ozawa approached the British Ambassador about the same time to say that they would like to see such an event, and the *Yomiuri Shimbun* (whose President was an associate of Ozawa) would support it financially. The political involvement was unnecessary, as we would have welcomed anyone prepared to put up sponsorship, but being Japan, it was part of the package. Our real problem was that the *Yomiuri* had its own preconceived ideas of what a British Festival would consist of, and although many of them were excellent and coincided with our aims, the Embassy had to establish from the beginning that this would be 'our' festival. Secondly, working with one newspaper company would create delicate problems in our relationship with all the other media groups on whom we depended, such as the *Asahi*. Some of the *Yomiuri*'s ideas were moreover impractical, such as borrowing the crown jewels, or unlikely to represent the UK, such as the pick of the National Gallery's Italian and French paintings. Having. said so, we were faced with finding good alternatives.

A 'festival' is a PR event, and it is often a question of presenting ordinary activity in an extraordinary context. We knew we could expect a good run of music performances, smaller exhibitions etc, but two or three major 'pillars' are essential to construct a bigger-than-usual edifice. It took more than a year to negotiate the magnificent show of 400 years of British art from the Tate Gallery, and much longer for the exhibition from the Science Museum, which had never organized an overseas exhibition before. But both institutions were able to offer unique loans because of gallery closures before moves took place in 1998, so the original plan for late 1997 shifted to the spring of 1998. It then became clear that many other events would fall in that year, such as the tenth anniversary of the Tokyo Globe Theatre.

Gradually, what had started off as a modest proposal or a two-to-three-month season of British events grew into a year-long festival. A joint committee was eventually set up in the Embassy under the chairmanship of Charles Humfrey (Minister in the British Embassy) to coordinate the overall impact of what became UK98, including commercial promotions, VIP visits and the key role of press and information.

∗   ∗   ∗

As we confirmed by a market survey in early 1998, although urban youth knows about British design, fashion and pop music, the image of Britain in Japan is still dominated by the traditional elements of Shakespeare, castles, the monarchy, bowler hats, rain, golf and bad food. We wanted to change that and the election of the Blair government in the year before the start of UK98 gave us a strong push in the direction of 'cool Britannia'. UK98 got a new lease of life with a message focused on the four Cs: Creative, caring, cosmopolitan and changing Britain. These themes went into a joint website which was in itself a 'virtual festival' and were pursued in practical terms by developing a grassroots element to the festival designed to reach local communities, and especially the young, through 'Britpacks', which JET teachers could use to illustrate everything from technology to cricket. We also found that we had struck gold in using 'UK' as it turned out to have positive, modern overtones, as opposed to the imperialistic image of *'Eikoku'* or the Peter Rabbit world of *'Igirisu'*.

Launched by the Blairs in heavy snow to the sound of Shooglenifty's Celtic rock music (and somewhat to the chagrin of HRH Prince Edward, whose planned visit three weeks later had thus been pre-empted by a politician), the UK98 festival broke all records over the year. Some 750 events in all, from automobile technology to the DV8 dance company, reached an estimated five million people across Japan, and took Japanese understanding of the UK to new levels. For example, of the thirty or so films shown in the largest ever showcase of UK cinema abroad, half later went on commercial release.

Japan is now truly a key market for the UK's creative industries. It is a long cry from bandy ballet and Iris Murdoch lecturing to a small number of uncomprehending aficionados. As Japan and the UK learn from each other, some convergence seems inevitable, and we increasingly see each other as 'normal'. There is a loss of exoticism, but our *differences* remain exciting. Perhaps the best compliment we can pay each other is still: 'I enjoyed that much more than I expected!'

8

Travails of the Teachers

ROGER BUCKLEY ● SUE HUDSON ● ADRIAN McGREEVEY
SUSANNA PFEIFFER ● SARAH JOHNSON ● PHILIP EVEREST

MANY THOUSANDS of young people from Britain have spent years in Japan as teachers of English. Some have also taught English literature and helped to spread understanding of British culture and history, but language teaching has been their main task. In the early post-war years they went to Japan at their own initiative or in response to job offers. Later, as the demand grew, the JET (Japan English Teachers) scheme was introduced and teachers were recruited in large numbers to assist in schools and offices. The scheme has undoubtedly helped many young British people to get to know something of Japan, Japanese people and Japanese culture. It has also contributed to improvements in the ability of Japanese people to speak and understand the English language, but as Mike Barrett (see Chapter 7) has pointed out, teachers of English in Japan have often been frustrated by the conservative attitudes of Japanese pedagogues and the rigidities of an examination system which puts the prime emphasis on grammar and syntax.

I have occasionally looked at Japanese multiple-choice examination questions for English language examinees. Sometimes I have concluded that there were two correct answers and even that none of the answers was correct. If I had been taking the examination I would perhaps have been failed by Japan's pedantic education bureaucrats. Nevertheless, the best Japanese students of English in, for example, the Foreign Ministry (Gaimusho) had a better knowledge of English grammar and syntax than some foreign diplomats with whom they negotiated agreements. I well remember lengthy discussions of linguistic points with Japanese officials involved in the negotiations on, for instance, the United Nations Status of Forces Agreement in the early 1950s and later, the Anglo-Japanese Treaty of Commerce and Navigation. They were right to emphasize the importance of clarity and to ensure that meanings were clear, but there are times when it is politically valuable to leave in vague phrases which can help in the presentation of the text to politicians and lobby groups. It seemed to us perhaps more flexibly trained British diplomats to be absurd to have an agreed minute for publication explaining a clause in the agreement and then sometimes an agreed record interpreting the agreed minute! Yet, I have to say that these negotiations made me focus very carefully on the meaning of words and phrases and I learnt something about my own language from my Japanese interlocutors.

In view of the large number of English teachers with experience of teaching in Japan, this chapter may seem rather thin, but many of those who contributed to Chapters 4 and 6 can equally be counted as teachers. It is also rather arbitrary to include in this chapter a contribution from Professor ROGER BUCKLEY who has written a number of books relating to Japan and the Far East, but his contribution here relates to the problems of being a teacher both at a language school and in a university.

SUE HUDSON went to Japan before the JET scheme was set up to work in a school in Shizuoka and her contribution shows how tough the work and life of an English teacher in Japan could be. The last four contributions are from JET scheme teachers and have been extracted from presentations which they made at a Japan Society lecture meeting in London on 18 May 1999. They give some interesting insights into life in modern Japan for young people. First, ROGER BUCKLEY writes:-

●

Two lines and a loan got me back to Asia. Answering the shortest possible ad in *The Times*, while finishing off a mini-thesis for Donald Watt on American journalists in Nazi Germany, led me to Tokyo. It was the autumn of 1968 and the euphoria of occupying the LSE and joining anti-Vietnam teach-ins, had left me slow to reckon with the near impossibility of finding work. After a perfunctory interview in Park Lane, I borrowed the money for the trans-Siberian and found myself a week later on the quay at Yokohama.

I was bound for the language mills. Since my qualifications for the position were zero and my knowledge of Japan would fit comfortably on the smallest of postage stamps, I had no objective reason to complain. I was single, starting to earn my living and answerable to no one.

Why had I signed on ? The economic factor came first. Teaching in Tokyo's Yurakucho Building conditioned my first eighteen months in Japan by giving me a living wage (six hundred yen per lesson) and dictating when I could be free (difficult on days when I had a split shift of morning and evening work). It was all very different from the briefing sessions, counselling and professionalism expected today. Provided I stuck fairly closely to the manual and avoided sounding off on too many political themes in class, I could hardly fail by the admittedly low standards of two generations ago. It was rote learning for the students and mechanical teaching for the instructors.

From the first weeks it was obvious that this neophyte was going to learn far more than he could possibly impart. My students were of all ages from retired executives keeping up their English for the fun of it to teenagers still in high school and dressed by their mothers. They were my collective teachers. From one middle-aged Japanese, who spoke English as if Russian, I heard of the fate of former POWs who never returned from their Siberian camps, from another I was instructed in the wiles of the advertising industry and from a third I was invited to see the stratifications of family life. Later, I would learn of the enthusiasm of corporate executives during the Occupation era to acquire American management skills; looking back on my experiences at the chalk face in the late 1960s I sense the same determination and enthusiasm.

Yet the working conditions frequently conspired to limit intelligent cultural contact. It would take a youthful Evelyn Waugh or a Tanizaki writing his Childhood Memoirs to do justice to the administrative shambles and single-minded profit motive behind the entire operation. Classes were forty minutes and there was only a five-minute break before the next began. We had to teach for far too long every day to survive. There was no safety net of any description. I came to dread the calendar – holidays such as Golden Week ate into potential salary. And even in a more normal month there was no guarantee of a full schedule; often we were faced with gaps in timetables that left us hanging around waiting for the next class. Twelve-hour days riddled with inconvenient breaks could only be endured by the desperate and needy.

It was the evenings and weekends that served as compensation for the factory regime. I lived in a six-mat room in Kasumicho on the road from Roppongi to Shibuya. It was the end room of a rickety building over a saw mill. The rent was 14,000 yen a month plus all the usual deposit and key money additions. When I wanted a bath it was a case of either the local *sento* (public bath) or the use of a shower in a fellow teacher's flat. The area was just short of being a slum, though it had the convenience of being central and well served with shops.

My immediate neighbours worked in the entertainment business and came home even later than I did. The crowded wooden two-storey buildings resembled the downtown Tokyo sketched by Ron Dore, whose book I took out from the old British Council library in Kanda. I was never going to be a sociologist but the manner in which the fish pedlar on his bike chatted up the younger housewives was a weekly event whatever the weather. Equally fun was the sight of the ancient bedecked tram that I saw clang down the road on its final journey to the knackers' yard at Aoyama. (The tram depot is now the headquarters of the opulent United Nations University and the pavement a few hundred metres from where I watched this spectacle would decades later be the Tokyo office of the International University of Japan.)

Just occasionally, I managed to escape from the Kasumicho-Yurakucho-Roppongi triangle. Two journeys stick in the memory bank. The first was in the summer when I was ordered to Karuizawa to help teach Princess Chichibu. I do not think my input was more than a couple of phrases on how to cope with the expected visit of Princess Margaret to open a British trade fair but it did let me roam for a fortnight. The other occasion was when I visited the Kansai and rudely accosted Yasunari Kawabata in an expensive antique shop in Kyoto. He had just won his Nobel prize and was clearly enjoying himself spending the loot. His face was even more arresting than the photographs had suggested and since I had been reading Edward Seidensticker's translation of *Snow Country* I blurted out my admiration in a mixture of present tense English and Japanese. (Later, I espied him and Yukio Mishima in a nightclub in Akasaka but the rock music and assorted groupies did not fit easily with my earlier recollection of the slight figure in *hakama* selecting screens in Gion.)

My first months in Tokyo remain a moveable feast. The work was slave labour but the assorted pleasures of the city for a European bachelor could hardly have been equalled. The transformation from unemployable postgraduate in Harold Wilson's Britain to the expat with money to spend appeared near total. Perhaps I had arrived with absurd expectations: having lived as a boy in Hong Kong I must have thought it would be a similar existence, but a week in the dingiest rooming house in Okubo (a dingy area near Shinjuku) instantly corrected all such illusions. Instead, I sat in the stalls and watched a newly affluent nation begin to break out of its post-war chrysalis. Even at the time I knew that I had been lucky.

*   *   *

In February 1957 the British Prime Minister wrote the briefest of brief congratulatory messages to the President of International Christian University. Harold Macmillan's thirty-five words to Dr Hachiro Yuasa were in response to ICU's request for British recognition on the graduation of its first crop of students. The fact that this harvest festival should have been formally recognized by the British government and that the slim subject file has survived the PRO's army of weeders is a remarkable testimony to the founding fathers of ICU. It certainly would not happen later. (I write in the week that ICU celebrates its fiftieth anniversary and I have yet to see or hear a word of Anglo-Japanese commentary at any level.)

Two generations ago, it was all very different. ICU, to quote the words of Sir Esler Dening in his letter to Oscar Morland of the Foreign Office's Far Eastern Department, '... is essentially an American-Japanese effort but in every aspect of its day-to-day administration emphasis is laid on its international character and ideals'. With a modicum of British staff and students in place, Ambassador Dening, who had himself spoken at ICU and taken visiting junior ministers to the Mitaka campus, appeared happy to endorse the new, experimental institution. He encouraged the Prime Minister to write to Dr Yuasa because he regarded ICU as '... a worthy attempt to instil the principles of international cooperation in a segment of the younger generation which may well exercise an influence in Japan in the years to come'.

By the time I joined ICU in September 1988, the era of the early visionaries and their enthusiasm was long dead and buried. Indeed, the place had little of the character of an 'experiment in Christian higher education' in Asia that its official historian had described in its first decade-and-a-half. Nor was there overmuch reality that I could see to the frequently evoked talk of 'the ICU family', though I was probably biased by the initial offer of campus accommodation that should have been condemned ages ago.

What ICU did have was seriousness – lots of it. It was evident in the faculty meetings, the divisional meetings, the departmental meetings, the library meetings and the scores of other meetings that clogged up the week. Instead of nasty, brutish and short committees, it was a case of gentle, consensual and interminable ones. Anyone with the necessary stamina could saunter through *Genji* or Proust in a few months of compulsory attendance at ICU's proud town meetings.

Yet it was equally obvious that the University had highly motivated and exceptional students. At least, at the undergraduate level – the less said about its unsuccessful attempts to get its graduate schools off the ground the better. From the start it was impossible not to compare the ICU student population with those at other Japanese universities and to remark on both the far superior English-language abilities of most students and their determination to excel. The best example of ICU's academic strength is the senior thesis required of all fourth-year students. Here I would supervise six to twelve students a term (we have graduation twice a year) and came across work that in some instances was certainly up to MA level. Much of this sophisticated and well-researched material centred on contemporary Asia-Pacific themes with, not surprisingly, a great deal of attention to Japanese foreign policy in the region.

The pleasures of the seminar room are not usually duplicated though in the large lecture halls. As with the on-campus housing, the University's parlous financial situation has left the main educational building virtually untouched since pre-war days. The result in the summer of having to require students to sit examinations in poorly-ventilated rooms bereft of any air-conditioning can be imagined. Classes in late June resemble a mixed *sento* (public bath house).

The other drawback that ICU experiences is equally unlikely to be changed. The structure is highly compartmentalized and it is well-nigh impossible to break down these carefully constructed academic and personal barriers. Reform or even the politest hint of possible change is taboo. Departments and divisions go their own merry way with little hope of introducing new courses or reconsidering teaching arrangements.

The University is Japanese. It is overwhelmingly so, despite its name, and on a scale that most outsiders continue to find surprising. The public at large has always assumed that ICU really is a foreign enclave on the lines of Deshima but the statistical evidence can hardly be ignored. The student body is 95% Japanese and all but a handful of teachers are Japanese. The administration and the general ethos reinforce familiar Japanese academic norms. This will not change. Internationalism, while alive since the university's founding after the war through joint Japanese and American religious initiatives, has to be understood within its Japanese environment. ICU – known to its student body from the start as 'isolated, crazy, utopia' – remains exceptional in its efforts to bridge cultures but it is hardly as radical as it professes.

SUE HUDSON writes about her *'Memories of Life in Rural Japan 1979-1983'*:-

●

I opened my eyes and found sunshine pouring through the sitting-room window of my new home in Mishima. I jumped up and there was the most glorious view of Mount Fuji and rice fields. All that was missing in my befuddled mind was a team of oxen pulling a plough, women in kimonos and a cherry blossom tree!

I thought I knew a lot about Japan but my four years living there and my subsequent involvement with a Japanese company have shown me time and time again that there is always more to learn, and that Japan continues to maintain the capacity to surprise.

I am not sure who was more surprised at my arrival in Japan; my school, my friends, my family or myself. Certainly, in 1979 it was not the career move that it has now become. Japan was still thought of as a land of paper houses, earthquakes, rice and robots. However, I had wanted to go to Japan since I was fourteen and nothing was going to stand in my way.

I arrived armed with two weeks' of intensive information about Japanese history, economics, and language. I also had 30 kilos of baggage and a bad case of butterflies. I had been chosen by the Japanese government to take part in a scheme that placed British graduates in Japanese High Schools in order to help with the English language teaching. I had asked to be placed in a school outside of Tokyo and was delighted to hear I would be going to Mishima High School in Mishima, Shizuoka prefecture. It was hard to find a map sufficiently detailed but eventually I found it lying at the foot of Mount Fuji, south-west of Tokyo.

My school kindly arranged an apartment for me and provided me with things that they thought I would need. This meant I had an odd mix of useful and useless items as well as some serious omissions, like curtains.

The apartment was in the middle of rice fields, near the school and with amazing views to the north of Mount Fuji and to the south the mountains of the Izu Peninsula. These mountains to the front and the back of my flat gave me such a strong sense of being in Japan and I never tired of looking at them.

I had arrived in a typhoon (though no one told me that that was what it was) and the next morning was the most fantastic, bright blue, hot day with a stunningly clear view of Mount Fuji. I could not believe that I could see this world-famous mountain from my own sitting-room window, but there it was, looking even more spectacular than I could have imagined. This view became a passion for me and even now on my return visits to Japan I look anxiously for Mount Fuji and only feel settled once we have become re-acquainted. I grew to understand how it was viewed as a goddess in the past, as it changed its mood with every season, day and hour.

*   *   *

The young woman English teacher who had been assigned to 'baby-sit' me overnight swiftly brought me back to earth. She told me that we would have to hurry up to the school where they were all waiting to meet me. Despite the fact that I put on my smartest dress she was most disapproving of my lack of tights or stockings. I had been warned that the Japanese were rather prudish but had not expected to come across it quite so early.

We arrived at the school and I was horrified to find I had to address the assembled teachers. I had no idea what to say, how to say it and whether anyone would understand me. My headmaster, one of the most impressive people I have had the fortune to meet in Japan, introduced me with a characteristic flourish, articulating clearly and slowly my full name, Suzanne Elizabeth Hudson. It sounded so strange, especially having come from the informality of student life. I tried to match the tone with a very simple self-introduction and was politely welcomed by the other members of staff. I could not judge whether I had been understood but I suddenly felt the first of many waves of 'foreignness' which I still occasionally feel even today.

I did not realize that I would have to do so many self-introductions but over the months I became quite a dab hand at trying to explain who I was, where I was from and just hoped that they would find me of interest. It was just as well that I was young, resilient and self-confident, as the school was quite tough, in fact I found out much later that the school had felt they needed a man for the job and were worried when they heard they would be getting a woman instead. I naively expected that my students would be interested in learning English from me and would be fascinated by my cultural background, neither of which proved to be the case.

Looking back now, I cannot believe how blindly confident I was. I think all of us on the scheme had been indoctrinated to believe we were 'the chosen ones', ambassadors for the country – which in many ways we were. However, those who had tried to teach us before we left for Japan had not experienced the life that I was to have in a regular, non-academic, rural school.

I found out rather quickly that my students were not particularly interested in the English language, nor did they seem to be impressed by me. The school was co-educational but the classes were not. I found I was the first woman teacher to be allowed to teach the boys classes and at times found the smell of fifty or so eighteen-year-old boys quite overwhelming. The girls' classes were quieter but I soon found that under those innocent-looking fringes were rows of sleeping beauties! The boys were more obvious in their lack of interest and shocked me by plucking their eyebrows and hair-line during my classes (it was the fashion at the time!).

In fact, considering the teachers were so strict it was amazing how persistent the students were in trying to bend the rules. The fashion at the time was for permed hair, both for males and females. It was forbidden in the school mainly because of its association with *yakuza* (gangsters) and anti-social behaviour in general. The length of school skirts was also prescribed yet I would find students in the staff-room on a daily basis being yelled at or even hit for having broken these rules. Boys with perms were sent home to have their head shaved and then regularly humiliated in the staff-room and around the school.

I was never very comfortable with the extreme severity with which the students were punished but my fellow teachers were very genuine in their belief that this was the only way to teach these children and that it was a way of showing their love for their students. I spent many evenings after school with small groups of teachers in the many *sunakku* (snack) bars in Mishima wrestling with how to deal with these rather wild boys and girls. Much later, I realized that it was important for these students to be brought into line if they were to stand any chance of finding reasonable employment. The rural society of Mishima did not have room for those who did not fit in.

Over the years in Mishima I taught hundreds of students, many of whom are still very vivid in my mind. However, my earlier classes were perhaps the most formative and instructive for me. One of the very first classes was a class of boys who unknown to me at the time, had a reputation for being a bit wild. I was brought in and after the usual instructions 'Stand up!' 'Bow' 'Sit Down!' I was introduced. I then went through the by now over-used self-introduction which was followed by me asking the class if they wanted to say anything. One boy at the back piped up:

'Remember Pearl Harbor!'. The rest of the class cracked up with laughter and the English teacher had to bring them all to order.

I was stunned but skated on. Afterwards, I was told not to worry about the boy's comment but to remember that he was the son of a local *yakuza* boss. Naturally, this worried me but over time I found that his background gave him the confidence to lead the class and when this was harnessed it worked in my favour. I also found that when he was working as a doorman at the local disco he could be very useful for helping me and my friends get in and find somewhere to sit. The deal was that he would help me if I did not mention to his teacher that he was working out of school hours. It was one of the few advantages to being '*Hudoson sensei*'.

*   *   *

Initially, my social life in Japan depended greatly on my fellow teachers and I resolved to invite a different group of teachers to my flat every, week in an attempt to get to know them better. My flat was fairly well equipped but, as with most homes in Japan at this time, I only had a two-ring gas stove to cook on. Having come from a country where four gas rings and an oven are the normal, I found the idea of cooking for six or seven people on just two rings rather daunting.

I decided that spaghetti bolognese was the only thing that could be done in these conditions (very English!) I later came to regret this decision as I had forgotten the tendency to make noise when eating noodles and was deafened by the sound of six teachers sucking their spaghetti! The local supermarkets were fairly impenetrable, stocking many items I did not recognize, and it was often guesswork when buying tins or packets with no pictures and only Japanese writing. I was shocked when I could not find items I considered basic, such as tinned tomatoes, button mushrooms and fresh cheese. However, I did manage to persuade my local supermarket to sell button mushrooms but felt permanently guilty if they did not all sell and so found myself living on mushrooms!

Food became quite an issue for me in Japan. I did not know what to order so I had to rely on plastic food models in the restaurant windows when ordering. I found that many of the cheaper restaurants relied heavily on deep-frying food, leaving food greasy and often with an overly heavy batter. They also used sauces too sweet for me; *mirin* (a sweet saké) and sugar were often used in savoury dishes. It was many years later in Britain that I was pointed to dishes in Japanese cuisine that I would enjoy and I have since become a real fan.

I was treated extremely well in Japan but in many practical ways I often felt I had been thrown in at the deep end and could have done with a little more guidance and help. I was left to find out how society functioned (often by making huge mistakes and only then being told). Most importantly, I had to learn how to deal with the ever-present bureaucratic thinking in Japan. At the local post office I had parcels rejected because they were not, to the clerk's mind, wrapped well enough. Over the years, however, I developed quite a good relationship with the main clerk in the post office who would take my ineptly wrapped parcels and repackage them! It really was a question of how to handle the situation; the head-on approach was definitely not the one that worked in Japan.

My frustration in these and other institutions was always further exasperated by my lack of Japanese and their lack of willingness to understand my attempts at Japanese. I carried two dictionaries with me everywhere and after a brief *chotto matte* would frantically search for the correct word in the dictionary. Usually, this would lead to understanding but I had my greatest problems when trying to pronounce words which had originally been foreign. 'Curtains' caused me hours of fun in a department store and it was only when I said *'mado no curtain'* (curtains for windows) that the assembled staff all suddenly understood, 'ah, *mado no curtain'* as if to say 'why didn't you say so before?'!

It was all very confusing and exhausting. There were several occasions during my stay when I thought I would have to pack my bags and return to Britain: moments when I really could not understand the differences in culture, when I did not want to understand the differences. I would eat vast amounts of chocolate (Japanese chocolate is surprisingly good) or drink huge quantities of Japanese beer (also exceedingly good) in an attempt to deal with these moments. I was also fortunate to have a few British friends dotted around Japan and we all spent hours on the phone, giving each other support and occasionally insight into the problems.

*   *   *

Over the years, I was fortunate to develop a group of friends in Mishima through teaching *arubeito* (part-time jobs). These classes allowed me to meet like-minded people who were genuinely interested in foreign cultures and wanted to learn English. I became good friends with many of them and found it possible to discuss my problems with them. They helped me feel a part of the community and eased my feelings of isolation.

My headmaster, Fujio Watanabe, was another great influence on my stay in Japan. I think he embodied the qualities of the Japanese culture that had so attracted me to Japan. He had read, in the original languages, most of the most important non-Japanese books on economics, philosophy or literature. He and I would drink together as *'nomi-tomodachi'* and he would inevitably start to sing German, English or old melancholic samurai songs. He was extremely knowledgeable about the traditional Japanese arts and introduced me to various Japanese *hanga* (prints) and ceramics artists. Above all, he was a humanist, educated, as he informed me, 'in that brief period of Japanese democracy' before the militarization of Japan and the start of World War II. He was proud that he had been a captain in the Japanese Army but equally proud that he had not killed anyone. He was one of the few Japanese I met who was not afraid to talk about the war and who shed tears when we talked about the lack of war memorials for the dead of World War II in towns and villages around Japan.

Mr Watanabe wanted the students of the school to have the opportunity to meet foreigners, to realize that we were also human and to open their minds to life outside Mishima. He felt that the students of the school would not necessarily learn more English but that the confidence that they might get as a result would be important for them. I am sure there were teachers who felt that I was an unnecessary luxury for the school and that I was being paid too much money for my age (wages are paid more according to age rather than ability). However, his support ensured that these matters did not become huge issues.

*   *   *

Obviously, being one of the only Westerners in the area had its problems, but being a Western woman was in many ways even more difficult. I had been living away from home since I was 18. I had grown up heavily influenced by the social movements of the 1960s and '70s and was, in my mind, a mature adult. I naively thought the young Japanese teachers would be the same or similar. I was wrong. I was disappointed that they did not offer to take me out to any local clubs or introduce me to any suitable young men. After all, many of them were the same age as me, and a few had even spent some time overseas, so naturally I thought they would have a similar attitude.

I had to rely on my own ingenuity to find suitable male company. For example, when my other British friends came to visit me we would go to the disco in the next town. We were all amused by lines of dancers all facing the walls of mirrors − not dancing together or even around a handbag! The confidence of youth allowed me and my friends to jump in feet first and ask the Japanese boys to dance. This was real cultural shock time! I do not know if they ever recovered from it, but it enabled me to meet a wonderful young man who kept me company for a number of years.

I was advised to keep my new boyfriend a secret and I had to learn how to act in a totally new way. Even when we were in different towns in the area we had to be aware that my students, their parents, friends or relatives might be there and they would know me even though I would not necessarily know them. I think that had my boyfriend been a Westerner it would have been more acceptable, but as he was Japanese it generated too many issues for local society to be comfortable with.

It felt odd going into such a seemingly prudish society after living for most of my life in such a permissive one. Initially, I found it difficult to adapt my behaviour and clothes to the rather strict standards expected in rural Japan. Sometimes, however, I had to rebel. In particular, I just could not get used to the idea of wearing extra underwear under a swimsuit – which seemed to be the norm for my school. In fact, I remember being amazed at the number of layers of underwear which the women seemed to wear. It was in such contrast to the bra-less life-style of the UK!

* * *

When I look back to my years in Japan I realize that my experience was very special because it was centred on what I regard as the real Japan, the conservative heartland of the country. Advertisers regularly use Shizuoka Prefecture as a testing ground for new products on the basis that it is the most representative prefecture in Japan.

I feel privileged to have experienced Japan at that time. Changes have happened that I would not have thought possible and are really interesting to see. Overseas travel and the media have been enormous catalysts for change, as has the change that comes from becoming an economically mature society with more time for leisure. The need for conformity has been challenged, though it still exists. The children of the teachers that I worked with are now young adults who turn up on my doorstep in London with backpack and no tour guide – unthinkable not so long ago.

I was really surprised by life in Japan, how different it was from my life up until that point. I am sure that friends, colleagues and students were equally shocked from time to time by my behaviour and who I was. However, what I think is the most surprising is just how easily we have all moved into a world where modem communications allow us to remain involved with each others' lives, despite being on the other side of the world. Direct dialling from Japan and the UK makes a phone call so easy and e-mail allows us to chat despite the time differences.

I only hope that the qualities that make a culture special will not be lost in a rush to conform to international standards. Japan, in particular Mishima and the Izu peninsula, still has many unique aspects which set it apart from other nations and though some of these aspects were difficult to adjust to, they were what made the experience so challenging and enjoyable.

THE FOLLOWING four extracts are drawn from the presentations made by four JET TEACHERS, on their return to the UK, to a Japan Society lecture meeting on 18 May 1999:-

●

ADRIAN McGREEVEY
[Wakayama, 1994-97]

B ritish people do not like to learn languages and Japanese people do not like to either... Japanese people, however, need to learn English. The fact that most of them learn English for up to seven years, with the majority not acquiring even a modicum of fluency, suggests that there is something behind the generalization that the system of teaching English in Japan is flawed...

At the beginning, the JET is usually involved in what are called 'self introduction' lessons, introducing themselves, and a little of their own culture. One point that did strike me, on entering a Japanese classroom, was the sheer number of pupils. On average, there are nearly 40 children in every classroom, which does not augur well for the personal attention that is required to bring out the latent potential of some pupils.

As the weeks went on, and as the job of teaching English began, I became aware of the 'teacher-centred' environment, where the pupil played the 'passive' role, and the teacher the 'active' role. As the months went by, careful observation soon gave way to frustration as I saw the pupils' evident lack of progress in foreign languages. I had seen the rapid progress made by the students I had taught in Spain and wanted to 'change' things in Japan. I took it on myself with a missionary zeal to 'convert' my fellow Japanese English teachers to the wonderful ways of teaching using a more creative, student-centred, speaking environment – emphasizing that this must occur when the Assistant Language Teacher was not in the room.

Realism, and I have to say, a hint of cynicism, set in as I spent more time on the JET programme, and realized I was not going to be able to wave any magic wand. Arrogance was also replaced by a more humble attitude as I realized my 'place' in the school hierarchy. I had to settle for making my lessons fun, and trying to impart elements of my culture and personality both inside and outside the classroom. This proved very fulfilling and I think a little worthwhile. However, there was still this lingering element of regret, that the system was structured in such a way that change would prove very slow and difficult.

Things will not change because of the entrance exams, at fifteen, to move into an appropriate high school, and at eighteen, for university. The need to assess and examine is, of course, fundamental to education everywhere but in Japan I feel that both the structure and content of the exams need to be reassessed.

Foreign language education is still based very much on the acquisition of grammar rules, often scientifically learned, with little emphasis on their application to the language. This is reflected in the examinations where there is very little oral assessment. . .

The Japanese youth in my school who dared to be different, by dyeing their hair or wearing hipster trousers, tended to be looked down upon, or at least treated with an air of suspicion. But I felt that these were the very ones who would most happily embrace other cultures and ideas. Unfortunately, the way language teaching is structured today they probably have next to no motivation to learn a foreign language.

I wish I could have done more to change things and I still believe that the system has a lot to answer for in not giving these young people the opportunity to learn to speak the languages which would equip them so well for life in the new millennium.

•

SUSANNA C. PFEIFFER
[Shiga 1994-96]

I was based for two years in central Japan, in the Kansai region, in Otsu which is the prefectural capital of Shiga prefecture. . .
I wonder how many of you will guess what this is?

Born in London in 1974, weighing as much as three apples, she likes baking cakes as well as generally liking 'small, cute things, candy, stars and goldfish'. In 1994 she was made the child ambassador of the United Nations Children Fund in Japan.

You would almost think she was a real person, and if she was real, she would surely rank amongst the top ten famous people of the world. . .

She is of course Hello Kitty. (You can even buy toasters that leave an imprint of her face on your bread whilst toasting!)

Hello Kitty statistics suggest that she is more than just a cartoon. Sanrio, the manufacturer behind the character reported last year that there are 13,000 officially licensed Kitty products on the market, with 600 new lines expected every month. . .

Tamagotchi, the electronic egg was the name of the virtual pet hatched in Japan, spreading across the globe in the mid 1990s. Tamagotchi – needing feeding, cleaning, looking after and loving – were aimed specifically at Japanese children and teenagers. It can be played with like a traditional toy, but more importantly it is an interactive experience, giving its owner lessons in how to relate to another 'being'.

Given the changing demographics in Japan that saw the birth rate decline to all time lows, many praised the Tamagotchi for providing the new wave of single children with substitute companions and encouraging socializing tendencies. Whether Tamagotchi succeeded in this respect has been fiercely discussed. Many now argue that the egg along with other electronic games far from encouraging interaction amongst peers, has isolated the users, who focus too heavily on their toys and thus miss real opportunities to interact...

No examination of modern Japanese culture would be complete without mentioning 'empty orchestra', or Karaoke which is also popular among teenagers and university students. Perhaps the most popular place to sing is the Karaoke box, a small room for hire where you go and sing in relative privacy. I am not sure quite what else happened there but my school had a rule that forbade its students from going to them...

The spending power of the young appears to be completely removed from the general economic malaise and declining consumption in Japan and is a fact that manufacturers cannot afford to ignore... Consumption is often seen as a Western import symbolizing Western capitalism. Many argue that the consumption frenzy that has gripped Japan during the last two decades will gradually erode traditional values which will be eclipsed by a modern Westernized version of Japan. This again is not something unique to Japan.

In looking at the trends associated with Japanese youth it can be seen that the reverse is true. Japan is no longer a sponge, absorbing Western ideas. Japan's youth is more globalized than Westernized...

In my experience, these phenomena have as yet done nothing significant to challenge the social fabric of Japan. The fundamentals of traditional Japan remain largely intact. School children still readily adopt the *senpai-kohai* (senior-junior) hierarchical relationship that will see them through their working lives. The sense of identity to the school, club, or, later in life, the company are still important to teenagers, giving them a stronger sense of belonging than other teenagers.

●

SARAH JOHNSON
[Gunma 1995-98]

I spent two years on the JET programme as an ALT (Assistant Language Teacher), then a year working in a private adult education school in Gunma prefecture...

My first experience of women in the workplace was in the town hall. My supervisor was not much older than me, and an office lady. This meant that she chose not to follow the career track so that she could leave the office at 5 o'clock, naturally on a lower salary. She performed the menial tasks in the section, made the tea, cleaned the office before work etc. It was still very traditional in my office that only the women made the tea.

There was only one female manager in the town hall, which is in line with national statistics which show that women account for only 9.3 per cent of managers. Part of me sympathizes with their situation for I could not blame them when I saw the demands made on men's time which required staying at work until late and relocating with the job, both of which are impossible if a woman wants to start a family.

On the other hand, I got annoyed that the women did not show more drive in challenging the system. I think there has to be a more balanced workload between men and women and that the pressure has to come from both sides. The women have to be prepared to push for more recognition and the men have to lose the macho image associated with work. This requires a great cultural change.

I was lucky to be invited to many people's houses and I often stayed over at my boyfriend's house. His mother was amazing. She was definitely the boss in the house and worked extremely hard. She juggled her job with the housework getting up at 6 o'clock every morning to make her husband's breakfast. He came home at about 9 pm, when she would have dinner on the table. She saw this as her duty because he was working so hard.

I know that a lot of young women have different expectations of their future husbands and a lot of younger Japanese men are becoming more home-oriented but I think that many middle-aged fathers and husbands sadly neglect their home life because of the cultural pressures to stay at work. . .

Although I realize things are changing, I found Japan to be a very male-dominated society and for me this was the most difficult thing about living in Japan. I was irritated by social pressures on young women to be cute and child-like, to carry bags with little rabbits or kittens on, to speak in high, child-like voices and to exclaim '*kawaii desu ne*' at every opportunity. On TV, especially in adverts, women were widely portrayed as being defenceless and infantile which frankly I found offensive. I knew a lot of mature, intelligent women and felt that in the face of these social and media pressures they had a constant uphill struggle to gain respect.

If it was only a question of taste in bags and clothes then I think I could live with cuteness but there is a darker side. Sexual obsession with young girls in pornography and the recent development of the alarming phenomenon of *enjo kosai*, 'compensated dating' or schoolgirl prostitution, indicate a range of social problems facing young girls: pressure to get designer clothes and bags amidst the current economic depression, the lack of a father figure in the family, their lack of self respect and morals fuelled by images seen quite openly of schoolgirls as sexual playthings. . .

●

PHILIP EVEREST
[Sendai 1995-97]

I went to Japan knowing little more than I had gleaned from the guide book sent to me by Sendai City which told me that Sendai is on the same latitude as Washington DC and the same longitude as Melbourne, information which left me none the wiser about my prospects for the next two years. . .

I assumed before I went to Japan that most of the younger Japanese would have started to reject these older traditions in favour of more Western pursuits that involved the individual rather than the group. But through observing situations such as the *hadaka-mairi* (procession of near naked youths) I realized that loyalty to the group held sway. The majority were graduate members of the same company or university classmates and it was not by chance that the groups carried banners showing their allegiance. I certainly felt great collective pride in this activity, particularly in the shared endurance of hardship. I suppose it was a kind of initiation ceremony or team-bonding exercise. They all appeared to enjoy the experience and were given a lift by the local population which was out in force to encourage and marvel at the exuberance (or some would say folly!) of the young.

These displays of traditional culture contrasted with my usual view of young people in Sendai. Freed from the restrictions of the classroom, my pupils would walk to the shopping malls on Saturdays and Sundays taking part in the very modern tradition of doing nothing in particular. To me, this occupation was an interesting one as I had quickly learnt that the average Japanese person was 'very busy' with personal time being at a premium. Usually, it seemed, the children did not shop a great deal but just wanted to relax downtown with their friends free from pressure from their family, teachers or any other person who could tell them what to do. . .

Although I witnessed isolated incidents of misbehaviour, I would not say that the Japanese children I had contact with showed strong rejection of authority. Indeed, compared with schools in England, I found the pupils I taught to be fairly placid. Their methods of rebellion at school were pretty obvious since they had a very strict set of rules against which to rebel. Boys enjoyed wearing their regulation uniform trousers low and pulled down, almost hipster-style. The way these low-flying trousers made them swagger around made for some memorably comic scenes.

Clothing rebellion for the girls went the opposite way with skirts hitched up to 1960s mini-skirt length, even in the coldest weather. The *de rigueur* accessory, for both indoor and outdoor wear, was the quintessentially English Burberry scarf. . . For both sexes the desired hair colour was a kind of dyed light brown known as *chapatsu*.

What can the British learn from the Japanese and *vice versa*? For me, the young in Britain have lost a sense of community and pride that I am fairly sure characterized my experiences in Sendai. The majority of young people that I came across had great pride: whether in their clothes, hair colour, hobby, community, club, company, school or country. I was completely unprepared for the dedication some of my students showed to their club activities. They would be at school most days of the year often from early in the morning until late in the evening. . .

On the other hand, I would like to see the Japanese young begin to question things more. Sometimes their allegiance to the group is too strong. The strict regime of their schools and clubs and the large amount of homework leave many children unable to enjoy their childhood. There are simply too many pressures on them to conform and perform, During my stay I was also concerned that there was always an element of compulsion, or of doing something because it was expected, or because it was ordered by the club, the teacher, the company or the family.

9

British Scholars in Japan

R.P. DORE ● ERIC CEADEL ● W.G. BEASLEY ● CARMEN BLACKER
GEOFFREY BOWNAS ● PETER SWAN ● IAN NISH ● RICHARD STORRY
LOUIS ALLEN ● KEN GARDNER ● PETER KORNICKI ● JOY HENDRY

THE WAR gave a major impetus to Japanese language studies and later to studies of Japanese culture in all its manifestations including Japanese society, politics, economics, literature and the arts. The development of Japanese studies in the University of London and elsewhere in Britain was explained by Professor F. J. Daniels of the School of Oriental and African Studies (SOAS) in his inaugural lecture as Professor of Japanese on 7 November 1963 (Bulletin No 41 of the Japan Society).

In December 1944 the Foreign Office set up an interdepartmental commission of enquiry on Oriental, East European and African studies under the chairmanship of Lord Scarbrough. Professor Daniels drew up proposals on the development of Japanese studies: these were largely adopted. This is not the place to review the problems, including inadequate resources and finance, which Japanese studies in Britain have had to face since then. Student demand has fluctuated while openings for graduates in Japanese were for many years very limited. Japanese studies in Britain could never compete with the United States, but it has compared reasonably well with the situation in other European countries and even in Australia.

The leading pre-war historian of the Japanese economy was Professor G.C.Allen who recorded his memories of sixty years in his memoir *Appointment in Japan* published by the Athlone Press in 1983. While he commented briefly on post-war Japan the bulk of his book is devoted to his time in Japan before the war.

Among the outstanding students of Japanese during the war was RONALD DORE. He was so successful in mastering the language that he was asked to stay on at the School of Oriental and African Studies during the war as an additional teacher to help with the tuition of the increasing numbers of service language students. He went on to take a first-class honours degree in Japanese and to specialize in the social sciences. He had to wait some five years after the war before he was able to make his first visit to Japan. In the following extract from his diary for 1950 Dore who came to Japan with the Frasers (see Chapter 4) gave his impressions and reactions to Japan in the penultimate year of the American Occupation:-

•

I had never been a diarist, but since the solid notebooks I have just dug out were bought from W. Straker, London, before I sailed for Japan in January 1950, I must have been prepared to find everything I encountered fascinating and worthy of record in the country whose language I had been learning for eight years. And a lot was. Despite having a University of London travelling scholarship to visit Japan since 1947, and later a more generous Treasury studentship, I had never managed to get a visa. MacArthur did not like academics, some of whom had been rudely critical of his orotund pretensions, though I believe the official reason was that an extra mouth to feed would strain the logistical resources of a food-short country.

So I waited. For two happy years I commuted between SOAS and the British Museum libraries, enjoying the pomposities – and the humanity, and just occasionally the wit – of Tokugawa Confucianists, frequently lunching with Hugh Cortazzi, at grave risk of severe indigestion from the terrible oil in which the SOAS student canteen cooked its chips. Finally, thanks to the initiative of Vere Redman it was arranged that I should be smuggled into Japan as the honorary unpaid secretary to the Cultural Adviser to the United Kingdom Liaison Mission to the Supreme Commander of the Allied Powers – i.e. cultural attaché to the Tokyo embassy, a post later translated into that of head of the British Council.

Edmund Blunden the current, much loved, occupant of the post was coming home, and in the early days of January 1950 I found myself on a boat headed down the Thames with the delightful couple with whom, until students finally became admissible and visible, I was to live for some months in Japan – George and Paddy Fraser and their nine-month-old daughter. George, a gifted poet, lively and discerning literary critic and sparkling conversationalist, was also something of a polymath. In a conversation somewhere off the coast of Malaysia about my research ambitions he said – because he had read what counted then as a major sociological classic about small-town America – 'What will you do? You can hardly write a Middletown all on your own.' I thought, but modestly did not say, 'Why not?'. He had set a thought ticking which eventually determined the major preoccupation of my eighteen months in Japan and led – Tokugawa education temporarily abandoned – to *City Life in Japan*, recently reprinted fifty years later [by Japan Library in their Classic Paperback series].

*   *   *

23 March, Tokyo. Landed at Kobe on the 21st. Wonderful sight coming slowly into the harbour at dawn, despite the vast stretch of factories with chimneys belching out smoke all the way up to Osaka. They are comple-tely overtopped by the vast mountains behind the town, steep and hairy with firs, but lots of grassland which gives them a smooth texture and shows up at its best when the evening sun casts shadows over all the cre-vices and hollows. Even in the middle of the town you can't forget nature – it's there every time you look up. Tokyo very different.

It was *Higan no chujitsu* (equinox) the day we arrived and the streets were practically deserted. They were working the ship as soon as we dropped anchor, though. (One of the stevedores said 'ee' for 'ii'. I thought it was supposed to be only in Tokyo they did that.)

Festively decorated streets. At least, most – though not all of – the shops had a *hinomaru* and some other flag. Neighbourhood flag? Seemed to be different in each street, anyway. I gathered from a news broadcast that there was some sort of *Kokki Aigo Kai* (Association for Promotion of the National Flag) holding meetings in Osaka to urge people to put out flags. Fifty years later there is a bill before the Diet to make flying the flag compulsory in schools. Three generations have passed and the failure to demonstrate orthodox patriotism is still equated with wallowing in the nation's shame, or using it subversively to denigrate authority.]

Also heard on the wireless a lovely cultured academic voice discussing Western painting from the neolithic cave drawings up to the Sistine Chapel.

Encounter with customs official. The typical 'Nip' of the wartime pos-ters; goggly glasses, teeth. We needed a 'Japan general' pass to replace our 'Kobe only' ones. I explained in Japanese against an insistent desire on his part to ask how many cigarettes and how much foreign money I had. I was cut short by 'I speak English. You speak English please'. Which I did. Twice. 'All right. You can go.' 'Yes, but where?' 'Where?' 'Where do I get the pass?' It took about three more repetitions before the message got home.

Afternoon walk through Motomachi. Still some brightly kimonoed ladies, but most of the men – bits of ex-army uniform scruffy cast-offs – clearly had not bought an item of clothing for years. Hadn't realized that ombued babies are covered by a sort of sleeved garment with a long low collar which comes around the baby's neck. Japanese babies not in the same danger of suffocation as the Chinese ones in Hong Kong.

Today to Blunden's farewell lecture at Todai. Place has a general air of unchecked dilapidation. The entrance to the main hall smelt and looked a bit like a country cattle market reserved for auctioning prize steers. Very pleasant and very skilled singing of English ballets and madrigals by a student choir organized by English teacher ex-Cambridge Madrigal So-ciety. The Japanese sitting next to me had wonderfully good English. The best I've heard from any Japanese, I think. Ex-FO now in the Economic Stabilization Agency. (Kakitsubo?) He was not impressed by the fact that

I know Japanese, not impressed by my interest in the country – almost 'more fool me'. A very salutary experience. It made me realize that I generally have a feeling of condescension to the Japanese I talk to. Why? the fact that I talk to them in English, perhaps, and therefore they are the ones who are at a disadvantage? But does it work the other way round when I speak in Japanese? *On va voir.* I noticed today, however, that I was talking in Japanese to a Professor on a footing of equality – or at least that was how it felt to me – which I certainly wouldn't have felt had I, young student, been talking to an English professor. Is it because of the universal Japanese deference which one takes at face value – but which it's probably insulting to presume on rather than giving the same deference back? Or do I have some sense of racial superiority that I acquired some long way back?

To return to Kobe as we saw it on the 21st. Tried to post letters at the Post Office and eventually found the right department. They kindly weighed my letters for me, but wouldn't sell me stamps – it was a *saijitsu*, a national holiday. But I could get them at a little shop across the street. (Which proved to be untrue.) Hard to imagine why a non-functioning post office should be open at all.

In one corner of Motomachi there were groups of students from Kobe-daigaku gathering signatures for a petition to protest against the dismissal of a certain Professor Komatsu. Slogans like 'The hand of authority has no place in the world of learning'. I asked one who Prof K was. He became all flushed and bothered and passed me on to another. Eventually 'Can I speak in Japanese?' Cleared his throat clearly as if to speechify. I cut in with '*amari muzukashii nihongo ja dame desu yo*' ('Not too difficult Japanese, though') which flummoxed him completely and he simply gave me their pamphlet, a mimeographed sheet absolutely cluttered with characters. Strong emotions about the wickedness being done, but no explanation.

Redman said last night – *à propos* the 'Can I speak in Japanese'? – that you can speak to a Japanese in fluent Japanese and it won't register, they still can't imagine they can speak Japanese back. The Japanese feeling of separateness. When they are talking to an Englishman they are the representative of 'we Japanese'. They will not criticize other Japanese as they would to a fellow Japanese, but they may apologize for having such a bad man among the Japanese people. R attributed all this to the long period of Tokugawa isolation. I said more likely to be the experience since Meiji brought *bummei kaika* – civilization and enlightenment – and the need to catch up with the West. 'We are behind. We must pull ourselves up to their standard. We must always show them that we are gentlemen too.'

*   *   *

24 March. In Kobe people were extremely kindly and helpful in pointing out the way and so on. Next morning at Tokyo station I was carrying a lot of luggage. A porter came up to take some. I said 'No it's OK, We haven't got any money yet.' 'Doesn't matter', he said, seized the bags, put them down in the appropriate place and disappeared.

The maid says *hanashi sureba ii deshita*' instead of *'yokatta desu*' as I've been taught to say. She talks of her mother as *okaasan* (which I thought was for other people's mothers) not *haha*. I lost status, though, by admitting that I did not change my underwear every day. Not what a pukka *tonosama* would do.

The Americans. They were everywhere in Kobe. They are everywhere around Marunouchi and the Imperial Hotel. There are far more American than Japanese cars on the road. Each train, crammed with Japanese, has a half-empty Allied Forces section. Do the Japanese resent it? No sign that they do. The Japanese conductor on the train seemed to behave quite naturally towards them. No sign of fearful deference. One young American who told me he didn't much like Japan nevertheless behaved quite naturally toward the conductor – gave him half his apple with no sign of condescension. [I remember continuing for some months to use the privilege my honorary status accorded of buying cheap whisky at the Ebisu army store, but I don't remember travelling in the apartheid car, though clearly I must have done at first.]

First sight of the palace impressive. The great moat with its smooth and in some places immensely high, banks and the pine trees dotted here and there on them. Spent the first afternoon at the Joruri – the *bunraku* up from Osaka. Fascinating. Especially the tasteful design of the sets, lovely combinations of pale colours, no gaudy clashes anywhere. The colour sense of the Japanese is amazing. The puppets behave with supreme naturalness, especially when manipulated by a master like the star manipulator Yoshida Bungoro. I hadn't realized how much the chief manipulator does become a star. Dressed in *kamishimo* [the starched shoulder-wing samurai garment] carefully chosen to blend with the colours of his doll and assisted by two black-hooded characters. The readers off to one side with the *shamisen* players roll and lunge about in their seats expressing all that actors do with their hands in their facial expressions. Funny diction. Short sharp rhythmical bursts, each at high speed – like some virtuoso competition for tongue-twisters.

*   *   *

26th March. *Chushingura* again. Kabuki. Not as good as the puppets. I had read most of the highlights before we went and one's imagination can provide scenes more impressive than those on the stage. The dark rainy night with Kampei sitting under a tree and espying a light in the distance, for instance, becomes a matt background excessively well lit with a chap lolloping down the *hanamichi*, lantern held aloft. Sets tawdry and shabby compared to the *bunraku*. I suppose the male females are graceful. They are certainly anything but beautiful. Not much correspondence between the original *joruri* text I had and what I heard from the stage. A lot of mixture of modern *'desu'* speech.

Passages of poetical description replaced by extravagant posturings of the actors. To please the groundlings to whom the original had become unintelligible? Most of the posturing is done with the limbs, though they nevertheless manage a fairly good range of facial expression even through the blanket of powder they put on their faces. The groundlings certainly are pleased. It is the done thing for young bloods in the audience to shout out (unintelligible) words of appreciation and encouragement at the really tricky bits. [Actually they shout the actor's name.]

The audience laughed, perhaps only just a nervous laugh, at the emotional scene between Kampei and his sister. Mrs. R. said that before the war people used to go to the Kabuki primarily to have a good cry. Handkerchiefs all along the row. I saw none, though everyone was tense during the bloody *harakiri* scene and appreciative at the end. Hard to feel attuned to the sentiments, though. The man cuts his belly and rejoices in the chance this gives him to add his name to the list of conspirators in blood and then expires under buckets of noble sentiment. Kampei is overcome with horror when he finds a dead man, but then forgets his horror completely when he discovers the man's purse. And the whole *motif*, of course, is simple revenge.

Discussed with Kanazawa, the Redmans' *boy-san* [am surprised that I did not comment on the fact that butlers became *boy-sans* when the Brits moved abroad], why *Chushingura* had been banned after the war. I suggested that it was because the notion of feudal loyalty was thought to be incompatible with democracy. His theory was that if the revenge story was allowed to be shown the Japanese would be spurred on to take revenge themselves against the Americans for their defeat in the war. Another of Kanazawa's ideas is that the *senzai-shitsugyo* (concealed unemployment) that everyone is worried about is due to the decline of black-marketing as an occupation. He also said that farmers are not happy under the new land laws; they find the taxes they have to pay heavier than their former rents. The price of rationed rice is now higher than black-market prices. Peasants are allowed to keep rice (twice as much as the town ration) for their own private use and that is what gets on to the black market. K has a thing about the younger generation. Under the New Constitution (which seems to be the root of all trouble) children seem to think that they have no duties towards their parents but nevertheless think that their parents have a duty to look after them and to send them to the universities.

The -*masho* 'let us' form of official exhortation: 'Let us all pay our taxes in full'. 'Let us make a beautiful and bright Japan', 'Let us love the fish'. The latter in the palace moat. To be translated: 'No Fishing'. . . .

*   *   *

7 April. Spent the evening with Haraguchi [President of Metal Miners Union] for whom I had interpreted at the founding conference of the International Confederation of Free Trade Unions in London. I've got to like him more and more. But what a contrast between his mild and pleasant personal manner and the aggressiveness of his manifestos in the union paper. And he did, as he boasts, take the Sumitomo strike to the point of stopping the pumps and letting the boilers go out.

Met other types at his office. A certain Kamiya very reminiscent of the British self-taught worker intellectual. He talked with real enthusiasm about the tin mines in Cornwall. But what kind of mines could they be, he wanted to know. He'd found reports of the rates of pay for porters and proppers, but no mention of cutters. Interesting about conservative villagers who won't use centrally distributed seed but insist on taking their own inferior seed from last year's harvest.

But resilience of Japanese family system remarkable, see absorption of so many returned emigrants from Asia. He reads Schopenhauer and the existentialists. Went on from restaurant to one of Haraguchi's favourite haunts in Kanda, ostensibly to have *tofu* though fortunately it didn't arrive. I had eaten far too much already. Beer and *sembei* while a waitress showed us a book of customers' poetic compositions. Mostly about *matsutake* mushrooms [of penis-like shape] or *nimotsu* [luggage, equipment] and about finding holes to put them in. Mock salacious embarrassment from waitress.

I was wrong: they do resent those empty American-forces-only cars on the trains, says Haraguchi. People's position on political spectrum easily defined. Do they use an honorific when they speak of the Emperor, and do they call the space in front of the Palace (where the big demonstrations are held) the Palace Front, or the People's Plaza?

*   *   *

9 April. Ueno Park. The thing that seemed to intrigue people most about Saigo Takamori's statue was the pigeon sitting on his head. Seems to be a regular speechifying spot. Students took it in turn to have five or ten minutes. One told a long story which started with a biography of Demosthenes and ended in a peroration which escaped me completely. Another made a little speech about stuttering. He used to be tormented by it, but found a teacher in Setagaya who cured him in a week. He is there to repay his teacher's kindness (*on wo mukuyuru*), express his gratitude and to encourage all stutterers and all relatives of stutterers not to be dismayed but to do something about it.

Toshogu in the most dilapidated condition imaginable and the inner part all shut up. Remains of the cherry blossom viewing parties not a pretty sight either; vast litter of paper and orange skins. But not of bottles. Some of the tramps seem to scrape a living out of them. One had an enormous basket on his shoulders full of them.

* * *

11 April. Chose the wrong day to call on Kaigo [Professor of Education at Todai with whom I had been swapping material on contemporary British education for Tokugawa material over the last two years]. He did not arrive till afternoon, but spent an interesting morning with some of his assistants and Shin Naka [a prolific writer on education in the 1950s]. Thin, emaciated, poverty-stricken air, but very cogent summary of the changes in the educational system. *Faux pas* when he told me about his latest book. I said I must look out for it which he took as request for presentation copy. He was very cagey about the Americans, though.

Not so Kaigo. He was caustic. They think a lot of committees are a good thing so now we have committees for everything. They report to the Mombusho [Ministry of Education] who then ask for the approval of SCAP. SCAP then mucks about with the proposal and the bureaucrats take it lying down and try to push the changes on the committees of professors. Occasionally they get direct contact when SCAP calls in American professors of education as advisers. Under the new private-enterprise/official censorship textbook system the big problems come with the social studies books. SCAP deems most of them unsuitable. All local governments now have education committees with, supposedly, extensive powers. But they just sit and wait for the Mombusho to tell them what to do.

* * *

18 April. Last night went with the Quines [John Quine was First Secretary in the British Embassy] to meeting of the local Seijo club. [The Frasers had been allocated a commandeered house in Seijo, salubrious suburb near a famous progressive school. Quines were other Embassy people in the district.] Arrived late towards the end of a talk by a large, genial but slightly dumb-looking Rotarian on the Goodwill Industries of America. The meeting was more or less run by a bright-eyed, earnest and God-how-smug Methodist local preacher called Fisher. How his eyes shone when, in summing up the talk he emphasized that all this good work had been done by private citizens of the United States without receiving a penny of government funds. His most revealing outburst came when Quine suggested, as a list of topics for future meetings was being drawn up, that one in particular, on the relationship of democratic institutions and the standard of living, might be made into a debate.'Yes', he said,'I can think of one or two others that could be divided up into two sides. This modem American literature, for example. Now some people say, for instance, that works like *The Naked and the Dead* are smart and cultural and others like me would say that it was just pornographic trash (uttered with great emotion) which ought never to have been published. And I'm not alone in that either, etc. etc. Phoney bonhomie, phoney internationalism.'We'd like to have a few more suggestions from the nationals.' What sort of Japanese is it – apart from crackpots like Fujisawa who thinks he'll get his 'Japanese spirit' books published in America – who belong to clubs like these where they are referred to as 'the nationals'?

*   *   *

So much for my first month. By my fourth month I had been legitimized as a student, found lodgings in what I later wrote about as Shitayama-cho – near the Hanazono lake between the zoo and the back entrance to Tokyo University, said goodbye to the Seijo Clubs and entered the student world. The sociologists took me along on one of their field trips, financed by the Mainichi Population Council, to a village in Ibaragi.

*   *   *

22 July. Komatsu-mura. Large relatively prosperous village. A lot of rice fields which people were weeding. Apparently they hand weed in this way three times and then let the water out of the field for the last stage before the harvest. Also a lot of *o-kabo* (dry-field rice) which needs a lot of rain. *Satsuma-imo*, the sweet potato, is a low and slightly purple vine. Soybeans still well-spaced small green plants. Nothing wasted. Some kind of bean grown on the banks between rice fields, also serves to bind the soil. Large fields of tobacco. The leaves are cut one by one and strung on a rope to dry individually before they are taken off to the government drying factory. The mayor says that the enforcement of the government monopoly is strict. Inspectors even poke about in the *irori* [fireplace] for the cigarette ends to make sure that the farmers are not smoking any home-made tobacco. (With a warrant? Rights of government officials not nearly as limited as they should be.) Punishments vary from fines – often very heavy – to withdrawal of growing rights. And, what's more, the old 'collective responsibility' device is still used. Growing rights ran be removed from whole *buraku* hamlets.

Interesting man the mayor. Former *Mainichi* reporter, in charge of the Seoul office at the end of the war, came back to his village where the family were largish landowners, still owning a lot of forest land which wasn't touched by the land reform. Good at explaining the family system [A lot of detail here about the 'main house' and 'branch house', intertwining of those family relations with landlord tenant relations, group rice planting etc.] 'When you *yome o morau* – get a bride – here it isn't the bridegroom that gets the bride, it's the bridegroom's family' is the sort of objective analysis one doesn't expect to hear in villages. Village mayor now a full-time job, not an honorific one as it used to be. Being a good mayor means successfully negotiating a reduction in the rice quota whenever there's some sort of 'bad harvest' excuse, so that there's more left for black market and gifts to relatives in the towns. Though now the boot is on the other foot; there's a glut of rice, black market price has dropped and they'd prefer the compulsory delivery quota to be higher. His main job this week to get the government to accept grade 5 wheat – spoiled by excessive June rain. Since the government decides how much they have to plant to wheat it's only fair after all.

Quite a welcome. A banner outside the temple where we're staying and outside the *yakuba*. 'Welcome to Mr Dooma, Professor Hayashi and group' [I recognized the absurdity of ranking any callow foreigner ahead of a professor, but not its personal dangers until I got back to England, was treated as a nobody again, and got depressed.] I was made to give a speech immediately on arrival and then besieged by people who wanted to exchange *sakazuki*. 15 in half an hour, but I wasn't the only one who got tipsy thereby. Most of the officials were equally drunk. The whole village office had taken the afternoon off for the welcoming party. Somebody had even been sent to Mito to buy some bread for the foreigner (tasteless and slightly sweet).

The temple is spacious. The sanctuary part is highly decorated with the usual over-gaudy artificial flowers and the golden lotuses. Priest is an odd old man with a constant worried expression who sits around either his own hearth or the one in the village office most of the day. His only duties seem to be to get up at half past six every morning, bang the gongs at the altar and gabble through the odd *o-kyo* (sutra) or two at an astonishing rate, At the back of the temple is a slow spring containing iron and sulphur – the White Cloud Hot Spring. Priest doubles as bath-house keeper. In the bath-house are some Kiyonaga and Kiyomitsu prints of naked women in bath-houses. Priest said he was out one day with the mayor when they saw them. Mayor suggested buying them. Priest demurred, bath-house is attached to the temple, after all. 'Go on,' said the mayor, 'It's all right. We live in a democracy now.'

Some points that emerged in the interesting conversation last night as we gathered on the bridge. Though they recognize the need for birth control [the subject of the survey] they resent the fact that the Americans are pushing it. A means of weakening the Japanese nation.

[The Korean war had started by this time] They confirmed that there were plenty of young bloods hanging around Shibuya, Shinjuku etc. who would be only too happy to jump on a boat and join in the war. Reminded me of the young drunk in a bar in Shibuya the other night. 'American soldiers are feeble. They need me to go and show 'em. I'm ready to give up my life for the Americans. What good's my life to me? (*kono inochi wa irimasen*).'

A lot of extreme pessimism. Matsushima, for instance, feels that it is all no good. The future is bleak for himself and for his nation, even though his reason tells him that there are things that can be done: reform of agriculture, developing Hokkaido, building up industry, etc. That's why somehow or other – apart from it being great to see the *Ame-chan* being driven down the Korean peninsula – the war makes him feel elated. Just because it's a big event that might change things. It's not so important how things change as long as they change.

Part of the general pessimism is the belief that eventually there will be a war. Which side will win? 'Russia' (from the Communist member of our group) Why? 'The Americans, with all that masturbation, no match for them.'

American policy towards Japan inept. Their post-war purges. Chucked out all the brains. They are bound to come back, and when they do they'll harbour deep resentments.

*   *   *

Not long after that the diary stops. Everything thereafter was written down in a notebook, separate entries with separate headings per significant point, on one side of the page only, to be later snipped into note fragments and filed under chapter headings for *City Life*. They remained after the book was written long stored in the loft and were recently transported by a young Japanese sociologist to an archive of material on Japanese social development in Tokyo.

ANOTHER British scholar to visit Japan in 1950 was ERIC CEADEL, lecturer in Japanese at the University of Cambridge. In his lecture to the Japan Society on 2 October 1951 he gave some account of his visit between June and October 1950. Eric Ceadel began his lecture by noting that although Japanese had not been taught at Cambridge University before 1947 the University Library had collections of Japanese books including those contributed by the scholar diplomats W.G. Aston and Sir Ernest Satow, but there were many gaps; consequently, Ceadel's main task on his visit was to buy books, which took over half his time in Japan. But he declared that '. . . the most enjoyable hours of my stay were spent with the professors and teachers I met from the Japanese universities'.

Fortunately, Ceadel found that the buildings of Tokyo University had survived undamaged by the war, whereas the salaries of professors and teachers were low '. . . even by comparative Japanese standards. Consequently, many professors have to supplement their salaries by doing other teaching in other universities, a system which places an undue strain on them and which detracts from their time available for research work'.

Ceadel was concerned by the feeling of isolation from Britain which he encountered and noted that for a long time '. . . no machinery existed permitting the import of British books and publications into Japan although American books and publications flooded in'. Thanks to the efforts of Vere Redman the situation had been largely remedied. (In 1948 Ron Dore and I had jointly written to *The Times* criticising the American authorities' unjustified behaviour on this score.)

BILL BEASLEY, it will be recalled (Chapter 1), had not expected to return to Japan after his service there during the Occupation. After his demobilization his research had increasingly focused on Japan and especially Anglo-Japanese relations in the nineteenth century. So, when he was granted a sabbatical year in 1950-51 he returned to Tokyo to carry out post-doctoral research at the Historiographical Institute (*Shiryo Hensanjo*) at Tokyo University. He went again in 1956-57 and for the first six months of 1963.

He received a warm welcome and was granted access to universities, libraries and archive collections. Access was never refused although '. . . occasionally the habits of bureaucracy might delay it':-

●

What is more, there were often more direct kinds of help, freely volunteered. In Kochi, where the prefectural library contained the family records of the former feudal lords, the professor of history at the university organized a team of students to copy the documents I needed (this being before the days of the photocopier). They were sent to me at intervals over the next few months. In Kagoshima the prefectural librarian detailed one of his assistants to help me during my stay, checking catalogue references (from an out-of-date copy acquired on an earlier visit) and bringing books to my desk to be inspected. The result was at least to double the work I could do in the time at my disposal. Nor was this kind of helpfulness only found in educational institutions. At the Ise shrines a priest, met previously on a train, invited me to the morning ceremonial, led me to a point where I could get a glimpse of the inner sanctuary (and turned his back while I took a photograph), then showed me shrine records of earlier centuries in his study.

It was at Tokyo's Historiographical Institute that I was given such help most often and over the longest period. It included guidance in the use of the books and documents housed in the institute's library; long discussions of Japanese history and historians; and introductions to colleagues and former students elsewhere, who could contribute to my research. One scholar, Jiro Numata, who was later to be director, taught me to read pre-modern texts (a skill that had not been part of my naval language training).

All the same, a willingness to help was not always matched by the availability of resources. The gradual improvement in Japan's finances in these years only slowly made its way into the humanities departments of the universities. Medical and science faculties acquired new buildings, or revamped old ones, but the faculty of letters, even of so prestigious an institution as the Historiographical Institute − originally founded by the government for the care and editing of archives − had to make do as a rule with what had survived the war. Salaries were pitiful, funds for new book-buying scarce, furniture old and rickety. In the winter, heating was negligible, at least in 1950-1. The room I shared at that time was large, concrete-floored, shabby. It had ill-fitting windows, which admitted icy draughts. Heating was provided by a single *hibachi*, supplied with a limited store of charcoal (it was still rationed). Working in overcoat and gloves, my thoughts turned to the literary image of the Confucian scholar, disregarding the cold while he studied the classics late into the winter night by the light of a single candle. Somehow it seemed appropriate to my situation.

By 1956 the *hibachi* had been replaced by an iron stove, its chimney led across the ceiling to the top of the nearest window. If one of the room's occupants remembered to give it fuel, it became red-hot. If not, it sometimes went out altogether. Scholars, it transpired, were not very good at tending such a piece of equipment. This did not make it a very wise arrangement in a building that housed a valuable, probably irreplaceable, collection of archives. Perhaps for that reason, by 1963 the iron stove had gone, replaced by a gas heater, free-standing in the middle of the floor.

From visits to universities and libraries outside Tokyo it appeared that this pattern was typical. Indeed, in some of the new universities, created at the behest of the occupation authorities, basic library provision itself was most unsatisfactory. Both staff and students had to look to the older centres for research facilities, adding to their overcrowding. Despite this, a very large amount of high quality scholarship was being produced. The cynic will no doubt draw the obvious conclusions.

The lack of library provision was exemplified here and there by the spectacle of students queuing, often outside the building, for seats in library reading rooms (a sight that brought home to me the degree of my privilege). Poor though many of these students were, they therefore had little choice but to buy a high proportion of the books they needed, at least the textbooks and standard works. The effect was to create a market of considerable size for academic books, both new and secondhand.

This no doubt helps to explain why they were remarkably cheap by American and European standards. Even so, the hardships the cost of book-buying must have caused to many students, together with the other unsatisfactory features of the higher education system – the almost total lack of scholarships, for example – may well have been a factor in the student unrest of later years, for all that it is usually put down to political discontents.

TRAVEL

Of a total of two-and-a-half years spent in Japan between the autumn of 1950 and the summer of 1963, more than half were spent in Zushi, a coast town a mile or two from Kamakura. The rest of the time was divided between Tokyo and a variety of travels round Japan. The travels, apart from occasional holiday trips, were mostly to the Kansai (especially Kyoto) and to the south and west, that is, the areas in which there were libraries, museums and historical sites of greatest importance to the study of the pre-modern past.

The usual means of travel in this period was the regular train or bus. Domestic airlines were still in an early stage of development (and some regional airports were regarded with distrust, to judge by local comment and insurance premiums). The Shinkansen (much more often called the 'bullet train'), though already under development, was not expected to be in service until 1964. Meanwhile, the least time-wasting way to get from Tokyo to Kyoto or Osaka was to take the night sleeper, a special express. This was luxury. Journeys to more distant destinations took longer and were much less comfortable as a rule. Kochi in southern Shikoku and Izumo on the Japan Sea coast were served by nothing better than a semi-express. The traveller, unless in a very great hurry, did better to break the journey in the Kansai.

In remoter regions still the facilities could be rudimentary. The last section of a journey from Fukuoka to Hirado in the early weeks of 1951 required the use of a very ancient steam train, the carriages of which proved on inspection to have been made in England in 1900. The interiors had been gutted, leaving only wooden benches round the outside shell to serve as seating. In the space so cleared in the centre stood an iron stove, which had to be fed with fuel by the passengers: a task they undertook with some enthusiasm, since it was snowing outside. The atmosphere that resulted was not only warm, but thick. Many of the passengers were fisherwomen, travelling home from work. Most were chewing dried fish.

In the larger urban areas there were then, as there are now, private railway networks providing a cheaper and more frequent service than was offered by the nationalized lines. Often they extended far out into rural districts. From Tokyo, for example, there was a private 'prestige' service to the Hakone and Nikko national parks; from Osaka one could go by express direct to Ise. Within the towns buses were almost everywhere replacing trams (though it took longer in Kyoto than in most places). Routes started as a rule from major railway stations. In these respects Japan has not changed a great deal in the last fifty years. Taxis, too, were numerous, though the standard of driving was more suspect then. Before the police drive to improve things for the sake of the Olympics, Tokyo taxi-drivers were known as *kamikaze* after the wartime suicide pilots. Private cars were few, most of them provided by the office or the firm, complete with driver. It was not until the 1970s that the family saloon was often to be seen, generally driven by the owner's wife. It was known in Japanese as *my-car*, to emphasize the significance of ownership.

Once away from the metropolitan centres life-styles could change within a very short distance, at least insofar as the eye recorded them. In Zushi, only twenty miles from Tokyo, it was possible in 1950 to hire a rickshaw at the railway station to take one home. Partly, no doubt, as a result of the Occupation, one did not have to go far to buy a selection of Western packaged foods, some simple drugstore items, or a variety of Western-style household needs; but for the more elaborate kinds of banking or medical services it was wiser to go to Tokyo or Yokohama. Even in so large a city as Kyoto one could meet with surprises. On one occasion, when calling at the quite palatial branch there of a major Japanese bank, the manager apologized for a delay in cashing a yen-denominated traveller's cheque, explaining that the staff had never seen one before.

In fact, while in Tokyo, Osaka and a few other cities the downtown area was almost wholly Western in appearance, Zushi and provincial towns throughout Japan had a quite different look. In them, the most substantial Western-style buildings were government offices, banks and schools. A few shopping streets had pavements; perhaps half the shops had glass windows and modern-looking counters, though even these used the abacus to total your bill; most town-centre buildings were not more than two or three storeys high, usually in an architectural blend of Japanese and Western construction, wooden-framed and plaster-walled. The overall effect was much more 'Asian' than it is today. Cars and buses on the streets had an out-of-date look by American and European standards, except for the very few that were imported. By contrast, electric power was available everywhere, evident in a network of overhead wires and cables. There was strip lighting in the shops, a rash of neon signs, though electricity was not used a great deal for household equipment. Our Zushi house in 1956 had an ice-box, not a refrigerator. Ice was delivered daily. The toilet had no flush or sewage, having to depend on nightsoil collection. Television arrived before there was any change in this.

When travelling it was not easy to find Western-style hotels of acceptable standard, so Japanese inns (*ryokan*) were the accommodation of

3. 'Simhat Tora' in the Coral Synagogue in Bucharest, October 1985. (Left to right) Chief Rabbi Moses Rosen, Ambassador Govrin, Emil Schechter, General Secretary of the Federation of Jewish Communities in Romania, and Ing. Theodor Blumenfeld, President of the Jewish Community of Bucharest.

•

As soon as I arrived at Keio I realized that I was going to be treated with a courtesy and consideration such as I had rarely enjoyed before. I was, in name, a graduate student, with a student card which enabled me to get into cinemas at half-price, travel on the railways at half-price and travel to and from between my lodgings and Keiō on a special student season ticket. But in fact I was given all kinds of privileges denied to the other graduate students – so much so that for the first few weeks I was completely bewildered. The professors and lecturers to whom I was introduced assured me that they would be glad to help me any time – any time, mind – I chose to come to their rooms. I attended a couple of lecture courses, and the lecturer would nearly always wait behind to speak to me after the lecture was over. Was there anything I hadn't understood, he would ask, because if so would I care to come to his room and discuss the points? There had, of course, been many things I hadn't understood – in fact in those early days there were very few things that I *had* understood. Sometimes, indeed, I had not understood enough to be able to frame any questions at all. But I would generally answer that there had been a few points I would like to ask him about, but I really would not take up more than a few minutes of his valuable time. We would go up to his room, where there would be yellow tea in a yellow kettle, which would presently be poured into small blue and white cups. There might even be some pink cakes – a present, the lecturer would explain, from a student. They might as well be eaten then and there. The 'few points' I had wished to ask about might take five minutes to discuss. But often, to my astonishment, they might take fifty. And even if they did take only five, other points might crop up so that it was often over an hour before I left. When I realized how long I had stayed I was always horrified – it was inexcusable of me to take up so much of a busy lecturer's time. But the lecturer himself always seemed quite unperturbed, and I always admired his unhurried courtesy under the circumstances.

Indeed, one of the most astonishing things about Keiō, and about Japan in general, was its time dimension. No one ever seemed to hurry. There was no sense of urgency, or of 'I'm sorry I can't stop now as I've got to rush off to my next appointment'. There was almost always time to drink a cup of yellow tea, and discuss what would be the best book for me to read on such-and-such a problem. This was all the more astonishing, since most of the professors and lecturers were so very busy, not only with their ordinary teaching, but also in writing articles in the innumerable Keiō publications, and in writing books and giving outside lectures. They had to work as hard as this simply in order to earn enough money to provide the necessities of life for their families, let alone buy books which a university teacher needs. That they should not only have suffered my interruptions, but even invited them, and prolonged them with cups of tea, made me feel very privileged indeed.

Because I was a student I was naturally brought into contact a certain amount with other students. Before I arrived at Keiō I had been looking forward with a certain amount of apprehension to my contact with Japanese students. From the stories I had heard I had imagined them to be alarmingly erudite about the West, and possessed of a divine discontent relentlessly urging them on to greater erudition. I had heard that they would bring one of their English poems before breakfast for correction and criticism. I had heard a story of a foreigner in a train suddenly accosted by a strange student who asked: 'Is Kierkegaard egoist?' And another story of an unsuspecting foreigner who found himself straphanging in a tram next to a student busy learning English words written on little cards. Glancing idly at the words that the student was learning he saw with a shock of horror the word 'floccinaucinihilipilification'. Plucking up all his courage he asked the student what the word meant, only to be told rather scornfully that everyone knew *that* word, as it was the longest word in the English language.

I saw that no preparation could be made for this ordeal. It was useless trying to 'revise' as though for an examination, for the questions might concern anything or everything in the universe. I should simply have to rely on the inspiration of the moment to guide me. Hence I was rather relieved to find that no-one ever asked me anything about Kierkegaard or even Kant. They wanted to know what I thought was the best way of preserving peace in the world, and what the British attitude to the Royal Family was, and who were considered the top ranking British novelists at present. But more than anything, they seemed interested in what I thought of them.

*   *   *

I often asked myself, 'Why are they so interested in what foreigners think of them?' What a contrast, I thought, to Oxford, where nobody ever wanted to know what foreigners thought. At Oxford one said to a foreigner: 'Hope you're settling down alright.' Or, 'Hope you like Oxford.' But never, never 'What do you think of Oxford?' Once indeed an American Rhodes scholar had the temerity to write an article in the Isis on what he thought of Oxford. Only very few people read it, and those that did thought it was rather a poor attempt on the part of the Editor to try to be funny. But I suppose that it is only natural that students who have suffered such a great upheaval, who have been ordered to reorganize so many of their ideas and values along strange and unfamiliar lines, should feel a lack of' confidence and a great desire for reassurance and encouragement from outside – from someone not in the same boat as them-

selves. I was asked for my opinion, not because I was in any way competent to give a wise one, but simply because I was an outsider. Perhaps if
Oxford suffered a like upheaval, we might conceivably find Rhodes
scholars consulted as oracles.

*   *   *

Almost as soon as I arrived in Keiō I was invited to join a small and select
student club, called the Pall Mall Club. It was called Pall Mall, I was told,
because its members all came from old and aristocratic samurai families,
and they had heard that Pall Mall was the most aristocratic street in London. The aims and objects of the Club were first, to enable the members
to become cultivated and well-mannered members of society, and second, to afford them opportunities for informal and friendly social intercourse. The president of the club was Morimura Ichizaemon, also a well-
known member of our sister the Japan-British Society. He was approaching his ninetieth year and was beloved and respected by everyone. He was
a kind of *genro* and great uncle rolled into one. He attended nearly all the
meetings, but always, with tact and delicacy, left before the end, so that
the members could forget a little about the first of their aims and objects
– becoming well-mannered members of society – and concentrate a little more on the seeond – informal and friendly social intercourse. One
of my friends, in particular, was a noticeably different person when he
was concentrating on the second aim from what he was when concentrating on the first. In the presence of distinguished visitors to the Club and/
or of Mr Morimura, his speech would be a model of the correct use of the
honorific language. In their absence, as when he would take me sightseeing in Asakusa, he would become a fount of quite a different but equally
fascinating style of speech. The Club meetings were a great pleasure to me
– though I was often made to feel very clumsy and mannerless, and that I
had a lot to learn with regard to the first of the Club's aims, by the beautifully brought-up female members.

CARMEN BLACKER was invited by the famous novelist Jiro Osaragi (see
below) to spend the summer in the tea house in his garden in Kamakura. Here
she began to develop her interest in Zen. This led to her spending a week
attending October *sesshin* at the famous temple of Engakuji at Kamakura:

●

The *sesshin* routine, the head monk explained to me, was as follows:
everyone got up at 2 am. Breakfast was at 3 am, lunch at 10 am and
supper at 4.30 pm. I could sleep in one of the smaller temples in the precincts, within two minutes walk of the monastery, but I could eat with the

monks. The head monk was a charming and sympathetic young man, and very considerate for the welfare of beginners. It was better not to overdo it at first, he said. I should not try to sit – that is to meditate –for more than eight hours a day, although it was true that the monks did at least eighteen. The first three days I should spend getting used to the position and the breathing, and after that I should be formally introduced to the *rōshi* and given a *kōan* or Zen problem on which to meditate.

The week I spent in the Zen temple, and the subsequent weeks and weekends, were among the most astonishing and certainly the most fascinating that I have ever spent. The first few days were completely bewildering – but, fortunately, I was not the only one to be bewildered. There was one other girl – Miss Oki – who was just as bewildered as myself. There were several male students too – but they slept and ate in a separate place and we did not see much of them.

The *Zendō*, or meditation hall, was a tile-floored building with two raised *tatami*-covered platforms along each side. On these platforms the monks sat and meditated, each monk having the space of one *tatami* mat reserved for him. The monastery was not full at the time, and there were a number of empty spaces – and it was here that outsiders like myself were assigned to sit. They were very strict about the sitting position. The strictly correct position is the lotus position – cross-legged with both feet on both knees. But I was told that one foot on one knee was almost as good – would 'do', in fact. An ordinary cross-legged position was no good at all. One's back and neck must be quite straight, and there should be a straight line between one's nose and navel. One's hands should be like Nikkō Bosatsu – thumbs together, fingers rounded as though holding an egg, and one's eyes should look at the spot in front of one known as *tanzen-sanjaku* – which is roughly at an angle of 45°. Also, very important, one must feel that all one's strength is concentrated in one's diaphragm. They did not insist on any particular technique of breathing – saying that if one's sitting position – *zasō* – was correct and one was really putting all one's strength into one's diaphragm, one would breathe correctly.

The *Zendō* discipline was to sit *kichinto* for twenty-five minutes, then walk round the cloister next to the *Zendō* for five minutes, then sit again for twenty-five minutes and so on. I remember the evening particularly vividly. At sunset one of the monks would strike the big bell and recite some *sutras* – and we would carry our cushions into the *Zendō*. For the first half hour or so we would sit in gathering darkness, the motionless figures of the monks on the other side of the hall would become black silhouettes, and then be almost lost in the darkness. Then, suddenly, there would be a piercing sound on wooden clappers and the lights would go on. We would all untwine our legs and file out of the *Zendō* for five minutes *kinhin* or walk round the cloister. The monks would go first, their robes bunched up to their knees, then the students. The cloister was lit by two or three lanterns, and in the grass plot in the middle was one tree, and to one side was the very beautiful building known as the *Shariden*, with two tiers of deep eaves which jutted out into the sky as one walked beneath them. After five minutes of walking round and round, the leading monk would strike the clappers again and back we would go to the *Zendō*. Before the lights were turned on the sitting was informal. Anyone could come and go as he liked, or move his legs as he liked. But after the light was turned on the twenty-five minute periods had to be strictly observed. One was not allowed even to move one's legs, however much they might be hurting. A monk would patrol up and down the tiled floor with a long flat stick called a *keisaku* over his shoulder. If anyone were sitting badly he would correct his position. If anyone began to get drowsy he would stop in front of him and bow, holding the long stick in front of him. The drowsy one would wake up and lean right forward with his forehead down. The sentinel monk would manoeuvre his back and shoulders into the right position and then give him eight terrific whacks on the back. The first time I heard it it gave me a tremendous shock – in the silent *Zendō* the noise sounded like the crack of a horsewhip. When the operation was finished both the striker and the struck would bow politely to each other. Subsequently, I myself got whacked several times – and though it hurt at the time, the pain never lasted and it had a strangely revivifying effect. If one felt oneself getting drowsy, one could always request to be whacked on the back by bowing to the sentinel monk as he passed by.

Sounds in the *Zendō* always had a strange quality about them. They were audible certainly. In summer and autumn there were the tirelessly reiterated calls of cicadas, and occasionally of a bird. There were noises of bells and wooden clappers, nasal voices intoning *sutras*, the murmur of straw sandals on stone. On rainy days there was the clatter of *geta*. But somehow the sounds were external, like waves lapping against the walls. Voices inside the *Zendō* had an abrupt, almost frightening effect – sometimes the sentinel monk would utter sharp reprimands and corrections, always in a compressed, fierce spitting tone reminiscent of snarling samurai in *chambara* films.

Meals were all eaten in silence, except for *sutras* chanted before and after. The fare was simple. For breakfast we had a mixture of rice and barley and a sour pickled plum. For lunch we had the barley-rice, some bean soup and yellow *takuan*. And for supper we had what was left over from lunch. Supper was not considered, strictly speaking, to be a meal at all, but something in the way of medicine to enable one to keep going in a non-tropical climate. Simple though the fare was, Zen table manners were very complicated. One's three bowls had to be arranged in a row, left one for rice, middle one for soup, right-hand one for pickled vegetables.

Between three and seven grains of rice had to be put on the table in front of one for the benefit of the hungry spirits. There were very strict and minute rules about the way the food was served, too – and the serving monks were often sharply reprimanded by the more veteran members. This diet was dull, of course, but the only thing I really missed was coffee. I would slip down to the village two or three times a day, and drink an extra strong brew provided in a little shop near the station.

After three days of sitting, Miss Oki and I were told that we were to have our formal interview with the *Rōshi* and would be given a *kōan*. The head monk told us what we must do – for it was very important that we should make no mistakes. We must make three bows – *sampai* – on the threshold of the *Rōshi*'s room, three more in front of him and, when we left, three more on the threshold, making nine in all. Each 'bow' had to be a regular prostration – forehead on the floor and palms facing upwards. The *Rōshi* was sitting in a beautiful sunny room in a yellow robe, a large staring Daruma in the *tokonoma*. Miss Oki and I duly executed our bows – then the *Rōshi* presented us with the *kōan* known as Jōshu's *Mu* – suitable, he said, as an initial exercise in *zazen*. This interview formally enrolled us pupils of the *Rōshi*.

You may have heard of this famous *kōan*. A monk came to Jōshū and asked: 'Is it possible for a dog to attain Buddhahood?' And Jōshu answered '*Mu*'. *Mu* is written with the character meaning 'not' – but in this case, we were told, it did not mean 'not'. It had no meaning at all. Our task was to find out why Jōshū had said it. I had known from the start that none of the *kōans* could be solved logically. They were particularly designed to train the mind to transcend logic – for the enlightenment – *satori* – to which they were a means was not a state into which logic or reason entered at all. One had got to realize, I had understood, that black *was* white, the part *was* the whole, and I *was* my boots or anything and everything else in the universe. But how one set about trying to 'solve' a *kōan*, I had no idea. What was there to solve, after all, when one's only material was a word without any meaning?

But that night I went to my first *sanzen*, and that helped a little. *Sanzen* is the name given to the formal private interview with the *Rōshi*, where he may ask one questions to see how one is progressing with one's *kōan* or one may ask him questions on points that are puzzling one. One of the monks warned me beforehand that it would be a *shinken shōbu* – a battle of real swords – and indeed it was. At 7 am in the *Zendō* there was a sharp command '*San*', and we all filed out down the flagstone path to the house where the interviews were to take place. We all sat in absolute silence in the room at the entrance of the house. When the *Rōshi* had finished with one person, he jangled a small bell, which could be heard far away at the other end of the house, as though over vast distances of space. The next person waiting then struck a bell in the corner of the room and walked

off to the *Rōshi*. The atmosphere was charged with an extraordinary tension, and I could see Miss Oki in front of me trembling. When my turn
came I followed the instructions, made one prostration on the threshold
of the *Rōshi's* room and another in front of him. I had been told not to
speak unless the *Rōshi* spoke. He said I must concentrate my whole mind
on *Mu* – so that everything else than *Mu* ceased to exist. Like this – and
suddenly his face became lost in concentration. Then he jangled the bell,
and I bowed and retired.

It was all very well, of course, to say that I must concentrate on *Mu* to
the exclusion of everything else. Actually it was the most difficult thing I
had ever tried to do. It would have been easier of course if I had been
given a word with at least a meaning attached to it – God, or love, or
charity. But to keep one's mind fixed on something meaningless is particularly difficult since distractions are so hard to keep out. *Mu* will change
into all sorts of protean shapes, and before long one finds oneself thinking of the shapes themselves. First of all I was bothered by the thought,
why *Mu*? Why not any other character, if it did not have any meaning
anyway? I then came to the conclusion that any other character would
have done equally well – but that the character for 'not' was easier to strip
of its meaning than the character for, say, 'dog' or ' horse'. Then I decided
that the point of using a meaningless character as the object of concentration was that it encompassed the whole of reality. A word with a meaning automatically carved out, isolated a little piece of reality and excluded
the rest. The word 'dog', for example, implied that the rest of reality was
'not-dog'. But a meaningless word did not exclude anything at all; it reduced everything to equality, or even to one. And that, I imagined, was
what I had got to realize, with the whole force of intuition, not merely by
vague speculation.

All these conjectures, I realize, may be quite worthless – but I tell you
them simply as illustrations of the difficulties a Westerner may pass
through in trying to understand Zen. After my first *sanzen*, I would go
to *sanzen* about twice a day. Sometimes the *Rōshi* never said anything at all
to me. He would simply go into the state of concentration for a few minutes – a wordless exemplification of what I was supposed to do. Som-
times he would ask me how I was getting on – 'Dō ja' – and sometimes
more specific questions. As for 'solving' the *kōan*, I knew that would take
me a very long time. The head monk told me it had taken him two years
to get through the *Mu kōan*.

I shall always remember how very beautiful the monastery looked at
night, when I came out of the evening *sanzen*. I would often sit under the
eaves of the *hondō* for a few minutes, and look at the curving corner of the
bell tower jutting out into the sky, the dark encircling mountains behind,
the white *kura* glimmering in the darkness, and the pool of light at the
door of the *sanzen* house. There were sounds of frogs and thin insects, the

occasional jangle of the *Rōshi*'s bell, followed by two strokes on the bell in the waiting-room. All these memories are still astonishingly vivid to me.

GEOFFREY BOWNAS was the first British scholar to study in Kyoto after the war, arriving there in 1952, as he describes in the following account:-

●

I arrived in Kobe on 1 November 1952, two months to the day after setting sail from Southampton in a P&O cargo ship. My visa had been issued in the summer by US State Department personnel in London, acting for the Occupation authorities in Japan. This went down not at all well with the newly-empowered Japanese immigration officers in Kobe.

That evening I reached Kyoto and the home of Professor Kaizuka, who was to be my teacher and in whose house I was to stay for the first few acclimatizing weeks.

Like every other major city in Japan, Kyoto had suffered hardship and shortage during the war and Occupation, though the suffering was perhaps not as acute as in the other six or seven largest cities which had all suffered heavy bomb damage.

Even so, Kyoto's opinion-formers had most of them in the early post-war days jettisoned Japanese values, as having failed Japan in the Pacific War, and had fetched up alongside a new set of Western standards. Kyoto's poets echoed the bleak, savage nihilism which drove Ryuichi Tamura, a leading member of the *Arechi* (*Waste Land*) School to write:

> For a single poem to be born
> We have to kill
> We have to kill many
> Shoot, murder, poison many whom we love[1]

With the end of the Occupation came the will and the stimulus to review the standards that had governed judgements since 1945. Towards the end of 1952, Japanese values were being revisited and reassessed and gradually put back in place alongside the newly-adopted Western standards until, by the middle of the decade, in 1956, the Japanese had 'settled down', as they put it (*ochitsuita*), and had created a synthesis with which the great majority could live happily.

Professor Kaizuka was himself going through this process; in his case, in his early sixties, it was (and still is) sometimes called *senzogaeri* – returning home to the values of our ancestors – after straying earlier in life to

---

1.   From Tamura Ryuichi, *Four Thousand Days and Nights*, Penguin Book of Japanese Verse, 1998, Geoffrey Bownas and Anthony Thwaite

alien standards. One of Japan's foremost authorities on China's early cultural history, Kaizuka *sensei* had studied and written widely on the cultures of the Far East. Now, he was returning to reassess the canons of Japan's culture and, from early in 1953 through the year, as he taught me he offered me the priceless privilege of being allowed to look into his own very personal thought processes as, with other opinion leaders in Kyoto, he reexamined and revalued the core canons of Japan's cultural heritage.

Kaizuka *sensei* was the most dedicated and inspiring teacher I have ever known: much of my own understanding of the early years of Japan's postwar journey and the essence of Japan's culture stems from his guidance.

Kaizuka *sensei* was born into a well-known Kyoto academic house. His younger brother was Hideki Yukawa, Japan's first Nobel Laureate. (Both were adopted into their wives' families.) He was a member of the quadrumvirate of outstanding scholars who spearheaded Kyoto University's primacy at the time. The others were Professor Takeo Kuwabara, a Rousseau specialist, who had had the temerity to publish a critique of *haiku* under the title *Dai Ni Geijutsu Ron (Second Class Art)*; Professor Kojiro Yoshikawa, whose studies of Chinese literature, and particularly the T'ang and Sung poets, were themselves literary feats; the fourth member was Professor Kinji Imanishi, Dean of Science, and pioneering mountaineer who later in the 1950s was to lead the team which made the first ascent of Mount Manaslu.

My arrival in Kyoto had lifted the number of British people living there to three. One was Welsh, working with an American missionary foundation. The second, who shall also remain nameless, was larger than life in every way. If Maugham had based a short story on him, one would have condemned it as too farfetched. At the time he was collecting various series (of Japanese literature in sixty volumes and so on) for American libraries; he knew all Kyoto's second-hand booksellers and diddled most of them. Collecting for Oxford's libraries as I was, his was an act I would have preferred not to have to follow.

*   *   *

From early in 1953 home for over twelve months was a newly-built two-storey *hanare* (detached house) in Fukakusa in Fushimi-ku, near Inari Shrine and six or seven stations down the line from Sanjo on the Keihan stopping train to Osaka. The *hanare* was beautifully built, with high quality lacquer and exquisite carvings by the local *daiku* (carpenter). The single large *tatami* room on the second floor had windows or openings in all four directions so that, in the sultry Kyoto summer, long before air-conditioning, you could catch the slightest breeze.[2]

In addition, my *hanare* had contemporary plumbing, boasting the only flush toilet in the community. In the evenings after work, fathers would dandle young children on their backs and loiter in Daimoncho, the lane leading past the house, waiting expectantly for the noise from my 'flushing toilet' (as it says in Japanese jumbo jets). Once I had obliged – often deliberately – they would dart back home, park the child and dash off to the bathhouse to be the first to announce that 'Bownas pulled again at 7.45'.

The community was tight-knit and was ideal for learning local and more general lore, such as the words of the *Hi no Yojin* chant which children shouted as they patrolled the streets and lanes on a late autumn evening -

Matchi ippon kaji no moto; hi no yojin (Beware of Fire!)
Sakana o yaite mo, hi no yojin
Tsuki ni ikkai entotsu soji; hi no yojin

Soon after I arrived, there moved in with me (or rather under me in the space under the house which was built on stilts at the front) a local stray cat which in no time produced a litter of six. One was a *mike neko* (three coloured fur cat) and people warned me that it would be a sailor's envy, since its fur would stand on end with the approach of a typhoon. Sure enough, as soon as the brood were capable of looking after themselves, young *mike* went missing – in the arms of a Kobe ship's captain, according to one neighbour.

Fukakusa posed language problems in those pre-television times when standard language was rarely spoken and local dialect prevailed. *Kyoto-ben* (Kyoto dialect) was widely spoken: Fukakusa-ben was a strong variant and, for safety's sake at the local barber or butcher it was as well to know the variants for key words such as 'back and sides *only*' or '*thick slices*'.

A regular visitor to the *hanare* – usually twice or three times in the month – was the *kuzuya* (scrap man), who would assemble his primitive hand-held scales and weigh the tins and other scrap metal items saved up since his last visit. I usually achieved ten to fifteen yen's worth, enough for a packet of the cheapest cigarettes or a ride on Kyoto's trams.

The *kuzuya* was something of an index of the state of the economy. Every piece of string, every sheet of wrapping paper, was hoarded. The status symbol in Kyoto in late 1952 was an electric iron: by mid-1954 – a very hot summer – it had become an electric fan.

Many commodities and food items, including rice, were still rationed. At Kyoto Station it was very easy to tell when a Hokuriku Line train had pulled in, for there would be a long procession of *obasan*, heavy bags of

---

2.   I am grateful to the Daiwa Anglo-Japanese Foundation for a grant in 1998 which enabled me to spend time in Kyoto, reviving and authenticating memories and, after forty-four years, visiting the *hanare*, which was just as I had left it.

black-market rice slung over their shoulders, dragging their way up to the restaurants and geisha houses of Gion and Pontocho.

1953 was the year of the firm establishment of Japanese patterns in a range of the arts; film was one of the areas where renewed confidence in Japanese values first began to show. Following the earlier lead of *Rashomon*, several examples of the classic Japanese film, including *Ugetsu Monogatari*, *Jigokumon* and *Tokyo Monogatari*, were produced in 1953. Among popular titles, *Kimi no Na wa* began in 1953 as a radio series: we would gather in cheap bars and make a single beer last for ninety minutes as the series unfolded and we escaped from reality, following the lead couple as they travelled the length and breadth of Japan. Later in the year, when it was turned into a film series, in addition to vicarious travel – which the average family could not afford – *Kimi no Na wa* set off all manner of fashions and crazes. In one scene, heroine Machiko wore a scarf over her hair, tied under the chin: in a matter of days, all over Japan, the *Machiko maki* was all the rage.

There was another indication of the return to traditional values and practices in the enthusiastic fervour with which Kyoto's big annual festivals were celebrated in 1953. First *Aoi Matsuri* in May, then it seemed as if the whole city turned out to watch the two main processions of the *Gion Matsuri* floats in July. Then, in October, for *Jidai Matsuri*, which celebrates the history of the city 'through the ages' since its foundation late in the eighth century, there were new costumes for everyone taking part in the long, majestically slow procession. Tremendous crowds watched the *Daimonji* bonfires in August and there was a record number of visits to Yasaka Shrine in Gion on New Year's Eve for *Otera Mairi*, to receive sacred fire for the slow-burning tarred rope which we twirled all the way home, keeping it alight to kindle the first fire of the New Year of 1954.

PETER SWAN, who had studied Japanese during the war and then joined the Museum of Eastern Art in Oxford, went to Japan in 1953 to study Chinese painting but expanded his studies to cover many facets of Japanese art. In a lecture to the Japan Society on 9 February 1954 he gave some account of his visit.

On arrival, he had arranged to go to the 'Shinagawa Temple', but when he reached Shinagawa he had difficulty in finding the temple. Eventually, at a police *koban*, he was told to take a train to Aomonoyokocho (literally 'the Cross Roads of Vegetables'). 'There followed by a group of ragged children I made my way to the temple situated in a little lane which I later learnt was part of the old Tokaido.' At last, he found the temple. His story continues:-

●

A large bronze Buddha stood in a dusty courtyard, impervious not only to the bustle around him but also to the numerous small children who crawled over him, standing on every possible foothold and making him look very much like a dignified god relegated to playing Pu-tai or what is called 'The Big Bellied Buddha' in some art circles. A man with a small cardboard stage fixed on the back of a bicycle in the courtyard was showing another group of wide-eyed children a play. All this stopped when I entered the yard, and there was a most uncomfortable hush ended by giggles from the older children and a sudden flight behind mothers' skirts by the younger. I made for the low wooden building at the back which looked somewhat derelict and quite unlike what I had imagined a temple should look like – no pagoda, no monks, none of that peace and tranquillity which one might expect. The young student who had expected me on the 12th had given me up and the place was thrown into complete confusion by my arrival. I was finally shown into what I later learned was the best room, where I awaited the arrival of the priest, the Reverend Nakata, an elderly, benign gentleman dressed in a purple robe, who hastened to greet me. I was later given to understand that I could stay in the temple until more suitable lodgings for a Westerner could be found.

There followed the most excruciating night I have ever spent. The priest and his wife and four sons had obviously seen somewhere an illustration of a Western bed, and had gone to considerable trouble to simulate one for my comfort. Two thin planks had been fixed between two boxes with the head about a foot higher than the feet. Over this, pall-like, were draped the *futon* and normal Japanese bedding.

It so happened that I spent only two nights there. By the third day there had been so much laughter in the place that I was told if I liked to put up with their poor household (and they were poor indeed) I could stay a little longer with them. I stayed there the whole eight months I was in Tokyo and a happier time I have never spent. Slowly I was transferred from the guest room to my own room upstairs, and from the cold guest chamber for my solitary meals to the back kitchen with the family, where I could tease and be teased with the other boys. I was completely accepted as one of the family.

PETER SWAN found an immense amount to do. He saw as many museums and private collections as he could in the time available. He found the introductions he had been given invaluable. He enjoyed visiting the bookshops in Kanda and Hongo and building up his library. He travelled as much as possible into the country districts and met art historians and scholars.'The scholars are,' he declared,'the finest people I met in Japan with the possible exception of the simple country folk. By our standards and indeed by any standards the scholars are miserably paid'. He particularly enjoyed Kyoto and Nara. There he was privileged to be able to visit the interior of the Shosoin:-

•

One sees the Japanese at their strictest in the art of preservation of the Shōsōin. To be allowed to see this ancient treasure house – the oldest in the world – on the two days of its annual opening is a privilege reserved for only the most influential. I was fortunate, through good contacts, in being allowed in for half an hour and was able with a guide and a torch to wander around these precious relics of the eighth century. As I left the doors were closed and the seals put on for another year. One of the most impressive things about the Shōsōin is its size and this, combined with its plain architecture added to the impressiveness of seeing this treasure house. I can understand how the objects have not yet all been sorted, even by what seemed to be an army of experts, all dressed like doctors in white smocks and masks and all busily engaged on them.

IAN NISH who had been in Japan during the Occupation (see Chapter 1) was a junior lecturer at Sydney University in the late 1950s and early 1960s. In that capacity he visited Japan every year from December 1957 to January 1963. He explains the purpose of these visits and how they were undertaken. The first visit in 1957 was especially significant because it marked the first return visit since leaving in the summer of 1948.

•

The purpose [of my visits] was to conduct research and this had to be done at my own expense. This was an interesting period in Japan's post-war development. But for me personally returning to the country which I had left in the summer of 1948, it was an opportunity to satisfy my curiosity and renew my quest for knowledge about one of the world's big countries. It offered the chance to make comparisons with the past and to assess the progress that had been made.

I travelled to Japan by air from Sydney. Since long-haul flights were shorter than they are today, it was possible to take in stopovers at Manila, Hongkong or Bangkok in each of which I had former students who were able to act as local guides. My most traumatic experience was in 1962 when my KLM plane from Sydney stopped at Port Moresby and picked up Dutch families fleeing from Dutch Timor which had just been invaded by the forces of the new Indonesia.

Planes arrived at Haneda airport. Since there was then no monorail, the journey to the city was (if I remember rightly) by airline bus. In the case of BOAC this took us to their office at Hibiya. The route was squalid and not the best kind of introduction to Japan. Having stayed previously in the Chugoku region, the outskirts of Tokyo with its urban sprawl were a relatively unknown area for me.

I stayed at the YMCA Hostel in Kanda for the first two years, because of its proximity partly to universities and partly to bookshops. The YMCA had been a subject that I had written about and I wanted to see how it worked in Japan. It was a common leave station for US servicemen from Korea.

Kanda is a district of bookshops, mainly second-hand, on the fringe of Tokyo's Quartier Latin. For the Japanese who frequent the area there is a sacred tradition of lengthy browsing and, it has to be said, buying more books than their houses can reasonably hold. I had a professional interest here because the Sydney University Library was anxious to build up its Japanese collection. More selfishly, it was possible for me to buy expensive pre-war books fairly cheaply because the pound sterling was still relatively strong. I was able in this way to build up a good personal collection of Meiji biographies.

Around 1960 I became a member of International House of Japan in Roppongi. In those days one had to take several trams: one from Marunouchi to Toranomon, and one from Toranomon to Roppongi crossing. The Yamanote-sen was miles away; and the convenience of the Hibiyasen was still a little way off. But considering the daily travel diet of a Japanese 'sarariman', this was a small price to pay in order to live in such an area, with an authentic Japanese garden. It was a great academic institution under the supervision of the late Shigeharu Matsumoto. In order to cultivate collegiality, they held weekly tea-parties for residents.

I was not a 'sarariman' but a wandering historian. My duties took me to universities and libraries. This was a period before the National Diet Library was created; and the national collection was dispersed and decentralized. For the Meiji archives I had to go to the Ueno Public Library; for the Shidehara papers to the Akasaka Detached Palace (*Rikyu*). For Meiji newspapers I had to visit the Shiryo *hensanjo* in Tokyo University. I also visited the Defence Agency archives in Ichigaya. Since my visits were always in the winter months, I had to shiver in these libraries because the days of over-heated public buildings had not yet arrived. But my prime place of research was the archives of the Foreign Ministry which were accommodated in a modest building at the rear of the ministry in Kasumigaseki – in marked contrast to the opulent building in Iigura nowadays.

One peculiarity about Japanese reading-rooms at that time – and still today – was that the level of desks and the height of chairs were suitable for a pre-war generation. They did not take account of the needs of foreigners or the post-war generation of Japanese who are now on average 1.80m tall. The old plush-covered chairs – lovely though they were – were not really suitable for the new generation of much taller Japanese.

So one worked in rather cramped conditions. No wonder one's re-
searches were often stopped at 11.00 and 3.30 to go to the courtyard for
physical exercise.

My position as an indigent scholar who had to be careful over his expenditure affected my attitude to transport. There was no question of my
driving a car. I had driven during the Occupation years in rural Japan and
had once taken the wheel from Yokohama to central Tokyo but never felt
tempted to repeat that experience. At the end of the 1950s roads in Tokyo
were being dug up in preparation for new undergrounds and presented
all manner of hazards . Those who experienced the improved facilities
associated with the Olympic Games and its aftermath are inclined to forget the years of difficulty over closed thoroughfares which preceded
them,

Fortunately, Japan is the country of the *densha*. Travel by tram seemed to
be part of the natural order for the Japanese in their cities. The trams
travelled slowly, noisily and grindingly round corners. Their drivers
who were monarchs of the road were not sparing in their use of their
bells to chastise anyone who happened to stray on to their tracks. Meanwhile the passengers queued patiently in hope. Watching them, we
thought of the Japanese as a patient, long-suffering race. How mistaken
we were.

Then there were the trains, at that stage under Japan National Railways.
They were efficient and lived up to their reputation for good time-keep-
ing. But the fares were still expensive for a foreigner. For me there was not
much money for travel; I only managed an annual visit to Kyoto where I
had friends at Doshisha University. I never at this stage managed to revisit
my haunts in Chugoku. Research and tourism do not combine easily.

As ever in Japan travelling on foot has its advantages. This suited my
budget. Japanese cities are places where it is difficult to find locations.
Even now pity the poor taxi-driver who is called on to deposit a passenger at an obscure or newly-opened restaurant. It is better by far to travel
on foot with plenty of time to study doorways. The Japanese are the
world's natural cartographers and are always happy to supply the traveller
with a good sketch-map.

Of course, Tokyo itself had plenty of scope for tourism. Tokyo in the
1950s offered a combination of the old and the new. Tokyo station at Marunouchi naturally attracted the Britisher. Frank Lloyd Wright's Imperial
Hotel was a worthy building, not as an ancient relic, but as an important
answer to a national problem, that of earthquakes. Its shops were spectacular; and its corridors could still be walked gratis. The solid Diet Building, opened in 1936, was an important symbol, though it attracted few
foreign visitors. I remember that I visited it around 1960 to listen to an
important debate on the country's economy. Invited by an official to take
a seat in the international press gallery, I stood on my dignity and expos-

tulated that I was not a journalist. But the official replied: 'When Japan's internal affairs are being debated, public galleries are full and foreign press galleries are empty. It is only when foreign policy is being discussed that the foreign press gallery is occupied.' I accepted my fate: for a day I was a lonely international correspondent.

*   *   *

It is always hard to assess the contemporary scene. Some have spoken of the 1950s as The Decisive Decade in Japan. I did not see it so. To be sure, the period from 1958 to 1961 was one of great economic advance and prosperity, leading on to Prime Minister Ikeda's plan to Double the National Income. But there was still an alternation of Boom and Gloom. Despite the Jimmu boom of 1954 and the Iwato boom of 1959-60, the speeches of the industrialists and bureaucrats regularly told of the difficult conditions and the discrimination they faced from consumers overseas and gave little sign of exporting successes and the economic miracle to come.

On the political front, it was hard to see Japan as a place of political stability. What influenced my thinking particularly was the assassination in October 1960 of Inejiro Asanuma, the chairman of the Japan Socialist Party, by a youth associated with a right-wing group. The fact that Asanuma was addressing a public meeting and the attack was carried to the nation by TV networks added to the horror of the occasion. So close and comprehensive was the coverage that it was possible to follow his glasses leaving his face. It forced me as a historian to ask the question: is Japan going to revert to the pattern of Government by Assassination, as Hugh Byas, The Times correspondent in Tokyo, had described the situation which he witnessed in the 1930s? On the one hand, it was a time of weak, though stable, government. On the other, it could hardly be said that violence was a major problem on Japan's streets. Certainly, the unions and the students had been militant and had organized politically-motivated strikes but their activities fell far short of a reign of violence.

No-one who was frequenting university campuses in the 1950s could be unaware of student activism. Student leaders were affiliated to parties of the left but to avoid direct identification with the political opposition in the Diet set up their own New Left party (not the Third Way). Protests culminated in 1960 with the *Ampo* demonstrations to stop the ratification of the revised US-Japan Security Treaty. I was not a witness to these major protests which (if memory serves) mainly took place in high summer. But anyone who studied placards on University student notice-boards at the end of the year could not fail to see posters which indicated the extreme militancy of the student body. The struggle in which the students were only one part failed; the treaty was revised and renewed. But the protest had a political impact. The broad support of the public for extra-parliamentary protest had a lasting effect on the political scene: it confirmed that the Japanese population had lost confidence in the established political parties.

*　*　*

Emboldened to generalize in my school textbook published in 1968, I said that it would be dangerous for a foreign observer to comment on the personal insecurity felt by the Japanese, were it not for the fact that so many of them had spoken and written about the lack of spiritual values in contemporary Japanese society:

> They claim that there is a search for direction which is felt be lacking. This is especially the case among the young who are not content with what they call a 'merchant culture' and 'merchant values': they profess to be trying to avoid being contaminated by the materialism which may to some extent satisfy, and certainly absorbs, their elders.'
> (*Story of Japan*, p. 223)

I did not return to Japan until 1966, some four years later. By this time the Olympic Games had taken place and been a successful shop-window. The Japanese had a new confidence. In terms of buildings, roads, public transport, there had been tremendous growth. I realized that in the period described here (1958-63), I had visited Japan during a time of regeneration; all around there had been hoardings and scaffolding, there continued to be hardship and some public amenities were still primitive. The prospect may not have been pleasing. But behind the scenes there had been invisible planning which had brought about an amazingly swift transition in Japanese society.

THE LATE RICHARD STORRY had been in Japan teaching at Otaru before the war. During the war he served with the Combined Services Detailed Interrogation Centre (India) (CSDIC (I)) and as a Major headed one of the CSDIC's mobile sections in Burma. After the war he pursued his studies of Japan and Japanese history and was appointed as a research fellow to St Antony's College, Oxford. He went to Japan on a number of occasions in the post-war years.

One of his visits in 1958 was the subject of a lecture which he gave to the Japan Society on 7 April 1959. He had arrived on 20 October 1958 and left on 6 January 1959. The purpose of his visit was to collect material about Prince Fumimaro Konoye who had been Japanese Prime Minister from 1937 to early 1939 and again from the summer of 1940 until October 1941. He was also able to fit in a visit to Hokkaido during this period. He explained:-

●

Most of the eleven weeks I was in Tokyo – living almost luxuriously in that cultural caravanserai known as The International House of Japan, on a hill in Azabu in grounds once owned by the famous family of Iwasaki. From my balcony I had, to right and left, contrasting views, symbolizing perhaps the ancient and eternal, and the modern and ephemeral. To the right, rising over a line of blue hills, was Mount Fuji. To the left, soaring vertically from the trees of Shiba, was that astonishing structure, the Tokyo Tower. This, as many of you may know, is actually a little taller than its counterpart in Paris. . .

At night, while the distant sounds might be those of an aeroplane warming up its engines at Haneda, or a ship hooting as it moves to its berth at Shibaura, or of the siren of a police car racing towards Roppongi, the noises close at hand are still those of the *geta* along the pavement, of the clap-clap of the night watchman on his rounds, of the noodle-seller playing that short, plaintive, unforgettable melody on his thin little flute. . .

At Okitsu, in November, I spent a night at the *Zagyoso*, Prince Saionji's villa by the sea. I travelled down from Tokyo, in the company of Mr Redman, to attend the annual ceremony to commemorate the passing of the last of the *Genro*. It is now more than eighteen years since he died. The villa *Zagyoso* is administered by the Saionji Memorial Society and it has been maintained more or less unaltered since the days when Prince Saionji himself lived there. On one side of the villa is the Tokaido and, on the other, a small garden facing the Pacific. Among those who attended the simple and impressive memorial ceremony in the *Zagyoso* was a distinguished Vice-President of the Japan Society, Viscount Hisaakira Kano. Also present were the Mayor of Okitsu and Prince Saionji's gardener; and the latter had many stories to tell – over the refreshments that followed the ceremony – of the Prince's daily life at Okitsu.

Almost opposite the villa and just across the Tokaido road and railway is the peaceful, sleepy old Seikenji; and if you pass through the grounds of this temple and mount by the path through the little cemetery up the steep wooded hill you emerge eventually into slopes covered with mandarin orange orchards. Keep on climbing and you come to a ridge that will show you, very suddenly, what is certainly one of the finest views of Fuji – seemingly quite close, like the view from Nagao Toge. . .

Not having seen Hokkaido in winter for more than eighteen years it was, I confess, something of a pleasure to realize that Otaru under snow looked much the same as in the old days – most people in rubber boots (or high *geta*) and fur caps, the children skiing home from school, the big Kushiro horses pulling the sledges along the streets, the icicles hanging like stalactites from the frozen, snow-covered eaves, the steel grey sky over the dark grey wintry sea. The harbour, it must be said, presented a rather dismal sight; for there were only a few ships where there used to be perhaps thirty or forty. The decline in shipping is due, of course, to the absence of trade with China and Korea. Otaru, commercially, is not what it was. Sapporo, on the other hand, has been transformed from something rather quiet and dignified, with an atmosphere almost reminiscent of an English cathedral city, into a very lively, bustling provincial capital. The spate of building, so evident in Tokyo, has flooded over the centre of Sapporo; and on every side there are new blocks of offices and shops. There is even a Sapporo Tower, with a high observation platform from which you can see what seems to be the entire Ishikari Plain.

IN AN ARTICLE in *Tsuru* (Vol. 3, No. 3, May 1974) entitled 'Japan: winter 1973-4: a triptych', RICHARD STORRY described a visit which he said was his tenth visit to Japan since he first set foot in Japan nearly thirty-seven years earlier. He was there at the height of the oil crisis. He recorded:-

●

The dryness of that season in the Kanto region was extraordinary. If, in the end, there was no shortage of oil, there was most certainly a scarcity of water. While the Japan Sea littoral and the Tohoku region were smothered by unusually heavy and persistent falls of snow, clogging roads and railways, bringing movement to a halt, Tokyo and Yokohama had day after day of cold, clear blue, sunny skies. From rooftops in Marunouchi and Azabu could be seen, even at noon on most November and December days, the cone of Fuji riding high above the Hakone hills, the best part of a hundred miles away. But it was a cone almost free of snow: a rare spectacle this, snowless Fuji in December.

January came, and still there was no moisture in the air. Electricity crackled from curtain, cushion, and white antimacassar. Door-knobs and light-switches delivered small sharp shocks.

Back in the autumn there had been talk of the prospect of another great earthquake shaking the Kanto region. Too much can be made of anniversaries; but older people could not forget that the Kanto Disaster had occurred just fifty years earlier. Vulgar prophecies of woe spread from mouth to mouth – like the rumours of a shortage of soap and paper that sent housewives on a buying panic in mid-November. Even dates for calamity were announced.

*   *   *

At all events, there were moments when one thought of *Mappo* – the end of a Buddhist age. Unscientific reflections, such as these, were enhanced, if anything, by what happened in Tokyo on the night of 21/22 January.

That evening the interminable drought was broken at long last. Snow fell steadily from about the time of the housebound rush hour. Caught without chains, wheels spinning, engines screaming, many an unwary driver had finally to abandon 'Cedric' and 'Gloria' in the storm. Across the city the humming spider's web of *kosoku doro*, elevated expressways, fell silent, closed by the police. Snow in Tokyo is always dramatic; and it is associated with at least three episodes of historic revenge – the vendetta achieved by the Forty-seven Ronin, the assassination of Prime Minister Ii Kamon-no-kami in 1860 and the military rising in the 1930s known as the *Ni-Ni-Roku Jiken* [26 February Incident].

The snowstorm of 21 January, 1974, witnessed no such scenes. But its swirling descent upon the city was marked by a most unusual phenomenon. It was accompanied by thunder and lightning as loud and pyrotechnic as any monsoon storm at the close of a sultry day. As a climax to a strange season this storm was appropriately bizarre.

Peace came with the morning, the harsher outlines of the city softened by the snow; the older monuments, the walls and watch-towers, islanded in white.

Those walls and watch-towers had been a focus of devotion, three weeks before the storm, on the morning of New Year's Day. The previous day, New Year's Eve, we had joined, through the goodwill of Japanese friends, a so-called 'O-*Shogatsu* Plan'. This was a kind of package-deal allowing one to enjoy for forty-eight hours the full treatment of traditional New Year festivities in a leading Tokyo hotel. Proceedings had begun with Year-end O-*soba*, cold noodles, eaten in company with the old and very young. For those who had joined the 'O-*Shogatsu* Plan' tended to be grandparents and grandchildren. It was a cheerful occasion, everybody happy in anticipation of the next day, the first in the Year of the Tiger. After this final meal we all retired to our rooms, to watch on TV the winding up of the Old Year and the ushering in of the New.

The outside cameras travelled from a cattle ranch in north-east Hokkaido to a community gathering near Kagoshima. Farmers, fishermen, housewives, in cosy domesticity for this one night at least, all chores done and next day's food prepared, spoke demurely and in a variety of dialects before a hundred million viewers. Then as the year closed, the great temple bells were struck in Kyoto, in Nara, at Matsushima, and by the Inland Sea; and with solemnity we entered 1974, while in London, Rome, and Paris the last of the sun was still red in the western sky.

* * *

Next day, in the blue and sparkling cold, we cross the Double Bridge, part of a multitude making its way to the patio within the walls facing the new Palace. This time we see a true Daimyo Procession – members of the

Yonezawa Han in full armour, with swords and halberds, winged helms, iron fans.

When the imperial family appears on the balcony the crowd responds with spontaneous but totally unhysterical warmth.

THE LATE LOUIS ALLEN studied Japanese during the war at SOAS. He was sent to Burma where he was at the time of the surrender. After the war he taught French at Durham until his retirement in 1988, but he kept up his Japanese and made a significant scholarly contribution to the history of the war in South East Asia and its aftermath. As he explained in an interview carried in *Japan Digest* in October 1990 Louis was one of a pair of translators and interrogators who were attached to British and Indian Divisions in Burma in the final stages of the war:-

•

As the war turned inexorably against Japan, these Japanese-speaking teams played a key role in the orderly surrender of military units in the field, first in Burma and then later across the whole of South East Asia.

The teams were the '. . . only people on the allied side required to change roles – from actually fighting Japanese on the one hand and then within a matter of days, and hours in some cases, to switch to friendly chat with them about surrender arrangements. In the aftermath of the surrender I reckon I got to know one element of Japanese life – the military element – in a way that nobody since has been able to get to know. . . a curious tiny unrepeatable moment of time.'

Louis moved into the Japanese surrender camps in Burma and spent some months there. 'Days before these people had been fighting us. Yet I never once felt insecure. I never felt we were under threat from any of them. They could have killed me at any time, but I never felt the least disquiet.' What happened, in fact, was that he formed deep, enduring friendships that he treasures to this day.

One of those was with Shinzo Tsutsumi, a naval lieutenant commander lost in Burma with 600 of his men. He had been told the British army had taken Rangoon and that there were no boats so he would have to hike to Moulmein for possible rescue, crossing two major rivers and hacking his way through hundreds of miles of jungle. During this epic journey, atomic bombs were dropped on Hiroshima and Nagasaki and the war was over.

By the time he was found by British forces all but three of his men had been shot, blown up, drowned or succumbed to jungle sickness. Louis Allen went to meet him and encountered '. . . the angriest man I have ever seen in my life. He was infuriated at what fate had done to him. He had fought his way through. He and three of his soldiers had come right through the British lines, hundreds of miles, and suddenly they had ended the war on him. He looked like Robinson Crusoe ... fierce unkempt beard, shaggy hair, quite unlike the Japanese officers we were accustomed to seeing: uniform hanging off him in rags, feet bound in rags. And he began to preach at me. "This war is all the fault of American economic imperialism" and all that sort of thing. Well, I said: "Possibly so, but as far as we are concerned the war is now over and a very special bomb has been used against the Japanese otherwise they would not have surrendered", and so forth. We did some hammer and tongs for a bit.

'We got into the boat to take him across to the surrender camp. It was an absolutely serene, beautiful Burmese autumn day and I was so taken with the scene that idiotically I began to whistle Beethoven's Pastoral Symphony. And the interesting thing was that this fury sitting behind me in the boat, just to show that he, too, was a cultivated chap, began to whistle Beethoven's Pastoral Symphony. So we crossed this Burmese river whistling Beethoven. Really an unbelievable moment.'

About twenty years later, Louis received a letter asking him to call at the Mitsui Building in the City of London and he did so. And there was Tsutsumi, 'clean-shaven, extraordinarily dapper, with a most expensive Savile Row blue suit behind an enormous desk looking out over the City of London. And I felt, "You haven't done so badly out of the war after all?" It was a symbolic moment.'

* * *

Unlike most of his colleagues, who shed the war instantly in August 1945, Louis Allen continued to be involved in what happened. 'It ate at me and absorbed me. I have wanted ever since to tell the war from the Japanese side. Almost nobody in Britain was doing it. I did that for the camps in Burma, a translation of Yuji Aida's *Prisoner of the British*, the end of the war negotiations (*The End of the War in Asia*), the fall of Singapore (*Singapore, 1941-42*) and the Burma campaign as a whole (*Burma, The Longest War*) ... the notion being that there are two people involved, ourselves and the Japanese, and you cannot do a story by telling one side.

'I don't want to be on either side. I want to see as close as I can the true story and tell it from both sides. It's quite difficult to do actually. It gets you a lot of enemies.'

* * *

What worries him is that the present unprecedented explosion in British interest in Japanese studies in some senses mirrors the panic reaction that occurred in Britain, America and India in 1942. 'The Japanese is a military superman. How has he defeated us? What is the tremendous secret? We must find it out. We must learn Japanese in order to discover this great military secret.

'Well, if you substitute today's industrial context for yesterday's military context . . . the Japanese has become the great economic superman. What is his business/economic/management secret? We must learn Japanese in order to find it out. So, forty years on, the adversarial approach is still embedded in the reasons why you might want to promote Japanese studies. And this seems to be a terrible risk.'

*   *   *

'A lot of my life has been spent in trying to document the Japanese role in the war in East Asia. But it seems to me that in order to know a nation really fully, you have to go beyond knowing the way it expresses itself in its laws, its military behaviour and its political systems. You have to know the way it talks about itself unconsciously and through its fiction.

'In other words, the fiction of a nation is as important as the facts of a nation if we want to know it properly. We certainly know the facts about Japan as we know the facts about America. On the other hand, the fiction of the nation, the way the Japanese reflect on themselves in terms of what they pretend they are, of what they imagine they are, we do not know at all. Our ignorance of Japanese literature is appalling.'

This is one of the reasons why Louis Allen thinks Lafcadio Hearn is so important to the Japanese, the British and the rest of the world alike.

*   *   *

What should British or any other non-Japanese readers of Lafcadio Hearn expect to get out of his stories today? 'They would get a notion, a very strong notion, that the Japanese, far from being economic animals, a totally materialistic-minded people, intent on material success, are an intensely spiritual people with a background which is not merely mythological but also supernatural . . . and in many cases, not just supernatural but superstitious too.

'The spiritual runs through both. It runs through superstition and the supernatural. The superstitious is, if you like, the bad end of it, and the supernatural the good end. But there is that element of Japanese life which is shown to you by festivals, temples and this kind of thing; it may be casual, it may be no more than ritualised habit, but they can't get rid of it. They can't shed it. It's real. Whatever they do in terms of weddings and deaths, if they are a totally unspiritual nation, they would have shed this sort of thing long ago. They haven't. And Hearn speaks to this.

'In him the material engineering triumphs of the nineteenth century in Europe are at war with the spirituality that he saw in Japan. That's the real conflict. And anyone who knows Japan now must see the conflict still there.'

THE LATE KEN GARDNER who had been a Japanese language student during the war returned to SOAS after the war and service in South East Asia. He took a first class honours degree in Japanese in 1949 and then became an assistant librarian at SOAS responsible for Japanese books. From there he went on to the British Museum where in due course he became Keeper of Oriental Printed Books and Manuscripts. Unlike Universities the British Museum did not provide 'sabbaticals' and it was not until 1967 that Ken was able to visit Japan. In a lecture to the Japan Society on 20 February 1968 he described his impressions:-

•

A nyone visiting Japan for the first time can confidently expect that his stay will be full of interest and enjoyment. The beauty of the country and the hospitality and courtesy of the Japanese people will make sure of that from the very start. But to anyone like myself, who has had the opportunity of working for many years with Japanese books and of observing Japan from the outside, through the medium of photographs and the printed page, the impact of a personal visit to the country is likely to be overwhelming...

The purpose of my trip was really threefold: to visit libraries and museums up and down the country, to discuss library topics; to search the shops of antiquarian booksellers and to buy any books or manuscripts of special interest to the British Museum; and to increase my own knowledge of the people, language and culture of Japan by travelling as widely as my time schedule would allow...

One of the best antiquarian libraries in Tokyo, now under the administrative control of the National Library, is the Seikado Bunko. There is a peaceful, leisurely air about this library, housed in a fine old building in rural surroundings, far from the centre of Tokyo. It has an impressive collection of early Chinese and Japanese books printed with moveable type, as well as many valuable manuscripts...

During those first two busy weeks in Tokyo I managed to visit most of the leading universities in the city and to spend a good many enjoyable hours in their libraries. In one day, for instance, I fitted in visits to Kokugakuin University, celebrated for its research on Shinto, to Meiji University, and to the biggest of all in terms of student numbers, Nihon University...

The day after that I spent entirely at Tokyo University, a miniature city in itself. The University Library, like that of many Japanese universities, is highly decentralized, which means that the central collection is sup-

ported by a host of departmental libraries scattered among the various
faculties and research institutes. This traditional system suits the professors, who like to keep their own teaching and research materials close to
hand in their own departments, but is deplored by the new generation of
professionally trained librarians in Japan. University libraries undoubtedly suffer from a lack of overall central control and a lack of coordination between the main library and the various branches. I also found
criticism of the prevailing system among Japanese universities of
appointing as librarian an eminent scholar in some field of learning
who may know nothing whatever about running a library.

KEN GARDNER naturally visited the National Diet Library where he received a warm welcome and was shown some of their antiquarian treasures.
He was greatly impressed by the Imperial Household's collection of precious
manuscripts. The Cabinet Library, he found, had a rich collection of early Chinese and Japanese literature. Another library full of wonderful early printed
books was the *Toyo Bunko* where he would gladly have spent a week. In Kanda he
called on many booksellers and spent hours '. . . weighing up the merits of one
book over another, and making my final choice of purchases for the British
Museum collection. Although I went from England provided with reasonably
generous funds for this purpose I could have spent the whole sum many times
over and still have left dozens of tempting items behind me.'

From Tokyo he travelled to Sendai, Aizu-Wakamatsu, Niigata and Kanazawa. From there he went on to Kyoto. Apart from sightseeing he spent many
hours in the libraries of Kyoto University and the libraries of Doshisha, Ritsu-
meikan and Ryukoku (Buddhist) universities. He then spent two weeks at the
library of *Tenrikyo* in Tenri, south of Nara where he said: 'It would be quite impossible even to sum up my discoveries.' He went on from Tenri to the Inland
Sea and Kyushu before returning home.

PETER KORNICKI, most recently Lecturer in Japanese at Cambridge University, explains how an Englishman became a Japanese professor:-

●

Owing to a set of entirely fortuitous circumstances I had the fascinating privilege in 1983 of becoming the first non-Japanese since the
end of the Pacific War to be given a professorial position at a Japanese
national university. Since the employees of Japanese national universities
are *ipso facto* public servants and since public servants are by Japanese law
required to be Japanese nationals, Japanese national universities had until that time been closed to foreigners, although this did not apply to
language instructors or to the many private universities. This arrange-

ment had come under considerable criticism on the ground that state universities in other countries did not apply such a nationality test to employees and that many of them employed Japanese nationals in senior and responsible positions. So in 1982 the law was changed to permit national universities to employ foreigners as professors, assistant professors and lecturers. The law did not, however, grant full parity of employment conditions, for it stipulated that in the case of foreigners universities would be required to stipulate a period of employment rather than granting them tenure as was the case with Japanese professors.

At the time I happened to be based at the Institute for Humanistic Studies at Kyoto University and the Director of the Institute, the late Mitsukuni Yoshida, a generous and entertaining polymath who had worked on the Japanese atomic weapons project during the war, asked me if I would be interested in the possibility of becoming an assistant professor at the Institute. Since I did not have any other job prospects on the horizon, the obvious answer was 'yes please'. I still do not know the full story behind all this. Certainly Kyoto University was manoeuvring to steal a march on the University of Tokyo (in English usage only the University of Tokyo is allowed to call itself the 'University of X', all the others being required to call themselves 'X University'!) by being the first to announce that it was to employ a foreigner, and the newspapers at the time made much of this, asking what had happened to Tokyo. Equally, the event certainly gave the Institute a lot of publicity in Japan. Whatever the case, I was sure that it was not for any outstanding merit of mine that I was appointed to this position, and at the time I felt somewhat embarrassed that more deserving Japanese colleagues did not have a chance to compete for this position, which had in effect been reserved for me.

After the official announcement there was an astonishing amount of media interest in the Institute's new employee, who was described as a 'brilliant young Englishman': since I am half Polish and was 32 at the time the second and third words were somewhat inaccurate and the first was way off the mark. There were many amusing consequences of the media interest. When a camera crew came to film an interview with me in my room at the Institute, some of the administrative staff came to check over my room to make sure there was nothing embarrassing there. I do not know what they were looking for, but they certainly did not care that it was untidy. What they did hurriedly take down from my wall, however, was an old poster I had picked up in Japan in 1972 when I was at Tokyo University of Education: it was a poster advertising a meeting of the dreaded *Kakumaruha*, the Revolutionary Marxist Faction of the *Zengakuren* student movement, supposedly one of the most violent of the student groups. The meeting had taken place eleven years previously, but it was still considered to be too dangerous for its presence on my wall to be shown on television. It was also disconcerting to be recognized in bars and for a short while it was difficult to have a private drink: even temporary celebrity is extremely tiresome and I was glad to be rid of it once the attention of the press had shifted elsewhere. The only benefit the press attention got me was a very embarrassed telephone call from an employee of the bank where I kept my account to say that the bank was honoured to have me as a customer and wished to present me with some wine. An hour or so later two timid bank employees, scarcely able to believe that I could actually speak Japanese, came to my door with a wooden box evidently containing two bottles of wine. Usually it is not plonk that is packaged in wooden boxes, I thought, as I expectantly prised off the lid. So what a disappointment to see two bottles of Manns Wine looking at me in the face: it may be one of the better Japanese wines, but it is not Chateau Latour.

I do not know how Japanese professors learn to be professors, but I was told hardly anything about my new privileges and duties except that I was entitled to two weeks' holiday a year. It was quite by chance that I discovered that I could go into any stationery shop in the vicinity of Kyoto University and walk out with whatever I wanted just leaving the name of the Institute, which would later pay the bill. I was only told of two duties. One was that I had to attend the regular staff meetings, at which attendance for all was compulsory and at which almost all present had booksellers' catalogues on their laps which they were looking through: I felt conspicuous at my first meeting as I found myself the only person who was paying much attention and I felt much more at home when I, too, had a bookseller's catalogue on my lap and occasionally raised my hand to vote without any idea of what I was voting for, like the rest. The other thing was that I had to impress my seal in the Institute's attendance register every morning at nine o'clock. On my first morning as an employee I found to my surprise that my name was the only one left without the impression of a seal beside it. Could it be that I was the last to arrive? The place seemed deserted apart from the administrative staff and I could not understand it; with my own eyes I saw some colleagues arriving later in the morning and collecting their mail so they had evidently not been in before and yet somehow they had impressed their seals in the attendance register. So, I cornered a friendly administrator and sought an explanation. It turned out that, in order to maintain the fiction that everybody was there by nine o'clock, every member of the academic staff had had a separate seal made which they gave to the office staff to impress in the register each morning before nine. Every member, that is, except me, and I hastily did the same.

The calculation of my salary seemed to cause the office many headaches, for it depended on my education and a whole range of other variables. The first difficulty was that I had not done a four-year university course like all Japanese graduates, for my course in Japanese at the University of Oxford had lasted three years. The initial proposal was to treat Oxford as equivalent to a Japanese two-year college, a very inferior form of higher education in Japan, but this was abandoned when it dawned on somebody that this would not be very good for international relations. Then there was my commuting expenses, which, I was surprised to learn, would form part of my salary. Since the old Japanese house I was renting was but half a mile from the Institute, I used to walk or cycle to work, but I was duly informed that it was not possible to record zero commuting expenses on the form that had to be returned to the Ministry of Education. I therefore had to find out the cost of a bus fare from the bus-stop outside my house to the stop near the Institute, an expense that would thereafter be part of my salary even though I never used the bus to go to the Institute. Similarly, whenever I made a research trip, say to a library in Osaka, I was not permitted to go unless I submitted a plan in incredible detail: every minute had to be accounted for, including the times of buses and trains, and my record had to contain a map of the journey. I soon learnt to make up all the details rather than spend hours poring over timetables, and it did not seem to matter.

The most bewildering difficulty I had was when I tried to take a short holiday in Hong Kong where a friend of mine was living, taking advantage of the leave I had been told I was entitled to. When I informed the office staff that I wished to take some leave, there was consternation: I was told taking leave was virtually unprecedented. The conversation went like this:

'But I am entitled to some leave, aren't I? I remember being told that.'

'Yes but nobody ever takes it, unless they are sick and need to stay at home.'

'Well, I would like to take some leave next month.'

'All right then, but where do you want to go? To Tokyo?'

'No, I want to go to Hong Kong.'

'My God, he is going abroad! This has never happened before.'

By dint of persistence I managed to get permission to go and I had a good time in Hong Kong, which was a lot further than Hokkaido but a lot cheaper to get to. But turning things over in my mind afterwards, I began to feel that I had not got to grips with the situation. My colleagues were all distinguished academics and their energy and output were prodigious, but could it really be true that they never took holidays? Again, I learnt the truth by chance. In fact, they were quite normal human beings who occasionally wished to take holidays, but such was the workaholic ethos to which they were pressured to subscribe that they had to disguise their holidays as work. It was only when a distinguished rural anthropologist was heading off to a certain European city, in what I shall call Ruritania to protect his identity, that all this dawned on me. He was going at Christmas time, when the libraries in Ruritania would certainly be closed; there was no possibility of doing any fieldwork in furtherance of his rural studies in the city; and, to cap it all, his wife was Ruritanian. This was evidently a holiday in Ruritania with his in-laws. The next time I went to Hong Kong I, too, disguised it, quite transparently, as a research trip in furtherance of my studies of Japanese literature, and nobody batted an eyelid.

I should emphasize strongly here that this is no exposure of abuses of the system. It was a fact that my colleagues did take few holidays even of the disguised kind. What was difficult to accept was that they were required to dress their legitimate holidays up as research trips in order not to spoil the Institute's, and the University's, workaholic record. It was fascinating to an amateur anthropologist to see academics in the Japanese system cope with what were to me the strange institutional constraints placed upon them, but no more anthropologically interesting than the manners and peculiarities of life in Oxbridge colleges, on which I should like to read the recollections of a bemused Japanese scholar.

At the end of my time there I was sad to leave the Institute. I had had the privilege of working with some formidably talented scholars and had enjoyed the exceptionally constructive and enquiring atmosphere there as well as free access to the superb library collections scattered around Kyoto University. My personal and academic ties with members of the Institute remain strong, and when in Kyoto I always drop by to greet former colleagues and the library staff. But my abiding memories are of these moments of puzzlement, and of the mental challenge it was to get to the bottom of them. And I have still got some of my pickings from the stationery shops.

JOY HENDRY, Anthropologist at Oxford Brookes University, published in 1999 (Routledge) a memoir entitled *An Anthropologist in Japan: Glimpses of life in the field*. This describes some of her reactions and experiences while undertaking field-work at Toyama in Chiba prefecture. The following are a few brief extracts:-

•

Toyama lies almost at the tip of the Boso Peninsula, a few degrees inside subtropical latitudes. This factor allows its inhabitants to cultivate fields of flowers while much of the rest of Japan is still waiting for the winter to pass. Tennis and golf are played here throughout the year, and in the summer long sandy beaches rarely fill with the hordes of bathers found nearer to the urban sprawl. The sea is cleaner, too, and the surrounding hills provide a cool retreat when the heat becomes excessive. A string of villages spread away on either coast, home to fishing families who help keep the nation's culinary demands supplied, and inland, beyond the developed area of golf-courses and other sports complexes, farmers grow carnations and keep cattle. Rice and vegetables are grown too, for this is a green and abundant piece of land.

*   *   *

Some five years before, I had spent six months living in Toyama, in a fishing community a few miles from the centre of the city. The south-bound train passes through the local station, and I was able to look out of the window and see the tiny house we had called home during that time. It was a white splash lodged between the fields of ripening rice and the darker green hills which lay behind. My children had been small. Callum had learned to walk there; Hamish had run down the road each day to play with his friends at White Lily Kindergarten. Our nanny had fallen for a local boy. She had also fallen off her bicycle into a rice field after having too much sake at the station bar.

This incident had brought about an interesting development in our relationship with the headmistress of the kindergarten in whose house we had lived and who helped in many ways with the research I had been doing on preschool education. It was just one in a series of impromptu events which add leaps and bounds to the sum of knowledge gained during fieldwork.

*   *   *

In fact it was this headmistress, Mrs Takahashi, or Mrs T, as we came to call her, who had provided direct inspiration for the new project on which I was about to embark.

She was a well-dressed woman, with an extraordinary presence, and she spoke, almost always, in formal and extremely polite language. She seemed to choose her words carefully, insinuating meaning far beyond a simple translation of the phrases, and I had often felt in a situation of competition when conversing with her. She had a way of putting people on their best behaviour, of keeping them in order, and she also seemed somehow to inspire most of her associates to work extremely hard – for her and her kindergarten, or on its behalf, though certainly not always without private complaint.

It was the language which had interested me at first. I had been attempting to notch up my own Japanese during that stay, using a book on the subject of *keigo*, which covers polite, respectful and formal language. However, while it helped me to get the phrases right, it failed to explain the range of possibilities which appropriate language could open up for influence and self-presentation. Officially, *keigo* is a way to express relative hierarchy; in practice it seemed to be much more, and this is what I hoped to investigate in the new study I was about to start. What exactly were Japanese people doing with these niceties of expression, layers of politeness and subtleties of meaning?

My previous research had involved much time spent with mothers and their young children, and I had learned that it is important to acquire these different levels of politeness as early as possible. Mothers took trouble that the tiniest of children should hear only the most exemplary language, and they would carefully repeat phrases appropriate for particular situations, sometimes even if there was no adult present to hear them. I had been told that those who learn later never quite achieve the same convincing facility with the use of these special polite forms, and since Japanese, like their British counterparts, judge one another by their manners of speech, this seemed also to be an important way to pass on social allegiances.

So here I was. I had received a grant from the British government, and I had arranged to spend nine months looking at this Japanese politeness phenomenon. Prior reading had made clear that there is considerable variation in the use of polite language, both regionally and socially, so I planned to spend a few weeks travelling around a little and discussing my project with Japanese friends and scholars.

*   *   *

Together we had pondered the best way to put the new project into practice. The study of politeness could be quite slippery, since declaring an interest might make people self-conscious, shrouding their normal behaviour with a front of unusual *politesse*, or impoliteness. Should I therefore invent another subject of study so that I could listen to people's language without their knowledge? It hardly seemed ethical. I would certainly need to get to know people so well that they could relax in my company. I would also need to see the same people in several different situations so that I could observe the way their language changed.

*   *   *

The house we were to live in was adequate for our needs, and once we were inside, with the doors and windows shut, it was quite charming. It had a small entrance hall, with a cupboard for the shoes in the usual Japanese style, and a surface on top which later became the showplace for the creations I brought home from my flower-arranging class. To the left, there was a well-equipped kitchen, with a table and enough chairs to accommodate us all for family meals, although the fit was a little tight for the less trim Western body. To the right was the bath-room and loo, and one Western-style room, with its own hinged door. Through beyond the kitchen were two rooms joined by a set of sliding doors, with springy *tatami* matting on the floor, and spacious cupboards along the whole of one wall.

JOY HENDRY was in Toyama when the volcano on Oshima erupted and caused earthquakes in the area in which she and her family were staying:-

•

During the course of the evening, we began to hear loud bangs at irregular intervals, and the house swayed and lurched from time to time. Takako went out to buy some supplies of bread in case there was a serious earthquake, she said, so we followed suit, and also filled our baths and buckets with water in case the supply got cut off. In our house we packed small emergency bags, with coats, sweaters, passports and the camera, as well as a pack or two of untouchable chocolate. No one else seemed to be doing this, but I thought we should be ready to run up the hill in case there was a tidal wave. We were not at all far above sea level. In the houses of my Japanese neighbours, people were soothed by the reassurance of the television broadcasts which had recently announced that the bangings we could hear were simply displacements of air. . .

The banging continued throughout the night, but I must have dozed off eventually, and the morning broke quiet and sunny. Out in front of the house, everything was covered in a fine layer of deep black volcanic dust. The bicycles, the washing line and each pair of swimming trunks had their own delicate sprinkling, sparkling in the sunshine. . .

An interesting TV programme was constructed around a series of interviews with the dispossessed families, asking them what they had brought with them and what they had thought about as they left their homes. From the point of view of a pair of foreigners with emergency bags at the ready, they seemed totally unprepared. Some had extracted the ancestral tablets from their household Buddhist altars, others had gone for a few clothes, or a change for the baby. One woman had rushed to make rice snacks for her family, and many children had brought their school books. On the whole, there was an air of being taken care of. Like our neighbours, they had put their trust in the authorities, allowing them to determine their fate.

10

Some Encounters with Japanese Writers

HONOR TRACY (Junichiro Tanizaki) • CARMEN BLACKER (Jiro Osaragi)
HONOR TRACY, LEES MAYALL, ANTHONY POWELL (Kenichi Yoshida)
LEES MAYALL (Yukio Mishima)
GEORGE BULL (Shusaku Endo & Graham Greene) • HUGH CORTAZZI
(Ryotaro Shiba)

HONOR TRACY gave an account in her book *Kakemono* (see Ch.1) of her meeting with JUNICHIRO TANIZAKI, so many of whose novels have been translated into English including *The Makioka Sisters* and *Some Prefer Nettles*:-

•

The next morning at half-past twelve Mr Junichiro Tanizaki, the novelist, drove up to the hotel in a smart Japanese taxi, accompanied by his brother-in-law, Mr Watanabe. He was dressed in a grey *kimono* and black *haori*, and on his head there was a flat cloth cap, such as might be worn by a gamekeeper. His car drawn discreetly up among the rhododendrons, where it could be in nobody's way, he surveyed the foreigners as they came and went with a beautiful air of benevolence. His manner to me was decidedly gracious because a few days ago I had sent him some caviare and, if there was one thing in the world that he liked better than modern French music, it was good food. We were going, he said, to see a lyric drama, the subject of which was the struggle between Yoshitsune and Benkei at the Gojo bridge in Kyoto, in the twelfth century. It was to be performed by an amateur school, or society, specializing in *Noh*.

Tanizaki was famous as a writer of extreme, if not morbid, sensibility and of a remarkably pure and classical style, but in appearance he more suggested an amiable boxer. He was a man of about sixty, sturdily built, with a cropped bullet head and, for a Japanese, an unusually aquiline nose, which was slightly flattened at the tip. Since I had been introduced to him as a friend of Arthur Waley, who had translated some of his work and for whom he had a great admiration, he had received me with the greatest kindness and with none of the usual fuss. He spoke his mind

freely and directly on all subjects, a thing very rarely found in Japan except among the simpler people, like the fishermen and farmers. Politics
he seldom mentioned, but only because they did not greatly interest him:
the Occupation, never, because. . . he was oblivious to it.

He was at present working upon what he considered to be his masterpiece, and wrote for five or six hours every morning on fine paper and
with a brush, in red or black ink. The beautiful and choice appearance of
every one of his manuscript pages was a matter of the greatest concern to
him. It was rumoured that there were writers in the world nowadays who
banged everything out on a typewriter, and the thought of it filled him
with aversion and foreboding. When first I had talked to him, he had told
me that he wrote very easily, with the words pouring out in a fine, disciplined stream, but afterwards Mr Watanabe had revealed that he could
often be heard growling for hours over a single page. His knowledge of
Western literature was considerable and his favourite authors were, or
had been, Anatole France, George Moore, and Synge: he was particularly
fond of the last, in the speech of whose peasants and tinkers he caught
echoes of life in the remoter and unspoiled parts of his own country; but
the older he grew, the less he could feel the spirit of the West and the more
he turned to the classical writings of Japan. As for writers like Sartre and
his school, they were incomprehensible to him, and if people wanted an
opinion of such works, he could only suggest they ask one of the students
of Kyoto University; at their age he too would have been willing and able
to furnish it, but that time was past for ever. But in spite of this professed
cultural insularity, he had the universal quality of an artist and was, altogether, the most approachable, humorous and responsive person I met in
the country.

He was much less of a domestic tyrant than most Japanese men, and
had a liking for the society of women which some of his friends thought
highly original. Nevertheless, he often had vehement disagreements
with his wife, being extremely temperamental and, as the years passed,
growing just a little crotchety and capricious. The present Mrs Tanizaki
was the fourth of a series. As a young man he had been apt, as someone
put it, to marry on the slightest pretext, but he had always behaved nicely
to all of his wives, and he had paired them comfortably off with literary
friends as, one by one, they were discarded. She was a handsome and
distinguished woman, considerably younger than he was, and it was
generally believed that she would manage to stay the course; but this
was a matter on which I was unable to form an opinion.

CARMEN BLACKER'S recollections of JIRŌ OSARAGI, published in the
Cambridge Review (April 1985) under the titele *A Room with a Gourd* recorded:-

•

On a Sunday in the spring of 1952, when I had been a student at Keio University for about six months, I went to Kamakura to visit the Buddhist temple Zuisenji. Zuisenji is now a celebrated *relais* for Buddhist vegetarian cuisine, to which gourmets from all over Japan flock to sample the mushrooms baked and served on a hot round stone, the chestnuts cooked with red rice, the green ginkgo nuts served on a bed of hot pine needles, the seaweed tea. But in 1952 it was still remote and inaccessible, requiring a longish walk through ricefields and up into the hills behind the town. The few visitors to the place went for the lovely view, which on certain autumn days revealed the violet silhouette of Mt Fuji, and for the unusual garden, said to have been designed by the eminent fourteenth century Buddhist ecclesiastic Muso Kokushi.

On this particular Sunday however an elegant party of men and women had assembled there to celebrate the unveiling of a *kuhi*, an aesthetic rock engraved, in cursive characters, with a haiku by the poet Kyoshi Takahama. Amongst them was a tall thin man, with grey windswept hair, who moved with a straightbacked animation and spring. That is the famous writer Jirō Osaragi, I was told.

Already by that date he had written stories, essays, a Nō drama, a story for children called *Kurama Tengu* and numerous novels, including *Kikyō* which had won a prize and was later to be translated under the title of *Homecoming*. He wrote regularly for the Asahi newspaper, and in consequence his name was familiar to every Japanese. He was one of the *bunjin* or literary men, for whom Kamakura used to be so famous before the war.

Later in the afternoon, the priest of the temple introduced me to this celebrated figure. 'How old is your father?' he asked rather abruptly. I replied that he must be about fifty-six. Just my age, Osaragi said. 'If I had a daughter she would be the same age as you.' He went on to say that he had a little tea house which stood empty for six days of the week. If I would care to come and stay in it during the hot weather of the summer vacation, he and his wife would be glad to put it at my disposal.

My amazement at this wonderful kindness to a complete stranger was even greater a few weeks later when I got a message from the priest of Zuisenji to the effect that Jirō Osaragi had been quite serious when he invited me to stay in his tea house. I was to telephone to discuss the arrangements, and move in, if that would suit, in the middle of July.

Osaragi and his wife themselves lived in a large house, set behind a wall and some trees, up a lane giving off the broad avenue in Kamakura which led to the Hachiman shrine. It was unusual in so far as it had no proper front door. The only entrance lay through the kitchen, which was closely guarded by a devoted cook-housekeeper, Itō-san, and several elegant maids. Through the kitchen one entered a beautiful large room, full of books and piles of prints and paintings, which gave on to a garden with bamboos. Here guests were received, meals eaten, future books discussed. The house also contained mysterious upper regions, where guests were seldom invited, and where Osaragi kept his immense library.

The tea house where I was invited to stay was set apart from the main house, in its own precincts and garden. Its principal room, to the size of eight mats, opened out completely on one side to a prospect of a pool with carp, a small arched bridge, a pine tree, a good many rare shrubs and flowers, and, unusually for Japan, a delightful lawn. Here, every Thursday, Mrs Osaragi gave her lessons in the tea ceremony.

But except for Thursdays, when I was to absent myself, this charming room was mine to work and live in. It was quite empty save for a small low desk, a flat cushion, and, piled in the *tokonoma* (the alcove), Osaragi's valuable collection of *suzuri* or inkstones. These stones he had collected over the years in all shapes and sizes. I recall immensely large ones, others scarcely bigger than a finger nail, others carved to the shape of birds or flowers or dragons. All were black, matt, and smooth as silk, many with the grey sheen, as though silver powder had been dusted over them, that is the mark of the special quarry in China called Tankei.

The rest of the little house, apart from a kitchen, bath room, and the anteroom needed for the tea ceremony, consisted of large cupboards full of other collections. Inside were dozens of long wooden boxes containing scrolls, scores of square boxes containing tea bowls or Sung celadon cups, piles of art books in English, French and German. It was a veritable treasure house, and the responsibility of living alone with so many valuable things occasionally filled me with anxiety. (Several years afterwards I found myself inhabiting the little house during the cold winter months, with a portable gas stove for heating. Every time I left the room, even if only for a minute, I was haunted by fears that a sudden earthquake might upset the stove, set fire to the straw mats, the paper walls and the thatched roof, and with them all the treasures that lay hidden in the deep cupboards.)

But no such worry marred my delight at the first sight of the eight-mat room. I could scarcely believe that it was to he mine to stay in for six days a week. As I sat looking out into the garden, I saw that the branch of a tree curved down over the eaves, and that by the open window was a flower called *yūgao*, 'evening faces', a kind of gourd which every evening was to bloom with new flowers.

The subsequent six weeks were among the happiest in my life. I was left completely free to come and go as I liked. I had a bicycle. There were interesting Buddhist temples to explore, and people in all walks of life who seemed ready and willing to talk. The sea was only a mile away. The transformation that the 'economic miracle', the Olympic Games and wealth were later to bring to the face of Japan was not yet dreamt of. Few people were rich and fewer possessed cars. Most of the roads were rough and untarred. There were no concrete blocks and no bullet trains. Instead, there was a sense of leisure, of an unhurried 'margin' to things. Small simple actions and scenes had a wonderful intensity and reality, a kind of magic which is now more difficult to find.

In the background during those weeks was always the kindly, learned presence of Osaragi. I would see him briefly sometimes in the morning when he walked over to inspect the garden and feed the carp, wearing a short kimono of pale grey hemp. From the arched bridge where he stood, scattering the carp food over the pool, he would make a brief salutation in my direction. Now and then I was invited to dinner, where always a feast of incredible elegance was served. The company included the beautiful Mrs Osaragi, who moved with the special grace that only long experience of the tea ceremony confers, old friends such as the Buddhist melon grower called Matsuda, and Han Takehara, a dancer full of the untranslateable chic called *iki*, and men from the Asahi newspaper. I recall conversations ranging over the Buddhist statues in Nara, the Paris Commune of 1871, the household sprite called *zashiki-warashi*, the incense sold at the famous old shop Kyūkyodō, the attempted assassination of the Czarevitch in 1891, and the provenance of the abalone which the company was eating.

He would also sometimes mention cats. He was well known as a lover of cats, and there were seldom fewer than twenty in the house. Sometimes the number rose to thirty or forty. In the kitchen they were to be seen stretched on shelves and dressers, and in all the other rooms, wherever the eye roved, it alighted on a cat. They were indulged and pampered in every way, allowed to tear the tatami mats and the paper *shōji* walls with their claws and scarcely a reprimand. I recall one cold winter evening several years later, seeing a pink electric blanket spread out on the tatami of the large front room, and nine cats, black, white and *mike* or three-coloured, stretched upon it asleep.

They were divided into two distinct classes. The large and glistening pedigree cats, acquired through Osaragi's own volition were 'inside' cats, and were fed inside the kitchen in a long row, each with its own personal dish. The rest were 'outside' cats, smaller and scruffier and fed in an even longer row outside under the eaves of the house. These were all cats which Osaragi had been kind enough to rescue when they were 'thrown away' by their owners. For in Japan unwanted kittens are not drowned, but abandoned by night on the roadside to starve, to turn feral, or in rare cases to be rescued and given a happy home. During that summer I was time and again woken in the early morning by loud piteous mewing. Another kitten had been dropped over the wall into Osaragi's garden, where its owner hoped it might join the large throng of outside cats.

In subsequent years, until his death in 1973, I stayed during several more summers in the tea house. He took a kindly interest in my studies and would often send over volumes from his library for me to read. This library I only saw once, in 1965 when he was ill and confined to bed. To visit him I had to pass into the mysterious upper regions of the house, and through the library. I could only briefly note the astonishing room, with thousands of books lining the walls and lying in piles on the floor. In a large adjoining room, he lay on a pile of *futon* on the floor. All round him, to a height of two or three feet, was a wall of books, which it was necessary to climb over in order to speak to him. They were volumes which he had been reading during his illness, and wished to have still to hand.

The last time I saw him was in a hospital in Tokyo, not long before his death. His conversation was as animated as ever. He spoke of the moss garden at Saihōji, the manner in which the Great Buddha of Nara had been constructed in the mid eighth century, the ghosts in the Nō plays of Zeami, and the Buddhist promise of release from the Wheel.

The little house had by then become so familiar as to be like a second home. To stay there brought always a renewal of the peculiar happiness, the sense of the joy of every moment of the day and of every small thing that happened. His death, and the death soon afterwards of Mrs Osaragi, meant the end of an era for me, the withdrawal of a kind and generous presence in the background that had animated my life and my studies. The cats were given away by Itō-san, and his library and other treasures moved to Yokohama, where a house has been dedicated to his memory. I have not walked up the lane to see what has become of the little tea house. Time and the bell have buried the day.

HONOR TRACY gave this account of her meetings with KENICHI YOSHIDA, son of Shigeru Yoshida, towards the end of the Occupation:-

●

Kenichi came to luncheon one day as he so often did, although not nearly often enough. He belonged to an interesting family. His grandfather was Count Makino, one of the grand old men of Japan, who was now spending a difficult old age in an obscure village across the Bay, in what Kenichi referred to bitterly as 'the sweet potato country'. His father was an astute and successful politician, the leader of the conservatives. Kenichi was a writer of considerable talent and wide culture, who could have had a career if he had been a little more supple in mind, but he did not at all get on with his father, of whom he would often speak with a frankness rare in a Japanese. He preferred to live penniless and to wear himself out as a literary hack. In his small house by the sea at Kamakura he sat feverishly writing day and night, turning out articles at a horrid pace for literary newspapers and small intellectual reviews. Once or twice a week he travelled up to the city to find new commissions or to collect, if possible, fees that were owing to him. He was getting on for forty now, and was of a most engaging personality. His eyes were still narrower and more tilted than was usual in his race, and there was a markedly ironic curl to his lip. In normal conversation he was gentle and inclined to diffidence, but in his cups he would burst forth in celebration of the glories of Japanese civilization and the Japanese spirit, soaring from one wild fancy to the next, in the beautiful, precise English he had learned at Cambridge. The next time we met after one of these sessions, he would rather sheepishly excuse himself for having talked so much nonsense, and we would speak kindly and encouragingly to him, and ply him with whisky, and in no time at all the magnificent performance would once more be set in train.

Today he had come on from one of his dunning expeditions through the frowsy editorial offices of the intellectual press, feeling tired and sad. He brought with him Mutsuru Yoshida, a man of twenty-five, with a delicate handsome face and a shock of silky black hair that continually fell down over his eyes, whom he introduced as an interesting new writer. Mr Yoshida said rapidly and at once: 'Please come to my house for a scenery viewing.' It was all the English he could find for the time being, and Kenichi explained, in his wonderful accent, that if it were possible to rake up a car I really should drive out to the place, which was about an hour's trip from the city, and view his friend's peach trees. While we sat down to a meal of Glorified Hamburgers with French fries, corn mush, grapefruit and raisin salad, and ice-cream swimming in chocolate sauce, which both of my guests appeared to enjoy, Kenichi told me more about the young man. He had done his war service in the Navy, and was aboard the battleship *Yamato* when it put out for Okinawa in the last naval operation of the war. The plan was simply to hold up, for a few weeks or days if possible, the invasion of Japan. There was fuel only for the outward journey, and no air cover at all. The crew sailed, knowing it was not meant to return, and when the ship was finally sunk from the air, only a handful of men were picked out of the water.

LEES MAYALL, Counsellor and Head of Chancery in Tokyo at the end of the 1950s and early 60s enjoyed meeting KENICHI YOSHIDA. I shall always remember seeing Kenichi no longer able to stand being frogmarched to the Embassy gate by an inebriated Lees to pick up a taxi to take him home one evening in 1961. On another occasion at a dinner given by Australian friends Kenichi, when the ladies had left the table, having seen the half-full glasses of wine left by them on the table turned to me and saying 'Silly to waste good wine' went round the table swigging the wine left in the glasses. Kenichi's high-pitched giggle and wit were unforgettable. Lees described his friendship with Kenichi in the following terms in his autobiography *Fire flies in Amber* (Michael Russell (Publishing) Ltd, Salisbury, 1989):-

•

We did make one real friend, Kenichi Yoshida, the son of the post-war Prime Minister. He was eccentric by any, not only Japanese, standards, but his English was faultless and erudite. He had lived in London when his father was Ambassador there in the early thirties and had spent three years at Cambridge. He did not always see eye to eye with his father and was on occasion very much in the doghouse. When in this condition he used to sit on the pavement outside the International Press Club at lunchtime, when all the foreign journalists in Tokyo assembled there to exchange news and views, with his upturned hat at his feet and a notice propped against it reading: 'Prime Minister's son – penniless.' This caused acute embarrassment to his family and presumably secured the restoration of his allowance or whatever redress he was seeking.

When we reached Tokyo he was editing with Yukio Mishima and one or two others the most high-brow literary magazine in Japan, but he also wrote for the popular press and his arrival at our house for a meal was always greeted with the greatest enthusiasm by our servants who were among his fans.

He was also a great expert on saké and his opinion was highly valued by producers of the wine. The only time I got into a real geisha house was under Kenichi's wing; the proceedings were charming and most decorous. We drank saké sitting on tatami mats overlooking the Sumida river. Kenichi indulged in no doubt witty conversation with the attendant geisha but my participation was limited to smiles and bows. It was like a rather cosy yet formal tea party in elegant surroundings. We kept up with Kenichi after we left Japan and saw him on his annual visits to England after his father died. He was staying with us in Wiltshire with his wife Nobuko only weeks before he himself died in Japan in 1977.

ANTHONY POWELL (see Chapter 5) had an introduction to KENICHI YOSHIDA from Lees Mayall:

•

The Council had already arranged that Kenichi Yoshida should interview me for the Tokyo Radio. This confrontation was to take place at 10.30 am, whether 'live' or not I am uncertain. When I arrived in the studio Yoshida was drinking a large glass of what I supposed, from its colour and the fact that the glass had a removable base like a *café filtre*, to be strong tea. He looked like a somewhat battered version of T. S. Eliot transformed into a Japanese man of letters; an impression renewed with equal force when we met a long after this in England. Yoshida held up the glass and asked me to join him in another. At first I accepted this offer, then withdrew when the beverage turned out to be one of those fine old nut-brown pegs of whisky (no doubt Japanese whisky) measured at a strength that would have knocked one out early for what was to be a day full of engagements. This morning pick-me-up, or perhaps an earlier glass, had already left a perceptible mark on Yoshida's manner. He gave a lively performance, during our duologue pausing in the middle to enquire: 'Well – how do you think it's all going?'

I was told later that Yoshida had a wide reputation for high-spirited toping, being at times deferentially referred to in Tokyo gossip columns as the 'celebrated writer and drunkard', respect thereby paid to his prestige in both spheres. Uninhibited newspaper references to the foibles of the eminent were rarer in those days than they have since become. As Inez Holden predicted in her novel of the future *Born Old: Died Young*: 'No editors would print the dull paragraphs of 1932 ... Gossip writers now referred frankly to sobriety, drunkenness, love affairs, gold-digging, lion-hunting, blackmailing and so on.' When told of such paragraphs proclaiming Yoshida's fame as a tippler I was reminded of a somewhat similar example of taking people as they come retailed by a brother officer during the war who had served in what was then called the Gold Coast. He said that he had read in a local paper the obituary of a popular African clergyman, in which, after listing the many good qualities of the Revd So-and-so, the obituarist added that devotion to religious duties was performed in the face of being 'all his life martyr to gonorrhoea'.

MANY OF US in the British Embassy met YUKIO MISHIMA although none of us knew him well in the way that Henry Scott Stokes or Donald Keene or Geoffrey Bownas did. Personally, I did not care for his conceit or his personality. LEES MAYALL did, despite the conceit, as the following extract shows:-

●

I liked Yukio Mishima who spoke fluent American-English and lived with his wife and baby daughter in a Spanish-style house in Tokyo to which he invited us from time to time. One room was entirely lined with his own books in Japanese and in translation in many other languages. 'This room', he said, 'contains the best books in the world – all written by me.' Those of his novels and memoirs which have been translated into English I have read and enjoyed, but his three-volume autobiography is to my mind less successful. He worried about what he considered to be the decline of Japan after the war and in protest killed himself in 1969 by committing *seppuku* – ritual disembowelment erroneously known to foreigners as harakiri.

GRAHAM GREENE's brief encounter with SHUSAKU ENDO is recounted by GEORGE BULL:-

•

For oddly different reasons the names of two not-so-long dead Catholic novelists from East and West are prominently, simultaneously, in the news. Because of two books dealing with his sexuality and the release of a quirky film based on *The End of the Affair*, the ambivalent nature of Graham Greene's Catholicism and his literary merits are being imaginatively argued about in Britain in early 2000.

Because of his growing international reputation and his widow's dedication, Shusaku Endo's memory is being enshrined in a remarkable memorial near Nagasaki. Between these two authors, by chance I once played the adventitious role of go-between.

Greene I knew from school days as a famous author, first through his books beginning with *The Power and the Glory* which (when I was sixteen) a Jesuit teacher urged me to read but not before I was twenty-one. With Endo I became friendly in the process of getting to know Japan as a journalist (first visiting the country with Maurice Edelman in 1963); then in some depth through running the Anglo-Japanese Economic Institute and making annual visits to Tokyo from 1988 onwards. I came to know Greene after I had been appointed along with him as a trustee of the Catholic weekly *The Tablet*, in 1976. Endo gave me an interview for *The Times* in April 1985, after I had been deeply affected by his soul-searing novels. Greene I met occasionally in London, chiefly to swap Catholic gossip. He would materialize infrequently at our trustees' meetings in the Garrick Club with mysterious suddenness like a risen Christ among the Apostles.

With Endo, when we spent time talking together in London or Tokyo (usually in French with which he was more at ease, having lived for a while in France after university in Japan) I explored either his own rather anguished literary, linguistic aims (though like Greene he inserted 'comedies' into his long run of novels) or the nature of the soul of the Japanese. He was always charming, courteous and generous, at one time writing an enthusiastic introduction to a book of mine, on the Vatican, in its Japanese translation.

Between the two great Catholic novelists I helped along quite a literary love affair, from infatuation to courtship and consummation.

Although writing squarely in the framework of post-war Japanese fiction, Endo was profoundly influenced by European Catholic novelists, especially Mauriac and Greene. He constantly re-read their novels. Given his religion, and his concern with sin and redemption, as soon as he won international recognition he was invariably characterized as the Graham Greene of Japan (where the number of Christians is tiny and their religion generally regarded as bizarre).

Endo, twenty years younger than Greene, shared with him attitudes and idiosyncrasies from professional purposiveness and relentless curiosity about the sources of human goodness and evil, to a tendency to tease and mystify and a conscious theatricalism. It was more than kindness of heart that prompted Endo to found a theatrical company in Tokyo to perform operas and musicals whose fifty or so members, aged from eighteen to seventy-eight, had to be '... inept at singing, clumsy at dancing, and bashful...' When the troupe performed *Madame Butterfly* in London a British amateur group put on one scene in competition and the Japanese Ambassador presented a bouquet for the worst performance.

In his last few years, Endo, as his widow recalls, would close one of Greene's novels, muttering how much he envied him his splendid gifts as a writer. The two often tried to meet, but managed to do so, by chance, only once. The score or so of letters to me from Greene and Endo respectively trace their efforts to get together and shed a flickering light on their personalities which had several traits, especially dry humour, in common.

Endo was always trying to arrange for Greene to visit Japan or to meet him somewhere in Asia. Endo's many friends included the Catholic novelists Shumon and Ayako Miura. But soon after I had interviewed him in London, for *The Times* in April 1985, Endo wrote to me saying that he 'felt rather isolated' because of the way Japanese critics regarded him, and that from Greene he had heard that 'it was not impossible for him to visit Japan'. Would I be able to come with him?

In his next letter, Endo announced that both he and Greene would be lecturing in Taipei and that Greene had promised to fly on to Tokyo, 'My friends and I are trying to make a schedule which will be easy and not a tiring one... I am looking forward to meeting him very much.' But on 9 April, Endo wrote to me that Graham Greene had sent a later saying he would not be able to go to Taiwan.'We are wishing so much to have him in Japan one day.'

The first ever letter Greene wrote to me, in April 1974, had thanked me for a review of *The Honorary Consul*, and said he had been most interested in an interview I had published with the then Soviet Ambassador to the United Kingdom – Lunkov – but as for himself '... I must admit I am not very fond of interviews'. Several letters on, in February 1987, knowing I would be visiting Japan, he asked me to give his 'warm regards' to Endo, and in February 1988 after calling himself 'an intense admirer of Endo' he added: I have met him once almost by accident at the Ritz Hotel and that is all. . . I have ordered a copy of *Scandal* but it hasn't yet arrived.'

I already knew about the meeting. Standing in the lift at the Ritz when Endo visited London in 1985 had been 'a tall gentleman with blue eyes'. Endo's interpreter telephoned excitedly to let me know about this the next day. But Greene never did visit Japan. Perhaps this was just as well, as he had a knack of arriving in distant parts just as some almost total, usually political, disaster struck.

In March 1986 Endo wrote to tell me how happy he was that Greene was receiving 'an honourable award' (the OM). In January 1990, Endo told me that he felt '. . . admiration and joy that Mr Graham Greene wrote such a wonderful novel at the age of over eighty. When you meet him or write to him, please convey that I am reading his books with great respect.'

The novel was *The Captain and the Enemy*. Endo himself was then working on what would prove to be one of his most important novels (*Deep River*), and had just returned from the experience of going 'deep into the unconscious' in India. He had sweated over the style and the content of a work which he feared would not be understood by Japanese readers, but in June 1994 he let me know that '. . . it has sold over 240,000 copies and is being made into a movie. . . being filmed in India right now'.

My letters from Greene over the years told me that he agreed the first in the TV series *The Shades of Greene* had been 'a terrible affair', that his agent would let me (as an editor looking for copy) see his short story called *A Really Bad Hotel*; that he was glad to hear that Malcolm Williamson retained 'a friendly memory of me'; and that he thought it was not worthwhile my writing a reflective book about his life and work as 'such a book' (*The Other Man*) had already been written: '. . . it is by a woman called Allain whose father I knew well and who belonged to the French Secret Service and was murdered in Morocco which is why I gave her permission. . .'. He invariably asked me to give his regards to Endo. In August 1988 he sent through me his 'admiring regards' to Endo, adding (in October) how interested he was to hear what I had told him about Endo's vivid impressions of Christianity in Korea.

Shusaku Endo's widow, Junko, recalls that after he met Greene in London he was 'leaping with joy'.

'He told Greene how greatly he had been influenced by his works and that he might even not have been a novelist had he not read his novels. . .' Greene told Endo that 'if he was interested in a Nobel prize' he would be pleased to introduce him to a 'very large and famous publisher'. But Endo refused to accept his offer as he '. . . wanted to be faithful to the other British publisher who had undertaken to get his first novel translated into

English and published'. (This of course was the courageous Peter Owen.) Greene also said to Endo that he had just a few years to live and hoped that Endo would continue writing 'Catholic' literature as if on his behalf.

In Japan, Mrs Endo speaks of Shusaku as having 'spent the whole of his life weaving the warp of faith and the weft of disease'. (In their married life of over forty years he was hospitalized for over ten years.) She says that he left her with three tasks: to let people know that death is not the end of life; to make Jesus Christ appreciated properly by the Japanese; to develop the programme of reform which Endo started to make Japanese hospitals more '... warm-hearted and friendly with regard to their patients, patients' families and friends'. Endo's christocentric faith was increasingly fortified by his perception of the creative nature of the suffering of the tortured Christ. Japanese Christians, he thought, might come to give to the West greater appreciation of the virtues of moderation, humility and benevolence.

On 13 May 2000 a museum to commemorate the Japanese novelist Shusaku Endo will be opened in Sotome Town, Nagasaki Prefecture, on a beautiful hill (famous for its sunset views) overlooking the East China Sea. Graham Greene will surely be there in spirit.

The museum to commemorate Endo will be on a site chosen by Mrs Endo after five municipalities had announced their candidacy. Sotome takes in one of the villages of 'hidden Christians' who kept but curiously modified their faith during centuries of persecution. On this village, Kurosaki, in his grim, spiritually disturbing novel *Silence*, Endo modelled the fictitious village of Tomogi. Designed by Jiro Hirashima to symbolize Japan's cultural gifts to the West, the Endo museum will contain a reading room, an exhibition hall, Endo's manuscripts and a collection of about seven thousand books, together with the desk and chair he used when writing *Deep River*. Junko Endo, who has been persuaded by Endo's publishers to write two books about her husband, would like visitors to go there to reflect in serene and beautiful surroundings by the sea on their own lives, and on the life and writings of a novelist who strove: '... to present to the incredulous Japanese, with their distinctly different spiritual background, a new face of the Christ and of the Christianity first introduced into Japan into the sixteenth century'.

Writing to me in 1991 '... as a good friend in England, a country far from Japan, who loves literature as I do' Endo had briefly touched on his own feelings about Japan's future. Japan's role, he hoped, would soon be to help the world's sufferers: 'We have seen and experienced too many cruelties and gone through too many hardships during this century.'

HUGH CORTAZZI met RYOTARO SHIBA during two visits to Japan. He writes:-

•

The first time I met Ryotaro Shiba was in early 1991 when I went to Japan to receive the 1990 Yamagata Banto Prize from the Osaka authorities. I discovered that Ryotaro Shiba had been one of the judges on the committee deciding on the award. I was interested to meet this famous author. He was totally unmistakable with his round face and shock of white hair cut in a rather pudding-basin fashion.

Shiba-san made a very generous speech at the ceremony marking the award and I had an interesting conversation with him afterwards. One of the other judges criticized some remarks I had made in my speech of acceptance when I had referred to some unfortunate aspects of Japan's past history including the Nanking massacre. Shiba-san did not endorse this criticism. His nationalism was of a different order. He was rightly proud of many aspects of Japanese history and culture, but was not an uncritical historian.

One evening, in Osaka, he and I were invited by the late Mr Hoji Shimanaka, proprietor and editor-in-chief of *Chuokoron*, to an excellent Japanese dinner in a famous Osaka restaurant. The purpose was for us to have a discussion on aspects of Anglo-Japanese history for publication in Chuokoron. In fact, we had a wide-ranging and fascinating discussion which covered, apart from the British part in the Meiji Restoration and the development of Meiji Japan, aspects of modern Japan. I recall that, as this dinner took place during the Gulf War, in my usual outspoken manner I made some sharp criticisms of the way in which Takako Doi, then leader of the Japan Socialist Party, had called on the Iraqi dictator, Saddam Hussein, in an attempt to arrange the release of some Japanese hostages. In doing this she had upstaged the UN Secretary General Perez de Cuellar, who had gone to Baghdad to try to broker a compromise solution, but had been kept waiting for two hours while Takako Doi chatted with the dictator.

The cuisine was excellent, but I noted that Shiba-san hardly touched any of it. He smoked incessantly, but seemed also to enjoy the saké.

Inevitably, our long conversation had to be edited down for *Chuokoron* and my comments on Takako Doi did not appear although they emerged in a *Bungei Shunju* piece in 2000.

I next met Ryotaro Shiba in 1994 when I was working with Antelope, a company which produces programmes for television and videos, on a two-part semi-documentary about the life of Ernest Satow in Japan, based on his own book *A Diplomat in Japan*. This was made in two versions, English and Japanese. The Japanese version included a discussion on film with Shiba-san.

Shiba-san was, in my view, an outstanding historical novelist and it is a pity that his only novel so far translated into English is *The Last Shogun* about Tokugawa Keiki.

Another Japanese writer whom I met once in 1970 was the late Mr Tomio
Tanaka, better known by his pseudonym KEITA GENJI, when I obtained
his permission to translate some of his short stories about the Japanese
'salaryman'. My translations first appeared in two volumes published by
the *Japan Times* in 1972. They were reprinted in 1980 in one volume under
the title *The Lucky One and Other Humorous Stories*. As I said in my introduction to my translation his stories provided 'an instructive guide to the
values and mores' of the employees of Japanese companies in the post-
war years. I was attracted to them because of their 'irony and satirical
humour'.

11

The British Part in the Tokyo Olympic Games 1964

DICK ELLINGWORTH • FRANCIS RUNDALL

DICK ELLINGWORTH had first been posted to Tokyo in 1951. He was appointed First Secretary (Information) in the Embassy in 1963 and was also given the job of 'Olympic Attaché'. This meant he was responsible for helping the British team in the Olympic Games which were held in Tokyo in October 1964. During his time in Belgrade before returning to Tokyo, the European Games had been held there. So he had some knowledge of the implications of such an occasion for the British Embassy, although the games were limited to track and field athletics whereas the Olympic Games in Tokyo included many more events. Ellingworth explained:-

●

The Olympic Games in Tokyo were of some political importance. Japan had been awarded responsibility for organizing the Olympic Games in 1940, the games which followed those organized by Nazi Germany in Berlin in 1936, but these had been postponed because of the outbreak of war in Europe and subsequently in Asia. Following her defeat, Japan was in no position to organize the next games in 1948. The International Olympic Committee eventually decided, following the coming into force of the Peace Treaty in 1952 and the economic progress achieved by Japan, to award responsibility for the 1964 Olympics to Japan. This decision was welcomed by the Japanese Government who determined to make every effort to make the Games a success which would enhance Japan's international standing.

By the time I arrived back in Tokyo in 1963, the city had construction works everywhere. War damage had still to be repaired; stadiums and swimming pools and other Olympic facilities had yet to be constructed; and communications in and around Tokyo had to be improved. During this period Tokyo was not a pleasant place to live in. Underneath many of the main thoroughfares work was in progress on the construction of an underground railway system and one had to drive, slowly and carefully, over temporary surfaces, often huge metal plates. There was dirt and debris everywhere and severe atmospheric pollution.

My position in the Embassy was in some ways an anomalous one, since I was responsible, on a day-to-day basis, to John Figgess, the Information Counsellor, and also to Sandy Duncan, the Secretary to the British Olympic Association, whose job was to prepare the ground for the British team. Sandy was not resident in Japan, but he made a number of visits and was an insistent correspondent. In due course, as Chef de Mission, he arrived with our team, shortly before the Games commenced. Fortunately for me John Figgess and Sandy Duncan realized the possible implications of my dual responsibility, and there were no insoluble problems, but there was a good deal of hard work, with time and effort being divided between two jobs.

My main job in the preparatory period before the Games was to persuade Sandy and other British sports visitors that Japan could do it. They were often appalled by the chaotic conditions in Tokyo and far from convinced that Japan could put all in order before the opening ceremony. They were worried also that, since some of the venues were outside Tokyo, it would be difficult to ensure that our competitors were being properly looked after. More generally, there was some unease still about Japan and the Japanese as a result of memories of the war. These were also the first Olympic Games to be held in Asia, far from Greek, or modern Swiss, associations.

These doubts and suspicions were overcome and most of the credit must go to the officials appointed by the Organizing Committee to deal with foreign visitors and teams. I remember especially the fine work of Mr Iwata, secretary of the Organizing Committee with whom Sandy Duncan established a good rapport. Members of the Japanese Self-Defense Forces were appointed to run the Olympic Village established for the athletes in the former US forces camp near the Meiji Shrine. They, too, quickly earned the good opinion and confidence of the British teams. We also persuaded Mr Iwata to agree to the appointment of 'uncles' to smooth the path of competitors, especially those in outlying areas. These were all British citizens resident in Japan, for the most part members of British firms such as Shell or Dodwells. Indeed, the British community's contribution was remarkably generous and wholehearted. John Besford, a British dentist working in Japan, who had been an outstanding swimmer, closed his practice down completely for several weeks and his staff – charming and efficient Japanese ladies – ran Sandy Duncan's office in the Olympic village. Sir Francis (Tony) Rundall, the British ambassador, supported the games enthusiastically.

I suppose that one of the reasons I was appointed – the first Olympic Attaché from the staff of a British Embassy – was the possibility that there might be political problems. Ninety-four countries participated, the most ever, and it would have been ninety-six had not Indonesia and North Korea withdrawn in a huff over the banning of some of their athletes. These were the only really political problems as such and I was in no way involved with them. My work as Olympic Attaché was largely administrative and in a general sense diplomatic. Most of this work was in the preparatory stages, since, once the games started, everything went smoothly and harmoniously. For Japan, the fine opening ceremony was a moment of deep emotion. The bearer of the Olympic flame on its last stage was Yoshinori Sakai, who had been born nineteen years earlier as the atomic bomb fell on Hiroshima. Symbolically, a new Japan was rising from the ashes of the old.

Although Britain did not head the final medals table, our athletes were very successful, especially in the track-and-field events. My own particular memories are of the gold medals won by Lynn Davies and Mary Rand for the men's and women's long jump respectively. I am still reminded frequently of the latter's achievement, as there is a permanent record of it on a pavement in the market place of Wells, where I now live. Mary came from Wells and had been a pupil at Millfield School.

British medals made a considerable impression in London and the team received two messages of congratulation from the Prime Minister at that time, Harold Wilson. This is not the place to tabulate in detail all the British achievements, which are recorded in the report prepared at the time for the British Olympic Association by Sandy Duncan. Like everyone else in the British community in Japan I was proud to be associated and was, perhaps, in some ways, closer to them, though the job had had only a remote connection with any real athletic achievement.

The British team's successes did not go unnoticed in Buckingham Palace and they were invited to a reception given in their honour by the Queen on their return to the United Kingdom. The British Olympic Association kindly invited me to be one of their number and the Ambassador gave permission for me to travel to London with the team on this occasion. So 1964 was a year I had cause to remember. After the Tokyo Olympics Japan and the rest of the world, Britain included, were somewhat more at ease with each other and I was grateful to have been a minor cog in the process which brought this about.

The British Ambassador at the time of the Tokyo Olympic Games was SIR FRANCIS RUNDALL. In a lecture to the Japan Society in April 1968 he gave his perspective on the Games:-

●

We were lucky enough to have the Olympic Games during our first year – which fulfilled a lifetime's ambition I have always had to see them. They could not have been better organized – Japan showed the world how the Games should be run and I am sure that they will never be better. Watching the athletics was for me the most pleasurable of duties, and I found that most of my colleagues felt the same. Nowhere else could one see some thirty to forty Ambassadors yelling their heads off – I think we triumphed and suffered almost as much as the competitors. But we were very sporting, and stumbled between the seats to congratulate the representative of the winner.

The Games gave us the chance to give our biggest party – over 900 indoors, which was about capacity for the Embassy Residence. We timed it deliberately for a short time before the Games opened, with idea that our contingent should have a chance to relax before they had to compete. And relax they did. I remember the lady swimmer stretched on the sofa, bravely trying to control the first Martini she had ever drunk, and a cheerful chorus of boxers and members of the Royal Yacht Squadron. The party was supposed to be from 6.00 to 8.00pm. We turned out the lights at 10.15 and eventually they went home. I like to think, though, that the party helped rather than hindered their excellent performance.

12

Britain at Expo' 70 in Osaka

LESLEY CONNORS ● LYDIA GOMERSALL ●JANET HUNTER
ANNE KANEKO ● PETER MARTIN

I HAVE GIVEN a brief account of the role of Sir John Figgess, the British Commissioner for Expo' 70 in Osaka, in my biographical portrait of him in the Japan Society's *Biographical Portraits*, Volume III, edited by Jim Hoare and published by Japan Library in 1999. The following contributions by four of the English young women (LESLEY CONNORS, LYDIA GOMERSALL, JANET HUNTER and ANNE KANEKO) who helped in the British Pavilion and by PETER MARTIN, who was the British Council representative in Kyoto in 1970, supplement my brief account and help to recreate the atmosphere of those months thirty years ago:-

●

Expo' 70 – Seven Months in Japan
by
LESLEY CONNORS, LYDIA GOMERSALL, JANET HUNTER and ANNE KANEKO

As students on Japanese Studies degrees in 1970, being given the opportunity to work at the British Pavilion at Expo' 70 for six months was a bit like winning the lottery. Since no period of study in Japan was scheduled into the degrees, this was an unexpected opportunity. At the same time Japan had been for most of us something of a distant prospect, and the thought of confronting the reality of the country, as well as of the Expo itself, was distinctly daunting. None of us had been beyond Western Europe and the United States, and some not even that far. Youth and inexperience strongly coloured our response to the *Banpaku*, and to Japan itself at that time. While some of the memories are sharp and clear, some of us felt that with so much focus on discovering ourselves, we probably failed in many ways to make the most of our time there. Moreover, much of the Expo experience stood in stark contrast to life outside it, and our responses were equally contrasting. The reminiscences below are put down with benefit of hindsight, and our interpretations now do not necessarily reflect our understanding at the time. Even so, for all of us this stay was our first exposure to Japan, and as such has been significant in the country's subsequent importance in our lives.

More than anything else, what initially struck us all was the 'difference' between Japan and our own familiar environment and culture. While this was something that we well knew in theory, and was exciting in prospect, the immediate sense of being in an 'alien' environment, where everything was different, from the most basic social customs or cuisine through to aesthetic values and literary traditions, was something that posed difficulties for all of us. While we were all happy to adapt to and experiment with what we ate, for example, the near impossibility of buying some of the basic British staple foods, such as cheese or cereals, meant not only an instant modification of diet, but also a recognition that 'Western' food was far from being the international norm. Prawns seemed to come with everything. We considered the Japanese version of other staples, such as bread and milk, distinctly unappetizing, and rumours circulated that Japanese milk tasted as it did because the cows were fed on fish! So, while we were comfortably accommodated in Western-style flats that would have been luxurious for many contemporary Japanese, and were in many ways insulated by our employment from the lives led by most Japanese, everywhere we went, every contact that we had with local people, did tend to reinforce a sense of difference. Where friendships were formed this became less prominent, but this awareness of difference, which will be familiar to many who have lived in Japan, was, if anything, heightened by our youth and generation. We had come from a Britain of miniskirts, the Pill, the Beatles, rock festivals, student protest, women's rights and unconventionality. Japan, by contrast, seemed dominated by conservatism and conformity, full of men and women who married when they reached the right age rather than when they fell in love, and where few women sought a career.

The gulf that we felt existed depended in part on disparities in economic activity and standards of living. While the economy had grown at a rapid rate during the 1960s, Japan in 1970 still appeared to us as the developing economy it still was. The purchasing power of our salaries (already a bonus for a student) meant that Japan was relatively cheap. We were the rich foreigners with yen to spend, a situation that was to be reversed within a decade. Although there was a tangible aura of energy about Japan, and it was apparent to us that the country had a rapidly developing economy and was going places fast, it was equally apparent that development had not been uniform. Back-street machining shops, cramped housing, scarcity of private cars and the evident importance of agriculture in the economy seemed closer to what we imagined non-industrialized economies to be like than to those with which we were more familiar. The huge numbers of farmers who visited the Expo, many of the older ones with bent backs from nutritional deficiencies, appeared to us not as the counterparts of our own prosperous farming community, but as 'peasants' deformed by years of unrelenting toil of a kind with which even the poorer members of the British working class were no longer familiar. Japan was very much a developing economy, very different from our own. We are now perhaps privileged in being able to remember it as such.

Something else that stands out in our memories is the enormous hospitality shown to us by Japanese, both within the confines of Expo and outside it. The willingness of many families and individuals to take us in to their homes and workplaces, to show us what they considered to be the best that Japan had to offer, and to explain their culture, customs and way of life, offered us unparalleled opportunities. In much of Japan *gaijin* (usually assumed to mean American) still had considerable rarity value, and while there was always that sense of being the freak or the curiosity, through Expo it brought us the chance to visit many parts of the Japanese archipelago, whether to see the pearl divers at Toba, the beef farms of Matsuzaka or the cormorant fishing at Gifu. It also placed us in situations where it was difficult to know how best to respond. At one celebration meal the yet to be totally dead fish designated for *sashimi* leapt off its plate into Lesley's lap, while the assembled guests looked on with horrified anticipation to see how the *gaijin* would react. With great presence of mind she replaced it on the plate, took a piece and ate it. The sighs of relief were palpable. Gifts were, as might be expected, also a common occurrence, and occasionally led to strange circumstances. The silkworm cocoons that unexpectedly hatched out in the warmth of the flat were just one instance. The extent of the hospitality extended to us inside and outside the Expo context was often overwhelming.

The welcome that we received, and which many of us have continued to receive, was always accompanied by a desire to know what we thought of Japan, and what our impressions of it were. This was our first experience of the commonly asked question, 'And what do you think of Japan?'. We probably for the most part responded to this question with a bland statement that we liked it, and were enjoying ourselves (not least, perhaps, because language deficiencies rendered a more complex response unfeasible). At the time it seemed a not unreasonable question, although the regularity with which it surfaced was conspicuous. The phrase 'gaijin complex' was frequently heard, particularly from younger visitors to the pavilion, and seemed to betoken a somewhat irrational feeling that Japanese were inferior to Westerners, but in what way was rarely articulated. In retrospect this concern to know what we thought of Japan and the Japanese, and to measure Japan against the Western yardstick, was perhaps an expression of the lack of confidence that many Japanese had in their own sense of nation, where they were going and what they were. The younger generation in particular was the product both of its parents' values and of the postwar education system. While economic growth had provided a national focus, by 1970 costs as well as benefits were becoming apparent (this was when we first encountered the word 'pollution'). The presence of Expo and the large number of foreigners it brought with it was a symbol of Japan's desire to open up, but also of her uncertainty as to her place and role in the international community.

The *Banpaku* itself, as the place where we spent many of our waking hours, was of major significance in forming our attitudes. The young Japanese women who acted as our fellow hostesses seemed not so different from ourselves. In the British Pavilion they mostly came from wealthy, influential families, had graduated from the Sacred Heart College, and spoke far better English than we did Japanese. Maybe most of them were just filling in between college and marriage, whereas most of us would have expected careers (in as far as we thought about what we might do after university at all), but this was not something that came between us at the time. Like most groups, they were diverse in personality as well as willingness (or unwillingness) to conform. In general, the staff of the pavilion were a varied but harmonious group, although on occasions I am sure our elders and seniors thought our behaviour outrageous. The singing of a lewd traditional English song at a pavilion party did not go down very well with some of those present. Being at the British Pavilion also exposed us to eminent visitors. Prince Charles was among those who came, while Michael Stewart, the then Foreign Secretary, attended for British Day. Other dignitaries included the Japanese Emperor, Emperor Haile Selassie of Ethiopia with his Nubian bodyguards, Imelda Marcos from the Philippines, and a number involved with cultural activities. On occasions we showed such visitors round, and in general had plenty of opportunity to observe them. The sight of Sir Peter Ustinov barking at Sir John Figgess' black labrador through a glass door is not easily forgotten!

This rather privileged and detached sphere of existence was in sharp contrast to the interaction with the majority of visitors to the exposition. From the start, the sheer numbers of visitors, the size of the queues (where people queued at all) and the congestion on the site and the transport networks leading to it was astonishing. In the 183 days of its duration, Expo '70 received a total of 64.2 million visitors. As *Banpaku* fever swept the country, it seemed that few wanted to miss out on the experience. Each day the number of visitors was announced on the news and some recall a sort of masochistic pleasure in hearing that they had visited on, say, a '62-*man*' day, a day when the number of visitors had been 620,000. The record was 800,000 one day in September. There were even deaths from heat exhaustion in queues to enter pavilions. No wonder it was dubbed *zankokuhaku* (brutal Expo).

While Expo staff obviously did not have to queue for access to the site, and had other privileges, coping with such a mass of visitors was not easy in either practical or emotional terms. The constant requests for signatures, the immediate seizure of any literature put out, however trivial, the apparent desire merely to obtain the Pavilion stamp on the Expo passport rather than taking any interest in its contents, seemed to render almost irrelevant our supposed role as ambassadors for our country and its exports. The desalination plant claimed to be at the forefront of British technology seemed irrelevant to most of our visitors, except that it offered a three-foot space underneath where elderly Japanese could eat their *obento* while taking advantage of the air-conditioning. Expectations of our behaviour as hostesses often seemed to preclude visitors' use of 'please' and 'thank you'. With more experience of Japan and a lesser sense of desperation Lydia might not have insisted on such niceties from one individual whose missing finger showed him to be a *yakuza*.

As foreigners we were invariably observed and commented on in the same way as the exhibits themselves. This raised the tempting prospect of seeing how long we could remain totally immobile, persuade the visitors we were actually statues, and then shock them with a sudden movement. The mass of visitors, the tendency of many to come in organized groups – for perfectly understandable reasons – , and their behaviour, left us with particular impressions of Japanese tourists as more interested in souvenirs than the experience of Expo itself, and expressing a strong herdlike instinct. The long hours of standing and being looked at, and the sheer numbers of sightseers involved, became at times intolerable, and we lived for our days off. We were consequently often less than sympathetic to our visitors. Our lack of preparedness for what we found ourselves doing, and our inability to cope with the pressures on occasions bred a contempt of which we should not now be at all proud. Many visitors, of course, were charming, and we can all think of memorable conversations of both a serious and lighthearted nature. We had the clear impression, however, that most were quite uninterested in the contents of the pavilion and those of us who worked in it – except in as far as a finger could be pointed to us as *gaijin*.

The denizens of other Expo pavilions with whom we talked clearly had similar stories to tell, and this common experience brought us together with them. Shared derision at the behaviour of some visitors became a safety valve. Even in the accommodation complex outside the exposition site, known to many, including the taxi drivers in Umeda, as the *gaijin dobutsuen* (foreigners' zoo), there was a sense of 'us' and 'them'. While we had a horror of the expatriate lifestyle and values, the *Banpaku* environment thrust us into the company of non-Japanese, and made it difficult to get beneath the surface in our interaction with the Japanese people themselves.

We found an outlet in laughter at apparent incongruities. All those who have spent time in Japan have found amusement in English language notices (and perhaps the Japanese do the same in Britain now), but the person who was responsible for the notices around the flats was a past master in this respect. Aside from the posters informing us in the same sentence that rubbish would be collected and prostitution was illegal in Japan, the English language *Manual for Living* told us that to light the water heater we should 'Turn to left at full stretch. If at first only to hear dim click, not to be alarmed'. The same reference guide informed us that if we should fail to find a phone number, we should 'go to the administration and examine it'.

What becomes clear with hindsight is that most of our visitors were as ill prepared for the extraordinary Expo environment as we were. *Banpaku* was not Japan. Heralded as doing for Kansai what the Olympics had done for Kanto, Expo was a world of unreality and artificiality, so detached from the real world that normal values and behaviour tended to be suspended. It imposed on both visitors and staff a context so distant from their normal daily lives, and one for which they were so unprepared, that both sides felt rather like fish out of water. The juxtaposition of the activity that went on in this Expo world and the lives of the young American soldiers on leave from the Vietnam War who sometimes stayed with us was almost surreal. In this context the opportunities that we had to explore Japan on our own were particularly welcome. Even where memories of Expo may be negative, memories of Japan itself are much more positive.

Our most cherished experiences invariably came from the time we had outside work, and the closer relationships formed with individual Japanese and families. Forays to local locations such as Mount Rokko in Kobe and Koyasan offered relief from the congestion of Expo and also an indication of the 'old' Japan that seemed even then to be fast disappearing. The more populated areas of Japan already seemed redolent of the characterless, fast-food outlet-dominated parts of the American landscape, and far from the traditional images of Japan and its people with which we had been brought up. It was easy to fall in love with the beauties of temples, shrines and castles, as well as with the stunning Japanese landscape, particularly since one rarely had to cope with the inconveniences that often accompanied the more traditional way of life. The impossibility of obtaining any Western food and drinks in some localities, for example, was the more attractive since it was not something that had to be coped with on a daily basis. It was easy for us all to have a romantic view of 'traditional' Japan. But 'traditional' Japan also meant meeting Japanese in a context with which they felt much more comfortable and confident than the frenzy of Expo. It meant finding out how some Japanese really lived, and what they really thought, including the Kyushu fisherman whose most positive experience in his life had been his involvement in

Japan's military campaigns in Malaya and his pride in getting hold of British rations. Such interactions compelled us to try and comprehend the 'difference' that so often stood in the way of better understanding.

Between us, we travelled widely over Japan, from Kyushu up to Hokkaido, often working double shifts at the pavilion to accrue a longer period off. While the trains were both convenient, and also offered many insights into provincial life, we commonly used hitch-hiking – then almost unknown in Japan – to get around. Some drivers stopped because they thought we were in trouble, while others disregarded us, either because they had no idea what we were doing, or else perhaps because they feared they would be unable to communicate with us. Often those who did stop would go out of their way to help us, not only deviating far from their own routes to take us where we were going, but helping us with finding accommodation, and guiding us round the local tourist spots. Some offered accommodation themselves, and Janet spent a night at the Tenrikyo complex near Okayama, after being given a lift all the way from Kobe. The best hitch-hiking story, however, must be that of Lydia, who, having temporarily been taken in custody for vagrancy, was given a lift all the way from Noshiro to Hakodate after the local policemen had flagged down a car with Hokkaido registration and instructed the bewildered occupants to take the misguided foreigner with them.

●

The Drum Major's Trews
by
PETER MARTIN

By the time the Osaka International Exposition was formally opened by the Showa Emperor (Hirohito) in the spring of 1970 I had been at post as the British Council's regional director in Kyoto for six-and-a-half years. In normal circumstances I should have been transferred in 1967, and being intensely reluctant to leave Japan I was delighted to be permitted to stay on in order to act as cultural affairs officer attached on a part-time basis to the British Pavilion, with responsibility for the cultural events arranged by the British Council in support of the British presence on the exhibition site. These ranged from performances by the Philharmonia Orchestra with Dame Janet Baker and other eminent British soloists conducted by John Pritchard, to concerts by a Welsh choir and a pop concert featuring the young woman singer Mary Hopkins, whose recording of 'Those Were The Days, My Friend' was a current hit.

Each participating country was allotted a National Day, on which to stage a spectacular display in the central plaza, and ours was centred on a brilliantly choreographed performance by the band of the First Battalion of the Scots Guards, complete with kilted pipers. The UK Commissioner, the late Sir John Figgess, desired the band after their plaza display to march to the British Pavilion where he would receive them, take the salute, and make a short speech of congratulations and thanks. The members of the band would then take a short refreshment break before forming up again outside the pavilion and marching back to the plaza where the dressing-rooms were situated. It fell to me to deal with the practical details in consultation with the Drum Major, who was not a Scot, but a Londoner who invited me to call him by his first name, Eric.

Eric was perfectly willing to lead the march to and from the pavilion, but the planners of the site had deliberately avoided straight stretches of roadway in favour of interesting twists and turns. So though it was probably not much more than a quarter of a mile each way, the route was so circuitous that he asked me to act as pilot, driving a few yards ahead as discreetly as it was possible to do in the pavilion's shocking pink electric buggy. (Each national pavilion had the use of one of these modified golf carts, the only vehicles normally permitted on the site.) When I demurred, Eric pointed out irrefutably that none of the onlookers would have eyes for me when they could point their cameras at a mace-wielding Drum Major resplendent in his dress jacket and tight tartan trews, followed by kilted bagpipers and other uniformed military musicians with a majestic bass drummer bringing up the rear.

The British National Day was blessed with brilliant sunshine, and the band's plaza performance was a huge success. As it ended I was duly waiting at the point where Eric extended his mace and wheeled off at the head of the fine body of men. His prediction that the pink buggy would go unnoticed by the crowds of onlookers was completely accurate, and my nervousness was soon replaced by a sense of euphoria as I negotiated the twists and turns between the plaza and the British Pavilion. We arrived there in splendid style, and Sir John did his stuff with the aplomb to be expected of a former colonel. He then invited the bandsmen to fall out for beer and sandwiches. Well pleased, I hovered in the wings, as it were, but shortly noticed that while the other Scots Guards were moving about, chatting and signing autographs, my new friend the Drum Major was standing with his back to the wall and an uneasy expression on his face. So I approached him.

'Everything all right, Drum Major?' I breezily enquired. His face contorted with misery, Eric responded with terse formality.

'No, Sah! Everything is NOT bloody all right! Me trousers have split right up the arse. And no way am I marching back with me backside hanging out. Sah.'

'Oh, dear. Haven't you got a spare pair, Eric?'

'Course I have. But they're in the bleedin' dressing-room, in't they.' This was a poser, but I was now confident that the shocking pink buggy held no terrors for me.

'Jump in the buggy, quick! I'll drive you back to the plaza, you can change there and I'll get you back here in time.' I brought the jolly little vehicle as close to him as I could and Eric sidled into the passenger seat, whereupon I put my foot down and headed back to the plaza at full speed (the electric motors of the runabouts were governed to achieve a maximum of about five mph). Our progress occasioned general surprise, since the Drum Major was sitting rigidly upright in his seat, his mace between his knees. Quite a few photographs were taken – I wish I had one myself.

I pulled up directly in front of the entrance to the dressing-rooms, and Eric furtively slunk inside, returning two minutes later wearing replacement trews and a broad smile on his face. The return march from the British Pavilion went according to plan, and a grateful Eric extended a warm invitation to me to drop into the sergeants' mess at Wellington Barracks for a pint on him at some future date. I often wish I had taken it up.

13

Death of the Showa Emperor, 7 January 1989

CAROLYN WHITEHEAD • DAVID POWERS

CAROLYN WHITEHEAD, from the vantage point of her residence at the British Embassy and status as wife of the British Ambassador, recounts the story of the death and burial of the Showa Emperor in January 1989:-

•

The Showa Emperor died on 7 January 1989. He had been taken ill at a birthday banquet in April 1987 and after an operation in the autumn of that year he had recovered sufficiently to resume official duties. He managed to appear again for his next birthday on 29 April 1988 and he and the empress spent the summer at their Imperial Villa in Nasu. But he continued to cause concern and lost a lot of weight. In September 1988 he suddenly developed a very high fever.

In the British Embassy opposite the Imperial Palace we found ourselves surrounded by the world's media. They camped along the moat by every gate, and ours, blocking the roads, polluting the atmosphere with engines ticking constantly, snoring on folding chairs, drinking Coke, eating noodles and covering themselves with pale blue plastic against the cold and the rain, their aerials and lights peering round like submarine periscopes. Every day the newspapers gave a detailed medical report of the emperor's condition and the whole country waited, prepared, for the inevitable news of his death.

The Showa Emperor had ruled Japan for sixty-two years, the longest reign of any Japanese emperor. He came to the throne at the age of twenty-five and lived through many turbulent years in Japanese and world history during which he changed from being almost a god to being the benevolent old man, steeped in marine biology studies, of whom most people had only the occasional glimpse. John and I met him a few times, the last most fortunately as late as May 1988, when he had recovered for a while, and when we had a ten-minute audience in the

Palace. Although eighty-seven years old he stood throughout the whole conversation, immaculate in morning coat, hair brushed down, his eyes almost shut behind his glasses in concentration in order to remember the message he wanted to convey. My knees shook and John thankfully did all the talking – in Japanese – but it was an experience, particularly in retrospect, we shall never forget.

The emperor is dead – so Prime Minister Takeshita informed the world. The sacred imperial regalia and state and imperial seals were conferred upon the new emperor, the government chose Heisei ('achievement of universal peace') as the new era name. 1989, according to our calendar, was in Japanese terms both Showa 64 and Heisei 1. A Cabinet meeting was held to determine the most suitable date for the funeral.

So began for us an amazing period of planning, discussion and diplomacy. After two weeks ambassadors and their wives were invited to an audience at 9.30 in the morning to pay their respects to the emperor's coffin and to meet the new emperor and empress. For the ladies the burning question was what to wear. 'Dark afternoon dress' threw us all into complete confusion. My friend Carmela, the wife of the Spanish Ambassador, extracted much more information than most by sending the Foreign Ministry questionnaires – hats? veils? shoes, shiny or dull? black? Eventually, it became clear that we should, in Japanese tradition, preferably be in black from head to foot. And so we arrived, strangely hushed and nervous, deposited from our sleek cars on to the Palace steps looking like a flock of old crows, eyeing each other up and down. After all our worries it would not have mattered what we had worn. There was the odd daringly rakish hat with net and the Africans quite naturally and respectfully wore their national dress, in brilliant golds, greens and blues.

In a large reception room and in silence we formed three long lines in order of precedence and the screens were drawn back to admit the emperor and empress, he in morning coat and she bowed and pale in her slender black dress, hat and veil. After a few imperial words and a handshake we walked through the beautiful, wide, gold-carpeted Palace corridors, one side all glass, suddenly noticing what a glorious day it was, the sky bright blue as only a Japanese winter day can be with two exquisite plum trees in full bloom in a courtyard of raked gravel. In a further hall white curtains draped the walls, a white carpet covered the floor and a huge white silk tent had been constructed to conceal the emperor's coffin. Here we had to bow twice in twos, retreat and bow again at the door, all under the gaze of two elegantly garbed priests in black and green, their pill box headdresses with stiffened squirls at the back. We succeeded nervously and carefully without bumping into each other and retreated, hushed and deeply moved as we made our way to our cars and back into the outside world.

The funeral day was set for 24 February. The British press predictably

made much of war-time memories and speculation centred around who
should represent The Queen. But the announcement was made quickly
that it would be Prince Philip and that Sir Geoffrey Howe, then Foreign
Secretary, would represent the British Government. It came as something of a shock to me that John and I would be the only other people
from Britain to be present at the funeral. Our house, which was large but
with surprisingly few bedrooms and bathrooms, had to be organized so
that the two visitors together with their staff could operate easily but
separately. Dinners and meetings were arranged, this being not only a
State Funeral but also a gathering of the world's royalty and political leaders. I worked out menus for Princes and politicians in one place and
policemen in another. And then of course there was the problem of what
to wear all over again. Carmela bought a new dashing hat of course and
worried whether it would be proper to wear her fur coat. The rest of us let
time pass and in the end the weather made up our minds for us.

Our younger daughter Jessica, in her gap year, had by this time joined
us from England. Because of the press of visitors in the house we started
the day with breakfast on a card table in our bedroom, Jessica still asleep
on the floor on a futon – having given up her bedroom to a Private Secretary. February is the coldest month of the year in Japan and the 24th
dawned grey with freezing rain. We all donned everything imaginable
from thermal underwear upwards to keep warm. Despite my 'World
Wildlife ' Prince I was definitely going to wear my fur hat. At 8.20 am
precisely John and I left for the Foreign Ministry to catch our diplomatic
bus, leaving our Rolls-Royce for our visitors' later journey. In fact, six
buses bursting with well-clad ambassadors and their spouses left the
Foreign Ministry on almost deserted roads. We travelled with the Italians,
very concerned because their official party spoke only Italian and were
insisting that they must have their 'brigata' with them – none of course
would be allowed in. At Shinjuku Gardens we came to a halt. The sky was
heavy and grey, a cold drizzle was in the air and we were each issued with
a transparent white umbrella and were led in crocodile through trees and
the mud, past galleries of press, to the clearing where the funeral ceremony would take place. We stood in overwhelmed silence at the sight
before us. Two open-sided white tents to seat 10,000 with a wide gravelled
aisle down the middle faced a wooden, specially-constructed funeral pavilion. We sat fairly near the front on folding chairs each with a cushion
and a blanket; our state and official visitors in the front rows were, so the
local papers later informed us, on leather chairs with cashmere blankets,
and the King and Queen of Tonga had specially strengthened seats!
Large television sets had been erected down the length of each tent so
that we all had a good view of the proceedings. We were much relieved
when we saw our official visitors arrive in time. President George Bush
represented the United States and, together with many kings, queens,

princes and princesses, presidents and prime ministers, headed the largest and most distinguished collection of delegates to assemble for a funeral in the twentieth century.

When the Showa Emperor's father, the Taisho Emperor, died in 1926
the Imperial coffin was carried through the streets on an elaborate cart
drawn by four sacred bulls. Behind the coffin a chamberlain carried the
emperor's sandals. As we waited in 1989 the procession left the Palace and
drove by car through the rain-swept unusually quiet streets of Tokyo past
silent crowds, many of whom respectfully folded their umbrellas and
stood bare headed as the hearse, a single gold Imperial chrysanthemum
emblem on its side, slowly passed, white pleated curtains drawn over the
coffin. Bands at intervals along the route played solemn music. At Shinjuku Gardens, however, the coffin was transferred to a black-painted palanquin curtained with yellow, hoisted on to the shoulders of fifty-one
members of the Imperial Guard. Dressed in black and grey trousers and
jackets of the style worn in the Heian period their load was so heavy they
had to shuffle in step, their black lacquer shoes hissing through the gravel
of the wide aisle. This sound was to be my abiding memory of the whole
day, as it was with Ambassador Toshio Yamazaki, Japanese Ambassador
to the Court of St James, who later sent me a copy of his haiku:

Sokaren	Emperor's coffin
saku saku susumu	passing away sha sha sha
hisame naka	in icy rain.

Behind them a bearer carried the emperor's shoes, followed by officials
with yellow and white banners representing the sun and the moon.
Others followed with sacred branches. Drums were beaten and priests
played haunting music on flutes. The sight was an ancient Japanese painting. The rain fell and a freezing wind blew through the tents as the coffin
was placed in the pavilion. Offerings of rice, duck, bean paste, fruit, vegetables, fish and bolts of silk were placed before the palanquin. Then
Akihito, the new emperor, standing slight but straight, delivered a farewell address to his father – a simple message of sadness – speaking in
everyday Japanese of his own sorrow and of the countryside, trees and
plants his father had loved and would see no more. The Shinto ceremony
over, the state ceremony began. A silence of one minute was observed
and the prime minister and other government representatives paid their
respects. Then the foreign dignitaries one by one went into the pavilion.
As Prince Philip and Sir Geoffrey Howe bowed to the coffin, John and I
had to stand and bow with them. It was a solemn and moving moment in
such a large gathering. This brought the ceremony to a close and our two
fortunate representatives left to the warmth and comfort of the car and to
drinks with Jessica. She has dined out ever since on her conversation with

Prince Philip as he arrived at the door asking whether he had time to take his thermals off before lunch!

Despite Hoka Hoka hand warmers in my gloves and even my shoes and the welcome blankets, we were extremely cold and were most envious of one of our colleagues who had been sensible enough to bring a hip flask of *umeshu*, plum wine, in his pocket! Uncorked, the smell was gorgeous but all pervasive, six rows in front and six behind. There was a long wait for the buses, but, once aboard, great joy, hot coffee and sandwiches had thoughtfully been placed in front of each seat. After the tension the journey back had almost a picnic atmosphere.

No event such as this can end without some form of reception and in the evening we were invited to drinks at the Akasaka Palace by the prime minister. Never have we been at such an event, with kings, queens and presidents at every turn. Step backwards and you clipped a royal foot or became tangled with a detective with wires in his ears. The hazard was keeping track of your own visitors, one of ours doing an efficient royal tour round the rooms among people he knew well, some his relatives, the other intent on 'funeral diplomacy'.

The Showa Emperor was buried that evening at the Musashi Imperial Cemetery near Hachioji in a hilly area west of Tokyo in a Mausoleum near to that of his father and mother.

DAVID POWERS who was BBC Correspondent in Japan at the time of the death of the Showa Emperor, recalls the event from a very different perspective:-

•

It all began with a quiet drink at the Irish Ambassador's residence. A reception was being held to dedicate the Lafcadio Hearn Memorial Library and, as one of the few foreign correspondents left in Tokyo, I had been invited along. To be honest, it was never going to make a story. For one thing, the 'Memorial Library' was little more than a bookshelf, and, however important Lafcadio Hearn may have been in shaping Western views on Japan in the late nineteenth century, there was no way he was going to muscle his way onto the news agenda in the middle of the Olympics.

It was 19 September 1988, and virtually the entire corps of correspondents resident in Tokyo had decamped across the Sea of Japan – officially in the hope of getting a good story at the Seoul Olympics, but mostly in the hope of having a good time. Little did they realize that their holiday was about to come to an abrupt end.

Still, for those of us stranded in Tokyo it was a good party, and the ambassador was a generous host – maybe too generous. Retribution came in the form of the merciless ringing of the telephone at 6 o'clock the following morning. I staggered into the next room, wishing I had gone a little easier on the whisky the night before. A distinctly unsympathetic Australian voice barked into my ear.

'We hear the emperor's dead and they're playing martial music on the telly. We need a report NOW!'

Folklore has it that once a journalist gets a story, nothing else matters and that the brain immediately goes into overdrive. What folklore omits to add is that if you have seen rather too much of the inside of a whisky glass the night before, there is a distinctly painful crashing of gears as what is left of the brain tries to find where overdrive is. It hurts.

I switched on the TV and, although there was no martial music (that *would* have been a story), it was quite clear the emperor was in a serious condition. He was eighty-seven years old, had undergone an abdominal operation less than a year previously, and was haemorrhaging badly. When I relayed that information to Australia, it turned out to be one of the shortest and most bizarre conversations of my career.

'He's not dead? Forget it!'

The producer slammed down the phone.

There was no time to ponder over this callous reaction. I should have been talking to my own editors in London. Why, I wondered, had they not been on the phone as quickly as Australia?

'Oh yes, David, we knew Hirohito had been taken ill,' came the reply, 'but we didn't think it was terribly important, so we didn't want to wake you up.'

Yet again, Japan had been put on the back burner. It was a constant frustration for most correspondents based in Tokyo, Europeans and Americans alike. News editors either seem to find Japan too difficult to understand or simply do not care. In their view, Japan belongs among business or feature stories. Even the massive trade imbalance between Japan and the United States failed to keep my American colleagues busy. The only Japan stories their editors seemed to be interested in all emanated from Washington or Detroit.

Sorely tempted to go back to bed and nurse my hangover, I patiently explained that the last surviving leader of any of the major combatants during the Second World War was lying gravely ill inside the Imperial Palace in Tokyo, and that by all accounts he had lost large amounts of blood. His prospects for survival did not look good.

'All right, David, I think you've made your point. Send us a report, but try to keep the blood out of it. It upsets a lot of people.'

Ironically, the clinical details that the BBC wanted me to skip over were all that the Japanese public were to learn about their head of state for the next three months or so. It seemed an unnecessary intrusion into what was essentially a private matter. Yet that was the only information coming out of the palace.

There was, undoubtedly, an unofficial taboo about reporting on the Imperial Family in anything other than reverential terms. It still exists to this day, unbroken except for a brief period in the mid-1990s when several magazines indulged in a bizarre spate of what came to be known as *kogo-bashingu* or 'empress-bashing' targeted at Empress Michiko. It is also true to say that until Hirohito was taken ill, the palace and its inhabitants figured little in the minds of ordinary Japanese. The bubble economy was taking off in the late 1980s, and people were too busy enjoying themselves and making money to think of anything else.

It had been more than sixty years since the previous emperor had died. Japan was a completely different country. The surrounding world had changed beyond all recognition. So, too, had the role of the emperor. It was surely a time for reflection on the past, time to look back on the disasters and triumphs Japan had gone through during the six decades of Hirohito's reign, and time to examine the controversy that still surrounds the role he did or did not take in leading Japan to war.

It was an open secret that plans had been drawn up well in advance for what everybody in the media – and many outside – knew as X-Day. What caught everyone out was that X-Day was such a long time in coming. For a media that had treated the emperor only with reverence while he was hale and hearty, it would have been too indelicate to have started digging over the past while he lay so ill. So they were left with only one option – to repeat the clinical bulletins over and over again.

Although Japan technically has a free press and there are no special restrictions on foreign journalists, the way most news emerges from government agencies, politicians and big business is subject to an even more pernicious system of control than the much-maligned Westminster Lobby. Like the Lobby, access is restricted to registered members. In Japan's case, the ostensible purpose of these press clubs, as they are called, is to disseminate news on a totally equal footing. Instead, those inside the press club actively collude to prevent each other gaining scoops, and those outside are forced to get their news second-hand – or, as the weekly magazines often do, simply make it up.

Officially, the Imperial Household Agency said it would be happy for foreign journalists to attend its briefings – the problem lay with the press club, which refused to let us in, apparently concerned that we would not act with sufficient dignity. Fortunately, the agency realized that refusing to speak to the foreign press on such an important matter of state was not an option, but instead of overruling the press club, it decided to give us separate briefings at 3 o'clock in the afternoon in a chamberlain's private office. The briefings were strictly off the record and conducted in Japanese only, with no interpreters allowed to be present. It was hard keeping up a rota of Japanese-speaking correspondents for so long, but it paid off.

The palace recognized that the foreign media had behaved responsibly, and gave us considerable access to the subsequent funeral and enthronement ceremonies.

By behaving responsibly, I do not mean that the foreign media ignored Hirohito's controversial role. Far from it. I remember reporting on a demonstration that marched its way down Koen Dori in Shibuya, one of the busiest parts of Tokyo. They were marching behind a huge banner that read 'Even if the emperor dies, you cannot erase the history of aggression,' and chanting a song ridiculing the emperor as useless. What was remarkable was the absence of helmets and face masks normally worn by extreme left-wing groups to prevent their recognition by the police. Equally forceful in his criticism of Hirohito's wartime role was the General Secretary of the United Church of Christ, the Reverend John Nakajima, who described the emperor to me in a radio interview not just as a war criminal, but as 'the war criminal'.

Important though it was to report such views, it was necessary to place them in context. The demonstrators on Koen Dori drew a few bemused stares, but most people ignored them. Japan was rich, peaceful, and as yet had not had its conscience pricked by the international row over whether or how it should contribute to solving a modern war. That was not to happen for another two years, when Iraq invaded Kuwait, provoking the Gulf War and ultimately prompting Japan to play a non-combat role in subsequent UN peacekeeping operations. While Hirohito lay ill, the government called for 'self-restraint', but that did not stop people enjoying themselves. They just did it more quietly, and the events of half a century ago were far from their minds.

When X-Day finally came on Saturday 7 January 1989, it started with another early morning phone call, only this time I had no hangover to contend with. My colleague, William Horsley, had been tipped off by a member of his family who had had difficulty sleeping and switched the TV on. The emperor was still alive, but the tone of the broadcast suggested the end might be near. William was on his way into the office, and he wanted me down at the palace as quickly as possible.

It was a bright, crisp morning as I rushed to join the small cluster of Japanese journalists standing in front of Nijubashi, the ceremonial double bridge leading into the palace. They were all listening to tiny pocket radios. I fumbled inside my bag to get out my own, but to my horror the batteries were dead. A young man next to me saw the look on my face, moved close to me, silently took one of the stereo car pieces out of his own ear, and placed it in mine just in time for me to hear a chamberlain announce the emperor was dead.

Apart from another small group of journalists camped out further down by Sakashita Gate, the vast Imperial Plaza was deserted. It was in the days before mobile phones, so I had a brisk walk to the nearest international phone to get my story back to London. I wanted to run, but knew I would have been too out of breath to broadcast. As I strode back across the plaza, someone ahead of me relayed the news of the emperor's death to a group of judo enthusiasts out for an early morning jog. They stopped, bowed towards the palace, and stood in silent prayer before resuming their jog. Immediately, helicopters began to fly overhead, and police reinforcements moved in to surround all approach roads.

After phoning London, I spent most of the rest of the day mixing with the vast crowds that thronged to the palace. Small, but highly conspicuous groups of extreme right-wingers swaggered through the masses. The red and white rising sun flags draped with black that they carried were just the same as those hanging outside virtually every building in central Tokyo, but they carried a sense of threat totally out of character with the rest of the crowd.

Certainly, they had nothing in common with the sixty-eight-year-old former signals officer who, oblivious of everyone around him, removed his hat and coat, drew up to attention, and at the top of his voice presented himself for the final time to his former commanding officer. Then he broke down in tears – genuine tears of affection for the emperor who had symbolized his nation through good times and bad. An old soldier who had fought for his country right or wrong.

Many young people told me they had come out of a sense of unity. Article one of the post-war constitution defines the emperor as the symbol of the Japanese people and their unity. Now he was dead.

It would be false, though, to give the impression that this teeming city and its suburbs of thirty million people had suddenly come to a halt. The shops remained packed with customers, although the interminable muzak was turned off, and some of the window dummies were dressed in black. As night fell, the streets were just as busy as ever, but there was no one outside the bars touting for business. All the neon lights were turned off, and there was an eerie hush in the air.

(For David Power's account of the funeral please see Chapter 14.)

14

The Start of a New Era

CAROLYN WHITEHEAD • DAVID POWERS

MANY OUTSIDERS hoped that the new reign would mark a break with the past and help to open up the Imperial institution to the people.

In one respect at least they were immediately disappointed. The antiquated system of era names was not abolished and Japanese dates would still be counted by numbering the years from the first year of the era even though no era has begun on 1 January. This inevitably complicates the calculation of dates of birth and events when translated into the generally accepted Western method of dating. The government decided that the new era should be called *Heisei* which might be translated as 'peaceful life'. The new era name perhaps reflected just as much wishful thinking on the part of those who chose the name as of those who called the reign of the previous emperor (Hirohito) *Showa* which might be translated as 'brilliant peace'.

Nevertheless, there were to be some possibly significant changes in the tradition-bound Japanese Imperial Household.

The British Embassy having said farewell to the Duke of Edinburgh following the funeral of the Showa Emperor were soon busy preparing for the arrival of the Prince and Princess of Wales for the enthronement ceremony as CAROLYN WHITEHEAD describes in the following piece about the enthronement:-

●

In the summer of 1990 it was announced that, after the traditional number of rice harvests had passed following the death of the Showa Emperor, the Ceremonies of the Accession to the Throne of the new Emperor (Akihito) would take place in the November of that year. The enthronement itself would be on the 12th and for three days afterwards a series of banquets would be held 'to enable guests to offer their congratulations'. The Prince and Princess of Wales would represent The Queen and John and I would go too.

After the domestic upheaval that accompanied the arranging of the funeral we were now much more practised for this kind of special event. Of course, many more staff would come from London to Tokyo than the last time and we had to use various houses in the Embassy compound as well as a local hotel. Again, the subject of dress was an early problem and this time the final decision was left to the Japanese Cabinet. After much consideration sketches were circulated of Morning Coat for men and 'Robe Montante' for the ladies. This latter showed a long dress up to the neck, with sleeves to the wrist asking us to show 'little exposure of skin'. The whole outfit was crowned by a circlet with a little crisp veil. I despatched the sketches swiftly to Kensington Palace. Although I was more than a little concerned about my own dress I knew it was nothing compared to the fervour that would be aroused by that of the other British lady!

The residence was once again prepared with the required plugs, hairdryers, office equipment and ironing boards. The grapefruit should preferably be pink. But it was I who caused near disaster when just an evening or so before their arrival I decided to watch a film on television in the main guest bedroom, it being at that time the only set that was bilingual. An annoying mosquito buzzed insistently around me and I picked up a spray and killed it, only to find I had used an oily repellant by mistake. The whole wall had to be repainted! So in this vein John and I presented ourselves at the airport at the beginning of an unbelievable few days. The Japanese Government had organized every detail with precision and each country's representatives were issued with a small motorcade. During the days that followed these little centipedes with flashing lights front and back were to be seen importantly bustling around the streets of Tokyo as we accompanied our guests on official visits and of course to the enthronement itself.

The ceremony was quite short and very simple. It was held in the State Hall of the Palace, its screens opening on to a gallery to reveal two large shrine-like thrones. Each throne was on a dais of black lacquer, with an ornate curtained canopy decorated with gold phoenixes and with mirrors. Broad steps led down to a large rectangular courtyard covered in fine white gravel, a cherry tree on one side and a citrus on the other. Seated round three sides facing the State Hall 2,500 visitors had an excellent view of tall silk banners in bright colours rippling in the sunshine against a perfect blue sky. Ceremonial swords, bows, quivers, shields, gongs and drums were carried in by bearers, attendants and guards who sat on stools wearing traditional costumes in black, red and deep blue, their stiff head-dresses tied under the chin curling suitably backwards. Then in complete silence we rose as the emperor slowly processed along the gallery with his chamberlains and took his place on his throne. His robe was rust-coloured like the first colour of the rising sun, worn over white trousers and wooden shoes with embroidered covers. His 'coronet' (eboshi) was plain black, the tall stiffened silk pennant the only one to stand upright. Behind him the empress followed to her throne, magnificent in the *'juni-hitoe'*, the ceremonial costume of ladies of the court, the glowing red layers beneath the white flower-patterned outer robe echoed by the brilliant green and red kimonos of her ladies-in-waiting. Her hair was drawn up and tied to hang down her back, an ornamental mirror with crystals at the front. The Imperial princes in stark black robes and head-dresses, the Crown Prince alone in bright orange, stood to one side. On the other, the princesses slowly moved into position, walking on their layered kimonos on the polished wooden floor, their outer robes purple and white and their hair, like the empress's, hanging in long tied bunches down their backs almost to the floor. With everyone in place the chamberlains drew back the curtains round the thrones and the emperor and empress rose. We all bowed and stood as the emperor proclaimed his accession in an imperial address. Prime Minister Toshiki Kaifu then gave a speech of congratulations on behalf of the Japanese people and led three cheers of *'banzai'* in which the Japanese guests joined. And then it was over as slowly and again in complete silence the emperor and empress left their thrones and walked in procession out along the gallery followed by the imperial family, chamberlains and attendants, the sight exactly like a painting from the *Genji Monogatari* scroll. The bearers and guards melted from the courtyard and a twenty-one gun salute could be heard in the distance.

As we all prepared to make our way home the emperor and empress changed into Western dress and travelled in procession through the streets back to the Akasaka Palace. The weather was mild and sunny, the car was open and the crowds could get a good view. We were particularly pleased to find that a Rolls-Royce had been specially built just for that day, an imperial chrysanthemum emblazoned on its side.

Our royal guests caused a great deal of media interest and the princess looked quite stunning in a pale blue version of the sketch I had sent her. In fact we were quite embarrassed to read in one newspaper that 'The Prince and Princess of Wales and 150 other dignitaries attended the celebrations'. Nevertheless, she was refreshingly normal around the house, chatty and giggly, always in jeans and sweatshirt and on one memorable occasion found by John flicking snooker balls on the landing in dressing-gown and tiara. Prince Charles was fascinated by everything, particularly the art and ceramics. He had only just recovered from a broken arm in a fall on the polo field and found sitting on the floor not too easy. Vice President Dan Quayle grasped his elbow in a particularly over-enthusiastic farewell at the residence door one afternoon which resulted in a loud 'Ouch!' The princess was not so interested in things cultural and found chopsticks rather challenging. The desperately raised eyebrow in my direction at the first mouthful of *sushi* was hilarious, but I felt bound to grin but swallow firmly! They were invited to the first banquet on the evening of the enthronement and together with the household staff and many other members of the embassy we saw off the glittering pair at the door. John and I thankfully had a quiet supper of *unagi* [eel].

The following days brought a hectic round of visits for us all, from remembrance service to museum and hospital, garden party to Honda assembly line, meetings with the embassy staff and the Japan-British Society, business forum to opera. The prime minister's banquet at the New Otani Hotel was an unforgettable occasion with its illustrious guest list, glittering dresses, beautifully understated kimonos, performances of Kabuki and Noh, delicious food and a most memorable Margaux wine.

With the last notes of *Salome* ringing in our ears, sung magnificently by the Welsh National Opera, we drove to the airport still in Black Tie and long dress. It had been a historic and momentous few days for us all, full of pageantry and incredible experiences. 'I hope the next visitor won't be so much trouble,' said Prince Charles as he climbed the aircraft steps. We certainly had no time to rest on our laurels – Prince Philip was arriving two days later!

DAVID POWERS of the BBC saw events from a quite different perspective and noted some significant changes as he describes in the following piece which he has entitled '*Beyond the Moat*':-

•

Keizo Obuchi was just about to leave the room after giving me an interview following an emergency meeting of G-7 foreign ministers in London in the summer of 1998. Flying halfway round the world for a meeting that had gone on far longer than anticipated seemed to have taken its toll on him, but he paused for a moment, dug his hand into his pocket, and as he fished something out, his face suddenly broke into a broad smile.

'Here, take this, it's something I've had made.'

It was a telephone card, and on it was a caricature of Mr Obuchi and the event that shot him to instant fame on 7 January 1989. In those days Mr Obuchi was virtually unknown, but fate had cast him in a role that would ensure that nobody in Japan at the time would ever forget his face again. As Chief Cabinet Secretary when Emperor Hirohito died, it had been his job to announce the name of the new imperial era, and his picture appeared on the front page of every newspaper the following day holding a sheet of paper with the word '*Heisei*' drawn on it in bold brush strokes.

Looking at that card brought memories flooding back of what Japan was like in the aftermath of Hirohito's death. Many people had predicted that the succession would bring with it a new style to the Imperial Family – greater openness, perhaps, less mystique hiding behind the moat and walls of the Imperial Palace. We did not have to wait long to find out. True to royal tradition almost everywhere, the succession was immediate. The emperor was dead. Long live the emperor.

Within hours of his father's death, Akihito had taken possession of the imperial regalia – the sacred mirror, sword and jewels wrapped in purple and gold brocade. It was a simple ceremony lasting just four minutes, and when the new emperor made his first public pronouncement, there was a stunning change. Unlike his father, he spoke in ordinary Japanese. It was still very formal and polite, but gone were the archaic expressions. Most symbolic of all, so too was the use of *chin*, the imperial 'we'. The emperor was *watakushi* just like the ordinary man in the street – well, almost, since most people refer to themselves as *watakushi* on only the most formal occasions. But after all, this was a formal occasion.

Perhaps, too, the emperor or his advisers had at the back of their mind the obscene joke circulating during the Allied Occupation after the war, when General MacArthur was referred to as *'heso shogun'*, General Belly Button. Phonetically, *chin* also refers to a certain part of the male anatomy, and the inference was that MacArthur was above the emperor. Never would the imperial 'we' have quite the same dignity again.

Anyone imagining, though, that the palace gates were about to be flung open, heralding a new era of the imperial family cycling through the streets of Ginza, was sorely mistaken. For a start, the emperor and his family were in mourning, and in addition to whatever their own feelings may have been, were to remain so officially for a full year. The only time they emerged into the public gaze during that time was, of course, for Hirohito's funeral on 24 February.

It was decided to give the funeral prominent coverage on that morning's edition of the *Today* programme on Radio 4, but the time difference between Tokyo and London presented William Horsley and myself with a logistical nightmare. The whole point of being a foreign correspondent is being there. The problem was that if one of us did go to the funeral in the Shinjuku Outer Garden, we would not be able to get out in time to make the programme. In the end, it was decided that William would anchor the coverage from a studio, while I would go to the Imperial Palace to watch the coffin leave on its final journey.

Even though it was impossible to attend the funeral service itself, I did get the chance to see the main preparations at first hand. About a week before 24 February, I joined a group of rather bedraggled journalists around Shinjuku Outer Garden in icy rain and mud to view the funeral hall. It was only six weeks since Emperor Hirohito had died, yet in that short time, a magnificent Shinto shrine had sprung up on what used to be a plain strip of lawn. The height of a four-storey building, it was topped with a sweeping wooden roof, beautifully carpentered and adorned with golden chrysanthemums, the crest of Japan's imperial household.

This was where the emperor's coffin was to lie throughout the two-and-a-half hours of open-air ceremonies. Concern that the weather might turn out to be just as bad or even worse on the day itself had necessitated the construction of facilities almost as elaborate for the guests themselves. Statistically, 24 February is one of the coldest days of the year in Tokyo, and the government was terrified that one of the heads of state, fourteen kings, queens or princes, or indeed any of the other foreign guests, might catch pneumonia. Consequently, electric heating was installed under the temporary floorboards of two massive open-sided tents, and each guest was to get a cashmere blanket to wrap round their legs. The very top guests, people like the Duke of Edinburgh, were – I'm told – provided with a personal electric heater under their seats.

But why put everyone to such inconvenience and discomfort, when right next door to the Imperial Palace stands the Budokan, Tokyo's equivalent of the Albert Hall, capable of seating 6,000 people in warmth and comfort? The answer, it seems, is that although the emperor of Japan is no longer regarded as divine, the symbolism of him being above all others had to be retained in the funeral service. It just would not do, a government official told me, to have the assembled guests look down on the coffin as though it were a spectacle.

The decision to go to the Imperial Palace on the day of the funeral itself involved an early morning start. For security reasons, the tiny group of journalists being allowed into the courtyard in front of the Chowaden Hall, the formal entrance to the Imperial Palace, had to be in place well before the obsequies were due to start. I had been there on several occasions before to see the imperial family appear on the glass-enclosed balcony at New Year and on the emperor's birthday. Normally it is just a quick walk across Nijubashi, the ceremonial double iron bridge. On this occasion, though, our instructions were to enter through Inuimon, the most northerly of the gates to the Imperial Palace.

The streets were deserted as the taxi dropped me off; the police checked my credentials, and then shook me to the roots by pointing through the gate and saying, 'It's down there. Just keep going straight ahead.' In spite of all the talk of security, I was being left to wander unaccompanied well over a kilometre through the palace grounds. It was a walk through central Tokyo like no other I have ever experienced. I was alone in a totally unexpected landscape. Unlike the neatly manicured East Garden alongside, an area open to the public most days of the week, the path from Inuimon leads past wilderness that has probably barely changed since the days of Tokugawa Ieyasu. It gave a completely new meaning to the concept of the imperial family living beyond the moat. It really was a world apart – so close to the brash, modern world of Ginza and Marunouchi, yet so far.

It was extremely uncomfortable in the bitter cold as I waited on the far side of the courtyard facing the Chowaden Hall. Nor did I feel particularly dignified. I needed both hands free to operate my tape recorder, so had resorted to ramming the handle of my umbrella down the back of my neck inside my overcoat to keep off the rain that threatened to turn to snow at any minute. Eventually, the coffin weighing nearly half a ton was brought out, and a shiver ran down my back as ancient court pipes struck up an eerie lament. It was a strange mixture – music unchanged for centuries and a motorized hearse. A twenty-one gun salute rang out as Hirohito embarked on his final journey.

Unlike the guests of honour waiting in the Shinjuku Outer Garden, we had no cashmere blankets or underfloor heating, so it was with an enormous sense of relief that I finally left the palace grounds. Not for long, though. I had taken up the offer of being allowed to witness a photo call after the funeral when the Duke of Edinburgh paid a courtesy call on the new emperor and empress in the Bamboo Room of the Imperial Palace. It was rather a strange assignment for a radio correspondent to go on. After all, I was not allowed to record anything, nor report any of the conversation I overheard. Still, it was in the warm and it gave me the chance to see inside the palace myself for the first time. The photo call lasted only a few minutes, but I have two lasting impressions: the exquisite simplicity of the interior of the palace; and the warm and friendly way the imperial couple came across, far more relaxed than they normally appear in public.

It was well over a year before I got the opportunity to go inside the palace again, this time to see the preparations for *Sokan-no-rei*, the enthronement. This was to take place next door to the Bamboo Room – in the larger Pine Room, where two thrones had been set up. Both were topped with magnificent golden phoenixes, their wings outspread above tall octagonal canopies draped in purple silk curtains. The canopy over the Emperor's throne was adorned with symbols representing the rising sun – not only the symbol of Japan, but a reference to Amaterasu-omikami, the Sun Goddess from whom the imperial family is said to have descended.

The Imperial Household Agency not only wanted to show off the preparations. They were also keen to point out what they regarded as an important change to the ceremony. When Hirohito was enthroned, his prime minister had stood outside in the courtyard, but this time the prime minister, Toshiki Kaifu, would be in the same room as the emperor and empress. Even such an apparently insignificant nod towards the changed constitutional status of imperial family, though, was enough to anger some extreme nationalists, who had sent a frisson through Japan earlier in the year.

In January an attempt was made on the life of the Mayor of Nagasaki, Hitoshi Motoshima, for suggesting Emperor Hirohito could have prevented the atom bomb being dropped on the city, if only he had ordered

Japan to surrender earlier in 1945. Then in April, shots were fired through the window of a room where a leading Christian academic was sitting. His crime in the eyes of the ultra-nationalists was to have signed a statement, along with the presidents of three other Christian universities, saying they feared the enthronement ceremonies would move Japan back towards regarding the emperor as a divine sovereign.

The ceremony in the Pine Room should have laid such fears to rest. Although it was a colourful and rather eclectic mixture of elements spanning more than a thousand years – with the emperor in Heian court costume, the prime minister in tails, and thrones that dated back little more than a century, the speech from the throne was unambiguous. The imperial couple ascended their thrones behind closed curtains. Then as the curtains were drawn apart, the emperor read a simple, short speech in which he pledged to uphold the constitution and to fulfil the role he is assigned by the constitution – in other words, to act as symbol of the state and of the unity of the people.

What attracted the real controversy, though, was the ceremony that was to take place ten days later. Even though 900 people had been invited into the palace to witness *Daijosai* – the Great Thanksgiving Ceremony – the main part of the ritual was performed away from the eyes of everyone except two handmaidens. For months Tokyo had been rife with rumours about the meaning of this secret ritual. Some versions were more lurid than others, but the common thread running through all of them was that this was when a mystical union would take place between the emperor and Amaterasu-omikami, and that he would emerge reborn as a living god.

I hoped to shed a bit more light onto this question by attending a special press briefing inside the Imperial Household Agency. The room was packed, but as far as I could tell, I was the only non-Japanese who had turned up. The Imperial Household Agency lies just across from Marunouchi, one of the main business districts of Tokyo, but it is just inside the moat – and once again I found myself in a completely different world. Palace officials described in the minutest of detail the special buildings that had been constructed for the ceremony and what each of the participants would be wearing. Yet when it came to the questions, all the Japanese journalists were interested in were even more details: how many centimetres high a particular ornament would be, which part of Japan had the wood come from. Fascinating, but unimportant details. Whereas journalists outside the moat were obsessed with the 'living god' controversy, those inside were obsessed with trivia.

Two hours had gone by, and the Japanese journalists were still bursting to ask more of the same. A ten-minute break was called, so I simply walked straight up to the Vice Grand Steward, Iwao Miyao, and said: 'Excuse me, there seems to be a lot of confusion in the minds of people overseas. What is the real significance of *Daijosai*? Does it transform the emperor into a living god?'

The Vice Grand Steward was not offended in the slightest. Without hesitation, he told me: 'I agree there are some scholars who believe that the emperor undergoes divine transformation during *Daijosai*, but that view is not shared either by the emperor himself or by Imperial Household Agency. The emperor makes religious offerings to pray for the nation's prosperity, but he doesn't become a living god.'

Mr Miyao's answer could not have been more straightforward. What a pity a few days later the Deputy Chief Cabinet Secretary, Nobuo Ishihara, told a packed gathering of foreign correspondents: 'The government is not in a position to make any comment as to whether the emperor does or does not acquire a divine nature.'

Who, I began to wonder, were living in the real world – those inside or outside the moat?

15

The Japan Festival in Britain 1991

MARTIN CAMPBELL-WHITE

THIS IS NOT the place to review the Japan Festival which took place in the United Kingdom in 1991. This was covered in reports in the Japan Society's *Proceedings* Nos. 118 (Autumn 1991) and 119 (Spring 1992), but this volume would not be a fair summary of *Japan Experiences* if it failed to mention this important event in post-war Anglo-Japanese relations and the contacts which developed in the course of preparation of the festival. It was a major event in the history of the Society as it marked our centenary.

Many people contributed to the success of the festival, not least Peter Parker, who chaired the festival committee in the United Kingdom, and David Barrie who was the festival's executive director. But there would not have been a festival if it had not been for the inspiration and enthusiasm of MARTIN CAMPBELL WHITE, then Chief Executive of Harold Holt, now Askonas Holt.

I shall never forget the day when he and Sir Ian Hunter gave me lunch and suggested a Japan Festival of a fairly modest scale. I immediately responded enthusiastically and the scope of the festival grew like Topsy. One idea suggested another. Performances of music and theatre (Noh, Kabuki and Bunraku) were complemented by numerous exhibitions. Martin Campbell White was involved in the majority of festival events, in particular Kabuki, Takarazuka and Sumo.

In the following two short pieces he describes his contacts with the Takarazuka and Sumo authorities:-

•

Takarazuka is a small city near Osaka. It is a terminus for the Hankyu local railway company which, in fact, built the city. There is an amusement park; there is also the complex of theatres, rehearsal studios and a school, all built by Hankyu and still owned by them, which forms the Takarazuka Revue Theatre Company. The place is unique in the world. What it does is unique as well.

In the early 1900s, Mr Kobayashi, the President of the Hankyu Company, decided to open a theatre and school for young girls to learn the art of acting and singing. Until that time, it was considered unacceptable for women to appear on stage. The worlds of Noh and Kabuki were a strictly male domain. A far-sighted action on the part of Mr Kobayashi: the theatre attracted the public, who travelled there on the Hankyu railway, stayed at the Hankyu hotels in the city and even took a turn in the amusement park before going to the show. Enlightened as well. Mr Kobayashi opened up a whole world to girls who had talents for acting and dancing. Competition to join, first the school and then after two years the company, was, and still is, intense. There are exams, interviews and aptitude tests; each April the results are posted at the entrance of the Takarazuka. I have seen fifteen-year-old girls collapse with grief into their parents arms, as they realized they were not part of that year's intake.

Girls, girls, girls, you hear me say! Where are the boys? Especially if there are to be stage shows. Well, quite simply, there are none; and never have been. The girls play the male roles themselves. This is an all-girl theatre company. Those who are normally a little taller and whose voices are pitched a little lower are groomed for the male roles. All a little creepy and just a touch sinister, I hear you say? Not in the least! Takarazuka performances — normally of musicals such as *Kismet, The Rose of Versailles* and modern Japanese stories — are touchingly pure and innocent.

This, then, is the background for an overweight, six-foot *gaijin*, who has heard about Takarazuka and is intrigued to enter the scene. I can truly say that my first experience of the theatre and its young performers was overwhelming.

The theatre is big. The audience is totally female and Japanese. The show starts at 11.00 am, so all the men are at work. Mothers and daughters; office outings; gaggles of giggling girls, whose amusement and incredulity are very visible on catching sight of this foreigner (and a man!) towering above them. Pretty unnerving for me as well! So, even before the show began, I felt in an alien environment. A visitor from outer space.

The Takarazuka performance is a breathtaking mixture of energy and professionalism. All the girls work so hard and are so well drilled. The plot is simple and easily understandable, even to this *gaijin*. The singers, taking the male roles, are credible both in their delivery and in their cross-dressing. The young girls in the audience indulge shamelessly in the hero worship of the their idols — always the males.

It is glitzy and strangely innocent. Certainly not high art; in fact, many intellectual Japanese ridicule the Takarazuka culture.

For me, it was a revelation, it gave me a further insight into a Japan that can provide a Westerner with a unique experience. So much so that I resolved to bring the company to London. This, I am proud to say, was achieved with great success in July 1991 at the London Coliseum. So I shall always be grateful for a very special introduction to a historic, but still vital part of Japanese culture.

*   *   *

My fascination with Sumo started on my first ever visit to Japan in the early 1980s. The May Tokyo *basho* (tournament) was in full progress and I became hooked. The eleven pm highlights on NHK TV became a 'must' and I determined to learn more about the sport – or should it be called ritual?

I could tell that this was the national sport. Baseball was imported from the United States. Sumo is tradition, grace and strength and uniquely Japanese. I was struck by formalities before each bout and then the speed of action. To a foreigner, the whole thing could be considered laughable: cumbersome, overweight Japanese wrestlers fighting for (normally) not more than thirty seconds in front of thousands of knowledgeable and passionate spectators, who sometimes included the then emperor.

So every time I visited Japan, I hoped to watch on TV one of the tournaments, which take place during the last fifteen days of each odd month. Three in Tokyo and one each in Osaka, Fukuoka and Nagoya. I became a Sumo fan. Slowly, an idea formed in my mind that a Sumo *basho* should be arranged in London. I knew that they had been to Madison Square Gardens in New York; I heard that there were plans to bring them to Paris. As we were planning a Japan Festival for 1991, we thought Sumo should be an integral part of the Festival.

We were fortunate that, in 1988, Channel 4 had decided to transmit edited highlights of the various Sumo *basho* in Japan. Lyall Watson gave an excellent commentary. Sumo developed a cult following in Britain. So the time was ripe for us to press ahead with negotiations.

A Sumo tournament was adopted as one of the central elements of the Japan Festival. Through the good offices of the Gaimusho (Japan's Foreign Ministry) in Tokyo and NHK (who were deputed to be our partners), we made contact with the Sumo *kyokai* (association) and explained what we hoped to do. We were not put off. The Sumo Association was fully aware of the regular Channel 4 programmes. So Hugh Cortazzi and I were bidden to the March 1988 Osaka tournament to meet the elders of the association. We had a very formal encounter which, in true Japanese fashion, accomplished nothing, but was nevertheless a crucial first meeting.

Negotiations progressed quickly. Three senior members of the association were sent to London to cheek out possible venues. Dewanoumi came with two aides; he was the number two in the Sumo hierarchy, and was to take personal charge of the planning. I took them round to view hotels and stadiums: Wembley Arena, London Arena and finally the Roy-

al Albert Hall. I will never forget the sharp intake of breath as the delegation first entered the Royal Albert Hall. They were impressed with its
pomp. This was to be the venue. A suitable hotel, the Royal Garden,
which was in walking distance from the hall, was chosen. So, almost
two years in advance, plans were laid for the first ever Sumo tournament
to be held in London. Another 'first' was that there had never been a five-
day *basho* outside Japan. All their other overseas visits had been for two
or, at the most, three days.

The planning for a Sumo tournament is complicated, especially for a
company like mine that normally presents classical concerts and looks
after some of the world's greatest musicians. At least we knew the Albert
Hall, since we had been presenting concerts there for over seventy years,
and our artists take part in at least thirty BBC Proms each season. So I
took the view that this should be a spectacular opera event. The wrestlers
(*rikishi*) were the *prima donnas*; the sets and scenery were the ring (*dohyo*) and
roof. We had arranged hotels for groups of a hundred on many occasions
so what was the difference?

Simple in theory; more difficult in practice. Language was a problem;
so we had to build a bilingual team. Negotiations were slow; everything
had to be translated for the Sumo *kyokai*. Technical requirements in the
Albert Hall meant that the *dohyo*, placed in the arena and weighing
twenty-two tons, had to be underpinned in the basement with many ac-
row pipes. The ring is built using a very special mix of porous clay, which
was difficult to find in the UK. The help of Kajima, one of the leading
Japanese construction companies, was invaluable. The traditional roof
that hangs over the ring had to be shipped from Osaka; its three-ton
weight had to be suspended from the roof of the Albert Hall. This had
never been done before. Would it work? Yes, it did!

The Royal Garden Hotel was requested to supply rooms with king-size
beds – some even had to be reinforced and lengthened. It is not uncommon for a Sumo wrestler to weigh over twenty stone and to be over six
feet tall. In fact, Konishiki, affectionately known as 'dump truck' weighed
in at over thirty-five stone and measured six feet one and-a-half inches.
By contrast, the smallest, Maenoumi, weighed a few pounds less than
me! To feed this bulk, the hotel contracted to supply food one-and-a-half
times normal consumption. After a great deal of discussion we decided
the menus would be Western. A sight to behold: thirty *rikishi*, their assistants, all in their traditional *yukata*, tucking into roast beef and Yorkshire
pudding. An indelible memory.

So plans progressed. Many trips to Tokyo. Meetings with the heads of
the Sumo Association. Finally, the contract was signed. We could look
forward to a five-day tournament at the Royal Albert Hall for four nights
– Wednesday to Saturday – and finally Sunday afternoon – 9-13 October
1991. This was a first in the hall's history.

An advance party came over in June 1991 to publicize the event and the Japan Festival in general. I took them to Edinburgh, Newcastle and Carlisle. Everywhere we went, crowds gathered to gawp at these gentle, graceful giants in their very distinctive traditional dress. Newcastle Brown Ale made a very big hit with them, traditional Cumberland and Westmorland wrestlers proved no match for them. The press coverage was enormous. They caused quite a stir at Epsom on Derby Day. So the build-up began in earnest for a unique event.

Thanks to Channel 4's excellent coverage of the tournaments from Japan, we already had a knowledgeable UK audience. There was a big demand for tickets – even for the ringside mats, which were £75 – and seats were reserved for the important sponsors – Hitachi, JAL, Nomura, Mercury and KDD. The famous boxes at the Albert Hall were extremely useful for that purpose. So by the time the main Sumo party arrived, each performance – with a capacity of 5,000 – was nearly sold out.

There were two groups which travelled from Tokyo to London – one via Anchorage and one non-stop. Some wrestlers were too large to use the facilities on a 747, so a pit-stop at Anchorage was very necessary. Even so, I shall long cherish the sight of a posse of *rikishi* in their formal attire making an unseemly dash for the toilets as soon as they disembarked at Heathrow. That evening, I had to greet the whole party during their dinner at the Royal Garden Hotel. Standing up to address Japan's finest Sumo wrestlers was somewhat intimidating. But we had made it thus far. And they seemed to be enjoying the food, judged by the speed with which it was consumed, and more was requested.

We had a formal reception welcome party in the main entrance hall of the National History Museum; there were unplanned comparisons with the vast dinosaur skeleton which dominates that area. The *dohyo* had been constructed in twenty-four hours, the roof had been suspended, the ring was blessed during a very formal Shinto ceremony. Everything was ready for the opening. When the *rikishi* paraded in the ring for the first time on that Wednesday evening, the audience (by then sold out) reaction was tremendous. I, for one, confess to a large lump in my throat at the very special moment. I am sure it was the same for the other twenty-five members of our team. It was an awe-inspiring spectacle from another culture that seemed totally right in the Royal Albert Hall.

Kensington Gore got used to seeing Sumo wrestlers trudging to and from the Albert Hall in their traditional garb, making clacking noises with their *geta* (wooden sandals). We learned to cope with the enormous media interest. We issued over two hundred and fifty press passes – mostly to Japanese journalists and TV personnel; the bouts were transmitted live on NHK satellite TV. Above all, we all learned to marvel at the skills of the *rikishi*. They were superbly fit and supple; they could do the splits in spite of their prodigious size. Their agility and athleticism were amazing. No wonder they are superstars in their home country. They deserve to be, for the way they dedicate themselves to their sport.

The tournament was a total success. It was almost irrelevant that Hokutoumi was the winner. The event was bigger than the winning. London had witnessed something unique that exists only in Japan, and which can still thrill an audience in the hall and on TV. We had been privileged to work with these marvellous, dedicated people. It was certainly one of the highlights of my career, set fittingly alongside the most memorable concerts of the Vienna or Berlin Philharmonic Orchestra. It was also a great pleasure and source of pride to have collaborated so positively with my colleagues in Japan. I had never worked so closely with Japanese before. I learnt a lot from them; perhaps they learnt a few things from us. It was an Anglo-Japanese partnership at its very best.

16

The Penetrating Eyes of British Journalists

HESSELL TILTMAN ● FRED EMERY ● WILLIAM HORSLEY
IAN DE STAINS ● HENRY SCOTT STOKES ● BILL EMMOTT

A GOOD JOURNALIST has a number of advantages over a good diplomat. He usually has ready access, not least because most politicians love publicity. He can ask to see anyone he wants; of course he may be refused, but the same is true of a diplomat whose government may be more sensitive to a rebuff. He can normally ask any question he likes and may be able to press hard for an answer, especially if the interview is on radio or television. But he has his problems. His 'stories' generally have to be topical and he can only rarely get longish 'think pieces' published (unless he works for, say, the *Neue Zuercher Zeitung*). He has to work to deadlines. Moreover, he must think of his audience or readership and, unfortunately, he has to pander to the whims and likes or dislikes of the proprietor of his organization.

The diplomat also has to think about the attitude and interests not only of his colleagues at home but also of his political masters. Few politicians like to be told home truths and unpalatable facts, but while a diplomat must try hard to ensure that his reports are read and his views listened to, if he trims and writes what his masters want to hear he will fail and, accordingly, deserves to be retired or sidelined.

A good journalist, too, will stick to his principles and fight for his right to report the facts as they are and not as his proprietor thinks they should be, but he has little or no tenure and if the editors back at home refuse to carry his reports or edit them down to meaningless snippets there is little he can do except look for another job with a better company.

Japan has never been popular with the owners and operators of popular media companies in Britain. They 'don't like the Japanese' and in many cases only want reports of a sensational kind which show Japan in a bad light.

The often appallingly silly way in which Japan has been depicted, if at all, in the popular media in Britain has frequently depressed and annoyed me, but my ire has to be generally directed at the prejudiced editors and proprietors not at the journalists in the field.

In the immediate post-war years *The Times* and the *Manchester Guardian* in different ways helped to improve British understanding of Japan. But the mantle of responsibility for fair reporting on Japan soon passed to the *Financial Times* and the *Economist*. The *Financial Times* has covered the Japanese scene, economic and political, with consistent and conscientious reporting. Sometimes, they may have got things wrong, but journalists are only human. The *Economist*, for its part, has provided in-depth and thought-provoking commentaries. The BBC has been fortunate in having a series of first-class correspondents.

The British journalists who have contributed to this chapter are or were all interesting and outstanding members of their profession. My only regret is that recent correspondents for the *Financial Times* in Tokyo are not represented. Perhaps I was not sufficiently persistent with my requests. This said, I am particularly grateful to the remarkable journalists who responded to my request to contribute pieces for which there can be no monetary award. For an amateur editor like myself journalists are a boon. They know how to write well and hardly need any editing.

This chapter rightly begins with a selection of comments made in a lecture to the Japan Society on 27 September 1955 by HESSELL TILTMAN who was the correspondent of the *Manchester Guardian* in Tokyo before and after the war and was justly considered in the immediate post-war years as the *doyen* of the press representatives in Japan:-

> Japan is still grappling with the after-effects of a national miscalculation which cost it an Empire, one quarter of its entire accumulated national wealth, two-thirds of its pre-war overseas markets and its entire pre-war merchant fleet, and reduced its territories to four small main islands which a century ago supported less than one-third of its present population.

'The inexorably mounting pressures of population' were, Tiltman observed, 'responsible for a shortage of more than three-and-a-half million homes required to raise housing conditions even to inadequate pre-war levels, for chronic shortages of school accommodation and increasing food imports'.

Tiltman thought that:

> The economic situation in which Japan finds itself is such that one would be justified – if one did not know Japan – in concluding that no alternative exists beyond an indefinite continuation of US dollar spending or a severe decline in living levels that are already low by Western standards. I say advisedly if one did not know Japan and the Japanese. For that nation is inured to calamity – natural and man-made – and has an ingrained habit of being at its best in adversity. It has faced impending national bankruptcy before, and somehow it never happened because a united, diligent and intelligent people decided it must not happen. So today in Tokyo, most foreigners who have known Japan longest and best admit the ser-

iousness of the nation's current plight, but decline to sell Japan short.

This led on to a discussion of Japan's significance in the world:-

In a word, one may dislike Japan and the Japanese; deplore the country's fecundity, fear it as a trade competitor; and, if you are so disposed, distrust the genuineness of its conversion to democratic concepts. What no-one can prudently do is to ignore Japan or discount its significance to the free world.

*   *   *

Interest in Japan concerning Great Britain appears to be permanently centred upon that country as a trade competitor – never as a customer. Yet for most years of this century to date, Japan has bought abroad more than she has sold. 'Cheap Labour' and 'dumping' are stressed, with, often, the underlying suggestion that if the Japanese are not closely watched and hedged in with tariffs, quotas and other restrictions, they are likely to revert to the unorthodox trading methods which resulted in so much resentment and bad feeling in the thirties.

*   *   *

But the true significance of Japan to the United Kingdom does not begin and end with trade rivalry – or even Japan's heavy purchases from the Commonwealth. Even more important in the international scheme of things is the fact – so rarely mentioned in this country – that eighty-nine million Japanese want to be friends. If, that is, you and the rest of the inhabitants of the United Kingdom will let them.

*   *   *

And so it may perhaps be worth a thought that in Japan, Britain has eighty-nine million friends – if it wants them and is prepared to be half-way friendly in return. If Britain is so rich in friends that another eighty-nine millions more or less makes no difference, then neglect of Japan would represent an understandable policy. But if the friendship of millions of the most hard-working, diligent, and advanced people on earth – people who revere tradition and accept austerity without complaint – is something to be valued, then it sometimes seems to me that Britain and its leaders might perhaps display a little more public consciousness of that fact.

Three further observations by Tiltman are worth recalling:

When I returned to Tokyo following Japan's historic stumble, the country lay prostrate, stunned and disillusioned. Amid Tokyo's cold, blackened devastation, only two things mattered – work and food. More than half the entire area of Greater Tokyo, the world's third largest city, was rubble and dust. More than sixty-five per cent of its factories, homes, furniture and clothing had been totally destroyed.

*   *   *

At that time I asked the late Yukio Ozaki, the Grand Old Man of Japanese liberalism who had sat in the Diet since the day it was established, how long he thought it would take to democratize Japan.

'If the Americans intend to persevere in the task,' he replied, 'then they may begin to see results in sixty years time, and in a hundred years may be in a position to judge whether the experiment will be successful. But I doubt if the Americans will persevere for one hundred years.'

*   *   *

Ten years after, it is still possible to say that the present at its most discouraging is definitely better, and more hopeful, than the past. And not only because a large proportion of the Japanese people staunchly support the Constitution, hate militarists, refuse to be intimidated by the police, have access to a free press – and answer back.

FRED EMERY was *The Times* Tokyo Correspondent from 1964-67. He recalled his experiences as follows:-

•

Communicating and corresponding from Japan in the nineteen sixties already seem light years away from today's instant internet. *The Times* had long sent resident staff correspondents, so had Reuters, but no other London newspaper did until the FT joined in after my arrival; the BBC relied only on occasional contributors. Feature articles sent by post were the preference of home offices, but we had a telex machine at home for sending news reports. The only serious interruption occurred when the local telephone company simply cut down the line, not knowing that it belonged to the international company (KDD), hitherto unknown in the suburbs, therefore, to the Japanese mind, like some weed to be removed.

The relative lack of interest in Japan by the mass media was the more amazing considering what was afoot. The country was about to 'come out' into international respectability with the staging of the Olympic Games. Japanese industry, already well known for its transistor radios, motorbikes, and supertankers, was – although it was hard to convince Western readers – about to storm world markets with electronics and, most important of all, cars. And in the region China was about to explode its first nuclear weapon, Indonesia was in uproar and Vietnam was aflame, although in 1964 the number of British forces in Southeast Asia still exceeded the Americans.

Possibly because Japanese governments were not as assertive as their manufacturers, or because Japanese tourists could not afford to travel beyond Hong Kong, the Western mass public, when they paid attention at all, thought of Japan and the Japanese as distant and inscrutable. Added to that were the undertones of cruelty resented then as now by British POW survivors.

The editor of *The Times*, Sir William Haley, had a deeper understanding of Japanese culture and literature, and was a personal friend of Japan's ambassador to France. He disdained mass media ignorance and wanted as much from me as we could print. It was a wonderful if daunting challenge.

The Times enjoyed probably falsely exalted status overseas, and in Japan this opened many doors. One of my predecessors started the extraordinary habit of keeping up with the Japanese 'top papers' by having *The Times* flag on the office car, the driver wearing a cap emblazoned with the company heraldry. With the flag flying, as if some ambassador, I was never once stopped by police, and we were always waved in unchallenged into the Prime Minister's forecourt or the Foreign Ministry.

More difficult than access, however, were language and comprehension. It was my first posting where I did not speak or read the language. And very few Japanese then spoke English. As a linguist, I found it difficult to accept that it would take years to learn to use Japanese professionally rather than simply colloquially. My first interpreter, of samurai-stock, found my approach too blunt, and either would not or could not put my questions in interviews. He did not tell me until afterwards, at which point it was rather difficult to go back. We parted company, in mutual incomprehension.

I suppose it was no surprise that when a brilliant Japanese foreign service officer interpreted my first interview with a Japanese Prime Minister, Hayato Ikeda, the exchanges caused a minor stir. I had asked him when, as many authoritative observers were predicting, we might expect Japan to take a more self-assertive role in world affairs. Shock horror. What a nerve, was the feeling those in the room conveyed. But Mr Ikeda smiled. And, if memory serves, he answered something like: why should we? No-one can deny that attitude has served Japan well in subsequent decades.

Asahi Shimbun colleagues in London had given me a send-off lunch, warning that I should find Japan's 'social capital' very inferior to Britain's. Indeed it did have its horrors, but there were also charms. Our first house in Harajuku was so supple that the slightest tremor would set the window panes jangling, the children crying and my wife ringing me at the office to ask about 'that earthquake' – which we, of course, on the sixth floor of a modern building had not noticed. The sewage also failed there leading to a call-out to experts at dealing with what the Americans called 'night soil'; but when the water failed one of my best features was produced on the visits I and my young sons paid to the public bath house. I realized then that many Japanese were not coming in because of an emergency but because they lived in such tiny homes many had no baths.

Industrial and downright criminal toxic pollution in the Tokyo Yoko-hama area in the summer was sometimes so dense that the police issued warnings for people to stay indoors. In those days Japan Inc. held total sway and environmental policy was non-existent.

But the greatest joy in Japan's weak infrastructure was to be had in the motoring holidays we took. Outside the Tokyo area roads generally were so bad, and there were so few cars that it was then bliss to get about, and the traditional Japanese *ryokan* was everywhere the norm – modestly priced and far superior to the jerry-built modern hotels. When we arrived without pre-booking their only concern was: could we eat Japanese? With the affirmative, efficient ladies would sweep our boys off to the bath, and then later serve what I remember as wonderful Japanese meals – sometimes followed by an attempted Western steak, just for good mea-sure! We loved our travels. Everywhere we were treated with hospitality. Once in Hokkaido my wife and I were recruited by the inn to be part of their dance team at a version of an *o bon* festival. The dance seemed inter-minable. But it transpired we were the first Westerners in the village since the end of the American Occupation.

The mass invasion of Japan by the world's athletes for the Olympics was a major event. Although there was no live television coverage (satel-lites were then archaically slow) there was major interest. *The Times* alone sent two sports correspondents. And with me covering full-time periph-erals like boxing, hockey and soccer, thousands of words poured over our telex each night, through the high-speed fingers of a US Army sig-nalman we hired (expensively) for the occasion.

The crowds of Japanese spectators were immense and respectful. It was the last time for a generation that the two Germanies competed as one, and the only hiccup was the North Koreans who arrived, but then declined to compete. The Olympics, remember, were still officially amateur, and the events themselves were flawlessly organized. It is arguable how much lasting impact derives for the host country, but I think the fact that these Games were Japan's first post-war appearance on the world stage did a power of good for the country's image, and its own self-respect.

If the Japanese government stayed quietly unassertive, my period saw the emergence of a more outspoken press, at least in foreign coverage. When in late 1964 and early 1965 both the Communists and the United States escalated the Vietnam war there was a strong response in Japan. The *Mainichi Shimbun* sent a team of correspondents to South Vietnam and their long series 'Mud & Flame' was emotional and ahead of the rest of the non-Communist world in criticizing the United States. The Japanese government was somewhat abashed and privately disowned the *Mainichi* as irresponsible. But the mark of independence was made.

As non-readers we correspondents had to rely on our interpreters to translate key articles in the papers, as well as on their English language daily versions – which of course were not at all the same thing. To try getting a feel for the mass of often fascinating magazine articles, of invaluable help was an English-language digest put out by the United States Embassy. Japanese-speaking foreign diplomats serving in Tokyo, as well as both Japanese and foreign academics, also were important sources. The business world, of course, could take care of itself, and usually had plenty of excellent English speakers. But occasionally what we reported they said was disbelieved back home. There was one instance of the head of Toyota telling us they would double production next year, and double it again the year after, and again the year after that. Commentators in Britain questioned it. Could we have misheard? Alas for British car manufacturers, if not purchasers, it was all too true.

I have to conclude with all the wonderful memories of Kabuki, Noh, symphony concerts, lectures at the British Council, the many wonderful meals given by Japanese hosts, a few at home, most in restaurants. Our initiation into *kamikaze* skiing. There was also the staged version of *Gone with the Wind*, only in Japan, as they say. In those days there was a self-confidence in Japan, a bit like the Victorian British, that they could do anything. It was a privilege to have witnessed it.

WILLIAM HORSLEY, who took a degree in Japanese Studies at Oxford University in 1971, was Tokyo Correspondent for BBC Radio and TV from 1983 to 1990. He is the co-author with Roger Buckley of *Nippon: New Superpower* (1990). He was impressed by the raw energy of Tokyo:-

•

In 1970, seen from Britain, Japan was like a distant star, exotic and mysterious – a riddle inside an enigma inside a zen *koan*.

I was a teenager when the Tokyo Olympics of 1964 amazed the outside world as a modern miracle. The newly-launched bullet train was a space-age symbol of this new Japan. The dry statistics already showed how Japan's economy was surpassing those of Britain and every country in Europe. How could a nation so devastated by war bounce back so quickly, with the inspired architecture of the sports stadiums, a confident show of pride in the nation's achievements, and a fine crop of Olympic medals? Japan was not only *an* unanswered question. It seemed to me then to be one of the most urgent questions in the world.

What first drew me into Japan's sphere was a chance visit in 1968 to an exhibition of Japanese art and design called *Fluorescent Chrysanthemum* at the Institute of Contemporary Art in London. I admired the clean lines of Japanese industrial design – the mixture of artistry and engineering skill in the way the Japanese were building ships and cars, bridges and skyscrapers. I discovered Japanese playfulness, in an animated film in which the flowing letters of the Japanese *kana* syllabary took on a life of their own. These images seemed to open up a new world with hidden springs of vigour and insight. It was the start of a life-long attachment.

At university, I switched from English Language and Literature to Japanese Studies, and felt something of the exhilaration of an explorer. In place of the humanist tradition of Montaigne and More, Hobbes and Milton, Cervantes and Shakespeare, Japan appeared as a society in which the individual had not escaped, or been set free.

In Japanese classical literature I found a world of great emotional richness and dramatic range, yet which stood aside from the great river of human experience outside Japan itself. In the plays of Japan's greatest dramatist, Chikamatsu, born less than thirty years after Shakespeare's death, there are echoes of the dramatic mastery of the Bard from Stratford-upon-Avon. Yet the defining feature of Chikamatsu's plays – written for the *bunraku* puppet theatre – was that they take place in a Japanese world that is literally sealed off. It was a claustrophobic world, with no equivalent of Prospero's Island, no outlandish or imaginary Albania, no Forest Outside Athens.

In the *jidaimono* – historical dramas and stories – the enclosed space of the Japanese setting provided fertile ground for tragedy. Throughout the canon of Japanese drama, from the age of the samurai to the present, many stories end in some variation on the same theme: self-destruction for those on the losing side, and who have infringed the society's norms of behaviour. The means of the exit range from the passionate love suicide or ritual *seppuku* (disembowelment) to the pathos-laden options of exile or escape to the life of a monk or hermit.

Faced with these discoveries I felt the need for some simple truths. Here, certainly, was one: Japan was, thanks to its particular history and geography, a land with few exits. The physical closedness of the country helped to explain the clannish behaviour, the highly-developed sense of hierarchy, and a language honed for hundreds of years in an exquisite array of meanings and coded signals.

History supplied the most important signposts. The story of Japan's entry to the modern world, in the one hundred years from the arrival of Commodore Perry's 'Black Ships' in Tokyo Bay to the San Francisco Peace Treaty of 1951 and Japan's new start after World War Two, is one of the most exciting episodes of history of any nation at any time. The more I learned, the more my amazement grew.

Yet I was not prepared, on my first visit in 1970, for the physical assault on the senses that was Tokyo. I remember the excitement as I walked for the first time in the drenching summer heat through the sea of people at Shinjuku Station, and out through the west exit into the noisy concourse there. The *Red Tent* theatre troupe of Kara Juro was performing one of its scenes designed to shock – half-naked bodies frozen in poses of controlled frenzy.

Kara Juro's actors, like the other 'underground' theatre troupes which were such a sensation then, had an elemental energy. They struck me also as a cry of protest against a new and stifling orthodoxy: the conformism of corporate Japan. In those days, though, Tokyo street life had a rough vitality which showed the battle for Japan's spirit under way. A few yards away from the site of the *Red Tent* performance was the dazzling bazaar of Shinjuku life – the commercial flags of the Kinokuniya bookshop, a hundred *yakitori* bars, and an almost solid throng of people. There were the sushi delivery men in their clattering clogs, doll-like teenaged girls in miniskirts, older women in colourful *kimono*, and swarms of male office workers – *sarariman* – in white short-sleeved shirts. In the air-conditioned coffee-shops willowy students bent over their paperbacks or comics. The Japanese bazaar was a feast to the senses and a challenge to the mind.

I stayed through the sticky heat of August that year with a couple whom I now count among my closest Japanese friends. Their small apartment was in Ikebukuro, in northern Tokyo, and in that confined, domestic setting I experienced an unforced generosity, and a quality of restraint which was a sharp antidote to the assertive ways that were considered normal back in Britain. To my impressionable young self, the Japanese seemed in some miraculous way to have mastered the art of self-control.

Much in Tokyo was strange, but one of the strangest things of all was the experience of first listening to the US Forces' Far East Network. The radio station for the US forces carried a mixture of light music, warnings to the GIs against the dangers of taking drugs or giving away military secrets, and news bulletins. These were delivered at the microphone in various southern and mid-western drawls. It was so wacky that at first I thought the whole thing must be an elaborate spoof, a take-off of the loud Americans abroad.

Then it dawned on me that this was for real, and that the Privates and Marine Sergeants at the microphone were just doing the best to inform and entertain the American troops in their bases around Japan. It was a moment to savour each night when, at midnight, a brash American voice announced: 'Out stations pause for a moment to denote the completion of one broadcast day and the start of a new one.' After a pause the voice boomed out proudly 'Ladies and gentlemen, our national anthem.' Then the radio tingled to the explosive sound of the *Star-Spangled Banner* – as Dong De-Dong Dong Dong Dong rang out over the streets of that sprawling Tokyo suburb, with its rows of uniform apartment blocks and its Japanese crowds, strolling back from the public bath or settling in before another day at the office or production line.

My first experience of the conflict in the soul of post-war Japan was a shock. It was anti-war day in the autumn of 1970. I found myself, one evening in central Tokyo, in what looked like a deserted battlefield before the clash of two great armies. Crowds of Japanese anti-Vietnam war protesters were marching snake-fashion, as in a traditional Shinto festival, chanting slogans against militarism, imperialism and the US-Japan Security Treaty, *Ampo*. A short distance away, as silent and disciplined as the warriors in some ancient Japanese epic, the riot police had fanned out to block a road. Their shields, helmets and armoured vests made them look like the troops of Darth Vader before a battle that would decide the fate of the Empire. I heeded the megaphone warnings to clear off before battle could commence.

In retrospect, I realize that what such scenes represented was the birth of a long-lasting consensus in the Japanese nation, twenty-five years after the defeat in World War Two. It was a consensus built on the interests of business, on the desire for a highly-ordered, prosperous society, and an alliance with the superpower, America. The street violence surrounding the renewal of the US-Japan Security Treaty before 1960, and again ten years later, was a showdown in which that conservative consensus prevailed over a motley band of left-wing forces.

The motives that lay behind the student revolt and anti-war movement are a vital part of Japan's modern development. After its defeat in World War Two, the country had changed course dramatically. Its leaders had embraced the protection of the United States as the best assurance against other supposed threats – that of republican revolution at home, and of expansionist Communism in China and the Soviet Union. The early

post-war soul-searching about Japan's actions in the Pacific war had been
brushed aside in the headlong pursuit of the new national goals. Many of
Japan's wartime leaders were back in positions of power and influence.
The *zaibatsu* business conglomerates had been re-formed and re-invigo-
rated, and were embarking on a worldwide offensive in the name of
peaceful commerce. Japan's thirty-year trade war with the outside world
had just begun.

Later, in the 1980s, I would devote eight years, as the BBC Tokyo Correspondent, to reporting the rise of Japan as an economic power and a
force in world affairs. I would discover the astonishing sophistication of
effort that underlay the mighty Japanese economic machine, as well as
the secret channels of patronage, and also corruption, which made the
wheels turn. This was a more calculating, power-conscious Japan. I admired much about it, but could not love it as I had loved the country I
had first come to know.

The decade of the 1980s took Japan through some dizzy extremes of
fortune. Japanese firms were accused of trying to 'buy the soul of America' with their high-profile acquisitions in high-tech industry and Holly-
wood. Japan became literally the banker to the world. Japanese leaders
had the satisfaction of hearing the British prime minister, Mrs Thatcher,
in a speech in Tokyo in 1990, extolling the 'unique combination' of
Japanese management expertise and British skilled labour in the many
Japanese-owned factories in the UK. But the time was marked, too, by
bruising trade disputes, by a series of political scandals in which Japanese
prime ministers fell in succession like tipsy guests in some dubious geisha
house, and at the end by a collapse of the bubble economy which sent the
stock market tumbling, and which has raised deeper doubts about Japan's
economic future.

My earlier experience of Japan helped me to see this new phase in perspective. I saw how the habit of defensiveness had now become the main
enemy of Japan's real interests. The Japanese had learned to defend themselves with spirit against colonization, but not to live on equal terms with
others. The merits of Japan's exclusive and refined cultural traditions,
which had long served to keep outsiders at arm's length, was now leading
it to a loss of balance.

The buzz-word of the 1980s was *kokusaika*, internationalization. But
each much-publicized government campaign for this *kokusaika* served
only to underline Japan's home-made isolation. Japan's ruling class had
itself erected a maze of barriers to trip up would-be foreign intruders into
Japan's business markets. With the increasing wealth, Japan's horizons
and its appearance were changing by the day. Yet the inner sanctums of
Japan's social conventions were jealously guarded. No-one seemed to
know any longer how to unlock them and to make the roads passable
again.

In those days the vice-minister of MITI, the Ministry of International Trade and Industry, was seen as someone with special responsibilities for safeguarding Japan's future. The mindset of the ruling elite was laid bare to me when the vice-minister travelled with me on a train along Japan's Pacific coast, and he earnestly explained why it was absurd to ask Japan to open its markets to the uncertainties of free trade and investment. As we watched the land speed by from the window of the Bullet Train he told me, without a trace of irony, that the well-manicured state of the paddy-fields showed Japanese society in miniature. Every inch of territory had been divided up and worked on in a spirit of collective harmony in ways that foreigners could not possibly understand.

I found myself on one of the many committees for *kokusaika* that were set up by the government. Mine was in the Home Affairs Ministry. Amidst stifling formality, rows of officials drew up lengthy papers about things like the need for more sister-city partnerships with other countries (in the West, not in Asia). The realities that lay at the heart of Japan's problem, including the widespread discrimination against non-Japanese – especially other Asians – in employment, housing, law-enforcement and business, were difficult to broach in such an atmosphere. Some of my Japanese committee colleagues shared my frustration. A delicious moment came when one of them, a liberal university professor, showed his impatience at all the humbug. He suggested that the best way of achieving *kokusaika* in the Home Ministry would be to send the ministry's own senior officials off to New Zealand, each with only a knapsack of food and a small amount of money, and leave them there for half a year. They would, he said, quickly learn what 'international' really means. The idea was, sadly, never taken up.

Japan's politics were, and largely still are, a closed book to outsiders, because they embody many private codes and protected hierarchies. I learned that although Japan was a parliamentary democracy in name, really important decisions were taken out of public view. Often that meant in the *ryotei*, the political restaurants where deals could be struck according to bonds of loyalty and obligation, not by accountable decision-making.

In my own field of journalism, I headed the association representing foreign journalists, the Foreign Press in Japan, and gained something of a reputation as a scourge of the *kisha* clubs – the exclusive press clubs set up by the Japanese press in every ministry and large organization, and which had long served as a filter against foreign intrusion into the worlds of Japanese politics and business. Whatever its other merits may have been, the system then was a sorry display of Japan's unwillingness to face the outside world. The *kisha* clubs' goal of keeping foreigners out had ludicrous implications. At one point, under sustained pressure, the club which controlled all reporting access to Japan's courts and judiciary system agreed to let some non-Japanese reporters have limited access to the courts. But a crucial precondition was proposed: that any foreigner who collected information in this way would not pass any of it on to any other foreign reporter who had not been there!

Japan has changed in many ways since then. More barriers have come down. There is more interchange with other countries than ever before, and both Japan and the world outside its shores are the richer for the more open relationships that flourish now. My own attachment to Japan is like a very old friendship. It involves moments of despair and neglect, but it is also a lasting source of companionship and pleasure.

IAN DE STAINS 'discovered' Japan in the 1970s as a producer-presenter for the BBC. Here he recalls some of his experiences, including dealing with the missing 'pineapple' as well as reviewing aspects of the Japan of today:-

●

I arrived in Japan in the mid 1970s, a fresh-faced enthusiastic BBC producer-presenter on secondment to Auntie's Japanese equivalent, *Nippon Hoso Kyokai*. The assignment was to be for two years. Almost a quarter of a century later, I am still here; less fresh-faced but none-the-less enthusiastic.

The flight from London (via Copenhagen and Anchorage, at eighteen hours or so then the quickest route) landed at Haneda airport at a little after 5.00 pm. So, it seemed, did all the other Jumbos in the world. The place was seething; the concourse a mass of shining black hair and apparently endless lines of Japanese businessmen. I took my place in line, one of only a handful of foreigners, and slowly inched my way forward, passport in hand, tired from the flight but excited by what lay ahead, anxious to get through customs to be met – I knew – by my predecessor William Horsley and – I suspected – by a whole entourage of NHK colleagues.

After what must have been the best part of an hour, I reached the front of the line and eagerly presented my passport to the official behind the high desk. He ignored the passport and looked impatiently at my carry-on luggage. 'Where,' he demanded, 'is your pineapple?'

For a single Monty Pythonesque moment I felt like saying that I did not know I needed one, but the helpful JAL ground staff led me away from plant quarantine and toward immigration.

Not, you might think, the most auspicious welcome and yet, as I now see, a perfectly fitting one. The intervening years have been filled with many such surprises: just when you think you have got a handle on Japan something happens to make you wonder.

It was William Horsley who, in my first few days on the ground, told me that if I wanted to write a book about the Japan experience, I should do so within the first six months. At the time I thought it a singularly odd piece of advice (and, incidentally, I am glad he did not himself heed it, for he would not otherwise have produced his own book). Now, however, I know exactly what he was saying. In those early days, if asked to record my impressions and voice my opinions, I would not hesitate. Today, faced with even this short contribution, I am caught up in what is a familiar predicament: each time I set down a thought, record an impression, come to a conclusion, a little genie at my ear whispers a dozen contradictions. Such contrasting sentiments are, in part, what has kept me here so long. Japan has been good to me. I am now on my second career here and feel privileged to be part of the Anglo-Japanese relationship at a time of such positive development.

It is hard to imagine now how little was known of Japan at the time I arrived. My task was to make radio and television programmes that would introduce the country and its culture to an international audience and the pursuit of that goal was to take me from the frozen wastes of Hokkaido to the seething volcanoes of Kyushu. What an extraordinary gift: to be paid to learn about the art of tea, the craft of *shibori*, the countless fascinating festivals and then to share such new enthusiasms across the airwaves. What a thrill: to meet such erudite figures as the Living National Treasures, custodians of the ancient arts of kabuki and noh or the movers and shakers of the *shingeki* movement. There were the electronic inventions of Isao Tomita and the impenetrable complexities of Toru Takemitsu and I shall never forget a series of interviews with survivors of the Hiroshima bombing; a frightening glimpse into a very hell.

My diaries and letters home were full of more private musings; reflections on the (often inadvertent) creative use of English in advertising slogans: 'Dr Zog's sex wax is good for your stick', 'Not to wear a rugger even if joining a team' and others too indelicate to mention. Or perhaps I regaled my friends with accounts of how colleagues entertained me in restaurant after restaurant that served up previously unknown delicacies, or the nightclub where all the hostesses were topless and rode unicycles. Such things seem tame indeed by today's standards.

For Japan today is a very different place. The old saw that nothing here ever changes is one of the most tired to issue from the mouths of so-called Japan hands. It never fails to amaze me that so much nonsense is spoken and written about Japan by those who, even if they live here (and many do not) do not read and write Japanese and yet claim to have an insider's knowledge. Reporters and analysts alike depend on second-hand information and translated materials and on such constructs make pronouncements about the state of the economy or the wisdom of the policies of MITI. The writer and commentator Eamonn Fingleton in *Blindside* has shown how often such experts have been spectacularly wrong.

For those willing to make the extra effort to see Japan as it really is – as opposed to the way they think it ought to be – the rewards are rich indeed. This is certainly true in business where I pursue my second career assisting British companies in their efforts to exploit the enormous opportunities of this very important market. Throughout the 1990s the United Kingdom has demonstrated a commitment to Japan that is the envy of many of our competitors. Government and the private sector alike have sought to understand the opportunities and to take advantage of them. We have come a long way.

I recall in the early days of this work the comments of the Japanese wife of a business associate who used often to play hostess to visiting foreign businessmen. They were, she said 'a lot of thick men in thick suits'. Not very complimentary but, sadly, true of many at the time. Today, however, our visitors are more aware; they, like British business, have smartened up their act.

So, too, have the politicians who come calling. I remember the sinking feeling I had when meeting a cross-party parliamentarians delegation in the late 1980s. One Member in particular was railing against the Japanese self-defence forces. Why, he demanded to know, did the Japanese need defences when their nearest neighbour was America! Fortunately, the politicians we meet these days are rather better prepared and many are only too pleased to address meetings of the British Chamber. It was after one such meeting that I was to encounter the handbag end of one former Prime Minister. Fortunately, my meetings with other former PMs – and, indeed, incumbent ones – have been much less fraught, and, indeed, subsequent visits by the handbag went off quite smoothly. Meeting members of the Cabinet at briefing sessions by British businessmen, I have on a number of occasions pondered on the fact that television plays such tricks. Some come across in the flesh as much more likeable and sincere while others are a sad disappointment: their on-screen charisma merely smoke and mirrors.

The number of visitors overall has increased; a sign that the UK's awareness of Japan is much better than it was. There is still more work to be done but it is encouraging to see so many of the captains of industry making regular calls here and understanding the importance of the bilateral relationship.

The year 2000 marks the 400th anniversary of Netherlands-Japan relations. While not wishing to detract from the importance of that, we should remember that the ship that brought the Dutch traders here – de Liefde – was piloted by a Briton, William Adams. I am certain that his arrival here was more dramatic than my own, but it was probably just as bewildering. In any event, I owe him a huge debt.

DAVID POWERS also worked for the BBC. He was BBC correspondent in Tokyo from 1987-92 and again in 1994. From 1994 to 1999 he was editor of BBC Japanese TV. For his experiences at the time of the death of the Showa Emperor and the inauguration of the present emperor see Chapters 13 and 14. HENRY SCOTT STOKES, now the Tokyo correspondent for the *New York Times*, arrived in Japan in the 1960s as correspondent for *The Times*. He has also worked for *The Financial Times* and wrote a biography of Yukio Mishima whom he got to know well. On 10 November 1999 he sent me the following piece:-

•

'How on earth can you write such drivel?'

This was the rhetorical question put to me. I do not remember John Pilcher pausing for a response. I do remember the half-circle of embassy officials including the editor of this collection, grouped about me in the ambassador's small office in the residence. . . Not long thereafter (or slightly before?) George Brown, Foreign Secretary, was to place his feet on the desk in that room, while he leaned back with a large glass of brandy at three o'clock in the afternoon, stirred on by a correspondent who represented *The Times* and wore a red tie.

'A red tie, my dear sir, what is *The Times* correspondent doing wearing a red tie?'

Brown leaned far back in the ambassadorial chair and puffed a cigar.

Thus my elders and betters tried to get me onto the straight and narrow. . . Thirty years on, I look back on that period as one of extraordinary excitement, interspersed with periods of complete boredom, as I struggled to manage a disorderly life (Sir John: 'what you've got to get into your head is that the most fundamental fact about Japan is *isolation* from the rest of the world, its historical *isolation*.' Oh, I thought, funny I overlooked that.)

What does one do, actually, if one knows nothing about a place and is in my trade? The first thing is to make a bee-line for the writers. These days they have names like 'Banana' (a first name, a lady's), and think up attention-grabbing titles ('Wild Sheep Chase'). In those days, in a post-1945 atmosphere, the thing was to be as Western, preferably European, as you could possibly be. We had a crypto-Kafka in Kobo Abe, who came to my house in Ebisu and took a great photo of me that I have lost; we had a Jack-of-all-trades in Yukio Mishima, who could be a Thomas Mann ('writers must look like bankers') at one moment, a Racine at another (his play 'Madame de Sade'), and a Schickelgruber ('My Friend Hitler', also a play) in his spare time; and we had a 'Graham Greene' in Shusako Endo, the one-lunged author of *Silence* (*Chinmoku*). I was to know them all, right up to their deaths, slightly.

But what did I learn *pace* Pilcher re Japan in the encounters with the novelist? That life in Japan was an incredibly, incredibly complex game of shields (to protect), and mirrors (to reflect) and fans (to dance behind). And that indeed the insular tradition, the geographical fact of isolation had led these extraordinary people to develop on their own in such an intricate fashion that, for them as for us, communication was fraught... Only now, do I find, am I meeting self-confidence, determined, even crusty Japanese who are gonna do things their way. Only now is the kaleidoscope nightmare of 1945 going gradually over the horizon. Only now.

And Britain and Japan in that era?

When I came here, first in 1964, I carried the burden of introductions from a cousin of my mother's, Oscar Morland, to the highest, excluding the imperials. My sense then – I spurned the introductions, which was another Black Mark – was that UK officialdom was on a very special track to the heart of 'Things Japanese', and that that track had been nurtured from its starting point in the Bakufu time ... to the present day. We Brits knew Japan far better than others in many respects, including the commercial. Our rivals, of the serious variety, were the Americans, the Germans, the French, the Russians and the Chinese in roughly that order, the usual suspects (today, the Chinese have moved up close to the top in that pecking order). The question was whether we developed the muscle that the Americans had, basing ourselves on our scientists – the one element in our country the Japanese most looked out for, then as now – our engineers and our artists and scholars. The jury is still out on this one, but the groundwork was being laid in the 1960s. Was it well done? I think probably yes. There was suddenly no time for generalists any more, the blessed Pilcher springs to mind – we all had to know trade (a natural for a Quakerish journalist). Are we getting there now, a bit, thanks to the groundwork finally begun thirty years ago? I think so.

Here, if I may put this in the record, is a piece of current writing by yours truly, published today, 19 November 1999, as my column in *Tokyo Weekender*, here and on our website (permissions not necessary):-

*   *   *

'Everything is changing,' a forty-ish ex-MITI Japanese consultant said to me the other day. I suspect he's right.

These are extraordinary times. For a start it's unusual that a mid career official – the person I quote above is Yoshiaki Murakami, president of M & A Consulting, a small Tokyo-based company that he created recently – left his ministry and set up his own business. Until now – this is a generalization I know – government was almighty in Japan and the *yakusho* (the officials) were little, tin gods. All of a sudden, the private sector offers superior attractions.

Murakami-san told me that to his knowledge he is the first government official ever to do what he has just done. Quit government one day and set up in business the next. To me this is just one illustration of a general point: all bets are off on the ancient proposition that Japan does not change. In my last column I doffed my hat towards someone who takes the view that, while there are changes going on, of course, still the essentials remain the same. I referred to Karel van Wolferen, whom I described as the ultimate guru on Things Japanese these days. *Le Japon eternel!* Actually, what is going on now in business is little short of revolutionary.

Hardly a day passes in Tokyo, if you are on a daily newsbeat, without a major M & A story breaking. So I am told by practitioners of the art of daily reporting. Not long ago he had to write three or four big M & A stories in one week, one of my friends mentioned. News people have become blasé about mega M & A developments – one bank trying to gobble another – to the point where they arouse no excitement.

The old notion of a System that ran the country ('Japan Inc') – the MOF ran the banks as is they were external bureaux of the ministry; and MITI ran all of heavy industry and a lot of manufacturing firms, as if they were subsidiaries – was always a bit exaggerated and now no long seems appropriate.

I remember the days when any slightest suggestion of foreign direct investment in Japan was regarded with inherent caution, bordering on paranoia, as if each potential investor was a Black Ship in the making. This was true as late as the 1960s, when Japan already had the second-largest economy in the world, and hardly seemed short of prowess in business.

These days foreign investments in Japanese firms, including takeovers, are seen as part of the natural order. Thus we had the British company Cable & Wireless taking over IDC, a telecom offshoot of NTT. Then there was the cession of Nissan Motor to Renault. Still more recently, at the end of September, the authorities decided to let the Long-Term Credit Bank be bought by Ripplewood of the US. Somewhat late in the day there is suddenly a bit of resistance – reminiscent of the past – to the last of these three moves, but the debate has so far been muted, not emotional.

Any one of these moves could have been greeted as a national catastrophe by the Japanese media in the not too distant past.

The most palpable signs of change, I would say, are to be seen at the grassroots level among small firms and startups. This is where the real excitement has been found since about a year ago – after a decade of flagging interest during which the OTC market (this is where the 'small cap' firms are found) sank to a 10-year low. There have been forty-fold surges in some funds invested in the tiddler stocks so far this year.

Not everybody senses the excitement, mind you. *The Economist* has just run a piece stating that 'Japan's small firms are losing both their youth and their vigour. . . In the year following the Second World War. . . most company founders were under 40 years old. Now most are over 40.' With all due respect – the last time I took issue with *The Economist* I got caned – it looks like the other way round to me. In a year's time there could he three OTC markets in Japan, according to colleagues who follow these things.

Three OTC i.e. start-up markets? Yes, firstly the current one, which is admittedly three parts moribund. Next, the Nasdaq Japan market, an idea that is being pushed by Masayoshi Son of Softbank and the Nasdaq people out of New York. Finally, there is a market planned with the happy name of 'Mothers', also for new, small companies.

Eighty per cent of new companies, in any country and in any period, tend to fail. But those that make it are heroes. That is the feeling out there today, down in Kayabacho, up around the Kabutocho, and over in Hakozaki where Mr Son has his office. And where do the entrepreneurs get their seed money from if, as we are always told, the banks will lend them nothing and venture capital is hard to come by?

From a great range of sources. Lest we forget Japan is banker to the world – financing half the $1 billion a day that America needs to keep going is all in the day's work. It's a staggering performance. Only a slight diversification of those flows – I admit this is a crude simplification – can finance all the future stars, the Hikari Tsushins and Fancis (this year's stars) of tomorrow, for ever and anon.

Could I have written this without being here in the 1960s? Of course not.

WHAT BETTER WAY to round off this section than a contribution from BILL EMMOTT, Editor of *The Economist* since 1993. Bill Emmott was Tokyo correspondent for *The Economist* from 1983-86, and wrote *The Sun Also Sets* (1989), *Japan's Global Reach* (1992) and *Kanrio no Taizai* (1996):-

•

I arrived in Japan almost by chance. Young and hungry for another posting as a foreign correspondent before I reached the hoary age of thirty, I was sitting in London as an economics writer for *The Economist* when word reached me that there was a vacancy in Japan. My paper always harbours a strong preference to send its own people to foreign jobs rather than hiring locally, perhaps on a slightly Jesuitical view that you need to get them young and shape them first, before sending them out into the world. But no one seemed to be available for the Japan job, even though it was seen as attractive, particularly because our then deputy editor, the great Norman Macrae, had since 1962 made quite a thing in our pages of Japan's importance and potential. So, after a week or two had passed and no one senior had been appointed, I tentatively volunteered, despite having never before travelled east of Suez, let alone to Japan. Somewhat to my surprise, I got the job.

All I had had before I arrived to take up my duties in early October 1983, was a one week reconnaissance trip. The highlight of that was that I was invited to join a dinner arranged by various people from the Foreign Correspondents Club, at the Chinzanso garden, during the firefly-viewing season. It was a convivial occasion, as journalists' get-togethers tend to be, but it did offer one portent of the sort of subject matter that would dominate the debate over Japan in the next few years. At the end of the dinner, a haiku contest was held. The clear winner, from Urban Lehner of the *Wall Street Journal*, ran roughly as follows:

Firefly
Tried to come here tonight
Non-tariff barrier

My real arrival, a few months later, was rather amateur. I landed in early October, speaking not a word of Japanese, and knowing virtually nothing about the country. Three days later, came the verdict in the trial for corruption of Kakuei Tanaka, arising from the Lockheed scandal. So, rather swiftly, I had to pretend to be an expert, appraising the consequences for Japanese politics of the trial, with the welcome help of the political analysts at various embassies, including that of Britain.

How could *The Economist* send out such an amateur? Well, from my point of view it was a great opportunity, and all learning has to start somewhere. From the paper's standpoint, and that of the reader, a different thing needs to be borne in mind. That even as late as 1983, and even in the business or financial press, the amount of space and time devoted to Japan was really quite small. It was not yet seen as the world's third great financial centre, nor even, beyond a small range of companies, as a great business force. That was to come, very quickly. But for the time being, the demand for and interest in articles about Japan was quite limited, and the correspondent could therefore confine himself to a relatively narrow range of topics, for many of which it was possible to find plenty of good English-speakers to converse with. Now, the range of topics is broader and the demands are much greater.

My sudden immersion in Japanese politics, three days after my arrival, did however lead me to make my first mistakes, which I later realized were educative ones: of assuming that in Japanese politics there would be swift and perceptible consequences of a trial such as this, and that my job was to guess what they would be. The truth was that such consequences as there were had long since already happened, behind the scenes, in a firm but gradual way. It was the end of a process, not the beginning of one.

This is one of the things that makes Japan frustrating for many journalists, especially – though not only – American ones. Newspapers, naturally enough, want news, and news is normally understood as something that arises from events, announcements, clashes, from new initiatives being launched or endeavours begun. News in Japan, however, is not like that. Even companies do not attempt, as in America, to create events or to make big announcements. To the naked eye, at least, nothing seems to happen. And when it does, much effort is expended by officials or company spokesmen on trying to explain that it has not really happened, or that it is not really as dramatic as it looks.

One consequence is that companies that act in a Western way have often gained a far better press than others, even when – perhaps especially when – it is not merited. I recall particularly that Nissan regularly got splendid write-ups, because that car company had a friendly and eager PR team who tried to create some excitement. Toyota, by contrast, looked the dullest of companies. It was painfully difficult to arrange a visit to Nagoya, and the team of top managers would merely emerge once a year for a press conference in Tokyo with the foreign press. They would sit in a line, all looking like rather dour thugs from the countryside, and do their best to say nothing interesting at all. So now Toyota is the world's greatest and richest car company. And Nissan is 36.8% owned by Renault.

Another consequence, though, was that at times a great mess was made when trying to adapt the Japanese pattern of things to try to appeal to the Western media. During my time this occurred repeatedly when MITI or even the prime minister himself, Yasuhiro Nakasone, tried to depict their real, step-by-step approach to trade liberalization as something that was happening in great leaps and bounds, in great headline-grabbing packages. They were desperate for a strong, clear message, especially in the American press since trade rows were growing nastier as the US dollar climbed higher against the yen and as the US trade deficit widened. Increasingly, the coverage of Japan became dominated by that issue, even in the non-American press, because unlike the Japanese officials and politicians, their American counterparts are past masters at creating drama and events.

Admittedly, Mr Nakasone was a godsend to us journalists, because he looked and sounded rather like a British or American politician: tall, smart, forceful, confident. In a political scene so static and impenetrable that it could never make good copy, he at least offered some colour and a story our readers might recognize.

But unfortunately the packages, and the prime minister himself, were misleading. This the journalists were quick to spot. For the second important lesson about the Western media is that they are extremely distrustful of official announcements, so it generally only took a day or so before they worked out that this dramatic new package was in reality simply an assemblage of small steps that had already been taken, or had long been planned, or in some cases, were simply theoretical possibilities and declarations of good intent.

Appearance and reality: how often do those words appear together in commentaries on Japan? But, cliché though it is, the basic task for a journalist did lie precisely in that phrase, in finding ways to see the reality behind the appearance. It was one, I am glad to say, for which I felt that working for an international weekly like *The Economist* gave me a big advantage, perhaps an advantage sufficiently big at least to neutralize the disadvantage of my initial ignorance and lack of command of Japanese.

For on a weekly I had time to dig and to delve, and to think about what was going on. And I had no need to become frustrated by the lack of events or happenings, unlike my daily or news-agency counterparts. Analysis was what I was required to offer, not news. This also meant that I cared not a fig about being excluded, along with all the other foreign journalists, from the *kisha* clubs of the ministries and big companies. I did not want to hear the spoon-fed 'news' in these clubs; and I especially did not want to suffer under some form of obligation to the sources of the news, in return for *kisha* club membership. It was far better to be independent.

Finally, probably the best thing about my position was that I worked for a British paper, by which I really mean a non-American one. In the climate of the 1980s, this was helpful for two reasons. First, that Japanese sources did not continually see me as a way to send their often rather clumsy 'messages' to the American political scene, nor did they see me as in some way an adversary. Second, that it made me far freer to choose what I wanted to write about, what I thought was important, from a Japanese or international point of view. The American press by and large saw all stories from an American angle: they could not write about an industry without looking for an aggrieved American competitor, and all foreign policy stories were essentially stories about American interests. By being British, and yet with an international readership, one was free of all that.

That freedom was, in turn, crucial for what I saw as the most important ingredient in understanding Japan, at least from the standpoint of an international journal in current affairs and business: a real, comparative perspective. By that I mean a perspective that seeks not only to find what is different about Japan, but also to find what is similar about it, and to use experiences and findings from other countries, whether in Europe or America, to cast light on what might be going on.

This was important, first of all, because of the strength of the crude 'Japan is different' syndrome. Too many journalists, reinforced by their sources both Western and Japanese, jumped quickly to the conclusion that Japan was a country apart. This is hardly a new phenomenon, but it was particularly potent during my time writing about the place because it was the era of Japan's great financial boom, the bubble that was to burst in 1990, and of Japan's apparently unstoppable threat to American hegemony.

The 'Japan is different' school was paramount in this period, because that idea both played to an understandable Japanese pride in their achievements and was a more acceptable explanation for Americans; if Japan were the same, it was liable to make Americans feel bad, but if it were different, they could more comfortably feel that it was simply unfair or had to be stopped in some way. The second importance of a real comparative perspective was related to that point: for Americans their only point of comparison was the United States, and Japan was undoubtedly not identical to the USA. It was crucial, therefore, to understand a bit about Western Europe, to see elements of the workings of Japan in France, or Italy or Germany, if one was to have a chance of working out what was going on.

Did I ever understand what was going on? Probably not. But the task was certainly made easier, and far more enjoyable, by the application of historical and international experience when seeking to decipher the reality behind the appearances. And being a journalist was the greatest privilege of all: observing everything as if from afar, a little distanced from the action but close enough to make it all out. Not quite Margaret Mead in Samoa, but with some of the same sense of discovery and of fun. And we all tried not to be as taken in as she was.

17

How Some Politicians Saw Post-war Japan

**JULIAN RIDSDALE • PATRICK JENKIN • KENNETH BAKER
DENIS HEALEY • DAVID YOUNG**

THIS IS NOT the place for a discussion of the reactions of British politicians in general to Japan. By the nature of their career in parliament it was inevitable that few British politicians have had more than a cursory knowledge of Japan, a country in which their duties precluded them from living. Large numbers of MPs from all the main parties did, however, visit Japan and a few managed to achieve more than a passing acquaintance with the country and its people. Two organizations are primarily responsible for this. They were, firstly, 'The British-Japan Parliamentary Group', founded and led for many years by Sir Julian Ridsdale, and the 'UK-Japan 2000 Group' set up in 1984 under the chairmanship on the UK side of Jim (later Lord) Prior. Both groups continue to work for better understanding between Britain and Japan. The 2000 group has, of course, had to change its name and is now the UK-Japan 21st Century Group. The UK chairman is currently David Howell (Lord Howell of Guildford). His predecessor who did much to develop the work of the group was Patrick Jenkin (Lord Jenkin of Roding).

JULIAN RIDSDALE who had been in Japan as an army language officer before the war and served as MP for Harwich until he stepped down in 1992, described in the following piece how he formed the British-Japanese Parliamentary Group:-

•

I paid my first visit to Japan after the war in 1960 to attend an Inter-Parliamentary Union Conference. On this occasion I took the opportunity to call on my old friend General Sugita whom I had known as a Major in the bad old days of 1939. General Sugita said to me: 'The trouble with your country is that you forgive but never forget. Will you do something to improve Anglo-Japanese relations?' I replied: 'Yes, I will, but must first consult with my friends who fought in the Far East. With their approval I formed the British-Japanese Parliamentary Group and was

Chairman of the group from 1960-1992 when I decided not to seek re-election to the House.

The British-Japanese Parliamentary Group was joined by MPs from the moderate right and the moderate left, but the group did not really come into proper contact with the Japanese until 1973 when I received an invitation from the Japanese government to take a group of British MPs to Japan. One member of this group was Walter Harrison, a warm-hearted Yorkshireman, who became Chief Whip in Harold Wilson's government in 1974 and who agreed to help me with the tour and the group in London.

This was the first of four delegations of MPs whom I took to Japan before 1979. The third delegation in 1977 included Margaret Thatcher and the fourth delegation David Howell, Norman St John Stevas, Norman Lamont, Cecil Parkinson and Winston Churchill. After we got back Margaret Thatcher commented that I had taken a strong delegation to Japan.

By 1978 the tours which I organized to Japan were reputed to be the best overseas tours for British MPs. One group, when Hugh Cortazzi was Ambassador in Tokyo, included Chris Patten and Richard Needham. Many who joined me on these tours went on to be Ministers and some to be members of the cabinet.

During these tours I had managed to get to know many current or future Japanese Prime Ministers including Eisaku Sato, Nobusuke Kishi, Takeo Fukuda, Masayoshi Ohira, Kakuei Tanaka and Kiichi Miyazawa. I met Miyazawa first in 1960. He has held every important post in the Japanese government. He has a great sense of humour and in the economic crisis of the late 1990s he weathered the storm with great wisdom. When John Whitehead was Ambassador he wanted to accompany me and my wife Paddy on our call on Miyazawa, but the reply came: 'Ambassador I can see you any time, but I want to have a gossip with Paddy and Julian.'

In 1981 I found myself on the Trilateral Commission which was again composed like myself largely from the centre right in politics. The Labour party was represented by the late John Smith.

In 1986 I formed an all-party group for 'Engineering Development'. The first meeting attended by ten engineers came to hear a talk by Frank Toombs who had been closely involved with Japan. He spoke to us about the importance of investment in the technical and scientific industries and the need to face the challenge from Japan. Although I started the group with a small membership, by the time I retired from the House there was a membership of some 150 from both Houses.

During my visits to Japan I did my best to promote British interests including, of course, Japanese investment in Britain. Japanese investment helped to build up our export base and encouraged British component suppliers to improve their standards. In particular, we wanted Japanese companies to undertake research and development in Britain.

One of my Japanese political friends was Masumi Esaki who brought a delegation to Europe which included other friends of mine such as Tadashi Kuranari. I arranged for the Japanese delegation to meet members of the British-Japanese Parliamentary Group and to ensure smooth communication I ensured that simultaneous translation facilities were available and that our MPs were well briefed on the imbalance of trade with Japan and the need to encourage Japanese investment and joint ventures. To follow the meeting I fixed a dinner with members of our group and added a few Welsh MPs. They were rather puzzled about why they had been invited, but I knew that the Welsh were good at singing! My Welsh ploy worked and we were treated to some of the best after-dinner entertainment ever. The star of the evening was Tadashi Kuranari, the staid and dignified Chairman of the Japan-EC League of Friendship, who enthralled us all, not by singing, but by giving a superb, and very artistic magic act. The songs sung by the British were not too bad, but nothing could ever match Julian Amery's version of the *Eton Boating Song*.

I did my best to help over the proposed Nissan investment in the North-East and worked closely with Edwin McAlpine.

Among my Japanese friends was Yoshio Sakurauchi who was for a time Japanese Foreign Minister and who enthused me about that Japanese phenomenon known as Takarazuka – the girls' 'opera'.

I was in Japan at the time of the Falkland Islands crisis when, sadly, the Japanese government failed to give us the support we needed. Hugh Cortazzi, who tried very hard to win Japanese support, asked for my help. I did what I could by an indirect approach to Sakurauchi and with other friends in the Japanese government as well as in the corridors of the Trilateral Commission, but despite our efforts the Japanese did not see the dispute in the same way as we did.

PATRICK JENKIN (Lord Jenkin of Roding) supplied the following piece entitled *On and Off the Beaten Track: A Light-hearted Reminiscence*, which covers a period of some thirty years; but still he wonders how far his understanding of Japan has advanced:-

●

Thirty years ago, Japan was virtually a closed book to all but a handful of British MPs. The horrors of the war in the Far East were still fresh in my memory. An uncle of mine by marriage had (just) survived three years on the infamous Burma Railway. My wife's uncle, the late General Sir Philip Christison Bt, one of Bill Slim's Corps Commanders, had become famous as the first allied general to defeat the hitherto apparently invincible Japanese army on land; and it was he who had taken the surrender of the Japanese in Singapore.

However, perceptions were by the late 1960s beginning to change. For me, the moment of truth came with an astonishing series of articles by Norman Macrae in *The Economist* in the 1960s. Japan was not only rising from the ashes of defeat; her economy was beginning to outpace the West's, and her exports were penetrating the world. So when it was suggested to me that, with a Labour colleague, I might visit the country to see this miracle for myself, I jumped at the chance. Eric Moonman and I wrote round to a few UK firms for financial support (in those days an unusual but entirely respectable course) and we were off. Of course, we had indicated our intentions to the Foreign Office, and the Embassy in Tokyo was forewarned of our arrival. The then Commercial Counsellor, one Hugh Cortazzi, was charged with the task of fixing up a programme, and we spent a fascinating ten days or so in the country.

Never before had I been in a country that *felt* so utterly foreign – and that was not only the language. I was starting from point zero and though we were given much help and advice, comprehension came but slowly. I have since come to realize that, on a scale of 1 to 100, a first visit of a few days may get one to point 6 or 7. It takes years of visiting and developing friendships to get any where near 20 or 25, and British friends who have lived in Japan have told me that a *gaijin* can never expect to get much beyond 50. The Japanese just think of themselves as different from the rest of us, and it is well nigh impossible for a foreigner really to become part of Japanese society. I have many Japanese friends, but in every case, friendship has only been possible because they have attuned themselves to my European culture, not because I have succeeded in tuning in to theirs.

It is important that the foreigner understands this. When the Japanese pharmaceutical regulators tell you that they have to test British drugs afresh before they can be sold in Japan, because 'Japanese rats are different', they really believe this! Of course, it is a convenient excuse for protectionism, but, underneath, in their hearts, it is true. The row over the ban on European ski exports to Japan because 'Japanese snow is different' is another example of the same mindset. And it only rubs salt in Western wounds to be told that the way round it is to try harder!

On my first visit, of course, I did not *begin* to understand this. I was a novice in a very strange world. But, with my companion, I was willing to learn. I have a clear recollection of sitting in Sir John Pilcher's drawing-roorn listening, as he strode up and down, to his enthralling account of the Meiji Revolution and of the history of the country from that event to the present day. As a former language student who had studied at Kyoto before the war, he was as close to an understanding of the Japanese character and culture as anyone I have since met, and I only wish that I had had a tape-recorder.

Other memories of that first visit that stand out include our being barred from a Japanese bar in Shinjuku with a guttural 'Japanese only!' (my companion who was Jewish called it racial discrimination, and threatened to complain to the authorities!); our first ride on the recently opened high-speed *Shinkansen* train to Kyoto; watching two elderly Japanese gentlemen bidding each other farewell for several minutes on a street corner late at night with neither being willing to be the first to turn away; standing by the lift in the New Otani Hotel when the doors opened to reveal about forty identical chattering, kimono-clad ladies on their way to a reception on the top floor; listening to the American wife of the British Council Representative in Kyoto describing the mixed nude bathing in a rural *ryokan* on the route of a three day mountain walk; visiting the Mitsubishi shipyard in Osaka, watching multiple heavy plate-cutting machines carving steel plates for giant tankers, and being, conducted round the Sony television factory in Tokyo by one Akio Morita [later Chairman of Sony, died 1999].

Meetings had been fixed with various bodies, both public and private sector, and one learned the importance of the ubiquitous name-cards. I used to arrange them in front of me in a semi-circle, with each card lined up with the corresponding person. I found it almost impossible to remember any of the names without referring to the cards. (In time, familiarity with Japanese names made it much easier to remember them.)

When we left Tokyo, we flew to Hong Kong on a JAL flight where every one of the other passengers was in a large package tour organized by Kinki Nippon Travel (it was on all their identical shoulder bags). It became clear that this was the first time that many of them had been out of the country or had even flown in an aeroplane. Although most were middle-aged, they were like astonished children rushing around the plane as they looked out of the windows, first on one side and then on the other. It was a glimpse of an unsophisticated society that was discovering that there was a world outside their own country, and we found it quite endearing (while admiring the skill of the pilot in keeping his plane on a steady course!)

An entirely different kind of visit came in 1983 when I was Secretary of State for Industry, and Hugh Cortazzi was by then the Ambassador. The main purpose of the visit was to take forward two important negotiations for inward investment projects − the Nissan proposal for a factory to build cars somewhere in Britain, and the Honda approach for a tie-up with Rover. The meetings with Nissan were friendly, but it was clear that the Chairman, Mr Kawamata, faced internal disagreements about the wisdom of investing abroad, and the firm was far from ready to move forward. Honda, by contrast seemed willing to advance matters and my role was to assure them that the deal they envisaged with Rover would have HMG's approval. At the end of a busy day of mixed fortunes, we retreated to Hugh's study for a contemplative drink and I suggested a haiku:

> We get fonda and fonda of Honda,
> But the kiss'n' with Niss'n is miss'n'.

Hugh pointed out quite rightly that it was nothing like a haiku; it had all the wrong rhythms and none of the traditional imagery of that unique form of Japanese poetry, but he was kind enough to agree that the Japanese guests who were coming to dinner at the Embassy that evening would appreciate it – and that they certainly did!

On that same visit, I had agreed to speak to a Conference in Osaka on the subject of the need to support small- and medium-sized firms. It was led by my opposite number, the MITI Minister, Sadanori Yamanaka. It was the beginning of a friendship which, I believe, was helpful some years later, when both of us were no longer ministers, in breaking the log-jam over the import of Scotch whisky. He had had a bad stroke and when I went to see him in his office, he was limping heavily. He was Chairman of his party's Policy Committee on tax reform – an essential step in freeing the market for imported spirits. In the course of a long chat, I remarked that he faced a particular problem in that there were many *shochu* producers in his own constituency (much of the opposition to imported spirits came from this very traditional industry).'You are very well informed', he said, and went on to tell me that he really wanted to understand the case for the Scotch whisky industry. I had come armed with the case, both in English and Japanese, and as I handed it to him, I asked that he might give it to the officials advising him on the issue.'No, old friend', he said; 'I will read it myself'.

Evidently he did, and the necessary tax reforms were enacted in the next budget. They proved deeply controversial, and in the ensuing election, my friend Yamanaka-san lost his seat. I treasure the beautifully turned tea caddy which he gave me at what was our last meeting. (I might add that I later read a telegram from the Scotch Whisky Association to our then Ambassador complaining that I had compromised their case by something that I had said on the radio!) Perhaps by then I had a better understanding of the Japanese character than I realized.

For four years, between 1986 and 1990, I was Chairman of what was then the UK Japan 2000 Group. This is not the place to attempt any assessment of that Group's contribution to the broadening and deepening of both understanding and contacts between our two countries. It has been the subject of many articles, notably in the Journal of Chatham House, *International Affairs*. What it did was to give me many opportunities to travel round Japan and to experience the warmth and hospitality of her people. I will end this essay by mentioning some of the experiences that stand out in my memory.

On one visit with my wife, we spent a weekend in Hakone. We stayed a night at a very smart *ryokan* overlooking Lake Ashi. We arrived after dark and were shown up to our room. The shutters were closed, the table was laid for dinner, and we were invited to change and bath before the meal was served. It was my wife's first experience of that most luxurious of Japanese experiences – the *onsen*. As we sat later in our *yukata* being served our meal, our sense of well being was magical. The table was removed, the *futon* were taken out of the cupboards and laid on the floor. and we went to sleep full of contentment. Next morning, we slid back the *shoji* and there was the lake glittering in the morning sun, and away at the far end Fuji-san raised her gleaming head.

We spent the day walking in the hills with our delightful guide and interpreter and in the evening came to another hotel. Stiff and weary, we ate and bathed and rolled into bed. Beside the bed was a card advertising a massage service. 'Yes,' I said; 'that's just what I need!' The young man arrived and I had a smooth but firm massage which eased the aches and pains.

'Me too,' said my spouse, and we rang again. This time a small, wizened, white-haired old man arrived who proceeded to subject her to what seemed to be an excruciating torture! He found every knotted muscle and stiffened joint and, to add to her agonies, I was unwise enough to fall asleep!

Next morning, it was as though she had never walked the hills. No stiffness, no aches, no creaking joints, not even any bruises!

On the same visit we were booked into a very small *ryokan* in Kyoto. Our driver could not find the house in the maze of small streets – it is not only foreigners who find Japanese addresses confusing. Eventually, he telephoned from a phone box, and the lady who answered told us to stay exactly where we were and she would come and fetch us. Her car arrived and she led ours into the maze and in due course to the *ryokan*.

We were the only guests; indeed, we were clearly regarded as very honoured guests, as we had been introduced by a former Japanese Ambassador in London; he was a particular friend of the eldest of the three ladies who ran the establishment. Her only anxiety was that we would not understand the rules of the *o-furo*. It is obligatory that one washes *outside* the bath, and rinses off all the soap *before* sinking into the hot water. We had been fully instructed on all this by various people before embarking on our journey, but it was with some difficulty that we persuaded the good lady that we did not need to be supervised! (On quite another occasion, visiting a British friend in his tiny Japanese house in Tokyo, I was conducted to the loo by the kimono-clad lady who had served our dinner: she insisted on staying to make sure that all was well! A bit inhibiting!)

Despite not understanding more than a very few words of the language, I found that I had acquired a reputation for knowing my way about. Accordingly, at different times I have led a study tour by the British Urban Regeneration Association, I led a team from the Groundwork Foundation, and I led a delegation from the Foundation for Science and Technology. With the first of these, we were being given a presentation by senior staff of the Tokyo Municipal Government on the City's urban regeneration policy. The English translation was being most expertly done by an interpreter from the Japan Travel Bureau who was travelling with us throughout our trip. It was quite technical, and at one point, an earnest lawyer in our party leant across to ask me 'Is our man getting this all right?' When I said that I did not know as I spoke no Japanese, he was shocked to realize that it really was a case of the blind leading the blind!

My most vivid memory of the Groundwork visit was when we were in Kumamoto, and we spent one evening in a Bierkeller in the city. One of our hosts had spent a year at university in Britain and had visited Edinburgh. He knew some popular songs and soon we were all singing along. Then he started on *Amazing Grace*. 'Stop, stop,' I said. 'Let's do this properly!' So we became a Pipe Band. Some were bass drones; others, tenor drones, and three of us sang the tune, trying to sound like the chanter of a set of bagpipes. The result was wonderful! The entire population of the pub stopped to listen and when we reached the end, they howled for more. So, we sang it again. Eventually, as always on these occasions, the singing became more and more chaotic, until we decided that it was time to get back to our hotel.

A complete contrast was provided when the 2000 Group were the guests of the former Governor of Kumamoto and his wife, Mr and Mrs Hosokawa. On a still, warm evening in the garden of their lovely house (the grounds contained a historic temple which dated back several centuries), we enjoyed many Japanese delicacies and many cups of saké, while listening to music played on five Japanese harps (*koto*) and two flutes. The musicians sat on the raised floor of the house open to the garden; some of us sat on the edge of the floor close to the performers; others listened from further back. The beautiful setting, the generous hospitality and that haunting music remain as perhaps the most memorable experience of all my visits to Japan.

The Kyoto *ryokan*, the Kumamoto bierkeller, and the Hosokawa party were a long, long way from the horrors of the last war. But even for those who fought, reconciliation is playing its role as peacemaker. When General Christison returned to Britain after the end of the war, he brought with him the Yamamoto family's samurai sword given to him by the defeated Japanese general. Nearly forty years later, a visiting party of Japanese veterans came to pay their respects to the aged Sir Philip. When he asked about his former adversary, they told him that both he and his widow were dead, but that he had left a son. 'Honour between soldiers has been done,' he said; and, taking the sword from where it hung on the wall, he gave it to them to take back to Japan. 'This sword should now go back to its rightful family owners', he said.

I do not know whether I have reached 15 or 20 or even 25 on my scale of understanding the Japanese; but I do know that I have been incredibly fortunate to have travelled to and in Japan so often in the last three decades, to have met so many interesting people, and to have seen so much of that fascinating country.

KENNETH BAKER (Lord Baker of Dorking) here recalls his first impressions of Japan and Japanese companies in the mid-1970s when already it was very obvious that Japan's economy was advancing full steam and companies had clear 'international' targets:-

•

I made my first visit to Japan in the mid-1970s when I was an adviser to the English software house, Logica. In those days computers were vast machines in air-conditioned offices and they were stored almost in temples served by high priests. Word processors had not been invented and mobile phones were unheard of but, nonetheless, computers had become a crucial element in all business activity. It was important to visit Japan since their government, through MITI, had a deliberate policy to expand and extend their country's technological capability in computing. They were trying to catch up with America where semi-conductor research and development had been spear-headed by the American Department of Defense.

MITI had introduced a scheme of government support for major Japanese companies to develop semi-conductors – computer chips: VLSI. I wanted to see how that scheme was working out in practice as the UK at that time had no nationally-led programme of research. The UK was slipping behind in the development of hardware which was particularly galling when it was recognized that the first working computer had operated at Manchester University at the end of the War. MITI's programme was an outstandingly successful example of how an enlightened government can help its companies to gain key positions in developing technologies, and this is exactly what they did.

I visited Fujitsu who were part of this scheme and, as this was the first major Japanese company I had visited, it was interesting to see their work and life-style. There was tremendous courtesy, great formality, but quite ruthless efficiency. They were very frank and open, explaining to me exactly what they were doing in chip development. They took me to their plant on the slopes of Mount Fuji which, by the standards of the time, had a very advanced layout and I learnt something of their employment policies. They were early users of robotic devices in the production line.

Those were the days when no one was ever laid off and when a Japanese employee had a job for life. It seemed to me to be an admirable social target but one that was not likely to withstand competitive pressures. There was a price to pay for their efficiency as I discovered the company maintained dormitories alongside the factory where their employees could live during the week. But then Japan was so clearly the top dog.

I found the attitudes amongst the senior managers absolutely fascinating. Mr Yoshikawa, who was then in charge of computer sales, looked upon IBM, their main competitor, as an 'enemy' and an enemy that had to be defeated. This feeling permeated throughout the company giving Fujitsu an embattled, marshalled sense to secure their competitive supremacy. I never came across this is in any American company. The Japanese were absolutely dedicated to winning and this attitude suffused their thinking day in and day out. It was rumoured that Mr Yoshikawa carried around with him radio tapes of Japanese martial music which he used to play to himself in his hotel at night to reinforce his spirits.

To me this was an interesting insight into the Japanese mentality. Having been defeated by America some thirty years earlier, this was Japan seeking its revenge and there was no doubt that this was a battle they were determined to win.

The other thing which struck me about the attitudes of Japanese companies in 1970s was how international they had become. They realized that they had to expand not only in America but in Europe and Asia. Fujitsu at that time did not have any major investments in the UK but wanted to forge alliances and this they did with ICL. They also forged an alliance in Germany with Siemens. The Japanese way of expanding is essentially through trust. They will not rush into a country with a huge investment but prefer to establish a personal relationship with people in an indigenous company and develop from that base. They realized they had to adapt their Japanese methods to a particular country but the country itself also realized that if it could absorb some of the Japanese methods, particularly in the production of hardware and semi-conductor technology, then they had a very great deal to learn.

VARIOUS POLITICIANS, Labour and Conservative, have referred briefly to Japan in their memoirs e.g. Lady Thatcher and Sir Edward Heath, but their references are rarely of sufficient interest to reproduce here. One exception is DENIS HEALEY's memoir (Lord Healey of Riddlesden) entitled *The Time of My Life*, published by Michael Joseph in 1989 and Penguin Books in 1990. He kindly agreed that I might quote from this book. Apart from the intrinsic interest of his comments their inclusion will, I hope, help to ensure that this chapter is not totally dominated by Tories.

DENIS HEALEY (Lord Healey of Riddlesden) who was the Labour party spokesman on Defence in 1964 visited Asia in April that year. As he explained:-

•

My tour started in Tokyo. At that time Japan was little known in Britain, and most people found the memory of its war-time atrocities a real barrier to understanding how it had changed since 1945. Indeed, the reaction to Prince Philip's attendance of the funeral of Emperor Hirohito shows that many still do. I found a country bursting with vitality. New roads and buildings were exploding everywhere through the middle of old ones. Tokyo trembled with the noise of drills and hammers. My dominant impression was of people swarming everywhere, as much in temple gardens of Kyoto as in the city streets of Osaka, and the majority were young. The gulf between the pre- and post-war generations was visible in the contrast between the older ladies. bowing low in traditional robes and sandals, and the independent young women in Western clothes, with a body language which proclaimed their independence.

The emphasis on material success reminded me of Germany; but the successful lived in conditions of unostentatious modesty, which was much more Swiss than German. Conspicuous consumption was reserved for corporate boardrooms, where the status symbol might be a drawing by Rembrandt or an etching by Picasso.

I found the language a much more difficult barrier to understanding than the cultural differences, of which so much is made. Any Japanese who could speak English well seemed to talk very good sense, and showed fewer prejudices than I had encountered in some other countries. Above all, I found the Japanese supremely rational in tackling their problems, and determined to find a consensus before taking a decision. This, in my view, is the secret of their astonishing economic success since the war.

I talked to many politicians, finding the Socialists too divided to make an impact, and the Liberal Democrats a collection of personal clienteles, rather like the Christian Democrats in Italy. Everyone was content with the 'low posture' in foreign policy; the militarism of the thirties seemed dead for good, not least because it had led Japan to catastrophe. China was seen as a potential market, not as a military rival. But the Soviet Union aroused real hostility because it had occupied the Kurile islands.

Later, Denis Healey as Chancellor of the Exchequer commented:-

Apart from Takeo Fukuda, who had served as a diplomat in London before the war, I found it difficult to make human contact with the Japanese ministers, none of whom spoke English. But I developed respect and liking for their officials, particularly those from The Bank of Japan, who spoke English well and usually talked very good sense.

The startling contrast between the social stability and economic efficiency of Japan, compared with the United States and Britain, led me to learn as much as I could about the secret of Japanese success. I accepted an invitation to the centenary celebrations of the leading Japanese newspaper, *Asahi Shimbun*, in 1979, and in 1986 became a member of the European Advisory Board of the biggest company in Japan, Nippon Telegraph and Telephones, a nationalized industry which was being privatized with glacial majesty, by the sale of ten per cent of its shares each year.

In 1979, despite my few days' visit in 1964 modern Japan was still largely a mystery to me. I had always admired Japanese art, particularly the coloured prints of 'the floating world' by Hokusai and Hiroshige, which made such an impact on French painting when they reached Europe in the middle of the nineteenth century. Post-war Japan first made its impact on me through the films of Kurosawa and the novels of Mishima. Despite his repugnant political views, Mishima seemed to me to combine the sensuous rapture of Colette and the cold rationalism of Montherlant in a disturbing cocktail which reached into the lower depths of the modern psyche. My recent visits to Japan with Edna have given us many pleasures outside the economic and political fields which were their excuse. Kyoto is an ancient city of inexhaustible beauty like Florence or Isfahan, particularly in the spring, when the cherry blossom foams pink and white among the temples. But how do we relate all this to the Japan of the compact disc and the microchip?

I had already learned as Chancellor, that consensus was the governing rule of Japanese society. No decision can be reached by government or private industry except after a long process of establishing a consensus among all who will be concerned with carrying it out. One reason why it can be so difficult to negotiate with Japanese is that once they have reached a consensus among themselves, they find it difficult to change their position by compromising with outsiders. However, faced with an external *fait accompli*, they are uniquely skilled in adapting to it by establishing a new consensus.

As Chairman of the IMF Interim Committee I had a personal experience of this when I negotiated the redistribution of IMF quotas in 1978. An hour or two after the genial luncheon at which I thought we had settled the matter, we were discussing the communiqué for the concluding press conference; I noticed a great commotion among the Japanese delegation. In the end their leader rose and said, greatly embarrassed, that he had misunderstood the decisions over lunch and wanted to re-open them. I suspected that he had just telephoned Tokyo, to be told that he had conceded too much, so I said: 'I'm afraid that the press is already assembled. We cannot keep them waiting any longer.' So that was that. I never heard another word of complaint.

The most important *fait accompli* to which the Japanese have had to adapt, however, was the constitution imposed an Japan by General MacArthur after its defeat. Carlo de Benedetti has said that the constitution of the United States was the last great political innovation of the Europeans. The constitution of modern Japan was the last great political innovation of the Americans.

At a meeting of the management consultants, McKinsey, I once attributed Japan's post-war success to its cultural and religious traditions. Not so, said Kenichi Ohmae, its Japanese board member, a nuclear physicist who has since become an international guru on business management; before the war Japan was as torn by social and political conflict as any country in the world. 'But after the war,' he said, 'we knew we faced an economic struggle for survival. So we got together and decided how to solve the problem.' In fact, only the Japanese could talk so naturally of getting together to solve a national problem.

However, without MacArthur's constitution the Japanese would not have been allowed to get together in that way; and due to him they were prevented from spending more than one per cent of their national income on defence. This limitation on its defence spending has been an essential factor in making Japan's economic strength acceptable to its neighbours. It has also helped its economic growth in many ways, particularly in steering Japanese research towards civilian objectives. Partly as a result, Japan's technological progress now exceeds that of the United States, and her national income has grown so much that, with only one per cent spent on defence, in terms of spending at current exchange rates Japan is already the third military power in the world, after the United States and the Soviet Union. It is worth recalling that the United States did not become the world's greatest military power until seventy years after it became the richest nation.

Japan's ability to adjust rationally to external shocks has been proved again and again since the Second World War. It took the so-called 'Nixon shock' of 1969 in its stride. The two OPEC oil price increases of 1973 and 1979 hit Japan harder than any other industrial country, but it adjusted to them faster than any other major power. Though its rate of growth is only half what it was in the early post-war years, it is still the highest in the industrial world. Its rate of inflation is the lowest. It has recently spent a great deal more on improving the quality of life for its own people. Central Tokyo is no longer the noisy building site I saw on my first visit; with its flowery patios and leafy pedestrian precincts it now compares favourably with the centre of most other great cities.

The country is still grossly over-populated, and excessive protection for the rice farmers means that far too little land is available for the rest of the population. My Japanese friends still define their three ambitions as 'Japanese wife, Chinese cooking, and Western-style house'. Moreover, the political system has failed to advance with the economy. The quality of Japan's politicians is far below that of its civil servants and business-men. The ruling party is an untidy collection of squabbling factions, rather like the Christian Democratic Party in Italy, and is no less open to corruption as the Recruit scandal has revealed.

Nevertheless, since these weaknesses are now widely recognized, I be-lieve they, too, will be surmounted, like the potential loss of competitive-ness caused by the rise of the yen. When the yen soared far above the value of the dollar and the Deutschmark, Japanese businessmen did not regard it as a cause for despair, as would businessmen in Britain. They regarded it as a spur to renovation, so as to add more value to their products. The rise of sterling during Mrs Thatcher's first term destroyed a fifth of Brit-ish manufacturing industry; since the yen rose, Japan has actually in-creased the share of manufacturing in its total output. Unlike Germany, it has accepted international advice by substantially increasing demand at home. It is also giving more aid to the Third World than any other coun-try, and is planning to increase its aid to more than $50 billion in the period to 1992. The shape of the nineties will depend in large part on whether Japan continues to use its economic and financial muscle with the same enlightened self-interest.

My fascination with Japan was aroused not only by its impact on the world economy. I have been equally concerned to discover whether Ja-pan's success has any features which might be transferable to Britain. One factor stood out above all others, and was very congenial to me. In every field of social and economic endeavour Japan insists on work-ing through consensus. It is no accident that since the war the only Eur-opean countries which have had a remotely comparable economic record are those which rely like Japan on consensus as the key to progress – Sweden, Switzerland, Austria and Finland. All are very much smaller than Japan, and all are neutral or non-aligned, though Sweden spends as much of her national income on defence as the average European mem-ber of NATO.

The key to Japan's postwar success has been what the leading British student of the Japanese economy, Professor Ronald Dore, has described as 'flexible rigidities'. Egoism is not the touchstone of Japan's economic morality; the Japanese do not believe that you can get an efficient society, still less a moral society, simply by the mechanisms of the market pow-ered by self-interest. Their society is a network of relations which impose responsibilities based on duty, trust and a sense of community. In the economic field these relationships apply between employer and worker, and between producer and supplier, no less than between producer and customer. A firm's obligation to provide lifetime employment to its workers is one example; if managers believe they must move out of a declining industry, they will not do so without first finding alternative work for their employees.

The rigidities imposed by this network of mutual obligations might have proved fatal to Japan in an age of international competition and rapid technological change. Japan has avoided paralysis by seeing that the state intervenes in both industry and finance to represent the residual public interest in the bargaining between organized private interests. Japan's behaviour during the stock market crash of Black October [1987] was a good example. By Western standards the Japanese stock market was more vulnerable than any other, because its stock prices were so much higher – NTT shares were actually sold that week at a price/earnings ratio of 162. But when the Ministry of Finance saw that the big institutions were all selling together, it intervened and asked them to start buying instead. They obeyed, so the Japanese market fell only half as far as that in New York, and had recovered all its losses within a few months.

Ronald Dore concluded his study of Japanese industry by pointing out that Thatcherism had failed by its own tests; despite its repeated attacks on the welfare state and the trade unions, despite its determination to end intervention in the British economy, it had not restored Britain's nineteenth-century dynamism. Would we not be wise, he mused, 'to ponder the Japanese example and ask ourselves whether we too might not do better by accepting that there is no road back to competitive individualistic atomized markets, and that we had better learn to live with organized capitalism'. I had come to similar conclusions, although I preferred the phrase 'market socialism', which is used in Sweden to describe its form of social democracy.

A BUSINESSMAN who became a politician and served as Secretary of State for Trade and Industry was DAVID YOUNG (Lord Young of Graffham). His memoir *The Enterprise Years*, published in 1990, included the following comments on trade and investment which form a bridge to the next section devoted to business relations:-

●

I decided to go on a trade mission to Japan and left in the Spring of 1988. . . The visit to Osaka and Tokyo went well as did the ministerial meetings. . .

One evening my host, Mr Tamura, the Minister for International Trade and Industry (MITI) and my opposite number, gave me dinner at an excellent Japanese restaurant. Over dinner I talked about our holding trade talks later that year in the UK. I suggested that we both invite about ten of our leading industrialists, and we could sit down over a weekend and settle any outstanding problems. There was not a flicker of interest. 'We could hold it at St Andrews,' I continued. At that I had all eyes on me.

A few weeks later, the Japanese Prime Minister was in London. We had been invited to a dinner being given in his honour at No. 10. When I arrived at the head of the line, the Prime Minister introduced me to Mr Takeshita. 'Ah, Lord Young,' he said, 'you have been giving Mr Tamura a great deal of trouble.' At this, the prime minister looked most concerned, shot me a glance, and Mr Takeshita continued. 'So many of our industrialists want to come to St Andrews with him for the golf. He simply cannot decide!'

The weekend was a great success. I heard a few days before we were due to meet that Mr Tamura had only taken up the game after my invitation. I suggested that we play as foursome partners, and the two businessmen we played against, one Japanese and one British, did their duty. With considerable effort on their part the day was saved, and they let us win. There was no doubt that the foundations were laid over that weekend for industrial cooperation between British and Japanese companies.

After the summer, I heard rumours that Toyota were considering manufacturing in Europe, with the possibility of an assembly plant in the UK and a joint venture engine plant in France. I wondered what I could do to make sure that they came here, when an opportunity was handed to me on a plate. The Nissan plant in Sunderland had doubled its production, and part of the new production was for export. They had invited me up to Sunderland on 1 October to drive the first Bluebird off the production line. A day or so before, I heard that the French were going to count these cars out of their Japanese-manufactured allocation, effectively banning them from entry into France. It was odd; only a few days before President Mitterrand had made a great speech about political union in Europe. Here, over two or three thousand cars, they were going to create difficulties.

The first car off the line was actually bound for France. My office telephoned, and as a precaution we asked them to change it for one due for the Netherlands. I flew up the night before to Leeds, and we started, appropriately enough, with an 'Opportunity Japan' breakfast, I then went to Sunderland and drove the first car off the line. I had written the day before to the Commission protesting at the French attitude. and asking the Commission to put it right. At the press conference I made a great song and dance about the right of Nissan to have its cars exported anywhere in the Community. 'Nissan is a Japanese-owned British company,' was the line I took, 'just as Ford is an American-owned British company.' I went right out an a limb, but I knew that our case was very strong indeed. Nissan had undertaken to source at least 80 per cent of parts in Europe, and were already just over 70 per cent. Who knew, or even enquired, what proportion of other cars manufactured in Europe was sourced locally? There was no actual agreement, but the cars were undoubtedly British under the general rules of the Community.

British Businessmen in Japan: Some memories of the Shell Oil Company 1952-72

PAUL BATES ● MICHAEL WINGATE ● NEVILLE FAKES

IN THE BRITISH EMBASSY in Tokyo we used, perhaps incorrectly, to regard Royal Dutch Shell as a British company. A majority of the company's expatriates were British, especially in the early days and it traced its origins to a British businessman, Marcus Samuel, who set up the firm of Samuel and Samuel in Japan in 1878 (as Neville Fakes who was Chairman and Chief Representative of the Shell Group of Companies in Japan between 1967 and 1972 has explained in his note on 'The Early Days of Petroleum in Japan' which is attached as an appendix to this chapter). It was also one of the few 'British' companies which had trained staff in the Japanese language.

PAUL BATES, who had served as a language officer during the Occupation (see Chapter 1) and had returned to Japan in 1951 before the Occupation formally ended writes:-

●

I returned to Japan in early January 1951 having spent the first two years of my service with the company in Singapore and Malaya. I arrived on a China Navigation boat in Kobe and hearing that if I stayed aboard, it would take a further week to reach my destination in Yokohama, I decided to proceed by train. At Sannomiya Station I found that I only had sufficient funds to purchase a ticket for a wooden seat on the overnight train and therefore had a rapid exposure to real life, not cosseted by the relative trappings of an occupying soldier. A memory that is still very clear in my mind is the sight of elderly men dressed in their *tanzen*, returning from visiting their family homes for the New Year, bowing deeply to Fuji-san as we passed in the clear winter light of early morning (very clear in those days!) with the snowcap brilliant white against the blue sky.

Having been away from Japanese completely for over two years, I was

IMAGES OF THE 1940s

1. Autumn 1945 - the black market in Tokyo   **2.** Bill Beasley (centre) with two American naval colleagues at their house in Yokosuka, late 1945

IMAGES OF THE 1940s & 50s

3. Peter Parker (left) and Pat O 'Neill wearing *yukata* in Atami, January 1946 **4.** GCHQ (Occupation headquarters) located at the Dai Ichi Building, Marunouchi **5.** Prime Minister Yoshida signs the San Francisco Peace Treaty, September, 1951 **6.** Shinichi Yonebayashi, long-serving member of the British Embassy staff, 1967 **7.** Oscar Morland, Col. John Figgess behind his right shoulder and Vere Redman, information counsellor, to left of Imperial Household Agency representative, prepares to present his credentials, 1959

IMAGES OF THE 1960s

8. Opening ceremony of the 18th Olympiad, Tokyo, October 1964   **9.** 40 yen stamp commemorating International Letter Writing Week, 1963   **10.** Stones from the Ryoanji Temple, Kyoto; the decade when 'Zen' was popularized in the West

11. Scene from Kurosawa's epic *Seven Samurai*, which in the 1960s inspired the making of the Western version - *The Magnificent Seven*.   **12.** The legendary 'Bullet' train came into service in time for the Olympics in 1964

IMAGES OF THE 1960s

13.

14.

15.

16.

13. British Week, September 1969. The Showa Emperor and Empress are shown an exhibit of British chinaware at the Budokan. Lady Pilcher is behind the Empress with Ambassador Shina and Sir John Pilcher between the Emperor and Hugh Cortazzi
14. Princess Margaret visits a Japanese department store accompanied by Hugh Cortazzi during British Week, September 1969
15. The new Imperial Hotel, opened in 1967   **16.** A marriage takes place on a TV game show, reflecting the growing Japanese affluence and exuberance of the early 1970s

IMAGES OF THE 1970s

17.

18.

19.

17. Hugh Cortazzi, Carmen Blacker and Duncan Fraser are interviewed by *Nikkei*, autumn 1969 **18.** One of the traditional public bath houses in Tokyo, now largely disappeared **19.** Typical street scene in Shinjuku

20.

20. An early group of British teachers at a ryokan (1978) on a Study Tour of Japan. From left to right: Colin New, Colin Cook, Graham Thomas, Brian Meadows, J. McWilliam

21.

22.

23.

21. Motorcade, central Tokyo   **22.** Tea ceremony at the Katsura Detached Palace, Kyoto   **23.** The Queen and Prince Philip at Tokyo Central Station after returning on the 'Bullet' train from a visit to Nagoya

IMAGES OF THE 1980s

24.

25.

26.

24. Prime Minister Margaret Thatcher is met off the plane by Prime Minister Zenko Suzuki and Ambassador Hugh Cortazzi, September 1983
25. Princess Chichibu watches a British craftsman demonstrating hand-painted chinaware at a Tokyo department store promotion of British goods, 1983. On the right of the princess is Elizabeth Cortazzi and David Wilkinson
26. Buckingham Palace carved in ice at the annual Sapporo ice festival, 1984

27.

28.

29

30.

27. Approach to the Fukagawa Temple, Tokyo, on the first 'lucky day' of the new year, 28 January, 1999. Courtesy *Nipponia*
28. Waiting for the next train, Shinjuku; photographed by Mike Blank
29. Memoir of Princess Chichibu, translated by Dorothy Britton at the princess's request (the first autobiography to appear in English by a member of the Japanese Imperial Family), was published by Global Oriental, 1996
30. Ambassador John Boyd greets Prince (son of Prince Mikasa) and Princess Takamado arriving for a British Embassy ball, 1995

given three months to revise at a language school in Shinjuku. As if the fallow period had given my intensive study in London a chance to mature I soon found my competence in the language improving far beyond its previous level. Perhaps the fact that I was no longer inhibited by the fraternization restrictions in the BCOF area and that my teacher included practice in the informal atmosphere of bars and the Shinjuku *yose* trying to understand the humour of the *rakugo* had some influence.

The office I eventually had to attend was on the top floor of the San-shin Building at Yurakucho which I recall provided a grandstand view of the only mass demonstration I saw in Japan, on the first May Day after the signing of the peace treaty. It was very peaceful to start with but as it made its way towards the Yurakucho crossing through Hibiya Park some more violent elements took over, resulting in the burning of a number of cars and GIs getting thrown into the Palace Moat.

Fairly early on I became a member of the Tokyo Club. It was then on the ground floor of an old red brick building that had survived the bombing. It was eventually sold and on the site is now the Kasumigaseki Building and the very superior facilities of the 'new' Tokyo Club. In those days it was far from plush. The bar was the most used facility – a stand up plain wooden bar with a fine brass rail. The members appeared to be mostly Japanese who had been educated in England before the war and Japanese-speaking foreigners – many born in Japan – as well as the remittance men who found it such a pleasant refuge from family disapproval. Two of the Japanese members I recall – one a Baron Inaba, a short man who always stood on the brass rail and had coxed his college eight at Oxford. His greeting on being introduced was – 'You can always remember my name – just think of "in a bar"'. The other one, whose name I cannot recall, had been a Viscount. He would say – 'I used to be a Viscount, now I am at a discount'.

*   *   *

In the early 1950s a couple of friends and I took advantage of Golden Week to travel from Kobe to Kochi and back. Having reached Kochi and started on the return journey we were travelling on a bus headed for Matsuyama. When making our way along an unsurfaced mountain road we came to a point where there had been a landslide and there was no way the bus could pass. The driver assured us that there would be another bus waiting for us on the other side of the blockage. It would appear that the blocking of the road was not a recent occurrence and that plans had been made by the bus company to deal with it. It was a fairly full bus and the driver instructed us all to take our baggage and walk across the blockage to the next bus, which would take us on our way

It was not an easy, or indeed particularly short, walk but probably easier for the three young foreigners with minimal baggage than for the somewhat older and more heavily-laden Japanese. When we arrived at the second bus we found the driver very relaxed with his hat off lounging in his seat smoking a cigarette. We settled into our seats and, as the other passengers started to arrive, began to complain to the driver about the poor service, having to walk so far and not getting any help with the baggage. The other passengers heard this, started nodding their heads and agreeing with each other that these foreigners had a point. The company should certainly have been more considerate towards their passengers! The volume of complaint began to rise and the driver took on a somewhat anxious look. He quickly stubbed out his cigarette, put on his hat – silence immediately descended and peace was restored!

*　　*　　*

After our marriage in Tokyo, my wife and I spent our honeymoon in the Fujiya Hotel at Miyanoshita. On the first evening while strolling through the hotel we met a couple, the man being someone whom I had met on a number of occasions in the course of business, the president of one of the larger shipping companies and a director of a company with which mine was associated. He introduced his companion as his wife. A very handsome woman, no longer young, and who behaved with all the demureness of a wife during the short time we spent having a drink together. We parted and our paths did not cross again during our stay.

Several weeks later, a delegation of staff from our associated company with whom I was involved business-wise came to my office and invited me to go out with them one evening for a drink. Not an unusual proposal and which I gladly accepted for an evening some days later. I recall that it was not the first bar we went to, but we eventually found ourselves in a very modest little establishment up a flight of fairly rickety stairs. A hostess guided us to a table and after we had been served drinks the madam of the bar came to welcome us. Despite the dim light I had a feeling of recognition and finally realized that we had met before in the Fujiya Hotel!

I found out later that the director of the company had instructed his staff to take me to that bar to ensure that I realized who his companion had been and that I would not be confused should I on a future social occasion be introduced to another lady as his wife. No sign of recognition took place in the bar and no reference was ever made thereafter to the incident. I always felt that it had been handled with great sophistication.

*　　*　　*

Doing business domestically in Japan, particularly in the medium/small enterprise sphere, an essential requirement was that one was able to perform some party-piece to maintain one's position at the many dinner parties which one attended. While a familiarity with, and if possible a competence at, the many little games that one played with the geisha was essential, the party piece really needed to be either a dance or a song. Since I have never been able to sing in tune, I eventually found that my party pieces tended to concentrate on dance.

In the mid-50s I spent a year working in the Kyushu Branch Office in Hakata. It was a tremendous experience. In those days 'before development' the island was very unspoiled. The people were most pleasant and enjoyed life to the full. A year without speaking much English was also of great benefit to my fluency in Japanese. It was also the period when I was able to spend some time improving my dance routine! Kuroda Bushi became my standard performance – particularly the *shinsaku* version.

Some years later when I was manager of the Branch in Osaka, I was invited to join one of the Rotary Clubs in the city. It was Osaka West and I had the pleasure and honour of being the only foreign member of that club. The knowledge of English among the more mature businessmen at that time was not very good and I became very useful for welcoming foreign Rotarians and engaging them in conversation during the lunches. I enjoyed my time very much – while the charitable objectives of the Rotarian movement were not strongly endorsed (charitable activity was a foreign concept in those days) no self-respecting president or senior vice-president of any company of size could be seen without the Rotarian badge in their buttonhole. Because the rules provide (in theory) for only one representative of any industry or profession to be a member of the same club, the atmosphere was extremely relaxed and lighthearted, with none of the inhibitions or status problems usually present when one met such executives in their corporate environment.

Osaka East and Osaka West clubs were both founded on the same day and each year on that anniversary they would alternately invite the other club to a party – with some entertainment! Inevitably as the years went by some rivalry developed as to the entertainment, which had to be provided by the members or their family. So on this occasion Osaka West persuaded me to perform the Kuroda Bushi (original – not *shinsaku*!). It seemed to go down quite well, albeit nerve-wracking for me, but my greatest pleasure came from the preparation which was organized by the president of one of the old family cake manufacturers of Osaka. This consisted of a number of sessions at his *machiai* being coached by his favourite geisha who also partnered me in the dance. He also insisted in having the *tanzen* and *tabi* made to measure for me. At almost two metres in height and size twelve feet, I think, Osaka East really had to try harder the following year.

MICHAEL WINGATE was another Shell expatriate who reached Japan just before the Peace Treaty came into force and stayed until 1956. In his book *Cherry Blossoms Never Change* (published privately) he gives an interesting picture of the life of a young expatriate working for Shell in Tokyo and Osaka in those days. The following are a few quotations from his book:-

•

Our life in Japan, when reviewed in retrospect, was almost perfect. I had an interesting and rewarding job, and we always lived in comfortable and well furnished houses. Food and drink were plentiful and we never wanted for anything whatever. The background to this idyllic existence was a never-ending succession of interesting and unusual experiences, which meant that literally every day had its highlights and diversions. There was never any boring routine, and we were constantly meeting and mixing with people from all walks of life and from every corner of the world.

One important such permanent piece of background of the utmost importance was the Japanese language. Very difficult for a foreigner to speak, almost impossible to read and write. But as time passed by, one automatically started to absorb it.

*   *   *

On arrival in Yokohama we lived in what was called the Bluff flats (though actually they were four Shell-owned terrace houses), located on top of a hill, overlooking Yokohama city. During this time I worked in the Shell Tokyo Branch Office and commuted daily by train from Yokohama to Tokyo.

We then moved to a very much superior house in the Negishi area of Yokohama, and I was transferred to work in the Yokohama Head Office. It was during this period that our daughter Diana was born.

We were then transferred lock, stock and barrel to Osaka in the Kansai region, some two hundred miles southwest, where we lived for the first three weeks in Shukugawa near Kobe, and I commuted daily to Osaka. We then moved ten miles or so nearer to Kobe, to a small village called Mikage, and I continued to commute to Osaka.

In April 1956, we set sail from Kobe for England, after a stay of exactly four years. David was by then four-and-three-quarters, and Diana was just two, having never been to England.

*   *   *

Well, here we are in Japan! After all these weeks of worrying, and after all the doubt that was in our minds, we now know the worst, and also the best.

We were met at the ship by the Chief Engineer from the office here, and were driven straight to our house! Most amazing we thought, because we both had visions of living in a hotel. But no, we start off straight in our own house, a huge place in comparison with anything at home.

It is one of a block of four terraced houses, not particularly beautiful from the outside, but absolutely excellent inside. There is a huge kitchen, with two sinks, gas cooker, enormous cupboards, a huge BTH refrigerator, a colossal lounge, dining-room, hall, cupboards galore, and upstairs there are three large bedrooms, a linen room, bathroom and lavatory. The house is completely furnished, with all cutlery, crockery, linen, curtains, carpets – everything except pictures and bric-a-brac.

The garden is a communal one shared by the four houses, all of which are occupied by Shell people, and all of whom we know already. In fact we have been having meals with all of them, while we get ourselves organized with shopping etc. Everyone is most kind.

Money matters are very complicated, – exchange control, income tax, etc. but as far as I can make out we can live on our cost-of-living allowance, and save all our basic salary. But whether that is in fact true, remains to be seen.

The house is one mile from the passenger docks, built in a district known as the Bluff, where all the foreign residents seem to live. Yokohama was badly damaged during the war, so everything is a complete shambles. But as far as I can gather the pre-war set-up was that the main foreign business premises, such as banks, traders, Shell etc. had their offices in Naka-ku (a district of Yokohama) . . . and it seems that all the expatriates working in these offices lived in these houses on the Bluff.

All the houses are very pleasant indeed, overlooking the city in one direction, and the ocean in the other, and life before the war must have been very easy and agreeable.

But the situation now is that many of the foreign business premises have been destroyed by bombs, though the Shell Office is still intact but in a shocking state of disrepair.

When we first arrived a few days ago, the house was completely bare, with no pictures or ornaments, and it had a rather empty and unlived-in feeling about it.

*   *   *

[They were invited next door to dinner.]
We both felt extremely tired, having had very little sleep the previous night, so we left at about ten o'clock and went to bed. We could not find any of the light switches, all of which seem to be outside the rooms, or in the most unlikely places, so we stumbled around for ages in the dark.

The following morning Doreen had to cook breakfast, much to her disgust having not done it for so long. After an awful palaver, because we could not find any saucepans or other important items required to make bacon and eggs, we finally succeeded and had it in the dining-room in great style. Meanwhile, David was in his usual place in the carrycot on the floor.

Promptly at 8.30am the servant arrived. and started to work. She is still with us and seems to be permanent, though she does not sleep in the servants' quarters, but goes home every night. Her name is Kiko-san, and she wears kimono, just like the chorus of the *Mikado*, and can speak no English whatever.

Soon after she had arrived on that first morning, another servant appeared, exactly where from we do not know, and she is now our cook! Her name is Masa-san and she lives in, using the servants' quarters at the back of the house. She is very good, she wears trousers and speaks quite a lot of English in a funny Japanese way. The result is that from our very first day we have been more or less organized from the point of view of basic living. These servants have asked for £8 per month each, which according to our friend Mary next door is the normal going rate.

*   *   *

Today, Saturday, we had lunch with Mr and Mrs Stewart. He is the Operations Manager, whom I met on my first morning in the office, and who is really my boss, or who will be when I get to the Tokyo Branch Office. They live in a simply splendid house in Negishi, about four miles from us, in a lovely area. They were both very helpful indeed and gave us a marvellous welcome. Their life-style is exactly what I had imagined expatriate overseas life to be like, and hopefully it will not be too long before we also can live like that. Lovely house, big garden, servants, waiters to serve the lunch, and all the trimmings of a gracious life!

WHEN Michael Wingate arrived in Japan in 1954 the head office of Shell was in Yokohama where he was introduced to REGGIE DIVERS, the Managing Director, 'a very senior person' as far as Michael was concerned, but his first job was to be branch engineer in the Tokyo branch office. He commuted from Yokohama to Tokyo by train on a season ticket paid for by Shell. He was driven to Yokohama station each morning with the Managing Director's secretary in her Ford Prefect as Divers himself generally worked from the Tokyo branch office. The journey to Shimbashi took twenty-five minutes. From there he walked to the Sanshin building by Hibiya where his office was on the seventh floor:-

●

In the basement of the building there is a restaurant called 'Peters' – not very Japanese-sounding, is it? but that is because it is German owned. It is very pleasant and we Shell expatriates have lunch there each day. There is a table permanently reserved for us and we have credit facilities whereby we can sign for our drinks and lunch and pay at the end of each month. In actual everyday routine, there is usually one of us out somewhere at lunch time, so on an average day there are never more than three of us at this table and we are able to swap experiences and learn from each other about life in this very strange and foreign land.

The Japanese staff have their lunch in the office and it usually consists of a small flat tin containing cold sticky rice (not unlike the paste you use with wallpaper!), and pickled turnips which they eat at their desks using chopsticks. For a drink they have Japanese green tea, which is quite nice actually, green in colour, very weak with a slightly bitter taste, which is drunk with no milk or sugar. This tea is provided at all Shell offices, depots and establishments free of charge for all the staff to enjoy at any time of the day, and whenever they like. The foreign staff, which means people like me and Freddie and Paul, have ordinary black tea with milk and sugar, at all times of the day.

And who makes and serves the tea you might wonder? We have an old woman, called 'Oba-san' (Mrs Old), who is a delightful character of indeterminate age, who spends all day serving out the cups of tea, collecting the empties and washing them up. She is always available by ringing a bell, of which there is a push button located at strategic positions throughout the entire office. When she appears in the general office, by command of the bell, the person who had summoned her will shout (Japanese people love to shout), Oba-san o-cha kudasai', which means 'Mrs Old, honourable tea please'.

The floors of the office are plain wooden boards, not very good, nor smooth, and when the Japanese drinker has consumed and finished his drink, what do you think he does with the dregs? He chucks them on the floor!

We also employ a full-time office cleaner, who is another old dear, who spends all day cleaning up the mess caused by the drinkers, sweeps up the cigarette ends thrown about by the smokers and clears up the litter left by the lunch eaters.

So that is my daily routine and as far as the job itself is concerned I am now getting more or less organized. After that first day, when I sat at my desk and had not the foggiest idea what to do, I have discovered how to tackle the immediate problems, have reorganized the Japanese engineers slightly and have cottoned on to the daily routine of Bishop and Bates with whom I have to work closely at all times.

The sort of thing I am responsible for is as follows. Bishop might decide that a new filling station should be put up in, say, Karuizawa, a town one hundred miles north of Tokyo. So he would ask Bates to find out what the probable sales would be and to seek a suitable dealer to operate the proposed station. Let's say that Bates finds a suitable dealer and discovers that the sales would be terrific, and that Bishop says, 'OK let's proceed'.

That is where I come into the picture, because my task is to find a suitable piece of land, no doubt entailing a visit to the site, accompanied by a Japanese legal expert. I have to arrange the purchase or lease and employ a contractor to design and build the filling station. I would then be responsible for the supervision of construction of the building and generally following the job through to completion. There are about thirty such projects in hand at the moment so that you can understand that I shall be very busy indeed when I get started.

*   *   *

Last night we were invited out to dinner with the big boss, Reggie and his wife Myla Divers. They live in the biggest and best house in the Shell Negishi compound and their lifestyle is something which I have only read about in books or seen on films. We were invited for 7.30, so we had a drink before starting off, in order to get some Dutch courage. We arrived at the mansion at 7.45 which is apparently the correct time to arrive on such occasions.

There were about fourteen other guests, mostly Shell people but there were also one or two British Embassy people, a Danish couple and a Standard Oil couple. The house has a huge entrance hall, an enormous staircase, a massive lounge, library and dining-room. Passageways and corridors galore lead to distant parts of the house.

The dinner was very formal with everyone in evening dress and we sat around for about an hour drinking cocktails. Eventually we were summoned to the dining-room by the Japanese manservant, who bowed graciously and said in excellent English, 'Ladies and Gentlemen, dinner is served'.

After the meal was finished all the ladies disappeared to Myla's bedroom, and the men stayed in the dining-room drinking port and discussing business and local affairs. When we had eventually reassembled in the drawing-room, it was eleven o'clock and we then proceeded to play party games – like charades, acting words, spelling things backwards, etc! This went on until about two o'clock in the morning. It was quite good fun but went on far too long, and when we finally arrived home we were both worn out!

SHORTLY AFTER he had settled in, Michael Wingate was sent on a visit to the Kansai accompanied by Dudley Sykes Thompson who came to fetch him by car:-

•

So we set off, along the Bluff road, down Daikan Zaka to the Moto-machi, over the creek, along Kaigan-dori and up to Yokohama Central station on the Tokaido main line, the car rattling over the never-ending potholes, and seeming to shake itself to pieces. But apparently cars in Japan in 1952 had never known what a nice smooth road was like. How they kept going was a complete mystery to me

We drove into the old-fashioned almost Victorian station entrance, and were met by an army of willing porters all vying with each other to carry our 'baggages' as they say. Putting our cases on their heads and running, before us with little steps, like the 'Three little maids from school' in Gilbert and Sullivan's *Mikado* to Platform No.2.

'I was interested in what you were saying about Japan being the best posting that you can have with Shell' I said [to Dudley].

'Well it is quite true. East or West Africa are no doubt all right in their way, but there is no culture. They are colonies, and contribute very little of their own. Singapore and Hong Kong are very exciting places, but again they did not exist even a hundred-and-fifty years ago. No, you are very fortunate to be selected by Shell to come here to a real nation, with a history as long and as interesting as ours, and you cannot fail to enjoy it.'

*   *   *

We left Yokohama at 9 pm and reached Osaka at 7.30 the next morning, the distance being about 350 miles. I slept very well, surprisingly, and woke at 6 o'clock to see the Japanese countryside whizzing past my window. This was my very first sight of the real country and it is very, very quaint indeed. It is all extremely tidy and neat, almost like a child's toy farm and every inch of the land that can be cultivated, is cultivated. . .

I had a very rewarding week in the Osaka Branch Office, spent mostly with Bill Drakeford, and sitting beside him at his desk, while he explained the whole set-up to me.

He was an extremely interesting character, about forty years of age and came from somewhere in Surrey, although he was born in Shanghai, where his father had a job in the Customs Service. He joined Shell in 1929 and no doubt because of his China background, was posted to the Shell Company of China, where he spent all his time in the head Office in Shanghai, a home from home!

But like so many others whom I would meet in the next four years, his whole life caved in and collapsed when the war came along. He was interned in Shanghai when the Japanese invaded and spent the whole war behind bars because he got caught up in illegal radio transmitting of messages to ships of the American navy. In fact, he told me that he was very lucky not to have been executed by the Japanese.

*   *   *

On the third day we went on an upcountry trip to a distribution depot at Oji, a small market town, about twenty miles away. We went in the office car with a driver and once again we were bouncing and sliding along the most atrocious roads imaginable. The car was an Austin A90, quite large, and it suffered the most terrible battering.

We slowly emerged from the crowded and noisy streets of Osaka and found ourselves driving through what was to become to me typical Japanese countryside. . .

We eventually reached Oji depot and were met by the Manager, a scruffy little man who needed both a shave and a haircut. He seemed to have very little work to do, and was gardening when we arrived. These depots merely consisted of a few oil tanks, one or two sheds, a railway siding and some tank lorries. Their role in the Shell system was to receive petrol and kerosene by rail tank wagon, store it in the tanks and then distribute it by lorry to the local filling stations and farms. All very simple and unsophisticated but still done today all over the world, although usually in larger depots of much greater storage capacity.

MICHAEL WINGATE was told by Divers that he should get a car, but in those days this presented many difficulties:-

We had never had a car since our arrival in Japan, because of the expense, complications, and difficulties. There was no such thing as a Japanese car in 1953 (strange as it may seem to someone reading this in the 1990s), except for a horrible little box on wheels called a Datsun. The only way of getting a car, therefore, was to import a new or second hand one from Hong Kong, or to buy one from a departing service- or businessman. This meant spending at least £1000 (a huge sum in 1953), if importing from Hong Kong. The alternative was waiting patiently for someone to leave and hoping to pick something up for about £500.

Eventually, he managed to buy one for £400 from a colleague who had returned to Britain, but this was the easy part. He had not taken account of Japanese bureaucracy:-

In order to transfer a car from one owner to another in Japan in 1953, it was necessary to go through a complicated bureaucratic procedure, by filling in umpteen forms and certificates, all in Japanese. Affixing to one of them, believe it or not, a tissue 'rubbing' of the chassis number, and engine number!

This was intended to substantiate the application, and to prove that the car really did exist, and it meant that someone (me), had to lie underneath the car in a most awkward position, to locate the number, and then to try and make a 'rubbing' of it. The same exercise had to be performed with the engine number, which was extremely difficult because engine numbers are invariably covered in grease and dirt! No wonder that the Japanese were so good at keeping records of equipment transfers from depot to depot during the war. I should add here that in my subsequent career with Shell, involving postings to many countries, some difficult, and some easy in their bureaucratic procedures, I never again came across that stupidity!

The whole process took three weeks and could only be effected by a Japanese member of the Head Office staff, who understood the system and could complete the forms. A bribe of one hundred American cigarettes was almost mandatory and the licensing office supervisor always expected to be given a bottle of Japanese Suntory whisky (the local brand of Scotch whisky, made in Kyoto, and surprisingly drinkable).

Meanwhile, the car stood stationary on the driveway of No. 3 Negishi and I spent many evenings polishing it up ready for the big day when the licence was issued.

But the great day finally arrived! I received the official papers and the official number plates. With great ceremony I bolted the plates on to the front and back of the car, to replace the existing plates, which had to be returned, accompanied, as the reader may guess, by three official forms of 'Renunciation of Registration'.

The whole family, including David, Masa-san and Kiko-san, then witnessed me getting into the car, starting up, backing into the service road, and then driving proudly up to our front door.

The Wingates had now well and truly arrived! We lived in a beautiful Negishi house with a 1949 Austin A40 parked outside the front door, a lovely garden and two good and loyal servants.

But did we have driving licences? – No!

How did we get them? Well we did in due course and the reader is invited to imagine the procedures involved! However complicated you may construct them, you will never be able to surpass the Japanese for their sheer brilliance of really professional bureaucracy!

BUT THAT WAS not the end of the story. When he was transferred to the

Kansai, the registration process had to be repeated. Fortunately for WINGATE, Uyeno Unya who acted as Shell's agents did all the work for him and Shell paid the costs.

When his wife was expecting their second child an unexpected problem arose:-

•

We had some more high drama yesterday. The doctor said that Doreen was anaemic and must have some blood immediately. 'Did I have the right blood group?' The answer is that I do not have the same group as Doreen, so he suggested that I approached some of our friends to see if they could help out. There is no such thing as a blood bank here! So I discussed the problem with friends and they suggested that I should seek the help of the Hullands – he is with Tokyo Babcock, and she is a nurse. I went round to their house, quite near us, but was told by the servant that '*Donna-san, Oku-san dete imasu enkai*.' Which means that they were out at a cocktail party. 'Where?' I said.

I eventually discovered that they were at an early evening cocktail party at a house a couple of miles away, at the residence of the British Consul. The matter was most urgent, according to the doctor, so I decided that I must go straight to the house and see if I could find them to ask for their help. To cut a long story short, I gate-crashed into this party (I knew some of the guests who probably thought that I had been invited!). I spoke to Beryl Hulland, who was deep in conversation with someone, and she was most kind and helpful. She said that Jimmy, her husband, had the same blood group as Doreen, and that she was sure that he would oblige. So there and then she rooted him out and luckily he had not had too much to drink, and he said 'Yes OK I will do it, but when?'

'Well, now!' I said, 'it seems to be urgent'.

So off we went to the hospital, and in a very dramatic manner Jimmy was put in a bed beside Doreen and connected up with pipes and wires, and the transfusion took place there and then. When it was all over, Jimmy went back to the cocktail party, and Doreen fell asleep!

*   *   *

When I look back on those days of the early 1950s it never ceases to amaze me how primitive communications were between Japan and England. There was air mail, but that took at least three weeks, because the air journey alone took a week as the aircraft spent every night on the ground, whilst the passengers stayed in luxurious hotels. Sea mail took three months. No Fax, no computers, no television and both business and private communications had to rely on these traditional, old-fashioned and antiquated methods.

THE SEMI-COLONIAL approach of the immediate post-war years had to change as the Japanese economy moved into top gear. Shell as a major world oil company was important to Japan not least because the Japanese were increasingly dependent on imported energy to sustain industrial development. But the Ministry of International Trade and Industry (MITI) was determined to keep the international majors on a short leash and ensure that Japanese oil companies gained an increasing share of the market. NEVILLE FAKES who became Chairman and Chief Representative of the Shell Group Companies in Japan in 1967 (staying until 1972) faced some difficult issues in developing Shell's business in Japan. Here, he describes his life and work in Japan:-

•

Immediately after World War II, my joining the Shell Petroleum organization in Australia gave promise of an international career in oil. Shortly afterwards, however, my hopes were somewhat blunted by being told in an interview with a senior Shell executive in London along with several other young graduates, that '... you chaps can read and write, perhaps some of you reasonably well, but now we are going to introduce you to the real world, in particular the world of oil'. This rather dry, sardonic introduction was daunting to some but, I must admit, to me was a challenge of considerable dimension.

After a year's training in the UK and two years experience in India, my transfer to Venezuela for a period of twelve years afforded the stimulating opportunity to acquire 'hands-on' familiarity with all major operational activities of the fully integrated Shell organization there.

A move to Singapore in 1961, as President and Chief Representative of the local Shell Group companies in the region gave us our first real look at the Far East. There, during our seven-year stint, we were to build a refinery in world record time, another in Malaya, initiate the development of the promising Sarawak oil fields, and steer the existing Brunei operation through the vicissitudes of the sensitive Malaysia negotiations.

Local governments were cooperative and understanding but none more so than in Singapore where trust between us developed quickly to the point where on the strength of a handshake with the Minister of Finance (Dr Goh Keng Swee), I would commit millions of dollars worth of materials etc. towards, say, the refinery project, much to the consternation of Shell's 'armchair' legal men who tried to insist on paperwork first.

How very different in Japan!

∗ ∗ ∗

At the London Head Office briefing prior to taking up residence in Tokyo, I was told that Shell Sekiyu had retained the services of an 'adviser', a senior Japanese of some standing with considerable local influence, of international reputation and who spoke fluent English. His name, Jiro

Shirasu. [For a different view of Jiro Shirasu see Chapter 24 below. Ed.]

This appointment, I was assured, had been necessary because of Shell's serious and prolonged differences on joint Board representation, policy and attitudes with the Japanese company Showa Sekiyu allocated to Shell as its refining partner. These problems, I was told, were to be resolved without delay. At the time, I recall idly wondering why Japan was so different that Shell needed a local adviser.

On my arrival in Tokyo in 1967, I was greatly disappointed to find our local organization was stagnating. An initial inspection revealed an urgent priority to upgrade certain refining facilities, inject finance, train operators abroad in new technology, improve refinery outputs to better balance market offtakes etc. etc. It was also clear that a first step was to develop a more understanding dialogue between the 50/50 refining partners so that Shell's representation on the joint Board could be improved from its two out of a total of ten. This apparently simple objective proved harder to achieve than originally thought.

My initial impression of our adviser at our first meeting was most favourable. Here was a gentleman of presence, of considerable charm and in spite of obviously not having achieved a great deal already in helping to solve Shell's local problem, gave the impression of wanting to cooperate with the new management. I felt reassured.

At subsequent meetings I felt increasingly dismayed at his meagre knowledge of the international oil industry. My many questions as to how Shell could quickly resolve its local problems and help Japan move forward in the oil business were avoided. However, my further queries as to why Shell were given only two out of ten Board seats did arouse his interest. Surprisingly, his explanations were not only fatuous but bordered on insult as he denigrated the efforts we were making to secure a more reasonable Board presence in accordance with what is considered normal. After all, we argued, the joint Company was quite prepared to accept Shell's financial and technical support. Why, therefore, did this not extend to significant voting rights? Surely this was unfair, even in Japan.

I began to feel uneasy about the role our adviser was adopting. Why was his behaviour so frustrating? Did it lie in some anti-British feeling? Not having had to deal with an adviser in my previous posts, I had naïvely assumed that such a person would be prepared to understand his employing company's point of view and to point out where we had gone wrong in the local context and to suggest how then to proceed.

Time-consuming and exhaustive meetings with Showa (none of which was attended by our adviser) failed to make headway. Finally, because our vote on the joint Board amounted to nothing, a new President was suddenly appointed after a quick overthrow of the previous incumbent. This new President could not be supported by Shell not only because of our perceived deception in the manner of his appointment but also because of his inexperience in oil matters. The intrigue surrounding our adviser now came into full focus.

My suspicions regarding his integrity in the way he conducted this affair were amply confirmed by a friendly outside source explaining that Shirasu had been obliged to meet a substantial favour to a long-time friend. Whether or not this was true, I cannot say, but circumstantial evidence would seem to confirm it. I confronted Shirasu with an accusation of treachery towards the company employing him and terminated his 'services' on the spot.

Needless to say, throughout this episode I kept MITI fully informed, principally through Mr Morozumi, not because I sought MITI's help which I well understood they could not give, however sympathetic they might feel, but because this episode was a factor of some significance in the progress of the oil industry in Japan.

At this point I must stress Shell's excellent relations with MITI. Invariably, I found Mr Morozumi received, with unqualified support, my suggestions for the energetic development of Shell's part in the development of Japan's oil industry. I could not have had a more satisfactory and stimulating relationship. On leaving Japan some five years later I was awarded the Order of the Sacred Treasure, Third Class, for outstanding services to Japan's oil industry.

The unsatisfactory Showa situation proved to be an impediment for some time but finally a realignment of joint priorities together with a decisive plan of action was eventually put in place. However, vestiges of the uneasy truce surfaced occasionally in the securement of a resilient competitive position in the industry. All in all, it was a frustrating and exhaustive time.

Even so, I did not feel completely isolated or alone in facing these problems. Though I had my own staff adviser, a Japanese of senior years, I felt the need to seek 'outside' counsel from one who could be expected to see our international point of view. So, in those early days, to avoid stepping on sensitive toes and to steer clear of unchartered waters, I was glad of the opportunity to discuss certain issues with the then Commercial Counsellor at the British Embassy, Hugh Cortazzi, later Sir Hugh as British Ambassador to Japan. As a fluent Japanese speaker, interpreter and scholar, together with his wide understanding of business values in many overseas diplomatic posts, his valuable guidance on procedure was greatly appreciated.

* * *

In order to understand the problems which we in Shell faced some knowledge of the history of oil in Japan is necessary. I should have preferred to include the basic background within my narrative, but as this is essentially a personal account of my time with Shell I have set out the facts as I see them in an Appendix.

Japan needed increasing quantities of energy for its fast developing industries. Along with other major oil companies Shell had developed a process by which natural gas could be liquified to a relatively small volume of liquid and transported in tankers. Early in 1968 I was able to approach MITI with the assurance that because natural gas was becoming available from the Sarawak/Brunei Shell oilfields in Borneo, and if satisfactory renegotiations could be finalized without delay, LNG could be delivered by Shell to Japan in less than three years. MITI were at first sceptical but Mitsubishi, Shell's partner, had secured considerable interest from several of Japan's large electricity-generating companies. Serious negotiations were started. Six tankers, were ordered together with supply and receiving facilities. In 1971, well ahead of schedule, the first shipments of LNG arrived safely in Japan.

The Japanese naturally hoped to find indigenous supplies of hydrocarbons. It seemed possible that there might be hydrocarbon deposits below the fairly shallow sea-bed in the western part of the Japan Sea in the vicinity of Tsushima island and the Korea Strait. To explore this possibility Shell and Mitsubishi formed on a 50/50 basis the Nishi-Nihon Oil Search Co. with Shell as the operator. We faced various legal and administrative problems which I have described in the Appendix. These were eventually solved and our joint venture company received permission to search for oil on the continental shelf in the vicinity of Tsushima. Sadly, after more than a year of diligent search at considerable cost all exploration drilling proved fruitless and was abandoned.

*   *   *

Post-war Japan has received enormous benefits from international technology of all types, processes, techniques, materials etc – all freely given. Industry personnel have been trained abroad and as far as the oil business is concerned, to their credit have responded well back in their own country. Many of the older Japanese oil executives, however, as well as certain sections of government in the 1960s maintained their suspicions – some even resentment – of foreign oil activity in their country even though, reluctantly, they had to admit there was no alternative and that the potential benefits were huge and virtually without cost.

At that time, it seemed difficult for many senior people to realize and accept that because Japan had no indigenous crude oil, their country was, of necessity, in the international oil business and dependent on other nations. It was therefore subject to the relevant dimensions of availability, operation, supply, finance etc. Such an attitude had held back foreign investment in the early years and in some cases led to certain oil majors looking askance at Japan, particularly when shareholders' interest might be better served by activity in other countries.

It is, however, fair to say that Japan's early 'special case, special treatment' mentality that indicated a lack of maturity in its exposure to international trade has now diminished considerably, though protectionist policies still exist in some quarters.

*   *   *

Shell had a shareholding in Mitsubishi Yuka (petrochemicals). Relations with them and with Mitsubishi Corporation as our Japanese partner (other than refining), were excellent. Not only were they internationally minded but their top management was skilled and competent, approachable and receptive, pragmatic and rational. I cannot speak too highly of them.

If a consensus on some particular issue could not be reached quickly by our respective work departments, a quiet word of explanation and recommendation from me personally as Chairman of Shell Group Companies in Japan to Mr Fujino, Chairman of Mitsubishi Corporation usually resolved the matter by his merely lifting the phone and issuing a command. Together by this means we 'cut corners short' in committing millions of dollars in our joint enterprises. Above all, he appreciated the immense value of time. If our managements were bogged down in lengthy and largely spurious arguments, it meant that very swiftly a competitive advantage was being lost.

Initially, there was a problem. On my arrival in Tokyo in 1967, I was most disappointed to find that Shell were being housed in cramped downtown quarters. They were totally inadequate for the greatly expanded operation that I had been directed to establish. The building in which our offices were located belonged to Mitsubishi and in the absence of any suitable alternative from them, I decided to break the lease and take adequate space in Mitsui's newly constructed Kasumigaseki Building. All hell broke loose. What a fuss! Mitsubishi threatened a legal challenge and relations deteriorated badly. Feeling sorry that my precipitate decision had caused a serious loss of face to the Mitsubishi man in charge, I made a courtesy call to his office to say I was sorry. Imagine my amazement when, after my apology, with tears in his eyes and a double handclasp he thanked me profusely and promptly withdrew the court action. From that moment on, relations with Mitsubishi prospered rapidly – an early lesson on how to do business in Japan!

Because Shell was the first tenant in Mitsui's new building, we were given the choice of floors and chose four at the 'node' position thereby minimising the disturbing effect of Tokyo's frequent earth tremors.

All my correspondence with MITI, MOF and other Government departments was translated first by a Japanese translator but then vetted by our ex-Jesuit Japanese scholar, one John Walker. He would check on my rather straightforward phraseology so that he could be sure that 'the right shade of meaning would be built into the letter.' Having dictated my draft letter in English in the early morning it would be typed in twenty minutes and the translators would spend half a day re-checking to ensure the 'feel and intent' were correct. By this time it was midday. The typist would then take most of the afternoon in setting it up with five copies on rice paper (a mistake on rice paper meant starting again because it cannot be rubbed out). Finally, my signature in a special book was needed to release my registered 'chop' from the security safe so that my secretary could validate the letter before handing it to a courier standing by to deliver it. A whole day for one letter. I used to chafe and smoulder at the delay! Roll on the word processor.

Having done well in Hindustani, Spanish and Malay in previous postings, I found Japanese strange and quite difficult. My Japanese language teacher was an elderly lady who, I found out later, for reasons of her own, preferred to use the feminine honorific for certain words. My innocent use of such phrases, especially at geisha dinners, would reduce everyone to smirks and laughter at my 'limp-wristed' vocabulary until I realised what was wrong.

Though my spoken Japanese was limited, with Naganuma's books as my bible and the assistance of several of my top Japanese staff, I was able to learn enough to give New Year and other speeches to gatherings of dealers (retailers) in our seven major centres as well as outlining policy changes, new developments, objectives etc. at staff functions. Always however, where necessary in business negotiations with Japanese companies, my interpreter was close at hand. From previous experience in other areas, I made great efforts in the early days to understand the translation of numbers and figures so that any later 'misunderstandings' could be avoided.

To know what really is going on in Japan is difficult for foreigners. The obliqueness of language, the enigmatic smile, the impassive body language, the tendency to say 'no' when 'yes' is expected, the reluctance of working level individuals to make the smallest positive observation until group consensus had been reached, even the off-putting energetic note taking of one's words by henchmen at meetings, the seemingly endless translations of simple and short English sentences requiring an answer – all this and much more prove formidable and exhaustive barriers to rapid progress. I used to liken such processes to a game of golf, i.e. a game of successive approximations.

It is at golf matches however that unexpected gems of information can be gathered. Under such less 'spot-lighted' conditions, one's Japanese partners seem more prepared to let their hair down.

An early lesson (from Mitsubishi), was that business decisions in Japan could depend on the careful consideration of any personal relationships involved.

Sometimes I used to feel that in order to comprehend how certain Japanese business decisions are reached, it was as if say, in a hi-fi circuit, a light would come on in a completely unexpected place when the button had been pressed. For a foreigner to try and trace the human circuitry involved is an impossible task.

One quickly realised too, that at geisha evenings, provided one stayed four or five cups of saké behind one's friends, much 'real' information could be gleaned by an attentive and appreciative ear.

My inclination to use a limited knowledge of the Japanese language suffered many a fracture but it was also amusing to observe the mishmash of English by some of my Japanese colleagues, particularly where prepositions were involved and where the 'ough' sequence was mis-pronounced in the words that carry it.

* * *

Although my family and I had previously visited Japan on holiday and had come away most impressed with the variety and excellence of Japanese handcrafts, five years residence in Tokyo and visits to almost every prefecture in the country gave us further opportunities to admire the wide spectrum of crafts ranging from Shoji Hamada's pottery to basket-weaving, flower-arranging, paper-making, lacquer work and many others.

To record and publicise this unique range of handcraft skills, Shell contracted with the Ian Mutsu organisation in Tokyo to produce a film that would show the various masters at work and reveal details of their exceptional talent. The film, entitled *Nihon no Kokoro* (The Heart of Japan) was dubbed in both Japanese and English and was widely shown not only in Japan but distributed to many Shell Group companies throughout the world.

There was considerable interest by 'golf mad' Japanese players in a series of films by the Shell Film Unit in London entitled 'Shell's Wonderful World of Golf' in which a local professional at his own course would play an internationally known celebrity.

Early in 1972, Shell Japan co-sponsored with the British Council and the Embassy, a visit by the Royal Shakespeare Company from Stratford. The interest in Shakespeare in Japan is quite extraordinary and large theatres were filled to capacity at every performance. Some Japanese students, whilst writing and reading English quite well but lacking some understanding of the spoken word, would use a small hand torch in the theatre to illuminate the written play in their hand thereby following the dialogue on the stage.

I had a long time interest in the works of Charles Dickens and a considerable collection of his first editions. My wife and I would organize a
'Dickens reading' evening from time to time at our Aobadai house to
which we invited several Professors of English from local universities,
interested friends and always the British Ambassador.

Somewhat resembling Mr Pickwick in stature, the then British Ambassador Sir John Pilcher would regale us with one of the great pieces
from the *Pickwick Papers*. Other readings would follow but those from
some of the Japanese professors, read in Japanese, were especially interesting. Pip's encounter with the escaped convict Magwitch in *Great Expectations* sounded not unlike Kabuki with strange sounds issuing!

The building of many ocean-going Shell tankers in Japanese shipyards
also gave us a unique opportunity to present a different face to the Japanese public. The launching of these tankers was always an occasion for
much fanfare. During the late 1960s and early 1970s, Shell's management
in Tokyo would donate one or more seeing-eye dogs for each of its tankers off the slip-way. Shell supported the British Embassy's efforts to
persuade local authorities that such seeing-eye dogs be allowed with
their owner on public transport. It took years to soften the opposition
of the authorities concerned.

The delivery of oil products to major consumption/distribution centres of Japan had to be made largely by coastal tanker, thereby avoiding
over-congestion of the country's busy road network. Such small tankers
operating in coastal waters adjacent to fishing grounds, oyster beds and
nori (sea-weed) productions involved the ever present risk of collision or
other mishaps that could result in a devastating oil pollution of the
waters. As domestic consumption of oil grew apace, Shell in particular,
with experience from operations in other countries took early steps to
formulate strict operating procedures, trained masters and crew in emergency measures and stored special crisis materials and equipment at several central locations in case of urgent need.

In 1972, in the Japan Sea near Niigata, a coastal tanker went aground
during bad weather. As oil began to seep from damaged seams, our
emergency crews sped into action. While floating barriers were raced into
position to enclose the leakage, worsening by the hour, an extra emergency apparatus was air lifted from Holland and in sixty hours was in
position.

After some anxious days, the spillage was satisfactorily mopped-up
and a potential disaster averted. The nearby fishing and *nori* areas were
protected and escaped damage.

*   *   *

Relations with unions were generally good with a sense of discipline and responsibility on both sides leading to respect for each other's position. On one occasion at Tokyo's main airport, after initial negotiations had failed to resolve a contentious issue, the Shell aircraft refuellers decided to strike for 24 hours in protest, but before the strike began the refuellers made arrangements with another oil company to supply Shell airline contract customers on Shell's behalf for the duration of the strike. In this way, the airline customers were supplied with fuel and their schedules maintained. The philosophy of the Union was that the dispute was a private affair between it and the Company and was not the fault of the customer. So why should the customer suffer? Such behaviour is most effective in moderating previously unyielding positions and the disagreement was soon settled amicably.

* * *

Prior to 1973, crude oil prices were relatively modest but when OPEC countries suddenly increased their prices by rises of over 100%, the resultant 'oil shock' dramatically altered every aspect of the oil business from exploration activity to market offtake.

Every nation, every business and every individual was now active in seeking ways and means of reducing consumption of oil products. The USA improved its energy efficiency by 25% over the years 1978-85 and its oil efficiency by 32%. Japan did even better with 31% and 51% respectively.

* * *

I always regarded my wife Audrey as my best PR assistant during our Tokyo days because in her usual energetic way, she was tireless in promoting Shell's local image. Apart from countless dinners at our house for Japanese friends, business acquaintances and visiting 'firemen', she organized annual tulip viewings for charity in our large garden where thousands of bulbs from Niigata had been planted in preparation. We averaged 300-400 people per night for four successive nights welcoming them with substantial finger food and drinks.

Another of her successes was the regular invitations to our house for the Japanese wives not only of senior but also fairly junior staff. We were astounded to find soon after our arrival that few such wives had ever before been invited to the No. 1 house.

On our first Christmas in Tokyo (and at all subsequent Christmases) the children of senior staff and wives were also invited to share our Christmas tree. This too broke new ground.

To familiarize herself with various aspects of Japanese art and culture, Audrey was active in a ladies' group 'Nadeshiko-kai' besides taking the opportunity to study the Japanese floral art of *ikebana* (Sogetsu), *bonsai*, *sai-*

kei, brush-painting, attending lectures and demonstrations. Her early 'kitchen' Japanese improved rapidly to the point where little escaped her during such excursions.

*   *   *

The bad times of frustration and disappointment in business, of annoyance and even resentment at the wearying circuitous and seemingly devious adventures required to reach a rather obvious objective, were balanced by the good times – an occasional few days of relaxation at our Karuizawa hideout travelling to and from Tokyo by the 'soft wind' (*Soyo-Kaze*) express, golf at the splendid courses including the annual MITI-Shell game at Hakone, visits with our daughters to the snow festival at Hokkaido, skiing at Teine Olympia, a weekend at the Kawana hotel on the Izu peninsula, visits to the Kyoto/Nara temples and gardens, fishing for *ayu* at Gifu, hot spring baths, a climb of Mount Fuji (also with our daughters) to see the sunrise and many such.

Our five years residence in Japan was one of hard work, many a frustration, many moments of uplift and exhilaration, but when all is said and done, a most rewarding and enriching experience.

British Businessmen in Japan: Developing Trade Relations

LEW RADBOURNE • DUNCAN FRASER

LEW RADBOURNE first went to Japan with the British Commonwealth Oc-cupation Force (BCOF) (see Chapter 1) and returned in 1949 as a junior expatri-ate with Dodwell and Company. He recalls those early years:-

•

D odwell and Company was a British trading firm which saw its origins in Japan during the Meiji era. Starting in Tokyo, which even then was sprinkled with debris-strewn bomb-sites and whose population was in a very deprived state, a comparison of expatriate conditions with those prevailing now is dramatic.

The cost-conscious management of British companies re-opening in Japan post-war, before profitability could be safely assumed as likely, seemed to me to start with their attitude to young bachelors. Often bil-leted with a married couple in the same firm until such time as escape could be contrived, the next best would be to share a mess with others in the same or other companies or small 'digs' in the Western (or Japanese-style) part of a Japanese house. Accommodation was normally rented although a number of houses were purchased at prices which even in today's depressed Japanese property market were ludicrously low. One of the classics must be Dodwell's purchase for a few 'thou' in 1949 of a 1000 *tsubo* (3,300 sq. m) plot to house one of the joint General Managers. I helped with interpreting during the purchase negotiations. The property was subsequently sold in 1988 for 57.1 million pounds!

During the first four-and-a-half years' service at Dodwell, I lived in a number of different abodes, one of which – a pleasant little house in Azabu near the Tokyo Tennis Club – had been bought for use by a mar-ried couple. When, however, the wife was thought to have become preg-nant and a survey of the property revealed that it was off its foundations and likely to collapse if jolted by a severe earthquake tremor, senior management immediately ordered Radbourne and one other bachelor to move in to avoid a waste of living space until other arrangements could be made.

We were subsequently moved to a large Western-style house in Oi-ma-chi, which the company rented, built pre-war in a style which would have done any Victorian proud as the owner's research had obviously been confined to English interior designs as illustrated in late nineteenth-century journals. The family who owned it had moved out of Tokyo during the war and left the property unoccupied and unheated for some years although all the heavy furnishing and drapes, including antimacassars, remained in situ. Five young bloods took up residence in what inevitably became known as 'Mildew Manor'. With variations in the mix, the hard core of the quintet were John Garrett, Russell Main, Desmond Reid, Pat Deveson and the author – if there had been an equivalent of Alcoholics Anonymous in Tokyo in the early fifties we would have driven them to despair!

*   *   *

With the yen at ¥1008 to the pound, a starting salary of £500 p.a., with allowances, enabled expatriates to live at an adequately comfortable standard, run a small car and employ a servant. When local allowances ceased during home leave (initially six months within a five-year contract), a protracted period during which to amuse oneself at home was not financially viable. Thanks to limited air travel facilities this meant that with a journey of five-six weeks, about half of the leave period could be spent on board a passenger ship or cargo vessel with the fare paid for by the company, which included board and lodging (drinks – at one's own expense, of course – were cheap). Eventually, a six-week per annum home leave pattern evolved for most expatriates with air travel essential not only because of the shorter leave period, but also because the availability of sea passages was reduced to virtually nil with the advent of containerized shipping and higher crew costs.

Emoluments for expatriates also improved enormously with the vital need to reduce the number of these in order to cut overheads. In 1950 the expat. staff ratio of Dodwell Japan was 20% (30 of 150 total staff). In the mid-eighties with the growth in business and the training and development of Japanese staff, the percentage of expats was a mere 1% (15 out of a total of 1,500 employees).

Marriage during the first contract period of five years was tacitly not allowed – after all, a married couple would require separate accommodation, a married allowance and usually a child/education allowance. Not expressed, but certainly there, was a view that young men on their first posting would probably fall in love with a Japanese girl-friend, as eligible daughters of expat families of marriageable age and other European spinsters were in very short supply, and marriage to 'locals' was still considered bad for the company and bad for business. A quarter of a century later, when interviewing a candidate for a job in the Far East, I had matured sufficiently not to blanch at his stating that before he could accept any offer his partner would have to approve the accommodation arrangements as she would of course be going with him overseas.

A number of the senior managers in post-war British commercial houses had worked in Japan pre-war – some since the twenties. Having had the good fortune to study Japanese at SOAS post-war before going out as an 'Occupationaire' I always envied those men for having been in Japan in a much more relaxed environment – no telephone trading, airmail or facsimile machines – but was amazed that in practically every case they spoke almost no Japanese and still moved only in a very tight European circle of social and sporting clubs. By comparison, given half a chance, my generation would be off into the wilds at weekends, sampling the varied joys of hot springs and visiting Japanese places of interest.

* * *

During the years of my association with Japan I experienced a great variety of forms of travel, from six-week sea voyages by troopship and, as a civilian, lengthy trips by P&O and Blue Funnel ships through both the Suez and Panama Canals. By air, a six-day flight by Sunderland flying boat which took off and landed daily at such ports as Augusta, Alexandria, Karachi, Rangoon and Hong Kong, arriving on shore to spend a civilized night in an hotel before proceeding onwards the next day. Adjusting one's watch by only about one hour per leg, resulted in nil jet-lag by the time of arrival in Yokohama. This service did not last long and was followed by long turboprop flights until the Comet arrived on the scene. That sadly ceased to operate in 1953, on one of the last flights of which I returned on a home leave at great speed. Today's non-stop flights, in one direction by what only seems like a long day flight, have become almost mundane and boring by comparison.

* * *

As far as work itself was concerned, Dodwell's activities were so varied that it was like working for a number of different companies. With spells in Kobe, Osaka, Nagoya and Tokyo, we handled everything such as the import of raw materials of all kinds, including bulk shipments of salt, which was controlled by the Japanese monopoly corporation as was tobacco. Also in the portfolio were machinery, consumer goods across a wide range of branded products, booze and the sale of MG sports cars to GIs.

Comparison of office conditions then and now is dramatic when one considers how it was in those days: a tiny paper-strewn office in Maru-nouchi, cooled in summer by one tiny electric fan; long-distance tele-phone calls were not made and the main form of communication overseas was by telegram – usually coded to cut down on costs, which were charged per word. During my last working days in the mid-1980s everything was highly computerized and communication with London was daily by international conference telephone. Alongside the commer-cial and economic strides, the improvement in individual standards from canvas-shoed clerks in threadbare clothing to the impeccably turned out white-collar executives owning their own motor cars still causes a slight gasp every time I set foot back in Japan. Since the era of virtual poverty one of the most distinguishing characteristics of present-day Japanese society is the comparatively small gap in wealth with the vast majority of Japanese considering themselves middle-class.

*   *   *

As my time in Japan was centred on the world of business, no recollection would be complete without mentioning some of the changes in this sec-tor over the years. Whether or not it was a stroke of good fortune, the early post-war years' policy formulated by the Ministry of International Trade and Industry (MITI) was undoubtedly one of the major keys to Japan's economic success. Instead of continuing with the pre-war strengths of Japan in textiles, pottery, toys and sundry goods, MITI's strategy called for concentration on steel, ship-building, heavy engineer-ing and of course motor cars and electronics. Initially, the latter cate-gories were protected by high tariffs whilst the industries developed technology and began the process of gaining export market share.

Dodwell's business was extremely mixed, falling into three main cate-gories: shipping, industrial equipment and consumer goods, in roughly equal proportions. Shipping was always a steadily rewarding area, being a very low investment business, acting as agents for major ship-owners and operators. The industrial area, from the early days of importing equip-ment manufactured overseas and shipped to Japan in wooden cases (not without difficulty), developed into a business where overseas know-how was purchased and the production subcontracted to Japanese manufac-turers so that pricing and marketing policy could be decided within Ja-pan and not from afar.

Prime examples of this policy were brewery equipment, where a li-cence to produce equipment and aluminium barrels for draft beer in kegs was purchased from GKN; manufacture was in Japan and supply to all major brewers such as Asahi, Suntory, Sapporo and later Kirin. Prior to this era bottled beer was the standard form of packaging and subsequent to the growth of 'Nama-biiru' ('draft' beer or 'raw' beer), the breweries went heavily into the canning of beer, witness the success of Asahi 'Dry', still calling it draft.

Other businesses pursuing the same licensing policy followed similar patterns such as equipment for high speed ink-jet printing and bag-in-box liquid packaging systems. In the consumer product sector most items had value added in Japan with the local gift packaging of groceries, confectionery, chinaware and wines and spirits. This was particularly so during the gift-giving seasons of O-Chugen and O-Seibo (mid-year and year-end) with packaging locally designed and produced to suit Japanese tastes. If ever the phrase 'the customer is always right' applied it certainly did in Japan. Our warehouses carrying stocks of Royal Doulton china-ware had to remain active over weekends so that sudden or unusual demands from retailers could be met immediately and not just ordered for delivery in a number of days' or weeks' time.

*   *   *

In the midst of all this there were illogical tariff and non-tariff barriers to the import trade, usually the result of the merchandise categories' coming under ministries other than MITI. For instance, before a licence to trade in surgical gloves could be obtained from the Ministry of Health, copious documents had to be submitted even down to floor plans of the sales offices showing the location of cupboards in which samples of the product were kept. Confectionery and biscuits were for years subjected to extremely high tariffs of 35% and 40% despite the fact that total imports were less than 1% of market consumption. The reason for this? Not to protect Japanese confectionery manufacturers but the producers of domestic sugar who faced tremendous competition from cheap bulk sugar imports. The Ministry concerned? – the Ministry of Agriculture (Norin-sho). (I do not need to point out the massive farming vote courted by political parties.) Subsequent to the Tokyo round of GATT negotiations tariffs eventually came down to more reasonable percentages.

The other saga that remains engraved on the hearts of importers was the 'parallel imports story' (heiko yunyu). Prior to 1972, branded products were only imported by sole agency channels but, with a drive to bring down prices by the government, the deregulation of imports led to the opening of other channels of supply by third parties. For some years the volume of parallel imports (PI) was small as 'pirate' importers found it difficult to obtain supplies, which the producers and sole importers naturally did everything to restrict. But in the 1980s the volume escalated after the Plaza Agreement as parallel importers were able to sell in bulk at lower prices without bearing the high costs of marketing, promotion, advertising and entertaining, and in many cases even resorted to under-invoicing so that tax and duty costs were lowered, making the on-selling price more competitive. At one stage over thirty, and almost fifty per cent, of total Scotch and Cognac imports were through the PI channels.

The inevitable result was that the market became confused and what was once a profitable and interesting business is now somewhat unrewarding. Contrast the loss-leader marketing techniques in supermarkets where well-known brands of Scotch can be purchased extremely cheaply, with Suntory's strategy of rigidly controlling retail prices so that wherever you are in Japan the price of a bottle of 'Old' is the same, and woe betide any wholesaler or retailer who tries to buck the system as his supply from the distiller would instantly be cut if he did so.

*   *   *

We hear a lot about Japan's trade unions' attitude to their employers making business life much easier than in Europe. This is mainly because so many unions are company-based as opposed to being national craft unions where all workers with the same skills are affected across the board, irrespective of the employer. Companies with staff numbers in excess of about 500 would normally establish their own company union. Dodwells with 1,500, of course, was in this category and in the early years the annual wage negotiations, the so-called 'Spring Offensive', would take days and nights to resolve. Many the time I returned home bleary-eyed in the early hours of the morning after a management committee/union collective bargaining session.

Although hours of debate would have to be gone through, both sides knew that in the end reasonable good sense would prevail because the only alternative to demands for excessive wage increase would be to bring the company down. Furthermore, although a white-collar operation, members of the management team would have come up through the ranks, having in their youth been on the other side as hot-headed union officials with a full understanding of how matters worked and how the union's honour could only be saved after much sweat and blood to prove to their membership that they had really done their stuff.

*   *   *

With dusk setting in so early in Japan (around six o'clock every day) I recall vividly in my pre-Olympics era the view from my Marunouchi office window in the evenings when the whole of Tokyo appeared to be sitting under an enormous blob of orange cotton wool – heavy pollution – compared with the now almost pure air that prevails there.

*   *   *

One of the abstract rewards of working in Japan was the loyalty of the company's team and the dedication which one became accustomed to expect whenever exceptional demands were made. Once, when we husbanded the Christie's auctions in Tokyo, the setting-up of the sale room and all the back-up necessities in the Okura Hotel required all-night work by the staff concerned before all-day duty the following day. The claim that the Japanese are by nature workaholics is not how I saw the scene. The phrase implies beavering away, head down at hard work for all hours and although working long hours was routine, many of these were spent in meetings, informal discussions, man management communicating, drinks after work and so on. I would prefer to think of this quality as belonging to 'timeaholics'.

* * *

Internal modes of travel within Japan have changed dramatically over the period of my time there. During the Occupation what seemed like only 10% of road surfaces were paved, and during my peregrinations around the Chugoku region the most lasting memory is of the bumpy jeep rides. On occasions when I travelled from Kure to Tokyo on duty it was usually by an overnight steam train belching out soot most of the way. Compare all this with today's expressways, and the quality of road surfaces even in the remotest areas, for example country roads in the San'in and Sanriku areas which I have visited on recent trips. There are now three bridges connecting the island of Shikoku with the mainland, compared with early visits by car from Kobe to the island in the 1950s necessitating a ferry trip to the island of Awaji, crossing the island and then another ferry into Takamatsu.

* * *

With the prevailing generosity which exists everywhere in Japan and nowhere more than in the countryside, I recall an occasion when, on one of the many bachelor weekends when we used to bushwhack around the Japanese countryside in an old 'banger', because of the state of the roads we finished up with two flat tyres and no spare. An elderly Japanese fisherman cycled past with his catch of the day's trout for his family dinner and, having continued for about two hundred yards past, he turned round and came back to present us with his whole catch because he thought that in our plight we might be in need of such sustenance.

Even as recently as during a trip to Kyushu in the autumn of 1999, one day my wife developed a toothache for which we thought some form of interim treatment would see her through the remainder of the journey. Whilst explaining the problem in Japanese to the pharmacist in a local chemist's shop I suddenly became aware of an elderly Japanese lady standing behind me taking in the whole story. Upon the completion of this she opened her bag and said 'I have just been to the hospital for treatment for a toothache problem and was given this prescription medicine by the dentist. Please accept some of the tablets so that your wife's toothache will get better. I can manage more easily as I live here.' This kindness did as much as the medicine, which the pharmacist also prescribed to cure the problem.

*   *   *

Despite the tremendous progress made in most sectors in Japan some have changed far less, the most outstanding being the general size of housing in Japan. Although the Denman 'rabbit hutch' quip, after initially being received angrily in Japan, has subsequently become a humorous way of referring to small-sized accommodation, the square metre statistic is still very small by advanced country status. Considering the population growth of something like 70-odd million forty years ago to today's 125 million, it is perhaps an achievement to have housed the additional people at all! What is also remarkable is that Japan's population is about half that of the United States while the land area is about 1/25th with 75% of it mountainous and 67% covered with forests.

*   *   *

In only fifty years life expectancy has increased from a mid-50 average to now close to 83 years for women and 77 for men. This, of course, is accounted for, largely, by greatly improved nutrition, an over-abundance of medicinal intake and careful health screening. I remember my driver in Tokyo taking a day off once a year for a check-up in the 'body dock' and sometimes asking for an extra half day for a liver biopsy, which was being included as part of the other routine medical monitoring.

*   *   *

Over the years I have come to believe that some of the stereotyped phrases describing the character of Japan are myths (or near myths). 'The nation works as a team and is orderly' – anyone who got even a distant flavour of the student riots in the nineteen sixties has seen another side to the Japanese character. The student outbursts were not really connected with academic problems but rather with political tensions stirred up by left-wing elements and centred on the Security Treaty which provided for the continuation of US bases in Japan. It seemed that people forgot all too soon that Tokyo University barely functioned for a year in 1968/69. Another classic 'Japan is dominated by its menfolk' – one would like to be a fly on the wall when the husband arrives home with his monthly pay-packet and see how much say he has in the division of his salary with his wife. In return for dedicated attention to domestic matters and the children's upbringing women are far more vocal in my view than generally thought. This is largely clouded by the male chauvinistic style which most Japanese men manage to get away with, much to the envy of many of their British expatriate colleagues.

*   *   *

During a visit to Japan in September 1999, part of which was spent driving around Kyushu (during the worst typhoon for eight years – No. 18!) I tried to re-visit the Inland Sea by taking a ferry from Beppu to Shikoku and then returning to Honshu via the new Seto Bridge. This plan was unfortunately upset by the typhoon so I have to be content until and if I can try again with the memory of my first journey through the sea upon arrival in Japan in May 1947 as a young Language Officer to join BCOF (British Commonwealth Occupation Forces) on the troop ship *Dunera*. Then, the Inland Sea was virtually unspoilt by industrial development and full of the most beautiful series of small islands I had ever seen – perhaps this memory should remain unsullied by what would today undoubtedly be a fragmented mix of natural beauty and modern progress.

Two factors which I vividly recollect of that sea journey were the beauty of Japan's unspoilt scenery and the *esprit de corps* of their people. The latter was demonstrated when we took on to the *Dunera* at Singapore a contingent of Japanese troops who had remained there after the end of the war. They were all in good physical shape and showed a discipline which put to shame the ragtag and bobtail bunch of post-war British servicemen which we comprised. When we inspected their quarters the standard of cleanliness they maintained working in teams and their personal neatness had to be admired. A thought then, which developed over years of exposure to Japan, to a conviction, was that 'these are a people to be reckoned with'.

*   *   *

I hope to see a reasonable part of the next half-century of Anglo-Japanese history, but I would certainly not do any deals to witness all of it in exchange for even a small part of the past. Nothing will ever match the variety, sense of progress and change – and fun! – of the last fifty or more years.

ANOTHER British businessman whose first visit to Japan took place before the war, who first worked in Japan with Jardine Matheson and Company (Japan) Limited and who ended his service there as Director of Rolls-Royce (Far East) Limited and manager for Japan was DUNCAN FRASER. He has entitled his story 'From Shanghai to Tokyo via South Africa: lumber, cars, aircraft and aero-engines':-

•

I was born in Shanghai in June 1923. There was a sizeable Japanese community there. I was struck by the *kimono*, *tabi* and the *geta* they wore and could soon recognize the differences between Japanese and Chinese even in foreign clothing, an ability which I sadly lost when I came to live in Tokyo.

My first visit to Japan was in 1933 when I accompanied my father on a business trip. We had an uneventful crossing on the NYK *Shanghai Maru* except for a diversion to check on an object in the sea. It turned out to be a dead whale. The stench stayed with us for a long time. At Nagasaki we were given a warm welcome by our Japanese host, a business acquaintance of my father. We stayed in his half-Western, half-Japanese house. My father gave me some pocket money and I was allowed to ramble around looking at Nagasaki Bay and trying to keep cool. Once I tried to buy a bottle of lemonade, but the old woman who ran the shop would not let me pay. She rubbed my hair between her fingers: she had probably never seen a blond boy before. One afternoon, I walked to a good viewpoint over the harbour and used my Box Brownie camera to take some shots of ships in the waterway. I was immediately pounced on by two policemen who kept me in custody until I was rescued by my father and our host. The policemen returned my camera but confiscated my film. Quite a daunting experience for a ten-year-old!

We had a lovely weekend at Unzen. We also visited Kumamoto where we stayed in a *ryokan*; this was my first experience of sleeping on *tatami*. I was much impressed by Mount Aso: this was my first sight of an active volcano.

I was in Shanghai in 1937 when trouble broke out between the Chinese and the Japanese and bombs fell in the international settlement. On the recommendation of the British Consul-General my mother took us children for a time to Hong Kong where I kept up my riding. There were no professional jockeys in Shanghai but I became a successful amateur rider on the flat and over the fences.

Early in 1941 I called on the British recruiting officer in Shanghai, but was told to return in June when I would be 18. In June I was told that I would have to wait until December before I could leave for India. I continued to serve with the 'Shanghai Light Horse'. On 7 December I was on sentry duty outside the offices of the *Shanghai Times* when a Japanese general visited the building. I presented arms and thought that this would be my last sentry duty before leaving for India. The following day we heard that the Japanese had attacked Pearl Harbour. Shanghai was in turmoil with Japanese troops and police everywhere. Four days later we were told of the sinking of HMS *Prince of Wales* and HMS *Repulse*. I wanted to get away and join up, but there seemed to be no way of escape from Shanghai.

One day, I was invited to lunch by Dr Gauntlett who was the official doctor to the British Consulate-General He told me that he was trying to find a way for me to leave occupied China. Subject to the approval of the Swiss Consulate-General, which was in charge of British interests, he was planning to put me on the Japanese ship which was taking British officials to Lourenço Marques as part of an exchange of diplomatic representatives. It would be my task with an Australian nurse, and a friend of mine, to help look after a judge of the British High Court in China who needed constant attention because of a mental disorder. On 17 August 1942 I boarded the *Kamakura Maru*. I said sad farewells to my father, mother, brother and sister who were interned by the Japanese for the rest of the war, while my father went into a prison camp.

The crew of the ship which carried some 900 British officials and civilians were polite and the food was excellent. As we enjoyed special status there was no blackout. One day, I left the judge in the bathroom and asked him to call when he was ready. When he shouted I went in and discovered that he had thrown all his clothes out of the porthole; as a result we made it a rule never to leave him on his own. After we had landed at Lourenço Marques I accompanied the judge by train to Pretoria and on by car to the South African mental hospital where he was to stay. I was sad to say goodbye: he had given me my chance of freedom.

Instead of going to India I joined the South African Air Force. In 1945 I lost my two engines over Italy, near Cingoli, and crash-landed with my 4000 pounds of bombs on board. Obviously none exploded. I have often suffered from serious spinal trouble ever since.

After I was demobilized in 1946 I joined Jardine Matheson and Co Ltd in London. I sailed back to the Far East on HMS *Victorious* and was back in Shanghai before the end of the year. In 1948 I went to live in Hankow where I found a bay horse which had been left behind by the Japanese troops. It was a wonderful jumper with a big heart. After a spell in Taiwan in 1951 I was posted that December to Tokyo to be responsible for the lumber department.

Accommodation in Tokyo in those days was very limited and for a couple of weeks I stayed in the house occupied by the Managing Director of Jardine, Matheson and Co (Japan) Ltd, at Mikawadai near Roppongi. From my bedroom window on a clear day, there was no smog and I had a fine view of Mount Fuji. Every morning before breakfast I would ride from the nearby stables of the American Army's Hardy barracks (later the headquarters of the Japanese Self Defense Forces) and went into the fields around Roppongi. (Hardly conceivable these days!) It took me five minutes in my Hillman Minx to reach our office opposite Hibiya Park.

The Japanese in charge of the lumber department was Nanjo-san, a splendid man. Unfortunately, the business was in the red and we had particular problems in Hokkaido. When I visited our office in Otaru and had been introduced to the office staff I went outside suitably clad but found myself on my backside slipping ten yards down the ice. At Otaru I had my first experience of a porcelain pillow. I spent nine days on that occasion in Hokkaido and soon got the staff working to clean up the storage yard which was a disgrace. The head of the Hokkaido office, Sasaki-san, with whom I had all my meals on this visit was completely open with me when we discussed the war. He had been a sergeant in the Japanese army in China and had sadly missed the chance of going to university.

My wife flew into Haneda airport in early April 1952 and we were able to have our meals at the old Imperial Hotel, designed by the American architect Frank Lloyd Wright, which had just been released by the American forces. Sadly, it has since been pulled down. Only the entrance hall has been preserved in Meiji Mura near Nagoya. On 9 April we had three wedding ceremonies, first at the Consular section in Yokohama, then at St Andrew's Church in Shiba, Tokyo. We also had to register our marriage with the ward office.

Our first house was in Shibuya in Takeshita-cho which we nicknamed Catastrophe-cho because so much went wrong there. When I woke up and threw back the curtains I was shocked to see not more than six metres away our Japanese neighbours, formally dressed, bowing at me pretending not to notice that I was clad only in pyjamas. They came straight up together from their bow and so did I. Down they went again and so did I for about five more times! I never opened the curtains again without a surreptitious peep to see if they were in their bedroom.

Our elderly maid had a disconcerting habit of descending onto her knees and knocking her forehead on the floor three times in quick succession. One evening I noticed that a champagne cork was lying on the floor from the night before. The next morning I watched her pick it up, sweep the floor and then return it to the same spot.

Our first Sunday lunch party was ruined by the overflowing night soil carts arriving at the same time as our guests. This meant an expensive lunch at the Imperial Hotel as we had to evacuate the house. Our first cocktail party was also a disaster as the floor slowly collapsed under the weight of our guests.

In those days I saw much evidence of Japanese poverty. Everyone was shabbily dressed; there were few cars and there was damage everywhere from the air-raids which Tokyo had suffered. For our part, despite the appalling state of the roads, we managed a second honeymoon in Nikko and Chuzenji.

At last that summer we moved into a house on the Bluff in Yokohama looking across the bay. It was now 24 miles by road to the office which could take up to 45 minutes, but it was a relief to be out of Catastrophe-cho.

Unfortunately, that autumn I developed for the first time in my life severe asthma. The American doctor whom I consulted found that I was allergic to almost everything and said that if I were an American he would have packed me off home. I tried everything I could think of to rid myself of my exasperating breathing problems, but nothing availed, not even moving into an air-conditioned hotel. So, sadly, I called one day on Eric Watts who had taken charge of Jardines in Japan and told him that I must leave Japan straight away. I left on 30 November 1952 and about two hours out of Tokyo all my symptoms had gone

I continued to work for Jardines in Hong Kong in the bulk trading department until one day Henry Sharp from Vickers-Armstrong (Aircraft) Ltd called and offered Jardines their agency in the Far East so long as Jardines could provide a man with an aviation background who would be totally dedicated to selling Vickers products. I qualified for the job. I first undertook a reconnaissance of the civil aircraft market. In Japan I had the assistance of Sueyoshi-san of Jardine Matheson's who was a graduate of Cornell University. We were also assisted by Daiichi Trading which had been split off from Mitsui and Co. as part of the Occupation's economic reforms. I prepared a presentation on the Vickers Viscount and met many of the top executives of Japan Air Lines who wanted to develop their international services. At Japan Helicopter Air Transport (later part of ANA) I found managers sceptical of British after-sales service. I did my best to reassure them. I also called on the Japanese Civil Aviation Bureau (JCAB) and always tried to keep in touch with officials there because I knew that they played a key role.

It was now time for me to be properly briefed in Britain both by Vickers and by Rolls-Royce. This meant visits to Derby where the Rolls-Royce aero engine school was and also to Weybridge for Vickers. I returned to Hong Kong that December with responsibility for seventeen countries from Japan in the north and Burma in the west.

In the spring of 1955 I revisited Tokyo where I made contact with what was to form part of the Japanese Air Self-Defense Force (ASDF). I also worked hard to promote sales of the Viscount aircraft.

An interesting feature of the Japanese aviation world at this time was the number of University Professors who became influential in the decision-making process. Among these were Professor Kimura and Professor Horikoshi who had been successful aircraft designers (Horikoshi had designed the Japanese Zero fighter). Both became good friends of mine.

In 1959 Nihon Aeroplane Co Ltd (NAMCO) was formed and the go-ahead given for the production of the YS-11 which was to be fitted with

Rolls-Royce R.DA.10 engines. After I had recovered from a cervical spinal fuse operation I stepped up my visits to Japan. In July 1959 I accompanied a high-powered delegation of experts from Vickers and Rolls-Royce to Japan. Once again I encountered concerns about British after-sales service.

In 1960 I spent nearly three months in Japan during a series of visits which led to ANA purchasing eight Viscount 828s and leasing two Viscount 744s. Nakano-san of ANA took a good deal of persuading that Vickers would and could provide good after-sales service, but our patience and persistence paid off. This is not the place for a detailed account of all the time consuming negotiations with teams from London and with lawyers in Tokyo, but I must mention John Ferguson Smith, the senior executive of Vickers, who was in charge of the negotiations and our American lawyer Wolf Rabinowitz who was most helpful. One amusing element in the negotiations concerned the number of loos in the larger 800 series. Vickers recommended two loos while the Japanese only wanted one. I spent the best part of a Saturday persuading them of my theory that if departure was delayed and passengers had consumed vast quantities of beer the second loo was needed to prevent an overflow.

We had to attend and give numerous parties including geisha parties where the geisha enjoyed playing (and winning!) childish games.

In 1959 Jardines wanted to send me to Singapore, but I could not see any advantage in the move although I got on well with the Singapore directors. Consequently, I submitted my resignation and although Hugh Barton, who was in charge in Hong Kong, tried to persuade me to stay, I was determined to go. We set out by sea for London where we arrived on 17 January 1961. I decided that Rolls-Royce would give me a much wider customer base than an aeroplane manufacturer. I visited the many scattered Rolls-Royce factories and did refresher courses on the main Rolls-Royce aero engines. I was also involved with the many visitors the company received from the Far East.

Early in 1962 I attended a series of meetings to assess the value for Rolls-Royce Aero Engine Division of having a permanent presence in Japan. I was strongly in favour, believing it to be essential to our long-term prospects in the Far East.

In June that year this was agreed in principle, but no firm decisions were made about how this was to be accomplished. In August I flew out to Tokyo as the Rolls-Royce representative with a team from the British Aircraft Corporation (BAC). While I was in Japan I was able to accompany the President of NAMCO to Nagoya to witness the first flight of the YS-11. I flew back to Tokyo in an ANA Viscount.

At the end of October 1962 Eikichi Itoh of C. Itoh and Co (now Itochu) who were associated with Rolls-Royce in Japan visited Rolls-Royce headquarters in Derby. This was the beginning of a good and fruitful friendship.

In early 1963 I did a sales report on prospects in the Far East and undertook a two-month reconnaissance visit with Mike Hartley who was in due course to be my deputy in Tokyo. I was taken aback in South Korea when the Chairman of a Korean airline told me he had never heard of Rolls-Royce. However, when he told me that he had also never heard of Pratt and Whitney I was somewhat comforted.

When we got back to Derby Tim Kendall asked me whether I would be prepared to take on the task of setting up a Rolls-Royce's office in Japan. My only hesitation concerned the debilitating asthma attacks which hit me in Honshu in November and December. Rolls-Royce told me that they would be happy for me to be out of Japan at the crucial season.

It took some months that year to arrange all the necessary paperwork before Rolls-Royce (Far East) could be set up. By the autumn all was in place and a press conference was held at which my appointment and that of C.Itoh as Rolls-Royce's commercial correspondents was announced

Early in 1964 I concentrated on getting to know the other divisions of Rolls Royce to whom I should be responsible for the Japanese market. These were the Motor Car Division, the Oil Engine Division and the Industrial Engine Division. I greatly enjoyed driving a Rolls-Royce Silver Cloud and was delighted to meet David (later Sir David) Plastow whose enthusiasm I found infectious. Eventually, when I was offered a Bentley to use in Japan, I successfully urged the division to let me have a Rolls-Royce. I knew that this would open doors for me which would be closed for a Bentley. The Japanese who are often snobs were rarely interested in the Bentley but were impressed by a Rolls. Back in Japan when I visited Honda's experimental factory Soichiro Honda, the founder of the firm, suggested that I drive his prototype Honda 600 sports car. I did everything with it except turn it over. Honda-san laughingly invited me to become a works driver. We became good friends.

I was soon in touch with Ishikawajima-Harima Heavy Industries (IHI) who eventually became involved in finishing off work on certain RR aero-engine components. I also saw a good deal of Tojo-san, a well respected aeronautical engineer working for Mitsubishi Heavy Industries (MHI) who was attached to NAMCO.

We still had not received formal government approval to establish a branch office. (That only came through on 4 November 1964 while I was on a visit to Peking. With my colleagues from Rolls-Royce we had a great celebration.) But we decided to risk getting approval, and took over the offices of British Petroleum conveniently located next door to C.Itoh. We worked out our first year's budget on a sheet of hotel paper. Fortunately, our forecast turned out to be accurate!

We moved from a rented house to a mansion block in Azabu and soon

began a seemingly unending round of entertaining our clients. My favourite restaurant was the Crescent, but I also enjoyed Chinese cuisine at
Sun Ya, named after one of Shanghai's most famous pre-war eating
houses. Among night clubs I patronized the Copacabana and the Mikado! I became a member of both the American Club and the Tokyo Club. I
used the latter on occasions for presentations. One club which had no
premises was the Tuesday Musical which never met on Tuesdays and never
had any music! It was a favourite with many of my Japanese aeronautical
friends.

As employees of Rolls Royce we had to be neutral between the competing British aircraft manufacturers, Hawker Siddeley and BAC. Mike
Hartley and I accordingly had to be careful to wear the right company
tie on the appropriate occasion.

We were soon absorbed in completing plans for a British exhibition at
Harumi in September 1965. We had three cars on show, the crowning
glory being a Mulliner Park Ward Drop-Head Coupé in Ming Blue.

On the first day of the show we almost had a riot on our hands as
people struggled to get a close view of the car. One man (perhaps a gangster i.e. a *yakuza*) asked whether the drop-head coupé could be armour-
plated and fitted with fixed, forward-firing automatic weapons. A more
sensible question came from a Japanese who lived in Kamakura. He
wanted to know the price and bought the car. I delivered it in person
to his home where it was duly blessed at his own shrine by Shinto priests.
Various members of the Imperial Family visited our stand. The guest of
honour from Britain was HRH The Princess Alexandra. Roy Jenkins, the
Minister of Aviation, who was in attendance, showed great interest in our
efforts to sell aero-engines.

The following February I had the privilege of visiting the imperial
garage. Here I saw not only the German bullet-proof car presented to
the Emperor by Adolf Hitler before the war, but also the Emperor's
two Rolls-Royce Phantom Vs. I was about to hop into the back of one of
them when I was firmly stopped. Only the imperial posterior was
allowed on the these seats. However it was necessary to give these
vehicles an occasional good workout. I drove the car down a hill at a
respectable pace. When I saw a crowd of people crossing the road I
stopped and had the pleasure of hearing an American tourist exclaim:
'Oh, Gee, Elmer, he even has a limey chauffeur!'

One of my tasks was to keep the Japanese aviation press, which was
enthusiastic and competent, informed. They gave us splendid coverage.

One day, I had an unusual visit from two members of the Soviet
Embassy. They brought me a bottle of vodka reciprocated with a bottle
of Johnnie Walker Black Label. They asked about the Spey engine and
said they wanted to buy one. I replied that we did not sell aero engines
on a one-off basis as we needed to be involved in the installation of the

engine. When they persevered I politely showed them to the door. Another day a wealthy Chinese businessman invited me to a drink and put the same suggestion to me and got the same brush-off.

In February 1966 an ANA Boeing 727 crashed into Tokyo Bay and all 133 people on board were killed. In March that year a Canadian Pacific Airline aircraft powered by Rolls-Royce Conway engines crashed at Tokyo airport. Then on the following day a BOAC 707, also powered by Rolls-Royce Conway engines, disintegrated in mid air after leaving Tokyo for Hong Kong with a loss of 124 lives.

These accidents had a serious effect on air travel in Japan, causing a marked dip in passenger growth. That same year I developed serious spinal trouble as a result of my aircraft crash in Italy in 1945. My asthma that December was particularly bad. So it was a difficult year. Nevertheless, we found ourselves increasingly busy. Mike Hartley and I took care of fifteen territories from Tokyo.

I had a fascinating experience when visiting the ASDF base at Miho in Tottori prefecture. Over a Japanese dinner in Yonago, the nearby town, General Minobe told me that he had been a naval pilot and had taken part in the sinking of the aircraft carrier HMS *Hermes* off Ceylon in 1942. He described the gunners on the ship as brave sailors who continued firing while their vessel was sinking. Eventually, there was only one of them left above the water line but he remained at his post and continued to fire his automatic weapon. General Minobe said he had never seen such bravery. He lost height, and circled *Hermes*, saluting in tribute to those heroic sailors as he watched the carrier disappear below the surface.

In 1967 it was apparent from Bank of Japan reports that Japan was moving from being a debtor country to being a creditor. We needed to step up our efforts to sell British equipment in Japan. For our part we concentrated on trying to persuade the Japanese government to adopt the Adour engine for their TX project, a supersonic trainer. But I wanted the British aviation industry to do more to sell ancillary equipment. I raised this with the Aviation Sub-Committee of the British Chamber of Commerce and discussed it with the Commercial Department of the British Embassy where Hugh Cortazzi was the Commercial Counsellor and an enthusiastic trade promoter. I was also in touch with Sir Richard Smeeton who was Chairman of the Society of British Aerospace Constructors and we worked hard to put together appropriate missions and exhibitions.

We were told unofficially that MHI would be the prime manufacturer of the TX and that the Adour stood a good chance of being selected. One day, I received a telephone call from the Defense Agency asking me to call on General Takayama, Deputy Director of the Aircraft Department of the Technical Research Institute. When Mike Hartley and I called he chatted about his self-designed gimmick to improve his golf: a normal golf ball with a light chain fixed to it. He opened the top right-hand drawer to show us an example. Then, quite casually, he opened the top left-hand drawer of his desk and took out a letter which he handed to me saying 'This might interest you'. It did! The letter dated 2 April 1968 cleared the way for the initial design of the twin-engined advanced supersonic trainer to be powered by two Rolls-Royce Turbomeca Adour Turbofan engines. This was a real breakthrough although, of course, there was an immense amount to do to bring the project to fruition.

Fortunately, the YS-11 was selling well and we became involved with many new customers visiting Japan. We were also receiving at this time initial approaches on the large RB-211 engine.

At the beginning of 1969 I was asked to prepare a programme for a visit to Japan by Rolls-Royce's Chairman Sir Denning Pearson, who was to be in Japan at the same time as Carl Kotchian, the President of Lockheed Aircraft Corporation who was working hard to sell the L-1011 to Japan Air Lines. (Sir Denning Pearson had to resign when later Rolls-Royce faced bankruptcy. Kotchian also had to go when Lockheed, Marubeni and ANA were involved in a bribery scandal involving Prime Minister Kakuei Tanaka.)

I was very much involved at this time in preparing for the planned British Week in October 1969 not least because I had become Chairman of the British Chamber of Commerce in Tokyo. Although British Week was primarily designed to promote British consumer goods, the Chamber and the Embassy were determined to feature capital goods as well and an exhibition of British Scientific and Medical Instruments was arranged at the Science Museum. British Week attracted many VIP visitors. HRH Princess Margaret and the Earl of Snowdon were the guests of honour. There was, of course, a ball laid on by the loyal societies and we all had a tremendous time.

1970 was the year of Expo '70 in Osaka. This was the occasion for a visit to Japan by the Prince of Wales. The Ambassador, Sir John Pilcher, asked me if I would lend our Rolls for the Prince's visit to Kyoto. I was delighted to comply and was amused when the Prince thanking me with a twinkle in his eye asked me why his mother's car was so much bigger than mine!

By now I felt that I had accomplished a breakthrough for Rolls-Royce in Japan and as my asthma attacks were worsening once again I decided, sadly, that it was time for me to leave. On 31 October 1970 I took a flight to Hong Kong. On the aeroplane, sipping a glass of champagne and forgetting my asthma, I looked back with happiness on my days in the land of the rising sun. I had been most fortunate to be associated with the sale to Japan of her first turboprop aircraft and then later on, engines to power the first Japanese supersonic aircraft.

In 1988 Dr Paul Shoda whom I had got to know so well in Japan and who had contributed so much to the Japanese aircraft industry invited me to Glasgow University when he was receiving the honorary degree of

Doctor of Science. He had read engineering and graduated in 1916. He was 96 and had played nine holes of golf at St Andrews on the previous day. He deserved the standing ovation which he was given.

20

British Businessmen in Japan:
Some Service Sectors

**MARTYN NAYLOR ● DAVID WILKINSON ● ANN WILKINSON
DICK LARGE**

MARTYN NAYLOR has spent much of his working life in Japan in public relations. He became honorary secretary of the Japan-British Society in Tokyo in 1968, a post which he continues to fill in 2000. His impressions of Japan in the 1960s and 1970s are a reminder of the important role played by the Japan-British Society:

●

FIRST CONTACTS WITH JAPAN

I was born in England, but my association with Japan began at the earliest possible date – in a small nursing home in Croydon where this event took place, the other two babies born on the same day were *both* Japanese! Whilst I cannot recall communicating with them, we were certainly put on view together, and I suppose I should consider them as my very first friends. My mother remembered one of them being from a Sumitomo family, and the other was probably the child of a Mitsubishi executive. Attempts to locate them during my years in Japan have been in vain, but it has always proved fascinating to reflect how I was fated to come to live in Japan.

There were other early influences that prompted my interest in Japan. As a student I stayed part of a summer with a Filipino classmate in Washington DC. His godfather, who was our guardian for the summer (in the absence of parents), made sure we paid the gas bill and behaved ourselves generally. He happened to be one of the most famous foreigners ever to visit Japan – the tall eminence that was General Douglas MacArthur. He inspired me to take a close look at Japan, which was the prime stop on my itinerary after graduate study in the United States. My fellow students at university in the US were mostly on the GI Bill, which

funded their studies after service in the Korean War: almost without exception, they told stories of the great times they had spent in Tokyo on R
& R from the front line.

Thus, when three years later I departed from Oakland Naval Base on a
freighter, the *President Harrison*, to take an appointment to teach economics at the University of Hong Kong, my first destination was Japan, where
I was to spend a month before moving on to Manila and later Hong
Kong. The only stopover between Oakland and Yokosuka (we were carrying 'naval supplies', which I only later discovered were mainly case upon
case of beer!) was Midway Island, and the wrecks of the proud Japanese
fleet were an uncomfortable reminder of the conflict that had ended only
fifteen years earlier. Suddenly, I questioned just how interested I was in
things Japanese. However, the three days of partying with the American
residents of Midway, who were satiating a four-week thirst following a
visit by Canadians who had drunk the island dry, allowed me to refrain
from questioning the Japanese, and gradually the hulks of the gigantic
battleships, which were a constant reminder of a needless war, prompted
within me sympathy for the many Japanese who had died so far from
home.

It was thus with real excitement that I looked forward to landfall in
Japan. Having weathered a typhoon the previous night, it was on a clear
August morning in 1960 that we sailed into Tokyo Bay with a glorious
view of Mount Fuji, the quality of which has never been repeated in more
than thirty years of residence. Owing to the typhoon, there had been no
time to pack my bags, and when the Japanese customs officials boarded
the vessel, their inspection involved rummaging through the chest of
drawers in my cabin. I wondered what progress there had been since
the time of Sir Harry Parkes; their only real concern was whether or
not I was carrying a sword!

The Yokosuka naval base was not the most salubrious point of arrival in
the country where I was later to spend most of my life, but, together with
a Korean girl, a mortician, who had been a fellow passenger, we took a
taxi past the girlie bars that were standard for any such American establishment, and at the railway station I had my first view of the real Japan.
Much to my consternation the Yokosuka Line seemed to speed through
the countryside and the suburban sprawl at a breakneck rate, and I remembered a very serious rail disaster in much this same area only months
before. However, we arrived at Tokyo station safely, after a journey during
which I was offered a seat in the overcrowded train by old ladies. I refused
again and again; everyone took great interest in me, and my first impression was of great courtesy and friendliness.

In Tokyo I stayed at the International House of Japan in Azabu, which
then had fewer modern conveniences than today, but the garden was
beautiful, and the rate was favourable. Before the opening of the interna-

tional hotels it was a great place to stay. Whilst I travelled around the city in a Fiat taxi (if I remember correctly the minimum fee was ¥40, compared with ¥70 for a Hillman taxi), I was not learning my way around. So I took to walking the unmade streets, down towards Tokyo Tower and round to Toranomon, where one could pick up the Ginza Line subway. Getting back to the International House was always difficult, and I called so many times at the Azabu police station that I was recognized by several of the officers when I stopped by five years later.

To see Japan outside the big cities, I spent two weeks staying with the Imada family in Otake, between Hiroshima and Iwakuni. Their son had been a classmate of mine in the US. The family lived in a fairly large house on the outskirts of the town, not far from the family factory where paper products were made. The Imadas were relatively affluent at the time, and they had a car, which set them apart from their neighbours. We drove in their brand new Toyopet along beautifully landscaped mountain roads with almost no other vehicles in sight; it would be nearly ten years before the hordes of tourists arrived with their exhaust fumes which quickly destroyed much of the carefully planted flora.

Much of Hiroshima had already been reconstructed, and I was amazed at the progress that had been made in the fifteen years since its destruction. The Atomic Bomb Memorial Park and the museum were amongst the early projects to be completed; the hospital which then housed so many survivors was a grim reminder of an event that should never be repeated. It was inspiring to see the extent to which the city had recovered; the determination to build a new life was clear from everybody I talked with. Nearby Miyajima was, of course, an oasis, and it was good to see this famous spot without the teeming visitors that would later spoil it. There were many Americans and their Japanese girl friends, given the nearby Naval Air Station. But most of the Japanese visitors on a working day were women, who in those days wore kimono or *mompei*.

This first visit to Japan convinced me that I had to return. With the start of Japan's plan to double the national income, it certainly did appear that Tokyo was the place to be for at least the next decade, although Japanese products had still not established their reputation for quality and the use of advanced technology.

WORKING IN JAPAN

At the University of Hong Kong I found a colleague who prompted my decision to return to Japan: the poet Edmund Blunden, who loved Japan as much as any Englishman, was another positive factor in convincing me that my future lay in Tokyo. As soon as my contract was up in Hong Kong, I returned to London, joining an advertising agency group, the London Press Exchange. In little more than a couple of years I was off on a six-month round-the-world trip to develop a plan for the expansion of the company overseas. Even before my departure it was taken for granted that I would make Japan a high priority market and recommend that I would be sent to Tokyo to open a window on Japan for my employer.

After two nights in New York, and one in Los Angeles, to consult with our American staff who had at least some knowledge of Japan, I was winging my way across the Pacific to Manila in a cramped propjet aircraft, with intermediate stops in Honolulu, Wake Island (being British I was required to stay on board the aircraft and could not stretch my legs!), and Guam. Manila was my first main destination, as I was to attend the First Asian Marketing Conference. It was my good fortune that the organizers for some strange reason attached me to the Japanese delegation, rather than the Australians or the groups from Hong Kong or Singapore. Thus I was to spend a week getting on and off buses, and participating in discussion groups, factory visits and banquets together with presidents and managing directors of a dozen of Japan's foremost manufacturing companies, most notably the president Mori of Toyo Rayon and the managing director Junji Hiraga of Toshiba. In our party there were MITI officials, and a handful of very senior bureaucrats who had been purged and jailed in the late 1940s, and had returned to industry by heading one of a number of 'inspection institutes'. Despite the gulf between our ages, this provided a tremendous opportunity to get to know several legendary leaders of Japanese industry on an informal and personal basis. These proved of great value when I was later to set up an office in Tokyo; and one great advantage was that, almost without exception, they spoke good English.

During the nearly four years that I spent in London, after my time in Hong Kong, I had made many Japanese contacts, mainly through working with the London office of JETRO. I met many of the younger members of Japanese companies in London and quite a number of the visitors who descended on the JETRO staff. Another point of contact was the *Wakatake Kai*, the junior group of the Japan Society, run by Michael Isherwood, a British staff member of Mitsubishi Corporation.

On my first night in Tokyo, in mid-September 1965, I attended a party given by the BOAC passenger service officer. He and others not unnaturally asked me whether I had flown there by BOAC. I recall that they were much distressed when I explained that not one sector of my route was served by their airline (my route had taken me to Prague, Moscow, Delhi, Rangoon, Pnom Penh (Hanoi was scheduled but the Americans had just commenced bombing that city), Canton, Peking, Hong Kong and Manila). I was at the party at the invitation of the cargo manager, who was a friend of a friend. In those days the British community was extremely close-knit, and it was not long before I felt I had met most of the British families in town. Without a family of my own it was good to be invited to join others for the traditional British celebrations. From the start I had numerous very good Japanese friends.

On arrival at Haneda I had taken a taxi to the Dai-ichi Hotel in Shim-bashi, a hotel I had found economical and in a good location on a previous visit, although the rooms were far from soundproof (it was a jerry-built structure that had gone up in the early years of the Occupation). Much to my dismay, the hotel was full, and they directed me to the Hotel New Otani, which had opened just prior to the Tokyo Olympics one year earlier. This proved remarkably fortuitous. Hitoshi Hara, a young management trainee at the hotel, proved extremely helpful and assisted me with the arrangements to find both an apartment and an office. Less than two years later, at the suggestion of my bosses in London he joined my company and we have now worked together for more than thirty-two years (1999).

Before moving into my own office, I was for two months given a desk in the JETRO office next to the Yaesu entrance to Tokyo Station. Tachi-bana, the department head who made space for me, was around fifteen years ahead of his colleagues in claiming that anything that could be done to stimulate Japanese imports would ultimately benefit exports, as trade is a two-way affair. It was useful to see how JETRO worked in their head office. Perhaps I managed to convince their research people that much of the material in their interminable questionnaires was irrelevant, and that they should give more thought to tailoring the questions more specifically to the subject at hand.

A large British exhibition at the Harumi Fairgrounds in 1966 was the first major effort to promote Britain in Japan. Machinery and equipment featured prominently, although the more obvious consumer goods, such as biscuits and confectionery and English tea, were also included. This seems to have been the British way of telling the Japanese that we recognized the immediate period of post war recovery was over, and that Japan was seen as a significant market for British exports that should be seriously developed. The success of the 1966 exhibition led to the planning of British Week in Tokyo, which came three years later in 1969. It coincided with the new policy of the Board of Trade to promote exports in a big way. Private enterprise was called upon to help organize the export drive through the newly-established British National Export Council (BNEC). We saw a great deal of Michael Montague, who was chairman of Valor heaters, and became chairman of BNEC's Asia Committee.

As the representative office in Japan of the London Press Exchange (LPE), an advertising agency, it was only natural that we should be drawn into British export promotion, and we had many regular tasks leading up to British Week in Tokyo (see separate account of British Week by Ben Thorne below). One of these was reporting back to The Board of Trade Journal with photos of the almost weekly visits of specialist trade missions, which over less than eighteen months numbered more than 50. These Monday evening get-togethers provided a splendid opportunity to meet Britain's top export salesmen in a relaxed situation at the start of their visit. My colleagues took photos of the key people, together with the ambassador. I recall on at least fifty occasions Sir John Pilcher [cf. Hugh Cortazzi's biographical portrait of Sir John Pilcher in *Biographical Portraits* Vol.III, published by Japan Library for the Japan Society, 1999] objecting to hiding his glass for the photographs. After his first drink, he usually resorted to his classic *kabuki* Japanese, learned as a language student in Kyoto in the 1930. He was a delightfully non-commercial ambassador, but a tremendous host with a great fund of stories, and unquestionably a fine diplomat.

The Pilchers had succeeded Sir Francis and Lady Rundall, who I remember best from Wednesday evening classes in Scottish dancing at the Residence. Whilst we stumbled around the ballroom, the Rundalls kept an eye on us, Sir Francis sitting in a high-backed chair reading *The Times*, and Lady Rundall knitting. I soon gave up Scottish dancing, after having ended a round at a St Andrews Ball in the midst of a circle paired with Sir John Pilcher who appeared to be almost as inept as I was. Sir John arrived in Tokyo from Vienna, where he had happily managed to get away just before a British Week, only to find himself wholly enmeshed in a very much larger event here in Tokyo! Whilst a 'commercial' embassy was a totally new experience for him and one he never completely felt at home with, I believe he ultimately found this promotion of Britain in Japan to be great fun, and he certainly enjoyed the many cultural exhibitions and other representations of British art.

THE JAPAN BRITISH SOCIETY IN TOKYO

Soon after my arrival in Tokyo I was invited to various events of the Japan-British Society, although in retrospect I cannot understand why it took me a year or so before I became a member. However, I was an easy foil when later asked by John Figgess (then Information Counsellor at the embassy) [cf. Hugh Cortazzi's biographical portrait of Sir John Figgess in *Biographical Portraits* Vol.III] to take on some of the leg-work. I was elected to the Council of the Society for the 1967/68 year, succeeding John Field as honorary secretary when he was transferred to the embassy in Moscow in March 1968. This is a post I still hold today more than thirty-one years later.

My mentor in the Society was Yoshitomo Tokugawa, who was by the mid-1960s a Vice-President. He had received an honorary CBE in 1967 for services to Anglo-Japanese relations, and he remained chairman of the programme committee of the Society until his death in 1993. When I agreed to take up the position of Honorary Secretary, I remember Yoshitomo saying he did not like frequent changes, and he asked me to remain in the post for a long time, my response being that I would do this for him 'for a quarter of a century'. When I attended his wake at his home in Tokugawa Village in Mejiro, I suddenly realized it was twenty-five years to the day since I had made this somewhat rash statement, and I was saddened not to have been able to have a gin-and-tonic with Yoshitomo at the Orchid Bar in the Hotel Okura, his favourite watering hole, and to have seen his smile when he understood I had kept my word.

Yoshitomo Tokugawa was a Vice-President of the Japan Red Cross and was the brother-in-law of the Society's Honorary Patron HIH Princess Chichibu, his wife Masako being a sister of the Princess. (Their family were the Matsudairas of Aizu Wakamatsu fame.) Princess Chichibu had succeeded her late husband, the next younger brother of the Showa Emperor, as Honorary Patron. She was invested with an honorary GCMG, one of the highest honours that HM The Queen can bestow on a foreigner, when in 1978 she completed twenty-five years in her capacity as Honorary Patron. The investiture was made during a visit by HRH Princess Margaret. The Society presented the Princess with an unique silver soup tureen at a garden party at the Residence. So that she could wear her newly-received order, the members of the Council of the Society entertained her at a white tie dinner, with some forty people seated in the splendour of the Heian no Ma at the Hotel Okura.

Princess Chichibu was a delightful person to have so closely associated with the Japan-British Society. She had a great sense of humour and brought grace and distinction to any occasion she attended. Born in England, the Princess qualified for a British passport, and her ties with Britain ran particularly deep. However, as a member of the Imperial Household, she led a restricted life and at least by the seventies she had been well protected from many of the realities of modern life. I remember the Princess being invited to a Charity Premiere for the latest James Bond film, that would aid the causes promoted by British loyal societies, and, not knowing the organizers, she agreed to attend if I would go, too. Just before leaving for the old Hibiya Theatre, she called my office to make absolutely certain I would be there to welcome her, and I duly introduced her to all involved; however, this being a very early preview, no one had checked the film, and James Bond was flitting from bed to bed in a way that we felt we had never seen before. There was much consternation as to whether this had offended the Princess, and I remember her staggering out of the cinema looking somewhat overcome, but, as ever, she graciously expressed her delight at the 'lovely picture', and we all went home feeling that although she may have found it a slightly rough and somewhat different experience, on balance it had been an enjoyable night out.

My first Chairman of the Council was Katsumi Ohno, who had been ambassador in London from around 1959 to 1964, during the period when the Treaty of Commerce and Navigation had been signed between our two countries. After his diplomatic career he held major posts with the Arabian Oil Company and with the Imperial Hotel. Although a diplomat of the old school he was able to adapt both to business and changed conditions in the modern world. As Chairman, he summed up both sides of a heated discussion and made a ruling in a manner that somehow kept all parties completely happy. His wisdom and full support made me, as an inexperienced honorary secretary, learn how to ensure the Council arrived at unanimous decisions. He was always a gentleman.

One of the most active Japanese members of the Council of the Society in the 1960s and 70s was Toshitatsu Maeda, who was head of the former Daimyo family from Kanazawa. (His ancestors had ordered the construction of the great Korakuen garden in that city.) His marriage had brought together two of Japan's greatest daimyo families, as his wife was a Kaga from northern Kyushu. Toshitatsu Maeda, who was a chamberlain in the Imperial Household, was influential in opening many doors to enable members of the Society to gain access to many places not normally seen by visitors, ranging from temples and museums in Sendai and Kanazawa, to the Grand Shrines at Ise, and even the former Imperial Stock Farm. Also, on his recommendation, we stayed at several almost legendary *ryokan*, at extremely reasonable rates. However, on the few occasions when something went wrong, and the Japanese side lost face before the British participants, he expressed his displeasure in no uncertain terms.

The person who left her mark most indelibly on the Japan-British Society was Dame Kazuko Aso, who for many years was a Vice-Chairman of the Council, and was the founder of the Elizabeth Kai, the ladies' group [cf. biographical portrait of Kazuko Aso by Phillida Purvis in *Biographical Portraits* Vol.III]. Kazuko lived an incredibly busy life, and was on many committees, especially for fund raising, but she was always ready to give of her time for a good cause, and she was an extremely active supporter of the Society's many activities. If one received an award, or something special happened, Kazuko always found the time to send a note of congratulation. She has been much missed by the Society in the three years since she passed away. At Council meetings, she made extremely sensible remarks, and I found that somehow she put dissenters in their place and unanimity was always easily reached if she was allowed to have her say. I could always count on Kazuko's support and as the years went by we managed to drop the mantle of conservatism, and a number of formerly controversial projects were adopted.

A sign of the changed situation of foreign residents in Japan is the disappointing level of participation of British members in activities during the nineties. In the sixties and seventies, at least one-third of those taking part in any event organized by the Society would be British, but

today 10% is considered a fair turnout. In the earlier years we tended to
have more time, and the programmes the Society offered were not only
welcome opportunities for the British community to get to know Japanese people, they also provided interesting ways of spending leisure time.
These were days before the fax machine and inexpensive international
telephone calls, but they were also days when most of us worked from
nine until five and had a great deal of leisure. Perhaps the 'old Japan
hands' worked inefficiently compared with today. They certainly had an
easier and less competitive time, with a market that had barely been broken open, and with businesses organized in a traditional manner, where
market share was protected, and where the expatriate manager could survive by following the hands-off style of business handed down to him by
his predecessors. Cocktail parties, dinners, lectures and outings used to
be welcomed and eagerly subscribed to, whereas now we are busy dealing
with the constant demands from head offices, leaving very little time for
our own leisure activities.

ONE OF THE most important service sectors for Britain in Japan was the
airline industry. Before Virgin Atlantic began to fly to Tokyo in the late 1980s
the main British company involved was British Airways, successor to British
Overseas Airways Corporation (BOAC). Cathay Pacific which was largely
owned by Swires in Hong Kong could also be counted as British in those days
before the return of Hong Kong to China in 1997 was negotiated. But Cathay
Pacific did not have rights to fly from Britain to Tokyo and were not therefore
direct competitors of British Airways. Their rights to fly to Japan from Hong
Kong were, however, regulated in air services negotiations between Britain
and Japan.

BA's manager in Japan between 1978 and 1987 was DAVID WILKINSON
who later became a consultant and executive adviser in Japan with Virgin
Atlantic. The following is an account of David's experiences in Japan:-

•

I had hardly any briefing from British Airways (BA) in 1978 before I was
transferred direct from Iran. It was left to the incumbent manager in
Tokyo to brief me in Tokyo but as he was urgently needed in his new post
in South Africa we had only a few days together.

We arrived on the Saturday in Golden Week. On the following day
having found our way to St Alban's Church by Tokyo Tower we walked
on after church to Tora-no-mon where we came across a Shrine festival
and realized that we were indeed in a different world.

We were puzzled by a label on our car (having apparently parked illegally). When we asked one of our local staff to settle the fine on our behalf I
was told that I had to settle it personally.

BOAC, as it was called in those days, had begun a flying-boat service to Japan (to Iwakuni) in 1948. In the early days staff costs were very low but staff numbers and salaries including bonuses had been allowed to escalate until they were among the highest in the world. In order to prevent further increases for some fourteen years no new staff had been taken on and retirements and natural wastage had been welcomed as a way of keeping a lid on costs. Despite this my first impression was that BA in Tokyo were overstaffed and that costs were too high. Unfortunately, we were unable to raise additional revenue by increasing the number of weekly flights because BA had entered into an arrangement with JAL under which the two companies had agreed not to mount further flights until their joint load factor had risen to 65%.

Another major problem for us was the rampant discounting adopted by all the airlines in Japan. Looking back, the whole situation seems comical with the airlines playing 'cat and mouse' with each other by advertising legal fares while all the time doing under the counter deals and watching out for 'King Cat' (i.e. IATA); occasionally, the Japanese government tried to catch the bad boys. The airlines, of course, denied all knowledge of discounting deals until they were caught out by proof of the purchase of a ticket by another airline. One airline in an attempt to hide their discounting opened a bank account in Indonesia to pay for discounts, but they were shown up by a disgruntled member of staff who presented bank statements to the Association of European Carriers.

When I arrived in Japan there were five expatriate staff in Tokyo. The number varied over the years at the whim of head office. There was, unfortunately, no company policy on language training and BA sadly never took part in the European Community's language and experience scholarship scheme. We could have greatly benefited from having expatriate staff competent in Japanese and with a knowledge of Japanese business practices. Despite this our expatriate staff were hard-working and interested in their job and worked well together

I had more problems with Japanese staff, although I am glad to say these did not involve dishonesty. I found that the company had tried to enforce Western ways of doing business when they should have been trying to adapt to Japanese ways. I discovered that the policy had been to promote local staff because of their knowledge of English rather than for their general abilities. In some cases the only merit some senior staff had was their ability in English. Gradually, I managed to alter the pattern and appoint people on grounds of their overall ability.

We had a number of difficult labour problems. The 'annual spring offensive' seemed to come round with unwelcome regularity. Each airline sent out to Tokyo negotiators allegedly expert in wage negotiations, but they did not speak Japanese and did not understand Japanese ways. They seldom achieved the kind of settlement they had agreed upon among themselves. The airlines rarely stuck to the formula agreed between them and after a strike or threat of a severe strike one or two would capitulate. Alternatively JAL or ANA, knowing what the other airlines were offering, would decide to make a higher offer to their staff and the other airlines would be forced to follow suit.

Our relations with head office were chequered. On the whole I was given reasonable latitude to do what I thought right, but occasionally someone high up in the organization would issue an edict which demonstrated a total lack of understanding of the local scene. One notable example was when it was decided on high that bonuses should no longer be paid. I did my best to point out that in Japan this would simply not be acceptable, but I was told that the edict had to be enforced. Inevitably, after a damaging strike, the edict was withdrawn. On another occasion the Chairman of BA gave an undertaking that no discounting of fares was to be permitted and everything would be done by the book. Only when BA's load factor had plummeted to 40% and BA had lost a fortune did head office relent. It took us a long time to regain market share.

I have never been able to understand why BA was so slow in taking up its options first on the Polar route and later on the Trans-Siberian. They seemed just to sit back and watch other carriers leading the way. When the penny finally dropped and they realized that the Japanese economy was booming BA altered their attitude and I am glad to say that BA caught up.

I arrived in Japan just before the move from Haneda to Narita. The Japanese authorities had made thorough preparations and I was frankly staggered by the efficiency with which this massive operation was conducted. Tons of equipment had to be moved and hundreds of staff reallocated, but the move was carried out without a hitch. This was despite the fact that, because of local opposition to the building of Narita airport, the move had had to be frequently postponed.

At an early stage I decided that a firm but non-confrontational approach was the best one to adopt in dealing with the Japanese authorities. When I was chairman of the airlines association in Tokyo we were occasionally able to help the authorities out of difficulties. At one stage local residents in the Narita area complained about items dropped from aircraft including bits of metal and blocks of ice. The Japanese did not have a budget to insure against such eventualities. So we included an extra clause in our policies to cover any damage which might be caused by such incidents.

Sometimes the Japanese authorities could be very bureaucratic and hidebound. On one occasion we had an urgent need to divert a 747 aircraft with 150 passengers travelling to London to go via Kuala Lumpur instead of Anchorage to pick up a further 200 passengers stranded at Kuala Lumpur as a result of engine problems. Because the UK-Japan bilateral civil aviation agreement did not cover flights to Kuala Lumpur our request was curtly refused. In fact, of course, there were no revenue earning passengers on board the aircraft to Kuala Lumpur and the Japanese decision was an error of judgement. When they realized their lack of common sense I am glad to say that we received profuse apologies.

Another example of Japanese bureaucracy at its most inflexible occurred when an aircraft in the take-off position was refused permission to take off because it was 23.02 and the curfew on night flights began at 23.00. This meant that BA had to find accommodation for some 280 irate passengers (mostly Japanese) and delay departure until 12.00 noon the following day as the crew had to have their stipulated rest time. The delay had a considerable knock-on effect on BA schedules elsewhere.

BA and later Virgin Atlantic fared well in the bilateral civil aviation negotiations. This was largely due to careful preparations and groundwork before the talks began. We worked closely with the British Embassy in these and other issues. Our relations with the embassy were always cordial and usually, depending inevitably on the personalities involved, necessary action was taken speedily.

I found BA and Virgin Atlantic generally good employers. My salary may not have been as high as that of many other expatriate managers. but it enabled us to maintain a reasonable standard of living and do the entertaining which was a part of the job. Of course Virgin Atlantic being a newer and smaller organization was less bureaucratic than BA and decisions could be reached quicker.

BA had a compound of three houses in Tokyo. The land had been bought in the days of BOAC around 1952 for some £2000 (for just under an acre). By the time I arrived in Tokyo it was a much under-utilized asset, but it was not redeveloped until 1990 because of delays due to objections from our neighbours. It took much patience, many months and considerable expense to settle these problems, but despite capital gains taxes BA made a good profit on their 1952 purchase!

I was, of course, a member of the British Chamber of Commerce in Japan, but it seemed to me that it never really made up its mind about what its role should be. Was it there to support British business in Japan or should its main purpose be to help business visitors to set up in Japan? Many of those already established in Japan did not see why they should devote their time to supporting potential competitors.

Outside the office I kept myself fit by playing squash and golf. I found that the time spent at the nineteenth hole was generally more productive in business terms than time on the course! I joined the American Club mainly for squash (there was also a squash court at the British Embassy which we could use) and swimming. We naturally supported the Japan-British Society. Other organizations in which we participated included the St George's Society, the RAF Association and the Royal British

Legion. We also helped charitable causes by assisting in fund-raising events. BA for its part backed promotions of British goods at Japanese department stores and any appropriate business events.

We made many friends and managed to visit most of the islands during our years in Japan. We greatly enjoyed our time in Japan and return there every year to see our friends.

DAVID WILKINSON had the support of his wife ANN who sent me the following reflections on life in Japan:-

•

D avid had joined BOAC as a trainee in 1954. We were married in 1956. I knew that we would spend much of our life abroad and I was happy to go with him anywhere. Our first posts could be regarded as 'hardship posts' and David spent long hours at the airport dealing with problems such as an aircraft which needed an engine change and coping with irate passengers requiring accommodation. Nevertheless, David enjoyed his job and I was happy supporting him and bringing up a family. When we had to move on I was generally sad to part from the many friends we had made.

The one country in which I did not want to live was Japan. My parents had friends whose lives had been tragically affected by their experiences in the hands of the Japanese military during the war. My heart sank when I heard that we were to be sent to Tokyo. As a Christian I recognized that I should forgive my enemies; sadly, I fear that I had only paid lip service to this precept in the case of the Japanese. I was torn between my loyalty to David and my bitterness towards the Japanese.

Our children were then at Haileybury and on our brief leave between our departure from Iran and going to Japan we were able to attend a service in the beautiful school chapel. The visiting preacher in commenting on his text from the Gospel according to St Matthew, chapter 25 verse 35 ("For I was hungry and you gave me something to eat, I was thirsty and you gave me something to drink; I was a stranger and you invited me in'), gave an account of the sufferings of British prisoners of war on the Burma-Siam railway. Amongst their Japanese captors was an engineer who had been assigned to oversee the technical side of the construction. He was a Christian and horrified and saddened at the treatment of the prisoners, many of whom were near to death through undernourishment and disease and yet were forced to work. At the risk of his own life he helped as many as he could. He would select each day one prisoner to whom he would secretly give a slip of paper with a sketch map directing the prisoner to his hut adding a warning to take care. When the prisoner reached the hut he would find a table below a simple wooden cross with a meal to sustain him. This story helped me to understand the real nature of forgiveness and made it easy for me to accept our posting to Japan. In Japan I made many genuine Japanese friends and greatly enjoyed our time there.

In Tokyo I worshipped regularly at St Alban's church near Tokyo Tower which became my spiritual home. Although St Albans is a part of the Episcopal Church of Japan (*Nipponseikokai*) there were regular services in English. The congregation was an international one and included some Japanese Christians who preferred to attend our services rather than those of St Andrew's next door which had an all-Japanese membership. The two congregations worked together to help old people's homes, hospitals and a home for lepers. In this cooperative work we overcame the inevitable language barriers. Although the Christian community in Japan is comparatively small we never felt that we were regarded as outcasts or oddities.

We soon settled down in Japan meeting many people from Embassies and business firms, British and Japanese. I became an enthusiastic supporter of the Japan-British Society and the Elizabeth-kai which helped to bring Japanese ladies into contact with British ladies. Through the Elizabeth-kai I made many Japanese friends. Looking back I wish I had learned Japanese but we expected to stay no more than three years although in the end we were in Japan for nine years. Instead of learning Japanese I taught English to various Japanese ranging from university students to teachers and housewives. This experience helped me greatly to understand many aspects of Japanese life, thinking and social attitudes. A number of those whom I taught took me into their confidence and spoke freely about their private and personal lives in a way that I had never expected.

The Japanese reputation of being 'unfathomably mysterious' was I found a myth especially in the case of Japanese women. Although they appear to be gentle and are taught to be genteel, I found that many of them are tough, aggressive and capable of being manipulative, yet warm-hearted, loving, generous and fun-loving. Thus in actual fact they are very like us!

Before we arrived in Japan in 1978 an association called 'Refugees International' had been set up to help the so-called 'boat people' who were refugees from the Communist regime in Vietnam. They arrived in places like Hong Kong destitute and emaciated. I became a member of the committee for 'Refugees International' and in due course became their fundraising director. We were soon involved in trying to assist other groups of refugees including those from the war in Afghanistan. Our task was a formidable one, not least because Japanese people were not accustomed to the concept of fund-raising for charitable purposes. The rebuilding of Japan after the devastation of war had absorbed all their energies. Few understood what it meant to be a refugee. We decided that it would be useless to seek permission to raise money through street collections. Instead, we raised money by organizing charitable events such as concerts including performances with Seiji Ozawa, conductor, Isaac Stern, violinist, and Yo Yo Ma, cellist. These won the support of members of the Imperial family, first Princess Chichibu and later the then Crown Prince and Princess (now the Emperor and Empress). Companies gave us generous support for instance through advertising in our concert programmes and sponsoring particular events so that all the money from ticket sales could go to charitable causes. As a result of these events we were able to donate some 26 million yen each year to alleviate the plight of refugees. Many of the contacts we made in these activities became real friends.

From the lavish initial party (including ice sculptures, kimono-clad waitresses, and mountains of food and drink) given to introduce us I realized that nothing was done by halves in Japan. Further experience confirmed this impression. I came to realize that in business and in friendship once a commitment had been made it was total and irreversible.

I often think of the Japanese engineer who helped some of our prisoners of war on the Burma-Siam railway!

WHILE ON THE Far Eastern staff of John Swire & Sons, DICK LARGE was first deployed in Japan in the late 1960s, initially with Cathay Pacific in the Kansai and later in Tokyo, where he was in charge of sales/marketing. Ten years on, and hard on the heels of the so-called 'container revolution', he presided over Swire Japan's international shipping/transportation operations, before retiring in 1982. After a further period in Japan as BAe's chief representative, 1991-94, he has been active in Anglo-Japanese affairs in London, chairing both the Japan Association and the Japan Festival Fund. The following reminiscences of his time in Japan span four decades:-

•

Already recognized, industrially, as a premier league player, Japan in the 1960s was an exuberant, if stressful, place undergoing a dramatic transformation in the sprint for economic growth. Accompanying this and a population explosion was a huge upsurge in air travel imposing an impossible burden on the industry's infrastructure. In Cathay Pacific Airways (CPA) all was frenetic, pell-mell activity as the company sought to extend its catchment area, opening ten prefectural sales outlets in two years – from Aomori and Sendai, south to Takamatsu and Kagoshima. Together with new markets and alliances – most notably with JAL, new points in Japan (CPA was the first international carrier to serve Nagoya) and new destinations beyond Hong Kong were served. Faced with a blatantly xenophobic mindset (it was thought obligatory for Japanese nationals to return home on the national carrier), airline staff nurtured good agency relations – the latter's employees sometimes being offered after-hours English tuition! – mechanization, training and marketing innovation. The rural influx and wholesale rebuilding programmes meant targeting the uprooted *'danchi*-dwelling communities (soon to emerge as the bedrock of Japan's new middle class) whilst, despite hassles with officialdom and numbing bureaucracy, multiple night-time charters to S.E. Asia were organized. The passengers, often from rice-farming areas, generally remained blissfully ignorant throughout of the carrier's identity

Surprisingly, the historically staid world of shipping and conferences proved hardly less challenging or innovative in the 1970s. The industry in Japan had earlier embarked on major rationalization moves, forcibly amalgamating many of the original twenty-two ocean-shipping operators (an operational 1 million g.r.t. per company being the benchmark). This draconian move greatly enhanced the competitiveness of the Japanese merchant marine as well as facilitating the containerization programme of the late 1960s/early 1970s. The complete integration of road, rail, sea and handling facilities necessitated a huge capital outlay on re-equipping (Overseas Containers Ltd (OCL) alone invested some £50 million) and rationalizing services through the formation of consortia with, in the case of 'TRIO', the British lines agreeing to work alongside NYK, MOSK and Hapag Lloyd on the Europe/Far East berth. For an industry traditionally dogged by inertia and outmoded practices, these were indeed absorbing times, not least because of the larger-than-life figures who helped fashion the change. Of the latter, none stood out more prominently than the former President and Chairman of NYK, Yoshiya Ariyoshi, the dominant figure in Japanese shipping for some thirty years. It was his personal magnetism, realism and humour, allied to a shrewd business brain, which helped ensure the success of the fateful meeting at Mitsubishi in 1966 between Ariyoshi and his visionary Ocean colleagues, Sir John Nicholson and Lindsay Alexander which set the seal on container service collaboration – with all the implications this was to have on the global conference system [cf. the biographical portrait by Hugh Cortazzi of Yoshiya Ariyoshi in *Biographical Portraits* Vol.III, published by Japan Library for the Japan Society, 1999].

No less enlightening, in some ways, was the post-'bubble' view of Japan in the early 1990s – this time with British Aerospace. This exposure to the hard-nosed, highly-political, often machiavellian world of defence and civil aviation marketing, in an environment at once dominated by the constraints of the US-Japan Security Treaty – dictated by Japan's somewhat ambivalent position on rearmament – and the hitherto all-powerful position enjoyed by the Boeing Aircraft Co, proved both fascinating and frustrating. Not unnaturally the Treaty had, over many years, spawned a myriad of cozy deals involving military aircraft, weaponry and technology alliances whilst Boeing's sub-contracting to Japanese industry, principally in the construction of the 747 and 777, together with the promise of future collaboration on 'YSX' (a phantom aircraft designed to appease the Japanese MOT's longstanding ambition to re-enter civil aircraft production on a commercially viable scale) had served, effectively, to freeze third countries out of the picture.

Given such high stakes, marketing strategies evolve over many years and are pursued with a dedication and ruthlessness that can seem far removed from the, invariably, more transparent, urbane world of airline sales and ship canvassing. One example must suffice. BAe's conspicuous breakthrough in 1991 in selling thirty 125-800 'search and rescue' aircraft to the Japan Air Self Defense Force (allegedly then the largest post WWII military contract ever secured by a non-US firm in Japan) caused ramifications across the whole spectrum of US/Japan relations representing, as it did, a startling departure in MOT/JDA policy and a threat to a hitherto virtual monopoly position. Small wonder that the US Chamber of Commerce in Tokyo trumpeted, almost hysterically, 'The Europeans are coming!'.

There have been other conspicuous European successes subsequently, and Airbus has long since changed the face of civil aviation market penetration, but deep-seated impediments/prejudices to sales by non-US aerospace companies in Japan remain. Thus in the field of technology transfers, the selection criteria applied by Japan in defence procurement exhibit a clear preference (for obvious interoperability, maintenance, logistics, 'tried and tested' reasons) for US equipment. Even when the US has refused the Japanese access to 'unique' technologies, available from Europe, sensitivities between the two countries over the trade imbalance and perennial strength of the yen, would still make the 'Buy American' slogan largely irresistible to both parties.

THERE WERE some interesting and amusing moments during DICK LARGE's varied career in Japan. The following are two examples:-

•

SHINTO LEGACIES

To recapture, faithfully, the unremarkable details of an episode which occurred some thirty-two years previously is a demanding discipline. The adage about the young having aspirations that never materialize and the old reminiscences of what never happened, rings all too true.

But I do recall that the invitation from our Japanese language tutor to join him one autumn weekend in 1967, deep in the Hyogo countryside, was eagerly taken up. Amongst other sylvan delights, we were, it seems, to witness a supposedly clandestine fertility festival at a little known Shinto shrine.

The festival was certainly well-attended. Included among those who had apparently prayed to the phallic deities for generations were infertile women and newlyweds – plus the usual assortment of lonely hearts club adherents, but as with many Shinto celebrations, our rural odyssey seemed to be mainly characterized by carousing youths bearing *omikoshi* shrines. Of these, some sported traditional masks representing the more explicit and comical allegorical personages involved. There was Okama, termed 'the insatiable, fat girl', Hyoko, 'the octopus-faced buffoon', and, inevitably, Tengu, the irascible, bawdy suitor with the ribald gesture and fearful visage. Indeed it was he who, wielding a beech switch and howling maniacally, suddenly materialized as our party threaded its way down the fields as darkness fell. Penetrating our ranks, he delivered my wife a painful thwack across the buttocks before careering on through the shrieking throng. Furious, I was at the time all for giving chase but was quickly restrained by our unflustered host who described the assault as a part of the ritual and much encouraged by the barren ladies present on the day. The relief which accompanied this revelation seemed misplaced when a few weeks later my wife discovered that she was pregnant! I subsequently recall the sisters at Kobe's Sacred Heart School, where she taught, expressing joy unconfined at the news. They had, they confided, offered up regular prayers to achieve the same end! But regardless of where the responsibility lay, our daughter Kate was safely delivered at Tokyo's Seibo hospital the following spring.

But that was not quite the end of the story. Kate's arrival was notable in other ways not entirely disassociated from this early brush with Shinto custom. During our first sixteen months in Japan our affection for sumo, as is customary amongst expatriates, had grown enormously. It was after all a golden age for Japanese wrestling being the era of the legendary Taiho and his co-*yokozuna* of heroic proportions, Sadanoyama, Kotozakura and the enigmatic, beetle-browed Kashiwado. Indeed, for many years prior to 1968, my own company, Cathay Pacific Airways, had co-sponsored the Fukuoka *basho*. Imagine our surprise and delight, therefore, when literally days after Kate and her mother left hospital to return to our new Shinanomachi apartment (overlooking the Meiji outer garden) we witnessed, amidst frenzied scenes, the installation in the flat immediately below our own of the newly-wed Kashiwado himself and his diminutive bride! I remember marvelling at the prodigious quantity of silver, bronze and glass trophies borne by retainers through the car park below and speculating on the sheer volume of treasure that could be squeezed into such a confined space.

Our meeting, not long after, had an inevitability about it. One Saturday morning our lift stopped at the fifth floor and a *yukata*-clad giant levered his gargantuan frame in beside us, dramatically brushing the ceiling and floors of the lift as he did so. Then, fixing his stern gaze at the bundle in my wife's arms, the man they regard to this day in Japan as a virtual deity stretched out his huge hands and, gently, adroitly, lifted our newborn to eye level. It was a heart-stopping moment! Only later was the full significance of that gesture – a *yokozuna*'s blessing no less – brought home to us and our daughter's life (she is now married with a child of her own) is happily testimony to this.

There is a postscript. Twenty-five years on, in 1993, and during our third tour of duty in Japan, I was privileged to occupy a ringside seat at the Kokugikan for the New Year *basho*. Perched precariously at the foot of the *dohyo* I found myself seated within touching distance of our daughter's 'benefactor', Kashiwado being by that time the Sumo Association's senior judge. It was with the greatest difficulty that I resisted the urge to lean across and re-introduce myself. No matter; in this family, as presumably in many others in Japan today, the legacy of Grand Champion Kashiwado, if not of Tengu, lives on.

IT'S JUST NOT CRICKET!

In the early 1990s, British Embassies and Consulates worldwide were tasked with drumming up support locally for Manchester's bid to host the 2000 Olympics. In Japan this entailed marshalling all available promotional resources in an endeavour, discreetly, to bring some influence to bear on government ministries and, specifically, on that country's two Olympic commissioners and vote-casters.

At the instigation of the then ambassador, Sir John Boyd, a Manchester 2000 Committee was established and expatriate businessmen co-opted on to it, myself included, in addition to one Gary Lineker, then under contract to a Japanese soccer team (with the improbable name of 'Grampus Eight'). A hugely popular figure in Japan, Gary was to prove an engaging and articulate emissary of this country throughout his time there, his presence, as Sir John recognized, adding a particular piquancy to Embassy gatherings.

The episode recalled here occurred in the autumn of 1993. A G7 summit was in progress in Tokyo with the British prime minister in attendance, an opportunity, reasoned Sir John, to have an impassioned advocate of Manchester's case meet privately with the two most influential Japanese. Which explains why on the evening in question a number of Committee members were found gathered in the ambassador's drawing-room with one commissioner, a Mr Igaya (Japan's only Olympic skiing medallist) awaiting Mr Major's return from his day's labours.

Unexpectedly, it was Igaya-san who raised the subject of cricket, which he had apparently witnessed at different times in his career, and we chortled at Ian Mikardo's alleged response on a US lecture tour, which had the unimaginative English inventing the game 'to give them some conception of eternity'! The Japanese can relate to this. (Fifteen years earlier we had grown accustomed to our Japanese neighbours (*besuboru* fans all) gazing incredulously over our garden wall in Meguro, where we had erected a cricket net, to applaud our young son's plundering of my over-pitched googlies.) So it was not long before we found ourselves kneeling around the oval coffee table the better to provide Igaya-san with a positional overview, with the ambassador intoning advice of the 'imagine, if you will, that this cigar-cutter is the wicket-keeper (catcher) and that the cigarette lighter is backward square leg', kind! Our guest, not lacking in humour, quickly entered into the spirit of things until this graphic exercise was interrupted by the sound of the PM's outriders approaching the embassy compound. Minutes later the doors were flung open and a slightly fatigued John Major burst in. It had been a long day. His demeanour soon brightened, however, when, on meeting Igaya-san, he learned of our efforts to explain some of 'clicket's' more bizarre rites. 'At last', he said, 'something I really know something about', or words to that effect.

Picture the scene. While his dinner guests waited impatiently in an adjoining room, the prime minister bade us all return to a kneeling position on the drawing-room carpet in a last-ditch attempt to unravel some of the intricacies of our summer game. It was, it must be said, a virtuoso performance, at the end of which he still managed the time to present Manchester's case fully and convincingly. Who of those present that night will ever forget the look of total disbelief on our Japanese friend's face as we later escorted him to his car?

Of course, Manchester's bid was destined to fail, though I like to think that at least one Japanese commissioner cast a vote in our direction. More importantly, a British prime minister, despite his well-chronicled shortcomings, had made himself known to our guest, and the rest of us too, as a sensitive, passionate and eloquent advocate of this country's position. He also demonstrated, what we had suspected all along, that here was an enthusiast and connoisseur of cricket who was, arguably, amongst the truly elite. Ask Gary.

GRAHAM McCALLUM was head of Swires in Japan from 1972 to 1978. He also worked in Japan for Swires during the years 1956-59, and spent six months with the company in the Kansai in 1953.

Graham has told me that as a shipping manager in the Kansai he had

... the most fantastic fun. My work entailed travel to all the lovely, out-of-the-way, ports throughout western Japan including Kyushu and Okinawa. The hospitality of Swire's sub-agents in these places was invariably charming and unselfish. The daily commute from my house in the suburbs of Kobe to the office in Osaka was, however, far from 'fun'. It entailed a walk from Nunobiki, a bus to San-nomiya station, standing up in a packed Hankyu line train to Osaka and then a jeep ride to Azuchi-machi. There I had to climb three flights of stairs to the office. In the heat of the Japanese summer this required stamina and determination. The din in the office with the windows open and the trams clanging outside was such that it was often impossible to hear what was being said on the telephone.

Like other British residents in those days Graham '. . . was appalled by the state of the main roads. The displaced blocks of road stone were serious hazards for even the most careful driver.' He enjoyed getting out into the then largely unspoilt Japanese countryside on week-ends. (In those days the week-end did not begin until Saturday afternoon.)

In the mid 1950s I was given the enviable task of testing as a car for Swire's Tokyo office a Toyota Toyopet saloon. This involved driving the car to Hakone and back to see how it stood up to the roads. My report had to go to head office in London who took the decision to buy the car.

[In the FCO at that time we would certainly have had to refer back to London any proposals for 'capital' expenditure although we would not in any case have been allowed to buy a Japanese made car! I thought that in British companies such decisions would have been delegated to the local manager!]

21

Manufacturing Investments

PETER PARKER • MIKE PERRY

THE IMPORTANCE and value of attracting capital investment to Britain was increasingly recognized by British governments from the mid-1970s onwards and the promotion of 'inward investment' became one of the most important tasks for the British Embassy in Tokyo.

One British businessman who became closely involved with Japanese investment in Britain was Sir Peter Parker. PETER PARKER began to study Japanese during the war. He first went to Japan as part of the Occupation forces and his experiences in and his impressions of Japan at that time are included in Chapter 1, 'The Aftermath of War: Occupation and Poverty'. After demobilization and Oxford University Peter Parker had a distinguished career in business including a stint as Chairman of British Rail. In the following essay Peter, now Global Adviser to Mitsubishi Electric, recounts his later experiences with Japan and ruminates about the future:-

•

I sense that Japan's next fifty years will prove to be as surprising to itself and the world as the last fifty have been. I witnessed the start of that first big surprise, just over fifty years ago. And nowadays I believe I am witnessing another big one on the way.

No one at the end of the war could have guessed the phenomenal things to come for modern Japan. Oddly enough – and it is very odd indeed – the nearest thing to any vision of Japan's future that I have found from the war-torn years of the 1940s is in the paperback OUP edition of *Hitler'sTableTalk*. Martin Bormann was responsible, for the record, and there is this eerie entry for 18 January 1942, evening: '. . . Japan will be one of the richest countries in the world. What a transformation! This country that as recently as a few weeks ago was regarded as one of the poorest. There are few examples in world history of a more rapid and complete reversal of the situation. . .'

*   *   *

After my service in Japan with the Occupation in 1945/46 my life did not
involve me with Japan seriously again until the mid 1980s. I had stepped
down from the Chair of British Rail and had a portfolio of industrial
interests to pursue. By that point I had forgotten much of my Japanese.
One of my ambitions was to reconnect with international business and
with Japan. The opportunity to do so in the most venturesome way had
me winging across the world to Tokyo.

Taking the chair of Mitsubishi Electric (UK) in 1984 was a controversial surprise all round in my business circles: to the Japanese themselves
who had never tried the experiment of a *gaijin*, a foreigner, as chairman in
any part of their affairs; to me, who had largely lost touch with Japan and
the Japanese since 1946; and to many friends with whom I discussed the
move. Some, straight out, condemned me as a turncoat. I was switching
sides: I was not so much a Trojan horse as a Trojan ass, letting the Japanese
in to British and continental markets. Some friends who had been
through terrible times in Japanese prison camps were puzzled, even dis-
gusted that I should treat and trade with the enemy. Others said there was
an urgent job of bridge-building to be done. I flew to Tokyo to decide.

I brooded over breakfast at the Imperial Hotel. I was alone and dood-
ling in my sketch book the view from my window of the Imperial Castle
wall. Its huge, rugged blocks of grey granite looked immovable, but reflected in the green moat below they danced with the lights of the se-
quined sun. The dark water was patched with white autumnal mist.
Part of the mist suddenly became a white swan and floated my way. A
haiku would have fitted the moment like a glove, but my Japanese was
too poor by then and I had business to attend to. I spent the day in discussions, discovering what Mitsubishi Electric did – everything from sea
to sky, from satellites and earth stations and power stations to semicon-
ductors and a vast range of the most advanced electronic equipment. It
had become one of the great electronic corporations in the world, a quiet
giant.

The head of its international activities was Yufu-san. William Blake said
Energy is Delight: Yufu-san was a delightful businessman with a vision
and ceaseless drive and charm, short, thin, and his dart-like shape aimed
accurately at export orders all over the world – if God had meant people
to fly he would have made them all like Yufu-san. His capacity for making
his colleagues feel braver than they really were and less lazy than they
really feel, had won contracts all over the global markets. And despite
my poorly-remembered, broken Japanese which lay in bits and pieces
in my memory, he understood my brooding over my decision.

That night Yufu-san and I dined together at a traditional inn by the
harbour with Takagi-san, a fine friend and the former chairman of the
Japanese National Railways, who shared with me at that time the record
for the longest term in the hot seat as head of a major railway system. We

talked late and reached that relaxed stage when, in customary style, a pad, ink-block and *fude* (brush pen) were brought to the table and we each tried to put something on paper. I remembered the white swan and the castle wall dismantled in its reflection in the moat, not so much a thought as a feeling still not formulated; that is how haiku are made. Pretty pusillanimous not to try. I thought. I wrote in seventeen English syllables about the castle wall dancing with flakes of light, the mist and that swan born of it. Next morning a messenger came early to my hotel room to tell me that Yufu-san had been thinking about the haiku: surely it meant that I had decided. He was right, I had. And I have lived on the busy frontier of East-West trade happily ever after.

This is what I said in my memoirs (*For Starters*) of ten years ago and I see no need for revision:

> I had three aims in taking the job: to establish more high-tech investment and more jobs in Britain; to encourage more collaborations in joint ventures, in research and exports; and to close the cultural gap between our two peoples. There are superficial similarities between the British and the Japanese, of which not too much should be made. We both suffer an unreliable climate, both enjoy a taste for tea, both celebrate royalty still, both are islanders and have a separateness which receives a mild shock when we drive on continental roads running into other countries – ours all lead to the sea. But still there is the gap of ten thousand miles of clouds and waves between us which the Shogun wrote about in the first letter between the two islands, to James I, almost four hundred years ago. And something more than the elements make us keep our distance. The British memories of war, the baffling obscurity of the Japanese language, and now their phenomenal, frightening rise to economic power and their sheer ubiquity – these make an explosive mix, just under the British skin, ready to erupt when some politician blows his or her top over a trade issue of maddening but temporary relevance. Or the Emperor dies. To shed our stereotypes of one another is going to take time and imagination, political statesmanship and, too often forgotten, good management in our international corporations that trade each way.
>
> British managers who work with Japanese are at a new frontier. In the give and take of cultures they have to learn to give and take time. I have learnt patience from Japan, sitting through the process of *nemawashi*, the careful root-binding of ideas to make it possible to move them. No macho Western manager wants to believe it, but the Japanese win by commitment and consensus. Their enterprise is management by committee, the country is a committee, and their management moves on the lines of a sumo wrestler. Ideas develop slowly, ponderously; action strikes like lightning. Also I have learnt that, contrary to managerial mythology in the West, the Japanese are not beautifully trained robots; they take risks with people. I spoke with Tominaga-san, then MD of MEUK, about job specifications, and he admitted that he was not in favour of them. 'If I say

exactly what to do, maybe that's all he'll do', said Tomi. Their attitude is
complex, full of contraries. Their management is highly detailed, yet it is
readier to live with unpredictability, ambiguity and uncertainty than we
in the West are. It may be stiffly respectful and hierarchical, about age
particularly, but it is scrupulous about listening to views and news from
every level, from the very bottom of the organization upwards; courteous and evasive about ever saying 'no' directly, but quietly certain about
what its objectives are: technically-based in its professionalism of management, but wonderfully realistic in admitting that the best management is an art; relentlessly competitive as between companies, both in
Japan and overseas, yet ultimately responsive to the fact that there is a
commitment beyond their corporate sovereignty. Where there is a national will, that is the way, and it was the national will that recreated
Japan post-war. Nothing was written in the stars to say they would ever
rise again as they did. The nation decided and worked with a unity which
is not to be as easily copied as their production technology can be copied
and as ours was once copied by them.

Takeo Fujisawa, co-founder of Honda, was asked to compare Japanese and Western management. He was as polite as he could be: it was
ninety-five per cent the same, and different in all important respects.
Five per cent may be a tiny figure, but revolutions are led by minorities.
In 1985 I wrote the introduction to a sort of revolutionary handbook,
one of the Penguin classics in management, *The Art of Japanese Management* by two Americans, Pascale and Athos. Their analysis of the components of success in any enterprise anywhere is arranged into the
inevitable checklist (if Moses were to come down the mountain today,
I am sure he would be presenting us with a checklist) and they reduce
their careful and exhilarating research into seven 'S's. The first three 'S's
are strategy, structure, systems. They call these the 'hard' S's and any manager worth his salt would agree; there can be no substitute for them. The
next 'S's are style, staff, skills, and super-ordinate goals: these are the 'soft'
'S's, and they are vaguer qualities that the professional literature often
rates as optional, decorative not decisive, mere froth. But that froth,
the authors argue, has the force of the Pacific – and in my opinion the
Atlantic as well. It may well be that in the world we are entering these
subtler qualities will have the power to make or break not just companies
but whole economies.

Of course, since these first impressions Japan has been on the rack of
recession, just about since the *Art of Japanese Management* was published.
But the analysis of their success is still relevant. Whatever it was that made
great Japanese corporations win through are characteristics which I find
equally evident in the best corporations all over the Western world. To
celebrate them is to celebrate the significance of excellent management
everywhere. The message is not that Japanese management is, or was,
supreme. It is that success in any enterprise depends above all on the
quality of management. What matters is not whether the management

is Japanese, American, British or Ruritanian, but that it is excellent.

Now it is impossible not to see Japan at the end of the twentieth century as reaching yet another crossroads. Still on the rack of recession, I am confident the economic recovery will come – this is a society immensely well educated and with a track record for change over a hundred and fifty years. But will recovery come quicker if they take the road East or by taking the road West and becoming more 'one of us'? I think this over-simplifies the situation. There are corporate changes that are already grabbing the headlines: smaller boards, the rise in shareholders' power, share options for management, internationalising accounting standards, the cut and thrust of mergers and acquisitions, the inevitable force of global markets and deregulation.

I am now a Global Adviser to Mitsubishi Electric and an admirer of the way that challenged corporation has been one of the earliest to respond realistically to its problems. One example, but there are others. At last, corporate Japan is grasping the bouquet of nettles which the future offers at the marriage of national economies and global markets. From what I can see and hear in corporate Japanese circles, its leaders are determined to change the way they have been going about their business. I believe the next two years will show results. Of course, I do not believe that Japan will change its culture as obviously as their growingly international businesses change theirs. The social values of Japanese society are deep and durable. That old house will stand for many years to come, with one wing Western style, the other still *nihon-shiki*. How I hope so.

BRITAIN, at least from the 1970s onwards, has worked hard to promote investments by Japanese companies, especially in manufacturing but increasingly also in research and development as well as service industries. In postwar Japan, however, British companies wanting to invest in manufacturing were for a long time forced into joint ventures. These were often unprofitable, at least initially, and faced stiff competition, cultural barriers and regulatory problems. MIKE PERRY (Sir Michael Perry), who headed Unilever's joint venture in Japan from 1981-83 and went on to become Chairman of Unilever and to lead various British campaigns to export to Japan, describes his and his wife's experiences in Japan in the early 1980s:-

•

Joan and I arrived in Tokyo in 1981, straight from a four-year stint in Buenos Aires, Argentina. We had come in a hurry because my predecessor as Chairman of Nippon Lever KK had died in office. This latter sad event had nothing to do with the stresses and strains of running a joint venture company in Japan, but was the consequence of protracted ill health.

For the two of us the opportunity to return to the East was greeted with delight. Eight years earlier working and raising a young family in Bangkok had established a deep and lasting affection for the Orient, and we eagerly grasped the chance to renew and expand the experience. With children by now being educated in England we were able to look for a home in Tokyo without the constraint of school commuting, and by good fortune found that most rare of properties in central Tokyo – a brand new semi-detached four-bedroomed house with a fully landscaped garden. The fact that the fully landscaped garden was only about three metres in length did not detract from the pleasure for George III, our Argentine-born blue roan cocker spaniel! We thus established ourselves in absolute luxury in Kami Osaki, within ten minutes' walk of Meguro station and ten minutes' drive from my Nippon Lever office in Shibuya.

Joan immediately threw herself into Japanese art. Her fascination for Chinese porcelain found new extension as she explored the beauties of Japanese ceramics, and her earlier introduction in Bangkok to Japanese flower arranging under the expert guidance of the British ambassador's wife, Betty de la Mare, was now given full rein. As a devotee of the Sogetsu school of *Ikebana* she acquired a source of providing and receiving pleasure which is life-long. For both of us the fascination of seeking to understand Japanese form, shape and structure in art has been one of the most enriching of experiences.

Life in a European-Japanese joint venture company at that time was equally enriching, but considerably more frustrating. By the early 1980s the worst forms of Japanese protectionism may have been starting to erode, but there was still a very long way to go. In the decades before that, joint ventures were the only feasible inward investment route, and the laboriously constructed partnerships which we all worked in were far from satisfactory. For Unilever, the strategic objective was to build a viable business in the world's second largest economy, both as an expansion opportunity in its own right, and as a source of learning from the Japanese economic miracle. Some of the world's largest producers in our core business areas of branded foods and household consumer products were Japanese and we felt it was desirable to seek to oppose them in their home markets as well as compete with them abroad.

As far as the first objective was concerned we had left it a few decades too late. Large and efficient competitors were already well established in all our key markets and the process of converting promising bridgeheads into successful, well-established businesses turned out to be a long and arduous one. In my time the most promising way forward was to build on our encouraging start in the packaged margarine market, which at that time was benefiting from the growing popularity in Japanese homes of bread, or rather toast, as an alternative for rice at breakfast time. It probably goes without saying that in countries where bread is not consumed as a staple, there is also very little market for products, like butter or margarine, to spread on it. By the way, this apparently self-evident truth never deterred the Unilever pioneers in decades gone by, who valiantly strove to sell their margarines in Far Eastern countries where the consumption of bread scarcely existed.

The other major success area for Unilever in the early eighties was in the perhaps unlikely area of toilet soaps. The twice-yearly Japanese custom of exchanging gifts with family and business contacts alike had produced an extraordinary industry focused around the Japanese department store. The important thing about a gift at *Ochugen* (mid year) or *Oseibo* (year-end) was that the recipient must know exactly how much money had been spent. To facilitate this vital social process, department stores produced twice-yearly catalogues of gifts neatly arranged by value in steps of ¥1,000. Such gifts were expected to be useful, and a specially wrapped presentation box of, say, a dozen tablets of a well known brand of toilet soap was especially acceptable. At the top of the range was a beautiful box of Lux Imperial, specially produced in Port Sunlight, England, and thus carrying the extra cachet of being imported. As evidence that I do not exaggerate is the extraordinary statistic drawn from consumer research, that the average Japanese home at the time possessed no less than forty tablets of toilet soap. Put another way, if all purchase of toilet soap were to cease forthwith the entire Japanese population could carry on washing and bathing to their heart's content for well over five years.

By far the most important lesson to be drawn from the business experience of Japan in the early eighties was to come to terms with the Japanese obsession for quality. Japanese products were successful in foreign markets because they were quite simply better. They were better because the fiercely competitive environment of the Japanese home market meant that only the very best survived the increasingly demanding scrutiny of sophisticated consumers. Japan may have been protected from foreign competition, but internally competition was 'white-hot'.

The early days of the Nippon Lever joint venture had been difficult. Our Japanese partners were a group spun off from one of the largest *keiretsu*, and the management team which had been seconded was of indifferent quality. Unilever supplied expatriate senior managers, none of whom had any practical experience in Japanese business or culture. The learning curve for everyone was a steep one, and in those early days Japanese competitors ran rings around us. By the time I arrived most of these early difficulties had been resolved, but the problem of recruiting top-class Japanese graduates or mid-career managers remained well nigh insuperable. Company loyalty and lifetime employment practices meant that young graduates seeking jobs looked first and foremost for long-term security and stability, neither of which could be guaranteed by a small foreign joint venture like ours. It would be another decade or so before the company could say that its middle and senior Japanese managers were even approaching international standards.

As far as the rest of our industry and Japanese bureaucracy were concerned, the attitude to companies like Nippon Lever was very simple in the early eighties. As a result of pressure from abroad Japan had been forced to accept, on very limited terms, the presence of foreign investors. That concession having been made, the principal task was to make sure that the foreign presence was carefully contained and circumscribed with as many restrictions to freedom of operation as it was possible to get away with. There is, for example, no doubt whatsoever that our Japanese competitors took collective action to ensure that our progress was limited, by means which in other jurisdictions might well fall foul of anti-trust laws. At the bureaucratic level protective measures were immutably in place to shelter local suppliers and to slow down the rapid implementation in Japan of proprietary innovation from elsewhere. Most of these anti-competitive practices aimed at foreign businesses have now been dismantled, but in the early 1980s they were a source of great frustration.

For Joan and me the personal balance sheet of our time in Japan is wholly positive. Frustrations in the office there may have been, but from the point of view of learning at first hand from Japan's enormous economic successes, and of experiencing at close quarters the richness of Japan's culture and the warmth of the many friendships we made, we would not have missed it for worlds. Since leaving in 1983 we have returned on a number of occasions, always with a sense of home-coming, and I have had the pleasure and privilege of working for a decade or more in London to promote Anglo-Japanese trade relations. It has been satisfying to watch the astonishing growth of trade and investment between Britain and Japan over the past two decades, and to observe with delight the goodwill and cordiality with which those relations are conducted today.

22

British Export Efforts:
Personal Reflections of a British
Trade Official

BEN THORNE

IN MY MEMOIR *Japan and Back and Places Elsewhere* (Global Oriental, 1998) I stressed the importance placed on export promotion especially from the mid-1960s onwards. The British economy was suffering from serious problems and the balance of payments was severely strained. Britain had to increase its exports. The Japanese economy, following Prime Minister Ikeda's call to 'double the national income', was growing fast and following Japan's accession to GATT and OECD the Japanese market was beginning, even if only gradually, to open up to foreign imports; but high tariffs on some goods, continuing quota restrictions and various non-tariff barriers made Japan seem to many British exporters an unattractive target.

The Board of Trade in London, encouraged by the British Embassy's commercial department, decided to back campaigns to persuade British exporters to look hard and long at the possibilities of doing profitable business in Japan. An important feature of this campaign was the decision to hold a 'British Week' in Tokyo in 1969. BEN THORNE who had seen through the 'British Week' in Hong Kong was appointed to head the British Week Office in Tokyo to prepare for this event. His dedication and enthusiasm made a significant contribution to the successes achieved in increasing British exports to Japan in this and subsequent campaigns. He followed up his work for 'British Week' by masterminding and managing the Tokyo Export Marketing Centre established in Tokyo in 1973. He then became Commercial Counsellor in Tokyo until he decided to take early retirement to develop his own business. What follows are his personal reflections, entitled 'UK-Japan Commercial Relations 1968-79':-

•

In 1950 I was sent by the Board of Trade to New Delhi to serve in a very junior capacity in the Office of the Senior British Trade Commissioner and from there worked my way up the ladder via postings to

Accra, Lagos and Hong Kong interspersed with some short spells in London working in both Commercial Relations and Export Promotions. 1964 found me in Hong Kong where the year after my arrival the Board of Trade decided to hold one of their large-scale 'British Week' trade promotions. Until then these big flagship events had been focused on consumer goods but this was such a good market for capital and engineering goods that the concept was extended. We were to hold an exhibition which ended up being entitled the 'British Engineering Display' thereafter known by the somewhat fatuous acronym 'BED' and I was put in charge of its planning and execution. Princess Margaret and Lord Snowdon came to open British Week, and BED in Hong Kong in 1966 and the whole thing was adjudged a success.

Hong Kong itself then became heavily engaged in the overspill of the Red Guard lunacy that was engulfing China, and as I was for some time acting Head of Post most of my attention was diverted to the struggle to retain Hong Kong's sanity. So I was greatly surprised, at the end of 1967, to receive a message from my boss in London inviting me to consider an urgent transfer to Tokyo where the biggest ever British Week was planned for the autumn of 1969 and I was first choice to be Director. It meant promotion, a real prize at that moment, but I had my doubts. To me, Japan was an unknown quantity; all I had to judge by was memories of wartime propaganda but, as I have recounted elsewhere,[1] I was finally persuaded to go mainly by my wife's desire to see this exotic place.

Although I was formally a First Secretary in the British Embassy and, indeed, the embassy provided most of my management level staff, there were bureaucratic divisions stemming from the Treasury's expenditure rules. Budgets for overseas fairs and trade promotions had to come from Board of Trade, not FCO funds. As a result, all the London policy-making and, possibly more important, the back-up staff were in the Board of Trade. All the costs of my separate British Week office plus the entire public sector funding of each event came from the Board of Trade; yet I and my staff were answerable to the ambassador in matters of administration and discipline. It was a set-up calling for much daily give-and-take on both sides and I am glad to say that throughout the eighteen or so months of preparations no serious disagreements occurred.

In retrospect, I firmly believe that the greatest credit for this belongs to the ambassador, Sir John Pilcher, who was wise and tolerant, realizing very well that his Commercial Counsellor had the fire and enthusiasm necessary to make a success of the operation, and he largely left his able lieutenant to cope with the motley Board of Trade crew of which I had the honour to be the leader in Tokyo. Hugh Cortazzi (for it was he) and I did circle one another warily at first but quickly came to recognize each other's virtues and settled down to a very satisfactory working relationship where I could translate his already vast knowledge of Japanese ways into arguments for doing things that were comprehensible to my Fairs & Promotions colleagues back at base. I recall only one serious disagreement with him and that was due to a misunderstanding about an administrative matter.

The team I led comprised two Japanese-speaking second secretaries and one Japanese commercial officer on loan from the Embassy plus one experienced Board of Trade officer of equivalent second-secretary rank. Locally, I recruited several Japanese female staff to run the office and a couple of retired Japanese businessmen as interpreters and contact men. Later, I was able with Hugh Cortazzi's help to recruit a highly, competent public relations manager who brought with him his own small team of staff. At the crucial final stages two more young second secretaries from the Embassy were engaged almost full time on the vast complex of the royal programme of which more later. I am proud to say that I remain in contact with many of the survivors of this happy band to the present day.

At that time the Japanese Government was just beginning to feel the first flickers of confidence that perhaps the economy really would recover from the effects of war and had made a small gesture to the rest of the world in easing financial controls by the tiniest amount. In Britain, both government and business in the guise of the CBI had for several years read the signals of industrial resurgence and were becoming restless at the restrictions on the import trade and international banking that both MITI and the Ministry of Finance (not to mention other vested interests which were the province of other ministries) fought to retain. We wished to exploit this tiny chink. One of our prime objectives in mounting British Week was to open a few more cracks in the protective structure in a way that could not be seen as hostile or offensive. We wanted to provide fun and a window on both British products and our way of life for ordinary Japanese people still starved of opportunities to travel and see for themselves, Looking back now I find it difficult to remind myself just how cramped and work-obsessed was the Japanese way of life at the end of the 1960s – a decade of liberation and self-discovery for people in Britain and elsewhere. Our attack would be gentlemanly and sugar-coated (literally in the case of confectionery!) but nonetheless determined and it had the support of large sectors of British industry represented by the newly-formed British National Export Council (BNEC). This body was the liaison between government (in the form of the Board of Trade) and the most important exporting sectors of our industries. In the field of exports it was more powerful than the CBI: well funded and, in general, capably staffed.

The BNEC Asia Committee formed sectoral sub-committees each led by a businessman with a personal knowledge of Asian markets including Japan. Most of these groups gave outstanding support in money and

time as our planning went forward but I must mention two of the leaders
who in my view made major contributions to success. First was Michael
Montague (later Lord Montague) chairman of BNEC Asia and chairman
of the Valor Company, at that time one of Britain's few successes in the
Japanese market. As the overall leader he was remarkably generous with
time, know-how and money. Norman Wood, a director of Associated
British Foods, was leader of the large and diverse food and drink sector
group. He was a senior and much respected figure in the industry, a born
leader by example who brought many of what today we call SMEs (small/
medium enterprises) to Japan for the first time. I had known both men
when in Hong Kong; indeed the only real advantage I brought to my
new role was an extensive acquaintance with British firms and their Hong
Kong representatives. Many of the firms also exported to Japan and it was
much the practice then to cover Japan from the Hong Kong operation. I
was also well known to the large Hong Kong-based British trading
houses like Jardines, Swires, Cornes and the two British banks, Hongkong & Shanghai and Chartered, which had long been active in Japan
plus the oil majors Shell and BP, and ICI. All of these threw their generous support behind British Week. So did our large airlines, BOAC and
Cathay Pacific, large shipping lines, P&O, Ben and Ocean and many another unsung hero.

From the Japanese side we needed all possible cooperation from several government departments, especially MITI and the Ministry of
Finance (in its guise as Customs), the Ministry of Foreign Affairs plus
the Tokyo Metropolitan Government, because many of the things we
intended to do were unprecedented. In Japan in 1968 that word tended
to be synonymous with forbidden. Fortunately, Hugh Cortazzi had been
at work for some time prior to my arrival softening up senior officials and
others. We already had the formal blessing of the Prime Minister, Eisaku
Sato, though I rather doubt whether he had any real idea what the scope
of the operation would be since at that stage we ourselves were groping
for a format. His name, however, opened many doors. And once we were
able to announce the roles of Princess Margaret and Lord Snowdon we
had the valuable support of the Imperial Family especially in the guise of
Princess Chichibu.[2] That lovely and charming lady had been born in
England when her father was a Third Secretary in London and later
was partly educated in the USA. She returned to London with her husband to attend the Coronation of King George VI. She had excellent
English and was friends with members of our Royal Family. She helped
to realize British Week in many quiet ways.

It was also essential to have the goodwill of the major business organizations and again the embassy had begun the process well in advance.
The work of explaining, cajoling and quite often apologizing in advance
for our temerity in even asking for impossible favours was to be a major

feature of the planning stages. In this area we could not have succeeded without the indefatigably persistent Commercial Counsellor who was already building relationships with Keidanren which would endure for decades.

When I arrived I had a totally blank sheet of paper. With the exception of Denis King, the Events Manager, who had come from the Board of Trade none of my staff had any real idea what a British Week entailed, whereas I knew nothing about Japanese business practices and, in particular, the retailing side which was of crucial importance to our success. A steep learning curve ensued and I had never worked so hard in my whole career. I found that there had been a British Store Promotion in 1965 and a further two in 1967 when the Commercial Department had more or less conned Mitsukoshi and Seibu into holding simultaneous so-called British Fairs that had been thought successful; so we were not on entirely stony ground. Hugh Cortazzi and I embarked on a ceaseless round of calls at top levels, especially on presidents and senior executives of the great department stores that soon emerged as the only medium then available for the increased sales of consumer goods that were our commercial objective. Somehow, we had to persuade a dozen store groups to reverse completely their normal habit and all hold their major store promotion of the year at the same time in September 1969.

By good fortune we had two aces to play. First was the ability of my colleagues in the Fairs and Promotions Branch of the Board of Trade to research and provide outstanding exhibitions, more or less free of charge, to cooperating stores and the second was that HRH The Princess Margaret had agreed to make an official visit to open the event and would actually tour those stores judged to have participated effectively (i.e. bought sufficient British merchandise specifically for the occasion). Suffice to say that every store in Tokyo took part and towards the end there was quite vicious in-fighting over which store should have which exhibition and, most of all, which store should receive the first Royal visit since that would get most if not all of the TV coverage.

The department stores were at the peak of their powers and in Tokyo accounted for more than 90% of all sales of imported manufactured consumer goods. They were rather grand but we had to make friends with very many of their senior executives because they had a rudimentary foreign goods buying system whereby so-called 'foreign managers' were responsible for dealing with all foreign suppliers. These foreign managers had little authority and even less knowledge of any merchandise. Their main role was to speak English to foreigners and keep them away from the merchandisers. My deputy, Bob Irving, loaned by the Embassy, was deeply engaged in the commercial arrangements with the stores and he and I spent many, many hours getting past these people to talk to the real decision-makers. That meant accepting much evening hospitality in the bars and restaurants of the Ginza and other celebrated areas of night life, for entertainment budgets were almost unlimited in those dizzy days of double digit growth. Bob was a naturally gregarious Geordie whose Japanese was fluent and uninhibited. He was well liked not only for himself but for his charming French wife Marie Rose and his three very attractive teenage daughters.

As we made progress in these relationships it became easier to persuade the stores to receive a regular flow of BNEC-selling missions from London and to give more access to real merchandise managers. It was a slow and uneven process, however, and two of the most progressive store groups were, thanks to the embassy's previous venture, Mitsukoshi and Seibu where the key personalities were Sakakura and Takao Mori. Some years later Sakakura of Mitsukoshi, having been passed over in favour of his rival Okada for president made unprecedented waves by deserting to Seibu in defiance of all lifetime employment practices. What is more, on the subsequent disgrace and downfall of Okada on corruption charges, Sakakura returned triumphantly as Mitsukoshi president.

These two groups were bitter rivals for the status of Japan's No. 1 retailer, a situation that we found both useful and at times delicate. Another positive factor was the existence of two store presidents who had long associations with Britain, both having studied at LSE in the 1930s. One, Itoh, the president and head of the founding family of Matsuzakaya, was fond of saying that the, other, Kosaka, president of the much smaller but prestigious Komatsu Store on the Ginza, benefited far more from his stay in Britain because he brought back a wife. Kosaka was indeed Anglophile and as the current president of the powerful Ginza Stores Association was able to bring considerable influence to bear. He was also owner of two hotels, the Fairmont and the Sanbancho (familiarly known within the embassy as the 'Sinbin' where I, in fact, spent my first forty-eight hours in Japan in company with a British troupe of dancers, the Bluebell Girls, who said they were too tired for sin!). These were only a few yards from the embassy and Kosaka gave valuable discounted (and sometimes free) rooms that helped with the pitiful subsistence rates allowed to our multiplicity of visiting officials. When we spent an evening doing the rounds of the Ginza bars and restaurants in company with Kosaka we would be treated like visiting royalty by the various *mamasan*. Fortunately, I was never allowed to see a bill! But I was introduced in this way to many an influential businessman. Mrs Kosaka suffered from severe arthritis but was a charming and attractive lady. They had two grown sons but neither took much interest in the business, one having gone to live in America.

Gradually, we reached agreement with store after store for purchasing targets, exhibition themes and contents, supplies of point-of-sale materials and a host of other details. One incident stands out in my memory. It concerns the large and powerful Hankyu Group which has its HQ in Osaka and was not then as prominent in Tokyo as it is now. Somehow it did not learn of the bandwagon that was building up in Tokyo until almost all these negotiations, including the schedules for the programme of store visits by Princess Margaret, were complete. Then President Noda heard that his Tokyo branch would be the only major store not to be visited by Princess Margaret. Emissaries were despatched and I had the difficult task of explaining that the visits were based on promises of additional buying. It was put to us that in order to save the face of the president and Hankyu collectively, the sky was the limit.

In such a situation nobody can resist the importunate and sustained pressure that a Japanese can mount and in due course a deal was done. Crisis! I found that the only possible slot in the Royal programme was for about fifteen minutes on a Monday morning and that could not possibly be changed. So Hankyu's will was put to a real test and to my astonishment President Noda negotiated with his staff unions and all others concerned to open the store on closing day. I believe that cost Hankyu a fortune but they received their visit. And it was the start of a very happy embassy relationship with President Noda which saw Hankyu running a series of British promotions that went on for decades. While I was Commercial Counsellor during the seventies my wife and I received a magnificent pair of the finest melons each year on the anniversary and I believe others were similarly remembered! Furthermore, the President made annual business visits to London and while there always went to Kensington Palace to sign the visitors book.

In parallel with the department store negotiations we were building up our programme of supporting events which were intended to ensure that the whole of Tokyo knew that the British were in town. This was razzmatazz of the most public kind and the star turn was intended to be the appearance on the streets of Tokyo of eight London buses. The famous double-decker red Routemasters were then as they are now a tourist attraction. But they were not designed for operation in Japan as Denis King, our imperturbable special events manager, soon discovered. In virtually no respect did those buses comply with Japanese regulations for public service vehicles, but we wanted them to trundle round Tokyo full of passengers. Worst of all, they were too high for a standard bridge and were liable to foul the tram power lines that were thick above Tokyo's main thoroughfares. Denis, therefore, trod every yard of the routes including the journey they would have to make from Yokohama, where they would be unloaded, to central Tokyo, where they would be deployed, a matter of twenty kilometres or so. He marched with a carefully cut pole before him measuring the clearance under every obstruction until he had verified safe passage for all their movements. He spoke not a word of Japanese so was accompanied everywhere by one of the local staff to explain that this *gaijin* was not mad.

Then began the saga of negotiating import clearance with Customs who took up an uncompromising stance. These vehicles were illegal and could not be imported, they said and they could not be moved. This seeming impasse went on for some ten months. Denis, Bob Irving and I had some of the most opaque meetings in our whole experience including one where we faced more than thirty Customs officials in their HQ, which broke off for callisthenics at intervals signalled by the ringing of a bell. We were never quite sure whether their object was to help or obstruct. I think that most of the credit for the final successful outcome, not only on buses but on venues for the equally popular five military bands and on matters like street decorations, was due to Mr Ishikawa, the head of the External Liaison Office of the Tokyo Metropolitan Government, a most charming, patient and helpful gentleman. I suspect, too, that the goodwill of Governor Minobe, an extremely powerful political figure at the time, had a benevolent effect all round.

It is amusing to recall the final Customs ruling in which our PR manager Tsutomu (Tom to all of us) Hara also had a hand. They ruled that import was permissible because these were not primarily public transport vehicles but mobile advertising units! We had to make special banners to drape on them to justify the ruling. Pragmatism of which any official anywhere could be truly proud.

Our eight buses carried 56,000 passengers during the ten-day operation, the crews cheerfully working flat out for long hours. At one point a single bus was carrying a large proportion of the imperial family together with the British ambassador. The seventy-six military band concerts in public places were listened to by an estimated 150,000 people and when one was unavoidably cancelled at the last moment we were inundated with complaints.

We called the third group of events 'Special Exhibitions' to differentiate them from the exhibitions in direct support of sales in department stores. Our manager for these operations was John MacDonald – young, a recently trained Japanese speaker and keen as mustard. His single biggest task was another of our apparently crazy concepts: an exhibition designed and created by the Central Office of Information which at the time provided all the technical exhibition services required by other government departments including the Board of Trade. It was called 'Britain in Tokyo' and was to be the flagship or centrepiece of the whole Week, For this event we chose the *Nihon Budokan* which is the HQ and spiritual home of Japanese martial arts, especially judo. It is a beautiful building situated in the Kita no Maru Park and close to the Imperial Palace. Needless to say, it took major negotiations to persuade the owners to allow their building with its hallowed *dohyo* or floor to be used for the first time for non-martial arts purposes. We agreed to build a temporary load-bearing floor so that nothing would touch the *dohyo*. That was very expensive but the end result was an exhibition, complete with Nelson's column and a Lord Nelson pub, that attracted not only large numbers of visitors but the emperor himself and many members of the imperial family. The PR spin-off was immense.

At all stages we consulted and involved local business, media and community organizations with the result that there were no negative reactions and only one local body refused to give us a facility we wanted to use. Another tough proposition was the use, on a paid basis, of Toranomon Hall for a series of fashion spectaculars. At a time when such choreographed events were unknown in Japan it was difficult to make the management see why they should alter time-honoured procedures. For example, they had seats in central positions that 'were always used for imperial family members' but we knew that our imperial guests would see next to nothing from there. We knew that their rather elderly seats were literally too small to accommodate the formidably large but absolutely charming and amusing Lady Pilcher, our ambassador's wife. It was not until a few hours before the dress rehearsal that the management said we could remove a section of the front row and instal comfortable armchairs! We never did persuade them that the glittering reception planned for the premiere show should take place in the foyer and they forced us to move all of the guests up several floors in slow and cramped lifts, a most frustrating and temper-fraying experience. Notwithstanding these behind-the-scenes tensions, the fashion shows were a huge success both with the audiences and with the media so that this week-long series of shows was a launch-pad for British fashion in Japan.

In all there were over sixty individual events ranging from a major Henry Moore exhibition at the Museum of Modern Art (the prospect of which, I suspect, originally persuaded Sir John Pilcher that a trade promotion might be a good thing) to a City of London pavilion in Hibiya Park; a Highland Games jointly sponsored by McVitie's biscuits and Seibu which helped to sell about a year's stock of biscuits in ten days; soccer and rugby matches; major sales of fine art, antiques and jewellery (including the first Sotheby's auction in Japan) worth some £2.5 million altogether; a Miss Tokyo Stores beauty contest (another first in Japan) allied to a visit by Miss London Stores, the premiere in Japan of the film *Battle of Britain*, a choice that raised many qualms but was received uncontroversially; eight major and five lesser 'cultural' exhibitions in the major department stores that were seen by some 2.5 million of the 12.5 million people who passed through those stores during the exhibition period; plus of course the events already mentioned and many more lost in the mist of time.

*   *   *

Just accommodating all the hundreds (thousands?) of the supporting cast was a logistical nightmare in a Tokyo far less well served by hotels than is the case today. One of the happier decisions was to house the bus crews in the then Akasaka Prince hotel, a modest building, together with the London Festival ballet corps. We had our doubts about compatibility but those bus men were real gentlemen and they all got on famously. The service attachés had given splendid support which resulted not only in two of HM ships being anchored at Harumi Pier but in the five military bands getting free accommodation on board. *Stromness* also carried a defence sales exhibition which was open to selected guests and the officers threw a grand party in best Royal Navy tradition.

In the later stages of our preparations we were desperately short of manpower in the office and 'Max' Bere, one of the Shell senior executives, suggested that his twin daughters Jenny and Jane would help out just for the experience. They were just eighteen years old, very attractive and wore the minutest mini-skirts ever seen in Tokyo. Suddenly, our office began to receive many callers and we conceived the idea of calling a press conference to publicise our proposed street and store decorations. The girls were sent up a couple of stepladders to hold up various banners and there was a scrimmage among the local media photographers to get the sauciest shots. The coverage received was extensive and thereafter Jenny and Jane were dubbed 'the bare twins'. They were very bright and cheerful girls – a great help in so many ways. This same manpower problem affected the two royal visit programme planners, John Dearlove and HRH Prince William of Gloucester, both Second Secretaries in the embassy, who became almost submerged in paper as the interminable guest lists, invitations, route plans and other documentation had to be prepared, printed and issued. It truly became a case of all hands to the pump as virtually the whole embassy became embroiled.

One near disaster befell when one of Japan's largest printers told us at the eleventh hour that they could not deliver the one million print run of the give-away public programme. I was perfectly beastly to them while Tom Hara used more Japanese wiles and somehow the programmes were delivered to the department stores and other outlets at the last moment. Without them nobody in Tokyo would have known where to go to see what. I have never since felt quite as confident about 'just in time' and Japan's vaunted ability to deliver.

*   *   *

At last, the great day dawned. The opening ceremony was to be at the National Theatre on Friday morning 26 September. On the stage would be Princess Chichibu and Princess Margaret, Masayoshi Ohira, Minister of Trade and Industry, Dr Ryokichi Minobe, Governor of Tokyo, Lord Snowdon, Sir John Pilcher, Michael Montague and a long tail. A few brief speeches of greeting and Princess Margaret rose to declare British Week open. We had added ceremonial touches like the Royal Marines playing suitable music outside and the trumpeters blowing a special fanfare inside. Also outside were the eight London buses drawn up with military precision on the forecourt ready to transport the several hundred core guests direct to the opening of the 'Britain in Tokyo' exhibition about a kilometre away. As the guests emerged they saw a huge model of our logo open to allow 3,000 special balloons to soar into the sky. Then it was on to the *budokan* where Princess Margaret performed another opening and toured the exhibition giving us some good TV coverage. One unrehearsed incident occurred in the Lord Nelson pub where some unruly British journalists tried to get a picture of Princess Margaret drinking in the bar. Instead, they got a picture of me trying to stop them! It appeared as 'Frock-coated British diplomats interfere with journalists doing their job' or some such caption although the Japanese papers took the line of criticising the offending British journalists. I have ever since wondered what whingeing, self-important, and usually third-rate journalists think the other party is doing when they take the 'doing my job' line.

Although this was the official opening day Princess Margaret and Lord Snowdon had arrived in Japan by normal BA flight on Saturday 20 September being met by the ambassador and Princess Chichibu and, after a day's rest, embarked on a maelstrom of engagements, some British Week oriented and some more formal. On Monday morning they began by meeting the embassy staff, then dropped into the Henry Moore exhibition for half an hour en route to the Palace where they made a formal call on the emperor and empress followed by a Court Luncheon attended by fifty guests. After a short pit-stop at the embassy to divest themselves of their formal clothes, they had tea with Princess Chichibu at the Akasaka Detached Palace before dashing back to attend an informal cocktail party at the embassy where they were under the scrutiny of the Press. Then they dined formally with Prime Minister Eisaku Sato at his official residence.

Next day, they were off to Kyoto by bullet train before 9.00 am where they did the statutory two days' sightseeing before, on Thursday, popping in to visit the British pavilion on the Japan Expo site at Osaka which would, in 1970, be our next venture in capturing Japanese hearts and minds. Then they travelled direct to Tokyo where that evening they would attend the so-called 'Principal British Week Reception' at the Okura Hotel. That was the bunfight to end all bunfights as three thousand invited guests fought to get there through traffic jams only to be faced with several hundred gatecrashers mingled with long crocodiles of ticket-bearers. It all worked out well enough and I was told by her Lady-in-Waiting that

HRH loved crushes. Finally, Princess Margaret and Lord Snowdon attended the Premiere of *Battle of Britain* before returning late to the embassy.

I have gone into the detail of the run-up for two reasons. First to show what gluttons for work our royal couple were, thinking nothing of a twelve-to-fifteen-hour day, and also to ask you to imagine the strain on the ambassador and his wife who were within perhaps a year of retirement and were expected to keep pace every step of the way right up to the royal departure after nine frenetic days. I can testify that their urbanity and humour faltered only once throughout British Week and that was after the end of the royal visit and in the face of great provocation by another far less enjoyable visitor, a pompous and self-important Lord Mayor of London who rather threw his weight about without having done his homework.

The only time that our Committee of Honour actually met so far as I recall was at the Opening Day Luncheon that Friday when a hundred of them, including spouses, were joined by Princess Margaret and Lord Snowdon at the Hotel Okura. But they had earned their lunch in many different ways. After that the serious commercial side of the visit began as Princess Margaret kept her promise to visit every department store that had pledged purchasing support. Altogether she visited fourteen major stores, spending up to forty-five minutes in each and she and Lord Snowdon between them also spent time at some dozen or so speciality shops and various minor supporting exhibitions. In between, they managed to attend a lunch for the Japan-British Society, a white tie dinner at the embassy followed by a reception for two hundred and fifty who could not be accommodated at the dinner, the Gala Fashion Show at Toranomon Hall and a Loyal Societies Ball with over five hundred guests at the Hilton.

*   *   *

The short-term results obtained from British Week were impressive enough in terms of extra sales and new exporters introduced to the market. I have provided a statistical summary[3] from my contemporary report that illustrates the achievements. The real impact, however, was in the long-term effect on commercial relations between our two countries. The policy-makers in London became aware that there were solid business benefits to be obtained in Japan and when, in 1973, the time was ripe for a further effort to widen the breach in Japanese protectionist attitudes it was possible to wheedle funds out of them. In another place,[4] I have described British Week as '. . . a catalyst marking the beginning of a burgeoning business relationship that has grown steadily and metamorphosed several times. From simple uncomplicated roots largely in branded consumer goods sold through old-established merchant houses, both British and Japanese, and retailed almost entirely by the great department stores of Japan, the relationship expanded during the early seventies into technical and industrial trade as well as the arts. . .'

Although the British Week office team was dismantled as quickly as possible, much of its know-how remained available within the embassy Commercial Department. In particular, the understanding of the inner workings of the department stores was a tool that could be used to construct an ongoing series of promotional partnerships for many years to come. Commercial department's relationship with DTI Fairs & Promotions Branch remained close and that was eventually, long in the future, to lead to expanded participation in Japanese trade fairs. At the time Japan's trade fair sector was rather weak and there were many areas in which segregation was practised – a glaring example was for many years that imported vehicles could not be exhibited in the Tokyo Motor Show. And when, reluctantly, the curtain was lifted it was only to the extent of allocating one small and not very attractive hall to imports. So the expansion of British participation in fairs of all kinds was a slow and irregular movement – partly because of barriers and partly because the Japanese fairs mostly were not of international standard.

By Spring 1970, I had taken up a new post in Fairs & Promotions Branch (F&PB) where I was head of a section dealing with the DTI's programme of participation in the big European fairs, especially in Germany, France and Scandinavia where we had large markets and good opportunities. It was a busy job requiring much travel in Europe so I had little contact with what was happening in Japan. That ended in autumn 1972 when Prime Minister Edward Heath visited Tokyo and met Kakuei Tanaka, Prime Minister of Japan. Heath was a former President of the Board of Trade and familiar with export matters. So when Tanaka gave him the standard Japanese line that British exporters 'did not try hard enough' in response to some enquiry about problems of access, Heath pricked up his ears. On return he sent a terse memo enquiring whether what the Japanese PM said was true and, if so, what should be done about it? This found its way eventually to my boss, the Director of Fairs & Promotions Branch, who had been involved to some extent in Tokyo British Week and he asked for my views.

There were at the time two differing lines of thought within the DTI about exports. One school took the view that money spent on export promotion was largely wasted and that the government's job should be to set the scene by negotiating in macro-economic areas such as GATT to eliminate protectionism and bilaterally in the same way where necessary. They were the intellectual 'heavies' who were ensconced in what they liked to call the 'policy' departments of which Commercial Relations & Exports (note the tagged-on afterthought) was the main centre for external commercial policy. The other school believed that there was an area in which business was at a disadvantage, especially in the case of small-to-medium firms, which could be ameliorated by carefully organized and modestly funded official support. One of the best examples of this was the planning of compact groups of participants at major Trade Fairs around the world. Fairs & Promotions Branch offered a package that made it possible for quite small firms to show their wares on an equal footing with the international competition. By buying space on a group basis, designing a smart basic stand, helping with freight and contributing towards travel costs, even minnows could be given a chance to catch the eye of the potential customer.

As the argument between the two sides could not easily be settled, it was decided to do research. Only two people in DTI had served in Japan, the other one being Tom Harris, a high-flier who had been given a six-month secondment to the embassy Commercial Department, while I was there. Tom was an activist rather than a theorist and thought trade promotion worthwhile. Tom and I were made a team and told to research the views and objectives of a broad cross-section of British exporters. We did that with great gusto and produced a vast report that offered a blueprint for a new trade drive into Japan. It was still difficult to overcome those who wanted no such thing. Our problem was that the only effective tool we could identify was based on the work of the existing US Trade Centre in Tokyo. Trade centres were anathema to all in Britain since the disastrous experience with a badly conceived static showpiece, launched in New York some years earlier and closed ignominiously after a short and useless life. Overcoming that hurdle was tough and the trick at the end was to find a new title. And so the British Export Marketing Centre was born with a generous enough budget to allow a quality image not to mention incentives enough to make export directors salivate!

Oddly enough, I had never considered that I would continue to be associated with the project in Japan because I thought the Diplomatic Service would want one of its own people. The fact that the budget would fall within the DTI vote, plus the lack at that moment of a suitable commercially trained Japanese language officer, combined to change the scene and I soon found myself in charge of the planning team which was drawn from the technical arm of F&PB dashing backwards and forwards to Tokyo in the search for a suitable building. From a hole in the ground on Aoyama-dori just beyond the Itchome crossing to the opening of the Marketing Centre by HRH The Duke of Kent in September was one of the most concentrated operations I have ever experienced. Innumerable people were involved including not only my highly effective technical colleagues from F&PB but the landlords of a building that they had never envisaged being used for such a purpose, their architects and constructors, the Embassy of course, the UK Ministry of Works, and many a Japanese bureaucrat since, as usual, the British wanted to break all conventions! I found myself working with a largely different set of embassy colleagues, including Sir Fred Warner, the new six feet seven inches-tall ambassador and a Commercial Department whose Counsellor, Peter Wakefield, had just been promoted to Minister and would be moving on.

By May 1973 all that could be reasonably done on a commuting basis had been done and it was time to have the new Director installed in Tokyo. There had been many weeks of tense negotiations behind the scenes between DTI and the Treasury over the terms and conditions for my secondment to the FCO. I knew that by this time there was nobody else in the frame and although I did not want to appear intransigent I was determined not to accept the usual 'second-class citizen' terms given to non-FCO people on secondment. In the end, the Treasury gave in and I was on my way forthwith. On arrival I plunged into a maelstrom of argument about my diplomatic status between the embassy and the Gaimusho who were extremely sensitive, for very good reasons of their own, about out-housed commercial and other non-diplomatic operations being cloaked under a diplomatic hat. So in the end I became two people with two separate offices, two titles and even two different *meishi*. Meanwhile, the hole in the ground was fast being transformed into the Pola Aoyama Building – a most attractive tall building of which the ground floor, originally intended as a double height banking hall, would be the British Export Marketing Centre with its own exhibition hall, conference facilities and state-of-the-art equipment!

Just to give one example of the kind of problems encountered, we wanted three-phase star/delta electric power facilities that would entail the installation of more capacity than had ever been put into a commercial building in Tokyo. Monster transformers and switchgear had to be installed in the basement area, almost with a shoehorn. The contractor's engineer in charge was a wonderful man who performed impossible feats daily and slowly we became a well-knit Anglo-Japanese team determined to be open on time. Meanwhile, the design and installation of the exhibition facilities were in the hands of a team from the technical arm of F&PB and a programme of events had to be worked up with the cooperation of suitable British Trade Associations. I had acquired a deputy, Alex McMillan, who was selected from a strong field of contestants in F&PB because of his wide ranging experience in building and operating overseas exhibitions and pavilions including the British Pavilion at the Expo in 1970. He was able to take care of a mass of detail and to control the Japanese contractors eventually chosen to build and dismantle the ten or twelve greatly differing exhibitions we planned to offer each year.

All through that summer we laboured, virtually on a seven-day week basis and far into many a night. It was fortunate that the embassy had been able to negotiate tenancies for both of us in a splendid new apartment block only five minutes walk away. It had the added attraction of being the only block to boast its own large outdoor swimming pool, a great boon to my wife and family when they eventually joined me.

As the deadline drew near we were into a situation reminiscent of the Royal Visit for British Week. Although the Duke and Duchess of Kent would have a shorter and less crowded programme there was the familiar scramble to prepare guest lists, write speeches, etc but we also had an exhibition and seminar to install and some fifty exhibitors arriving from Britain, a hitherto untested customs clearance drill and, to top it all, the BBC sent a news team to cover the opening. The BBC was our nemesis. Claiming to know what they were doing, they linked their equipment into our massive power system and blew every fuse in the building half way through the speech by the Duke of Kent! That would not have been so bad if we had not been making a full multi-screen recording of the whole proceedings that could be used for the succeeding several evenings to show to further audiences who could not be accommodated at the actual opening. We were left with only part of the Duke's speech and nothing usable of the speech by Yasuhiro Nakasone, then Minister for Trade and Industry.

This disaster struck on a Friday evening and we had a weekend in which to recover the situation. The Duke of Kent could not re-record his speech in the remaining time but we found a specialist studio who were able to enhance what we had to a barely acceptable standard by working the whole weekend. Mr Nakasone was superb: he invited us to come to his weekend retreat and record him again which was done. By Monday we had a passable presentation though I am glad that HRH never saw those reruns. The BBC, I am sorry to say, just slunk away.

After that distinctly hair-raising start, the Centre quickly got into its stride. Some outstanding exhibitions were mounted and BEMC in Aoyama dori became a place to which Japanese businessmen were happy to come in considerable numbers. We had a highly effective publicity operation based on direct mail for which we built up our own mailing lists. The contractor for this was none other than the same Tom Hara of the British Week team, now running his own PR company and happily blending our ideas on promotion with Japanese practice. Every exhibition began with a Centre reception hosted by the ambassador who made a suitable speech: the large and influential local trade press came regularly for a drink and to report on what was in the exhibition hall. Any newcomer firm was provided with capable interpreting staff though the established people used their agents.

All exhibits (including some really large pieces of engineering), were collected in the UK, packed and shipped by F&PB, and delivered to the door of BEMC by our highly efficient handling contractors Odawara Unyu. Getting the exhibits delivered in Tokyo's congested traffic was in itself a masterpiece of cooperation involving the local police, Customs who allowed our containers to roll up unopened from the container port, and Alex McMillan's exhibition contractors who had to install everything. In the first five years of operation I do not think we were ever late, nor did we lose a single item!

It had been recognized from the start that a new section would be needed in London to act as the sales team that would make sure that British industry was aware of and made use of the marketing opportunities available. So much of manufacturing industry had for so long had a distinctly jaundiced view of the protectionist nature of Japanese government policies that it required a major effort to change attitudes. Thus was born the Exports to Japan Unit in the DTI which, led mainly by recently returned members of the Commercial Department, has had a long and successful history of enthusing exporters and broadening understanding of the Japanese market right up to the present day.

The full-time staff of the Centre was little more than half a dozen people: Alex McMillan, my deputy; his assistant, a locally engaged Japanese-speaking British lady, Lydia Parry,[5] who had studied the language at Sheffield University, worked as a guide in 1970 at the British Pavilion at Expo Osaka, and was employed by JETRO in London when I 'acquired' her to help set up the Centre; two male Japanese who were rather a disaster, one being a total alcoholic foisted on us by a (non-British) oil company and the other quite demented – they had to be quietly removed; and finally but most important a core of young nearly bilingual Japanese women who quickly learned to handle all the complexities of our operations and to help Alex to deal effectively with our contractors.

At least some of these are still loyally serving the embassy in some capacity now that the Centre has faded into history. One in particular, Mrs Hariyama, a trained architect, provided the link that took all the Centre's exhibition know-how into the Commercial Department when the Centre, its job well done, closed. That was the point at which Japanese trade fairs became of international class and as acceptable for British exhibitors as any European venue.

Once the Centre was fully into its stride, I had far less than a full-time job. I was paid the great compliment of being invited to take over as Commercial Counsellor and coordinate the management of the Centre with the large and active Commercial Department. There were two first secretaries, one handling a consumer goods section and the other the technical/capital goods industries. Each had a team consisting of Japanese-speaking British second secretaries and locally recruited Japanese commercial officers who focused on specific market sectors and aimed to build up quite detailed information for the benefit of visiting British businessmen. These came in large numbers, either individually or as members of mission groups sponsored by a variety of trade organizations and partially funded by the DTI. Missions were of two basic types: vertical, e.g. from one industry like a dozen furniture makers; or horizontal, e.g. from one location like Birmingham but otherwise unrelated. Both kinds had advantages and disadvantages. Altogether we handled some fifteen or more groups a year all requiring introductions, briefings, interpreting arrangements etc. These were in addition to the Centre exhibition groups who also needed much the same kind of support services from the Commercial Department. In the course of this work a valuable interpreting resource was created in the form of a register of competent people who worked on a fee scale set by the embassy.

At the same time, there was a need to pay attention to the small but important group of resident British businessmen. They varied from heads of fairly large operations such as the oil majors, banks, trading houses, shippers and ICI to small one-man businesses and had formed themselves into a British Chamber of Commerce (BCCJ) many years before. The Chamber had endured many vicissitudes but been much encouraged by the Embassy in recent years and its members looked to us for support in various ways. Responsibility for much of this was theoretically shared with the Economic Counsellor but he had few people or resources and a wide range of Japanese government and financial sector contacts to cultivate. I tried to include leading Chamber members in all our activities whether related to the Centre or to other parts of the commercial operations and the Ambassador and Minister also kept in close touch. This, allied to a little financial help from London, allowed the Chamber to grow and, eventually, to take a leading role in the formation of a suitable European Union body that secured some recognition from the Japanese authorities. Today the BCCJ is a thriving institution.

In the later seventies HMG began to consider the possible advantages of encouraging Japanese industrial investment into Britain. It seemed an unlikely gambit at first but with Japan's rising costs and strong fears of protectionist barriers as the EU emerged the mood changed with well known and documented results. Inward investment became a new major area of work both in Whitehall and in the embassy where it was entrusted by Sir Michael Wilford, who had succeeded Sir Fred Warner as ambassador, to an enlarged Economic Department. By now my own very long stint in Japan made me think of pastures new and in early 1979 I decided to take early retirement and see if I could contribute to Anglo-Japanese commercial relations from a private sector viewpoint.

NOTES:

1.   see the Preface to *Biographical Portraits Vol. III*
2.   see her autobiography *The Silver Drum*
3.   see Appendix
4.   see Preface to *Biographical Portraits Vol. III*
5.   Lydia married Stephen Gomersall, an embassy language student, and they have maintained their links with Japan, Stephen being appointed British Ambassador to Japan in July 1999.

BRITISH WEEK in TOKYO 1969

PARTICIPANTS	VISITORS	SALES
19 Dept. Stores	12.6 million	Yen 1.86 billion (£194m)
17 Supermarkets	N/a	N/a
352 Specialty/Small Shops	N/a	N/a
EVENTS	VISITORS	
Dept. Store Cultural Exhibitions	2.5 million	
Band Concerts	150,000	
'Britain in Tokyo' Exhibition	120,000	
City of London Pavilion	90,000	
London Bus Passengers	56,000	
Hi-Fi/Home Appliances Show	50,000	
Soccer & Rugby Games	40,000	
Highland Games	30,000	
Fashion Spectaculars	25,000	
London Philharmonic/ Festival Ballet/Julian Bream Concerts	18,000	
Visitors to HM Ships	10,000	
PUBLICITY COVERAGE		
Press Cuttings	2,600	
TV News Items	6	

23

Banking and Financial Services: A British Commercial Banker in Japan 1980-85

IN THE FIRST twenty years or so after the end of the war British banks had only a limited role in Japan. British overseas banks such as the Hongkong and Shanghai Banking Corporation and the Standard Chartered Bank, which had opened branches in Japan before the war, were permitted to reopen but the Japanese Ministry of Finance (MOF) did not allow them to expand their operations or to benefit more than marginally from Japan's economic growth in the late nineteen fifties and sixties.

Local managements were plagued by labour troubles and the banks' head offices never seem to have regarded Japan during this period as much more than another overseas territory for their operations. The managements of the banks in Hong Kong and London had yet to recognize that the strategic changes in their areas of operations had made 'colonialist' attitudes outdated and irrelevant. The big four British commercial banks (Barclays, National Westminster, Midland and Lloyds) did not even have representative offices in Tokyo in these early decades after the war.

I can remember as a young third/second secretary in the British Embassy in Tokyo in the early 1950s being invited to a party at the grand residence in Yokohama of the manager for Japan of the Hongkong and Shanghai Banking Corporation. The atmosphere was colonial (if I recollect correctly almost all the guests were expatriates) and anachronistic.

The situation by 1980 was vastly different as PETER HAND describes in the following piece – 'Reminiscences of a banker in Japan 1980-85':-

•

The plane climbed steeply from Kimpo International Airport, banked left over the new National Assembly building on the southern bank of the Han River and headed south for Tokyo giving a good view of Seoul, the city in which my family and I had spent almost four years.

It was September 1980 and I had been posted by my employers, Grindlays Bank, to take over as General Manager Japan with concurrent responsibilities for the bank's branches in Korea and Taiwan.

I could look back with some satisfaction on my time in Korea where I had started the bank's operation literally from scratch, finding premises, employing the staff and building a profitable business base. When we first commenced activities in Korea in 1977 we were the tenth foreign bank to obtain a licence, the largest being Citibank which was a major shareholder of Grindlays; by the time I left a further thirty foreign banks had arrived.

As a fast industrializing country Korea had needed foreign capital and foreign banks were given much encouragement to help in this task. Banks were granted a US $/Won swap allocation to enable the generation of local currency for domestic lending most of which had the added comfort of a bank guarantee and a fixed Won/US$ exchange rate. We broke even after six months and over the next four years established a large off-shore business base in London, Hong Kong and Bahrain from which latter office support was given to the fast growing construction activities in Saudi Arabia and the Gulf.

I pondered on what might lie before me in Japan where the bank was a relative newcomer with a single branch in Tokyo which had only been opened for business by Geoffrey Bignell in 1974. In 1980 there were sixty-four different foreign banks in Japan of which eighteen had offices in Osaka.

I took control of the branch from the late David Murray-John who prior to this assignment had run British Oxygen's operation in Malaysia and had been one of the first recruits from British industry to the bank under a scheme initiated by our former Chairman Lord Aldington.

I made the usual courtesy calls in Tokyo – to the British Embassy to meet the Ambassador Sir Hugh Cortazzi and his Financial Attaché Chris Elston and to the Ministry of Finance and the Bank of Japan as well as calling on our customer base, other British banks and Japanese city banks.

During the period of taking over the branch my predecessor had introduced me to that great necessity of all bankers – convivial watering holes. These ranged from the Tokyo Kaikan, the Imperial Bar, the Oak Bar of the Hotel Okura to a bewildering number of establishments in Ginza and Roppongi at which I had been persuaded to put down bottles of whisky with my name written in katakana on them – many were never re-discovered!

My office comprised six British staff and seventy-two Japanese staff and was located in the Tokyo Yanmar Building in Yaesu opposite the rear of Tokyo station. The underground car park had direct access onto the expressway system that enabled me to commute to my house in Shibuya in about thirty minutes – an enviable commute in any world capital. The

office conducted on-shore and off-shore commercial banking operations, foreign exchange dealing, merchant/investment banking business
and a growing volume of shipping (hull finance) business.

Initially, my driver would call at the house at 7.30 am and take me to the
office but later I decided to drive to the office and meet him there. If I had
to attend a late evening appointment I followed my predecessor's arrangements in allowing him to go home to Yokohama in the car which
he would drive to the office the next day and I would come in to work on
the Ginza line.

I noticed on a number of such days that he seemed fairly exhausted and
on occasions fell asleep at traffic lights. I had presumed that this was due
to the journey time to and from his home but when my operations manager, who lived in Yokohama, was trying to hail a cab outside the YCAC
late one evening in pouring rain, he was surprised to find my driver behind the wheel of my car – the drive home concession was cancelled.

My first business meeting was held in Osaka. We called on a civil engineering company which had been awarded a contract in Zambia where
Grindlays had a strong branch network and where I had worked in the
early 1970s. At the end of the meeting, of which I had understood not a
word, I asked my senior Japanese Manager what had transpired and he
informed me that I had agreed in principle to grant them a facility of US
$5 million – the following week I commenced Japanese lessons!

The British Banks in Japan ranged from all the clearing banks, the
main merchant banks and other British international banks such as Standard Chartered and Hongkong Bank who were both long established
with offices in Tokyo and Osaka. Grindlays fell into the last category with
the bank's main strength being in the Indian sub-continent, the Middle
East, Africa and Europe. The bank's presence in the Far East (apart from
a brief foray into Shanghai in the last century) had only seriously begun
since the acquisition of the Dao Heng Bank in Hong Kong in the 1960s.

The British clearing banks built their initial business on the back of
their UK customer base and tried to provide such customers with facilities in Japan. As most British companies operated in Japan on a joint
venture basis this was not always possible as the dominance of the Japanese prime bank often dictated otherwise. Grindlays like other British
banks strove to bring the expertise of the City of London to the Japanese
market and we were active in making available to Japanese companies the
established capital market capabilities of Europe coupled with funding
from the new markets of Singapore and Hong Kong.

Unlike the situation I had left in Korea the role, or the need, for commercial foreign banks in Japan was much less clear. Japan was clearly
'over-banked' in terms of numbers of branches available to serve the public. Major Japanese banks appeared driven by balance sheet size and to
this end most foreign banks were prepared to grant substantial loans to

offshore subsidiaries of Japanese banks at those month ends which were crucial for the calculation of Japanese bank 'league tables' but at those periods which did not affect their own liquidity back home.

The over-capacity of Japan's domestic banking sector had been further compounded by the permitted domestic expansion of second tier and regional banks, some of which had even been granted authority to expand overseas when it was questionable that their business even warranted the authority of an office in Tokyo or Osaka. It subsequently transpired that the new business written by many of these newcomers was less than wise and often either related to real estate or had been secured by it. This activity subsequently was to trigger the overall banking crisis of the late 1990s and will undoubtedly lead to a sharp reduction in the number of Japanese banks and branches as mergers and absorptions are 'arranged' by the monetary authorities.

To put all this in a global context, the early nineteen eighties saw many international banks also operating on a strategy which seemed to encourage the philosophy of 'big is beautiful' and too often the criteria for 'big' had been set to measure success by either the number of branches or by the countries of representation. In due course most international banks focused their attention on earnings rather than asset size and in particular on the return on shareholders' funds or the return on risk assets.

In my five years in Japan while the number of foreign banks increased by 23% from sixty-four to seventy-nine operating a hundred and fifteen branches, loans and discounts grew by less than 5% and deposits only rose from ¥12.4 trillion to ¥15.2 trillion. However, during that time Tokyo did see the rapid development of the money market with resultant increases in Call Money and Call Loans. The calculation of market share was not a greatly revealing activity as the combined assets and liabilities of foreign bank branches amounted to less than 1% of bank deposits in Japan and a mere 3% of bank loans.

I recall a conversation I had in 1981 with the general manager of a British clearing bank who told me that on a recent visit to Japan by his chairman he had been asked why they were so small in this market and why they could not, for instance, acquire the Mitsubishi Bank. He had explained to his chairman that (at that time) they would not have received authority to take over a city bank and even if they were it would neither assure profitability nor guarantee that the underlying business, if profitable, would still exist after takeover.

Most Japanese city banks being the core members of their *keiretsu* groups held substantial property assets and many of their loans were granted against the security of Japanese real estate. Each year as property values escalated such property was revalued in their books and the annual increase often treated as income. When in the early 1990s property values collapsed it took companies some time to appreciate that the underlying business was often operating at a loss and had been doing so for a considerable number of years; this fact had been clouded by the property 'gains' or, if known, quietly ignored. This position led to a fundamental reassessment by the stock market of those factors affecting corporate profitability in Japan with a resultant sharp decline of share prices.

At the time I arrived in Japan foreign banks alone were allowed to grant foreign currency loans to Japanese companies up to a limit set by government authorities. Due to the very tight fiscal policy at the time the demand for this product, known as the impact loan (because of the impact on the balance of payments), was strong.

The Ministry of Finance, which received constant requests for increases in the limits allowed for this business, eventually indicated that this business would be deregulated. Foreign bankers were overjoyed to hear this news but their elation soon changed when it became clear that in order to 'treat all banks on an equal footing' Japanese banks would henceforth also be allowed to transact the business. Overnight the loan margins on loans collapsed as the major Japanese banks bid for the business or took back loans they had formerly placed with foreign banks on behalf of their own customers.

All foreign banks in Japan were continually faced with the difficulty of attracting new business and had the ongoing struggle of earning sufficient income to cover the particularly high cost base they faced; the demise of the impact loan was thus another hard-felt blow.

This need to cover costs undoubtedly led to an increase in business in certain sectors that would not have been countenanced elsewhere. An example in point was the sharp increase of yen lending by foreign banks to the so called *sarakin* companies. It was especially difficult at that time for individuals in Japan when faced with the need for short-term funds to obtain personal finance from domestic banks with the result that many people had little choice other than to approach these personal loan companies.

The companies, which themselves were undercapitalized and had a tainted history with regard to their methods of business and the steps used to obtain debt repayment, set about improving their public image. They recruited recently retired senior bankers and government officials who were then used as the day-to-day contacts with the foreign banks. Foreign bankers were entertained with dinners and golf days designed to demonstrate the more caring face these salary loan companies wished to portray both to the public and to their potential sources of funding.

Many foreign bankers entered this business but privately accepted that the security offered, normally a charge over the receivables in a branch of the company, was at best comfort and in reality almost impossible to realize should the need arise. I gradually withdrew from the business I inherited and decided to concentrate our resources elsewhere.

One other piece of business which had been written for income reasons was a yen denominated syndicated loan to a government in West Africa, the lead manager for which was a major Japanese city bank. I arranged a meeting with the Japanese bank and expressed my concern with the business. It became clear that they had little up-to-date knowledge of the borrowing country and seemed unaware that the domestic currency of the country concerned was the US dollar and appeared unfazed by the country's total absence of yen income. Following a *coup d'état* when the country's finance minister, who had signed the loan agreement, was assassinated my worst fears proved well founded.

The safety of lending in Japan was a much discussed subject as was the concept of 'Japan Inc' where the risk of lending to a Japanese corporate was sometimes equated by the lender to the risk for lending to Japan itself. I considered there was nothing to warrant changing my bank's normal credit criteria when assessing Japanese risk – as with any dynamic economy companies flourished and companies failed.

Long-serving foreign bankers informed me that they considered the collapse of Ataka & Co in the 1970s had marked a watershed for foreign lending in Japan. Prior to the Ataka demise if those companies forming part of a *keiretsu* group got into financial difficulty any foreign bank in their picture had normally been repaid by the Japanese prime bank in order to facilitate more easily a 'Japanese settlement'. The sums involved for Ataka were too great for this to happen and foreign banks involved probably suffered their first experience of major corporate bad debt in Japan.

After that time it became clear that any corporate lending in Japan quite rightly carried risk which needed careful assessment and also the lender was well advised to make the Japanese prime bank aware of the business being written. The responsibilities of a company's Japanese prime bank were far more onerous than those associated with a Western company's first-tier bank relationship and needed to be clearly understood.

In early 1983, during the mainly fraudulent failure of the medium-sized trading company J. Osawa & Co., it became apparent that the Japanese bank which most lenders had understood to be the prime bank was either not so or was not willing to accept the additional responsibilities of that role. This had dire results and the company collapsed almost overnight with most lenders suffering loss as a result.

In 1983 my Head Office introduced a new computer system based on the IBM 399 and eventually we made the changeover in Japan. Late one evening while holding a meeting with my computer manager the machines started up with the discs whirring. I enquired what was happening to be told it was my London office taking off the daily balances.

I was dismayed to hear this news as it effectively prevented me from 'massaging' the monthly profit figures: like all overseas operations it was always helpful to be able to keep a bit back for a rainy day. Changes in technology are not always welcome!

As I have mentioned, the historic strengths of the bank lay not in the Far East but in South Asia, the Middle East and Africa. Japanese civil engineering and trading companies were also conducting an increasing volume of business in those areas and I thus decided to concentrate on the provision of facilities to our Japanese customer base outside Japan.

From 1981 I made regular visits with my senior staff to India, Pakistan, Bangladesh and the Gulf with encouraging results and in the following year we placed senior Japanese staff in Delhi, Bombay, Abu Dhabi and Bahrain. This move was rewarded with substantial volumes of new business written outside Japan and I was more than able to justify to London the necessity of maintaining a significant operating presence in Japan where decisions relating to overseas business were normally made.

I found myself obliged to spend an increasing amount of my time in Taiwan during the next two years as a result of the difficulties faced by banks in Taipei following the collapse (quite often fraudulent) by a number of major companies. The operation was eventually restored to profitability after a period of much pain and the removal of the Taiwanese General Manager.

In 1984 the Australia & New Zealand Banking Group made a bid for the business of Grindlays Bank and I was instructed by my London Board to pre-advise the Ministry of Finance and to obtain from them their clearance in principle as at that stage no Australian bank had been granted a banking licence in Japan. The bid eventually succeeded and the ANZ Bank Representative Office in the New Yurakucho Building was merged into my branch and their Chief Representative, Neil Cleland, lost the somewhat comfortable status as Representative for Japan to became my deputy.

From that time the actual business conducted in Tokyo significantly changed. We decided to offer Aussie and Kiwi dollar deposits to the Japanese public and greatly expanded the foreign exchange dealing capabilities of the branch. With the help of possibly the bank's two most experienced Australian dealers we became market leader for the bank's two domestic currencies of the Aussie and Kiwi dollar and were also rewarded with a great expansion of trade-related business.

Throughout this time I remained an active member of both the British Chamber of Commerce and the Japan British Society, as well as continuing to serve on the EC Banking Sub-Committee. While wearing my new antipodean hat I also joined the Australian Chamber of Commerce in Japan and got to know the ambassador, Sir Jim Plimsole and his staff.

For the next two years I made frequent trips to the bank's head office in Melbourne as well as visiting the other major cities of Australia and New

Zealand. My staff in Tokyo became more cosmopolitan with officers from Britain, Australia, New Zealand and (the head of my shipping department) Hong Kong. Japanese staff also enjoyed the new experience of working for periods of duty in Melbourne and Sydney.

So much for my life as a banker in Japan; now to my family. When I first arrived I was accompanied by my wife Jacqui and sons Timothy (seven) and Luke (four) and we all moved into the bank's house in Shibuya.

The boys started school – Timothy at St Mary's in Setagaya-ku and Luke close to my house at the local Matsumura Yochien where every morning dressed in a light blue smock and matching hat, he would join the 'crocodile' of small children which passed my house en route to school.

Jacqui enjoyed *Elizabeth kai* meetings and became an active member of St Alban's Church where she sang in the choir. I bought her a small car, a Toyota Corsa, which had non-automatic gears (at her request) and as a result had been very difficult to obtain. While she could never read much Japanese she felt able to drive in Tokyo provided she could occasionally see known landmarks such as the Tokyo Tower.

We were members of the Tokyo American Club which the boys enjoyed for swimming in the summer and we often used for Sunday lunches. I was also a member of the Kawasaki Kokusai Country Club where I held a *gaijin* membership. This was much used as it only took me thirty minutes to get there from my house and as such was one of the closest golf clubs to the centre of the city. I frequently played in the Saturday competitions with Derek Fair and held my annual office competition at the club. I spoke to Derek in Tokyo in May 1999 and he told me that, sadly, the long expected takeover of the course for municipal building had now occurred.

Shortly after arriving in Japan I purchased a cottage near Toji beach to the south of Shimoda to which we used to enjoy escaping once a month. If I was to return to live in Japan I can think of no more ideal spot from which occasionally to escape from the concrete jungle of Tokyo.

Luke's Japanese progressed much faster than my own as he was the only *gaijin* boy at the school. On return from my office one night my maid informed me that Luke was in trouble, having apparently insulted the wife of one of my neighbours. He had been playing in the garden with a ball which had frequently gone over the wall. Initially, Mrs Watanabe had returned it but eventually refused whereupon he climbed up a stepladder, peered over the wall and told her of his displeasure in no uncertain terms.

I bought some flowers and went next door to apologize in my poor Japanese. Mrs Watanabe thanked me and said how shocked she had been to hear such language from someone so small and asked where he had learnt it. I could truthfully reply that it had not been from me.

We all enjoyed the summer sports days held in the compound of the British Embassy and the many other occasions when we were entertained at Ichiban-cho. All British businessmen and their families based in Japan considered themselves extremely fortunate to have these facilities in Tokyo.

Some weekends the boys and I would cycle to the nearby Yoyogi Park which offered ample space for ball games and many other leisure activities. In my youth I had been keen on model aircraft and we used to make and fly planes at Yoyogi Park where a model club – Air Friends of Yoyogi – gathered each Sunday. No engine-powered models were permitted so the majority of planes were gliders, rubber powered or launched by catapult. As Yoyogi Park is not without trees I found it useful to have the services of my agile sons to act as retrievers.

In due course both my sons left Japan to start at prep school in England and Jacqui used to go back and forth for half terms interspersed by the boys' own unaccompanied visits on the British Airways school specials.

I travelled one January to London with Timothy and his friends Roger and Peter MacDonald who all attended the same school. The plane broke down in Anchorage and being the fortunate holder of an American multi re-entry visa I managed to arrange for us all to be checked into a hotel where the boys were more than happy to stay up most of the night watching the novelty of multi-channel American TV. I discovered downtown Anchorage is made up of one and two-storey wooden buildings and can best be described as a frozen Wild West.

Eventually, in late 1985, I was appointed Regional Director Far East for the Australia & New Zealand Banking Group to be based in Hong Kong where I was to look after the bank's operations in nine countries including Japan.

I look back with pleasure on my time in Tokyo and the friends we made there. The difficult business climate, at least for bankers, was more than compensated by attractions of the country, the culture, the food and the courtesy of the people. There surely can be no major city where one's family can feel safer and the efficiency and cleanliness of the public transport system puts most others to shame.

Few overseas postings can match the quality and excitement of living in Japan and the five years we spent there flew by too quickly leaving too many things undone and far too many places still unseen. I hope in future that one day I may have the time to see those parts of rural Japan that at the moment are only names in my imagination.

24

Experiences of Some British Merchant Bankers

EDMUND DE ROTHSCHILD ● HUGH TRENCHARD
CHRISTOPHER PURVIS ● JOHN NAISH

N.M. ROTHSCHILD traces its links with Japan to the early Meiji era. In 1937 all direct dealings by the bank with Japan were broken off. Contacts were resumed in 1949 and Rothschilds became correspondents for a number of Japanese banks. Soon after his arrival in London Takashi Ihara who became Financial Counsellor in the Japanese Embassy after the Peace Treaty came into force in 1952 was invited by N.M. Rothschild to lunch at New Court and friendly relations were established. As a result to quote EDMUND DE ROTHSCHILD in his memoir *A Gilt-Edged Life* (John Murray, 1988) '. . . we were more or less besieged by Japanese banks and securities houses desperate to re-establish connections in London. So we advised them on opening up London branches' and Edmund '. . . used regularly to accompany Japanese bankers to interviews at the Bank of England'.

In this process Edmund de Rothschild got to know Tsunao Okumura, then President of Nomura Securities and a friend of Hayato Ikeda, the Japanese Finance Minister and later Prime Minister. Nomura Securities soon became the bank's most important business associate in Japan. Later, when N.M. Rothschild began to fear that there was a danger of their 'trying to do too many pieces of business with too many people' in Japan they decided that Nomura Securities should remain their 'Number One contact' in the investment field.

In 1962, at the instigation of Okumura, a group of top Japanese businessmen invited a delegation of senior bankers from the City to visit Tokyo. Before setting off for Japan Edmund de Rothschild decided to learn a little Japanese and mugged up a short speech to give on arrival. This caused some 'suppressed amusement' as he had used a woman's style of Japanese.

Edmund records that '. . . every now and then I would get over-confident and run into difficulties'. On one occasion when he was in Tokyo with a young colleague he is alleged to have '. . . insisted on ordering breakfast room-service in Japanese. Feeling rather smug, his [young associate's] story went, I sat back and waited – for almost an hour. Eventually, there was a light tapping at the door; I opened it, and there, standing before me, were two beautiful kimono-clad ladies bowing politely and saying, "You ordered geisha girls?".'

Edmund ended his report on his first visit to Japan '. . . with some simple observations on the Japanese women I had encountered'. 'The primitive attitude of some Japanese men to women was brought home to me when, some years later, I was in Japan with my wife Elizabeth, and together we went to a party given by Tsunao Okumura, who was then seriously ill with cancer. The moment came when he wanted to talk to me about some piece of outstanding business, and so turning to Elizabeth he said, "Woman, leave the room". She was sufficiently startled to do so but it was by no means the last I heard of it.'

During the delegation's tour of 'the Imperial Gardens' Edmund came across the most magnificent camellia tree he had ever seen. Although not in flower it was laden with seed. Thinking of his own magnificent collection at Exbury Edmund asked one of the guides if he could be permitted to take some seeds. After much consultation he was told that unfortunately this would not be possible as 'the seed from this very special camellia tree was used exclusively to make hair oil for the Empress. Not to be put off, I then did something which I strongly discourage visitors to Exbury from doing, I dropped my camera-lens and stooped down to retrieve it in my handkerchief, scooping up a few seeds from under the tree in the process. But I got my come-uppance in the end.' After a seventeen-year wait the camellia seeds bloomed at Exbury but turned out to be '. . . no more than a fine strong strain of the common or garden *camellia japonica*'.

Edmund explained that as he was 'getting a little stout' he was allowed to sit at a table. In 1964 when N.M.Rothschild were managing a Eurodollar bond issue for Hitachi with the First Bank of Boston '. . . a pretty little geisha girl came up to refill my sake glass. "Rothschild-san," she said to me, "I don't call you Rothschild-san; I call you Spoilt-child-san because you have so many parties."'

N.M. Rothschild launched The Pacific Seaboard Fund and later 'Tokyo Capital Holdings' of which Edmund became Chairman of the supervisory committee. This meant that he made at least one visit each year to Tokyo. These visits often included seminars e.g. with the *Nihon Keizai Shimbun*.

Edmund notes in his memoir that 'On my first and almost every, subsequent visit to Japan, I used at some point to have meetings with the Japanese prime minister of the day and his minister of finance.' However, all his time was not taken up with business: 'Whenever possible on my visits to Japan, I used to try to fit in a few days for sight-seeing or plant-hunting around the country.' Tsunao Okumura also used to take him '. . . to play golf at the 300 club outside Tokyo; but one Friday afternoon, when he asked me what I would like to do for the weekend, I said that I should very much like to make an expedition to Beppu, a hot-spring resort on the north-eastern coast of Kyushu'. Edmund's choice of Beppu stemmed from a conversation over a game of bridge with Ian Fleming and his James Bond book *You only live twice*.

As a result of his close involvement with Japan Edmund de Rothschild took over the chairmanship of BNEC's Asia Committee from Michael Montague in

1970. In 1973 for his outstanding services in the fields of finance and relations between Japan and Britain he was awarded the Grand Cordon of The Sacred Treasure by the Emperor on the recommendation of the Japanese Government.

ALL THE MAIN British merchant banks wanted to get a piece of the financial business which they saw developing in Japan. Two of the most important British merchant banks in the 1970s and 1980s were S.G.Warburg and Kleinwort Benson. At this time their independence as British financial institutions was not threatened by takeover bids and both, determined to develop business with Japan, sent out to head their offices young and able bankers.

HUGH (VISCOUNT) TRENCHARD arrived in Japan as the representative of Kleinwort Benson in March 1980. CHRISTOPHER PURVIS arrived in Tokyo as the representative of S.G.Warburg in May 1982.

First, Hugh Trenchard's account:-

•

I arrived in Japan as the representative of Kleinwort Benson ('Kleinworts'), the merchant bank, in March 1980.

My involvement with Japan had started three years earlier in London, quite by chance. A former colleague who was at the time seconded from Kleinworts to our then joint venture with Fuji Bank, Fuji Kleinwort Benson (the predecessor of Fuji's overseas investment banking arm, Fuji International Finance) suddenly decided he did not like the city and unexpectedly resigned in order to run a restaurant. I was appointed in his place as deputy general manager of the joint venture. The head of the operation, or general manager, was Toru Hashimoto, who is today Chairman of Fuji Bank and my opposite number, the other deputy general manager, was Tomoshiro Kamio, who has been appointed President of Fuji Securities which is Fuji's domestic investment banking arm.

I was supposed to teach my Japanese colleagues what I knew about the British investment banking scene. This, of course, did not take very long! I think I learned rather more from them than they did from me. In 1978 Hashimoto took me with him to Japan. This was my first visit to the country and I was instantly fascinated by almost everything I encountered. Looking from my Palace Hotel window on my first night in Japan at those incessantly flashing red lights on the tops of buildings I remember clearly thinking how very different and strange Japan was to anything I had experienced before. We had dined at Tenichi, the tempura restaurant, which was then, as now, a safe choice for inexperienced *gaijin* (foreigners). I can still hear the ringing chorus *'irasshaimase'* as we entered the restaurant.

I spent two weeks in Tokyo, based at Fuji Bank's headquarters in Ohtemachi. I was looked after with great courtesy and care by Hashimoto and many of his colleagues. We visited many of Fuji Bank's corporate clients on courtesy calls and at the weekend I was taken to an *onsen* (hot spring resort) outside Tokyo.

I completed my two years' secondment to Fuji Kleinwort Benson in the spring of 1979 and returned to international corporate finance at Kleinworts. In May that year I was asked to move to Tokyo on a posting which was supposed to be for two to three years. Even though I had enjoyed working with the Japanese in London and had been fascinated by my brief immersion in Japanese culture I had not anticipated going to live in Japan which was not quite a mainstream expatriate posting at the time.

Anyway, having decided that two years was not so long, Fiona and I resolved to make the most of it and so it was that I came to take up my duties at Kleinwort's representative office in the Kokusai Building in Marunouchi on 1 April 1980.

There were just three representatives and three secretaries in the office then. The senior of the three secretaries, Mrs Watanabe, was office manager as well as being my secretary. Watanabe-san represented the continuity of the office, as she had been its mother figure since it was opened. She was totally loyal to the firm and addressed herself with complete commitment to every task she undertook. Nothing was ever too difficult for her. She lived in Kamakura, as she still does, about an hour by train from Tokyo. Once, before having a fax machine at home became normal, I was in the office late on a Sunday afternoon trying to send a fax but the paper was jammed and I could not fix it. I rang Watanabe-san to ask for help but insisted it was not important and she did not need to come to the office at 7.00 pm on a Sunday evening. An hour-and-a-half later I was having my dinner at home when Watanabe-san telephoned me from the office; in spite of my insistence that it was not necessary and was well beyond the call of duty she had felt obliged to go to the office and fix the machine.

This was typical of her and illustrates well the devotion to duty which, to some extent even today, but certainly then, many Japanese possessed in abundance. She had of course firm ideas about the standards that should be maintained by Kleinworts' staff in Japan and which activities were acceptable for representatives. Antony Stanley-Smith, my predecessor, had once wanted to buy a motorcycle and had asked Watanabe-san to investigate models and prices but uncharacteristically she continued to forget to do this. Eventually, he challenged her: 'Mrs Watanabe, is it that you actually do not want me to have a motor bike?' She replied: 'Mr Stanley-Smith, I think perhaps it might be better not.' The chief representative in Japan of Kleinworts should not be seen by the clients riding a motor cycle, that would certainly not present the right image. Later, as the office grew, Watanabe-san ceased to be my secretary but continued to manage the office and rose to the position of *somubucho* (head of the general affairs department), which is the pivotal position carrying responsibility for the administration of a Japanese company.

I had a three week handover period during which Stanley-Smith took me round to meet our principal clients, both customers of the Fuji Bank such as NSK (Nippon Seiko), Oki Electric and Marubeni and members of other *keiretsu* or industrial groups such as NYK Line, Mitsubishi Heavy Industries and Sumitomo Electric. The Japanese business world was much more formal than Britain's and has relaxed somewhat in recent years although I believe that the building of long-term relationships remains an important element in building a successful business.

*   *   *

One of the early dilemmas that Kleinworts faced in Japan was to decide on its Japanese name. Apart from the fact that Kleinwort Benson transliterates into katakana, the phonetic Japanese alphabet, in a somewhat clumsy fashion, Kleinwort Benson Limited would mean nothing to most Japanese. The correct Japanese corporate name had to be written on the back, or front if you prefer, of the visiting card, or *meishi*, which must be exchanged with due ceremony on first meeting. Most Japanese companies' names explain what they do or what they make. However we could not be 'Kleinwort Benson Merchant Bank' because the Japanese had no word for merchant bank. Thus, we became Kleinwort Benson Ginko (Kleinwort Benson Bank), which name we used until we were later licensed as a securities company by the Ministry of Finance and were required to change our Japanese name to Kleinwort Benson shoken kaisha Tokyo Shiten (Kleinwort Benson Securities Company Tokyo Branch). Japanese companies' financial needs were substantially met by their commercial banks' provision of almost unrestricted lines of short-term unsecured borrowings; there were no 'merchant banks' in Japan.

One or two years before I was posted to Tokyo Andrew Caldecott, who was my senior boss and had responsibility for the Tokyo office in the early years, had come out to address a seminar attended by senior financial officers of Japanese companies on merchant banking. Caldecott had a good understanding of the limits of the knowledge of the participants about the subject and pitched his talk accordingly. He was, however, disappointed when the first question to emerge after he had spoken for an hour was 'Mr Caldecott, what is a merchant bank?'.

None of my predecessors had spoken more than rudimentary Japanese and had not attempted to use it in business. Indeed, I was advised not to bother to learn the language. It was widely held in the expatriate community that the Japanese did not like or trust *gaijin* who spoke a little Japanese; they would be most unlikely to speak it well and would sound funny so it was much better that they should not try. I was told that as an Englishman I should speak English. Initially, I accepted the advice not to learn the language but in less than six months had realized I could not be more wrong. Having little or no grasp of the language was hugely limiting in terms of one's ability to communicate, establish relationships in business or socially, to understand what was going on around one; in short, to live a relatively normal life. I therefore started to learn the language although I never had time to attend an intensive course, rather I had to make do with two lessons a week with a teacher who visited the office. I was not very conscientious about doing my homework and so did not make the progress my teachers expected of me although after around three years I found myself able to use the language for business and from that time my progress accelerated somewhat.

After two years in Japan it was clear that my posting would be extended; staff numbers grew little in my first four years. What administration there was was handled competently by Watanabe-san. I spent most of my time visiting large and some smaller Japanese companies to establish our credentials as an underwriter and distributor of their equity and debt financings in the London capital markets. We also established a niche as the leading sponsor of Japanese companies listing their shares on what was then called 'The Stock Exchange in London'. Toshiba, Honda and Fujitsu were among the first three companies to list their shares and we handled all of them. It later became more difficult to persuade companies of the merits of listing in London because, with the establishment of SEAQ (Stock Exchange Automated Quotations system) companies could have their shares quoted and traded in London without complying with the burdensome reporting requirements involved in obtaining and maintaining an official listing. I remember, some years later taking Makoto Iida, then chairman of Secom, to the Stock Exchange to encourage him to list Secom's shares. Sir Andrew Hugh Smith and his colleagues received us courteously and then proceeded to demonstrate the SEAQ system and showed Iida-san his company's quotations on the screen. Iida-san enquired how Secom would be traded differently if it listed. The answer, that admission to the Official List would make no difference to the manner in which Secom was quoted and traded on the SEAQ system, convinced Iida-san that Secom was in fact already 'listed' in London and that there was little additional merit to be gained by obtaining an official listing at substantial cost.

Among our clients in the early 1980s were many Fuyo Group companies such as Nippon Seiko (now NSK), the bearings manufacturer, Marubeni, the general trading company, Oki Electric and Nippon Kokan (now NKK) the steelmaker. There were, however, many other clients which were members of other groups. In particular we enjoyed a close business relationship with NYK, the shipping line. Its former chairman, Yoshiya Ariyoshi [See Hugh Cortazzi's profile in *Biographical Portraits*, Vol.III, published for the Japan Society by Japan Library, 1999], was one of those who adopted me when I arrived in Tokyo in 1980 and Fiona and I attended his last azalea-viewing party at his home the same year. Ariyoshi-san was a traditionalist and introduced me to his favourite 'secret' restaurant in Akasaka, whose proprietress was a former geisha. Ariyoshi-san maintained that the geisha industry was distressed and, as an important part of Japan's cultural heritage, warranted financial support from the government.

On another occasion Ariyoshi-san arranged a boat trip round Yokohama harbour for me and a dozen other bankers whom I had been invited to nominate, together with the long-serving mayor of Yokohama. After the boat trip, he entertained us all to lunch at a neighbouring hotel and, to my embarrassment but also amusement, made a speech in which he said: 'Mr Mayor, the City of Yokohama should borrow money in the City of London, it should borrow from Kleinwort Benson.' Unfortunately, by the time the City got around to borrowing internationally, Kleinworts had withdrawn from debt markets.

There was a great deal of business entertainment in those days. In a typical week one might have dinner with a client twice or three times, almost invariably followed by a visit to a bar or club in Ginza where one drank interminable weak '*mizuwaris*' or '*sodawaris*' and occasionally had to sing. The Japanese custom is that you generally sing alone. Once I had to sing the *Eton Boating Song* in a bar in Akasaka in duet with the late Lord Rothermere, who was reluctant to perform solo. Other than the first verse neither of us could remember the words very well.

The wives were always excluded from the business entertainment, but there was also a great deal of social activity among the expatriate community. We generally managed to include some Japanese friends when we gave a dinner party at home. We also occasionally entertained business clients at home especially when the chairman or another senior director was visiting from London. On these occasions we tried, often unsuccessfully, to persuade the clients to bring their wives. I felt many Japanese businessmen felt uncomfortable to be with their wives in a social gathering, particularly with foreigners. However, the traditional custom of the ladies leaving the gentlemen in the dining-room to continue drinking appealed to them greatly.

*   *   *

By early in 1984 it was clear that the British merchant banks would have to have a presence in the secondary market in order to protect and develop their successful capital markets businesses in the primary market. This

meant that the merchant banks needed their own stockbroking business.
At the same time the countdown to 'Big Bang' had started in London and
the traditional demarcation lines between the various financial services
businesses had started to break down.

I was thrilled to be asked to begin negotiations with the Ministry of
Finance in order to upgrade our representative office to an operating
branch office. A branch office had a minimum staffing requirement of
twenty-two and both in order to meet this qualification and in order to
sell foreign securities to the Japanese financial institutions which were
growing rapidly as the 'bubble' started to grow, we increased our staff
both by secondment from London and by local recruitment. Unlike
the heads of many other foreign financial services companies I was determined to lead the negotiations with the Ministry of Finance myself,
believing, probably optimistically, that my Japanese language ability was
up to the task. In the event the negotiations made slow but steady progress until early in 1985 when the news arrived from London that Kleinwort Benson had agreed to buy Grieveson Grant, the stockbroking firm.
Grieveson Grant already had a representative office in Japan headed by
Simon Grove who had once served as assistant naval attaché in the British
Embassy in Tokyo and who speaks Japanese fluently. Grieveson Grant's
chief saleslady and Grove's effective deputy was the unique Makiko Shir-
ai. Unusually for a Japanese woman in the securities business, at that time
a rarer species than today, Shirai-san was very happy to join in all the
evening entertainment with the clients. She developed the business of
selling British gilt-edged securities to the Japanese life insurance industry
and remained a leading player in the business for several years.

It was decided that the representative offices of Kleinworts and Grievesons should merge in May 1985, some months ahead of 'Big Bang' in
London. Grievesons had filed its own application for a licensed securities branch. The Ministry refused to process either application until one
of them was withdrawn. It was eventually decided that Kleinworts'
application would stand as it was the acquiring entity. I was asked to stay
on to complete the negotiations with the Ministry for the securities business licences and to become the General Manager of the branch.

The offices merged in May 1985 and the licences were issued on 1 November that year. We were able to open for business on 2 December. The
next two-and-a-half years were periods of steady expansion and when I
finally returned to London in August 1988 staff numbers totalled more
than 190.

This period was an immensely challenging and exciting time. It was
not easy to build a single corporate culture and establish a single effective
image for a British-owned business in Japan which was part merchant
bank, part stockbroker but whose staff and clients were mostly Japanese.
I believed that, as far as possible, and without compromising our stan-

dards and principles, we should adapt our working practices to those of the Japanese market-place. We were able to develop the perception that we were easier to deal with than most of our competitors and I believe this was the reason why Kleinworts was able to punch above its weight in Japan until the end of its history as an independent investment bank. There was great pressure on expatriates arriving from London and elsewhere to learn and to be able to operate in the Japanese language. At the end of my tenure of the office as general manager of Kleinworts' Tokyo Branch twenty-three out of our twenty-eight expatriate personnel spoke at least passable Japanese.

In spite of the expatriates' communications skills they did not always work well with the Japanese staff members. The young British expatriates would not readily report to Japanese department heads and the reporting relationship between a young Japanese staff member and his British boss was often equally unsatisfactory. I sometimes wished that I could divide the office into two parts with a glass wall which would provide complete transparency and free exchange of information. The expatriates would work on one side applying British or Western working practices and the Japanese would operate in their own way on the other side. I think, however, that it was right to persevere and develop the hybrid organization that we did.

The very meaning of 'company', or 'kaisha' in Japanese, is different in the two cultures. The Japanese company is a tighter knit organization and the expectations of and obligations held by employees with regard to the company are different and generally more onerous. This distinct feature of Japanese business is now diminishing as practices evolve into something closer to 'Anglo-Saxon capitalism' but significant differences remain.

In Japan, China and Korea, the use of personal seals (hanko) in executing any document is much more important than a mere signature even if someone other than the owner has affixed a seal. Kleinworts' internal audit department tried, unsuccessfully, to eradicate the authentication of dealing tickets by use of personal seals. To use a seal improperly or without authorization in Japan is a much more serious crime than imitating your colleague's signature on a document which was in no way considered unusual or something to be discouraged!

The bubble was blowing up and although many market commentators predicted it would burst and inflated stock market prices would collapse, most Tokyo-based expatriates did not believe that the eventual collapse would be as devastating and as far reaching in its consequences as it ultimately became. In the late 1980s many of us believed that we would before long be earning greater revenues in Tokyo than our head offices were in London.

In order to improve the quality of our local staff we started a programme of graduate recruitment direct from Japanese universities. The Japanese academic year ends in March and graduates all start work with their chosen companies on 1 April.

Recruiting the right kind of young men was much more difficult than finding good women graduates. In 1987 we wanted to recruit five male graduates and five female graduates. A shortlist of applicants eventually emerged and I asked a panel of Japanese and British managers to examine them. What was striking was that the evaluation of the graduates by the Japanese assessors was almost in reverse correlation to that by the British assessors! The Japanese proverb, 'The nail that sticks out must be hammered down' perhaps explains the main reason for this. What all agreed on, however, was that the quality of the female applicants was much higher than that of male applicants. We were unable to find more than four male graduates that we could employ and all of them had scored less well than all of the six female graduates that we agreed to hire.

As head of Kleinwort's operations in Japan I was frequently expected to attend both funerals (usually of former chairmen and presidents of our client companies) and weddings (usually of staff members). I was often asked to make a speech at the latter, eulogising the virtues of the newly-wed to his or her in-laws! On one occasion I acted as 'go-between' or *nakodo* which was a rare honour for a *gaijin* and meant that Fiona and I were asked to preside at Mr and Mrs Tsuga's wedding ceremony and celebration. This was a company wedding and the couple considered that the company had brought them together. As the representative of the company I was perhaps the logical choice to act as *nakodo*. At first, the couple's parents were not particularly happy about it but in the end actually seemed quite pleased. True to tradition, when the couple's first baby was born, Mrs Tsuga brought the infant to our house in Shirogane to show Fiona.

To attend a wedding was expensive as the standard present is to give unused consecutively numbered banknotes in traditional presentation envelopes. The same practice is followed at funerals. As branch general manager, I was normally expected to give ¥50,000 (c. £250) at a wedding or ¥30,000 (c. £180) at a funeral.

My last major task for Kleinworts in my first Japanese posting was to obtain membership of the Tokyo Stock Exchange which enabled us to play on a level playing field with Japanese securities companies. We started trading as a member in May 1988 as one of the second main batch of some twelve new foreign members. It was a source of some satisfaction to me that on the first day of trading, Kleinworts was second to Salomon Brothers in terms of total value of orders received and second to another competitor in terms of the number of orders received. I have always considered that these results meant that, on balance, we came first.

Although I was away from Japan from September 1988 until February 1993 I continued to visit regularly from London. Despite the fact that the stock market bubble had burst and prices were falling, 1990 was a very active year for our mergers and acquisitions business. We advised five Japanese companies on investments in Britain or Europe in that year.

It was a very different Japan that I returned to in the spring of 1993. Confidence had been shattered and most foreign houses were losing money, as indeed were the Japanese houses. The factors that eventually forced a complete restructuring and consolidation of the banking and securities industry were already in place although their full force and effects were not to be widely understood for some time. The excitement of building something new with exciting growth prospects was not there and this time, as president of the Japanese company, I was to concentrate on maintaining our excellent relationships and representing the company externally. I was privileged to serve as the first non-Japanese director both of the Japan Securities Dealers Association and of the Bond Underwriters' Association of Japan, which has since been absorbed by the former. I also served under Graham Harris as a member of the Executive Committee of the British Chamber of Commerce in Japan and as a Vice-Chairman of the European Business Community. Thus, in a sense, I felt that I had a foot in both camps.

CHRISTOPHER PURVIS who worked for S.G. Warburg in Japan in the 1980s reflects on his experiences:-

•

I arrived to live in Tokyo in May 1982, armed with Greek and Latin texts of Homer and Virgil, which had been largely unread at Oxford and which I thought would while away long evenings in a strange land. Little did I realize the extent of the coming transformation of Tokyo during the 1980s into a major financial centre and one of the most lively cosmopolitan cities in the world.

There were very few *gaijin* in Tokyo at that time. Each of the major firms had a single representative at most: Hugh Trenchard of Kleinwort Benson, John MacLaren of Barings. The Americans were no different. But all this was to change. Although we are inclined to complain about the slow speed of change in Japanese financial markets, those of us there at the time sometimes felt we were hardly keeping pace.

I had been selected to go to Tokyo because I already had some knowledge of Japan. After joining S.G. Warburg & Co., I had found myself working for Andrew Smithers on the investment management side of the business. I was sent off to the United States to encourage US pension funds to invest internationally and to Japan to find investment opportunities. Andrew introduced me to the books of Sansom [Sir George] and Morris [Ivan] and encouraged a wider appreciation of Japan. I took over from Andrew Dalton, who wanted to return to London to enter politics; happily for Warburgs he remained with the firm and was to come back again to Tokyo later in the 1980s.

My visits to Japan in the late 1970s had introduced me to Warburgs' many friends. I was despatched by Siegmund Warburg up to Karuizawa to meet Jiro Shirasu [cf. comments by Neville Fakes of Shell in Chapter 16]. Siegmund had met Jiro in 1962 and was convinced by him that Japan was a country to be taken seriously. Although they spent not many days in each other's company during their twenty-year friendship, they became close; and Jiro's help and advice was to play a critical part in my life.

I made some attempt to learn the language before I arrived to live in Tokyo. However, my teacher, Junko Kirkbride, widow of a Canadian whose novel *Tamiko* is well worth reading, was so delightful and interesting on so many subjects that we talked for hours in English. But the interest was sown. I battled on in Tokyo with Ihara sensei; but it was the *mama-sans* in Akasaka who, after midnight, were my most effective teachers.

Warburgs' business with Japan had begun in 1963 with the first financing for a Japanese borrower, the Metropolis of Tokyo, in the eurobond market. The Hamburg firm of Warburg had had a long Japanese history, having played an important role in the financing of the Russo-Japanese War of 1904-5 with a sterling loan – again at a time when Japan's economic prospects were not obvious. It was still the case in the early 1980s that financings, particularly on behalf of the government guaranteed borrowers, were the most important part of our business. My job was to develop further the relationships with them; Warburgs was the only house at that time to be in the syndicate group of all government guaranteed bond issues.

The investment banking community was tiny and we enjoyed friendly competition for quite a narrow range of business. We would bump into each other on the steps of the Japan Development Bank or the Ministry of Finance, all knowing who the next issuer would be. There were few secrets in Tokyo.

Even then the markets were developing and new business opportunities were becoming apparent. In 1982 the first issues of bonds with warrants attached were made in the international market. The warrants were detachable and became a very exciting way to invest in the rising stock market. They were highly geared instruments and could provide great returns for investors. They also led the way to the development of futures and options in the Japanese market.

We were already managing money for non-Japanese in the Japanese equity markets and we saw the opportunity to manage money for the

Japanese. Most funds were at that time invested either passively through cross-shareholdings or for the purpose of building closer business relationships. We believed that this would change and we formed a joint venture with Dai-ichi Seimei, the second largest life insurance company, in investment management. Later, we were to form both an investment management company of our own to manage pension funds and a mutual fund company.

Soon after I arrived, we acted for British Oxygen and for Merck (a leading American pharmaceutical company) in the two important acquisitions of Osaka Sanso (oxygen) and Banyu Seiyaku (pharmaceuticals). We imagined at the time that this might be the start of a major trend of mergers and acquisitions; but we were ahead of the game: it was not until Cable and Wireless acquired the telecommunications company IDC and Renault its stake in Nissan in 1999 that we might say that Anglo-Saxon capitalism was arriving in Japan.

As a representative I was not allowed to transact business. We decided soon after my arrival that we should apply for branch status, so that we could develop our own business in Tokyo. The financial market was a closed shop and nothing would be made easy for the newcomer, until he finally became a member of the club. After eighteen months of preparing papers for the Ministry of Finance and answering questions about every detail of our business in London, I was telephoned by our case officer and asked what the 'G' of S. G. Warburg stood for; 'Why, George, of course; we are British.' It was the last question I received from the Ministry and we got our licence; neither of us knew whether the other was joking.

The relationship with the MOF was key to everything we did. They had considerable latitude in what could and could not be done. It was imperative to have the best lines of communication. Once I was telephoned by an official to say that a certain type of swap transaction that we and other banks had been proposing would now be allowed. We launched a deal immediately; the CSFB representative saw me at a party late that night, amazed that we had done it: he had not received that call.

We were surprised by the speed with which we were invited to apply for membership of the Tokyo Stock Exchange. In early 1985 it was announced that foreigners could join, but there would only be room for six firms. We spent many months developing the arguments for our membership. This was not easy in our case because 'Big Bang' was only just occurring in London. Until that time merchant banks could not become members of the London stock exchange because of the traditional split in the London market between the activities of underwriting, trading and selling securities.

Jiro Shirasu took the closest possible interest in this process, never ceasing behind the scenes to press the case for Warburgs. He and I became close during that year; his two projects were our stock exchange membership and my marriage. On 29 November the *Nikkei* (which was usually accurate in its publication of leaks from the MOF) ran as its lead article the names of the six lucky firms, and our name was not included. I was in London that day and received two calls: Jiro had died and, contrary to the *Nikkei* report, we had received membership. Later that day I asked my future mother-in-law for permission to marry Phillida.

I was always of the belief that it would be the market-place that would force the liberalization of the market. This was correct: in the late 1990s it has been economic pressure that has led to a radical opening up of the market. But the whole process has taken longer than I expected.

While I have always been a proponent of liberalization, my position was somewhat compromised by the fact that we had invested so much in becoming members of the Japanese club. This was an important competitive advantage and was not to be thrown up overnight.

I had reservations about the interference of British politicians in the liberalization process. Attempts were made to negotiate with the Japanese authorities on behalf of British firms. I took the view that this was fruitless: London was already the most open market-place in the world; we could not prevent Japanese firms coming to London because they were already there (a minor exception was some delaying tactic with the opening of the London branch of a regional bank). The next negotiating tactic was to link the discussion of the next round of Stock Exchange seats to other industries. Michael Howard, then a minister at the DTI (Parliamentary Under Secretary), visited our offices. I did not want him to give a press conference on Warburg soil on the importance of Barclays becoming a member; the meeting took place in our lobby.

There were some significant differences in the way the Americans negotiated with the Japanese. In the mid-1980s the MOF felt that it was important to hear directly from the representatives of foreign firms. The representatives of the six foreign members of the Stock Exchange were invited to regular lunches. These were intended to provide a channel of communication and for the MOF to understand better what our concerns were and I took the view that they would be useful. One American turned to another in one such lunch and said in a loud voice: 'Do you think that I am being rude enough?' Although there was an interpreter, our hosts were well able to understand. British firms at that time took the view that there were some advantages in differentiating ourselves from this type of behaviour.

Once in the club there was a strong feeling that you would be looked after. I became a member of the 'Ginseikai', a monthly lunch club of the heads of securities companies associated with banks. Lunches could be agonizing: interpreters were not allowed and my night club Japanese sometimes let me down. In 1990 I joined the Stock Exchange membership committee, the most powerful body of the exchange. There was an annual weekend outing of the heads of all the member firms of the Stock Exchange to a *ryokan* in Yugawara. We were joined for dinner by ladies from Atami. As the youngest I was always placed beside the most senior, Yoshihisa Tabuchi of Nomura and Yoshitoki Chino of Daiwa. There were no other foreigners; other firms either had Japanese running their offices or the foreigners simply did not come. I thought it was important (I had been elected to the club and should now participate), and indeed it was fun. Chino was always particularly kind. But one could see that this was a very traditional industry and it was going to have to change; the only question was when.

Some British firms formed close ties with Japanese banks, Morgan Grenfell with Tokai, Kleinworts with Fuji. We were closest to the Bank of Tokyo, and we had our joint venture with Dai-ichi; but these were not exclusive and we tried to develop business with all the successors of the pre-war *zaibatsu*. Toray was our longest-standing industrial client. Kohei Sakamoto, senior managing director in the early 1980s, became a dear friend and he is now an adviser to Issey Miyake. I used to call frequently on vice president Uchiyama of Nissan to encourage him to finance the Nissan plant in Sunderland through us; he was keen to talk about the girl in the embassy, with whom he played tennis, who was similarly encouraging him to invest in Britain. He, too, died just weeks before I became engaged to Phillida.

Such relationships were critical to success. They were demonstrated by such events as chairman Shoda of Nippon Credit Bank calling on me in our small office in Yurakucho to pay his respects on the death of Siegmund Warburg. Toray had stood by us at the time of the oil crisis when other companies were quick to bow to pressure to boycott names on the Arab blacklist. The life of the investment banker in Tokyo was one of constant calling on companies, lunches and dinners. We were developing new financing and investment techniques; but the relationships were still critical to success.

One day, in 1988, I was delighted to find that we had transacted an equity sale to a leading life insurance company with whom we had had no previous relationship. I immediately assumed that this breakthrough had occurred because of the brilliance of our research or the fineness of our pricing and rushed to congratulate our head of sales. I was the next day visited by the insurance company to thank me because we had decided to give them some insurance business, a decision we had taken on commercial grounds. Two steps forward, one step back.

As financial markets developed in Tokyo and as the stock market rose, the Japanese financial firms took on great importance on the global scene. By the late 1980s the Stock Market capitalization of Nomura Securities alone was greater than that of all Australian companies. Inevitably,

some began to believe that they could walk on water. It was also a time of
ambitious planning. The idea developed that there were three major financial centres and the firm with global pretensions had to be strong in
each. It was unsurprising that there were rumours in the press of a tie-up
between Warburgs, Morgan Stanley and IBJ; but there was nothing in
them.

*   *   *

As we went from a representative office to a branch with offices in Tokyo
and Osaka, the system of operating the business was transformed. To begin with, I relied completely on Miss Sogi, our secretary who pulled all
the strings. I was shortly joined by a young colleague, Nick Hanbury-
Williams. It was a free and easy environment . We had considerable latitude in the types of business we were able to pursue (he concentrated
mainly on the investors and I on the borrowers). There was little planning, and there were no internal management meetings. I would set off
to Kansai on a Thursday night to see our clients there with a view to
arriving at Matsubaya, a cheap family-run *ryokan* in Kyoto, for a weekend
of exploring temples. We did lots of business; our costs were low; and we
had fun.

We were assisted in this feeling of freedom by the wonderful Kawagu-
chi-san, a freelance cook, who came to organize many aspects of our lives
and become Japanese *obaasan* to our children. While we did our fair share
of dining in restaurants and singing in bars, I preferred a more English
form of client entertainment with large dinners in my home, Chateau
Hattori in Akasaka (apartments were often given wonderfully grand
names; mine became known to friends as Shatty Hatty), and singing
round my piano rather than the *karaoke* machine.

By the time I left Japan in 1992 we were the largest British employer in
Tokyo. The business had become part of a global investment bank with
large sales and trading activities as well as corporate finance and investment management. An increasing amount of time was spent in management rather than with clients. In 1991 we found ourselves facing losses as
the stock market levels (and more importantly volumes) fell. During
those ten years there was a major shift from the small relationship-based
team to a major business, which required management and, when the
profits declined, laying off of staff.

A turning point came on Good Friday 1987 when a team left us to join
Barings. Staff, both Japanese and *gaijin*, could be wooed away by other
firms. Competition became more intense and we would have to pay up
for good people. It became apparent that the successful firms were either
those with a small cost base and a specialization, or those with breadth in
trading as well as advisory capability. The style within our firm changed,

just as it was also changing in London. This was a sad but inevitable development. While it caused strains and stresses at the time, and although it completely changed relationships both within the firm and with clients, I welcomed it. No business can stand still.

As the business grew, we recruited heavily from the universities. I was a strong believer in the need to develop our own culture in Japan by recruiting directly from university. We had some success, particularly in attracting excellent girls. I took great delight in the fact that one of ours, after only a few years, received remuneration greater than that of a typical Japanese chief executive. The young men were more traditional; I enjoyed encouraging them to give up their white shirts and blue suits and become more adventurous in their outward and inward thinking. I encouraged everyone to call me by my first name; the Japanese custom of addressing seniors by their title is a small symptom of the stifling of imagination in the young. Persuading my Japanese colleagues to take two weeks' holiday at a time was yet more of a challenge; I managed it by calling on our insurers to make it a rule.

Our early days as a trading business were only made possible by the excellence of our Japanese staff. Masaharu Ono, whom we had known for many years at Nikko Securities in London, joined in 1983 and he in turn lured on board Tadashi Jitoku, who made us the envy of other foreign firms in the efficiency of our 'back office'. It was they who put us into shape to open for business as a branch in 1984 and as a Stock Exchange member in 1986. Shortly before we started trading, our head of settlement was poached by a newly-arrived British investment banker, who had little sympathy with any idea that we should try not to poach from each other. It was a rude awakening; and we, too, hired from other firms. But loyalty continued; after I left in 1992, with some recent losses in my wake, Yuichi Kamina, our head of sales, handed in his resignation and appeared at my London home with a beautiful lacquer tray, with a phoenix depicted on it.

With so many young people in our office there were plenty of weddings, many of which were *shanai kekkon* (marriages between two members of a company's staff). This meant that many were inflicted with woeful speeches in Japanese from the *shitencho* (head of branch office). Those were the days of long wedding ceremonies; it could be a terrible shock to find oneself trapped at a dinner, proceedings having started five hours earlier. Most of these ceremonies were held in hotels, but some were Christian. One or two took place at St Andrews, the Japanese-speaking Anglican church by Tokyo Tower, sister to St Albans which we regularly attended. There were also many funerals. I followed the custom of going to those of clients. But the greatest sadness was the death of Ono-san who bravely struggled against cancer to be able to see the start of our stock exchange trading. It was a great honour to lead his family and friends in saying goodbye at his funeral.

There were several office moves. The most ambitious was to a newly-built office in Showa Dori when we became members of the Stock Exchange. It was remarkable the way in which pieces of furniture that had been selected a year earlier were delivered at the exact moment predicted at the time of ordering. Things were not always straightforward. In order to guarantee that our telephone lines were installed on time we were told that we would have to buy several million yen's worth of telephone cards. We duly did so and were still handing these out to clients as gifts years later!

Jiro Shirasu introduced me to the world of Shimbashi and the geisha district in Nagoya, which had the atmosphere that Shimbashi might have had fifty years earlier. His favourite tea house was Shinkiraku, whose *tatami* rooms were vast (and cold in the winter). Hanbury-Williams, Shirasu and I made an expedition to Toyota City with his intrepid driver, Akama-san. The stated purpose of the trip was to visit Dr Shoichiro Toyoda and to see the factory. Indeed, this must have been the only time that a Mercedes has been on the shop floor of a Toyota factory as Shirasu had announced, probably for effect, that he could not walk. But the real reason for the trip was to see some old friends in the tea house in Nagoya. They were delightful. Shirasu did not draw a distinction between business and pleasure. Thus his Warburg parties always had a sprinkling of people from other worlds: film or fashion. When he died I inherited in a miraculous way the friendship of his family and friends. Masako, his widow, had shown no interest while he was alive in Jiro's banking friends; but once he died she became like a mother to me. Kazuko Aso, daughter of Prime Minister Yoshida and such a great friend to Britain, showed me particular kindness. Tokio Nagayama, who had worked closely with Jiro at MITI after the war, rang me immediately after Jiro died and offered to take on the mantle of business adviser.

There were challenges in operating in what was considered by most London colleagues a strange country on the other side of the world. The Japanese business by the end of the 1980s was a significant part of a global business. But few in London had much sympathy for the place. It was always a challenge persuading good people to come to Japan. There were, however, some who did take Japan very seriously. Eric Roll (Lord Roll) came to Japan in the 1950s for negotiations about sugar, long before he joined Warburgs. David Scholey (later Sir David), Warburgs' chairman, did not come until 1984, but was an immediate convert. Martin Gordon had been involved in Japan since the early days and had many close friends in Japan. He came to live in Tokyo for a couple of years in the 1980s as our senior director for the whole of Asia.

In 1986 Warburgs merged with several other firms including the government broker, Mullens. Our new colleagues came from a great tradition: two hundred years of co-operation with the Bank of England in the issue of government debt. A wonderful pair, Dinwiddy and Marriott, arrived in Tokyo from this firm to peddle their wares. I invited them for Sunday lunch the day after their arrival (it was something of a custom to have large lunch parties with roast lamb and mint sauce); and they arrived bearing some 1963 Taylor's that had been decanted the night before in London so that it would not get shaken up on the journey.

Investment banks and makers of perfume have a habit of listing the names of cities where they have their offices or shops. And it became the custom for Tokyo to be a key member of that list in the late 1980s, joining London, Paris and New York. Musicians seem to follow the same pattern in their choice of venue, again motivated I suppose by the search for handsome fees. Thus it was that in the 1980s we were able to enjoy a plethora of concerts given by the greatest talent. To begin with these were in the Tokyo Bunka Kaikan or in Showa Women's College; but fine new halls were built while I was there, Suntory in Roppongi and Orchard in Shibuya. Frequent visitors were Jessye Norman, Yo-Yo Ma, Menuhin, Tennstedt and Sinopoli (whose series of all the Mahler symphonies was packed with an enthralled audience). But it was not just a question of the top artists putting on performances there; sometimes musical history was made in Japan. I remember Seiji Ozawa conducting Messiaen's *St Francois d'Assise* in Tokyo Cathedral, not long after its composition (Messiaen was teacher to Akio Yashiro, whose family became great friends of mine). Leonard Bernstein came when he was already ill and conducted an extraordinary performance of Mahler's 9th symphony as though it was a farewell to the concert platform. For me the most astonishing event was the visit of the Royal Opera in 1992, when Tokyo audiences were able to see all three Mozart da Ponte operas on successive nights in the Schaaf productions conducted by Haitink and Tate, a treat that had not been available in London.

Another indicator of economic booms is the growth in restaurants; and the 1980s for those of us who lived in Tokyo was a decade of putting on weight. Ogawa-ken was a miraculous mixture of East and West, and in the late 1980s there opened a restaurant called Hotel de Mikuni which produced quite simply some of the best French food in the world. Sotheby's held wine auctions in Tokyo and there were some great tastings. A memorable evening was spent with Anthony Barton who gave a vertical tasting of Leoville Bartons (a great St Julien, but so drinkable that it must be my desert island wine), finishing with the glorious 1982s.

I managed to live for ten years in Japan without ever playing golf. Indeed, I am no sportsman and was not inclined to join the typical weekends of *gaijin* bankers wind-surfing at Akiya or waterskiing on Lake Yamanaka-ko. Many foreigners rented *besso* in the hills at Minakami. I resisted this in the belief that it was good to get away from the British at weekends. A *gaijin* place I did enjoy visiting, however, was the Grindlays Bank *besso*, a scruffy hut literally on the beach of a small cove just west of Shimoda. Even I did enjoy occasionally getting on the 7.00pm train from Ueno on a Friday night to go on a skiing weekend. In the early 1990s one was able to take the newly built Niigata *shinkansen* and be on the slopes by ten o'clock and back in one's bath in Akasaka at eight that evening.

Recreation in Tokyo occasionally brought its frustrations. I could not bear the inability of those in authority to show any flexibility regarding their rules. I once was in the swimming pool at the New Otani carrying my two-year-old child. The attendant asked me to take off my sunglasses because it was against the rules to wear them. I pointed out that we were alone in the pool, I was literally standing still and they were plastic. On his insistence that I take them off I hurled them in my frustration against the wall to prove my point and stormed off thus wasting several tens of thousand of yen entrance fee.

It was, therefore, also important to escape from Japan from time to time. 1985 became an *annus mirabilis* for Warburg's business in Singapore. This might have had something to do with the fact that Phillida Seaward had been posted there from the economic section of the embassy in Tokyo. I would catch the Singapore Airlines flight at seven on a Friday night, which in those days stopped in Taiwan and did not arrive until three. Phillida and I would then get into her red Mazda RX7 and drive up to Mersing to catch a boat to Rawa at dawn. Uchiyama and Shirasu played their part in my marriage plans; but Saturday breakfast on the beach also helped.

The 1980s were a remarkable decade in the development of financial markets in Japan. It was a decade of great excitement. But the quintupling of the stock market, based on rising property prices, led to what appears in retrospect an artificial climate. The fact that everyone was making money meant that there was little pressure for change. The foreigners, too, found it difficult to believe that this would not go on for ever.

But in December 1989 the Bank of Japan raised interest rates. The stock market was just under 40,000. We did not pay much attention; but it was the beginning of a long bear market, which would bring even greater changes to Japan at the end of the 1990s.

HILL SAMUEL was a British merchant bank for whom I worked part-time between the end of 1984 and the end of 1991. JOHN NAISH was one of the main advocates in Hill Samuel of Japanese financial markets. As he explains in the following piece he was a frequent visitor to Japan and later headed Hill Samuel's office in Tokyo:-

•

I had become interested in Japan as a teenager when Dr Blount, a colleague of my father's who was a veterinary surgeon, used to talk enthusiastically about his visits to the country and gave my parents some Japanese prints. My involvement in Japanese business began in the early 1970s with the London merchant bank Hill Samuel. After a while, dealing with the London offices of Japanese companies and banks, I was seconded to Hong Kong in 1974. From there I began travelling regularly to Tokyo and on my return to London at the start of 1977, I became, in effect, Hill Samuel's representative in Japan, albeit from a London base. For the next few years I would spend alternate six-week periods in Tokyo and in London. I came to know the Palace Hotel extremely well.

From the 1960s Japanese organizations had been major borrowers of eurodollars. The still quite new market for this off-shore currency was centred on the London-based banks. Hill Samuel was lending substantial sums to Japanese corporations as well as arranging bond issues for them in the international capital markets. In 1965 it had worked with Yamaichi to arrange for Canon the first issue of eurodollar convertible bonds (debt convertible by the investors into equity). The capital markets were at that time too small, however, to accommodate the voracious appetite for funds of Japan's rapidly expanding economy. Bank lending was of crucial importance to Japanese companies.

Medium-term loans were good business. The Japanese authorities did not allow Japanese banks to lend to Japanese companies in this way. They could introduce loans and would almost invariably add their guarantee to enhance the credit quality but they could not provide the funds themselves. Competition among non-Japanese lenders was in any case limited at that time and consequently profit margins were high on what were very good loan assets.

The way in which restrictions were imposed by the Japanese authorities contrasted with the way the UK authorities imposed theirs. In the UK, if there was no provision against it in the rule book, you could do it. In Japan, if there was no specific provision, you could not. Furthermore, it seemed interpretation of the rules by the bureaucrats of the Ministries was much more important than the rules themselves.

Despite progressive liberalization during the 1970s and 1980s, the frustrations of dealing within this system cropped up from time to time. Quite late on towards the end of this period, a colleague of mine, well-known in the bank for his original ideas, came up with a bright notion which would allow Japanese companies to raise funds internationally at lower interest rates than it seemed the market required. Before going too far down the path with any one company, we thought it prudent to check things with the Ministry of Finance. The senior officer asked why we needed to discuss anything since after a recent bout of liberalization measures, things were so free. We explained the idea, concluding by saying we wanted to mention it to the authorities before embarking on a marketing campaign with it. The long silence ended with an apologetic intake of breath through teeth. Rules did indeed exist, they would indeed be broken very sorry but. . .

Gradual relaxation of the regulations was, however, a feature of Japan as its international presence increased and its economy evolved. This was accompanied by rapid growth of the international debt and equity markets during the 1970s which enabled Japanese companies to reduce their dependence on the banks for their financing needs and thus the influence which banks could exert on their activities.

Japan had adopted the US policy of demarcation between commercial and investment banking and securities business. All financial institutions were keen to increase their size and influence. Competition between the banks and securities companies was keen. As the sway of the banks reduced, the power of the securities companies increased.

The merchant banks had big names in the world of international finance but as organizations were quite small. Successful marketing depended on having good relationships with the introducers of business – the banks and, increasingly, the securities companies. The Japanese market was too vast for the limited marketing resources of the merchant banks to cover adequately.

Building relationships took time, patience and money; returns would not be immediate. It was not possible to fly into Tokyo, do a deal and fly home. Japanese institutions needed to know that you would be around for long enough to make it worth their while to get to know you. In addition, most business meetings would be with executives who recommended to their seniors which foreign houses to work with rather than with who actually decided this. Executives at all levels of influence had to be comfortable with you. If not, the consensus would not be reached and the marketing bid would fail. Relationships like that take time to develop.

All of this was anathema to the much shorter-term needs of Western organizations and business development in Japan was as much about keeping head office on side as it was about getting out and about among potential deals. Very few visiting businessmen could conduct meetings in Japanese and misunderstandings compounded the frustrations for representatives such as myself when introducing expert visitors from London. Patience simply had to be the watchword if a marketing strategy was to succeed.

Some foreign banks used the need for taking a long-term view as an excuse for dodging what should have been a short-term decision. A careful analysis of their business would have shown that never in the longest of terms would they have made a satisfactory profit. Very few foreign organizations, however, seemed able to have a long-term plan which they would then follow through. The concept of long lead times was just too much to bear. Taking the wider perspective of head office, this may well have been correct but it was trying for those in the field.

In the mid-1980s, the City of London embarked on a restructuring of its finance industry in preparation for the so-called 'Big Bang'. Banks bought stockbrokers and/or stock jobbing companies to give them the securities trading expertise which the old London system had denied them. They aimed to cover the spectrum of finance. As far as their Japanese ambitions were concerned, they saw their enhanced securities activities as enabling them not only to service better the needs of their corporate clientele but also to exploit the rapidly growing capital export activity resulting from the vast increase in Japanese individual and institutional wealth and liquidity.

The Tokyo stock market was booming. Frenetic levels of turnover were leading to silly statistics emerging like the entire outstanding stock of a company changing hands in a few days.

Competition was hotter than ever and the feeling was developing that to have any credibility at all in the Japanese market you had to have some permanent representation. Hill Samuel officially opened its representative office in 1985 staffing it with its own executives, those from Wood Mackenzie, the stockbroker it had acquired, and with a limited number of new recruits. My colleague, Donald Rushton, was moved from New York to become the first Tokyo representative and I continued my shuttling between London and Tokyo although with shorter visits.

By the time Donald's tour of duty had finished and I had succeeded him in 1988, Hill Samuel had itself become a victim of Big Bang. It had abandoned its securities trading activities and had been purchased in the October of 1987 by the TSB Group. The, much smaller, Tokyo office was to focus on three different areas: introducing potential users of Hill Samuel's more esoteric financial products, placing yen financings with Japanese institutional lenders and promoting cross-border merger and acquisition opportunities among Japanese corporations wanting to expand overseas. Whilst there was still a great deal of money flowing into Japan, there was also a lot flowing out.

For the most part I enjoyed considerable autonomy and support from London. It has to be admitted that credibility was not helped by the irritating and wasteful tendency for TSB's head office to mandate US banks to arrange its own yen financing needs without even giving the Tokyo office a chance to compete. It always seemed to me like buying a lot of DIY equipment and then leaving it unused in the tool-shed whilst paying others to do no better a job. This sort of thing was however exceptional. My prime contact point was Donald Rushton and my immediate superior was Tim Frankland who had been involved in Japan for almost as many years as I had. Both were fun to work with and understood the requirements of the Japanese market. In addition, Hill Samuel had recruited Sir Hugh Cortazzi as a non-executive director. As ex-ambassador to Japan, he of all people knew what was required and could always be counted upon for support when it was needed.

Hill Samuel's business in Japan went reasonably well and continued for a few years after my own time in office ended. Whilst I was there, however, it was becoming clear that Japanese respect for size as a measure of success and reliability gave the American investment banks a considerable advantage over their smaller European competitors. The Americans had the foresight to invest heavily in their Japanese operations and the wherewithal to make it feasible. At the same time, the Japanese miracle was coming to an end as the 1980s bubble burst. Other opportunities were coming to the fore.

*   *   *

It was not all business! I was often invited to spend Saturdays and Sundays with Japanese I had got to know while they were in London.

They were hospitality personified. Drinks parties, dinner parties, visits to places of interest with their families or sometimes just sitting at home with them talking. I used to wonder if we in the UK would have shown the same degree of concern to help a visitor escape from the monotony of hotel life.

And of course there was always golf.

On a Sunday afternoon when my boss, Tim Frankland, was also visiting Tokyo, we went to ride on the tram at Waseda. After a few stops we got off and walked through the narrow village-like streets which seemed to be everywhere in Tokyo. We spotted a golf shop where the discounts were unbelievable. It was closing down because the young golf professional owner was moving to California. Three woods, nine irons, a putter, and a bag for half the UK price. These became the Hill Samuel golf equipment, permanently resident at the Palace Hotel. I used them about twice a month when I was there.

The golf day is an event: an early start, a snack half-way round, a hot bath and drinks at the end of the game and the slow drag home. The manicured courses of, probably, twenty-seven holes laid out in three sets of nine surround club-house facilities most English clubs could only dream about.

I was taken to play at many courses. One friend, with whom I had played regularly whilst he was based in London, introduced me to Tsuru-gashima. Another friend not only took me to play at Shonan, of which he was a member, but also arranged for me to be introduced to and join my home club at Strawberry Hill in Twickenham, located no more than half a mile from where I live. He had lived in London in the 1960s and knew the course and some of its members well. Yet another took me regularly to the various clubs in which his company held a debenture. He was a particularly generous man. Although I suppose this would have been called business golf, the bank did only a little business with his company and these days on the course were really just social affairs.

Most of my friends lived a little way from the centre of Tokyo which made visits more difficult. One very good friend lived (and still does) in Minami Aoyama, one of the nicest and most central residential parts of the city. He would also invite me to golf but because he lived only a short taxi-hop from my hotel, I would be a regular visitor to his house for dinner. He and his wife had lived in London in the early 1970s and had kept up to date with British current affairs since their return to Tokyo. They both have a terrific sense of humour and I always enjoy their company.

I became interested in Japan's history. This may have been because it did not require me to remember the English history I had learned at school. It is only over the past 150 years that Japan's activities have become intertwined with our own so I could start again as it were. Not that I have made a great start since either but there are some terrific characters to learn about – like Takeda Shingen, whose death and whose look-alike were the subjects of Kurosawa's film *Kagemusha*. Oda Nobunaga, Toyotomi Hideyoshi and Tokugawa Ieyasu are three others. I was amused by the parable of the silent song-bird. It is said to illustrate the character differences of these three. Oda's violent killing it if it would not sing, Hideyoshi's forcing it to sing and Tokugawa's ultimately successful patience in waiting for it to sing.

*   *   *

Travelling around the country was not cheap but I always enjoyed trips to the countryside. In the summer of 1982 I had to visit Shimoneseki. I was en route to Hong Kong and broke my journey to call on some friends and to visit some regional banks' headquarters. One bank arranged to take me to the caves at Akiyoshi. These vast subterranean caverns are the third largest of their kind in the world and the temperature is a constant seventeen degrees all year round – inside was much more comfortable than out in the September heat.

Everybody has stories about the first time they felt an earthquake in Tokyo or the first time they saw Fuji. During one of my early visits I was taken to see Fuji-san. Over the two or three-hour car journey, my hosts told me all about how wonderful it would look and so on and so forth. When we arrived, mist and low cloud greeted us. It was impossible to see more than a few yards. 'Yes, but from here,' said my host drawing a wide arc with his arm in the foggy gloom, 'you must be able to imagine . . .' I assured him I could.

Once I had started living in Japan, I decided to photograph and to video as many sites and views as possible. On clear winter days, especially when a stiff breeze had blown away the pollution, if you went to the top of my apartment block you had a wonderful view of Fuji. I still have the video I took in January 1990. Fuji is silhouetted against the winter sunset. I was frozen taking the video and caught a heavy cold but it was worth it.

Not every weekend was filled with entertaining and on quieter Saturdays and Sundays I used to cross the road from the Palace Hotel to the Imperial Palace Gardens. Walking inside the great dry stone walls is like entering another world. Twenty-five years ago there were few tall buildings visible from within the Gardens and it was hard to believe that you were in the centre of one of the world's great cities.

I am not a linguist but never found my lack of Japanese much of a barrier. As a discipline, I would try to learn one or two phrases on every trip and this was useful for dealing with the basic situations of life like giving directions to the taxi driver. But although the Japanese themselves have no reputation for other languages, sometimes there were unexpected exceptions.

It was just after cherry blossom time and I was returning to my hotel after a morning meeting in Kasumigaseki. I climbed into a taxi and, doing my best impression of Japanese, asked the driver for the Palace Hotel. He turned around and politely enquired of me as Jeeves might have of Bertie Wooster: 'Excuse me, sir, but where would you like to go?' He and his wife had been studying English for years by radio. He had never visited England but spoke the language perfectly. I commented that Tokyo could look lovely at that time of year and could only smile when he replied: 'How awfully kind of you to say so, sir.'

Hill Samuel's office in Tokyo which opened in 1985 was located in Kasumigaseki, just up the hill from the Tokyo Club. This operates in much the same way as any London club. Quiet, a place to read newspapers, meet for lunch or to have a drink. I was fortunate enough to be able to join. There were some interesting people to meet and some good stories to hear. I used to eat there at least once a week and probably more. I hope I will always keep my membership. I invariably look in when I visit Japan.

I suspect that it is only when you live in rather than visit a city that you learn its distinctive sounds and only when you leave that you recognize what they were. The summer whir of cicadas, the winter drone of the sweet potato-seller, the perennial sharp caw of the crows and the night-time chanting reminder to switch off oil heaters are all in my memories of Tokyo. But most of all, and unique, from my experience anyway, were the five o'clock chimes.

Although an obvious landmark in the day, nothing much changes at five o'clock in Tokyo. Nobody seems to stop work and go home or break for a cup of tea. And yet every day on the stroke of five, the chimes sound. I would notice them on Saturdays and, most especially, on Sundays when they would awaken that 'end-of-weekend feeling' I have had since I was at school.

The friendliness of the people, the safety, the punctuality and the orderliness of the place form the backdrop to my memories of Tokyo. I reckon that if I could not live in Britain I would choose to live in Japan.

25

Investment Management and Broking: The Experiences of Two Old Hands

ERIC ELSTOB ● DUGALD BARR

ERIC ELSTOB, as he explains in the following piece, has had over thirty years of close contacts with Japan, beginning in the 1970s with the Foreign & Colonial Investment Trust:-

●

I first went to Japan in April and May 1969, as a twenty-six-year-old, working for the Foreign & Colonial Investment Trust. Foreign & Colonial had been one of the very first British institutions to invest in Japanese equities, traditionally because the deputy chairman Charles Wainman was an expert on camellias, and on a trip to buy specimens had bought a few shares as well. One of them was Sony!

By 1969 it was felt that more professionalism was due. So Jeremy Paulson-Ellis who worked at the stockbrokers, Vickers da Costa, and I were summoned by Charlie Wainman and Ralph Vickers, Jeremy's senior partner, and we were told that we were going to Japan for two months to learn about the markets. To be precise we would be working for six weeks. We were then ordered to take a fortnight's holiday, for which our respective employers would pay. The only conditions were that we had to promise never to stay in a Western hotel, and always to use public transport. That was the old City. It formed the habit of a lifetime, to use my weekends to travel around Japan, rather than drinking whisky in a plastic hotel. For Charlie and Ralph were wise old birds; and during the rest of my career I have won instant goodwill from my Japanese contacts precisely because I had travelled around and enjoyed their country.

In those days the only young Westerners in Japan were American servicemen and their families. On our holiday we met a group of American schoolgirls in Beppu; and arranged to go out for the evening – but they never showed up. Next morning we ran into them again; and learnt that their teacher had forbidden them to go out with dubious European play-boys!

It was on a boat on the Inland Sea that I achieved the summit of my sexual career. Jeremy and I were sitting on the deck with our sleeves rolled up in the hot sunshine, when a whole class of Japanese schoolgirls in their sailor uniform surrounded us, asking by signs for our autographs in Western script. Any old bit of paper was produced for us to sign; and its proud possessor then withdrew giggling. After a bit I felt my forearms getting badly sunburnt, or bitten by mosquitoes. So I slapped down, to find that I had trapped a little girl's hand. There was much giggling and almost tears. The girls had each been tweaking out a blond hair, which we then saw them sellotape next to the signature.

Although neither of us had close family who had served in the Eastern theatre of the war, I was still apprehensive about being in Japan. Yet I have never felt so safe in a foreign country. The obviously genuine helpfulness of all whom we met was only negated by the lack of a common language. Inevitably, we made our pilgrimage to Nagasaki; and the dignity of the museum left us both silent for the rest of the day. The image which I can never forget was the three milk bottles, unbroken but fused together by the heat.

The young Japanese stockbrokers who were detailed to look after us were the brightest and best of their firms, the only ones who had con-versational English, which they were keen to improve by epic drinking bouts. Next morning there was more tea drunk than in any British office, but to some degree as a hangover cure.

Even though investment analysis in London was by today's standards amateurish, in Japan it was non-existent. Equipped with the *shikiho*, a thick paperback of corporate statistics, we visited company manage-ments to discover that these statistics were complete nonsense. When I asked a question about a major subsidiary, the director in charge would disappear to return with all the internal financial statements. These showed that the subsidiary was sometimes making more profits than the parent company, nothing of which was consolidated into the pub-lished figures. Indeed, our interest in them was seen as rather odd. After watching these young Westerners buying large lines of shares, our Japa-nese friends asked us to explain why. And then they tried to sell these cheap shares to their own clients, but for many years with more success to foreign funds than to their own insurance companies.

We benefited from the confusion that makes Westerners appear older than they are to Japanese, just as all Japanese appear younger to Wester-ners. Senior Japanese were immensely generous with their time to us. Akio Morita of Sony must have been the most outstanding; but there were many more at his level who often gave up evenings to these young Westerners.

Language was often a problem. Trying to learn Japanese and do a full day's work has defeated me and most others who were not living there and so totally immersed. I treasure one very smart dinner party, where even the geisha were finding it hard work to get hosts and guests together. The interpreters had given up; and concentrated on their whisky. As the most junior I was sitting at the far end of the table on the guests' side, while the chairman of our hosts sat the centre on his side. Somehow it emerged that he had been a naval cadet on exchange in Kiel in the thirties, and my own father was a sailor. So he and I ended up, in total breach of etiquette, singing *lieder* and German scout songs together, enjoying ourselves greatly, while everyone else just sat in silence.

We stayed at the Okura Hotel, which is next to the American Embassy, and almost part of the compound. The spirit of 1968 was alive and well in Japan. Indeed, the quality of Japanese student rioting was well up to the French. Taxi drivers would approach the hotel from the back, and we guests scampered in through the kitchen.

Since then I have always stayed at the Palace Hotel in Otemachi, with its big, old-fashioned rooms, and restricted enough for the staff to recognize all their regular customers. It is a pleasant walk from there to Nihonbashi where all the brokers had their offices and to the Bank of Japan. There is a clear class distinction among top international hotels in Tokyo. The Okura retains the prestige of presidents and sportsmen. Grandees use the Imperial, presumably with some vague sub-conscious memory about Frank Lloyd Wright, although his hotel is now two re-buildings ago. If you want to meet the serious foreign and indeed local businessmen in town, the private breakfast room at the top of the Palace is without question the best club, with its views across the gardens of the palace itself and, a tribute to the reduced pollution in Tokyo over the last decade, often of Mount Fuji.

The smogs in Tokyo were atrocious. To an Englishman it was the Novembers of my urban boyhood in the 1950s with a visibility of ten feet. This has improved dramatically. The great pan-Tokyo traffic jam, however, has lasted at least thirty years, regardless of new subways and fly-overs. Whenever I had a very senior Brit making his first visit to Japan, I could see how he subconsciously registered the Japanese as coolies; and my cure was to sit with them for an hour or so in a traffic jam, as I watched how the scales fell from their eyes and they realized that this was an industrial society like the USA or Britain.

* * *

Visiting companies in the Japanese countryside is always great fun. Foreigners do not appreciate quite how much of Japanese industry is scattered around in the provinces. On a visit to Hamamatsu I admitted to my host how delicious I found eel; and when we left a miniature Sargasso Sea of differently cooked eels was thrust upon me as a gift. Matsushita Kotobuki has its main factory on Shikoku, so a visit there could end with a visit to the handsome castle of Matsuyama.

Too many foreign businessmen see only the grey urban landscapes of industrial Japan. They fail to find the wild and breathtakingly beautiful countryside of mountain and forest. To have seen the magnolias flowering in a leafless forest, to have seen the wisteria flowering in the treetops in summer, to have seen the thin snow cover the dark green moss in a country shrine, such is also Japan. One of our young staff, Peter Douglas, took our chairman and myself off for a day's hike through the forests beyond Nikko. The trail was almost overgrown; and we met only four other hikers all day. At lunch we sat drinking a bottle of Indian champagne, which Peter had provided, beside an abandoned wooden shrine reverting back to forest whence it came.

In the world of finance and investment Japan has in my working life always shown a conservatism wholly at odds with its manufacturing industry. It may be that the wealth thrown off by industry was so immense that it carried for decades a superstructure of inefficient banks and protected insurance companies. We listed the Foreign & Colonial Investment Trust on the Tokyo Stock Exchange in 1987, when the bubble market was in full strength, and any professional investor would have been diversifying his portfolio. Although investing abroad in a collective vehicle was precisely in line with any rational policy from the MOF, it proved impossible to get Japanese investors, particularly professionals, to buy our shares, in spite of a performance which held up well against the Tokyo index. Of course the relative performance during the bear market of the 1990s was off the graph. Yet the analysts who came to our presentations were only there for the beer; and slept through most of the speeches. As they were all wired up to the simultaneous translation, I developed a technique for capturing the attention of my audience by occasionally banging the microphone on the reader's desk to emphasize a point. The result was galvanizing.

In 1994 I was lecturing to a group of some thirty Japanese investment managers; and when I asked them how many had personal computers at home, a rather shame-faced four, which included the managing director, put their hands up, at a time when my own office had leased personal computers to any its staff who wanted them. This has now changed with a vengeance; but Japan lay a good five years behind the West, although companies like Fujitsu were already supplying the rest of the world with hardware.

In the small group of foreigners investing into Japan in the seventies, and it is frightening how small that group was and what economic power it wielded, each individual stands out as a personality: John Clay with his first in Sanskrit and Old Persian, Ed Merner with his futon, long before they became fashionable on the East Side, and going the other way Haruko Fukuda. After a long week presenting the Foreign & Colonial Trust in Tokyo and Osaka, we all retired to a smart *onsen* to relax. The actual pool was beautifully landscaped with azaleas in flower and clusters of rare bamboos. My chairman, John Sclater, Peter Douglas and I were wallowing naked in the boiling water, when Haruko wandered into the garden, and greeted us warmly. The speed with which John grabbed his flannel to cover his modesty was a tribute to the fast reactions of an excellent shot. Sadly, Haruko's photograph was not technically good enough to be included in the company history.

In my generation the Anglo-Japanese financial mafia was literally only a few dozen in the Western investment world; and of course we all knew each other, all the details of our private and commercial lives. In the 1980s a whole new generation came along, drawn by the explosive growth of the Japanese stock market. Now we are seeing in my friends' children the first generation of world citizens, often Japanese mothers and Western fathers, born into intellectual families where cross-cultural experiences are encouraged and valued, where Chinese New Year is as natural a festival as Christmas. Life cannot be easy for them at school with the envy of the stupid and the less privileged; but these are the elite which will have to run the world in the new millennium.

DUGALD BARR writes: 'These sketches of some Japanese episodes from a twenty-five-year City career are necessarily abbreviated. They would make little sense without a brief introduction. In June 1969 I was recruited by Vickers, da Costa, a London stockbroking firm which had pioneered the concept of investing on the Tokyo market, to resuscitate their Japanese research. Three years later I opened their Tokyo office, the first of a London broker. Returning after a year, I moved after a short interval to a larger firm, James Capel, to start their Japanese department accompanied by Haruko Fukuda (Joint Chairman of the Japan Society, 1995-2000). Over the next ten years we built up what was easily the largest business of any foreign broker in Japan. Big Bang and a change of ownership led to a role change when I turned my hand to fund management. I ceased direct involvement in the Japanese stock market in late 1992. Except for one year in Tokyo, I was based throughout in London; but the following recollections deal with my experiences when in Japan':-

•

On my first day in the City, I was presented with a set of company accounts in Japanese (*eigyo hokokusho*), and told to produce a considered evaluation of the firm. My ignorance both of accounting and of written Japanese was total. A Rosetta Stone-derived approach – though finding a company which reported the same figures in Japanese and English, as it were, was not easy – led to 'Barr's Shorter Anglo-Japanese Financial Dictionary' and partial solution of the second problem. Spoken Japanese, however, remained both inaccessible and irrelevant until I was finally permitted to visit Japan nearly two years later. Meanwhile, the investment community had been treated to my musings on the Japanese economy and stock market unsullied, in unconscious imitation of the great Ruth Benedict, by any actual experience of the place.

My first visit to Japan, with live clients, took place in May 1971. Dinner at Hannya-en on the first evening was magical, with the startling appearance of my first geisha and the garden softly illuminated. The next morning was work, not too strenuous since my role was clearly to be seen but not heard as I was introduced to the wondrous world of the *kaisha homon* [company visit]. Starting with a small company called Nippon Electric, the next two weeks were spent visiting companies large and small, stagnant and entrepreneurial, modern and antediluvian. In the evenings, brokers' strategists took us to dinner and earnestly explained the situation of the economy and stock market. More senior figures were less earnest and relationships were cemented in the classier cabarets of Akasaka. A suitable contrast came through a kind friend's introduction to John and Delia Pilcher, and a long and convivial lunch at the embassy was the start of a lasting friendship.

The weekend introduced me to the enduring pleasure of travel within Japan. With the ideal companion, the most courteous and quizzically humorous client I ever knew, I first tasted *ryokan* living in Kyoto. Naturally, we 'did' the obvious sights – though I suspect we may have seen some places I have never revisited, such is the astounding variety on offer. In Takamatsu I witnessed the most delicious definition of the broker-client relationship when John Huntsman declined an invitation to join us in a scalding bath (too hot for some locals): 'I'm not in the habit of bathing with my broker!'

Vickers, da Costa had the generous habit of financing a week's holiday following a 'maiden' visit to Japan, provided it was spent in educational wanderings in no great luxury. So it came about that on the Friday night I found myself, after a fraught journey, in a hot spring resort at the very southern tip of Japan. (Shortly after take-off from Osaka to Kagoshima, the ANA hostess had proudly announced: 'We shall shortly be landing at Osaka International Airport...') The *ryokan* had been predictably less than ecstatic to find a *gaijin* turning up at around 11 pm. I sat in my *yukata* fending off their fishy offerings as rain belted down, wondering what in the world I was doing there. Next morning saw me hastening back to Kagoshima and a train and bus odyssey through Kyushu, the Inland

Sea coast and Kansai. Kyoto revisited seemed already familiar. By the time the *shinkansen* whisked me back to Tokyo I was a veteran.

The Tokyo office was conceived eighteen months later, amid a panic that deadly rivals would steal a march and establish one first, which would never do. (Ironically, the rivals, my future firm James Capel, had no such intention – and indeed it took Margaret Thatcher, more than ten years later, to bounce my reluctant partners into doing so – but that is another story.) On a weekend in Hakodate with Scottish clients, we were marooned by a typhoon. During the 200-kilometre taxi ride to Sapporo to get an early morning plane to Tokyo, where Jeremy Paulson-Ellis was due to apologize to MOF for daring to denominate a fund in yen, three of us drew lots. Though the principal purpose was to introduce the Japanese to British equities, gilts, gold and other dubious concepts (which they were to have little difficulty in resisting), it made sense for me to be the one to set up the office. Within the week, I had returned after putting my affairs in order in London.

This was one of these exhilarating moments when one's old routine is shattered. It was bliss to be one's own boss and start virtually from scratch. The Fuji Bank were painstakingly helpful. The bureaucratic procedures were awesome. NTT in particular were a nightmare, and clearly had learned 'Catch-22' by heart. There was a phase when visitors emerging from the lift were greeted with the sight of the temp and myself, sitting on beer cases donated by an expectant fourth-echelon broker, with four separate telephones on the window ledge – the only place NTT was prepared to instal them. Of course when one rang they all would. Furniture and fittings mostly came from Mitsukoshi, whither I would dash in spare moments. What Japanese I have was learned the hard way in negotiations with shoals of elusive salesgirls. (The delaying tactics of gift-wrapping items like staplers were especially appreciated.)

The office was on the 'wrong side of the tracks' in Koamicho, just over the river from the Tokyo Stock Exchange. This was an indisputably good thing. In those days all the brokers, except Nikko, had their head offices in Kabutocho, or at any rate in Nihonbashi, and this gave it its particular flavour of a 'securities souk'. I grew very fond of the tranquil and old-fashioned atmosphere of Ningyocho, where I sometimes took visitors for *yakitori* and saké. My smarter English friends in merchant banks, trading and shipping houses all worked in Marunouchi. I was delighted to relax with them occasionally in the Tokyo Kaikan, but would not have changed places for the world.

I was also pleased eventually to find a spacious apartment in Yonbancho. Though near the British Embassy this was also a virtually *gaijin*-free zone. Mercifully, however, the flat was built to *gaijin*-friendly dimensions. It was a peaceful quarter with many large houses and gardens, now swept away for apartment blocks. As a long-standing naval enthusiast I appreciated the tiny Togo *koen* (park) next door, with a statue of the great man. (The midget submarine in the Yasukuni shrine nearby was also the source of some wonderment.) From the Palace View, as it was misleadingly called, to Koamicho was a quick drive in the Cedric I bought when Jaguar were unable to supply their product within six months and six times the UK retail price. Thus I could easily go for a week without seeing another foreigner: sometimes, indeed, I could become almost resentful when spotting such a person, say in Ginza. In the office I had been fortunate to find as my assistant one of the two Japanese I have ever known with perfect English, the temp had become perm (for the time being), and the delightful Mr Ebina took care of Cedric during the day.

With the infrastructure in place a grand party in the Heian-no-ma of the Hotel Okura was now *de rigueur*. Organizing it, and an all-day investment seminar beforehand, was taxing, surreal, but enjoyable. The great and the good came, the ice statue of a bull prophetically melted, and I appreciated the bill (sample: 'Item: Girl; Unit Cost: ¥5,000; Quantity: 14. . .' etc.). I even enjoyed signing my first ever cheque for millions.

Meanwhile all opportunities had been taken to explore the country. Fortunately, a very great friend, Robert Woods, was in Japan for P & O at the same time. Memorable expeditions were made with Robert and friends and relations to Hokkaido, to the Japan Alps at Christmas (no, ski boots and *tatami* do not go well together), to Kyoto and the closer Nikko, Hakone and Kamakura. Clients and 'visiting firemen' also needed to be chaperoned. Having a sabbatical from investing *into* Japan, I was spending little time visiting Japanese companies except when accompanying clients (when I still seemed to end up doing all the talking). Visiting Japanese institutions with Vickers' own experts gave me a new perspective and valuable contacts. In late March my mother came out and explored Tokyo by herself for a week, imperturbably tackling the subway the morning after a two-day flight via Singapore: for her second week I took time off and we drove over the Japan Alps to the Japan Sea coast, down to Kyoto and then home. I was enthralled by the beauty of Ishikawa, Fukui and Kyoto prefectures, the coast road in those days being 'unimproved' and little frequented. Nine years later we were to complete the journey, driving north to Wakasa-wan and along the San-in coast to Hagi and Shimonoseki.

*   *   *

After moving to Capels a routine of two or three visits each year of about a fortnight each became established. These were principally to visit the management of companies our clients owned, companies we thought might be worth recommending or which just sounded fun, or provided a good 'mix' of industries. Arranging this was a complex and frustrating exercise – calling incidentally for good topographical knowledge – and the final schedule might owe much to chance. Nevertheless a good balance was usually found. So in the morning we might visit a major insurance company in Marunouchi, followed by a small electronic instrument-maker along the Chuo line, a supermarket in Meguro and a private railway in Shibuya. This kept me alert as I desperately mugged up questions for the next interview in the limo. If I could end up near the hotel I was delirious with joy, for at six o'clock sharp young brokers would be in the lobby to drag me off to dinner. Usually at that point I was well outside the Yamanote-sen, if not actually in Nagoya. After dinner there was telephoning the office, often doing a day's work, and writing up reports if the visits warranted it. (There was one memorable week when Haruko Fukuda and I spent every night till dawn, selling the NSK sterling convertible. After midnight: 'Could you please ring him back a bit later?' was hardly music to the ears.)

There were factory visits too, usually requested by clients, as I found I learned far less of use through these than in a conventional interview. Were I an engineer it might have been different. Nevertheless, the clinical efficiency of virtually umanned production areas, contrasting with the armies of paper-shufflers in any office, was good for impressing visitors. One highlight in the Seventies was coming across a Fujitsu Fanuc robot, Jiro, busy assembling his younger brother Saburo. The world of Arthur C. Clarke was drawing closer. It was also instructive to realize that robots could work without the lights on! You always learn something.

Of course, we also visited the Ministry of Finance, the Bank of Japan, the economic institutes *el al* to get a handle on the macro economy. However, I always found that it was through visiting this cross-section of companies that one appreciated best what sort of shape the economy was in. A theme would emerge, often on the plane home as one began to order one's thoughts (there was never quite time for that on a visit). As much could be learned through incidental observation as through formal questioning. Companies which moved from modest, workmanlike premises to glossy new palaces with platoons of receptionists were invariably a sell (often, simply because the Japanese broker used up most of the allotted hour by taking us to the old office). Curiously, this did not seem to apply to name changes: Hayakawa Electric was none the worse for the change to Sharp, nor Teikoku Dempa reborn as Clarion.

The Japanese craze for crazes also had a corporate dimension: one year, I remember, almost every meeting room was adorned by a stuffed pheasant. (One company president, who claimed to go shooting with ex-Prime Minister Takeo Fukuda, presented me, and a surprised but gratified junior broker, with one each, in heavy glass cases.) The courtesy and hospitality shown to inquisitive strangers was, in most cases, amazing. Union flags over the front entrance always predisposed us most favourably. Quite often, especially out in rural areas, we were the first foreign investors to visit and then usually found *ourselves* being interviewed for an hour or more by management who had never seen such specimens before.

A kindly word must be said for the Japanese brokers who usually arranged these meetings and supplied interpreters. The latter were often very young and overawed by company management as well, no doubt, as irked by impatient and know-all *gaijin*. They had a difficult job and on the whole coped well. After the intense concentration of an interview one hoped to unwind a bit, hearing their opinions and, I hope, helping their own career development. (Not a few went on to become president of their company.) In those days we were of course clients of the Japanese brokers, among their most important sources of commission; thus we knew everyone in the industry, while the Japanese normally knew only their own colleagues. It was fascinating to follow old friends' career paths all over the world, though the thinking of personnel departments at *jinji-ido* time (musical chairs) was sometimes impenetrable.

Companies, in general, were remarkably free with information (accompanying clients often hissed 'You can't ask that!', but one could and did – one reason I really preferred to go alone). This was perhaps more true in the 'good old days' when one could usually meet the president of all but the starchiest ex-*zaibatsu* companies: excellent relations were formed with such men as Itoh of Ito-Yokado or Inagaki of Pioneer who would speak with great frankness. With the crush of supplicants for interviews latterly one was lucky to be fobbed off with a pair of apparatchiks from the *keiri-bu* (accounts department), each minding the other's words. The flavour of the company and its decision-makers was diminished.

Sometimes the flavour was more pronounced than usual. There was the company president in Gunma-ken who insisted on driving us himself (in his Nissan President, of course): with that vehicle's prehistoric roadholding it is unsurprising that we ended up in the ditch. There was the visit to a film production company which segued into a session of the censorship board appraising its latest effort – not one for eyes easily embarrassed. On a descent into Sumitomo's Hishikari gold mine I was encouraged to break off the world's richest ore with my bare hands. I never, I think, had a bath with management of an investee company (though I did with a broker). I did once wake up in a in a remote Fukui-ken *onsen* to find an inebriated Japanese asleep in the bath; but he was much more surprised than I was.

These are just a few of many such episodes. I have perhaps been tempted to dwell too much on the comical, but it *was* a highly entertaining, as well as stressful and often frustrating, way of earning one's living; and better understanding is often gained through the comic aspects of life. Stockbroking, in essence, is a business of ideas – at its simplest, a buy or sell recommendation of an individual stock; but that makes little sense without an understanding of the wider market context. A British broker in Japan, especially in the earlier days, had a broader remit: to convey to his clients an understanding of the culture and investment climate within which their decisions would be made. Attempting that was perhaps presumptuous – everyone knows that 'understanding' Japan is a chimaera – but brought with it many most rewarding experiences.

I was lucky to be in near the start of overseas investment into Japan, a trail blazed by Ralph Vickers and John Clay and a small band of far-sighted Scottish and London institutions. There was still a feeling of discovery and solidarity, and most of the participants knew each other well. Not a few of my closest friendships date from shared experiences working and playing in Japan – and others have miraculously survived them. (Driving around Hokkaido, my passengers eating giant hairy crabs in the back. . .) I was also able to find that Japan, too, was populated by a remarkable variety of individuals and make fast friends with many of them.

The sheer numbers of City people involved in Japan now make this a vanished era. It is probably an illusion that the industrialization of fund management with screens and indexation and quartiles has diminished the human element: nevertheless I am glad to have experienced Japan when I did. At that time alone could one have known virtually all the participants – Japanese brokers, British brokers and investors from all over the world – all embarked on an adventure of mutual discovery. It was enthralling to seek, with colleagues and clients, to fathom the mysteries of Japan; it was equally rewarding to see the Japanese move confidently into the wider world, and to witness the transformation which look place within three extraordinary decades. It is beginning to seem a long time ago now.

*   *   *

It is a source of regret that I never learned the language properly. In the beginning, as mentioned earlier, I was confined to deciphering written Japanese, as far as was relevant for the task at hand. When I suddenly arrived in Japan, the spoken language became of immediate importance: but time was sorely lacking. Having acquired a tape recorder and set up my system in my Okura room I went to Maruzen and bought an impressive pack of about ten tapes with accompanying textbook exercises. Having a reasonable ear for languages (a classical education in this case perhaps less relevant), I assumed this would he a doddle and polished off the first three exercises. A week later I had another free evening, revised exercise 3 and did exercise 4. Two months later I had another spare evening and revisited 3 and 4, and may have progressed to 5. . . When in the 1980s we were competing with other firms for the best graduates to send to join the City throngs in Tokyo, I was more than a little envious, not only that they could demand substantial one-on-one language tuition, but that they had the time for it. Of course, they were then far better equipped for the job.

I did, of course, make some headway on the practical, 'total immersion' basis and could get around adequately and enjoy many of the pleasures of wordplay and vile puns the language can offer those of a certain mentality. Being able to read street signs, name-plates, notices etc. does seem the absolute minimum for navigating a normal existence. (I have a theory that it is easier for almost anyone – Japanese reader or not – to drive in Japan than anywhere else: first, *kanji* road signs are almost always easier to distinguish at a distance than *romaji*, and you need only memorize their rough shape for the period you need that destination; second, the traffic moves so slowly that there is plenty of time to think anyway.) Unfortunately, I find the 'active' ability to write *kanji* atrophies fast, though it has surprised me how the modest competence in character recognition and the spoken language stays despite little recent use. For reasons of pure intellectual satisfaction, however, I am disappointed not to have made a serious study.

It is not hard to avoid adding to the reams of amateur sociology aiming at 'understanding the Japanese'. In the first place I think it rather presumptuous. In the second it may be either unnecessary or even counter-productive for practical purposes: remember all the 'Oh, Japan is different' rationalizations of unsustainable price-earnings ratios both before and after the stock market debacle. A paradox is that this does seem to be a people whose attitudes and behaviour lend themselves to generalization: but anyone with any acuity will find himself shortly qualifying any general observation with its diametric opposite. Where theories can be so swiftly reconsidered there is little point formulating them in the first place!

In identifying and disagreeing with several of the well-known 'consensus' myths I am in danger of generalizing myself: but I cannot resist it. First of all, the 'homogeneous' myth. I 'bought' this for about my first ever hour at Haneda Airport, where all Japanese were about five feet tall, with neat short black hair and crisply-pressed white short-sleeved shirts. Since then the variety has amazed me: of physical, even racial, type; of demeanour, of character, of attire, of speech. Even among a relatively coherent sample such as company management the individuality of personalities has been what has always struck me most forcibly. Second, the 'polite' myth. It is probably true that there exists a plane of kindliness and helpfulness among many Japanese that is seldom encountered elsewhere. There can also be a dimension of arrogance and of rudeness, whether boorish or sarcastic, that is hard to find anywhere else. (The words:

'Frankly speaking. . .'* often seemed to be used to give the speaker licence to say something of breathtaking offensiveness.) This is not really
a criticism, just an antidote to a rather facile and saccharine myth. Other
myths which may hold good in some cases, but in very many cases do
not, are the 'far-sighted, long-term-oriented Japanese'; the 'cautious, prudent Japanese'; the 'ascetic, minimalist Japanese' and many other stereo-
types. They do exist, but so, in at least equal strength, do their opposites.
This variety and these contradictions are what make Japan really rewarding – just like anywhere else!

---

* Editor: One leading Japanese Ambassador amused me by always saying 'Frankly spoken' instead
of 'Frankly speaking'!

26

Banking and Financial Services: A View from the Bank of England and Treasury

CHRIS ELSTON ● SIR GEOFFREY LITTLER

BEFORE THE 1970s neither the Bank of England, nor HM Treasury were represented in Japan. There seemed to be little scope for British financial services in the closed Japanese market. But Japanese membership of the OECD began to force gradual changes to the Japanese financial fortress. There was also increasing internal pressure for change. Japanese companies wanted access to foreign loans and the Eurodollar market which was much freer than the securities market in Japan.

In the following account CHRIS ELSTON who joined the British Embassy in Tokyo as Financial Counsellor (or attaché) in 1979 recalls his time in Japan as the Bank of England representative:-

●

I arrived in Tokyo in November 1979, the third in a line of Financial Attachés seconded from the Bank of England. The position had been instituted in the early 1970s, largely, I believe, on the initiative, in consultation with the FCO, of the then Governor of the Bank, Gordon (now Lord) Richardson.

This type of embassy secondment was, at that time, unusual for the Bank. The thinking behind it was that it was obvious in the early 1970s that Japan was a growing economic and financial power; being in a distant time zone there was a need for closer contact and communication on financial issues; and, more importantly, the Japanese financial system was differently structured and regulated from those of other major countries and so called for closer study and understanding.

In fulfilling this role it was expected that the work of a Bank of England secondee, with a background and training in financial markets, would benefit not only the Bank, but also the FCO and other Whitehall departments, with an increased flow of more focused information and analysis than could be achieved by a diplomat. Diplomats – perhaps with excess modesty – used to hold that an FCO man could not be expected to be able to develop and maintain the required range of financial contacts or to understand adequately the intricacies of international financial markets. There was also in the Tokyo embassy a nuclear energy attaché, seconded from BNFL, with whom I tended to develop some fellow feeling. He did for the United Kingdom's nuclear energy interests what the financial attaché did for our financial interests. I cannot help feeling, however, that the diplomats' self-deprecatory stance was rather more applicable to his role than to mine.

Nevertheless, the ability to make meaningful contact, on a basis of mutual understanding, with a range of financial institutions in both the public and the private sectors, was an important aspect of the role. And it became more important as the issue of liberalizing and opening financial markets to foreign firms became, in part, a political one.

*   *   *

On my arrival in Tokyo I found that the then Minister, Sidney (now Sir Sidney) Giffard was on home leave and that he had kindly bequeathed to me his direct copy of *The Times*, an offer which I accepted gratefully. He had also – rather bravely, I thought, but with a generosity typical of the man – offered me the use of his private car while he was away. This kindness, however, while I was still unaccustomed to Tokyo traffic conditions, I circumspectly declined.

My nearest colleague work-wise in the embassy – in fact the fine chap had been deputed to meet me on arrival at Narita – was the First Secretary Economic, who at the time was on secondment to the FCO from Barclays Bank. The then ambassador, Sir Michael Wilford, while he maintained that he wholeheartedly approved of this sort of cross-fertilization, used to say that he preferred bankers coming into the FCO to diplomats being seconded to banks. Diplomats, he thought, could inadvertently lose banks millions of pounds while bankers were unlikely accidentally to start wars.

Sadly, my Barclays colleague had to return before long to his bank where he went on to much greater things. As a result, I took over the economic as well as the financial reporting, which went back not only to the Bank and the FCO, but also to the Treasury, the DTI, ECGD (Export Credit Guarantee Department) and elsewhere. It may also have been found to be of some use in the embassy itself, as well as in parts of the British business community in Tokyo. The main interest in my role in the generality of the embassy, however, tended to centre on the financial attaché's view of where the yen/sterling exchange rate was heading – in order to judge the best time to bring in hard-earned sterling in exchange for usually insufficient yen.

The world's central banking community is a close-knit one and it is certainly true that the Bank of England had – and, of course, still has – very close and cordial relations with the Bank of Japan (BOJ). The BOJ has long had a representative office for Europe located in London. In Tokyo they accordingly attached importance to the presence of a Bank of England attaché in the British Embassy. As a result contacts in and dialogue with the Bank of Japan were smooth and easy, from Governor Maekawa, a charming man who received me in his office virtually in my first week in Tokyo, downwards.

At that time there was only a handful of financial attachés at other embassies and most of those tended to originate from their respective Finance Ministries rather than central banks (although the French had at least one from each). Interestingly, the Deutsche Bundesbank did not have a representative in Tokyo until, I believe, 1983.

Each month the financial attachés of the G10 countries – or the approximately eight of the G10 with financial representatives in Tokyo – took it in turns to organize lunches at their homes to which a senior Japanese figure was invited to address us. On one occasion a particular attaché's home was so difficult to find, even with a detailed map, that the embassy driver must have circled the area half a dozen times before we finally fetched up at the correct house. I remember arriving just as a sumptuous lunch was ending and the Japanese guest was about to start his presentation.

With the Bank of England held in high regard there were good relations with a wide range of contacts not only in the BOJ, but also in all the relevant bureaux in the Ministry of Finance (MOF), the Economic Planning Agency, and MITI. This was less true of the Ministry of Foreign Affairs (MFA) which was rightly considered more the realm of the professional diplomat. Nevertheless, early in my stay I remember accompanying Ambassador Wilford to an MFA ceremony to conclude a tax protocol, which for reasons of timetable pressures could only be held at breakfast time. Sizable quantities of cold saké were still consumed in mutual toasting.

The diplomatic process inevitably meant inheriting from one's predecessor a range of both business and social contacts, with whom it was one's duty to strike up a mutually beneficial rapport. Equally inevitably over time the contact list evolved – some of one's Japanese colleagues retired or were consigned to the outer darkness of, say, Sapporo for a spell. But, of course, one was introduced to their successors and one added new contacts in new areas as others moved off. And those who were sent to Sapporo and elsewhere always came back to Tokyo, often at a higher level, and the contact was renewed.

Indeed, the Bank of Japan's branches scattered throughout Japan presented the opportunity, which the BOJ were pleased to offer, of calling on one's colleagues outside Tokyo. On this basis I visited at various times Kumamoto, Kobe, Kyoto, Nagoya, Niigata, Mito, Oita and Sapporo, with calls on the local banks and other financial institutions, as well as industry – all with a view to gauging the economic and financial pulse of Japan.

Back in Tokyo there was regular contact with the head offices of the city banks and the main securities companies. At that time the banks and securities houses seemed large and amorphous. They were – or at least considered themselves to be – highly regulated. In fact this was probably more the after-effects of history and habit than of actual detailed regulation. They had graduated from a regime of stringent formal direction to one of more informal guidance. But old habits died hard and they were still very much in the hands of their respective bureaux in the MOF – a system which later led to wider problems.

In general, the man in the Japanese street was not outstandingly well served by his banking system, which was bureaucratic and lacked the stimulus of adequate domestic competition. With the extremely high Japanese personal savings ratio, however – partly the result of habit, partly of social forces and the absence of an adequate social security system – the banks and securities companies were more than well served by their man in the street.

In the early 1980s external finance was still highly regulated – much more and for longer than it need or should have been given the strength of the economy. But in 1983, with the first relaxations of exchange control, it was just beginning to ease.

If only I could have recognized them at the time the seeds of Japan's later problems were there to be seen. The banking sector was large, powerful, complacent, shielded largely from internal and external competition, living off capital derived from ever-appreciating equity and property portfolios, cosily ensconced in cross-shareholding *keiretsu* relationships and regulated by bureaucrats who ruled with firmness, but who got too closely involved with their charges, partly through the pervasive *amakudari* system (literally 'descending from heaven'). Sadly, I do not recall reporting that this was a bubble that was waiting to burst.

Another aspect of the financial attaché's role was to liaise with the British financial institutions present in Tokyo and where possible to promote their interests in trying to develop their business in the Japanese market. All four of the main British clearing banks were represented in Tokyo at that time, together with the two 'ex-colonial' banks, HSBC and Standard Chartered. The latter two had a reasonably solid base in their traditional field of trade financing, but all had difficulty breaking into the still heavily protected – informally, if not formally – retail and corporate lending market. In those days if a Japanese company came to a foreign bank for a loan, often introduced by his domestic bank, the foreign banker had cause to be suspicious. The opacity of Japanese accounting practices and financial information made sensible banking a difficult business. It was often said that the biggest asset in the balance sheet of one of the British banks was the manager's golf club membership. In those days it was almost certainly the most profitable.

It also seemed that the British banks at that time were not too sure what they wanted to do in Japan or how much in the way of resources they wanted to put into penetrating the market. The managers very often came to Tokyo from former colonial-type postings, with no specialist knowledge of Japan and usually with no Japanese language skills. It was difficult for them to hire high-quality Japanese staff and much reliance was placed on senior Japanese advisers, usually former bureaucrats, but sometimes ex-commercial bankers.

These handicaps and conditions applied to most of the foreign banks in Japan, not just the British. They applied less, perhaps, to the US banks who had history and political and economic muscle on their side and were able to put a far greater level of resources into their Japanese operations. Spending now was always for expected – or at least hoped for – benefit in the medium to longer term, but in time it gradually became clear that those benefits were less and less likely to accrue in the commercial banking sector.

In the late 1970s and early 1980s the British investment banks, too, were dipping their toes in the Tokyo waters. Here there was more scope for future success since the Japanese investment banking sector was relatively under-developed. Ultimately, the availability of seats for these institutions on the Tokyo Stock Exchange (TSE) became a political bargaining chip for UK banking licences for the big four Japanese securities companies in London. This issue was eventually satisfactorily resolved and big inroads were made by foreign banks – particularly the large US investment banks – into TSE turnover, at least until the bubble burst.

The embassy received a good flow of senior UK bank visitors, usually chairmen on a Far East tour to rally their troops, nourish their correspondent banking relationships and make their number with their Japanese regulator. Briefings were given and views exchanged with the ambassador on the Japanese economic and financial scene. On one occasion the visitor was Robin Leigh-Pemberton (now Lord Kingsdown), the then Chairman of NatWest Bank. Two days after he visited the embassy Mr Leigh-Pemberton's appointment as the next governor of the Bank of England was announced. On hearing the news the ambassador's main concern was whether we had offered our now even more distinguished visitor lunch (we had, and he had declined – honour saved).

In those days – probably less so in recent years – there seemed to be a constant stream of lavish bank receptions. These celebrated anniversaries, the opening of new offices or on at least two occasions during my stay the dedication of new head office buildings. These always provided a good opportunity to maintain acquaintances, make new ones and generally keep up with gossip. One such which was always enjoyable was the IBJ (Industrial Bank of Japan) reception which was traditionally held on Boxing Day. It provided an excellent opportunity to swap the excesses of our domestic Christmas celebrations for a completely different atmosphere. Another enjoyable occasion was the annual Mitsui Bank garden party in the summer at the Mitsui villa. And yet another the annual cherry blossom party hosted by the Japanese Prime Minister at Shinjuku-*gyoen*, which always managed to get its meteorological and botanical timing right.

On another occasion, by way of contrast, I was asked by the Bank of England to represent our governor at the funeral ceremony for a former governor of the Bank of Japan. I duly contacted the Secretary's Office of the BOJ to ascertain the correct procedure, dress, etc. I assumed morning dress would be in order but was told firmly that a dark lounge suit was all that was required. Not only was I the only Westerner attending the funeral; I was also the only one not wearing a morning suit. I imagine the BOJ Secretary's Office had considered such attire not very Western.

* * *

When I was first asked by the Bank to accept a three-year secondment to the Tokyo embassy, the Bank looked for a response in two days. This sort of move no doubt comes naturally to a professional diplomat, who in the perhaps unusual event that he or she has a choice can probably give a quick answer. In the Bank I had worked briefly on the Japan desk in the late 1960s and had not expected to be reunited with things Japanese. In my – and my wife's – initial thinking we saw all the potential problems and few, if any, of the benefits. As a result we were at first inclined to say no and I missed the Bank's deadline. After a week or so, however, all the problems were mentally set aside and the benefits brought to the fore. One of the attractive prospects was the opportunity to renew acquaintance with a number of BOJ colleagues who had worked in London. About ten days later, therefore, with the offer still open, I accepted, and in fact stayed in Tokyo for one year longer than the initially proposed three.

We have had, needless to say, not the slightest regret. I can safely say that the decision changed permanently the direction both of my professional career and of our family and social life.

It is clear that Japan is not something that you can pick up and put

down. Once immersed it stays with you for ever. On my return to the
Bank in 1983 I took over, from one of my predecessors in Tokyo, the role
of adviser in the international division covering Asia and Australasia. I
continued in this role until the disbandment of the Bank's international
division in 1994 and it provided a marvellous opportunity to get to know
at close quarters over a lengthy period the most vibrant and, to me, the
most culturally interesting area of the world. Our contacts with Japanese
colleagues continue, both privately and in the Japan Society and for my
wife in the *Nichiei Otomodachi Kai*. Moreover, Japan, and Asia more generally, must have seeped into the blood of our children, all three of whom
have been or are still working in Japan and other parts of Asia. In short, I
consider it an immense privilege to have had the opportunity to see both
Japan Inc. and the FCO from the inside and to get even the merest inkling of what makes those two equally intricate and fascinating institutions tick.

HM TREASURY, although not represented on the staff of the British Embassy until the late 1990s, became increasingly involved in the development
of financial relations with Japan. British financial institutions were determined not to be left out of the race to acquire profitable niches in Japan's slowly
liberalizing financial markets and pressed the British authorities to take a more
active role in supporting their interests. British financial institutions feared
that as a result of understandings finally achieved after tough bargaining between United States and Japanese financial negotiators all the best opportunities would be preserved for American banks and financial institutions.

The task of leading British negotiations with the Japanese, which began in
1983, fell to Sir Geoffrey Littler (then second permanent secretary in HM
Treasury from 1984 until his retirement in 1988).

In a lecture to the Japan Society on 16 November 1993 GEOFFREY
LITTLER gave an account of the negotiations for which he was responsible.
The following is the bulk of his interesting talk, which provides the official
background to the previous chapter recording the experiences of British merchant bankers in Japan:-

•

It was for me a fascinating and novel experience, and an entry to a world
quite different from anything I had ever known before. . . It was also a
time of quite dramatic events and changes in the international financial
scene and, even more strikingly, in the role and conduct of the Japanese
financial economy.

I had never visited Japan, and I had at that time, I suppose, about the
average educated Englishman's knowledge of Japanese history, culture
and society – which means, sadly, almost none at all! I had met no more

than a handful of Japanese, almost entirely Ministry of Finance officials and ministers and Bank of Japan officials – entirely in the course of business meetings of the Groups of Five and Ten and in the Paris-based OECD and the IMF. I had found them personally extremely courteous, even effusively so, but reserved to an extent which makes the traditional Englishman's reserve a pale shadow. They were very assiduous at meetings, often with a remarkable command of the English (or sometimes American) language, but along with many European and American colleagues I found most of them liable to stick to formal statements and reluctant to venture opinions in informal debate. In short, I had a lot to learn.

* * *

In 1983 and 1984 some extraordinary foreign currency relationships had developed, especially between the US dollar and the yen, but also between both those currencies and the main European currencies. To most of us in Europe, sitting in the middle, the over-valuation of the US dollar was the most striking feature and, given the growing US current account deficit, it looked dangerous and unsustainable. European (and even more Japanese) traders in the dollar area were enjoying a bonanza, but our authorities were increasingly worrying about growing imbalances and the threat of trade distortions.

There was also a widespread feeling that the Japanese yen was undervalued – in relation to European currencies as well as the dollar: and this was strengthened by concern about huge Japanese surpluses in visible trade with most European countries, and of course a long history of European worry about the combination of Japanese trade protection and highly successful trade competition.

The United States Treasury was inclined to see the yen as the main problem and had embarked in 1983 on bilateral discussions with the Japanese authorities – for which they sought and gained moral support from European governments – focusing on the general issues of under-valuation of the yen and trade restrictions by Japan. These came to be known as the 'Dollar-Yen Negotiations'. But of course these negotiations were being watched jealously by other countries, particularly in Europe, all happy to encourage general pressure on Japan, but some concerned lest the United States should take advantage of their negotiations to secure preferential national benefits.

There came a point in the early summer of 1984 when we noted in the Treasury in London that parts of the US/Japan negotiations were touching on the national interests of US financial houses in licences and other facilities to operate in Tokyo. They assured us that they were seeking better treatment of non-Japanese houses generally, but they naturally knew best and emphasized the needs of their own US houses. Nigel Lawson, then Chancellor, at once asked me to explore the possibility of engaging in some parallel talks ourselves, and our interest in this was heightened when, quite independently, a couple of British houses wrote in to say that they were facing difficulties in Tokyo and to enquire whether the government might be able to help.

We took the opportunity of the annual Summit meeting, held in June 1984 in London, to broach the subject with our Japanese colleagues. I talked with my opposite number, then Vice-Minister Tomomitsu Oba, and Nigel Lawson talked with Finance Minister Noboru Takeshita.

Our proposal for bilateral talks was met with a ready acceptance amounting almost to enthusiasm. I was agreeably surprised by this, since we had made it clear that we would be presenting quite a list of demands. Perhaps, I reflected, they just welcomed a change from having their tables banged by their American counterparts!

At the outset we proposed and it was agreed that our negotiations would aim at a rather lower key of publicity than the US talks; that we would have small teams; that we would in the first instance focus on certain limited areas of bilateral 'finance ministry' interest, to be defined in advance, that we would probably find it useful to meet about twice a year; and that an important longer-term purpose of the series of talks we envisaged would be to get to know each other's work and concerns more closely.

It was also agreed that Oba and I respectively would lead the two teams. The two of us arranged that, during the next of our regular international meetings we would – as the venue happened to be Paris – have dinner privately together to settle the programme and other arrangements for our first round of talks. These preliminaries can be not only extremely interesting, but also important in setting the atmosphere of discussion. Several points remain strongly in my memory. There was no problem over the agenda. The fundamental issue was that the British financial market had for some time been relatively open to all foreign participants, including Japanese houses, in conditions which were competitive but in general equally so for all participants. By contrast the Japanese market was for both formal reasons (licences and similar barriers) and informal reasons (long-standing market practices) difficult to access for non-Japanese, including British, participants.

I had a first shopping-list of key demands developed with the help of our own houses in the run-up to the talks. Top of my list were licences for securities firms: I also included interest in future rules for professional investment management (a particularly strong British interest), foreign exchange dealing, and complaints about the onerousness of some banking supervision. Oba had found a number of points on which Japanese houses sought improved treatment in London: banking licences for leading Japanese securities houses, primary dealership in the gilt-edged market, and admission of Japanese securities houses (fifty-four of them, I think) to the London Stock Exchange. I don't think either of our lists caused much surprise to the other side.

Much more trouble arose, however, over the composition of our respective teams. I proposed to use our local financial Embassy man in Tokyo (economizing on travel costs, but mainly because he was steeped in local knowledge and spoke some Japanese) and also to have with me from London a Bank of England colleague and one from our Department of Trade, reflecting our shared responsibilities for the matters under discussion. This caused brief consternation, and I realized both that responsibilities were much more concentrated in the MOF in Tokyo, and also that the problems of inter-departmental jealousy in Tokyo went beyond my British experience of bureaucratic in-fighting! In the end, as I recall, my Bank colleague was deemed to be working under my complete direction, and I think we pretended that the Department of Trade man was seconded to the Treasury for the occasion. The Bank of Japan was invited to provide a senior observer: MITI did not join in! Happily, it all worked out quite comfortably in practice.

We also agreed to have the first meeting in Tokyo and settled dates. When I confirmed to Oba that this would be my first ever visit to Japan, and added that I was very much hoping to be able to spend a week there and see something other than the hotel and the meeting-room, he immediately showed huge enthusiasm and begged me to fix a particular Tuesday afternoon and Wednesday in October, but to fly out to arrive no later than the previous Sunday afternoon. I agreed and he contacted me later to say that everything had been arranged for me to pay a short visit to Kyoto on the Monday and Tuesday morning, coinciding with the occasion of a great annual historical pageant and procession.

In keeping with our low-key approach, we had not thought the talks warranted a public announcement. But it was not long before news of them broke – in a Japanese newspaper. Oba kindly phoned to warn me, commenting that it was difficult to keep this sort of thing quiet in Tokyo. I later discovered why. On the main floor of the MOF in Tokyo there is a room set aside permanently for the press, quite close to the offices of the Ministers and Vice-Ministers, and journalists are always to be found there. When I told my Treasury colleagues about this, they blanched at the thought!

My last memory of this preliminary period is of the extraordinary interest of the Japanese financial establishment in our talks. I received a number of inquisitive but friendly approaches and invitations and began to develop a much wider span of acquaintances in Japanese financial circles. I also began to suspect – a view which became a conviction – that there was a significant element in the Japanese financial establishment of people who positively wanted a more open Japanese market. and were disposed at least up to a point to wish me well!

It had been clear to many inside observers that the Japanese engaged in the 'Dollar-Yen Negotiations' did not like the aggressive style adopted by the American team. For various reasons, including personal preference, it seemed to me to be worth trying for a more constructive atmosphere, without being in any sense a soft touch. I was convinced that development of the Japanese market itself would in any case in time undermine many of their restrictive practices, and that this would indeed he necessary if Tokyo was to develop and take its rightful place as part of the global investment markets of the future. From several private discussions, I had come to suspect that many influential Japanese people had similar views. I decided to build on this theme wherever it might help. I am sure it was a good decision.

* * *

I was royally received at Narita Airport. Koji Yamazaki, who had been the MOF minister at the Japanese Embassy in London until very recently, and had become a most helpful and valued friend with whom I had discussed some of the arrangements for our talks, had returned to Tokyo to a senior position in the Customs department, and he had put himself out to arrange an impressive welcoming party! It was so impressive that, as my Embassy colleague finally escorted me to the Ford car to drive us to Tokyo, he paused and apologized for not bringing the Rolls-Royce!

Early on the next morning Koji Yamazaki collected me at my hotel and together we caught the Shinkansen to Kyoto in time to spend a couple of hours in the Palace Gardens watching the pageant and procession, which I found enormously interesting as well as a colourful spectacle. There followed a formal tea ceremony, a short visit to the Gion theatre, a superb dinner with geisha entertainment, a night in a genuine old *ryokan*, a morning of visits to the Palace buildings and to two magnificent temples, then a quick rush to the station where a small band and red carpet greeted me. It was an overwhelming succession of new experiences and I can never be sufficiently grateful to Oba and Yamazaki and my Kyoto hosts for arranging it for me.

We began the talks in the afternoon back in Tokyo, with a series of formal, prepared statements. That first session was all a bit 'sticky', and I found it impossible to promote any general debate of the kind I wanted – especially with the vitally important Head of the Securities Bureau, who seemed severe, cold and even hostile.

That evening, Finance Minister Takeshita entertained the two teams to dinner at a famous geisha restaurant. It became an immensely merry party. I gave an enthusiastic account of my visit to Kyoto and at one point said how interested I had been in the development of weapons and fighting in Japan in medieval times, which seemed very different from what happened in Europe. To my astonishment, our Japanese colleagues fell about laughing and the Minister dug in the ribs the Securities Bureau Head. Oba kindly explained to me that this happened to be a subject on which the Securities Bureau Head was an expert. It broke the ice completely. Having hardly spoken at the dinner before, he now came out of his shell – no longer cold and hostile – and proved to be a most entertaining person.

The next day our talks went much better! The atmosphere was warmer, and we had some lively discussion and debate which helped both sides to a better understanding and led to what I believe was a satisfactory outcome.

On the question of licences for British houses in stockbroking there was a clear breakthrough, in a couple of cases immediate. It was agreed that certain controls on banking operations were too onerous and should be relaxed, and this was indeed done soon after. We were able to explore what kinds of arrangements the Japanese authorities might introduce to liberalize the rules for professional investment management, and arrange to have further opportunity to discuss them in advance. We partially clarified some misunderstandings which were preventing Japanese securities houses from carrying on banking in London, and arranged for a visit to London by the Head of the Securities Bureau which later completed that process. Most importantly, we had set a pattern of exchanges which could obviously be developed more deeply in future. It was undoubtedly a promising beginning.

*   *   *

Later rounds of talks took place approximately twice a year, once in Tokyo and once in London.

We worked slowly through the original, later slightly extended, shopping-lists, with pretty regular progress, although with some hiccoughs and at a pace which was certainly at times a test of patience. I regularly had the tactical problem that my shopping-list was the bigger one. This reflected the starting-point that there were simply more restrictions in Tokyo than in London. For all the substantial progress I was able to make, there was still some unfinished business of this kind for my successor at the end of 1988, although by then nearly all the British houses anxious to operate in Tokyo had been admitted to do so.

There were one or two really difficult barriers. Most troublesome was the question of membership of the Tokyo Stock Exchange. The problem that was alleged was lack of physical space – I and my team were taken on visits to the floor of the Exchange to see for ourselves that all the boxes were full and there was no room for more boxes. Underlying this was the fact that this limitation, in a private monopoly body, had led to monopoly price – I should perhaps say an astronomical price – for Stock Exchange seats which in principle could be traded. From my perspective, we had in London an equally venerable private London Stock Exchange, whose floor had however been effectively eliminated in the course of one week after 'Big Bang': most deals were now done electronically in any case: and we could not believe that Japan was not capable of developing similar electronic mechanisms and therefore had to limit Membership to the physical capacity of an old building. But it took a long time to break that log jam.

As time passed we widened the scope of our agendas at successive meetings, particularly in three directions:

• the UK added its voice to the US demands for liberalization of the restrictive regime of control over savings and interest rates on savings and a variety of financial instruments, which segmented and protected particular markets and made business difficult in practice for foreign participants:

• we spent more and more time talking about developments and problems in our respective markets, their implications and possible repercussions, and increasingly found ourselves exchanging ideas as between colleagues confronting similar problems:

• we also exchanged views on a growing number of international problems, seeking ideas on which we could not only agree together, but then go on to plan concerted action for wider international discussion – I believe this has been a growing element in some of the more recent talks since my time in them.

The success of our series of talks prompted a considerable fashion: Germany, France and Italy – I think in that order – gradually set up somewhat similar bilateral meetings.

DIRIGISME – SOME BROADER COMMENTS

For whatever reasons of history and social structure and behaviour, the shape of authority in Japan has been one of the strong and closely-knit and often quite detailed central direction, much fortified by two things: the high quality of many individuals in the major ministries (only three other countries in my experience have quality at all comparable); and the deep and close relationships and the constructive cooperation between the ministries and their 'customers' in industry and commerce and public life. This can facilitate enormously effective joint action when common purpose is identified. . .

The power and range of responsibility of the MOF are large. The sense of personal responsibility among senior – and also among relatively junior – MOF staff is very strong. Internally, the responsibility of middle-ranking division and bureau heads is recognized by their senior colleagues: to get results it is often not sufficient simply to persuade the most senior man – you must also persuade others with personal responsibility.

The pervasive and detailed entry of the MOF into all aspects of financial business in Japan is well known. In the matter of licences, the idea of general authorization of a defined type of institution seemed unnatural to the MOF – much more natural was to subject every applicant to meticulous individual inspection and approval, and to ration approvals. Supervision was often on a scale approaching that of a major audit. All change seemed to have to be limited to small incremental steps which could be tightly controlled and monitored, the idea of loss of control being the ultimate nightmare. This notorious line of 'step by step' changes led to some very odd rigidities.

I particularly remember the occasion when it was decided to grant precisely eight licences to foreign 'Trust Banks' and it emerged that there were precisely nine well-qualified and eminently respectable applicants. We did succeed in getting the original eight changed to nine, but it was a triumph achieved at the expense of turmoil in a MOF quite unused to responding to external pressure in that way. Similar 'rationing' of concessions came up in other contexts. And I have already spoken of the extreme example of the limited size of the Tokyo Stock Exchange.

I must emphasize that a great deal of this was by no means action against foreigners: it had for long applied to limit opportunities for Japanese newcomers. But the foreigners were less used to accepting it – and of course as very late and unconnected newcomers they were especially hampered by it.

The whole approach is *dirigiste*, with a deep conservative and self-defensive quality, particularly when faced by any outside challenge. I would normally expect this to prove a source of potential weakness in an environment of rapid change.

It therefore interested me enormously to see how the Japanese authorities reacted to changes which they came to recognize as unavoidable, and even desirable, when those changes would clearly undermine past practices and methods of control. Let me give two instances, on quite different scales.

FACING CHANGE

Modern Japan owes many features of its law to post-war 'guidance' (if that is the right word) by the United States. One such feature in financial affairs is Article 65 of the Securities and Exchange Law of 1948 which follows the US model of forbidding banks to engage in securities business. This does not apply in many other countries and was inconvenient for certain UK and other European houses, where the potential conflicts of interest are recognized but are dealt with in a less prohibitive way.

To my surprise, satisfaction and very great interest, my MOF counterparts did not simply rule out my request for consideration of the UK banks with securities operations. The Japanese are certainly great pragmatists! I soon found myself engaged in a fascinating discussion of how we could together develop definitions and structures which would get round the problem. It took time, and a good deal of ingenuity which the MOF itself and our individual houses contributed. We were all very sensitive to the need to respect the spirit of the law, but together we found a way – or a variety of ways!

Soon after, the Japanese authorities – and in this they were ahead of the US – began to explore ways of liberalizing their law generally on this point. I think they had begun to see the need, and were probably under pressure from some Japanese houses, before we achieved our own arrangements. Typically, the authorities put huge effort into prolonged and detailed consultations with all parties concerned in Japan, exploring as they went operational and supervisory implications, and seeking a national consensus on the best forms of change before reaching decisions. They also studied with their usual care the experience of other countries, including what we could offer. It all took a long time, certainly longer than I would expect with any similar process of change in the UK, and I am not convinced that such long gestation produces the best results.

A very much deeper change was involved on another front. Much of the US pressure, backed by my own team – and by German, French and other teams who later joined in with their own bilateral talks – focused on the traditional tight control of channels of savings and interest rates available, all of which formed part of a general system of detailed knowledge and control of all monetary movements by the MOF and the Bank of Japan, and at earlier times contributed to the sustained mobilization of relatively cheap financing for Japanese industries.

It must have been in 1986 or 1987 – it was after Toyo Gyoten had succeeded as Vice-Minister – that we had a long discussion during one round of talks about methods of monetary control. My colleagues and I recognized that liberalization of the kind we and others were pressing on Japan would have uncomfortable results for the authorities. First, there would be a period in which it might be difficult to track useful statistics – the old pattern would be changing and the new one not yet established and understood: not surprisingly, the MOF instinct was to take this as slowly as possible: my argument was that transitional periods are especially difficult to handle and should be traversed quickly, to curtail the period of difficulty. Secondly, control of a liberalized monetary system has to be achieved by general influences from the centre (broad interest rates, etc), and not by detailed direction of individual types of transactions. This was a particularly tough nut for the MOF to swallow, calling for a less *dirigiste* form of supervision and control, and one in which the relative authority and importance of the Bank of Japan and the MOF could be affected.

There is still some way to go, but the pace of change has been faster than many of us had expected, and the way the Japanese authorities have adapted to the change has been an impressive example of realism and pragmatism.

REACTIONARIES AND PROGRESSIVES

I have to tell you that I like Japanese individuals better than I like Japanese systems of administration – and I suspect many Japanese would agree with that sentiment.

I mentioned earlier that, as I came to know more individuals in Japanese financial circles, I first suspected and later became convinced that many were looking for change, and saw the restrictiveness of the traditional system as a limitation, rather than a protection. I found this attitude especially among those with international experience, and perhaps also among the more successful and self-confident. I even found it among quite a number of MOF and Bank of Japan officials. I have found it also often linked with unease about the Japanese political system and its structure.

In the nature of things, my acquaintance is a selective one – most of my Japanese friends are engaged in some aspect of finance, they speak English, and most have experience outside Japan. They may well be unrepresentative.

But they are influential: and I remain convinced that there is a significant body of influential Japanese who are much more internationally minded than would have been imaginable even a generation ago, and who see the future on their side.

27

Army and Navy Officers in Japan

JOHN FIGGESS ● PETER DEAN ● JIMMIE ABRAHAM ● MIKE FORREST

OFFICERS from all three services have done stints in post-war Japan as service attachés (service advisers during the Occupation years). Their tasks were initially to observe the demilitarization of Japan and then, following the Peace Treaty in 1952, develop contacts with the gradually expanding Self-Defense Forces. In recent years, one of their main duties has been to promote defence sales from British manufacturers to the Self-Defense Forces.

Until about 1980 a few youngish military and naval officers were sent out as language students. This gave them on later appointment as service attachés unrivalled access. Sadly, despite efforts by me and others with the Chiefs of Staff, the service authorities decided that the schemes were too expensive in budgetary and manpower terms and thus Britain no longer has service attachés in Tokyo trained in the Japanese language.

I have quoted extensively in Chapter 1 from the account given by John Figgess (at the time a Lt Colonel, later Colonel and appointed a KBE in 1969) about his time as assistant military adviser to the United Kingdom Liaison Mission to SCAP. I have also given some account of his service later as Military Attaché in the British Embassy in the biographical portrait I produced about him for *Biographical Portraits*, Vol. III (published for the Japan Society by Japan Library in 1999).

On 28 September 1969 JOHN FIGGESS, who had just returned from Japan after serving seven years as Information Counsellor in the Embassy, gave a talk to the Japan Society on the theme 'Japan: The New Affluence'. In this he declared that '. . . modern Japan is probably as near to being a classless society as exists in the world today'. He reported that '. . . the nation is well fed, well dressed, and well equipped with appurtenances of our age'. He noted the development of the 'leisure boom' exemplified by increased expenditure on travel and sports. He added: 'One person in twenty-five now owns a motor car . . . Housing lags behind however . . . Wage scales are by no means low . . . Planned parenthood . . . tends to limit families to two or at most three children.'

Figgess went on to refer to the growing problems of congestion, air and noise pollution and disposal of rubbish. He noted the move from the land to the towns and the development of *san-chan nogyo* (i.e. farming left to the three old people, grandma, grandpa and mum).

He spoke also about the recruiting campaigns of big firms 'plagued by labour shortages'. He noted that the high population density in Japan '. . . imposes a terrifying degree of conformity on people'. 'Although nearly everybody is better off financially than ever before, life for most people in today's affluent Japan is fairly circumscribed and tends to follow a set pattern which varies astonishingly little between one individual and another.' In conclusion, Figgess read out his translation of '. . . an amusing little story satirizing the whole concept of this mapped out existence' which he had come across in *Shukan Asahi*.

I have mentioned in Chapter 1 that in 1945 as a prisoner of war PETER DEAN was in Japan when the Japanese surrendered. He returned to the country in 1959 as Military Attaché and successor to John Figgess. Colonel Dean, as he had become, gave an account of his service in Japan in an article which appeared in The Japan Society *Proceedings* No 120 in the autumn of 1992. He was sent initially in 1959 to Kamakura to study the Japanese language:-

•

There Mrs Naoko Nishi and her family took us under their wing, and introduced us to the culture of Japan. They were most generous in their friendship, so that I soon became intrigued and fascinated by the beauty of the country and by its totally different life-style.

Thanks to the perseverance and patience of my teachers, together with the help of our Japanese domestic staff, my interest increased and my family could not have enjoyed a happier time. I shall always be thankful for the efforts of my teachers to help a rather bone-headed student of the language. Our house and gardens were tucked in a valley within walking distance of a Buddhist temple at Zuisenji (at Kamakura), which was built as though it was part of nature itself. . . Our eldest daughter attended the local kindergarten. When her end-of-term report arrived we learnt that 'individualism' was not considered a desirable attribute.

As my knowledge of the language progressed, I established close bonds with Mrs Nishi and Mr Nakazato who told me much about the war from the Japanese side. Both had experienced bereavement and hardship; both were ashamed at the Japanese treatment of Allied prisoners of war. Once, while wrestling with the translation of a Japanese text given to me by Mr Nakazato I found that it dealt with his own war-time service in China and New Guinea as a corporal in the Japanese Imperial Army. Only later did he tell me that he was captured by the Australians and became a prisoner of war in Australia. For the first time we could share our experiences for till then nobody had mentioned that I had been a prisoner of the Japanese. Perhaps because of our shared experience an even closer bond was established between us, a bond only severed by his death. Like me, he still felt the disgrace attached to surrendering in wartime but had no remorse and spoke with gratitude about experiencing a new way of life in Australia. However, he never accepted a Japanese government war pension and for this gesture I greatly respected him as a man of honour and a true patriot.

From conversations with a number of young Japanese it soon became evident to me that they had no knowledge of the unfortunate incidents which had happened during the war, and had learnt little from their censored school history textbooks. Several of them had travelled abroad and had heard very different tales of Japanese Imperial Army behaviour. They felt ashamed and were keen to know more of what had happened during the Pacific War.

Apart from the close links with my teachers it was not easy to get to know many Japanese except as casual acquaintances. To be invited into a Japanese home is rare, even between Japanese, which I found unfortunate. The Japanese rarely give candid answers to questions whatever the subject under discussion. This may be due partly to a lack of open debate in the Japanese educational system, but it is also a cultural phenomenon where ambiguity is preferred to clarity, and allusive expressions are more usual than direct reference. I had been told that the Japanese have no sense of humour. This is not true, but humour directed against themselves is generally resented.

One day, while waiting for my teacher, I asked my daily help, a married lady, to peel a peach for me. Mrs Fujiwara seemed surprised by my request and asked me to repeat what I had said. Then, in typical Japanese female behaviour she covered her mouth to hide her laughter and scampered out of the house, meeting my teacher who was on the way in. I was surprised and abashed to learn that my pronunciation of the Japanese word for peach – *momo* – had been mistaken for the word thigh – also *momo*. So I had asked the lady to strip her thighs. I was made to learn the correct pronunciation of *momo* and forced to repeat it many times. The word soon got around the neighbourhood in which I lived, and there was much kind ribaldry of which I am reminded when I visit Mrs Nishi's family.

After some months during which I only had the opportunity of speaking with my teacher I was advised to practise in the local community. My first attempts were most frustrating. I found that I had difficulty in being understood and that people replied either in halting English or with blank looks. It was not until I ventured into some bars that I had more chances to practise my spoken Japanese. The effect of imbibing Kirin beer, together with the flattering attention of the bar hostesses, raised my morale and gave me a false idea of my fluency. From this experience I was to learn how easy it was to fall into the trap of using female words, and that the words '*o jozu desu ne*' (how fluent you are!) were expressions of politeness rather than the truth.

After nearly a year in Kamakura we moved to a semi-Western-style house in Azabu in the hustle and bustle of Tokyo. Shortly after joining the embassy staff we were invited by Sir Vere and Lady Redman to a drinks party where I was introduced to a Mr Yoshitomo Tokugawa. During our conversation he asked me if this was my first time in Japan. Deciding that truthfulness was the best policy I replied that my first visit was in January 1945. My hostess, rather taken aback, said that I could not have been in Japan then as it was during the war. Mr Tokugawa then asked me if I was in his camp as he had been commandant of a prisoner of war camp in Tokyo. I knew that his was a show camp for International Red Cross visits. Later experience showed that while some Japanese may not appreciate plain speaking they do respect foreigners for it. I had several opportunities to observe Japanese reaction to plain speaking during my visits to units of the Self-Defense Forces. Dealing with members of the same profession was easier and there was also the advantage that over a period of time mutual trust was established.

*   *   *

The Japanese Commander-in-Chief of the Ground Self-Defense Force when I first moved to Tokyo was General Ichiji Sugita who had been Intelligence Officer to General Yamashita during the Malaya Campaign and was interpreter at the surrender of General Percival at Singapore in 1942. General Sugita had also spent some time in Changi jail after the war because of his links with General Yamashita who was executed by the Americans as a War Criminal. General Sugita was a fine officer and very-pro British. I was lucky that he was Commander-in-Chief during my stay in Japan. A few months after taking over as Military Attaché I was summoned to Sugita's office for a private meeting. He told me that he was aware of my background as a prisoner of war, and apologized for the way we had been treated as prisoners. He also expressed the hope that I would help him to dispel any feelings of rancour between our two countries. It was fascinating to hear from him what went on during the surrender meeting in Singapore, and the story of the campaign from the Japanese side. He was writing a book about this period and asked me whether I could help him with some details from the British side. Later he introduced me to a number of ex-officers who had taken part in the campaign. I was also told that should I have difficulty in visiting any unit in the Ground Self-Defense Force. I was to phone his office. I shall always be grateful to General Sugita for his understanding and we have kept in touch ever since.

During my time at the British Embassy in Tokyo, Service language students were attached to Japanese military units as part of their training before taking their interpretership exams. This proved to be an excellent way of fostering good relations with the Japanese forces as well as giving us an insight into the strengths and problems of the Self-Defense Forces. After their attachment language students were asked to write a report and one of these reports, written by Major Ken Collins, became a classic on the Ground Self-Defense Forces. General Sugita asked me if he could see it, if possible, warts and all. So I decided to agree and as a result every officer in the Ground Self-Defense Forces was made to read it on the order of General Sugita.

Since retiring from the army I have noticed that today many academics and officials whose duties take them to Japan are fearful of upsetting Japanese feeling when so-called 'sensitive' matters are raised. These matters include the behaviour of the Japanese imperial army and the role of the late emperor during the last war. I feel that this attitude is mistaken, for the Japanese are realists and respect honest opinions when backed by common sense. Furthermore, they do take notice of foreign criticism and act on it if at all possible. I noticed during the war that the late Emperor's influence appeared to be extremely important but it was difficult for me to find out what in fact was his role as Commander-in-Chief of the wartime Japanese forces. It seemed that the workings of the Imperial Palace were shrouded in mystery, and that the emperor's role was unquestioned. On the death of Emperor Hirohito this question was aired in the British media. A number of Japanophiles rallied to his defence but I think that, at present, it is too early to come to a conclusion. Much of the information needed to make a fair judgement about the emperor's wartime role is still unavailable and as long as this is the case this matter remains a grey area.

On the British side many questions remain unanswered, particularly about our wartime intelligence of Japan's military capabilities. It seems amazing that two infantry divisions, one Australian and one British, were sent to reinforce the defence of Singapore when it was obvious that the battle was lost.

JIMMIE ABRAHAM (Captain H. J. Abraham, RN,) was Naval and Air Attaché in Tokyo 1969-1972 as well as UK Naval and Air Representative, United Nations, South Korea. One of his main embassy tasks was to promote defence equipment sales. As the following account shows, entitled 'The Advantage of Having Three Hats', ingenuity was sometimes required:-

•

'Regret to inform you Hawker Siddeley Harrier crashed last Friday. It cannot be in time to participate in Japanese International Air Show.'

So read the signal from the Ministry of Supply that arrived on my desk in the embassy early Monday morning on 4 October 1971, just two weeks and five days before the first truly International Air Show in the Far East was due to open.

The Harrier was to be the top attraction over all other countries attending, which included large contributions from the Americans, Russians and French as well as twenty-eight British and fifty-four Japanese firms. This unique aircraft had just entered squadron service with the Royal Air Force and it had great potential for overseas sales. To drive home this potential the Minister for Aerospace, Mr Frederick Corfield and the Commander Far East Air Force, Air Marshal Nigel Maynard, were to attend the show.

'Loss of face' dominated my thoughts, not only for Britain but also the sales prospects to the Japanese Navy. I had been much encouraged by their interest in the Harrier for their large destroyers then under construction.

The Japanese simply would not understand why the Harrier did not appear. I felt top-level action was required and drafted a signal to the Chief of Air Staff in London which was approved immediately by the Ambassador, Sir John Pilcher.

Air Chief Marshal Sir John Grandy turned up trumps and replied by return. A Royal Air Force Harrier from the Operational Conversion Unit at RAF Station Wittering would be taken apart and flown out in a RAF Bristol Transport aircraft providing I could find a suitable airfield for the Harrier to be put together again.

A Japanese base would have been difficult to arrange in the time available and my only hope was the Americans. Fortunately, the American Air Attaché had become a good friend and his house was within walking distance of mine in the suburbs of Tokyo.

I felt an approach on the national net using embassy offices might be embarrassing for my American colleague and to avoid a potential conflict of [sales] interest, I used our United Nations hats to make the initial soundings at his house over a whisky. Much to my surprise he said there would be no problem – just send a letter and now let's enjoy the whisky.

Within two days I received a letter saying that hangar space and accommodation for officers and men would be provided at the United States Air Force Base, Yokota, and I was asked to signal the aircraft's time of arrival and any ground equipment required.

The RAF Bristol Transport with its Harrier and ground crew left Wittering on Monday 18 October and, after several stops for fuel, arrived at Yokota on Sunday 24 October. Next day, the Harrier was put together again and on Tuesday it was ready for a test flight by the display pilot, Squadron Leader Profit, who had flown out by BOAC over the weekend.

On the Wednesday, he practised his display at Yokota which enthralled the Americans and then flew the aircraft down to Nagoya to prepare for the Air Show. Next morning, he put on a special demonstration for a live early morning television programme.

The Show opened on Friday 29 October.

During each of the six days of the Show, Squadron Leader Profit gave two displays to reveal every facet of the Harrier's capability. He also had a bad weather routine which proved invaluable because low cloud and poor visibility restricted flying on two days when the Harrier was the only high-performance aircraft to fly.

The highlight was at the end of each display, which aptly culminated in a Japanese bow to the audience of many thousands whose automatic appreciation was to bow in return; it was a wonderful sight from the ground, and must have been very gratifying for Squadron Leader Profit.

MIKE FORREST (Captain Michael Forrest, RN) was Naval Attaché from 1981-84 and was the last Naval Attaché who had been a Japanese language officer. The following contribution records his association with things Japanese. It is supplemented by some interesting comments from his wife, GAIL FORREST:-

●

At the end of our time in HMS *Devonshire*, the training cruiser, all of us cadets had to state our preferences for where we would like to be sent as Midshipmen. A group of us decided that this was the time to go as far afield as possible and so we put down for the Far East Fleet. So it was that in November 1952 I had my first sight of Japan as I sailed into Sasebo harbour aboard HMS *Glory*. I knew nothing at all about the place other than information gleaned from wartime reports and from the twelve-part serial story 'A Sword of Nippon' in the 1914 *Chums* annual. I was struck by the beauty of the coastline of western Japan. As we went into the landlocked harbour I could see little villages with heavy tiled roofs down at the water's edge and then in Sasebo itself. A few hundred yards inshore of the buoy to which we customarily secured there was even a little island complete with tiny shrine and stunted pines. From the very first sight it looked different.

HMS *Glory* had come to the Far East to be the nucleus of the Carrier Task Group operating off the west coast of Korea. The pattern of our lives was an eleven-day patrol off the Korean coast, where our aircraft attacked supplies and carried out interdiction and close air support, followed by about a week in Sasebo for ammunitioning or a week in Kure, near Hiroshima, which was our administrative base. Everyone looked forward eagerly to the passage to Kure. It began with the transit of the Shimonoseki Straits between Honshu and Kyushu, narrow, winding, crowded with ships and boats of all sizes and with a tidal stream that ran at anything up to eleven knots. After this we went along swept channels marked by buoys (the Allies laid about a hundred thousand mines in the Inland Sea during the war) past rocks with stunted pines and terraced islands with a fishing village here and there. A Midshipman's life did not give much scope to explore, particularly in Sasebo.

Our buoy was two and a quarter miles from the landing place, and as Midshipman of a boat running an hourly service, frequently calling at other ships on the way, there was barely time to snatch a meal. A day's duty was 1230 to 1230. The last boat back from shore left at 0200 and we were back in the boat before breakfast to supervise cleaning. After a day's duty the rest of the boat's crew had twenty-four hours off, but the Midshipman spent the time in an ammunition lighter, supervising the unloading. There was less to do in Kure and we did sometimes have the chance to walk out through the suburbs and climb hills round about for a prospect of the island-strewn Inland Sea.

The Japanese economic miracle had yet to make its impact felt. The long journey from our berth in the former Japanese naval dockyard was made by rickety three-wheeled taxis, clinging on tight as they bounced through potholes that sometimes looked big enough for them to hide in. The town looked poor. Most of the women were still wearing the baggy *mompe* trousers that had become the norm during the war. Of course in both ports we headed for the bars in the evening. In those days the pound sterling was worth 1000 yen and a large bottle of beer cost 200 yen. Add to this the fact that we were at sea for half the month and the result was that, even as Midshipmen, we had enough money.

In those days of post-war poverty the bar owners were so keen for our patronage that no charge at all was made for the company of the girls who poured your drinks, danced with you, showed you innumerable tricks with matchsticks and always beat you in the game where holes are burnt in a paper stuck over a glass until a coin on it falls through. They were completely unlike girls we had come across before. But then the great fascination of the place was that everything was so different. The fields, the houses, the boats, the bowing, the whole atmosphere of life struck one as utterly alien. I was conscious of a complete lack of knowledge of just what these differences were.

Out of curiosity I bought a book called *Japanese in Thirty Hours* and started to work my way through it. I will never forget the time I first tried out my Japanese. I fixed a girl in a bar with an earnest look and said, '*Tabetai* (Want to eat)'. She blinked and then looked blank. I tried again more emphatically. She looked at me hesitantly then shot away like a startled rabbit, but a few minutes later she appeared with a plate of sandwiches. I was hooked. I decided that if it was at all possible I would come back as a language student and find out more about this mysterious but beautiful country.

*   *   *

So it was that in the autumn of 1961, when I had passed the Preliminary Examination after some years of studying Japanese as a hobby, my wife Gail and I sailed for Japan from Hamburg aboard MV *Shizuoka Maru*. On our arrival in Tokyo we were taken under the wing of Lt. Cdr. John Calderwood, the Assistant to the NA. We were to stay with him for a short time while he shepherded us through the initial formalities, showed us around and gave us some tips about life. However, before all this could be accomplished Gail had to be rushed to hospital with a threatened miscarriage. The hospital was run by an order of French nuns, but the duty night midwife was Japanese and spoke not a word of English. I did my best to interpret, but it was not really my field!

The upshot was that we stayed nearly three weeks with John Calderwood before Gail was allowed to travel carefully to the house that had just been vacated by the previous language student. As the journey seemed to have upset the baby again we called out a Japanese doctor, who gave Gail an injection. We thanked him and said we would see him the next day. He looked shocked and said that it was his golf day. I rang up the Austrian doctor, Dr Eitel, who had looked after Gail in Tokyo and asked what was to be done. 'Well, Mr Forrest, you go out and buy a syringe and the medicine and you inject 3cc into your wife's buttock every day.' The first syringe I bought had a needle too small for the viscosity of the liquid and as I pressed home the plunger the syringe came apart and the liquid turned into a cloud of spray. I bought a syringe with a bigger needle. A few days later I broke my left hand playing rugby and from then on I had to inject one-handed. Poor Gail suffered agonies, but the baby was carried to term and he is now thirty-seven years old.

We were living in the outskirts of Fujisawa on the Pacific coast outside Tokyo Bay. Military language students had to live outside Tokyo, which had too many distractions and a ready-made anglophone society. We rented the larger part of an L-shaped house. It had a table and chairs on wooden floors in the study and the kitchen, but apart from that it was a completely Japanese-style house. The bath was an *o-furo* and we slept on a *futon* spread on the *tatami*. Everything about a Japanese house was new to us and living in one was a bit like playing a children's game. We were guided by our housekeeper, Chiyo-san.

On arrival in Tokyo I had not the foggiest idea of the system by which I would learn Japanese. I found out that I would not be attending classes in a language school. There were a number of teachers who were approved by the embassy and who undertook the work of teaching diplomatic and military language students. They travelled round from house to house, which meant that a lesson period had to be long or else the teachers would spend too much of their day in fruitless travelling. This resulted in three-hour one-on-one lessons, a demanding – and initially mentally draining – system. There was little chance to coast or daydream during a one-on-one lesson, especially when given by Japanese teachers with their strong ethic of conscientiousness. It was up to the language student to decide which teachers he would employ and how many formal sessions he would have with each per week. I expect that if I had devised too undemanding a timetable there would have been a quiet word in my ear from Colonel Figgess, the Information Counsellor and former Military Attaché who was the supervisor of language studies, or a loud word from Captain Ritchie, the Naval Attaché and my direct naval line superior. Not that there was any question of wilful backsliding on my part. I was burning with eagerness to get to grips with the language.

I was told that whatever else I did there was one teacher I must employ because he was able to cover the military aspects of the language. This was Mr Nakazato. He had been taken prisoner in New Guinea and gone to POW camp in Australia. He had made good use of his time there by learning English, even though he had to write out his notes on toilet paper. He had clearly enjoyed his time in Australia. However spartan the accommodation it must have seemed like heaven on earth after the jungles of New Guinea. I was mightily disconcerted on his first visit to the house because the words poured out of him in a high-pitched torrent. I wondered how I would ever be able to cope, as his speed of delivery was way above my 'white-out' speed at the time.

The amount of effort Mr Nakazato put into his lessons was enormous. He carried round with him a tape recorder that was like a pile of bricks so that he could play things like excerpts from news broadcasts for oral comprehension. He brought cuttings from newspapers and magazines that he had scoured for suitable articles. He also brought pieces that had been copied out by hand by his wife. There was a particular reason for this. As a potential liaison officer it was essential to be able to read handwritten Japanese. One paper of the final examination was indeed always hand-written. He and his wife would pick out an article where a number of the key words recurred frequently and then with consummate skill she would write them more and more cursively, leading the student by degrees right through to the most difficult 'joining-up writing' form of *sosho*.

Mr Nakazato was vastly patient and good-humoured. He would take you through something again until the penny dropped. If you looked blank after reading a sentence he would say, 'Do you understand all the words?' If not, he would paraphrase and explain them. If that failed you could look up the words in a dictionary. If the sentence was still incomprehensible he would say, 'Read it again' – and again and again and again. This always worked eventually because the speed of reading the sentence became faster and faster with repetition until the whole of the sentence was taken in as one piece. It is a method that I use to this day for comprehending the meaning of things like enormously long and convoluted sentences in technical patents. It has never failed me. Mr Nakazato only ever used one expression in English (lessons were conducted entirely in Japanese) but he used it with relish. The Japanese word *hiyori* is an unusual reading of its constituent characters and it means very good weather – what we naval pilots used to call 'eight eighths blue'. This word seemed to turn up surprisingly frequently in the articles he brought. I would purposely misread it and look puzzled, whereupon he would smile gleefully and say, '*Hiyori*. Air Marshals' weather'.

During our first meeting Mr Nakazato said that I must also take lessons from Mrs Nishi. If we call Mr Nakazato's task that of teaching me 'applied Japanese', Mrs Nishi would teach me 'pure Japanese'. She would teach me the richness of the language and introduce me to the literature. She duly called one day soon afterwards and we agreed the times for lessons. Then something happened that utterly nonplussed me. We had been sitting in the armchairs in the living-room but, when the interview was ended, to my consternation and horror Mrs Nishi knelt down on the *tatami* literally at my feet, bowed her forehead to the ground and expressed her thanks in the most honorific language. I was too aghast to do anything but just sit there. I would have been even more aghast, as a lowly Lieutenant, had I known at the time that her father had been Colonel of the 1st Regiment of Cavalry and later Army Minister and Governor of Korea and that her husband had been a Major-General when he was killed.

One of the things I did with Mrs Nishi was to work through eight volumes of the Naganuma Standard Japanese Reader. These progressively introduced all the characters in current use and in volume six covered *bungotai*, the literary form. This was supposedly obsolete, but such was not the case in reality. It was still the form normally used in naval signals, which I had to be able to translate and indeed to interpret on the spot. It is also still very much alive in some business communications. In my work as a translator since leaving the Royal Navy it has proved invaluable to be able to read both *bungotai* and Japanese that was handwritten for Japanese eyes. Mrs Nishi also gave lessons to Gail, who was by now determined to be able to communicate on her own account. Mrs Nishi was a mentor for Gail in other ways, too. Together with her friend Mrs Hashimoto she provided an entree to the world of Japanese arts and crafts, particularly during our second year, by which time Gail had acquired a perfect accent, a sharp ear and a somewhat ungrammatical fluency.

Both Mr Nakazato and Mrs Nishi independently recommended the same third teacher for conversation practice. I had also heard his name from Chiyo-san and other students. It was therefore a surprise when he appeared in our *genkan* and said, '*Watanabe desu*' – the equivalent of 'I'm Smith'. I was told that he was a member of the Crown Prince's suite and this was presumably why he was using what we all knew to be a pseudonym. Three hours of conversation was a daunting prospect, but he was a wonderful talker. He could hold my unflagging attention even after the latest of nights. He was also patient and encouraging in an amused and lordly way. I had him for one session per week on a mutual trial basis, but one day as he left he said, 'You are getting better. From now on I shall come twice a week.' I think he liked coming to me because he had been a naval officer during the war and it was with him that I read the whole of '*Rengo Kantai no Saigo*', the story of the Japanese navy in World War II.

*   *   *

Those were my three teachers and they remained my teachers throughout the two years. During the first year I could only have them at times that had not already been booked and this meant that the seven three hour sessions each week (three with Mr Nakazato, and two each with the others) included a class on Saturday morning. In the second year I was better organized, having two classes from each teacher spread from Monday to Thursday. This does not mean that I only worked for four days per week. Far from it! Although I say it myself I was a most diligent student. After all, I was now being paid to do what I had done for years as a hobby. What it did mean was that Gail and I could go out and about more and venture further afield without having to readjust the study programme.

The other teacher to whom I must make an acknowledgement was Chiyo-san herself. We spent a great deal of time chatting to her. I believe that she spoke some English, as I heard of her working for non-Japanese-speaking families at other times. However, she was unflaggingly dutiful in all things, like most Japanese of her generation, and she expected us to be the same. I never heard one word of English pass her lips in two years. I was a language student and therefore I was to converse in Japanese. She applied this rule from day one to Gail as well, sweeping her up into the general task of working for a language student. Of course this meant that Gail gradually became familiar with the normal Japanese for everything to do with things like shopping, cooking, the house and babycare. It was a great bonus.

In the summer of 1963, towards the end of my time, a short but vital part of the course was five weeks of *Taizuki Kimmu*, an attachment to the Maritime Self-Defense Force (MSDF). I went first of all for one week to the air base at Tokushima on the east coast of Shikoku. The heads of each department gave me detailed classroom briefings and tours. I was therefore able to learn not only the way in which the Fleet Air Force was organized but also the correct terms for everything to do with the organization. Next came the best two weeks of all in the minesweeper/hunter *Tsukumi*. I joined her in Yokosuka in Tokyo Bay and sailed to the far end of Japan to take part in a major minehunting and sweeping exercise off the entrance to the Shimonoseki Straits. On completion of the exercise, we sailed in through Shimonoseki and made our way through the breathtakingly beautiful island-strewn western part of the Inland Sea, through Nakanoseki and on through Kaminoseki into Hiroshima Bay and so to Kure. It must be one of the most beautiful passages in the world.

What a transformation there was in Kure! No three-wheeler taxis, no enormous potholes, no *mompe*. All was bustle, new buildings and prosperity. The difference from the scene ten years previously was staggering. This was the burgeoning Japanese economic miracle in action. On leaving Tsukumi I returned to Yokosuka and joined the destroyer *Uranami* for my final two weeks of *Taizuki Kimmu*. After the all-action fortnight aboard the minesweeper the pace aboard *Uranami* was slower. The first week was taken up with day-running from Yokosuka, a complete spring clean of the ship and a holiday. I went round the ship copying down the names of all the compartments from the tallies over their entrances. This was the sort of detailed knowledge that could only be acquired on this sort of occasion. I buttonholed anybody who failed to avoid me and talked to them about their duties. Eventually we sailed round to the Inland Sea for some daytime exercises – useful for my naval Japanese. I was also given a key to the Operations Room safe in which there were copies of the basic NATO tactical and exercise publications with Japanese on one page and the English facing it – another fruitful study tool.

After supper one day I gave what I think was my first lecture in Japanese, entitled 'The Present State of the Royal Navy', to the assembled officers of the four destroyers in company. This five weeks of *Taizuki Kimmu* was a matchless opportunity to acquire linguistic and service knowledge. Twenty years later I mentioned it in conversation to two Japanese admirals. They looked amazed and one of them said, 'It would be unthinkable now'.

*   *   *

I was constantly being surprised in Japan and an unusual surprise occurred at the end of my time in Uranami. All the officers took me to dinner at a restaurant ashore on my last night. A very large fish was selected from the fish tank for preparation into various dishes. First of all the whole fish was presented as *iki-zukuri*, where slices of the best flesh are cut off to be eaten as *sashimi* while the body of the fish is still nervously twitching on the dish. After this it was borne away and used to prepare soup, grills, *tempura* and so on. I thought of England and ate my *sashimi*.

The captain had been rather stiff and reserved towards me, but now his face changed like the sun coming out from behind the clouds. He leaned towards me, smiling, and said, 'The reason we accept you is not because you speak our language but because you eat our food.' He went on to say that they had many American visitors in Yokosuka and prepared the best food they had for them but they would not touch it and asked for fried eggs. Well, that was another thing learned. The food on board had been completely Japanese throughout and I had enjoyed it all. The only difficulty was managing to find room for the three full bowls of rice at breakfast necessary to keep me going until lunch.

The food is one of the excitements and enjoyments of Japan. Every railway station is surrounded by dozens of wonderful little eateries. Armed with that nonpareil of books *Eating Cheap in Japan* and the ability to read menus in Japanese the world is your *kaki age* – or *aji tataki* or *dobin mushi* or *hiya yakko* or whatever.

The MSDF was set up on the model of the USN, but I soon found that the appearance was only skin deep. Virtually all the officers from senior Lieutenant upwards were ex-IJN (Imperial Japanese Navy) officers and it was to the IJN that they looked for the ethos of the new force. True, the discipline was gentler. The emphasis was on encouragement to conscientiousness, diligence and *esprit de corps* with the aim of building a service that would be a worthy successor to the IJN. There was an atmosphere of earnestness that pervaded the ships.

One thing that struck me was that when items of the daily routine were broadcast they normally ended with the words 'go fun mae' (five minutes before). If you were not in the correct place five minutes before the time stated on the routine you were letting the side down. Another small thing was that at the broadcast 'Kokki keiyo' at 0800 personnel inside the ship as well as those on the upper deck turned aft and stood to attention while the flag was hoisted. I listened in amazement to a Leading Seaman giving a lecture to the mounting's crew about the underwater trajectory of the hedgehog anti-submarine projectile. Earnestness. Diligence. At the tail end of one afternoon at Tokushima Air Base all the junior ratings had to march round and round the parade ground in a big circle singing the old military songs like *Doki no Sakura, Umi Yukaba* and of course the *Gunkan* march.

The other thing I soon found out was the special regard for the Royal Navy that had come down from the IJN to the MSDF. I was truly on a pig's back. The IJN was set up by missions from the Royal Navy soon after the Meiji Restoration. The grandfather of Margery West, NA's secretary, had been a member of the main naval mission. Every year the NA and his staff were taken out to lunch by Admiral Yamanashi, who had stood by the building of Admiral Togo's flagship *Mikasa* in Barrow-in-Furness in 1902. The new personnel in the MSDF came into a force inaugurated on the lines of the USN but the officer corps looked back to the great days of the IJN and set a high store by the old links with the Royal Navy.

*   *   *

For the first three months of our stay in Japan Gail was virtually house-bound for fear of a miscarriage and after our first son was safely born on 20 January we had a tiny baby to look after. I was determined to use this six months or so to work really hard and try to achieve real competence in the language. It was just as well that I did. We still had a sizeable fleet East of Suez and Captain Ritchie had persuaded the programmers to send a large part of it on a late spring cruise to Japan. He had arranged forty-one ship-visit weeks. There had naturally been a great deal of long-term planning with the ports concerned, but face-to-face meetings were expected to settle the final details as the time drew near. It was a physical impossibility for NA to satisfy all these demands for meetings, so in April 1962, about six months after arriving in Japan, I was despatched to Kyushu to make the final arrangements in Beppu and Kagoshima.

It was quite a daunting task for a Lieutenant in his first year as a language student. I think some of the people at the meetings thought I was the NA because I did overhear someone remark how young I looked to be a Captain. If only! The normal form for these meetings was something like this. You would be conducted by the local government official assigned to be your escort throughout your stay into a conference room where long tables were set out in a hollow square. You and your escort seated yourselves at one table and round the others there would be twenty-five to thirty Japanese all seeking the answers to their own questions. They came from various sections of the city administration, mirrored by Prefectural representatives if it was the seat of a Governor, police, customs, immigration, port authority, MSA/MSDF, Chamber of Commerce and so on. I see from my working diary at the time that I had noted down twenty-seven headings that I knew needed to be discussed and I am quite sure that others arose.

Two matters that invariably required to be handled with the utmost tact and good humour were the status of the unofficial Chinese laundrymen and the matter of landing shore patrols from the ships. The meetings were intense and lasted over two hours. I was grateful for every minute of study that I had put in to date. (I did not fully appreciate then just what an advantage it was to be able to hold the meetings in Japanese. That came home to me in 1969 when I was sent ahead to make the final arrangements for visits by six ships to ports around the eastern end of the Inland Sea. One day NA rang from Tokyo to the office I was using in Kobe and said, 'Get down to Wakayama. They expected a meeting and they are upset.' When I entered the conference room there I could sense the hostility, but when I started to conduct the meeting in Japanese the atmosphere lightened within minutes.)

The good news was that except when being grilled at the meetings you were an honoured guest of the city, well fed, shown all the sights and lodged at the best hotel. The Shigetomi-so in Kagoshima had been a villa of the Shimazu feudal lords and on the night that I stayed there a group were rehearsing on a stage in the grounds outside my window for a performance of local song and dance. This was the continuation of former annual performances for the lord's family. I felt very grand.

I made the trip down to Kyushu by train, a journey of over twenty hours. Soon after we left Tokyo the attendant brought me the card of a gentleman who said he would like to talk to me. It turned out that he was a company chairman on his way back from a meeting in Tokyo and he was feeling expansive. We went to the restaurant car for a beer and there he called over two girls from a neighbouring table to teach me children's songs to sing to my baby son. All the way to Nagoya, where he got off, our host bought the beer and he and the girls taught me songs. It was a jolly way to pass a couple of hours on the train and I still remember the songs.

I had wondered about the mechanics of going to bed, but when the attendants had converted the seats into bunks all the men left the carriage while the women went to bed and drew the bed curtains. Then the men returned and went to bed in their turn. Gail and I also travelled about as much as we could in our little Renault car. There were still far more Japanese-style *ryokan* than Western-style hotels. They were not the expensive relics of a bygone age that they are fast becoming now but the normal place to stay. There was still an abundance of female staff, presumably still largely drawn from the women whose potential husbands were killed in the war. Two of them took you under their wing on arrival, brought you your tea and saké, organized the bath, served supper and breakfast in your room, spread the bed and made sure that you were well looked after. Travelling by car was often slow and stressful, but the cares of the day soon faded away once ensconced in the cosseting environment of a *ryokan*.

Fujisawa was a nondescript place, but Kamakura was steeped in the atmosphere of old Japan. Every year there was a historical festival with a period costume pageant of the leaders of the Minamoto clan who established the Kamakura Shogunate and their wives and retainers. There were performances on the stage at the shrine to Hachiman, the God of War. A famous film star came to dance the dance of Shizuka Gozen, the wife of the renowned general Yoshitsune. I listened to a narration accompanied on the *biwa* (Japanese lute) of the whole of the *Shuzenji Monogatari*, which I had just ploughed my way through in Book 8 of Naganuma with Mrs Nishi. Kamakura was the setting for a period of the history of very old Japan and one was led quite naturally to a study of Japanese history. Of course Mrs Nishi and 'Mr Watanabe' lived in Kamakura. Where else?

* * *

I am not in a position to give a balanced judgement on the merits and demerits of the two-year language course. I do not know what was covered during the year at SOAS which I skipped, having taken the Preliminary Examination under my own steam. None of the teachers had formal teaching qualifications. During the time in Japan the classes were conducted entirely in Japanese and there was little formal and structured instruction in Japanese grammar and syntax. I learned mine on my own from Vaccari's grammar book, using Latin as a datum reference, and this proved to be adequate. What the course did lack was structured instruction in interpreting. That is something that was probably still in its infancy in those days, unlike today when interpreting courses are offered by several universities. There was virtually no interpreting training as such in the whole course. No technique was taught and the acceptable end standard was sentence by sentence consecutive interpretation. There was, for example, no instruction or practice in the technique of note taking.

When interpreting as a naval officer for naval officers in the context of something like a ship visit this was no great problem, particularly if one could be fast and unhesitating. However, this is not always acceptable at higher levels, where the principals expect to deliver a whole train of thought without interruption. Interpreters are taught on modem courses how to deal with this. There is the story of a renowned interpreter who listened to a tightly argued point for fifteen minutes and then gave it all back perfectly with only the word 'but' on his notepad. This sort of ability is not given to the normal human being, but I was privileged to witness an example of what modern techniques can achieve.

A few years ago I was with the JDA (Japanese Defence Agency) Administrative Vice Minister for his call on the Permanent Under-Secretary of the FCO. The latter developed a particular point for at least five minutes, going round it, going down side-tracks, tacking back and forth. Thank goodness my Japanese counterpart was in the chair. He sat calmly making notes and gave the whole thing back perfectly. It was a real *tour de force*. I have been forced to fill notebooks with scribble that I could not read even one hour afterwards when interpreting at that sort of level, but I never had any formal training or practice in doing so. Not that I was aware of any lack at the time, as I had never seen top flight interpreters in action. Nevertheless, in retrospect it was a shortcoming in the course, particularly as the final examination was at that time called the Civil Service Interpretership Examination.

During the years after my return to England in 1963 I was from time to time required to act as escort officer and interpreter for visiting groups of MSDF officers and JDA civilian officials. Then at last in January 1981 I returned to Tokyo as the British Naval Attaché. It was a very different life-style in every way from that of a language student. This time I was not leading the life of an academic civilian in a Japanese-style house in a pro-vincial town. This time I was a military representative working in an of-ficial environment and living in a Western-style house (bought by Sir Hugh Cortazzi during an earlier appointment) in the heart of an enor-mous capital city. There was not, on the surface, a great deal of 'Old Japan' in evidence. The main requirements of the job were to represent the Roy-al Navy at official functions, be the source of any necessary information inside the embassy, keep the Ministry of Defence informed about the state of the MSDF and help with defence sales. The main success in sell-ing to Japan in the naval field has been the marinized Rolls-Royce gas turbines that power nearly all the MSDF's destroyers. This began with the sale of the Tyne and Olympus engines in about 1967. I was escort offi-cer and interpreter for the MSDF officers who, accompanied by KHI representatives, went to Rolls-Royce Ansty for the final talks. On the way back on the train the jubilant chief of the KHI London office came over to me and said, 'When we get back to London we are going to have a celebration dinner, just the Japanese, but you are an honorary Japanese tonight.'

We went to Annabel's in Berkeley Square and had a memorable dinner of astronomical cost that began with caviar and ended with the best bran-dy in the cellar. I must say that one of the fringe benefits of interpreting is the food. All the parties concerned with the engines worked hard on mutual bonding and to keep this project ongoing in the face of fierce competition from the alliance of General Electric and IHI and of busi-ness disagreements between the companies.

Each year there was a week when representatives of Rolls-Royce, KHI, MSDF and the Royal Navy spent most of their working and relaxing time together. During my time as attaché the Japanese made the decision to go on from the Tyne and Olympus and buy the marinized Spey engine. The KHI men concerned appeared at the embassy and swept me along with them literally to bang on the Ambassador's door to tell him the good news. Other such success stories were few. It was Japanese policy to make their own defence equipment whenever possible, purchasing only the know-how from abroad.

The MSDF had developed enormously in the amount and quality of its equipment and in the scope of its operational experience since the early 1960s. It was working steadily towards achieving the force levels defined for it in the National Defence Planning Outline. These included forces allocated to each of the five districts, flotillas of minesweepers and submarines and large numbers of shore-based fixed and rotary wing anti-submarine aircraft. The showpiece of the MSDF, however, was the Fleet Escort Force. This was to consist of four flotillas, each of eight modern destroyers that carried a total of eight anti-submarine helicopters among them. This force was tasked with defending the sea lanes out to 1,000 miles. At the time of writing these force levels have been achieved and AEW (Aircraft Early Warning) cover is being provided. The things that still need to be provided to make the MSDF a fully capable ocean-going navy are Sea Harrier air defence fighters to destroy the air threat before the release range of air-to-surface missiles, more supply ships to provide underway replenishment of fuel, ammunition, food and spares and nu-clear-powered submarines for sea denial.

The MSDF is now a big navy, much bigger than the Royal Navy. The emphasis has been on the teeth, but the tail has not been neglected when it is a matter of prestige. On a visit to Tokyo in 1996 I was invited by a former Chief of Naval Staff to attend the Self-Defense Forces Day reception hosted by the Defence Minister. The name of the venue was unfamiliar and when I arrived there I found that the Ichigaya Kaikan, which might loosely be called the SDF clubhouse and was a nondescript building, had been pulled down and replaced by a palatial hotel on the scale of Tokyo's international hotels and called the Ichigaya Grand Hills.

*   *   *

There was not a lot to bring old Japan to mind when driving through Tokyo in the early 1980s. There had been much rebuilding in reinforced concrete. The trams were gone. Standing in the foyer of Tokyo Station twenty years before I had watched thousand upon thousand of women commuters coming from the trains in workaday *kimono*, but in the 1980s only a few elderly women were to be seen so dressed on the trains. The *kimono* had ceased to be a normal daytime dress. For eighteen months we provided a home for two of the daughters of Captain (later Vice-Admiral) Terai. One was at university and the other coming to the end of high school. Their father was sent to command an air base in west Japan and we were asked if we would take the girls in so that they could have continuity in their education. They had little time for traditional Japanese customs and attitudes. The elder one declared that she had never worn a *kimono* and never would.

With this connection and the historical inter-naval links and being able to speak Japanese I was given very friendly, even at times privileged, treatment by many of the MSDF. It also led to some quite startling confidences. One little example that may be told concerns a Rear-Admiral whose department I used to visit about every three weeks. He sometimes called me into his office for a chat. One morning he was complaining about the Chief of Naval Staff and said, 'He was shouting at me again this morning. I had my letter of resignation in my pocket – I carry it all the time – and I took it out and told him he could have it any time.' Presumably, he felt that he could unburden himself to someone who was uninvolved and would be discreet.

GAIL FORREST WRITES:

When we sailed from England in 1961 to join M.V. *Shizuoka Maru* in Hamburg I had never left the country before; there were no school visits to Europe when I was young. My experience of the Japanese people was limited to one person known as Ta-chan, the son of the Japanese ambassador to the Vatican, who spent two months living with us in Weymouth to help Mike with his language studies. Faced with a six-week 'cruise' to Japan, Mike intended to teach me Japanese on the way. However, I was perpetually seasick, being pregnant at the time, and had no aptitude for learning languages; I had given up French in the third form. By the time we landed in Kobe all I knew was 'good evening' and 'your bath is ready'.

We arrived in a typhoon and travelled to Tokyo by train to lodge with the assistant to the Naval Attaché until we moved to a house in the country. Unfortunately, I was taken ill and the baby threatened to arrive far too early. The next three months were spent mostly in bed. For convenience sake we decided to take over the house of the previous language student, on the banks of the river that flows out by Enoshima, next to the road and Enoden bridges leading to Katase. Thus Fujisawa was our nearest town but Kamakura was not much further away.

This was a very frustrating time for me. I was desperate to set up the equipment needed to look after a baby but every time I tried to get to the shops I was taken ill again. Mike has already talked about the medical situation and the injections I had to suffer to keep the baby in place. Chiyo-san was very competent and ran the house for me but only spoke Japanese and repeated and repeated and mimed things until I understood. When I went to the shops I found people expected me to speak Japanese and gradually my vocabulary extended to cover food and clothing. I loved the hairdressing parlours. I used them as a chance to practise my language and thought the service was wonderful – free neck massage, shampoo warmed in trays of hot water before being applied and such time and care taken with my long hair which they put up in various styles.

The traditional house with *tatami* floors, *shoji* and *amado* took some getting used to. During the hours spent in bed I was tormented by insects of various kinds and large sizes. I already had a phobia about spiders and this was not a good place to be; some of the large black hairy ones that jumped drove me to hysterics. Then at high tide seasons river crabs would invade the house and I had to sit on my futon with a household broom to drive them away. The cold of that first winter was a terrible shock. No heating of course and we resorted to an oil heater in the baby's room to keep him at least warm. This really upset our landlord who insisted on large sheets of asbestos and a wire cage being placed around the fire and often when I was getting out of bed for the night feeds I would meet an apparition in a long grey night shirt and night cap coming through from his part of the mansion to ours, checking on the fire. The bathroom was icy cold, covered in white tiles and I dreaded my visits there.

When travelling I never got used to the idea of communal bathing and found the scalding water difficult to cope with, although often ladies would help by adding cold water in one corner of the bath for me. I could never see either how one was meant to dry oneself with a tiny strip of cotton towelling in a freezing cold ante-room. However, one had to be philosophical and this was part and parcel of the life-style and was more than compensated for by the beautiful scenery and sites we visited.

Once the baby was born, through the good offices of the American and British Naval Attachés, in Yokosuka hospital, I learnt to drive and then life opened out for me. I attended *sumi-e* painting classes at the local convent with other foreigners and flower arranging classes but my Kamakura *bori* classes consisted of half foreigners and half Japanese. Through this class I made friends with Japanese living in the area and once my language skills reached a certain level I was able to go, taking a *bento* (lunch box), to an all-day class in *roketsu-zome* (wax-resistant dyeing) where I was the only foreigner.

I found the day very long and draining, even lunchtime was not a relaxation for me. The language classes I had been taking with Nishi *sensei* really helped me and gave me the confidence to go out and practise and being English I did not mind making mistakes and hopefully learnt from them. The miserable lonely months before Peter was born were forgotten and life was very interesting, especially when Mike and I were able to travel around the country together. Some of the experiences were very hard. Our nearest contact with other English people was at the YCAC (Yokohama Country & Athletics club) in Yokohama where I could obtain library books and meet other people living in the area. However, roads were so bad and maps very difficult to decipher that every time we set off we seemed to get lost in different places. The feeling of inadequacy was somewhat lessened when Nishi *sensei* confessed she had driven to Tokyo to visit a nephew, got lost, given up and returned to Kamakura without finding him.

*   *   *

We spent New Year up in skiing country in Nagano prefecture leaving the baby with Chiyo-san but on our first long trip down the Tokaido we took him with us, heating bottles in a machine that Nakazato *sensei* gave us that worked off the car battery. We took the ferry to Shikoku and were held up one day while workmen and women blasted a new section of the road around the island. Some of the rocks hit the car but we were safe. One night was spent in a hotel, not a *ryokan*, in Takamatsu; after feeding the baby I left the packets of food on the bedside table and woke to hear a mouse climbing up my sheets to reach the food. On another journey we were delayed around the area of Lake Biwa and could not make Nagoya in time for nightfall. We saw lights at the top of a mountain pass and found a small *ryokan*. The owners at first refused us admission but then granny heard the baby crying and insisted that we be taken in. We often found that having a baby with us helped open doors and made us the centre of attention. After a wonderful meal during which the baby was looked after by the family, I needed to visit the toilet. I found the room and put on the slippers and to my surprise the room was quite large and very cold, the hole being in the middle of the room. I returned next morning in daylight and to my horror found out where the draught was coming from. The hole was over a huge drop, out on a platform over the sheer side of the mountain, no need for refuse collectors! Taken with an attack of vertigo I crept along the walls back to the corridor vowing never to return.

Journeys in those days usually involved several punctures due to the unmade-up road and one's schedule was often disrupted. Another trip to the north found us completely lost with night falling, but we found a Catholic church and an American Franciscan priest who let us sleep on his floor. Next morning two Italian priests called and we all spoke Japanese to each other, before we set off on the right road to our destination.

We had very little contact with the embassy as we were meant to stay in the country to learn the language. However we did accompany the Naval Attaché on a trip to the south west, which was very enjoyable and I was able to interpret for his wife in simple conversations with Japanese naval wives. The sightseeing was very interesting and we were privileged to stay at a monastery on Koya-san. On a similar trip, the following year, with the new Naval Attaché, I was pregnant with my second child and was taken ill while we were in Kyoto. I ended up in the local Baptist hospital where I had to rely on Mike to wash and look after me. As he was busy with interpreting for the official visits and it was June, I was rather smelly by the end of the week. The doctors diagnosed an ectopic pregnancy but we dissuaded them from operating. Eventually, I was allowed to return home by train on the overnight sleeper and be treated by my own doctor, who found a cyst which did not affect the baby's development.

From time to time, I was called up to Number One house (the ambassador's residence) for a particular function. One such occasion I remember was the visit of Sir Alec Douglas-Home, the then Prime Minister and his wife. I felt a very 'up from the country' wife and my temper was not improved by one of the embassy wives holding my hand and asking me to queue with her before being presented to Lady Douglas-Home. Lady Douglas-Home was, in fact, absolutely charming and very tired from the effects of the official visit and just wanted to relax, all the fuss and protocol seemed to be so ridiculous. I am afraid I usually found excuses not to attend functions although I was an enthusiastic member of the Elizabeth Kai as it allowed one entrance to facets of life in Japan.

I found the weather very trying – too cold in the winter and too hot in the summer. I also developed allergies to the mosquitoes who lived and bit me in the area where we lived. Our second year was spent in a newer but still traditional house off Omachi in Kamakura and it was great fun being near the town centre and setting off pushing Peter in a pushchair and investigating the lovely town. I loved Japanese food and found it very healthy so we had no problems there. Being unable to read was very frustrating but Mike would write out place names for me for buses and stations and I was not shy of asking for help.

*   *   *

My second time of living in Japan was when Mike was the Naval Attaché and we were forced to live in an official residence near Shibuya in Tokyo. However, our position entailed a large amount of travelling which was always very interesting. I was fortunate enough to find another wonderful teacher as Nishi *sensei* was retired and still living in Kamakura. Atsuko-san was a graduate of Keio and her husband a professor at Todai. Gradually, she extracted my ungrammatical memories and forced my Japanese into some semblance of correct language. Often I could repeat parrot-like what I had heard from naval wives or the female public at the shops, on buses etc. but did not know what I was actually saying. Due to her patience and efficiency I was able to pass the Civil Service lower grade Japanese exam and for my oral examination I was interviewed by the late emperor's interpreter. I decided to go in on the attack and keep the conversation within bounds that I knew I could talk about, travels, family and hobbies etc., rather than wait for questions I might not understand or be able to answer. After the allotted time the gentleman held up his hand and said, 'Mrs Forrest your time is up', and I had passed.

During the last two years of our stay Atsuko-san introduced me to a friend who was a weaving teacher at the Ochanomizu Bunka Gakuin (cultural institute) in Tokyo and, although she did not speak English, after a having tea with me to observe my language skills she agreed to have me as a student. Of course it was not until the first class, when she wrote instructions on the board for our notebooks that she realized, to her consternation, that I could not read! However, the rest of the class consisted mainly of young girls who were willing to write out the notes in *kana* for me. I graduated from weaving in one colour wool, through two and three colours in cotton and linen but never reached the heights of silk as we had to leave Japan. The other students graduated on weaving their first silk *obi*.

I continued to weave when I returned to the UK and took up spinning; I still correspond with my *sensei* and have exhibited at her annual exhibitions. At this class and at parties where I met Japanese wives I often heard comments that I seemed to be more of an old-fashioned Japanese than they were. Of course most of them were from Tokyo, lived in flats and used modern convenience foods, whereas I had lived in a *tatami* house and had had a middle-aged housekeeper twenty years earlier, who had taught me the old-fashioned ways of running a home. For example, I used a wooden plane to obtain *katsuobushi* (grated bonito); they used cellophane packets of *'insutanto'* flakes.

During our trips to naval bases and air stations around Japan I was left with the naval wives, many of whom did not speak English. Usually, I was asked what I would like to do while in a certain area. Due to these opportunities I was able to visit textile, ceramic and lacquer workshops all over the country, from Hokkaido to Kyushu, as well as seeing the usual tourist sites.

Mike's deep knowledge of Japanese history always enlivened our travels and the stories he told of old battles, sieges and feuds and treachery were so much more real when one could see the actual sites where they took place, stories like those of the crabs at Dannoura and the last stand of the White Tigers at Aizu Wakamatsu in the north. The arts and textiles of Japan became my passion. I was never so interested in Buddhism, or Shinto arts and sites that we visited, whereas the lives of historical persons, their homes and possessions shown in castles and museums really fascinated me.

The fact that we both spoke Japanese, ate the food and loved living in the traditional manner meant that we enjoyed our travels and were able to visit out-of-the-way places. I hope that I am making good use of my experiences by now teaching young undergraduates in England a course of Japanese Art and Design, having completed my MA dissertation on a Japanese costume subject. We still keep in contact with many friends and often have visitors from Japan. Our second son made Japanese classical literature his speciality at Oxford. He returned to Japan to attend Tokyo university (Todai) and now teaches Japanese literature at a university in America. Friends of his use our home as a base when in England, too, so our life is still enriched by our experiences of Japan.

28

Two Scientists in Japan

BILL WILLIAMSON ● CLIVE BRADLEY

BILL WILLIAMSON did two separate tours as Atomic Energy Attaché at the British Embassy. His account of his work and life in Japan is a reminder of an important facet of Anglo-Japanese relations which is sometimes over-looked:-

●

At my grammar school in the 1930s I was taught that the atom was the smallest indivisible particle. At Mingaladon outside Rangoon in 1945, I realized that I had been misinformed. Atoms were being split in the bombs which were dropped on Hiroshima and Nagasaki.

In the late 1950s I joined the United Kingdom Atomic Energy Authority (UKAEA). In 1965 I was Manager of the reactor operations school at Calder Hall and was asked to take a small team of experienced reactor operators to Japan. Our task was to assist the Japanese staff in the early operation of the Tokai-mura nuclear power station. Construction was complete and the commissioning of the station had just begun.

The Japan Atomic Power Company (JAPC) had been established in 1957. It was financed by the electricity supply utilities, the large ex-*zaibatsu* groups and the government. Its objective was the introduction of commercial nuclear power to Japan. That aim was achieved by the purchase from the British General Electric Company (GEC) of a Calder Hall-type nuclear power station.

Both contractor and purchaser of a multi-million pound project like a nuclear power plant are under considerable pressure to meet contractual targets – the contractor to avoid financial penalties and the additional costs of overrun, the purchaser to obtain as early a return as possible on his substantial investment. There were long delays at Tokai during the construction and commissioning periods, which added to the pressures on the site staff. The turnkey conditions in the contract for the sale of the plant did not help. JAPC assumed, rightly, that it was the responsibility of GEC to construct, commission and hand over a fully proven plant.

GEC expected participation by the JAPCO operational staff in the commissioning trials and run-up to full power.

After a brief introductory visit to the site, I recommended that it was in JAPC's interests to adopt the UKAEA policies, that the JAPC station superintendent should take responsibility for site safety now that the reactor had gone critical, that he should chair the commissioning committee and that his staff should take over operation of the plant during commissioning tests. But who, I was asked, would foot the bill if there were to be an incident attributed to mal-operation? I replied that GEC still had responsibility for preparation of the commissioning and operating instructions. So I was asked to return to the site to implement the regime I had advocated. This was easier said than done, but nevertheless achieved.

The delays during the commissioning of the Tokai nuclear power plant were almost entirely due to modifications to the Calder Hall Chapelcross reactor design which it had not been possible to prove in the UK. My three-month stay in Japan was extended at the request of the Japanese until the plant had been fully commissioned and licence to operate at full power had been obtained. My wife and ten-year-old daughter Jane joined me at Tokai in June 1966.

*   *   *

We lived in a brick-built two-storey house adjacent to the Tokai Club, provided by the nuclear industry to accommodate guests visiting the area for short periods. Jane attended a small school on the GEC staff compound about a mile away. A coach was provided twice weekly to enable foreign wives to shop in Mito city. In those days, however, we still needed to visit a supermarket in Tokyo to find imported foods and fresh and frozen meats which we took back to our home in Tokai in boxes of dry ice.

We used to drive to Tokyo in the elderly Toyopet kindly provided for my use by JAPCO. Our destination was the Imperial Hotel, the famous Lloyd Wright-designed hotel full of character and corridors and comfort. It had withstood the disastrous 1923 earthquake which had destroyed much of Tokyo. It was demolished shortly after we left Japan to make way for a much more economic, much less attractive high-rise building.

We discovered Akihabara, the fantastic square mile packed with shops selling all sorts of electrical goods, clocks and watches, cameras and binoculars and radio and television sets, all at prices well below those on offer in down-town Tokyo, well below, too, those of equivalent articles of much lower quality in the UK.

The JAPCO station superintendent, Yoshio Usui, asked me on one occasion what we would like to do away from the site. Perhaps I surprised him by expressing the wish to climb Mount Fuji and also to be invited to a Japanese family home. Both wishes were realized. I climbed Fuji-san accompanied by a JAPCO staff member and still have my stick, stamped at each stage and at the summit, to prove it.

The same staff member Shinsaku Takahashi invited us to his apartment to have dinner with his wife Teiko and two children. We invited them back to visit our Tokai home with its carpeted floors and Western furnishings. More invitations followed, probably at the insistence of the young Japanese wives curious to see for themselves how we lived and behaved one with another. But there were also the 'Tokai bachelors', men whose wives had remained in the family home, partly, at least, in order to ensure that the education of their children should not be interrupted.

Ultimately full power operation was attained and the final commissioning tests completed. It was time for me to go too. It was also a time to celebrate.

I had invited JAPCO and GEC staff and others to a farewell party. The others included the daughter of a local doctor who had become a friend. She and another girl arrived in a large Mercedes car. I advised them in a fatherly way of the dangers of drink and driving and suggested they leave at 10.00pm before the party became too boisterous. At 10.00pm as I accompanied them to their car, I was surprised, and a little worried to see four young men, members of the JAPCO technical department, making their way to their own car. A little later, three cars pulled up outside a bar on the main street of Mito city – the Mercedes, the car belonging to the JAPCO staff and my old Toyopet. We discussed the situation on the pavement outside the bar. I insisted that the daughter should seek her father's permission for an extension to the evening's entertainment. Eventually, I won and we went our separate ways. The following morning I was at Tokai railway station to catch the 8.31 train to Tokyo. Just as the train was about to move away, the manager of the technical department came to the door where I was standing with window down and said with a very straight face, 'She was 27, you know!'.

*　　*　　*

By 1967, on my return to Britain, seven of the nine Calder Hall-type power stations ordered by the electricity supply industry in England and Scotland had been commissioned. Their early performance and problems were monitored by a UKAEA/Central Electricity Generating Board (CEGB) Committee which met periodically in London. It was agreed that I could represent the Tokai mura nuclear power station on the committee. Annual collaboration meetings were arranged to enable physicists and engineers, employed by JAPCO, to meet their opposite numbers at Calder and Chapelcross in order to update them about developments in the nuclear industry here. I was one of the UK representatives.

When JAPCO ran into cartridge cooling pond problems at Tokai, I was asked to go to Japan to advise how similar problems had been overcome in the UK. (All nuclear power stations have cartridge cooling ponds where spent fuel, highly radioactive, is stored under some 20 ft. of water.) It was necessary to clean up the pond water and remove all the radioactivity it contained arising from corrosion of the fuel element canning material. Thereafter, I advised that the ponds be emptied and that the walls and floor be repainted under health physics control. The advice itself introduced another problem. Where was the highly active fuel to go? Discussions followed between JAPCO and UKAEA production group's commercial department. They led to the first of what were to be many reprocessing contracts and the transport of the fuel elements by sea to Windscale.

At the end of 1970, I was asked to return to Japan for a three-year tour of duty as nuclear attaché in the British Embassy. I embarked upon an intensive briefing programme which included two weeks only at a language school in London. At the end of the course I was able to say in Japanese that I had a pencil and it was a red pencil!

My wife and I spent a very busy and interesting three years in the Embassy. The nuclear power industry in Japan was growing rapidly and tremendous changes were taking place in the country as a whole. By 1971, the UK had generated more units of electricity by nuclear power than the rest of the world, including the United States, put together. Teams of UKAEA specialists visited Japan to talk with their counterparts in the Japanese nuclear research institutes about progress in the development of advanced reactor types. There was a potential customer in Japan for a commercial Advanced Gas-cooled Reactor (AGR). Sadly, the Dungeness B AGR had encountered severe design problems and its construction programme was far behind schedule.

Meanwhile, Japan had been authorized to pioneer the use of US-designed water reactors on behalf of the electricity supply utilities and had ordered a Boiling Water Reactor (BWR) power station to be built at Tsuruga. Without waiting for the results, the utilities led by Tokyo and Kansai Electric Power Companies embarked upon their own nuclear power programmes based upon BWR and Pressurized Water Reactor (PWR) power plants.

British Nuclear Fuels Ltd (BNFL) which had formerly been UKAEA production group had a commercial interest in the fuel cycle for these power plants, firstly in the conversion of natural uranium purchased by the utilities to a state and stage required for the manufacture of their fuel elements and secondly in the reprocessing of spent fuel.

The ponds at nuclear power stations are of limited capacity and reprocessing provided not only the opportunity for removal of fuel but also the return of plutonium and depleted uranium which could be reused in the manufacture of new fuel elements. Japan had a small reprocessing plant under development. When the ban on the reprocessing of nuclear fuels of American origin, imposed by the Carter administration, was lifted, BNFL negotiated a contract with JAPCO for the reprocessing of spent BWR fuel from Tsuruga.

The reprocessing contracts with BNFL enabled JAPCO to demonstrate that nuclear fuel could be transported safely in Japanese waters – a factor of considerable importance since all the Japanese nuclear power stations are coastal, all have small ports used during their construction and all therefore have the potential to move irradiated fuel by sea to their own reprocessing plant when it is built, instead of having to transport it by road or rail.

* * *

I returned from Japan in 1973. BNFL, which had been very active negotiating contracts for the reprocessing of nuclear fuel irradiated by the utilities in Japan, asked me to return to Japan in 1980 to take up for a second time the nuclear post in the embassy.

Shortly after our arrival in Tokyo, we saw on our television screens old friends from JAPCO apologizing for a nuclear incident at Tsuruga. Routine testing by the station staff had shown that there had been a small leak of radioactivity into Tsuruga Bay. The amount of activity released was negligible and harmless. The incident had been correctly reported. It nevertheless made headlines in the press and was the leading item in TV and radio news bulletins.

Investigations by JAPCO showed that 'active liquor' had found its way into a clean drainage system which discharged into the bay. The 'liquor' had come from a spillage some time earlier which had been cleaned up but not reported.

The nuclear industry in Japan cannot tolerate such adverse publicity. The company had to be punished mainly because non-reporting of the earlier incident might have resulted in loss of trust between the power station staff and the local authority. The president had to go. Senior staff were demoted by one grade. The plant was ordered to be shut down for some months with the consequent loss of generation income.

Visitors from the UK were not as frequent as those during our previous tour but they were more business-orientated. Representatives from Urenco, the Anglo-Dutch German company were promoting their enrichment service. Purpose-built ships carrying heavily shielded flasks were regular visitors to Japanese power stations picking up fuel for reprocessing in the UK and in France.

Within the embassy, I attended the weekly meeting of senior staff chaired by the ambassador. At one of the meetings I had to advise that there had been a small nuclear explosion in Tokyo. When the panic had subsided, I explained that the Japan Nuclear Forum had been distributing bags of potatoes, lightly irradiated to aid preservation, to passers-by in the Ginza. I had been offered a bag and had given half to my secretary, Jemima. She had told me that morning that the potatoes had burst during cooking. My investigations had shown that the potatoes were not at fault. It was a clear case of operator error.

In 1982 Mrs Thatcher, then British Prime Minister, who came to Tokyo for discussions with the Japanese government made an official visit to Tokai mura. This was a great success but entailed an enormous amount of preparatory work by me and my friends in JAPC and BNFL. BNFL re-routed the *Pacific Swan* to enable it to be tied up at Tokai for the visit. The President of JAPCO, Minoru Okabe, and President of the Japan Atomic Energy Research Institute, Fujinami, could not have done more to welcome Mrs Thatcher to their sites.

The end of my final tour of duty in Japan was fast approaching and appropriately it was to be the end of my career in the nuclear industry. I retired after we returned to our home in Bassenthwaite in May 1983.

*　　*　　*

We have paid two return visits to Japan since my retirement. The second in 1998 was for the closure of the gas-cooled reactor at Tokai. We were honoured to be specially invited guests for the occasion along with P.T. Fletcher and his wife. P.T. was the managing director of GEC, the company responsible for the design and construction of the plant. It was a memorable and emotional occasion. After thirty-two years' service, the reactor looked immaculate; the operators carried out an abnormally precise shut down procedure to perfection. The cherry blossoms were in full bloom; the demise of the reactor foreshadowed the fall of the flowers.

We learned that JAPCO had been given one more pioneering role. They were to decommission the plant fully in order to make the site available for yet another more modern, more economic plant.

We have had many Japanese visitors to 'Morningside' (our home in Bassenthwaite), some elderly others young and energetic, often the sons or daughters of colleagues at Tokai so many years ago.

An elderly professor came to stay with us, interested in the privatization of the electricity supply industry in this country. He came with his wife and they wished to visit a ruined church. So we took them to Sweetheart Abbey in South West Scotland, marrying them at Gretna Green on route! The name of the minister on their marriage certificate was, of course, Williamson.

Last year a young student who had stayed with us on two or three occasions came with her husband. She was on her honeymoon having been married less than seven days earlier. We enjoyed watching the wedding and the reception on the video cassette they had brought with them. It all looked very expensive and I thought sympathetically of the parents who had had to foot the bill.

CLIVE BRADLEY (Dr C.C.Bradley) was Counsellor for Science and Technology in the British Embassy in Tokyo between 1982 and 1988. The post of Science Counsellor had been established in the 1960s. It grew increasingly important as the Japanese economy expanded and Japanese research and development came to the fore. The Science and Technology Counsellor in the embassy was responsible not only for reporting on scientific and technological developments but also for promoting British science and technology. Clive Bradley provided the following account of his time in Tokyo:-

●

I spent six enjoyable and rewarding years between 1982 and 1988 as Counsellor for Science and Technology in the British Embassy in Tokyo. We lived in a Western-style house in Ichigaya, which we rented from the President of the Toyota Motor Company. Our children, nine and twelve at the outset, came with us and attended the Sacred Heart and St Mary's schools in Tokyo. Tokyo was a wonderful city for children who were safe (and perhaps too free!) to roam wherever they liked using the excellent subway system.

The Science and Technology Section consisted of six people with two seconded from the UK (myself and my first secretary). Our offices for the first four years were in the Diamond Hotel behind the embassy. Subsequently, we moved to a splendid new building in the embassy compound. Establishing a strong presence for S&T in the embassy was a priority for me and I suppose at times led to a few 'turf wars' but we were accepted at the same level as the other sections as full contributors to the embassy's burgeoning work. Through successive FCO inspections the number of S&T staff eventually reached ten in recognition of the importance of Japanese science and technology and contributions we had made and would make in the future.

In Tokyo there was a strong network of science counsellors and attachés from the different embassies and we made many close friends through this. There were regular lunches in a Roppongi restaurant to exchange views. Many Japanese individuals were invited, including on one notorious occasion a journalist who subsequently wrote in a newspaper about our 'clandestine' activities since often counsellors from the Eastern bloc countries attended as well as US military attachés.

I came from a background of government research and was seconded by my department (Trade and Industry) to the FCO. My predecessor, Graham Marshall, had been very successful particularly for his reporting of research and development in Japan's electronic industry. I decided to build on this but also to widen the coverage to other sectors. Although as government servants our main responsibility was to inform the ambassador and, through him, government departments of the latest developments in policy and broad trends in science and technology in Japan, the most rewarding work for me was direct reporting on the details of science, technology and engineering which I sought from Japanese government departments and research institutes, universities and industrial laboratories.

Starting in the 1980s Japanese technology began to make its presence felt worldwide. This was due to their ability to turn developments into real products which customers wanted. The ever-increasing large-scale integration of electronic circuits, or 'chips', was being led at that time by the Japanese, although the Americans did not take this lightly. The population of robots in Japanese factories was far outstripping those elsewhere, as was the development of opto-electronic devices (eventually sought by the US military). Foresight in the development of liquid crystal displays for computer monitors led to the revolution of the laptop and notebook PC and other portable devices. The super-computers built by NEC, Fujitsu and Mitsubishi were beginning to challenge the monopoly of the Americans like Cray. Also the world's first really true high-definition television was being developed by NHK (the Japanese equivalent of the BBC). All these and a myriad of other exciting developments had to be followed.

My discipline is physics which can cover a multitude of sins but enabled me to gain a reasonable insight into a wide range of electronics and engineering in Japan. I do however wince a little at the attempts I made to report on genetic engineering, recombinant DNA and other biosciences. However, we were concerned at the time that the level and ambition of the Japanese pharmaceutical industry was well understood in the UK so that the brightness of one of our industrial jewels might not be dimmed through superior competition as had happened to many parts of our electronic and mechanical engineering sectors. I cannot express my gratitude enough to the many Japanese individuals and companies who received visits from me and other UK people with great courtesy, always making sure that as far as possible we were satisfied. We had, of course, to extrapolate a little on the information given to us to be as up to date as possible!

Perhaps the most stimulating part of my time in Tokyo was the opportunity to brief very many leading people in politics, government and commerce who visited the embassy. By the early 1980s science and technology in Japan was already impacting on UK opinion-makers and a high proportion of visitors to the embassy requested briefing from me and my section. Also, through the efforts of my excellent Japanese staff we enabled these visitors to see at first hand the latest developments and to meet their opposites to exchange views. To build on the relationships we developed I proposed to the DTI that they should organize and support well-targeted missions to Japan containing leading experts in their fields. These missions became known as OSTEMS and they have continued to be very successful up to the present time. In return for financial support the mission members give presentations on their findings at a seminar on their return to the UK as well as producing reports for wide circulation.

As Sir Hugh Cortazzi has referred to in his book, *Japan and Back and Places Elsewhere*, an S&T agreement with Japan was very much on the agenda of the FCO in the 1980s for good diplomatic reasons as well as practical ones, but the DTI while accepting the need to develop more intensive S&T cooperation with Japan preferred multiple informal arrangements. The Japanese authorities were very keen from the beginning. The dilemma was not resolved until 1992 when an agreement was signed which placed a seal on what was already an extensive and growing body of cooperation across government, industry and academe. Another very real outcome of building relationships in the 1980s has been the decision by several Japanese companies to invest in R&D laboratories in the UK starting with Canon in 1989 and continuing with Sharp, Kobe Steel, Yamanouchi, Hitachi, Toshiba and many others.

In the period to 1985 an important embassy activity was our support to the Central Office of Information for the UK Pavilion at Expo'85 at Tsukuba which was a landmark for exhibiting the world's latest technology, by participating countries and particularly for Japan, by industrial companies. I was deputy to the British High Commissioner for Expo'85, Brian Hitch, and we had many issues small and large to deal with before this very successful UK pavilion was finally established and subsequently visited by the Emperor of Japan.

There were lighter sides (perhaps not so light at the time). One was the memorable visit four weeks after my own arrival in Tokyo of the then prime minister, (Lady) Margaret Thatcher. As part of her programme she had asked Clive Sinclair to demonstrate his pioneering PC in Japan. This was scheduled to be in the embassy prior to a dinner in honour of the Japanese prime minister. All went well until with three minutes to go the monitor (a TV in those days) went blank. Bernard Ingham whom I knew well from his Department of Energy days became very concerned with over thirty journalists and reporters covering the occasion and said that if we could not solve the problem in two minutes he would have to head off the two PMs. We tried everything without success until the Sinclair engineer realized that he had switched the TV off by accidentally pressing the remote control in his top pocket. We just made it and although the music of Mrs Thatcher's 'you see Mr Suzuki, we also make computers' was ringing in my ears I made a mental note never to be involved again in a demonstration for a prime minister.

During the same visit Mrs Thatcher was entertained at a factory near Mount Fuji belonging to Fujitsu Fanuc. This was at the time of a very strong push for inward investment in the UK. Over lunch she made the proposal to the President of Fanuc that if he built a factory to make robots in the UK, in return she would give him lunch at Number 10. I remember thinking that it would have to be an extraordinarily good lunch. We also had nervewracking moments with the visit of the Princess Royal and her then husband, Captain Mark Phillips. The lady-in-waiting (or rather her assistant) left behind the present she was due to give to the President of Fujitsu during a visit we arranged to their computer factory at Numazu, some 100kms from Tokyo – a serious matter in Japan! However, thanks to the Shinkansen the assistant was able to return to Tokyo, retrieve the present and return to Numazu in time for the traditional exchanges.

We did a great deal of entertaining at all levels to foster links which on the whole was most enjoyable. My wife Vivien, while writing out name cards for a dinner which we were giving at our house for six members of the House of Lords, complained to me that my career as a scientist had not prepared her for such matters.

I was a regular attendee at meetings and lunches held by the British Chamber of Commerce in Japan and at one event Ray Giles, the Beecham representative, and I had the idea of setting up a S&T action group for the chamber. Subsequently known as STAG this had its first meeting in my offices and became well known for a number of publications about science and technology in Japan and later the *Gaijin Scientist*.

I cannot praise enough my staff in the embassy whose work so much contributed to putting the S&T Section on the map as far as our visitors and customers in the UK were concerned. They have continued this under several of my successors. The many visitors we had were almost all very responsive, even if I had to nudge them occasionally to ask questions and listen to the answers rather than using valuable time talking of their own experiences. I believe we made a very important contribution to UK/Japan relationships and helped British industry and commerce in a very effective way.

After Tokyo I become Head of the Advisory Council on S&T in the Cabinet Office and ultimately Managing Director of Sharp's R&D company in the UK. My connections both British and Japanese made while in Tokyo were of great value in both these two changes in my career.

29

Bridging the Professions

PHILLIDA PURVIS

PHILLIDA PURVIS lived in Japan during the 1980s and experienced a number of different roles, which she describes in the following 'Reminiscences':-

•

The strength of my interest in Japan has, I believe, something to do with the fact that I lived there in three different 'roles' and developed a wide circle of friends and acquaintances in each. The Japanese take pleasure in categorization and are especially willing to be categorized according to their particular roles. They even use clothing as a tool to encourage this, with the salaryman in sombre suit and white shirt, the gardener in combat jodhpurs and *tabi* and the pregnant woman in maternity tent and ankle socks – almost from day one! I lived in Japan for nearly ten years over three periods. During each I had more than one occupation and was, I felt, categorized according to what that occupation was. In each persona I went to different places, met different people and was treated differently. Life for me as an expatriate in Japan was, therefore, unfailingly rich, varied and rewarding.

I arrived in Japan in the dual role of student and diplomat. I was attached to the British Embassy in Tokyo but spent the first year continuing my Japanese language study in the embassy language school in Kamakura. I did three home stays during the year, the first in Kofu, in Yamanashi prefecture. The only other Western foreigner there at that time was a missionary teaching English. Nothing I did went unobserved or unreported by well-wishers to my host. The local paper had advertised who this was. Running short of cash I found that no-one had heard of the Hongkong and Shanghai Bank, whose chequebook the embassy had already fixed me up with. Only the Sumitomo Bank claimed to know about credit cards and yet my Visa card did not seem to work with them. Of course my host came to hear of my quest for cash (only to buy him and his generous family gifts) and presented me with a million yen, until such time as I might repay him!

The following Easter I learnt Kyushu-*ben* in Oita, sweated it out in a mud bath and climbed a volcano. In the summer I was the only *gaijin* dancing, with my host family, in Tokushima's magnificent Awa Odori in the local jargon *odoru aho ni miru aho onaji aho nara odoranya son son*, (since you look like a fool dancing and you look like a fool watching people dance, you may as well be the fool dancing!) Although this was already the nineteen eighties I was still a novelty outside Tokyo and given a lot of attention. I was young enough to be called *ojo-san*.

Back at base I continued to study Japanese at the embassy's language school at Kamakura Yama with the wonderful teachers Ujihara, Toshishige and Haga, from conversation with whom I learned so much about Japan and Japanese thinking. I lived underneath the Ofuna-Enoshima Monorail, in the house, built as an artist's studio, at the bottom of the garden of Omura 'Roko', who had himself for years taught embassy language students.

I had no idea how to cook Japanese food; so I lived on rice and vegetables, or the cheese brought down from the embassy 'Gatehouse' shop. Cheese or bread (other than 'doorstop' white) were not to be found in Kamakura. My everyday conversational language skills improved dramatically during a six-week hospital stay, following a walking accident near the Karuizawa *besso*, holiday house of the Hongkong and Shanghai Bank. I saw what it was like to be a patient at a Japanese hospital and how keenly the Japanese medical profession dispense sachets of powdered medication.

Once at the embassy I dealt with officials mainly from MITI and the Ministry of Health and Welfare who met me with mild surprise but always treated me with avuncular kindness. A junior female diplomat was no threat but one deserving of compassion. I believe I achieved less formal and more useful relationships as a result. I am still friends with two former Chairmen of the Economic Planning Agency's Office of the Trade Ombudsman, ever since I had to represent, at one of the many meetings I attended, a British calendar exporter whose tasteful, artistic, nude models were unacceptable for Japan. All the ministry representatives, as well as the diplomats from other countries with trade complaints were always men. The Japanese were hugely embarrassed that, to demonstrate prejudice against the British calendars, which were banned from import, the complainant required me to display far more offensive and explicit material which he had found available in abundance in Shinjuku! As well as tackling these so-called non tariff barriers (NTBs) those were the days of bringing industry associations together to negotiate voluntary restraint agreements (VRAs), of promoting industrial collaboration and, of course, of welcoming the newly-fashionable ministerial visits, all of which I was involved in organizing, writing up and interpreting for.

I lived in a comfortable, centrally located flat and drove everywhere in my red sports car, with diplomatic blue plates, without ever being stopped for random police checks or letting the parking meter overrun. It was a privileged existence and, as single Western women were not then in abundance, I enjoyed more than my fair share of invitations and attention. I even met my husband to be, at the top of the Yurakucho Denki Building. Another advantage of being a relative rarity in Japan in the early nineteen eighties, before the British service sector boom a year or two later brought many British expatriates into Tokyo was of being introduced by friends from home to any Japanese they had ever met. Some of these brought me friendships which I could never on my own have made. The dearest friend, 'Tomo', of my mother's friend showed me immense generosity up until his death. He was Yoshitomo Tokugawa. His friends' kindness towards me continues to this day as if they had inherited the mantle of benefactor from him.

I left Japan for a posting in Singapore and returned, two years later, married. To all my husband's friends and contacts I was now *okusama*, wife. I was adopted by his Japanese friends to whose key player, Jiro Shirasu, he had been introduced from England. The doyenne of this circle, to whom we came to owe an enormous debt of care and hospitality, was Mrs Kazuko Aso, and its other members still remain our closest Japanese friends today.

I took up the offer of a job teaching international relations at a private university. I was elevated to *sensei* but was not permitted to test or chastise the students who all but ignored my efforts to talk about Japan's role in the world. I regularly had to endure what must be described as *seku hara* (sexual harassment) on the commuter train through Kasumigaseki during rush hour on my way to the university. Most weekends, taking advantage of the free domestic flights my husband's many business trips back to London attracted, we went to different parts of Japan by plane, or by train, and explored the remoter mountains and beaches, potteries, temples and *onsen*.

*   *   *

After two years back in London we elected to return to Japan and I became a *ryugakusei*, postgraduate foreign student at Tokyo University, on a Japanese Ministry of Education (Mombusho) scholarship, researching the development of Japan/ASEAN relations, under Professors Seizaburo Sato and Akio Watanabe. Inside the seminar rooms or outside in the canteen or Komaba campus' notorious *ryo* dormitories the students, mainly from China, Taiwan, Korea, Burma and the Philippines all had heated debates about Japanese foreign policy. Despite these being in their own language the Japanese postgraduate students contributed the least. Around us the campus was full of signs deploring Japan's proposed involvement in UN peace-keeping forces as inappropriate for a 'peace-loving' nation with a peaceful constitution. The anything but peaceful campaign swamped us at home, too, as we lived beside the Defense Agency (*Boeicho*), in Roppongi.

As well as the departmental and university libraries I spent many happy hours in the National Diet Library to which I cycled, and the convenient and comfortable International House library, preparing for *happyo* presentations or articles. Much of my focus concerned Japanese ODA (Overseas Development Aid) and I came to meet JICA (Japanese International Cooperation Agency) technical experts and a few small NGOs (Non Governmental Organization). I helped to found an international students club at Tokyo University, which created close lasting friendships for me with a Russian chemist, a Chinese physicist and another Chinese key figure in the Freedom and Democracy for China movement. At the same time I represented in Japan the main UK Gap year-out providers, GAP and Project Trust who wanted to set up in Japan. I talked to schools, hospitals and community organizations all around the country to try to find volunteering opportunities for British young people. I soon learned the Japanese overall view of voluntary work. I met some of the precious few people from voluntary organizations who knew the value of this sort of volunteering experience by young people for promoting international connections and understanding. They were beacons for me.

Tokyo at the end of the eighties was awash with expatriates. Some British wives were able to pursue their professions locally but for the most part work was not easily found. They therefore spent much of their time arranging children's play dates, attending exercise classes, planning trips to exotic destinations in the region or entertaining. At many of the parties the only Japanese faces to be seen were of the occasional Japanese girlfriend of a foreign banker; for the rest there was little difference from a London drinks party. I knew myself to be lucky to have learned Japanese and to have a wide circle of Japanese friends and an occupation.

My other major persona at this time was as *oba-san*, mother. This was most clearly defined at the local ward-run play-school (*hoikuen*) which my children attended. I tried hard to conform, never failing to write a notice of their temperatures, ablutions, food-intake and bedtimes, putting them into the right nappies (*nuno*), embroidering pictures of their appropriate groups (*gumi*) and apologizing hard for the disruption my children caused when they could not sleep during nap-time (*hiru-ne*), as they had been to bed at 7pm, up to four hours earlier than their classmates. I have also had the ultimate experience of Japan for a *gaijin* woman – I have attended ante-natal check-ups and given birth, unrelieved of pain, in two different Tokyo hospitals. This was the most unifying experience for British women in Japan.

These various incarnations in Japan have shown me so many of the good things of the country. I have friends of every age, from many parts of Japan and from every walk of life – literally the princess to the pauper, the suicidal road-sweeper, the blue-contact lens-wearing hairdresser, the concert pianist, the priest, the politician, the old country doctor, the Ka-buki actor, the alcoholic, the forklift-truck driver, the kamikaze pilot. It is a wider spectrum than I know at home. Japan is my home from home, and yet it never ceases to surprise me.

30

From Diplomacy to Commerce and Back

MERRICK BAKER-BATES

MERRICK BAKER-BATES was first a diplomatic service language student in Japan. He later became Commercial Counsellor. He then transferred to commerce for four years before returning to the diplomatic service. His last post was Consul General in Los Angeles. Here he describes his various lives in Japan:

•

In August 1963, about half way through a New Entrants course at the Foreign Office, I was summoned to the Personnel Department and invited to acquire a hard language. This, I learned later, was a way of sparing young married men the struggle for existence in the London area on a salary of £725 a year before tax. The languages on offer were Chinese, Arabic, Amharic, Persian and Japanese. China at that stage of the Cold War sounded grim. I did not fancy spending most of my time reading between the lines of the *People's Daily*, punctuated by picnics at the Great Wall. As for Arabic, I had already heard about the rigours of the Middle East Centre for Arabic Studies (MECAS) and was wary of a return to a boarding school atmosphere, albeit in the mountains overlooking Beirut. Amharic I had never heard of, despite an expensive education; and I knew next to nothing about Persia. So, *faute de mieux* and not wanting to sound negative, I opted for Japanese.

It was a leap into the dark. I was ignorant about the country and my aptitude for languages, beyond some conversational French, was unproven. Nonetheless, a couple of years of language study sounded agreeable enough: no school was involved, the teachers came to one's house and I was assured that there would be plenty of opportunity to explore the country. A few days later I received a letter confirming that I had been 'selected' as a student of Japanese and was to proceed to Tokyo by the 'Approved Route'. I was just twenty-four and had been married four months.

That 'Approved Route' turned out to be a memorable five-week voyage with my new wife aboard the P & O liner *Chusan*. We were a group of six from the FO, two married couples and two bachelors. Before long we enjoyed a little celebrity for our prowess at the weekly quiz. Absorbed in the excitement of immediate surroundings I gave little thought to Japan. In Singapore, however, picking up a copy of *The Times* I saw an article, which to an aspiring student of Things Japanese made dispiriting reading.'Tokyo rebuffs' the correspondent complained, 'the first impression is one of overwhelming ugliness. In endlessly monotonous vistas, unmemorable buildings crouch under a sky scarred by a grid of overhead cable. . . . In the caverns of the largest city in the world there is a terrible and deadening failure to communicate. Tokyo, furiously flourishing, with all its raucous vitality and avidly eclectic enthusiasms, still stonily withholds itself from alien apperception.' Worse, I read that those foreigners whom I was soon to join suffered from feelings of vulnerable isolation and were divided into obscurantists or haters – obscurantists in order to enhance, with the myth of the 'real Japan', their own uncertain status; and haters because they were trapped.'I float and drift as my grip on reality is insidiously prized loose', the writer concluded, 'Europe is unimaginably far away'. If that interpretation was correct, I reflected, I would have to shut my eyes and think of England pretty often.

*   *   *

First impressions were far from favourable. Arriving in late October, we were driven away from the quayside at Yokohama in pouring rain over bumpy roads, picking our way around seemingly endless roadworks and always surrounded by dense, anarchic, traffic. The gardens and teahouses of the guidebooks were not on our route. The Sanbancho Hotel, home for our first few weeks in Tokyo, catered almost exclusively for foreigners in what I came to realize was the efficient, sanitized, American way – eggs over easy, squeezy bread rolls, plenty of iced water and not a chopstick in sight. Moreover, getting around without a word of Japanese in a city, which was almost totally unplanned and had no detailed map which we could read, was obviously going to be a challenge.

We had only one Japanese contact in Tokyo, a telephone number provided by a friend in London who explained that his godmother was Japanese and liked to meet British visitors. I put the name of Mrs K Aso into my address book without further thought. A few days after our arrival I telephoned to ask if Chrystal and I might call to introduce ourselves. After just managing to make myself understood to the first person who answered, I was greeted by a second voice in perfect, almost cut-glass, English. Evidently this was The Godmother. I explained my connection and she kindly invited us to tea. Having as yet no car of our own, and not daring to try a taxi, we asked if an Embassy car could take us to an address in Shibuya. Expecting a kimono-clad lady in a wood and paper house, we were amazed to find ourselves deposited in front of what appeared to be a stockbroker Tudor mansion.

The Godmother, looking chic in Parisian style, was warmly welcoming. She gave us tea and cakes and told us to make sure that we joined the Japan-British Society. She exuded an air of affable authority, which ensured compliance with her wishes, and, of course, we joined. It was only a week or two later, on mentioning this visit to someone at the embassy, that I realized we had spent an hour in the company of Mrs Kazuko Aso, *the* Mrs Aso as I was told by a colleague, daughter of the former Prime Minister Shigeru Yoshida, political hostess, internationalist, anglophile and one of the most remarkable Japanese of her generation. After that we met her quite regularly 'BB-sans' she always called us, and we enjoyed several amusing experiences together. But that tea with Mrs Aso taught me something, blindingly obvious in retrospect, that had not been mentioned on our New Entrants' Course: never instigate a meeting knowing nothing of the person to be encountered.

*   *   *

We had to grapple with the language at once. After all, I had only two years to learn almost as much about their language as the Japanese did during basic education. The embassy's senior language teacher, Mr Nakazato, arrived at the hotel to give my first lesson. He said nothing on the way up to my room in the lift. We settled into chairs facing each other.

'My name is Nakazato', he said.

'How do you do?'

'Watakushi wa Nakazato desu. Anata no namae wa nan desu ka?'

'Sorry?'

'No English please. *Anata no namae wa nan desu ka?'*

He never spoke to me ever again in English. It took what seemed an age, I think about ten minutes, to realize, after he had put the same question a dozen times or more with gestures, that he was expecting me to reply *Watakushi wa Baker-Bates desu'.* This first effort in Japanese was greeted with a smile and *'yoroshi'*, which I took to be some form of OK. After that, the lesson moved slowly and painfully forward to other topics: my nationality, my profession, my wife and our families etc.

That first encounter with the Japanese language lasted three hours. My head throbbed: I was totally exhausted, as much by my teacher's energy and enthusiasm as by the realization that I faced two years of very hard grind. As he was about to leave, Nakazato-san produced two pieces of paper on which were written the phonetic syllabaries of *katakana* and *hiragana*, with their pronunciation in Roman letters. I guessed that he expected me to be able to read them by the next lesson in forty-eight hours' time. Aptitude for languages? I groaned inwardly. Europe seemed unimaginably far away.

Once our Ford Cortina with its reinforced suspension and sump protector had arrived (somewhat pretentiously painted in 'ambassador blue'), we ventured onto the Japanese road system – or rather lack of system. Our first trip was to Hakone some sixty miles from Tokyo. Encountering a traffic jam of seemingly endless proportions on the outskirts of Odawara we decided to break the journey and take a look at the spectacular castle. It turned out to be a reconstruction, built only three years earlier and containing displays of cameras, transistor radios and chewing gum.

The scenery at Hakone was certainly more memorable, but the struggle to get there, or anywhere outside Tokyo, on narrow overcrowded roads was a deterrent to sightseeing. In the film *You Only Live Twice*, which had its premiere in Tokyo, James Bond nonchalantly jumps into his sports car declaring that he will be in Osaka within four hours. That brought a guffaw from the audience. More likely the journey down the Tokaido would take a couple of days. Rail was the sensible way to travel. Even as late as 1980, when a considerable number of high-speed roads had already been built, the Japan National Tourist Organization's official handbook still guided the foreign traveller around the country by train. Our first long trip by train was on the *Matsukaze* express down the Japan Sea coast to Karatsu in Kyushu. We soon realized that foreigners were regarded with uninhibited curiosity and were always assumed to be Americans. Our fellow passengers seemed to have no qualms about squeezing in beside us for photographs, commenting on my blue eyes and stroking my then flaming red hair – the colour of devils as I later discovered. When it was hot the men carefully removed their trousers, hung them over the luggage rack to preserve the creases and sat cross-legged in their *sutekeko* cotton pants.

*   *   *

The embassy found us a house in Akasaka in a quiet side street. In the background, however, was the round-the-clock construction of the Akasaka Mitsuke overpass. And in the distance loomed the Hotel New Otani nearing completion. Next door lived a well-known kabuki actor in a large and beautiful Japanese-style house. We did not rub shoulders with him or indeed any other neighbour. After a few weeks I began to get restless. Our Japanese conversation continued to make slow and painful progress, largely because outside the lessons we had very little opportunity to practise.

On the day that Cassius Clay knocked out Sonny Liston, I consulted Nakazato-san. He made two recommendations; move to the suburbs and take the plunge into a bathhouse. Those were the places to meet people and chat. Getting out of our lease and finding new quarters would take time, so one afternoon I tried the option of the bathhouse. For a government regulated fee of ¥23 I was able to get what felt like a good scalding in a huge tub, under the benevolent gaze of the natives. On my third visit I met Ryuichi Yano, a first year student at Nihon University whose father ran a hardware store in Hitotsugi dori. Afterwards Chrystal made us supper. Although he spoke no English somehow we conversed far into the night. I thought the dictionary would fall to pieces. Later, he introduced us to his friends. We explored Tokyo and travelled together outside. Confidence grew as a new world began to open up to us.

Through an advertisement in the *Japan Times* we found a house in the suburb of Shimouma, owned by a retired German engineer who had lived in Japan continuously since 1927 and wanted to spend a year in Europe. The house had three small *tatami* rooms and a delightful wooden bathtub, but no mains sewerage. We were connected to the 'honey cart' once a week, manned by two cheerful fellows with a tennis ball on the end of their suction tube. Herr Muller's housekeeper decided to return to the country but not before introducing Mrs Gotoh, a friend who would do our washing in the bathtub and some other household chores. Within a couple of weeks, however, Mrs Gotoh had resigned. As consolation before she left, she presented us with a second-hand washing machine.

Down the road, introduced by Mrs Gotoh, we rented a garage. Finding the car washed by an unknown hand, Chrystal repaid the compliment with a Victoria sponge cake and took it round. A nineteen-year-old student turned out to be the car-washer. He lived with his family and the twenty-odd students who lodged with them. I took to having breakfast with Hisao and his family once a week sitting around the *kotatsu* (foot warmer). Conversation (using that, by now very battered, dictionary) started to bubble merrily. Through Hisao we met the neighbours. Far from the Japanese stonily withholding themselves from alien apperception, as *The Times* correspondent had claimed, my wife and I found that we were constantly in and out of our neighbours' houses and they were regular visitors to ours. Chrystal taught English to small groups of students. In return she learned some of the intricacies of Japanese housewifery, papering *shoji*, squeezing *nigiri*, beating *tatami* and sewing *futon*. Before the arrival of a gas boiler we burned refuse to heat the bath. I took up mah-jongg, becoming a devotee and often playing into the small hours.

Against this domestic background our lessons continued, six hours a day, five days a week with four different teachers. We visited the embassy infrequently, to collect mail or occasionally to make a spot check on the monthly accounts or 'weed' unnecessary papers from old files before they were returned to the archives in London. On one occasion my eye fell on a draft despatch of some ten years earlier, the work of one of my now senior colleagues. Through the entire text the ambassador had drawn lines in red ink with the comment: 'This is an example of how *not* to draft a despatch, please speak'. Letting bygones be bygones, I stuck it in the shredder.

Every three months or so I acted for a week as Duty Officer, dealing among other things with urgent telegrams arriving outside office hours. My first 'Emergency' telegram appeared at about 2am and as I drove in to receive it from the Communications Officer I speculated about what could be the purport of a message deemed so urgent that it had to be deciphered and read within an hour in the middle of the night. There was a sense of apprehension as I turned the dials on the lock of the strongroom door, being careful – as I had been warned – not to leave fingerprints on the numbers in case potential spies could thereby break the combination. I never understood how that was regarded as a serious possibility. The telegram, however, was an anti-climax. It was from our embassy in Teheran and concerned the type of hat to be worn by Princess Alexandra (who was then in Tokyo) when she met the Empress of Iran in a few days' time.

The embassy was built to impress. Within its eight-acre compound, on the site of a park formerly belonging to the Tokugawa family, were thirteen houses and the Chancery all built in the early 1930s in a style described as concrete Queen Anne and allegedly earthquake proof. As if in deference to Britannia's requirement for peace and quiet, the rattling city tram crossed the road in front of the embassy returning to resume its normal course once past the outer walls. It was replaced by a bus shortly after we arrived which motored resolutely straight past the gates. Having been spared bombing during the war, the embassy was, from a distance, a sight on the itinerary of tourist buses. We paid a peppercorn rent of six silver yen agreed in perpetuity in the late nineteenth century. At the prevailing rate of exchange this amounted to around £16.00 a year. As Tokyo land prices soared in the 1960s there were complaints in the Diet about our privileged status until a revised, but still very reasonable, formula for calculating the rent was agreed in the 1960s.

One Sunday, permission was given to shoot a scene for Cary Grant's latest film *Walk, Don't Run*. Grant played a businessman in a hurry who had lost his passport. Bounding up the steps in quest of a replacement, he was accosted by a Chancery Guard.

'Important business: I need to see the ambassador.'

'So do I,' replied the guard, 'and I've been here two years.'

There was more than a grain of truth in this exchange. The ambassador worked in cloistered calm at his residence. He travelled about in his black Rolls-Royce Phantom motorcar flying the Union flag. During the hot summer months he decamped in this vehicle, like some latter-day colonial governor, to Lake Chuzenji over three hours away in the mountains. Official papers were taken up at regular intervals. In Tokyo the ambassador presided in the only suite of offices benefiting from air-conditioning. Other buildings were served with electric fans. In deference to the heat, the office closed on Wednesday afternoons during the midsummer period. Until 1968, however, the residence did not boast a shower, this being regarded as an unnecessary luxury by the representative of the Ministry of Works.

Inside the compound the atmosphere was friendly but often formal. Some people still occasionally wore black jackets and pin-striped trousers. Paper being an important tool of the diplomat's trade, there was a bewildering array to use. The ambassador wrote in red ink on blue paper. He was addressed in writing as HE and always on blue paper. Lesser mortals wrote on white of various sizes depending on the nature of the communication. There was airmail paper of many shapes and colours for the diplomatic bag. There was paper for draft letters and draft telegrams. But incoming telegrams as well as those outgoing were retyped on different coloured paper. Someone discovered a cache of 18,000 sheets of mourning paper left over from the death of King George VI. In the interests of economy and not anticipating the demise of a monarch for many years, we cut off the black edges. The Royal Arms were emblazoned on almost everything, a subconscious reminder that we held our appointments at Her Majesty's pleasure. Even the toilet paper – very British Bronco – had the words 'Government Property' stamped clearly on every sheet. There was no forgetting our employer even in the most intimate of circumstances.

We had only a hazy idea of our role at embassy functions. Arriving at one of our first receptions at the residence to greet the ambassador and his wife, we moved away hand-in-hand. 'NOT together!' cried the ambassador's wife, directing me towards the ballroom and Chrystal to the drawing-room. Not long afterwards at a reception for the Foreign Secretary R.A. Butler, language students were detailed to accost guests and escort them to the receiving line. Each had to be introduced loud and clear. A Japanese man entered looking nervously around. Eagerly I bore down upon him. Despite his unwillingness, I managed to drag out his name and bring him to the receiving line where the Foreign Secretary, the ambassador and his wife were waiting. 'Mr Watanabe,' I bawled and retreated. He passed down the line shaking hands sheepishly. He was introduced to the Minister, steered towards a Counsellor for a few words, thence to a First Secretary and finally to the bar set up at the back of the ballroom. He did not need a drink. He turned out to be the Japanese Foreign Minister's chauffeur who had come to find his car ticket.

After dinners, ladies were invariably invited to retire upstairs by the hostess whilst the men smoked and drank port. No member of staff could leave until all guests had departed. And there was always a certain nervousness about whether the guests would actually arrive. Japanese ladies seemed prone to 'colds' all the year round, which often prevented attendance at the last moment. Second helpings at the Ambassador's table had to be taken with care. On one occasion we had enjoyed a chocolate mousse in the shape of Mount Fuji, surrounded by its five lakes of blue sugar on which perched small chocolate boats. Greedily I dug in for a second time only to realize too late that out of the thirty-odd diners I was the only person to have done so. As my spoon and fork rapidly worked on the mousse, silence fell upon the room. Suddenly, the ambassador intervened: 'When you're ready, Merrick, we'll move into the next room.'

*   *   *

During the 1960s the Foreign Office and the Board of Trade began to lay greater emphasis on the role of embassies in promoting British exports. In Tokyo this change was symbolized in the disappearance in 1965 of the ambassador's tennis court and its replacement by a prefabricated building to house the Consulate and Commercial Department. This structure cost some £20,000 and was supposed to last at most five years. Before long commercial work expanded to take over the whole building, which by the time I returned for my second tour in 1976 had been weakened by earthquakes and was a distinct hazard. In winter our offices were heated by electric fires and during earthquakes the plugs gave off sparks as they moved in their sockets. Eventually, after a life of over twenty years, the prefab disappeared to make way for a new and elegant building.

As a First Secretary in the Commercial Department and later as Commercial Counsellor, I knew that trade and investment lay at the heart of the Anglo-Japanese relationship. Our job as diplomats-in-trade was to introduce British businessmen to commercial opportunities in the Tokyo area and, strongly supported by our Japanese colleagues, we were good at it. Despite what one sometimes read in the newspapers about diplomats being out of touch, in Japan at least our export promotion work was much appreciated by the overwhelming majority of the British businessmen. Many came to Japan in a sceptical or suspicious mood. I like to think that we in the Commercial Department, most of whom had been language students and spent some years in Japan, helped to allay those feelings. We had to steer a careful course between understanding and interpreting the Japanese and not appearing to be too much influenced by them. However, criticism, sometimes ill-informed, was often just around the corner. After I bought a Honda Accord, a visiting MP wrote to the President of the Board of Trade to demand that I should drive British. The ambassador had to point out that the only new British cars then meeting

Japanese specifications were Rolls-Royce, Bentley, Jaguar or Lotus. A
First Secretary could only drive what he could afford.

*   *   *

The drawback of being a diplomat-in-trade was that one was only an
adviser not an active player in the commercial game. We could take the
horses to the waters of the Japanese market, but getting them to drink
deeply for the long term was a much more difficult proposition. I wanted
to get involved with business, rather than simply be a facilitator. And I
wanted to work with Japanese on a more equal footing than was possible
in the hierarchical atmosphere of an embassy.

My opportunity came when I was asked in 1981 to become the General
Manager of Cornes and Company, an old established trading house in
Tokyo owned by the Wheelock Marden Group in Hong Kong. The
Chairman was Peter Hewett, an Englishman who had lived in Japan since
1947 and made his fortune trading in a wide variety of products ranging
from Rolls-Royce motor cars to Marmite. I spent a month sitting at the
feet of this remarkable entrepreneur. He smoked about sixty cigarettes
and drank the best part of a bottle of John Begg whisky each day amusing
me with his witty and often penetrating comments on business, politics
and the personalities around him. Peter left for six weeks' leave in Britain
and Ireland. Sadly, within a month he was dead at the age of sixty-three.

The new Chairman was Tatsuo Takahara, known to all as TT. A former
purser in the Japanese Imperial Navy with a penchant for palmistry, TT
had joined the company shortly after the war and had built up the Insurance Department as its main profit centre. A much-respected figure in
the London insurance market who had been awarded an Honorary OBE,
Takahara had observed Peter Hewett's idiosyncratic management style
over the years and to some extent modelled his own upon it. Both men
ran the company as if it were a personal fief.

With my background of Civil Service parsimony, I took some time to
grasp that it was acceptable to spend money in order to make it. We
spent ¥20 million on Peter Hewett's memorial service in Tokyo and when
I ventured to query the need for that amount of ostentation, TT cut me
short with a characteristic wave of his hand: 'Merrick, our customers will
be there and watching us.' As General Manager I had to authorize expenditure. I found it refreshing that we could buy equipment, travel abroad
on business and invest large sums in new ventures without the need for
bureaucratic submissions, which had been such a feature of life on public
money in the Diplomatic Service. So long as the company made money –
and those were the boom days of the 1980s – there was no reason to stint.

I was surprised to discover that our business at Cornes was hardly affected by the notorious Japanese trade barriers so widely publicized in

Britain and become such a feature of the embassy's work with the Japanese Government. The reason was that over many years the company had adapted to the environment in which it traded, complying with, and not complaining about, the often pettifogging regulations and making sure that its principals abroad knew what to do. Besides cars and consumer goods, we sold agricultural machinery, defence equipment and high technology products of all kinds. Being a comparative minnow on the Japanese trading scene (albeit a company with several hundred employees), Cornes was not seen as a threat to the *sogo shosha* (general trading companies such as Mitsui and Co. and Mitsubishi Corporation); so we were able, like those birds which live on the backs of the rhinoceros, to profit by our relationship with them and frequently collaborated on business ventures. We were aiming at the niche markets and that approach paid handsomely.

Some in the company could not understand why I had left the highly esteemed (in Japan) bureaucracy to join the murky world of commerce and with a smallish firm like Cornes. Besides the fun of making money, the main attraction lay in the greater understanding of the Japanese character and way of thinking which my move made possible. This was particularly so in the case of Gestetner (Japan), our joint venture partner, where we were confronting a very difficult market and fighting to survive. Before joining Cornes for an unofficial secondment of four years, I consulted Sir John Figgess, a former diplomat and at that time director of Christie's. He encouraged me to take the plunge, but warned that I might not sleep so well at nights. There was certainly some truth in that. We worked a sixteen-hour day and I had no superiors to carry the can for me. But the compensation was getting to know my colleagues in a way not normally open to foreigners in Japan and in learning an enormous amount from them. The word teamwork acquired a new dimension. We were allies in the struggle to sell and survive which brought me to understand the pressures inherent in their daily lives and greatly to admire their dedication to the job and the ingenuity with which they carried it out. I learned, too, that one did not sell products in Japan so much as persuade one's customers to buy. Personal relationships and personal service were paramount, that much I knew from my days in the embassy. But the extent to which we took those commitments was a revelation. Many books have been written about the secrets of Japanese success in those days. My experience with Cornes and Gestetner showed me that there were four essential ingredients: the high standard of education, the work ethic, low interest rates and an infinite capacity for taking pains.

Those four years in the private sector were undoubtedly the most stimulating and interesting of my working life, not least because my job and those of my colleagues depended largely on the outcome of my efforts. I had more direct responsibility than most British civil servants ever have and I was stretched to the limit both mentally and physically. In the course of that experience I became emotionally involved with Japan and its people in a way that I had not thought possible. I do not think that I went native – the diplomat's ultimate nightmare. But I proved, to my own satisfaction at least, that Japan did not rebuff those who really wanted to understand its heart.

'So, why on earth did you come back to the Service?', asked, the man who signed me on again at the Foreign Office in January 1986. 'Don't you miss your Rolls?' Sometimes, saddling up for the next cocktail party or re-drafting another submission, I had regrets about pulling up my roots in Japanese business. But, no, I did not miss the Rolls.

31

'Early Days in the Kansai'

SYDNEY GIFFARD

SYDNEY GIFFARD (Sir Sydney Giffard, British Ambassador to Japan 1984-86), after completing his time as a language student, was sent to the Kansai to gain experience as a Vice-Consul. In the following piece he describes life in the Kansai at that time:-

•

Early days for me, I mean, in the Kansai. For the Kansai as a centre of powerful interests, capable in combination of exerting a compelling influence on national policies, in 1953 time was already running out. Osaka was still host to the head offices of major banks, industrial corporations and newspapers of national importance; and Kobe was, as it remains, despite the city's recent, tragic, natural disaster, one of the best endowed deep-water ports in Asia. But the progressive centralization in Tokyo of all the machinery of government administration, of decision-making at every level, was already beginning to seem inevitable. The pride of Kansai people and institutions was sensitive to this process, but it did not diminish the constructive energies of the leaders of society in the region, many of whom played most distinguished parts in Japan's postwar reconstruction.

These great men (great women were rarely visible, though there was abundant evidence of matriarchal power) were often good enough to make themselves easily accessible, even to a mere vice-consul. The days of the director's limousine were not yet, and one would meet chairmen and presidents on the morning train, especially if one commuted on the Hankyu line, rather than on the Hanshin or the *Kokutetsu* (JNR). When we lived in Mikage (which we did after a short time in Kitano-cho in Kobe, looking out over the harbour from a house arguably qualifying as an original *Ijin-kan* (foreigner's house)), we were close neighbours of two very eminent business leaders, both as it happened also prominent in the Japan-British Society of the Kansai. Their hospitality was as instructive and enjoyable as it was generous and both personally and professionally rewarding. Others were to be met at an informal luncheon club, on Thursdays, in the Gas Building on the Midosuji in Osaka. It was a privilege to have the opportunity to enjoy the company of so many interesting people, in relaxed circumstances. (I have always had the impression that pedestrians walk more casually and slowly along the street in Osaka than they do in Tokyo.)

Life was fairly easy-going also because our offices, both in Kobe and in Osaka, were staffed generously, certainly by today's standards. The gradual shift of emphasis from Kobe to Osaka was criticized by some members of the British community, the majority of whose interests, and lives, were centred in Kobe. The three British banks (Hongkong & Shanghai, Standard Chartered and Mercantile) were strongly established in both cities, but the shipping and trading interests were more thinly represented in Osaka. Two of the British concerns with substantial numbers of expatriate staff (how times change) were Dunlop and Lloyds Register of Shipping. While most leaders of the European communities, like their Japanese hosts, lived in the steep residential districts overlooking Osaka Bay between Kobe and Osaka, there was a sizeable foreign enclave in the James Estate, at Shioya, to the West of Kobe. Occasional fancy-dress balls were held there, and some European consuls would celebrate their national days at the Shioya Country Club. I always expected to meet Davidson and Sadie Thompson there, or even Maugham himself. The Kobe Club was a fairly exclusive affair, the Kobe Regatta and Athletic Club (KRAC) less so, The King's Arms not at all. At the KRAC, cricket, soccer, hockey and baseball were in competition with the swimming-pool. For tennis, one was likely to be invited to the newly-installed all-weather court at the Mercantile bank manager's house at Shukugawa, with curry and pink gins giving its true meaning to the weekend.

With any luck, on one or two Saturdays or Sundays every month, one could visit Kyoto or Nara, and the chance to become more than superficially acquainted with temples and shrines, palaces and gardens, hills and rivers, villas and museums and their endlessly fascinating collections of paintings, sculpture and porcelain must rank as the outstanding advantage of a posting to Osaka/Kobe, since nothing remotely comparable would be found anywhere else. Nearer to home, if one lived in Mikage, was the Hakutsuru Museum, offering in small compass a superb introduction to the fine arts of China and Japan. Intrigued by a small cup of early Tang silver, with a hunting scene chased round the exterior, I asked the curator whether it was unique. He said there was one other companion piece, in the British Museum. But, he added, they tended to polish it, so it would not last for ever.

Despite the proximity of these treats, and although, as already noted, we were not under strength, there was plenty of work to be done. HM Consulate-General Osaka/Kobe, as we became, was charged with the representation of the interests of some other Commonwealth countries, besides our own. There was a good deal of consular work, especially in connection with shipping, with which the Honorary Consul in Moji assisted. Commercial work was beginning to take its modern form, and was at this time particularly concerned with the promotion of a constructive relationship between the British and Japanese textile and pottery industries, chiefly in regard to design. There was enough scope for information work to absorb any spare capacity, in pursuit of contacts with the national and local press, in meeting the requests of English-speaking societies in schools and universities, in helping to service the Japan-British and the Cambridge and Oxford societies of the Kansai, and in the projection of wider British interests and objectives generally. The cultivation of acquaintance with distinguished Japanese industrialists, academics, officials and journalists led to rewarding and lasting friendships. I do not mention names here, not so much from a sense of piety as because they come flooding into the mind in unmanageable volume. So even Dennis Enright and the Japanese Chairman, Yujiro Iwai, who had the imagination to lead Konan *Daigaku* (university) to invite him to take up a residential appointment, must now remain anonymous.

The demands of the working day precluded all, except sometimes the Consul-General himself, who was able to invite guests to his house in Shukugawa, from returning home for lunch. Apart from occasions at the Gas Building, we enjoyed the choice of numerous simple Japanese restaurants, including one in the precincts of a nearby temple, where vegetarian dishes of great delicacy were served in a cool *tatami* room, shut away from the street noise. Very rarely, one could afford to go to a barge-restaurant, moored off the Nakanoshima, for oysters.

The New Osaka Hotel, of genuinely recent construction, also provided an easy refuge. One lunchtime, I joined half the population of the city there, to gaze at Marilyn Monroe and Joe Di Maggio as they walked very slowly through the lounge for our benefit. We were like minnows watching two great white whales. After work, one was seldom tempted to spend the evening in Osaka. Exceptions were when it was possible to obtain tickets for the *Bunraku* theatre, where we were extremely lucky to have seen unforgettable performances by Yoshida Bungoro, almost blind towards the end of his career, as perhaps the greatest principal puppet-operator of all time, unfailingly capable of moving an audience to tears.

A factor which kept us busy was the need to carry home leave. With three months due after a tour of duty of two-and-a-half years, if one travelled by cargo-passenger ship, the whole business could take six months. When I first went home, I asked a contemporary friend, who had gone into the Treasury, whether it was sound economics, to pay us to do nothing for quite so long, on the grounds that the air fare would be more expensive. 'In our view', he said, 'you chaps don't do much anyway.' In fact, these voyages, of which I enjoyed three each way, enabled one to gain some knowledge of other countries. Besides, how else would one have found the time for a really concentrated reading of Waley and Sansom ? The system also enlarged one's professional skills, since the long absences of colleagues meant that every vice consul had to be able to play in any position on the field. The locally-engaged staff, both Japanese and British manfully underpinned the long learning process.

A certain gentle pressure of work, added to the pressing attractions of Kyoto and Nara, militated against longer and more distant expeditions. We did get to Miyajima and to Ama-no-Hashidate, to Hikone and Kura-shiki, to Ise, Kashikojima and Nagoya. But all the marvels of Kyushu, and most of the Japan Sea coast had to wait for later years. I was sent to the old naval base at Maizuru one January, because there was a rumour that a Red Cross ship bringing prisoners of war and civilians detained in the Soviet Union since 1945 had picked up a solitary Briton. So far as I could discover, when the ship docked at five o'clock on the coldest morning I have ever experienced, there was no such person. But scenes on the quay were memorable. Banners held by representatives from every prefecture provided rallying points for the reception of the repatriated mass of bewildered people. I recall vividly the sight of two very old men, brothers I supposed, dancing together in the joy of being reunited at last.

I also had the good fortune to visit the four capital cities of the prefectures of Shikoku, in preparation for a tour by the ambassador, and then again accompanying him. My clearest recollections are of the castle at Matsuyama, with Governor H., directly descended from the former *daimyo*; of the Ritsurin *Koen* (park) in Takamatsu; of the Sansuien at Kochi, which ranked for me with the great Japanese inns of Kyoto; and of the beautiful, wild mountains and valleys of the island's interior, and their jade-green rivers. Crossing the Inland Sea on return from my first visit, I was puzzled by the appearance of a number of what seemed to be new islands. These proved to be huge piles of debris, the shattered components of several villages in Wakayama Prefecture, which had been devastated by a typhoon, their remains washed down by the floods.

Among the people of Shikoku, I never sensed the strange undercurrent of violence which the novelist and Nobel Prize winner Kenzaburo Oe has evidently experienced. Nor did I ever detect feelings of hostility towards foreigners anywhere in the Kinki District. The only occasion in that period when I felt less than welcome was, unsurprisingly, when I chose to wander alone one evening through the streets of Hiroshima. For daily life in the main residential area between Osaka and Kobe, centred on Ashiya, one was provided with a description by Junichiro Tanizaki, in 'The Makioka Sisters', which is in my view the greatest of his novels. The Makioka family are the lasting representatives of the Kansai, in life as in literature.

Soon after I was posted back to Tokyo, I received a message that a highly distinguished banker,who had been one of the most senior figures to participate in the lunches at the Gas Building, wished to call at my house. I could think only that this unexpected request might have to do with the introduction of some young person who might wish, for example, to practise his or her English. But, on arrival, my visitor explained that he had been asked to make a discreet enquiry about the possibility of a visit to London by the Foreign Minister of Japan. The government thought it was time that the first postwar visit of this kind should take place, but was anxious that a formal proposal should await an intimation that it would be welcome. So, as soon as my caller had left, apparently content that the insistence on confidentiality was understood, I hastened to report to the ambassador, who at once despatched a telegram to put the idea into operation. He was so clearly not surprised as to leave me wondering if he had been expecting the approach. The contriving of discreet enquiries was a fine art in Japan.

It was all long ago. I have considered how best to mark the distance in time. To return to the point of departure of this note, it was in the summer of 1953 that an armistice was at last concluded in Korea. HMS *Belfast*, now for many years dedicated to the reception and instruction of civilian visitors, at her final mooring on the Thames in London, paid an official visit to Kobe. Another way of illustrating the gap is to recall that, if one planned to motor from Kanto to Kansai in those days, it was as well to allocate three mornings and three long afternoons of driving time, and to spend two nights en route, the first probably in Shizuoka and the second preferably at the Gamagori Hotel, then still one of the five outstandingly enjoyable Meiji/Victorian hotels in Japan. Much has changed, but some impressions and sentiments have not, and affection for people and places discovered in the Kansai in the early nineteen fifties is among the latter, as others have confirmed to me. Memories cause one to reflect on the nature and purposes of diplomacy as a career. It is not all instant noodles.

32

The Reactions of Two Young
Language Students in the 1950s

DICK ELLINGWORTH • BRIAN HITCH

THE PRE-WAR Japan Consular Service sent selected new entrants each year to study Japanese. As a result, a corps of Japanese-speaking consuls was created. The Foreign Office realized that Japanese-speaking officers would be needed after the war in the embassy, and in consular posts in Japan and as soon as circumstances permitted the practice of sending out each year young diplomats to study the language was revived. The first of these was Peter Westlake (the Rev. Peter Westlake, CMG, MC) whom I succeeded in late 1951 in the United Kingdom Liaison Mission to SCAP (in 1952, after the entry into force of the Peace Treaty, the British Embassy).

I was not a language student as I had obtained a degree in Japanese from SOAS before entering the Foreign Service in 1949. The Foreign Office, rightly or wrongly, did not think that I needed further language training although I was forced to pass all the Civil Service Japanese language examinations. At my final interview at the Civil Service Commission before I was eventually accepted for the Foreign Service I recall that I was told that the Foreign Office were not interested in any knowledge of Japanese I might have acquired as they preferred to train their own staff!

The next two language students were Dick Ellingworth and David Symon, new entrants to the Foreign Service. They were sent to Japan in early 1951 to study Japanese as Third Secretary language students. DICK ELLINGWORTH explains:-

•

Although we had been posted to Japan as language students, both of us already had some knowledge of Japanese, having studied language for a month or two at the Army Intelligence Corps Training Centre in Karachi in 1946 where we had been pupils of the beautiful Go sisters. When, to our chagrin, the course there closed down, we both transferred to the Intelligence Corps from the Royal Artillery and were eventually posted to serve in field security sections in Japan. Having spent a year in

Japan with the Occupation forces we returned to the United Kingdom on demobilization and then spent three years at Oxford, studying subjects far removed from Japan. When we joined the Foreign Service in 1950, the Foreign Office, uncertain, apparently, about what to do with us, attached us temporarily to the Information Research Department, where we were somewhat bemused to find ourselves involved in anti-Communist propaganda.

This episode did not last long and we were sent to study Japanese at the London Berlitz school. Our teacher there was a Mr Rawlings, brother of the actress Margaret Rawlings. He was an expert in phonetics and explained the positions the mouth and tongue should form in order to pronounce Japanese vowels and consonants.

Eventually, towards the end of 1950, we embarked on the MV *Antilochus* at Birkenhead for the long sea voyage to Japan. David Symon and I used this interval to good effect and had learned or re-learned a substantial vocabulary and several hundred *kanji* by the time we eventually disembarked at Yokohama. At Karachi we had learned the *kana* syllabaries and some characters used in Japanese primary school textbooks (*shogakko tokuhon*). We found these books a good foundation, providing, as they did, many insights into Japanese psychology and culture as well as being linguistically useful. For grammar and colloquial Japanese we had used the books of Arthur Rose-Innes. We had kept these books little imagining that we should be using them again in a few years' time.

Arrangements for our studies had been made by Peter Westlake under the supervision of Arthur de la Mare, the Head of Chancery, who had been a member of the Japan Consular Service and had studied Japanese before the war. But once our teaching arrangements had been settled we were left very much to ourselves and our course was quite unstructured in contrast with the more developed and supervised regime developed within the Embassy in later years.

Our three teachers were Colonel Isobe, a retired and ageing ex-army officer, Mr Kano, a retired teacher, and a Mr Yamada whose background I do not recall. They were quite a good choice. Isobe-san had been a friend of General Piggott and was a cheerful and amusing conversationalist, quite good at choosing texts to study, but not so good at explaining grammar or idiom. Kano-san was a mine of information and could rattle off the names of the old Japanese provinces, or give historical summaries of past Japanese events, all without thought or hesitation. We learned much from him, but not so much about the structures of modern Japanese. For reading we studied the Naganuma *Tokuhon* (readers).

I think that both Isobe-san and Kano-san became genuinely attached to us. One of my most prized possessions is a bronze writing set given to me by Isobe-san. Kano-san's devotion lasted long after we had left Japan. Following David Symon's tragic death as the result of a skiing accident in Japan in 1964 he called on David's parents in Scotland to express his condolences in person. Yamada-san left less of an impression on me. He was a pleasant but slightly colourless man, introduced to the embassy, I think, by the Imperial Household Agency (*Kunaicho*).

At first we shared a Japanese-style house with some Western-style rooms in Isarago in Shinagawa ward which was some way from the Embassy compound. The house had a charming small garden and was in an area which had been spared the worst of the bombing. Nearby was Sengakuji with the tombs of the famous forty-seven *Ronin*. There were other houses with gardens and we even saw wild pheasants living unmolested in the area. We had two maids and a cook. Furniture and crockery were provided. So we were very well, indeed luxuriously, established. We were without cars, but soon learned to find our way round Tokyo on the trams and by other means.

David used his time to better effect than I did, joining the Tokyo Madrigal Singers under the leadership of Kei Kurosawa, who with his son Hiroshi (Peter) also organized a small recorder-playing ensemble. Kei who had been at Cambridge between the wars had served briefly at the League of Nations. His family's office equipment business on the Ginza had fortunately survived. David was a dedicated member of the group both as a singer and player of the recorder. The Tokyo Madrigal Singers paid their tribute to his memory by performing *The Silver Swan* by Orlando Gibbons at his Memorial Service.

I did not have any such regular recreation, but I did make some memorable visits away from Tokyo. Japan had been permitted to join UNESCO before the Peace Treaty came into force. I got to know Professor Ohnishi, a UNESCO enthusiast. He invited me to go to Kyushu with him on some UNESCO project and under his guidance, staying at simple Japanese inns (*ryokan*), I got to know something of ordinary Japanese life. Later, I went to a UNESCO conference with some Japanese students at Sugadaira, a skiing resort. Many of these students became good friends with me and others in the embassy.

Because of our war service and years at Oxford, David and I were already in our mid-twenties by the time we took up full-time Japanese language study. In theory we were supposed to have two years to study the language, but as things worked out we had little more than one year. This was a pity as although we both had a reasonable facility with the language our knowledge was more superficial than it would have been if we had had the full two years we had expected.

The embassy was short of staff. We had moved into Number 6 house in the compound in the second half of 1951 where on his arrival Hugh Cortazzi joined us. We were thus easily available for various part-time tasks, such as the compilation of data on important Japanese personalities. As we wanted to earn our living we readily accepted these commissions and became more and more involved in the work and life of the mission, at first under Sir Alvary Gascoigne who had the rank of ambassador, then under George Clutton, the Minister, as Chargé d'Affaires, and finally under Sir Esler Dening, who arrived as head of mission with the rank of ambassador in late 1951, and became ambassador *en titre* to Japan in April 1952 when the Peace Treaty came into force. In those days the diplomatic corps was a small one. So receptions and dinners were less frequent but more enjoyable. Among the senior staff at the embassy were Vere and Madeleine Redman, John and Alette Figgess and Arthur Goodman with his wife, a Polish countess; they were all particularly kind and hospitable to us:

THE NEXT language student appointed to Japan was Sydney Giffard. He was soon followed by Bill Bentley. Sydney and Bill were both married as were Cliff Hill and Brian Hitch.

BRIAN HITCH, who arrived in 1955, has sent in the following piece, entitled 'Attitudes 1955':-

•

It would have been difficult to be more ignorant of Japan than I was when the factory chimneys of Kobe loomed out of the dawn haze on a cloudless December morning. The boat journey had taken sixty-nine days from Rotterdam, days which a grateful government counted as working time – or anyway not as holiday. The factory chimneys brought home more vividly than any amount of reading might have done that this harbour was unlike any of the British harbours we had spent time in on the way: Aden, Penang, Port Swettenham, Singapore or even Hong Kong.

The year was 1955. Only much later did I try to put that in perspective. It fits nicely. Ten years previously Japan had, deservedly or not, suffered two atomic attacks. Tokyo, as well as the atomic cities and as well as most other cities for that matter, lay devastated. Ten years after 1955 Japan woke up to the idea that, having just invited the world to a well organized Olympic Games, for which superhighways and the bullet train had been built, the country had 'arrived': the war was finally over for the purposes of everyday life even if at a political level there was any amount of outstanding business with the Soviet Union, with China, with South East Asia, in Okinawa, with the constitution and so on.

So 1955 was neither one thing nor the other. And this meant that a newcomer from a country still very conscious of having won the war and somewhat less conscious, even after India in 1947, of having lost an empire, had real problems of perception, problems which the young Japanese faced the other way round. I had been sent to Japan as a Foreign

Office language student, committed to meeting as many different Japanese people as possible. But few were of such interest to me as the budding Japanese diplomats of my own age. It did not need much imagination to see that there was much to be gained on both sides from getting to know one's 'opposite numbers': my seniors in the Embassy encouraged these contacts with their greater awareness that friendships formed in one's twenties could last a lifetime. And so it proved.

What did we – the younger British not only in the Embassy but those who were in Japan doing other jobs – think of the Japanese? Allow a personal interjection. I came from Cambridgeshire. The whole regiment was captured at Singapore and many of my father's generation in my small town were put on the Burma/Siam railway. But the same newspaper that had printed columns of names in 1942 wrote an editorial when I was sent to Japan. The editorial, written no doubt by an older person to whom the ten years 1945-55 seemed shorter than they did to me, concluded that I should never forget the past (how could I?) but that it was time for a new generation to start again with a new relationship. The clichés of small-town journalism if you will. But somehow the right editorial at the right time.

That is my first answer to the question what I thought of the Japanese: my origins coloured my early attitudes. But I was all the same not so unlike the GIs of 1945 of whom it was often said that they came, they saw – and were conquered. I was conquered by the friendliness and often the hospitality of the Japanese; I was almost masochistically overwhelmed by how much there was to learn, not just the language which was my job, but – for want of a better word – the whole culture.

Yet I do not believe now that I approached this strange new world from an inward attitude of equality. I cannot now avoid the confession that I felt superior: not winning-the-war superior, but superior because we were richer and had a shiny new British-made MG, because we spoke as natives the world language which the Japanese seemed to struggle rather ineffectively with. The Japanese did not always help us there! Politeness stopped them from often probing the carapace of our smugness and they were very adept at remaining in learning mode even in situations where they ought to have been doing the teaching. So they were not going to bring us down a peg. It was up to us to absorb a few lessons: give or take a month or so, this was the time when Japan's shipbuilding production capped ours as the number one in the world and when Germany's motor vehicle output became number one in Europe. It was the time of the Messina conference to which Britain sent a middle-ranking official who concluded as his masters hoped that this European business was not for us.

Both at a personal and official level in Japan at that time we tended to associate with the Anglophone community: Canadians, Australians. New

Zealanders – and above all the ubiquitous Americans, who (much to my initial shock) thought, as did most Japanese, that the war had been just a Japan-American affair. As a language student I held that this group of countries was taking the acquisition of Japanese seriously whereas the Europeans seemed occasionally to have some young person turn up who was disposed to give study a bit of a try and see how it worked. Grossly unfair, probably. As a Cambridge graduate in French, German and Italian, why did I not mix with the Europeans more'? When, with the Treaty of Rome in the air, both young Japanese and young European diplomats gently hinted that there might be something in this Europe for the empire-less United Kingdom (I have specific conversations in mind) why did not some alarm bells ring? I neither knew then nor do I know now.

This first five-year experience of Japan thus changed my attitudes overall, though not of course to the extent of making me think that most of my education had misled me or that my country's foreign policy was mostly wrong-headed. Perhaps apocryphally Mrs Thatcher is reputed to have said that the trouble with diplomats is that they can see the other party's point of view. To which any professional diplomat would retort that such is their job. My re-education never led me to accept Japan's justification for its militarism from Manchuria onwards; many Japanese did not accept that either. But I was re-educated to see colonialism in a more critical light, a re-assessment in which K.M. Panikkar's book *Asia and Western Dominance* was crucial. Rejecting as impossibly hypocritical any thought that Japan's mission in Asia was morally superior, I could nevertheless see that Japan had not been playing a discernibly different game from us and others in seeking by force a place in the sun, meaning in those days privileged access to raw materials and control of markets. On a personal level things changed too. My wife and I had our children baptised, but we were gradually finishing with Christianity, partly I am sure as the result of seeing ninety million people who seemed to run a society as good as ours without it (though with superstitions of their own!).

Learning a language can never be done in a vacuum. Even in this day and age of tapes and language drills the time comes for free conversation with a teacher. In Tokyo in 1955 free conversation ruled the day! I am not sure that many of our teachers knew the rules of grammar, or even if they did, how to put them across to those of us on the other side of the enormous linguistic gulf. But they were interesting people and if one tots up the hours spent with them during two years of full-time language study, especially as one became gradually more fluent, it is obvious that no interlocutors shared their thoughts more intimately. So my view of Japan today must still owe much to a lieutenant in the Russo-Japanese War and a wind-tunnel engineer who had been, that most shameful of

things for a Japanese, a POW in the hands of the Australians. These hours
and hours of conversation practice are of course a two-way traffic and I
sometimes idly wonder whether any organization, not necessarily Japanese, started off a (pretty worthless) file about a fledgling diplomat on the
basis of what our teachers had to say.

Friends at home seemed to admire me (and my wife perhaps more!) for
going through this exotic and truly mind-boggling experience with success: success measured, I should like to think, less by passing the Civil
Service Commission's little hurdles than by surviving the culture shock,
the new environment, the unfamiliar way of life. I could see why my wife
deserved admiration for producing two children so far from home and
family support. I never saw any reason why I should be admired: more
appropriately envied for the extraordinary opportunity given me. I was
being paid for learning a new language and rather more than I had been
doled out on a state grant and Open Scholarship, which was how I had
learned languages so far! Admiration would be better reserved for the
Japanese students doing my job the other way round. Take for example
the first Gaimusho (Foreign Office) students at Cambridge where the
university had for some years after the war banned Japanese for reasons
I explain with my own reference to Cambridgeshire above. They surely
had a harder life: lack of hard currency was among their problems. Apart
from occupying the moral high ground at that time − as I may mista-
kenly have seen it − we in Japan had all sorts of infrastructural support
totally lacking the other way round: we went to foreign doctors and den-
tists, we read English-language newspapers and when all else failed we
expected educated Japanese to meet us more than half way with their
knowledge of English. Certainly not a level playing-field.

Coming fresh from the student musical life of Cambridge, where for
two years I had been organist of my college, I was keen to find things to
join in actively in Tokyo, the first preference being Japanese music. Alas, I
could not get on with it and even after many years my small interest in it is
cerebral and not emotional. Instead, I was astonished − as are some visitors to Japan even today, though they should know better! − at the popularity of Western music. It had been around for nearly a century after all
and had taken on more, it still seems to me, than among other cultures,
Arabic, Indian or Chinese, for example, similarly exposed to the whole
mix of Western colonialism. Professor Michio Akimoto of the Tokyo
Fine Arts University allowed me access to a small but serviceable pipe
organ, unfortunately a long way from my house; other friends actually
lent me on long loan a clavichord, a spinet and even a harpsichord at
different times.

Yet it was the Tokyo Madrigal Singers which gave me the greatest fun:
close friendships, and travel to Kyoto, for example, where we stayed for
the first time in a temple. Pianos and symphony orchestra perhaps, but

who would believe that a specialist choir for, largely, English Elizabethan music would exist in Japan? The Singers were founded in 1929 by Keiichi Kurosawa as soon as he returned from taking his degree at Trinity College, Cambridge. The association with the British Embassy was close from the beginning, but not exclusive by any means. Operating discreetly, the Singers survived the war and when I arrived I was delighted to find a soulmate in the conductor's son, Hiroshi [Peter], the same age as myself. These people were pioneers in a way that is hard to imagine now that the recordings of Mr Masaaki Suzuki's Bach Collegium are by some reviewers preferred to those originating in Germany. In 1950 Mr Kurosawa demonstrated the recorder to officials of that most conservative of all ministries, the Ministry of Education: such a curiosity. Now the number of Japanese schoolchildren learning the recorder has been conservatively placed at two million. Things were moving fast: air travel brought the Vienna Philharmonic Orchestra to Tokyo, conducted by Paul Hindemith, the forerunner of by now hundreds of such visitations; but for the Anglo-Japanese community, and not only, the tour by Benjamin Britten and Peter Pears in the spring of 1956 [see Chapter 5] was the highlight. Mr Kurosawa interpreted and at one of our practices the male ranks of the madrigals suddenly found themselves somewhat reinforced.

In all foreign communities clubs spring up which are by their nature designed only for the foreigners: those of one nationality perhaps (though of course the British needed to commemorate more than one saint) or of one language. That was where the Tokyo Amateur Dramatic Club came in, uniting the British with, overwhelmingly, the Americans and the other Anglophones. The standard was quite high. I wangled myself a small part, but was not asked a second time. I had to rehearse a scene between one of the twins in *Twelfth Night* (me) and the sea captain. I remember chiefly the lack of similarity between myself and the beautiful young woman who was supposedly my twin and also the unstoppable hilarity which overtook me and my partner every time we were called up by the producer. That partner was, many would still say, the most distinguished of post-war British Japanologists, the late Ivan Morris.

After nearly half a century one's memory can play tricks. Surely the Japanese must have infuriated us sometimes, or we them? How about that taxi driver in an inferior Toyopet (yes, Toyopet) who unable to bear the sight of a young foreign woman (my wife) in an MG, overtook her and slammed on his brakes? How about the Japanese who, confronted with a knowledge of Japanese unsurprisingly better than their knowledge of English, either refused to respond at all or who persisted through thick and thin in inflicting a kind of Japlish on us? It can all be explained in historical perspective, but was maddening at the time. Yet that experience now occupies a few bytes only of memory against megabytes storing kindnesses shown me way beyond any obligation;

not to forget the loyalty and friendships which have been the hallmark of my (and many other people's) relationship with Japan. My greatest benefactors are mostly dead; just occasionally I can attempt to return a fraction of the favours received in the direction of a younger generation, who are not allowed to know my motives.

33

The Beginning of a Long Association: John Whitehead Remembers

JOHN WHITEHEAD

IN THE 1950s the British perception of Japan continued to be of a far-away exotic (even tropical) place that had hardly any relevance at all, other than in opera or because of war memories. For the time being, however, the British Foreign Office maintained the excellent tradition of sending language students to such distant places. In 1956 one such student was the future ambassador, JOHN WHITEHEAD. Here he 'lifts the veil' on those early days, partly prompted by the letters he wrote to his parents about his 'Japan experiences':-

•

It was August 1956. I was in Piccadilly shopping for long johns to wear when I went skiing in Japan. At the age of twenty-three I was excited at the prospect of a spell in what everyone in Britain knew to be a tropical island situated variously in the northern or southern hemispheres with a splendidly exotic capital called Tokyo, full of Madame Butterflies. It was not quite like that, warned a former language student, and he was right. The shop girls got their laughs and I got my long johns, one of the first in a long series of encounters with my own countrymen and women about that country which still continues to surprise and baffle many, even the so-called experts-on-Japan hands.

Setting out from Southampton on the P&O ship *Canton* was the culmination of a whole series of chance encounters and happenstance, advice from friends, some good, some not so, reading the odd book, and fortuitous timing.

The autumn of 1956 was an almost cataclysmic period. In the five weeks it took to reach Japan it seemed as if much of the world had changed. There was the uprising in Poland, the attempted Hungarian revolution, brutally repressed by Soviet forces, and of lasting significance from the British point of view the Suez debacle. Three months earlier I had leant out of the Foreign office windows overlooking Downing Street and had seen John Foster Dulles roundly booed as he came to No. 10 to talk to Anthony Eden in the context of the Second Canal Users Association meeting in London, a meeting provoked by Nasser's nationalization of the Suez Canal which in turn owed much to Dulles's abrupt *volte face* over American aid for the Aswan High Dam. My passage through the Suez Canal that October therefore took on a particular significance in my mind; as it turned out our ship was one of the last passenger liners to go through before the invasion and the blocking of the Canal for an extended period.

I flew the last leg to Tokyo to be met at Haneda Airport (Narita was not even thought of) by Brian Hitch. It took probably more than an hour through very dimly lit and much potholed streets to reach the embassy by car and the haven of Bill and Karen Bentley's house in the compound where I spent my first night before starting a five-week spell in the then two-storey Fairmont Hotel overlooking part of the moat surrounding the Imperial Palace. After such an extended journey I was keen to get started on the language and asked Brian whether I would be going to 'the university' on the following day. I was quickly told that language teaching was carried out by a small number of Japanese teachers who came to one's house two or three times a week; one of these was good (Nakazato); the others – 'well. With a bit of luck I might be able to start with Nakazato in a few months, and in the meantime . . .' In any case it would be sensible to get myself properly administered and settled in first.

On my first full day in Tokyo, 16 November 1956, I had been invited by the head of Chancery, Ralphy Selby, and his wife Juliana, to lunch in one of the large houses in the compound. I was a touch overawed about how the conversation would go. I need not have worried. He was an experienced diplomat; I was young, rather raw and a touch fiery in argument. Suez came up almost immediately after the initial courtesies were over and we found ourselves on the opposite side on many points. A distinctly animated lunch conversation was eventually brought to an end by Juliana Selby breaking in to enquire whether I could do Scottish country dancing. I said, 'yes', to which she replied , 'Good. 6.30 tomorrow evening then, and bring your plimsolls.' The lunch was over.

First impressions of Tokyo were somewhat bewildering. It was not the exotic capital city that I had been half imagining. Large areas were entirely made up of wooden buildings; the centre of the business section, Marunouchi, was built wholly of red brick, of which Tokyo Station is the sole remaining example. Streets, even in the centre around the Imperial Palace, were comparatively narrow, although the Plaza outside the Imperial Palace itself (of which only the Library Wing remained standing) was extremely large and impressive. It was there that I first noticed the

Japanese habit of clothing the trunks of smallish trees with a yellowy girdle of straw matting during the winter.

There were tramlines on many main roads in the city, radiating from Hibiya crossroads; up past the embassy and on to the Yasukuni Shrine and along Yasukuni-dori; up Aoyama-dori and to Shibuya and beyond. It was only eleven years since the end of the war, eight years before the Tokyo Olympics. No expressways; only one main subway line from Shibuya to downtown. There was little traffic – mainly buses and trams, heavy lorries driven by madmen and taxis whose drivers were a little closer to sane on that scale. Small Datsun taxis started at 60 yen, larger Toyopets at 70. It was 1,008 yen to the pound. To be fair, the state of the roads was so bad that traffic had to drive all over the road in order to avoid potholes or broken concrete slabs. But the experience threatened to have long-term consequences and it was only in the late 1960s that improved surfaces and the sheer volume of traffic forced a measure of lane discipline on the majority of drivers.

Most of the language students before, who were still in Tokyo, were married – Sydney and Wendy Giffard, Bill and Karen Bentley, Cliff and Cicely Hill and Brian and Margot Hitch. Only Richard Burges Watson ('one s, no hyphen') was a bachelor like myself. The Giffards, sadly, departed for the UK, a nine-week voyage round the Cape I recorded, perhaps inaccurately, in one of my letters to my mother, in January. Bill and Karen Bentley threw black tie dinner parties for ambassadors and lesser mortals in a very glossy life in No. 9 House in the embassy compound. Cliff and Cicely Hill, he a pipe smoker, she with masses of blond tresses, were quite arty with large very modern paintings on their walls. Brian Hitch was a great musician, any keyboard from organ to clavichord, and he blew things occasionally. Richard Burges Watson skied and played bridge well and travelled a lot around Japan. And so it was good that he and I should set out on my first trip outside Tokyo on my first weekend in Japan in his rather bulbous but very sturdy Chevrolet. The roads outside the city were unpaved and of very variable quality, as they remained for the most part until the 1970s. When I returned to Tokyo for my second tour in 1968 I took Carolyn, my wife, to see some of the surrounding countryside by car; but she cried out that the road had stopped (at the end of the tarmacked stretch) and since she was seven months pregnant we decided on discretion and postponed the journey.

No such inhibitions with Richard, although the roads served up two punctures on the way to the Pacific coast of the Chiba Peninsula. For a newly-arrived Westerner this was a highly evocative trip, thickly wooded countryside with lots of bamboo and clearings for rice-growing in paddy fields, and then the sea with a flat shore for many miles gradually becoming more hilly. There were masses of fishing boats and here and there a group of women helpers who hurtled into the sea with a steel rope, attached it to the boat and laid wooden slats or sleepers in the sea and on the first part of the sand so that the boats could be hauled up on to the beach by means of a small engine which wound in the steel rope.

We stayed in Ubara just south of Katsura in an inn looking over the small harbour with fishing boats returning with their catch. But my first experience of a Japanese inn was not encouraging and gave little foretaste of the enthusiasm to come. Eating, bathing and sleeping all presented serious problems. Our three meals there were entirely made up of fish – eleven different sorts by my reckoning, most of them raw and in my view at the time virtually all inedible. The soya sauce which accompanied them did not commend itself, neither did the rice, and I found the saké 'a somewhat watery substance'. All in all I commented to my mother that 'just at the moment I cannot really say that I like Japanese food; it remains to be seen whether I get used to it or not'! Bathing I approached 'with very mixed feelings'. On this particular occasion I waited for the Japanese guests to leave before (horror of horrors) 'a judicious amount of cold water enabled me to ease my way in and sit there, not daring to move'. And as for sleeping it was the pillow 'as hard as the biblical stones' which meant that when I woke in the morning I was 'only partially rested and full of aches and pains'. On the Sunday evening, having returned to the Fairmont Hotel after a highly eventful weekend, I took two aspirins, two large whiskies, a substantial steak and sank gratefully into a tepid Western-style bath before sleeping soundly in a Western bed. Only three days down with four years to go; I wondered how I could cope with Japan!

*   *   *

First, get on with your ambassador. There were three during my first tour: Sir Esler Dening, Sir Dan Lascelles and Sir Oscar Morland. The first two were bachelors, while Oscar Morland was married to Alice, a well-connected, very experienced and thoroughly bubbly lady who was a perfect partner for Oscar and was the mother of four sons, one of whom, Martin, was an almost exact contemporary of mine in the Service. Esler Dening was in his last few months before retirement by the time I arrived in Tokyo. He had been born in Sendai, knew Japan extremely well, was perfectly correct with me and invited me to a newcomers' lunch and my first black tie diplomatic dinner in my first two weeks. Apart from that, as a language student I saw rather little of him. Dan Lascelles was in Tokyo for barely eighteen months before he took early retirement. He gave the impression of being more interested in music (about which he knew a great deal) than people.

After stints in Ethiopia and Afghanistan Dan Lascelles seemed to find ninety-four million Japanese a little too many for his liking and so took to the hills and to his excellent hi-fi equipment. Unlike in the cases of the other two ambassadors I had the pleasure of being Oscar Morland's private secretary for a year. He knew his Japan well, spoke Japanese and liked the Japanese people. But he was somewhat shy and of a nervous disposition, smoking a great deal to steady himself. This was where Alice Morland was so helpful with quick repartee and a ready laugh. In the summer they went up to the ambassador's villa in Chuzenji, above Nikko. The younger members of the embassy took it in turns to visit Chuzenji with a 'box' containing diplomatic papers which it was deemed the ambassador should see, drafts that he should approve and letters that he should sign.

Latterly, a road was built around part of Lake Chuzenji which ran behind the villa, but in the 1950s those who came by car had to embark in a boat from the town of Chuzenji and reach the villa on the other side of the headland by water. It made a welcome break from the heat and humidity of Tokyo to take up the papers in this way and spend the night there before coming down the next day.

The Morlands also knew the Asos very well. Mr Aso's companies (coal mining and cement) were based in northern Kyushu just south of Fukuoka. Unfortunately, he died comparatively young but Kazuko, his wife and daughter of Prime Minister Yoshida who did so much to put Japan back on its feet after the war, survived well into the 1990s. In the 1950s and 60s private secretaries still travelled with the ambassador on tour and in 1959 I accompanied the Morlands and Kazuko Aso on an extended visit to Kyushu, a trip full of new experiences, a lot of laughs and many happy memories. She was to be a wonderful friend and support for life.

During my two years as a language student I travelled a great deal – my natural curiosity and wish to visit, for example, the end of a peninsula because it was there, combined with what I saw as an essential part of getting to know Japan. I went up to Wakkanai, the northernmost tip of Hokkaido, and down to Kagoshima in southern Kyushu. A group of us went to northern Hokkaido in February to see what winter was really like. We found out just north of Asahikawa when a blizzard halted our train for hours. We were lucky to have a wood-burning stove in the middle of our railway coach.

After the first few months in Japan I bought a second-hand Morris Minor which did me well but suffered much. Travelling by car was an ordeal as much as an adventure. Average speed was twenty miles an hour, maximum a hundred-and-twenty miles in a day. On Monday morning the car would have to go into the embassy garage. Its steering column would frequently need to be realigned after shaking *gata gata* on appalling dirt roads with occasional places where one had to build the road before proceeding. *Ippaku* (a night at a Japanese inn with dinner and breakfast included) was ¥700 at a little more than ¥1,000 to the pound. A beer was ¥50. Everybody sensible drove a Hillman. The Japanese, we thought, did not know how to make cars, at least not ones with comfort and style. We learnt better soon enough. By the 1980s the average speed could still be twenty miles an hour because of traffic jams on the expressways: from *gata gata* to *noro noro*.

In all I estimated that in my years as a language student I covered about twenty thousand miles round Japan, nearly half by car, the major part by third-class train. I chose to go third class partly out of natural frugality (it was unbelievably cheap, particularly with such a favourable exchange rate – something like 13 shillings, 65p, or ¥650 for two hundred miles) and partly because of the much better chance of having Japanese conversation than in second class: 'One misses much of the local colour if one goes second class with the businessmen and the other foreigners' was how I primly put it at the time. My aim was to talk generally to almost anybody sitting opposite (many of whom tucked their legs up under them on the seat) '... and if that brought no real response I would produce a guide-book in Japanese of the area through which we were passing. If the truth were known I could only understand about half of what it was all about, but it looked impressive and usually brought some sort of reaction.'

On one journey on the Japan Sea Coast from Kashiwazaki opposite Sado Island down to Fukui and Maizuru, I almost got more than I had bargained for. My opposite neighbour was so amazed at this foreigner who could make some headway in his language that he called to his friends elsewhere in the carriage and I found myself performing to twenty-two of them! As a member (albeit very humble) of the British Embassy and with the ability to read quite a number of *kanji* I found myself bombarded with the books or magazines which they were reading for me to sign 'for surely he will be Foreign Secretary in three years at this rate'! Little did they know.

My party piece fortunately did not last too long because the coast as one came towards the Kurobe river was magnificent: 'Many of the villages along this coast are typical of what one would imagine a Japanese fishing village would be like. Old wooden houses built on the sides of very steep slopes with boat houses tacked on to the bottom of many of them. Narrow streets and lots of trestles with nets and fish drying on them. Old women and young boys in students' clothes sitting squat-legged and bent double, busying themselves with the mending of nets, the making of boxes or the sorting and packing of fish. Old men with bath towels (*hachimaki*) tied round their heads, tight-fitting trousers and those typical Japanese split toe stockings (*tabi*) so that *geta* can be worn. In one village there was an old school which looked like a fine traditional English thatched barn or farmhouse, with a bell and belfry standing outside it. Out in the countryside there were lots and lots of persimmon trees all well laden with the bright yellow-orange fruit, and strings of persimmon hung from windows on sticks.'

My letters at the time were full of descriptions of various journeys to different parts of Japan but the area which clearly struck me then as being one of the most impressive was the stretch 'from the Kurobe Gorge down into the Shirouma, Tateyama and Yarigatake ranges of mountains, some of which go up to more than ten thousand feet.'

It was November 1957. I was on a very roundabout way to Kyoto to see a splendid Heian Period exhibition to mark the sixtieth anniversary of the opening of the Kyoto Museum It included some of the *Genji Monogatari* scrolls with their 'ceiling off' stylized paintings; I had arrived in Japan a year earlier, just in time to see much of the *Genji Monogatari* paintings (c.1150) at the Nezu Museum in Tokyo – 'the first time they have been on display for perhaps two hundred years' as the local press reported at the time. And after Kyoto I was fortunate enough to get into the Shosoin in Nara which was '. . . only open by special invitation to a handful of people each year at about this season. It was specifically stated that the purpose of opening up the building was to give the treasures which were housed in it an airing and not necessarily to put them on show. If there was bad weather the building would be closed regardless. The opening and closing was done in the presence of an imperial messenger from the court in Tokyo.'

And in late 1958 an Australian called David Sissons and I made a visit of a few days to Shikoku. It was amazing that we were able to leave Tokyo at all since much of the area was flooded after a typhoon. 'The railway between Tokyo and Yokohama was flooded but just passable. Our train was the first express to get through, using hand signals and even with a man running along in front of the engine at one stage. We took a boat from Kobe to Kochi, a much more pleasant place than I had been led to believe with a wonderful natural harbour a mile or so up a delightful estuary. We went to the Ryugado caves, full of stalactites and stalagmites, but particularly noteworthy as they wind inland for the best part of a mile and the exit is about two hundred feet above the entrance. That night we travelled on a very small boat, about three hundred tons; the 'accommodation' was merely *tatami*, a pillow and a blanket at an additional cost of ¥ 30 (three old pence).'

It was a thirteen hour journey to Shimizu close to Ashizurisaki the most south-westerly tip of Shikoku. We passed '. . . one of the most deserted areas that I have seen in Japan, with scarcely a sign of life except for several little fishing villages tucked away behind one or other of the rock bastions along the coast. The ship would go almost up to the breakwater separating the harbour from the open sea, when a small boat would put out from the shore and take off any passengers, baggage, mail or freight for that particular place. These were wonderful little places [parts of them I found out later were pretty smelly], just the sort of area about which to write a book.'

Our near-circuit of Shikoku finished in hair-raising style. From Awa-Ikeda, almost in the centre of Shikoku, we set off by bus up the Iyadani gorge: 'This was a frightening ride of about three-and-a-half hours in a ramshackle old bus with a driver whom one could not completely trust, and with twice the standard number of passengers in it. The road at times was scarcely as wide as the bus, and it gradually got dark. On the one side there was sheer cliff and on the other an equally sheer drop of anything from fifty to two hundred and fifty feet.

'We eventually arrived at our destination, which was a minute village called Icho where there was reported to be a reasonable inn. The old girl told us that the maid had a day off; she served us up some cold rice and really revolting fish and vegetables (she apologized that the fish was black!) and there were mosquitoes galore. In addition to which it was mighty cold; however the bath was quite enjoyable and the scenery the next morning made up for a lot.

'This was really rugged gorge scenery, dotted with houses in incredible spots and cultivated areas hanging over tremendous drops of sheer rock. We walked further up the valley for two or three hours and on the way passed an old vine bridge which had been constructed by an ancient clan living in seclusion on the south side of the river. Some workmen told us that when the road was really bad just after the war about twelve to fifteen lorries a year went over the edge and were wrecked below. The situation was much better now and the number was down to two or four. Fortunately, no buses had been known to go over the edge!'

But it was at about that time that tourist buses came off the road and rolled down slopes in various parts of Japan with sufficient frequency that some of the coach companies took to sending their drivers to temples to meditate for a while.

*   *   *

I played rugby football in Kobe, climbed Daisen on the Japan Sea coast, went skiing at Shiga Kogen. But the most memorable and worthwhile trip came in the summer of 1957. The younger members of the Embassy took it in turn to visit the nearby Foreign Service Training Institute to lecture to new entrants to the Japanese Foreign Service. Each year those new entrants spent ten days in the Kansai studying their own culture at first hand and visiting some industrial plants before going abroad to represent their country. It was a splendid arrangement; and it was even better when the Gaimusho suggested that someone from the embassy might like to join the trip in return for the time and trouble we had taken over the lectures throughout the year.

I was the lucky one to go. This was an intelligent man's tour to Nara and Kyoto with a few industrial asides to Kobe and Osaka. The balance of purpose in the trip – whether to equip young diplomats with a deeper knowledge of their own culture the better to be able to spread that knowledge to people who had never visited and knew little about Japan, or whether to imbue in them a great certainty of their Japaneseness – was never entirely clear. So it is easier to fudge and declare that both purposes were in view and achieved.

For a foreigner like me it was a very special opportunity to visit the shrines, temples and gardens as well as the industrial sights away from the superficiality and patronizing (of foreigners) which was (and alas still in large measure is) the stock in trade of many tour guides and a lot of the Japanese who think like them or who do not bother to think. The 'do you eat raw fish' syndrome or 'have you slept on the floor' was a cast of mind that dogged one, unnecessarily irritatingly, throughout one's time living in Japan. But the Kansai trip gave me one of those rare opportunities to get to know quite well fifteen almost exact contemporaries in the Japanese Foreign Service.

Over the years geography and the demands of our careers have meant that in many cases we have loosened or lost the ties created in that summer, but others are still in touch and stay as good friends even though we may meet rather infrequently. The old saw that one makes good friends before the age of forty and good acquaintances thereafter is perhaps inevitably reinforced in the case of British and Japanese because of geography, culture and mindset. I had no way of substantiating either point at the age of twenty-four but I was, almost unwittingly, adding well to my store of under-twenty-five Japanese friends.

Physical exercise and sport were important then as, to a lesser extent, now. And in this field, too, the opportunities for making good and lasting friends were many. To run the three miles around the moat of the Imperial Palace is more of a solitary occupation, although to see hordes of the dedicated Japanese and some foreigners who do it at lunchtime almost every day one might scarcely credit such an assertion. I did my first circuit in 1956 and my last shortly before I left Tokyo finally in 1992. The embassy was ideally placed except for the final uphill grind from Takebashi or, less frequently in a clockwise direction, from Sakuradamon.

In more sociable vein I played rugby and occasional cricket at the Yokohama Country and Athletic Club (YCAC), taking wickets but making few runs, mostly for teams which must have been pick-up sides and which have long been forgotten.

Rugby football was a somewhat more serious pursuit. Japanese teams were centred primarily on the university campus, although there were some good corporate teams as well. What they gave away in size in those days (rather different, although not entirely, now) they made up in keenness, fitness and the ability to travel fast in the posture of an oblique stroke. The resident foreigners' sides were of variable quality, experience and fitness. Half-time slices of orange were for a few replaced by a sizeable glass of sherry to see them through to the final whistle. Not only were there the Interport (Yokohama/Kobe) fixtures but we also used to play against Japanese sides including an All-Kanto team.

There was the occasional visit by an Oxford or Cambridge side but the memorable visit in 1959 during my first tour in Japan was by a combined Oxford and Cambridge team led by John Herbert, Cambridge and three caps for England, who handled a lively, hard-playing, hard-drinking group with great skill and a maturity way beyond his years. This side acquitted itself well on and off the field, which was just as well since I had been given the job of embassy minder as the team visited the Kansai and Kyushu to play games against All Japan sides. It was on that trip that firm friendships were made with a range of Japan Rugby Football Union players and officials, of whom Shiggy Kohno (of BBC fame), Bob Taka-shima and Bu Okumura stay particularly in the mind.

It was at almost exactly the same time that the Oxford Eight came to row against Keio and Waseda. They also did well for Britain. But part of the requirement for those resident in Tokyo and Yokohama (and in those days sizeable parts of the business element in the British Community were still living in Yokohama) was to ensure that the teams were made welcome after matches had been played or races rowed. At the time I was camping in the flat of a more senior member of the embassy staff (he was probably nearly twice my age) and I can now see that my not infrequent returns at four or five in the morning after forays to the Blue Lagoon in Yokohama or wherever must have irritated him considerably. 'Young man,' he said, 'one of these days you will find that you pay for this.' He was probably right, although at that stage I was not in the mood to concede the point. Fortunately, the frequency of visitors fell off sharply after that and I moved out to my own house in Akasaka Fukuyoshi-cho where I often fell asleep at a much earlier hour to the sound of revelry and the *samisen* from several *geisha* houses nearby.

I decided that, with music as a major interest, I would try learn to play the *samisen*. Japanese musical notation, and learning in a very rudimen-tary way to sing nursery songs and *naga-uta* as well as to play an instru-ment at regular lessons with a trained Japanese teacher while we knelt opposite each other on the *tatami* seemed to me to be a good way of dis-covering something about another aspect of Japanese culture. And so it was for a year or two no matter how painful the posture or the sounds which I managed to produce. I still have some of the books of music, although the *samisen* which I bought at the time seems to have been lost in the recesses of our loft. It was certainly one of those things which, looking back, I am very glad to have done, however imperfectly.

The Tokyo Madrigal Singers and the choir of the German-speaking community in Omori also featured at that time. The former was a remarkable group, mainly Japanese, but with a sprinkling of foreigners, first established in the 1920s by Kei Kurosawa after he returned from Cambridge where he had been a leading light in the musical world. Madrigals, part-songs and Christmas carols sung with great gusto in any number of different languages were their stock-in-trade. When Kei Kurosawa died his son, Hiroshi [Peter], took on the conductor's role. This remarkable group has recently celebrated its seventy-fifth anniversary: a great tribute to the Kurosawa family who apparently continued to meet with some of the singers throughout the war and kept the tradition of English madrigal singing alive.

The German choir I had a brief relationship with, although for a year or two quite an involving one. Bach, Buxtehude and Schütz were the main focus, essentially cantatas. We would travel to several parts of Japan, particularly where the German influence was strong, and give concerts. There was a preponderance of Germans in the choir whereas in the Tokyo Madrigal Singers the great majority were Japanese. Neither group exceeded twenty-five members. The German choir stays in the memory not least because for a few months after the departure of the founder-conductor, Dr Schmidt, I was asked to take over his role. There was a certain piquancy in finding myself directing a mixed group of Germans and Japanese and trying in a mixture of imperfect German and Japanese to lead them in the singing of Bach and Buxtehude.

* * *

The late 1950s were a period of quite dramatic typhoons which hit Japan. There are typhoons which pass through Japan pretty well every year. Nowadays, flood prevention and other measures are sufficiently good that few people are killed even in the worst storms. But in 1958 and 1959 there were three typhoons of particular note, for various reasons. The one which wreaked such havoc in the Shuzenji, Heda and Toi area in the north of the Izu Peninsula was a classic case of a combination of rather unusual meteorological events and rudimentary flood control.

As always there was plenty of warning that a typhoon was approaching, was expected to pass over the Izu Peninsula in the late afternoon and probably to come straight through Tokyo about supper time. Several of us congregated in mid-afternoon in my house, generally reckoned to be a sturdier model than many, and with a fair supply of drink and food we settled down to await developments. Supper-time came but nothing happened, although it was raining quite hard. The typhoon had stalled as it reached the coast of Izu and stayed there for three whole hours. The deluge of rain was apparently unbelievable, rivers burst their banks and most of the hillside between Heda and Toi was washed down into the sea taking with it much of several villages and killing two thousand five hundred people. The following year brought the even better known Ise Bay typhoon during which the sea wall of Nagoya was breached and five thousand people were killed. Between the two we had a typhoon which brought sixteen inches of rain to Tokyo in twenty-four hours, flooded much of Chuo-ku and the downtown part of the city and caused the moat between Miyakezaka and Sakuradamon to overflow. The carp in the moat went with it and it was left to policemen to try to catch them as they floundered in the tramlines.

*   *   *

My two years as a language student were very full, quite apart from language study. The British Embassy was the scene of mass protests on several occasions in those days, whether it was over nuclear tests on Christmas Island or British forces going into Jordan at a particularly tense time in the Middle East (in 1958). Part of me longed to be involved in the embassy work to a much greater extent and to stop being 'an everlasting student'. But there were exams to be passed, which they were with – much to my relief – a degree of room to spare. And there were lots of interesting Japanese and foreigners to meet, not least at a group which was known for obvious reasons as The First Thursday Club. Japanese Foreign Service officers such as Otaka and Otsuka, bankers such as Shijuro Ogata, academics such as Ayako Ishizaka, together with a clutch of British and Canadian diplomats were regular attenders. We would take it in turns to give lectures on a subject of our choice. And into this club came a diminutive girl called Sadako Nakamura. The daughter of a Japanese diplomat, she had just returned from Berkeley, California, where she had acquired a PhD; and she gave a lecture on 'White Elephants and Ivory Towers'. I do not remember the subject matter, but it was one hell of a title and stayed in the mind. She married Shijuro Ogata and has been the UN High Commissioner for Refugees for most of the 1990s.

It was also a time not only for visits to Kabuki, Bunraku and very occasionally Noh; it was a period when one visited down-at-heel cinemas to see amazingly good films: *Kumo no Sujo* (Spider's Web Castle in the Macbeth style), *Botchan* (a Japanese classic by Natsume Soseki about a schoolmaster in Shikoku), *Donzoko* (about life at the bottom of the heap), *Kome* and *Naruyama Bushiko* (about old ladies and others in Japan's middle ages when food was scarce being taken piggy back – *ombu* – up to the tops of mountains and left to die). And I commented in one letter that *Bridge over the River Kwai* had been well received in the Japanese press.

Japan was not at this stage on the international circuit for many foreign orchestras or other musical groups, nor was there much theatre as we know it in the West. There was a shortage of both concert halls (only at

Hibiya and Ueno) and theatres. So I was ready, a few weeks before Christmas 1958, to return to Britain via Hong Kong, Beijing, Ulan Bator, Irkutsk, the trans-Siberian railway, Moscow and Leningrad, my first break from Japan in more than two years apart from my four days in 1995 with the diplomatic bag in Korea.

34

Cypher Officer, Language Student, Vice-Consul

EDDIE RIPLEY

EDDIE RIPLEY'S account of how he took up the study of Japanese and of his early experiences as a vice-consul in Yokohama shows both his persistence and his sense of humour. His postscript on foreign words in the Japanese language (*gairaigo*) is a reminder that the Japanese penchant for adopting foreign words often makes Japanese even more difficult for the foreigner, although it has to be said that if you pronounce a foreign word in a Japanese fashion you may be understood. I recall my wife asking me shortly after we arrived in Tokyo together what the Japanese was for 'cream cracker'. Not having a clue I suggested *'kureemu kurakka'* and it worked!

The Sanbancho Hotel which has long since disappeared was popularly known in the embassy in those days as 'The Sinbin', although I do not think it ever was what in Japan is termed a 'love hotel':-

•

On 14 July 1958, I was serving as a twenty-one year old cypher officer in the British Embassy in Baghdad. I could not have foreseen what fate had in store for me that day and the enormous impact it would have on my life. But it led to my spending twenty years of my Foreign Office career serving in Japan and a further eight years in London – firstly working in the Exports to Japan Unit and later as Head of the Japan Section of the Invest in Britain Bureau.

That day in Baghdad was at first like any other day. It was very hot and as I was on early duty I was on my way to the embassy in the embassy car. Suddenly, in the road ahead appeared a howling mob of Iraqis who apparently were nor taking too kindly to Europeans. There was no place to turn round and the car was quickly surrounded. My driver ran away, and I was dragged out of the car. After being subjected to a severe beating and losing all my clothes and my watch, I was then taken, naked except for the blood pouring from wounds to my head and face and a serious knife wound to my arm, by two soldiers through the mob to my home and released without any explanation. Two weeks later, after lengthy negotiation with the Iraqi Revolutionary government, it was agreed that the embassy ladies and children and any other staff requiring urgent medical treatment could leave Iraq.

On arrival back in London and after a short period of hospitalization with my wounds healing nicely I went to see the FCO personnel officer who understandably felt that after such a terrible experience I would perhaps prefer to serve in London for a few years. No, I assured him, I really wanted to go abroad again, but I did not want to go to Europe because it was too close to London. 'So, is there anywhere you would particularly like to go?' I was asked sympathetically. My immediate reply was 'Japan'. This response was greeted by the personnel officer in a kind of voice one would have expected had I asked to go to the moon. At that moment I knew virtually nothing about Japan except that our two countries had been at war and that two of my uncles had been killed in Burma. My family was totally prejudiced against Japan and the Japanese. And yet at that moment I knew precisely why I wanted to go there. It had nothing to do with language or culture or even visiting an 'exotic' land with strange temples and 'a famous volcano called Mount Fujiyama'. 'Because it is the furthest post from London and I cannot afford to become homesick.' I replied in all seriousness. Needless to say some days later I received confirmation of my posting but when I told my mother that I was going to Japan her reaction was less than enthusiastic.

*   *   *

I left Southampton on the SS *Canton* in late September 1958 bound for Yokohama. Unfortunately, it transpired that I was 'urgently' required in Tokyo and I would therefore have to disembark at Singapore and fly the rest of the way to Tokyo via Bangkok (overnight stay) and Hong Kong (two-hour fuel stop) where I saw Japanese people and witnessed bowing for the first time. I arrived on 19 October 1958 at Haneda Airport and was met by a colleague, Stanley Wright, who attended to the immigration and customs requirements.

My first impression of Japan (admittedly in the dark) was that it was a town and country-planning nightmare. There were narrow streets with no pavements with little wooden shops and houses of all shapes and sizes on both sides. The streets were packed with a motley array of vehicles from bicycles to three-wheel motor cars all seeming to be vying with the crowds of people for the limited space in which to move. In the main streets, which were badly lit, to add to the mayhem was a clutter of mainly small taxis and large trams. It seemed that the train stop islands had been specially designed and located to impede the movement of any other form of transport.

But what I remember which impressed me most of all on that trip from the airport was that Stanley appeared to speak Japanese like a native. He also told me that if I wished really to enjoy my time in Japan I should attempt to learn Japanese. I soon came to appreciate this wise advice. The average Japanese, with the exception of very few, could not speak English. To make matters worse there were no street names, houses were not numbered, and there were no places or buildings with names in English except for the remnants of the Occupation such as 'A Street' or 'Fifth Avenue' which I later found were pretty useless as the Japanese did not understand them. On all the telephone and electric power poles in the labyrinth of side streets in areas where foreigners lived there could be seen as many as twenty little wooden arrows attached to each on which the foreigners' names had been printed. It was particularly worrying for somebody like myself recovering from the experience I had had in Baghdad. I was terrified of crowds and I had visions of staying in my house and never going out of the door for the whole of my tour for fear of getting lost and not being able to seek directions from anybody.

Despite being assured by Stanley that I would soon get used to life in Japan, especially if I took the trouble to learn Japanese, I was too embarrassed to mention that before leaving London I had bought Yanada and Dunn's *Teach Yourself Japanese* which had just been published, and that I had already attempted to teach myself some '*Nippongo*' on the boat. My main embarrassment was that, sadly, the sentences I had studied so hard did not seem to sound anything like the way he pronounced Japanese. (Come to think of it I have never heard a Japanese pronounce *Nihongo* as *Nippongo*.) The way he pronounced '*jidosha*' and the way I thought '*zidoosya*' should be pronounced were just not the same; neither did words such as '*enpitu*', '*teeburu*' and '*nooto*' which appeared in the very first lesson. But the most disturbing for me was the name of a place called '*Tookyoo*' in the book, which I was later assured, was not pronounced '*Took you*' even in Japanese.

Despite the initial setbacks I had caught the language bug and was truly keen to learn Japanese. And there was the bonus that my not daring to go out on my own gave me plenty of opportunity to study my book. Stanley, who really was a very talented Japanese speaker, took the trouble to explain the different forms of *romaji* and recommended I should learn Japanese using the Hepburn system even if for no other reason than that it was the system used in the most authoritative English-Japanese dictionaries such as Kenkyusha.

For the first six weeks I stayed in the original Sanbancho hotel (there have been two more since and they, too, have gone) near the embassy until I could find more suitable accommodation. My mental condition and fear of crowds made every day a nightmare getting to and from work. I peered out of the front door of the hotel and, making sure there were not too many people about, I took off towards the embassy and its welcoming safety. I did the same back to the hotel when returning for lunch and in the evening. Many people could not understand my fear especially as the Japanese were in no way anti-foreigner or threatening. Indeed, they were always very pleasant and kind, and, as the months went by, this helped to cure my nerves, although I did have a few tense moments.

When I did go out it was always with somebody else, and if I was going to a party I would avail myself of the embassy transport pool cars which provided cars in the evenings to take staff to and from parties at a very low cost (¥25 per mile): even cheaper if the cost could be shared with colleagues. Taxis were not expensive (flagfall yen 60-80 depending on the size of the taxi) but the drivers generally had no idea where they were supposed to be going even if they were handed an address in the Japanese language.

Many times it was like a mad paperchase as the foreign passengers recognized a name on one of the little arrows. The poor driver was totally bewildered by the shouts of his almost hysterical passengers waving their arms about indicating the way they thought he should be going. To add to his misery he had to suffer the incomprehensible instructions being shouted at him: 'Stop here! Now right! No, not left you idiot. No, not left I said right! Stop! Back! No! Are you deaf? Back, and then right!!' And the classic remark: 'Can't you understand simple English?' It was not so surprising that taxi drivers would prefer not to pick up foreigners if they had a choice.

To add to the taxi drivers' woes there were also those who 'spoke enough Japanese to get about'. Instead of directions in English they used the basic but woefully mispronounced Japanese words '*mee-gee*' '*hee-daari*' '*masoogoo*' and '*koko stoppu OK Arry Gateau*' and the name of such exotic places as 'Ayo-yarmy rock Chomey' (Aoyama Rokuchome) or '*Kinny Kinnear*' (Kinokuniya supermarket). I often wonder what an English taxi driver might have said to his passengers speaking to him in an equivalent form of English let alone in a foreign language.

*   *   *

At the end of November 1958 I moved into a Western-style wooden bungalow in Yotsuya 4-Chome. It was comfortable and comprised a good size living/dining-room, bedroom, kitchen, bathroom and flush toilet. There were also 'maid's quarters' consisting of a four-mat *tatami* room and a Japanese-style toilet which did not have a flushing mechanism. My foreign-style toilet, however, did have a flushing mechanism. This intrigued me until the first time the so-called 'honey-bucket brigade' arrived to clean out the system and I realized that my foreign-style toilet flushed into the same cesspit as the maid's toilet. So much for modern technology!

Kanda-san and Mitsuhashi-san, the two embassy receptionist/ 'fixers' arranged for me to interview a maid who would work for me. As a cook/ housekeeper she would be paid yen 10,000 per month on a six-day week basis. I was assured that Kobayashi-san, who had worked for the embassy for nine years, spoke excellent English. Her English was indeed good but limited. She not only introduced me to new English words like 'Bacon Fot' and 'Freeding Ko' to describe types of weather but let me into the first 'secret' of foreigners understanding Japanese customs and habits. She often demonstrated the technique of nodding the head and smiling. She did this most of the time whenever I spoke to her. It suggests that the listener understands what is being said, but does not in fact mean that the listener actually understands what is being said. In many cases the listener does not understand a word of what is being said and inevitably it can lead to difficulties!

There is an apocryphal story illustrating the kind of linguistic problems one could face. A maid was working for an embassy security officer who spoke mainly in pure Cockney rhyming slang. As can be imagined the poor woman picked up a lot of cockney vocabulary, which she understandably assumed was the Queen's English. Everything was fine until he left Japan and his successor moved in believing the maid spoke English well. However, he felt he was not getting his message through to her despite asking the maid slowly and clearly several times without success to telephone the local shop and have some beer delivered. In his frustration and exasperation he telephoned a colleague and explained the situation. His colleague laughed, said he would explain all later, and then spoke to the maid. The beer was duly delivered a few minutes later. He was later told about his predecessor's English and it was suggested that in future all he had to say to the maid was 'Hey Sunshine. Jump on the Eau de Cologne (phone) and order a dozen pigs (ears = beers)!' Wisely, he decided for the sake of future arrivals to teach her a more standard form of English.

I was gradually becoming adjusted to life in Tokyo. However, as there were no signs in English anywhere, I became more and more fascinated by *kanji* although initially this was more from the artistic than the pragmatic point of view. The shape of the *kanji* and the order and number of strokes were particularly interesting. The first *kanji* I ever attempted to copy was *Asahi Shimbun*, the name of the newspaper the maid used to read. Indeed, when I discovered that a large *kanji* such as *'Shin'* was made up of three small *kanji* I was convinced that learning *kanji* would be simple! Poor fool! Oh how easy to be lured into that trap!

By the end of February 1959, through lack of guidance, I was still not making any real progress in my Japanese studies. Even the odd word and sentence I practised with the maid did not sound right which was not so surprising in view of the textbook I was using. I went to the Kitazawa

Bookshop in Kanda (Tokyo's Charing Cross Road) to browse and by chance I came across a copy of *Japanese Conversation Grammar* by Oreste and Enko Vaccari. It explained, for me at least, Japanese grammar clearly and simply. But its most important feature was that the translation exercises were in English/Hepburn Romaji/and *Kanamajiri*. The vocabulary listed in each chapter was also in the three styles. This enabled me to practise translations of the sentences between English and Japanese and also learn *kanji* and *kana*. I finally started to make progress and within a few months using a system I had devised myself I was able to read and write both *kana* syllabaries and was starting on basic *kanji* using an exercise book used by Japanese junior schoolchildren. I later bought a book called *Kanjirin* which I learnt much later was a pre-war publication compiled by three Germans. It contained many *kanji* no longer in use or which had been simplified after the war. Nevertheless, I spent many happy hours learning to write difficult *kanji* which would be of no use to me in my career, especially those which were now no longer being used.

I was making some progress albeit limited in Japanese. I had heard in the embassy about the various Japanese language examinations but I thought this was for official language students only. I did not realize that it was possible for even junior officers like myself to take them. Every year since the 1950s the FCO has trained four students in the Japanese language – two administrative stream officers and two executive stream officers. Between the 1950s and the 1970s the students spent two years in Japan receiving individual tuition at home from a team of three or four Japanese teachers. From the early 1970s the students spent one year in a UK University (Sheffield or London) followed by one year at the embassy language school in Kamakura. Clerical grade officers were not selected. I was also unaware that to encourage others in the embassy, including clerical grades, to study the Japanese language in their own time, the FCO would meet the cost of a hundred hours of formal tuition. One was, of course, expected to sit the lower standard examination for which on passing one received an overseas language allowance of £60 per annum (yen 60,480 in those days). It was at the beginning of 1960 that I first heard about this tuition and made enquiries. The lower standard examination was due to take place in May. I was able to obtain some previous examination papers and after studying them I was confident that my knowledge of Japanese was of a level that I could sit the examination and stood a good chance of passing.

*   *   *

When I heard that I had passed I was allowed exceptionally to apply for the hundred hours' tuition so that I could try for the Intermediate level (providing a language allowance of £100 pa which was a major incentive to me). I was also refunded the cost of the set books which were Rose-Innes' *Conversation Grammar* (an old-fashioned book written in the 1920s containing quaint sentences illustrating the various 'levels' of Japanese from 'plain bloody rude' when speaking to your menial staff to the 'ultra polite' honorific style when replying to questions from a *daimyo*). There was also the first volume each of Naganuma's *Reader*, *Word Book*, and *Kanji Book*. I was allocated a teacher, Mr Yonemura.

Mr Yonemura's reputation was that he had been an outstanding teacher in the embassy since long before the war. However, sadly, being of advanced years, he was clearly well past his sell-by date. He had the habit of asking his student at the beginning of the lesson if he might have a glass of whisky purely for medicinal purposes to keep out the cold etc. At the diplomatic price of 5 shillings (yen 250) a bottle compared with £10 on the domestic market, he could hardly be refused. The first thirty minutes of the lesson were quite useful but the second half left something to be desired. I was regularly asked to read aloud a page from the reader whilst Mr Y listened with his eyes closed. It did not take me too long to realize that he had dozed off. He was clearly suffering from the soporific effect of good Scotch whisky when drunk in largish quantities in a warm room.

I finally had to complain to Leo Pickles (HM Consul) who was the language officer in charge, that HMG funds, not to mention my time, were being wasted. Leo then apprised me of the second 'secret' of understanding the Japanese. Although a Japanese might be sitting at a concert, in the cinema, or at a seminar, with his eyes closed and audibly snoring, he is not asleep, but carefully listening to or concentrating on every sound or word. In fact, I discovered that, contrary to popular belief, if a Japanese is sitting with his eyes closed and gently snoring he is fast asleep and therefore temporarily partially deaf like the rest of us.

As an extension of this belief I recall it being pointed out to me that the Japanese, unlike foreigners, had the amazing ability to 'relax' on buses and trains but be able to wake up at the right bus/tram stop or station. As somebody who had 'slept through' my station in England on more than one occasion especially late at night, I did a study of this and I discovered part two of the 'secret', to which our attention is not usually drawn. In Japan unlike England before every stop the conductor or guard makes loud announcements in a strange nasal voice always mentioning clearly the name of the stop and reminding passengers not to forget things etc. Any human being would have to be stone deaf or unconscious not to hear those announcements and wake up. The 'street cries' of the guard/conductor on trains, trams and buses were as much a part of Japan as those of the different vendors selling anything from roasted sweet potato, goldfish, chestnuts, *soba*, and *tofu* to bamboo laundry poles. Sadly, thanks to modern technology, they have either disappeared completely or the natural human voice has been replaced by tape recordings or even CD. But they are still as loud!

But I digress. After 'squealing' on Mr Yonemura I was begged to continue with him. The embassy owed him a great debt of gratitude for his long and devoted service. The truth was that he needed the money. His pension was minimal, any savings had been lost to post-war inflation, and as he was not exactly popular with the serious full-time language students he was dependent on his income from the unofficial language students. I have no doubt that he must in his day have been a great teacher and I never will understand why, if HMG owed him such a large debt of gratitude, he could not be paid a proper pension making allowances for the war years. A few lessons later I decided to test my teacher's hearing whilst he was just resting his eyes by reading the page of *kanamajiri* from the top left corner of the page to the right instead of right to left. Complete gibberish. As I expected he did not even twitch until I coughed loudly and he knew it was time for him to leave. I eventually took the intermediate exam in 1961 and passed. It had taken me eighteen months of teaching myself and only six months of formal part-time tuition to reach the level a full-time language student reaches after six months' tuition. But it had been a labour of love. It was at this point that fate once again stepped in.

*   *   *

In June 1960 Ann Morgan, a new secretary had arrived in Tokyo. I was immediately attracted to her although there was little opportunity for me to meet her because I had been temporarily moved from the main embassy building to the Consular Section in the Sankei Building next to Tokyo Station. By an amazing coincidence the three senior members of the consular staff – Leo Pickles, (then Consul-General), his deputy, Eric Owen (Consul) and Derek Bakes (Vice-Consul) – were all absent at the same time with illness. I was on duty in the embassy on a Sunday morning. The Head of Chancery, Lees Mayall, came into the Registry, and effectively told me to stand by to go to the Consular Section the next day as Acting British Vice-Consul. The ambassador issued me with an authority to sign visas but not British passports. I did not return to the main embassy until September. By October Ann and I were starting to go out together; in February 1961 we decided to get married and at Easter we announced our engagement.

But there were some complications. The first of these was that I had been due to leave Japan in September 1961 at the end of my tour. This was postponed until October because Prime Minister Harold Macmillan was due to visit Japan in September and his visit would understandably generate an enormous amount of cypher work. My plan was to return to

London, and see Ann's parents to discuss when and how we could be married in the UK. Thanks to the postponement I was able to sit the intermediate level exam, as I could not return to England as planned. Following Ann's father's advice we decided to marry in Japan in July 1961 and return to the UK together in October. In the event we returned on the SS *Cambodge* in November.

One day in early 1961 Lees Mayall had called me into his office. He had heard that I was keen to learn the Japanese language and that I was planning to take the intermediate examination. He asked me whether, if I passed the exam with a reasonable mark, I would be interested in becoming a full-time language student. As I did not think it was even possible for a Clerical Officer to be considered I could not believe what I was hearing. At that time I am sure that nothing had been officially discussed with or agreed by the FO. Clearly Brian Hitch (now in charge of the language students) and Lees Mayall had decided it would be worth a try.

Ann and I were married on 7 July and 8 July. In those days foreigners could not be married under local law. We were legally married in the Consular Section by the Acting Consul General, Eric Townsend, and the next day were married in the Franciscan Chapel Centre in Roppongi. Lees Mayall gave Ann away and he with Mary Mayall hosted an unforgettable champagne reception in No 4 House of the embassy. The Chargé d'Affaires, Edward Warner, was the guest of honour. The day was the hottest on record with temperatures rising to 38.9 degrees centigrade. It was just as well we had decided to spend our honeymoon touring Hokkaido. We were taking advantage of specially priced 'Honeymoon' tickets on JAL. As part of the deal there would be a special souvenir ticket in red and gold signed by the captain of the plane.

In accordance with the British tradition we were pelted with rice when we left No 4 House. As we got out of the car at Haneda and went to check in, hundreds of rice grains cascaded from our clothes much to the amusement of everybody. But most embarrassing for us! The plane had barely taken off from Haneda when the American captain made an announcement in English, which attracted very little attention because there were no more than five foreigners on the plane. It was a different story when one of the crew made the same announcement in Japanese and one of the stewardesses pointed us out to the passengers. It was met with enormous happy smiles and many good wishes of '*o-medeto gozaimasu*' (congratulations). As newlyweds this, too, was most embarrassing! On the return journey a week later we suffered a similar embarrassment. The announcer informed everybody that we were returning from honeymoon, which attracted an entirely different response, and which needs no explanation. After thirty-eight years we still have not decided which of the two was the more humiliating,

The exam results finally arrived. I had passed with a good mark and true to his word Lees Mayall wrote to London. They agreed in principle but as I had already reached the Intermediate level it was suggested that I need only do one year as a student to reach Higher standard. Fortunately Hugh Cortazzi, one of the FCO's leading Japanese linguists, who had by this time taken over responsibility for the language programme, submitted a very forceful case to the powers in London. He pointed out that language students reached the intermediate level after six months full-time tuition and therefore I should be a student for eighteen months. The FCO compromised by finally agreeing to fifteen months but they had not calculated the time I would start after my return from leave and the date of the examination in the autumn of 1963. I went on leave and returned to Tokyo in February 1962. Yet again fate had struck. I was a full-time language student.

*   *   *

But things were not easy. The lease on the house in Yotsuya had expired so that on our return we had to stay in the Sanbancho hotel and go house-hunting, which took several weeks. I was also in effect an additional full-time student and all the teachers' time was already taken up with the four regular students. I was therefore unable to get regular lessons during the daytime and I was forced to grab a lesson here and there with whomever of the teachers – Mr Nakazato, Mrs Nishi and Mr Imaizumi, was available. The senior teacher, Mr Nakazato, with enormous dedication, however, arranged to give me occasional lessons late on Friday evenings from 8.00 until 10.00, or on Saturday afternoons from 2.00 until 4.00, and on National holidays. He also left me reams of translation homework to work on. Later, in the heat of the summer, as the other students took leave I took advantage of their lesson time. In September 1962 three new students arrived but I now had my regular daily lessons.

As part of their Japanese studies today the students enjoy a two-week homestay with a Japanese family well away from the large cities. Not only do they experience family life but are also able to study and practise Japanese in a totally Japanese environment away from the big cities where no English is spoken at all. In the 1960s for whatever reason we did not have this arrangement but the students in their second year were called upon to do interpreting work from time to time. In the summer of 1963 the British Far East Fleet was visiting Japanese ports under the flag of Admiral Sir David Luce. In the Naval Attaché's Office in the embassy, Lt Cdr Mike Forrest, a qualified Japanese language speaker [see Chapter 25], was coordinating the whole visit. He was nominated to assist the Captain of HMS *Alert*, the admiral's flagship, when it called at Wakayama and continue with the ship until it reached Tokyo to meet up with the admiral. I was nominated to be his assistant and look after ship's chandlers, immigration officers, and similar people who come on board ships when they are in port. I felt confident enough to do this!

Despite having already lived for four years in Japan I was not exactly sure where Wakayama was even though I had travelled quite a bit. I was assured it was a very easy place to get to. Tokyo to Osaka and change onto the Wakayama Line. Although the *Shinkansen* was still a year away, trains, albeit slower, were just as punctual. I had just seventeen minutes at Osaka to change trains. I searched everywhere for a sign indicating the way to the Wakayama Line without success. Panic started to set in. I saw a man standing a few yards away from me and decided to seek his help. I said in absolutely perfect and polite Japanese: 'Excuse me my man, but would you please be so good as to tell me from which platform the Wakayama train leaves?' My question was met with a totally blank expression before the man, waving his hand in front of his grinning face, said 'No shpeeky Ingrishu!' I mildly protested and in perfect Japanese said: 'I am speaking Japanese. Please listen.' I repeated my original request. Again it was met with the wave of the hand, the toothy grin, and 'No shpeeky Ingrishu'.

As a student I always carried a note-pad with me. Whenever I saw *'kanji'* I could not read I wrote it down in my note-pad, preferable in context, and looked up the meaning later. I took my note-pad and wrote my request in Japanese, which I showed to 'No shpeeky Ingrishu'. Immediately he responded in the most amazing torrent of words, none of which was immediately recognizable to me as Japanese except possibly for *'Wakayama ka?'* and by his waving his arms in a general direction of 'over there'. I thanked him profusely and ran off in the direction he had indicated and caught my train with about a minute to spare.

As I sat down gasping for breath with my large suitcase beside me the other passengers without uttering a word looked at me quizzically as if I had arrived from outer space. In the thirty minutes on the train to Wakayama I had the opportunity to reflect that after four years in Japan, with effectively two years of full-time study of the Japanese language the Japanese could not understand me and I could not understand them! I was a failure! I could only console myself with the thought that there was probably a Japanese able to speak perfect English trying to understand and be understood by somebody in Newcastle or Birmingham.

It is worthwhile noting that for many years, wherever I travelled in Japan outside of the Tokyo area, oral communication was always a great problem. I was told that this was basically because most Japanese believed that foreigners could not speak Japanese. Therefore even if they recognized the foreigners' words as Japanese they were not prepared mentally to accept it was Japanese. I found this hard to believe but there must have been a lot of truth in it.

As a result of my experience in Osaka I was on the point of resigning myself never to being able to speak Japanese. When I arrived at Wakayama

Station Mike Forrest met me with the awful news that his wife, Gail, was seriously ill and that he had to return to Tokyo immediately. I was now to be chief interpreter for the captain of HMS *Alert* during his calls on the governor and at the official dinner and look after the various visitors to the ship. Panic started to set in! Fortunately, I was saved by the subsequent appearance of a *Nisei* (second generation Japanese American) who worked in the prefectural government building as an interpreter. He was going to do the difficult bits such as interpreting the formal speeches. However, at the official dinner I sat between the governor and the captain. The governor mumbled lengthy sentences in the local dialect, that I reduced in the translation to such a degree that the captain at one point said 'Surely that is not all he said!' I tried to explain the circumlocutory style of Japanese but it came back to haunt me when the captain's circumlocutory sentences in English I interpreted in my truncated style of Japanese. But the saké flowed, the food was delicious, and both became the subjects of an animated discussion on the relative merits of Scotch whisky and Suntory whisky, roast beef and Yorkshire pudding and *sashimi*.

As I continued to be employed in the Embassy I like to think that in the heady atmosphere of the occasion my obvious limitations as an interpreter were soon forgotten. I was able to make up for my limitations however the next day dealing effectively and efficiently with the callers who were talking about more mundane things like ship's water and other supplies, as well as accompanying some of the ship's officers around the local bar district.

*   *   *

I passed the higher standard Japanese examination in September 1962. This created a problem. There were no jobs in my grade demanding the language skills at the level I had reached. After the FCO had invested so much money in me surely they had to have me use it. I could hardly be posted back to London or elsewhere. So a job was created for me as British Vice-Consul in Yokohama. After all I had spent three months in Tokyo in 1960 doing consular work so I was already experienced! I could not have asked for a better job. Consular work covered such a wide range of duties, which I am glad to say the Consul, Reg Brereton let me get on with. However he coveted two particular duties. The most important was to pander to the senior British business community when they needed a new passport or to have a signature certified. In those days Yokohama was very much a dormitory town for the foreign (particularly British) business community in Tokyo. The second was dealing with the Consular Corps.

My duties included dealing with the fifty or so British registered ships, which called in at Yokohama/Kawasaki and Shimizu every month and involved crew changes each month, and acting as a go-between between the local authorities, i.e. police and immigration and the ships. On many nights I was invited, under the terms of the Japan-UK Consular Treaty, to Yamate police station to witness one or more drunken seamen, lying in their own vomit on the floor of a cell and totally incoherent. After obtaining details of the individual's real nationality, which could take some time because many claimed British nationality even if they were Danish or Chinese I would return the next day with somebody from the ship or the shipping agent. A fine would be paid, or compensation paid for damages to the bar owner whose bar the seamen had attempted to destroy or whose employees they had intimidated. Many times I witnessed these people each with a screaming hangover, with vomit-soiled clothing and stinking of alcohol, swearing on oath and before several witnesses that they had not been drinking and could not therefore have been drunk and disorderly. They had however been cruelly beaten by the 'secret' police to the point where they had lost their memory. Fortunately, such people were, of course, in the minority but as usual they took up a lot of valuable time; the large majority were responsible seamen able to go ashore and take advantage of the facilities of the Missions to Seamen and other seamen's clubs.

To some sailors Yokohama became a holiday camp. If a seaman had simply missed the sailing he was placed in the Yokohama Immigration Detention Centre until somebody somewhere could arrange repatriation. The shipping agency generally did not want to meet the cost. Fortunately, most British masters repatriated the genuine cases as distressed British seamen. The troublemakers and 'ship jumpers' were another matter. Understandably they were not very popular and many masters were loth to take them for fear that these men would upset their good crews. Consequently, a long wait was inevitable but the seamen very seldom seemed to mind, because they could sit around all day being well fed and doing nothing except read, write letters, play table tennis, and demand visits from the British Consul to sort out one or another case of alleged cruelty or suffering.

The next most important duty was issuing visas mainly to the Americans living in the consular district who wanted to visit Hong Kong. We had one problem with the writing of dates because the Americans always wrote their date of birth month/day/year unlike the UK where it is day/month/year and their nationality according to their ancestry. Thus we had 'Dutch/Irish/Scotch' or 'German/Norwegian'. This begged to be made fun of.

'So I see from your application that your birthday is 3 October 1936.'

'No Sir! It is 10 March 1936.'

'But I see here it is 3 October' (Look of total confusion spreads across the applicant's face.)

Closely studying the application: 'I see that you are not an American citizen.'

'Sir?'

'It says here that you are Latvian/Danish/Irish.'

'Yes Sir, my paternal grandfather came from Latvia and he married my grandmother who was Irish and . . . But I am an American!'

We also issued visas to Japanese businessmen making business trips abroad. The visa application in those days asked two embarrassing questions. The first was whether the applicant had served in the Japanese military forces. The second was the amount of funds they would be taking with them. In the first case not a single applicant seemingly had ever served in Hong Kong, Singapore or Malaya. All, however, had served in Northern China on the Russian border. They were totally convinced that had they served in a war theatre involving the British army they would automatically be denied a visa.

As for foreign currency they were limited to so many dollars a day and could not exceed a total of (say) $1,000 for the whole trip. Generally this was in US dollar Travellers Cheques. Yen was a useless currency outside of Japan, but thanks to the black market, dollars and pounds could be had at a premium and Japanese businessmen had no choice but to avail themselves of this facility. The official rates were Yen 1,008 = £1 and Yen 360 = $1. The premium rate was Yen 1,400 and Yen 450 respectively. The applicants fell between two stools. They could tell us the truth, which revealed they were contravening the foreign currency regulations and they feared (totally unfounded) we would report them. Alternatively, they could lie and we could refuse the visa on the ground of insufficient funds to maintain them while in a British territory. They always ended up by telling the truth.

My knowledge of Japanese came in useful when dealing with the shipping agencies and the local authorities. I was also able to read the daily newspapers. But there were times when my ability to read Japanese was particularly useful. In a port city such as Yokohama there were numerous interracial marriages mainly involving British sailors. The Japanese lady had to produce a copy of her family register (*koseki tohon*) which provided full evidence that she was not married or that any previous marriage had been legally terminated. It also showed details of her parentage, any children etc. The British side had to produce his passport, his birth certificate, and a certified document to show that the banns had been read in his parish in the UK; he also had to swear an affidavit stating that he was free to marry. If he had been previously married he had to produce a copy of his divorce decree absolute. Each couple had to be interviewed and invariably there was a serious language problem. Neither could speak the other's language apart from basics and therefore I was obliged to question the couple on various points. Many times the answers came as a surprise to one partner or the other. Invariably it was previous marriage or children, which caused the biggest problems.

One day, a couple called to give notice of marriage. She was clearly much older than he was. They did not have a communicable language. He was born in 1938; his fiancée was also born in 1938. At least she had told me in Japanese that she had been born in Showa 13. From her appearance this was clearly untrue. I studied her family register and sure enough her birthday was in Taisho 13 (1924); she was married and divorced and had a son aged 18. I was in a dilemma. Clearly if he was aware of these facts he might change his mind and I had no right to influence or guide him. He was an adult. But I felt I had to tell him something. As he could not speak Japanese I read out the contents of the family register to the woman. When I stressed 'Taisho 13' and not 'Showa 13' and the fact that she was divorced etc she started to bow her head and hold a small handkerchief over her mouth. The man asked me what I was talking to her about and I replied that there had been a couple of minor errors on the application form. As soon as I crossed out 'single' and wrote 'divorced' and then the year of her birth as 1924 instead of 1938 he became a little angry and pointing at her shouted 'Why you no tell?' The woman started to cry. I then suggested that perhaps they should go away for a few days and discuss the matter and come back again when all was decided.

Looking back now it is very sad that many British and no doubt other nationals believed that interracial marriages under local law in Japan were not valid in their home country. As a result desertion was quite common and many a time the deserted wife was left pregnant. The husband did not realize that the 'bit of paper in Japanese' with an official translation was a legal document, which was lodged at Somerset House. In the above case the couple went through with the marriage but the husband was loyal for no more than a year before leaving his wife and Japan for good. I heard later that he had gone back to the UK to get married. I am sure that he and his new bride were more than a little surprised when the bigamy case came up.

There were also humorous moments. One day, I heard from the public office a loud stentorian voice demanding to see the consul on a 'very personal and confidential matter'. A few seconds later a huge lady with a shaven head and dressed in saffron robes barged into my office pushing my assistant summarily to one side. She spoke in a most refined albeit booming voice and introduced herself as Peggy Kennett from Gloucestershire. She was a Buddhist Abbess and she had been living in India and she had now moved to a temple in Tsurumi on the outskirts of Yokohama. She sat down and proceeded to tell me in a hushed but somehow still booming voice that she was the only female amongst twenty or thirty monks in the temple. There was now a whispering campaign against her by people in the neighbourhood that she was providing them with sexual favours and her reputation was being damaged. One would have to look hard to find a more masculine or less feminine person than Miss Kennett and my mind rioted. Trying to maintain a concerned face I asked her to confirm that it was not true before I contacted the police. But apart from involving the police there was little the consulate could do to stop neighbours spreading salacious rumours about her. Of course, if she had any suggestions. . . . . . I nearly fell off my chair when she calmly asked me to issue a formal 'virginity certificate' with the consulate seal on it! When I asked what she proposed to do with it she replied that she would stick it on the gate to the temple for all to see! That would quieten the gossips.

I attempted to explain in the best pedantic bureaucrat manner that consuls could only certify those things that we knew to be true or that we had satisfactory evidence to prove that something was true. I could certify that Joe Bloggs was Joe Bloggs, for example, because I had known him personally for a reasonable period of time. But in any case he had produced as evidence his passport which I knew to be genuine etc etc. Under the circumstances as I was not a doctor and I could not certify that the lady was '*virgo intacta*' I could not produce such a certificate. However, if Miss Kennett would care to go to the Bluff Hospital and be examined by Doctor Len Kitson, who was personally known to me as a Doctor of Medicine (he had delivered two of my children), and whose signature I well knew I would be delighted to issue the necessary certificate. She agreed and I telephoned Dr Kitson who agreed to see her immediately.

Miss Kennett departed and about one hour later returned trium-phantly waving the certificate. I had no doubts what it would say. We prepared a beautiful consular certificate on crested blue paper, to which was attached with red ribbon the doctor's certificate with a translation in Japanese, and bearing a bright red wax seal with my signature below. It was a classic example of the bureaucrat's art and nobody would ever say a word about Miss Kennett's sexual habits after reading it. She was de-lighted and left just as the phone rang. It was Dr Kitson. I thought he was going to tell me that something was wrong with the certificate. But all he said was 'I have been thinking. That certificate I issued could be invalid by now'. (Pause) 'But I doubt it. I really doubt it'! 'So do I Len, but thanks for letting me know.'

*   *   *

Despite my having the title of British Vice-Consul Reg Brereton often referred to me as his Cockney office boy when speaking to certain mem-bers of the community. Fortunately, Ann and I were active members of the Yokohama Country and Athletic Club, which he was not, and there-fore we were well known. It was just as well because when other members of the Consular Corps asked Reg Brereton why I was the only Consular

official in Yokohama who did not attend the monthly Corps lunches, and
he attempted to tell them that I was too junior, they knew better and
insisted that I should attend.

The consulate business hours were from 0900 until midday and from
1400 until 1600. As far as Mr Brereton was concerned anybody arriving
one second late had to wait until the office next opened. Needless to say
there were emergencies which had to be dealt with but it would have to
be akin to murder before he would deign to deal with it. One day, a British businessman turned up in a taxi at 12.05. The doors were locked. He
signalled to one of the Japanese staff who let him in. He had arrived at
Haneda Airport to discover his passport had expired. He had to catch the
plane to attend an important business meeting in Hong Kong. Fortunately, he had passport photographs and while he completed the application I prepared the passport. I was not permitted to sign passports, so at
12.20 I went into Reg Brereton's office and I asked him to sign the passport. He refused pointing out that he only signed passports at 16.00 after
the office had closed. I explained the circumstances and again he refused.
I pushed the case and angrily he snatched the passport from my hand,
saying 'Who the hell do these people think we are? Their servants?!' I
replied 'Well, as a matter of fact, that is exactly what we are.' Muttering
under his breath he signed the passport; I ran out and handed it to the
man and he jumped into his waiting taxi and left. A week or so later Reg
Brereton received a warm letter of appreciation and thanks. The man had
caught his plane and the meeting had been successful. Without Reg Brereton's appreciation of the facts and his taking urgent action it would have
been a disaster. The letter was quickly forwarded to H M Ambassador in
Tokyo for the 'kudos file'.

POSTSCRIPT

A nybody who has seriously studied the Japanese language will have
been aware from the very beginning of the large number and range
of foreign words, which have been imported into the language. The majority of these words seem to have originated from English although
there are also words of German and French origin. It is reasonable to
assume, therefore, that a large segment of Japanese vocabulary will be
that much easier for an English-speaking person to learn. To appreciate
fully the number and range one only has to delve into the Kenkyusha
Japanese-English dictionary under 'P' where such Japanese words as *'pur-
ashitikku'* or *'puropera'* appear. I can easily understand why perhaps new
scientific or technical words can be so easily absorbed into the language
but is there any justification to use word such as *'puraido'* (pride) and *'pe-e-
so-su'* (pathos) when perfectly good Japanese words are available.

Contrary to popular expectation, imported foreign words help to make Japanese even more difficult than it already is for any foreigner, English speaking or otherwise, to learn. Take, for example, the English word 'close-up' pronounced with a hard 's'. This has entered Japanese meaning the same as the English 'close-up' but with a soft 's' i.e. pronounced 'cloze-up' which has an entirely different meaning in English. In view of the Japanese difficulty in pronouncing the English 'th' sound, 'close-up' has occasionally even been heard as 'clothes-up'. However, it is not just in pronunciation that difficulties can arise. When I was a Japanese language student, at the beginning of the 1960s, the hardest test of reading ability was not to read aloud a few paragraphs from a Japanese book or newspaper in a way that suggested that I could actually understand what I was reading about: it was to read out loud to my teacher a text which was virtually made up of imported words. The imported, words were written in *katakana* separated here and there by essential Japanese words such as *'suru'*, or *'no'* in *hiragana* without which a sentence could not be formed. In fact, it was infinitely more difficult to read such texts than even *'kanamajiri'*. More times than not, even when I could read *katakana* fluently, I did not actually fully understand what I was reading despite being assured that the words were imported English. The difficulty was not always the words themselves; after all, one could guess at words such as *'ka-me-ra'* or *'te-re-bi'* although it was less easy to understand words such as *'bo-ri-yu-u-mu'*. Nor was it particularly difficult to read *katakana*. It was the Japanized versions of the imported words, which proved to be the stumbling block. I recall the most famous example at that time was *'genesuto'* which was an abbreviation of *ge-ne-ra-ru-su-to-ra-i-ki* (general strike). There were numerous others which I will not go into here.

Abbreviating words or rather abbreviating compounded words is common in the Japanese language. Thus *'Tokyo ni agaru'* (to go up to Tokyo) was abbreviated to *'Jokyo suru'* although that does not strike me as being particularly shorter but it is. It is, however, reasonable that very long imported words should be abbreviated provided everybody knows what the original words are. For example, *'pa-su'* in Japanese can either mean 'pass' as in examination, or as in bus pass, or calipers (do not ask me), or to pass as in card games. It is also the accepted abbreviation for para-aminosalicylic acid!

Abbreviation can be a good thing. It saves breath when in conversation except where you have to stop to explain what the abbreviated word means. In a way it is like people who choose to pepper their conversation with trendy London rhyming slang. It definitely loses something when the speaker has to explain that 'to go for a ball down the frog' is omitting the rhyme words 'ball (of chalk) down the frog (and toad)', which rhymes with 'walk' and 'road' respectively. But I digress. In Japanese even more difficulty is created for the student when a real Japanese word is joined to an imported word. One example is *'poketto gata'* (pocket size). But then the word *'poketto mane'* (pocket money) made up from two foreign words could, if the Japanese word *'mane'* (imitation or to imitate) was used, mean imitation pocket. The same logic applies. The best possible example of an abbreviated import plus Japanese compound word however must be *'karaoke'* which has become an internationally known *'Japanese'* word! Its origin is the joining of *'kara'* (empty) with *'orukesutora'* (orchestra) which together means 'empty orchestra'. Nobody has satisfactorily explained what an 'empty orchestra' is but who cares? We all know what it means.

Then there are cases where we have two foreign words with different pronunciations e.g. plateau and Plato, both expressed in Japanese as *'purato'*. Nor can we overlook such words as 'connection' being abbreviated to *'ko-ne'*. The list goes on.

I am proud to say that my colleagues and I studying Japanese nearly forty years ago took a dim view of this abuse of the Japanese language. We decided that it was only right and proper that wherever possible we would only use real Japanese words. Clearly *'Rondon'* had to stay in but *'kamera'* and *'rekodo pureya'* could go to be replaced by *shashinki* and *chikuonki* respectively. Admittedly, when we used such words it occasionally caused eyebrows to be raised, but we assumed our deep knowledge of pure Japanese was simply an object of amazement or incredulity. We decided to carry this forward to our translation homework. If we did not know the word in Japanese we would look it up in our dictionaries. There were always one or two Japanese definitions but many times there was the corrupted English (or French or German) word, which understandably was anathema to us and therefore could not be used under any circumstances. One student had the misfortune of looking up the word for 'concrete' as in 'a concrete building'. In his dictionary he found two words – *'gutaiteki'* and *'konkuriito'*. Naturally, he chose the former and wrote *'Gutaiteki na tatemono'*. Our teacher clearly did not appreciate fully our idealistic approach to his language. My colleague's explanation to justify his choice of words in the translation, that buildings are tangible solid things and are not abstract, fell on deaf ears.

From November 1966 until April 1977 I was not in Japan. During that time I did not find many Japanese speakers in my postings to London, the USA and Belgium, at least none that wished to speak to me in any other language than English. I therefore had no opportunity to stay in touch with the Japanese language during that time. In May 1977 I attended the British Embassy language school at Kamakura on a one-month refresher course. This meant that I had one month to re-learn about 2,000 *kanji* and a basic Japanese vocabulary running to several thousand words. I admit I did take advantage of using many imported English words. Unfortunately, many had not even entered the Japanese language which meant that, at times, people did not understand what I was saying, but it was worth the gamble.

I later moved to Tokyo and started work in the embassy. I moved into a house in Tomigaya in Shibuya. On the first day I realized I had no milk in the house. My colleague, who lived nearby told me of a small *yorozuya*, located at the bottom of the hill, which sold milk. I soon found the store and knowing the Japanese word for milk I asked the old shopkeeper in impeccable Japanese whether he had any *'gyunyu'*. Presumably by way of confirmation he said in Japanese 'You mean *"miruku"*, don't you?'

'Yes' I replied.

'Certainly' he said and shuffled off towards a refrigerator at the back of the store from which he produced a carton of milk. Thanking him I paid the yen 180 and left thinking to myself that perhaps in future I had better use the new word *'miruku'*.

A few days later, I called again at the same store and asked the same old man again in impeccable Japanese for some *'miruku'*. The old man's response was 'That's *"gyunyu"* you mean, isn't it?'

'Yes' I replied biting my tongue, for fear of saying something I should not.

'Certainly' said the old man once more digging out a carton of milk from his refrigerator. I paid the money and left, this time muttering to myself that it was clear the old fool was poking fun at a foreigner's funny Japanese. 'There's ingratitude. I was only trying to speak his language' I thought.

A few days later, my wife and three children arrived from London. It was not long before one evening she told me that she was short of milk for breakfast and asked me whether I could go to the local store and buy two cartons. Down the hill I went to the store. The old man cheerfully greeted me. 'Danna-san, Good evening'.

'Good evening' I replied. 'May I please have one carton of *'miruku'* and one carton of *"gyuunyuu"*?'

'Certainly' said the old man, automatically heading for the refrigerator before suddenly stopping after realizing what I had said. With a big grin revealing a mouth full of rotten teeth he turned and said *'Danna-san! Share o-jozu desu ne!'* (You are good at playing with words).

For the next three years we exchanged pleasantries and regularly chatted until after a long time of not seeing him I heard that he had passed away. Suddenly, the little store closed and was replaced by a *'koin randori'*. Somehow to me an imported word like *'koin randori'* never did have the same ring as good old-fashioned 'Yorozuya-san'.

Gairaigo has haunted me on several occasions during my twenty years of service in Japan. I have one particularly humiliating memory and even today it makes me blush when I recall it. I have always had an interest in traditional Japanese popular songs such as *enka*. In the 1970s there was a song I thought was called *'shikuramen no kaori'* which I particularly liked. However, the title confused me because I could not understand why anybody would wish to write a song about the smell of a type of *ramen* (noodles) from 'Shiku' (wherever that may be in Japan). I had heard of *Sapporo ramen*. Perhaps *shikuramen* was similar. I asked a Japanese friend for advice. At first he thought I was joking. God knows I wish I had been. He quickly realised where I was going wrong and he suggested that perhaps if I thought of *shikuramen* as an English word instead of *shikuramen* (as I was incorrectly pronouncing it) that might help. The penny still would not have dropped had he not given me the clue that it was obviously a flower. I was able to decypher the word, but to this day I still do not know how 'cyclamen' can be pronounced as *shikuramen*.

35

Language Student, Commercial Officer, Information Officer

ALAN PINNELL

COVERING a span of some twenty years, from the end of the 1960s to the late 80s, ALAN PINNELL picks up on the memorable moments of his years in Japan, culminating in the visit of the Prince and Princess of Wales in 1986. He concludes with the truism that 'the longer you work with Japan and the Japanese, the less you understand. That is the continuing fascination of Japan':-

•

O ur connection with Japan was entirely fortuitous. Certainly I would not claim to have had a lifelong, burning ambition to go to Japan; and Tokyo would not have been my first choice of overseas posting. While I had all the traditional images of Japan – *geisha*, Mount Fuji, cherry blossoms and so on – I also thought of it as a vast, over-crowded city where people (we were told) had to wear face masks to combat the pollution.

We arrived in Japan [myself, my wife, Tina, and my two daughters Mandy (then nearly four) and Julie (nearly two)] in November 1969 following a three-year posting in Lahore, Pakistan. My next posting after Lahore was to have been Vientiane, but happily for us the FCO inspectors got there first and cut the job I was to have done. I was therefore somewhat in limbo, awaiting a new posting, when a vacancy opened up on the Japanese language course. By the time confirmation of the posting to Tokyo came through, we had only a few weeks to get there. Our baggage took longer, having been sent from Lahore to London, where it was redirected to Tokyo, arriving several months after us.

By comparison with our time in Lahore – an interesting but difficult posting, especially with two small children – arriving in Japan was, to us, like a posting in wonderland. I well remember the sense of amazement and excitement we felt as we travelled by car from Haneda, where the international flights then landed, into the centre of Tokyo. The expressway (still rather rudimentary by today's standards) and the bright lights, the shops and the sheer numbers of people we saw, were beyond anything we had seen before. Soon after our arrival I described our first impressions in a magazine:

> We felt that we had been dropped, without warning, into the twenty-first century... Even after recovering from the initial shock of arriving in this vast metropolis, one retains an overwhelming impression of thriving, bustling, almost frantic, ant-like activity.

On arrival in Tokyo we were taken to the Sanbancho Hotel, just along the road from the British Embassy, since converted into Tony Roma's Restaurant. There we met two of the other three language students I would be studying with, and their wives: Peter and Judy Denison-Edson, and Tony and Susan Millington. Interestingly, but I am sure entirely coincidentally, all of us have since left the Diplomatic Service.

We learnt Japanese in what turned out to be an interim period between two different systems. Before we arrived the Japanese teachers had travelled around Tokyo to give their lessons in the individual language students' houses, mostly on a one-to-one basis. Possibly because getting around the increasingly congested city had become more difficult and time-consuming, it had been decided that the new intake should study in one centralized location, more on a group basis but still with a good number of individual classes. For the first year we were in a suite of rooms rented from Sophia University in Yotsuya, opposite the New Otani Hotel. In the second year, classes were held in the Denison-Edsons' house, just behind Aoyama-dori.

It was said that the Head Teacher, Mr Nakazato, could teach Japanese to a donkey (a reflection on his teaching skills rather than the aptitude of his students, we hoped!). He was indomitable, and, although not beyond the strategic use of anger at our stupidity when appropriate, was at most times unfailingly patient. He was assisted by a number of part-time teachers, principally Mr Omura, a very old-style, traditional Japanese gentleman, and Mrs Nishi, who tried to teach us *shodo* (calligraphy) – with, I am afraid, abject failure in my case – and the hidden arts of reading Japanese cursive script (*gyosho*), in which I had similarly little success.

A year or so after I finished the language course the system changed again, so that the language students did a first year at Sheffield University, and came to Japan only in their second year, to study at Kamakura away from the distractions of Tokyo and the embassy. I suspect that those who did a year in the UK before coming to Japan had a better grasp of grammar and the essentials of the language than we did, while those of us who did a full two years in Japan had a better grasp of everyday usage and vocabulary. Probably, over a period of time, the differences evened themselves out. Whatever the merits of the individual systems, I am glad I did my two years in Tokyo.

Mr Nakazato had one teaching method which seemed to us very en-lightened. He said that we should practise our Japanese in the bars of Tokyo and spend time talking to the customers and the bar hostesses. We were happy to comply, so with official blessing (and even our wives' agreement, which spoilt the fun a little), we made regular forays into the bars of Shibuya and Shinjuku (Ginza and Akasaka being well beyond our means). We often caused much merriment by attempting to engage in conversation using a combination of rudimentary Japanese and phrases learnt from the editorial columns of the *Nihon Keizai Shimbun*, which formed the main texts for our lessons!

Such innocent pleasures are, I think, now almost gone in Japan, de-stroyed by a combination of *karaoke*, which makes it impossible to have a conversation in a bar without having a microphone thrust in your face, and the fact that most bar hostesses are now from other parts of Asia with little or no knowledge of Japanese.

One of our more interesting duties as language students was to inter-pret for Royal Navy ships making goodwill visits to Japanese ports. I did this twice, once for a minesweeper visiting Kure, and once for HMS *Al-bion* visiting Kobe. Our duties were twofold. The most important, and the real reason we were there, was to interpret for the captain's official calls on the local mayor and other dignitaries and at other official meetings or functions. The second, more informal, duty was to accompany the offi-cers on their 'runs ashore', to guide them round the local watering holes and interpret for them in their social chit-chat (which certainly extended our vocabulary). I was always rather puzzled why the officers needed this personalized service, when the other ranks seemed to manage more than adequately by themselves!

*   *   *

A practice which I suspect went back many years to when the Foreign Office first sent language students (or Student Interpreters)[1] to Japan in the nineteenth century was the 'Month in the Country'. For each of the two years of our study, we had to leave Tokyo during the summer and stay with a Japanese family for a month. For my first year (1970), I split my month into two, and spent some time in Yamagata, and some in Hokkai-do. In both cases I stayed with farming families. Although it cannot have been easy for them to have this *gaijin*, unaccustomed to Japanese ways and with only a rather basic grasp of Japanese, staying with them, they both made me very welcome, as any who knows the Japanese would expect. My main difficulty in Hokkaido was that, having been assured that every-one in Hokkaido spoke *hyojungo* (standard Japanese), the grandfather in the family had in fact emigrated from Yamagata in the early years of the century and still spoke with the region's characteristic *zu-zu-ben*, whereby (as it seemed to me) every 'su' and 'tsu' sound came out as a 'zu'. This made it almost impossible to understand him – rather like confronting a novice English-speaker with a Geordie accent!

The next year (1971), I went to Miyazaki, in Kyushu. I was again rather dispirited by my lack of progress in Japanese when, on the ferry from Kobe to Beppu, I found I could not understand what a group of schoolgirls were saying to me (maybe just as well!). Later, I realized that they were speaking *Kagoshima-ben*, another hard-to-understand regional dialect.

It was in Miyazaki that I had one of those embarrassing experiences which befall all newcomers to Japan.

On my first night I was – naturally – invited to take my bath first. I found the water in the bathtub scalding hot, but knew better (I thought) than to add cold water. So I slowly lowered myself in, inch by inch, until I was fully submerged and boiling like a lobster. Having stood it for as long as I could, I got out, dried myself, put on my yukata and presented myself fresh and red to the family. The husband took the next turn in the bath. When he reappeared, he said to me: 'My word, Pinnell-san, you really like your baths hot, don't you? I had to put some cold water in before I could get into the bath'! Of course, having established that I liked scalding hot baths, I had to endure the same medieval torture every night I was there, rather than admit that I had got it wrong the first night.

Away from Tokyo, we were treated like local celebrities or perhaps, more accurately, local curiosities. We were interviewed and photographed for the local newspapers. I even merited a half-page spread in the *Hokkaido Times*, which reported that my lifestyle was '... completely Japanese, eating rice using a bowl and chopsticks, reading the Japanese newspapers and watching television sitting on a *zabuton*'! It was in Miyazaki that I was called, for the first and, I think, only time, '*takahana*' (meaning 'high nose'), though we could not escape cries of '*Gaijin da yo!* (he's a foreigner!) wherever we went.

Apart from the benefits of the 'Month in the Country' for consolidating our Japanese skills and seeing Japanese life at first hand, the experience also gave us valuable opportunities to travel around Japan – opportunities which became much scarcer once we were ensconced in our jobs in the embassy. Travelling on Japanese trains was an experience in itself, and although I found that the split-second punctuality for which they were famous abroad did not apply to all of Japan's railways, they provided an excellent opportunity to people-watch, and to see how the Japanese went about their daily business. Two incidents remain in my mind. One was travelling on a crowded train in northern Japan where every seat was taken except the one next to me, even though there were many people standing. Perhaps I really did smell of butter (*bata-kusai*). The other was when the old lady sitting next to me insisted on sharing her green tea and *o-bento* box with me because – stupid foreigner! – I clearly had brought nothing to eat or drink with me. Such were, and maybe still are, the contradictions in Japanese attitudes to foreigners.

One other abiding memory of travelling on Japanese trains, then and later, was of Japanese businessmen taking off their suits and hanging them up when getting onto the train, sitting for the journey in their long-sleeved vests and long-johns, and then putting their uncreased suits back on again before getting off the train. (By the time I returned to Japan in 1982, this sensible but immodest custom seemed to have died out, as I did not see it again then.)

The wives and families of the language students also took advantage of this month to see more of Japan. In each of the two years we were away they rented a cabin at Nojiri-ko, a resort originally established by American missionaries near Mount Kurohime in Niigata Prefecture. This began for us a long association with Nojiri-ko, where we spent many very happy summer holidays away from the heat of Tokyo.

* * *

Our first few years in Japan were a time of left-wing student activism and riots against the US-Japan Security Treaty. Barely a week passed without some demonstration snaking its way around the Diet building, or along Aoyama-dori, or around the centre of Shibuya, near where we lived. On many occasions Tokyo seemed like an armed camp, with huge numbers of riot police in battle gear stationed around every corner and down every side street. Often the air was filled with the smell of tear-gas and the roads were scorched with the remains of Molotov Cocktails (*kaenbin*). One Sunday morning we awoke to learn, from the local news, that we had been 'liberated' by a group of left-wing students rioting in Shibuya. The immediate effect of our liberation was that we could not get out of the area! A more tragic outcome was that one policeman from our local *koban* (police post) had been killed.

But the rioting apart – and, after three years in Pakistan, we were not unfamiliar with civil disturbance – life for myself and for my family was good. Though the range of foodstuffs, and especially foreign foodstuffs, was not nearly so wide as it is now, we never felt at all deprived and Kinokuniya, in Aoyama-dori, supplied most of our household needs. (Interestingly, when we returned to Japan in 1982, we could no longer afford to shop in Kinokuniya, and had to move downmarket to Peacock.) Even after the initial novelty had worn off, we still enjoyed visiting the Japanese stores to marvel at all that was available. After trying to shop in the sparsely-stocked markets of Lahore, we were like children in a candy store.

Unfamiliarity with many of the Japanese products on sale, and an in-

ability to work out what the Japanese on the labels actually said, sometimes led to embarrassing results — as when a Japanese guest asked politely why we kept moth-balls in the toilet. We had thought it was toilet
freshener.

For our two daughters, joined by our son Mark in 1972, Japan was a
paradise where children and their needs came first, and everything
seemed designed for their delight. The only danger they were in was suffering from inflated egos, especially outside Tokyo where they were invariably photographed and greeted with cries of *'kawai-iii ne-eee'* (how
sweet). Mandy and Julie got a good — if rather American-oriented — education at the International School of the Sacred Heart, which they enjoyed (so much so that when we went back to Japan in 1982 Julie
returned to do her GCSEs and her International Baccalaureate there).

Despite valiant efforts, my wife Tina never learnt more than a few
words of basic Japanese, partly (she says) through an innate inability to
learn foreign languages but also (I think) through over-dependence on
me as her ever-present interpreter. But she nevertheless led a very full life
in Tokyo, working among the foreign community, and was one of the
founders and later Director of Tokyo English Life Line (TELL). Later,
after we returned to Japan in 1982, she was part-time Pastor of Yokohama
Union Church and also set up *Welcome Furoshiki*, a welcoming service for
newly-arrived foreign families in Japan.

*   *   *

Although I was not much involved with the visit of the Queen to Japan in
1975, beyond doing some interpreting at official functions, the visit did
provide the occasion for another of my more embarrassing experiences
in Japan. Before the visit, some of the Japanese speakers in the embassy
were despatched to different parts of Japan to talk to local groups about
Britain and the monarchy, so as to create a grass-roots awareness and
understanding of the forthcoming visit. As I recall it, we were given a
basic script, but had to produce our own speech text for each occasion.

I was assigned to speak to the ladies of the *Fujin-kai* (ladies' group) in
Nagoya. When I enquired whether they wished me to speak in English or
in Japanese, I was told: 'Both, as most of our ladies do not speak English,
but we have some English ladies who do not speak Japanese'. Due to
inexperience and an eagerness to please, I did not demur at this impossible request. The result was that, first I had to translate my English text
into Japanese — a task I would never now embark on — and secondly, and
disastrously, I tried to give the speech one paragraph at a time, alternately
in Japanese and in English. Since I was unable to build up a fluent flow in
either language, I stumbled my way through the speech as my audience's
faces grew more and more blank and uncomprehending. I learned then

the true meaning of wishing the ground to open before me and swallow me up!

My other recollection of the visit was the Queen's departure from the Akasaka Palace at the end of the visit. I was in the last car of the motorcade, and had the curious experience of seeing the Japanese Emperor bowing to me, a mere second secretary, as we swept out of the Palace gates.

Our first tour of duty in Japan coincided with the Japanese 'economic miracle', with constant double-digit growth which made Japan the envy of the developed world. Yet I have to say that one of my first impressions, when I started work in the embassy's commercial department, was that it was a 'miracle' that Japanese business worked at all. The efficiency for which Japanese manufacturing was famed worldwide did not, I soon learned, extend to business, the service sector or the bureaucracy. One Japanese friend, with whom I swapped English and Japanese conversation every week, taught me the phrase 'okurazu, yasumazu, hatarakazu' – don't be late, don't be absent, and don't work. This was obviously a caricature, and my friend himself would often return to work after our evening conversations to complete some 'urgent' project. But the long-hours culture did not seem to be matched by commensurate levels of efficiency, a situation summed up in another phrase current at the time, 'cho-jikan, tei-noritsu' – long hours, low efficiency.

I will not dwell here on the work of the commercial department and the opportunities, and frustrations, of promoting British goods in a market which had been, until quite recently, all but closed to foreign imports. It was a time when British companies were beginning to make inroads into the Japanese market, although it was a constant frustration to us at the embassy that so few major companies thought it worthwhile to establish a permanent presence in Japan – at a time when Japanese companies were steadily encroaching on the British market. I remember a visiting representative of a major British 4-wheel drive vehicle manufacturer saying that their customers were quite prepared to wait several years for delivery of their precious vehicle and that the company had nothing to fear from the Japanese. Not long after, their markets worldwide were overrun with Japanese look-alikes, not so good, maybe, but available and at reasonable cost.

My time in the commercial department also saw the beginning of the treatment of Japan as a special case, deserving of extraordinary export-promotion efforts. This led, among other developments, to the establishment of the Exports to Japan Unit in the DTI, in which I served for two years after my return to the UK, and the opening of the British Export Marketing Centre in Aoyama-dori. [See Chapter 22.]

We left Japan in 1976, after an unusually long six-and-a-half-year posting. These were the formative years of my children's lives, and to a large extent for us as a family. They felt that they were leaving their home, not going home. In contrast to the excitement of our arrival in Tokyo, our journey back to Haneda was a tearful one.

*   *   *

We returned to Japan in 1982, to my new assignment as First Secretary (Information) – a post now more accurately named Head of Press and Public Affairs. I will simply highlight here some of my main impressions of my second tour:

- By the early 1980s, Japan's high growth rates had moderated and could be seen, in retrospect, to have been not so much a 'miracle' but the normal process through which a developing economy – as Japan was in the 1970s – must pass.

- Apart from the many physical changes in the Tokyo landscape – including the sad loss of many of the old Japanese-style houses and their replacement by high-rise apartment blocks – there were other changes, mostly for the better. Tokyo was a greener, cleaner city to live in, and the horrendous air pollution of the 1960s and 1970s had gone, though the traffic congestion had got even worse.

- Compared with my previous time in Japan, the number of foreigners who spoke Japanese – and, indeed the number of foreigners in Tokyo and other major cities – had increased very considerably. It was no longer unusual to hear other foreigners speaking Japanese, and at least in the big cities the Japanese themselves no longer thought it so odd for a foreigner to speak Japanese. Outside the cities, however, foreigners continued to be treated with a mixture of deference and amusement.

- The number of British company representatives had also increased considerably, not from the manufacturers we had wanted in the 1970s but from financial institutions, taking advantage of Japan's increasing wealth and the very slow opening up of its financial markets (though Japan's equivalent of the 'Big Bang' did not come until much later, in the 1990s). The opening up of the Tokyo Stock Exchange to foreign membership was the big issue of the day, though ironically many of those who fought hard for membership in the 1980s relinquished it in the 1990s, having found the costs too high and the benefits too slow in coming.

- Japan had become a very expensive place to live. When we arrived in Japan in 1969, one pound had bought 864 yen. By the time we left in 1976, the rate was around 600 yen. On our return in 1982, it was 430 yen, and continuing to fall. Although the overseas allowances paid by the FCO had of course been adjusted to take account of the weakening pound (and strengthening yen), our impression was that they had not fully kept pace with the changes and that we were, in real terms, worse off.

- By the early 1980s, cracks were beginning to appear in Japanese society. There was increasing violence in schools, and increased affluence had produced pressure for ever more conspicuous consumption, resulting in high personal and corporate indebtedness. We were of course seeing the beginning of the 'bubble economy' which burst at the end of the decade.

- Along with this increased, but ultimately destructive, prosperity, there was among the Japanese a new self-confidence; some might even say arrogance. Japanese young people were beginning to show signs of individualism, though in a rather Japanese, group-oriented way – as evidenced by the *take-no-ko* dancing together in Yoyogi Park on Sundays, all being individualist together!

- Despite all the embassy's and the DTI's export-promotion efforts – and of course the efforts of many British companies – Britain's burgeoning trade deficit with Japan still dominated the bilateral relationship. However, against this gloomy background, there were two bright spots. The first was the increasing level of Japanese manufacturing investment in Britain (around twenty-five companies at that time, employing some six thousand people). The second was increased collaboration between Japanese and British companies, notably Fujitsu/ICL and Honda/Rover (or British Leyland, as it was then). These developments were in due course to bear abundant fruit in the more healthy and mutually-beneficial bilateral relationship which we now enjoy.

- In my own area of work, one major task was to try to dispel the myth of the 'English disease' – shorthand for Britain's poor economic performance and record of stagflation throughout the 1960s and 1970s. Under Mrs Thatcher, Britain's economic performance was being transformed, but still the myth persisted. We therefore worked with the Japanese media to bring home to them – through briefings, sponsored visits and so on – the realities of Britain's changed economic circumstances. Often the harder task was with the British press. On one visit to Japan by the then Foreign Secretary, Sir Geoffrey Howe, their main concern was whether he had worn his brown suede shoes to the meeting with Japan's Foreign Minister, rather than the substance of the talks.

My own swan-song from Tokyo and from the diplomatic service was the visit of the Prince and Princess of Wales to Japan in April 1986. Working with the Buckingham Palace Press Office and the Ministry of Foreign Affairs, I was responsible for the arrangements for the British and the Japanese journalists covering the visit. Not surprisingly, the British press corps found themselves outnumbered – and often outmanoeuvred – by the hordes of Japanese journalists when it came to getting the best positions for photo-opportunities. We did what we could to help them, but our efforts were not always appreciated and tempers often became frayed. I can still hear the voice of the *Sun*'s photographer, Arthur Edwards, crying out for 'Just one more shot, Alan' as we tried to usher the 'rat pack' (as they were not-so-affectionately known) away from the royal presence. But since one good photograph of the Princess which no-one else had could be worth tens of thousands of pounds, their frustrations were understandable.

Just before the Royal Visit, the Tokyo Economic Summit had involved me in the arrangements for the British and Japanese press to cover the British delegation led by Mrs Thatcher. I therefore left Tokyo, and the diplomatic service, in a veritable flurry of activity – exhausting at the time, but an interesting and exhilarating experience.

I have been fortunate to have been associated for so long with such a fascinating country and its people. It is a truism that the longer you work with Japan and the Japanese, often the less you understand. That is the continuing fascination of Japan.

---

1. Editor: The 'Month in the Country' was my proposal when I was in charge of language students. In the pre-war Consular Service language students had more free time and there were consulates in places such as Nagasaki, Hakodate and Shimonoseki where they could work (and perhaps study). In the early days it was not easy to find host families.

36

Two British Embassy Heads of Chancery who were not Japan Specialists

LEES MAYALL • NICHOLAS BARRINGTON

LEES MAYALL (Sir Lees Mayall) who had joined the diplomatic service before the war might, by those who did not know him well, have been written off as a typical Foreign Office toff. His second wife Mary was the sister of Lord Harlech, British Ambassador in Washington. He had known both Burgess and Maclean and his leg had been broken as a result of an incident involving Maclean in Cairo, but his loyalties were not in doubt. He enjoyed the good things of life and was full of curiosity. He became an amused and amusing observer of life in Japan when he and Mary went to Japan in 1958. They stayed until 1961. In his memoir, *Fireflies in Amber*, published in 1989 by Michael Russell (Publishing) Ltd in Salisbury, shortly before he died, he described his reactions to Japan:-

•

I had never been east of Suez before we went to Japan and I was immediately entranced by the beauty and the strangeness of the country and its people. The Japanese are quicker than most people at finding out whether you like them or not and if they decide that you do like them, they make every effort to be nice to you. Mary and I loved them from the start and this was at once appreciated. . .

*   *   *

Our principal work in Tokyo consisted in keeping a sharp eye on the way in which the Japanese Government was going to work the new American-imposed democracy. It soon appeared that the Japanese did not regard the result of a democratic election and its reflection in the composition of the Diet as the final answer. Mr Kishi's right-wing Liberal Democratic party, which had a very large majority in the Diet, did not like to use that

majority to force through controversial issues. To do so would have made
the party feel guilty of imposing the 'tyranny of the majority'. In spite of
the democratically expressed will of the voters of Japan such action
would not have been regarded as democratic by Mr Kishi's or any subsequent Japanese Government. Indeed, the 'tyranny of the majority' is
still a dirty phrase today.

We also had to push British commercial interests and do our best to
secure an entry for British goods into a Japanese market which remained
obstinately closed to them, although the balance of payments between
our two countries was heavily in Japan's favour. Japan had virtually no
indigenous motor-car industry at this time but there was a factory turning out small Hillman cars under licence. Imported cars had to pay a
swingeing duty of more than 100%. Japanese shipbuilding was however
developing rapidly and in 1960 Mary and I saw on the stocks in a Nagasaki shipyard the skeleton of what was to be an 85,000-ton oil tanker.

When I was on leave the following year I described this to two important British shipbuilders who first of all said that I must be mistaken and
then that a tanker of such a size would not be economically viable. When
the ship was launched a couple of years later there was the usual outcry
that British commercial concerns had not been alerted to the possibility
although the commercial department of the embassy had reported on it
to Whitehall as early as 1960.

One of my own concerns in Tokyo was to finalize an agreement on
claims made against the Japanese Government by British firms and individuals for damage done to them before war actually broke out in 1941. I
had been a member of a British delegation which met a Japanese delegation in London at regular intervals to discuss this matter during the years
I was in the Far Eastern Department of the Foreign Office. The Japanese
delegates were only surpassed in negotiating skill, obstinacy and ingenuity by their British counterparts who had the added strength of being
convinced of the justice of their cause. We finally reached agreement in
Tokyo and accepted a sum very considerably less than our original claim
but which was considered more or less reasonable in the circumstances.

*   *   *

In 1958, when Mary and I arrived in Japan, the Japanese were only just
beginning to realize that they could bring a blush to a sensitive American
cheek by talking about the appalling after-effects of those bombs. Once
this aspect had been appreciated the Japanese were not slow to exploit it
and the family of any nonagenarian who died of natural old age were
quick to produce evidence that strontium 90 had been diagnosed in his
body and to demand compensation.

I found, however, that the attitude of the Japanese towards foreigners and particularly towards the English and the Americans was extremely tiresome. Either the Japanese man-in-the-street regarded us as completely alien and probably bad or wrong beyond hope of redemption or he regarded us as superhuman and endowed with unearthly qualities of wisdom and experience. Hardly ever did he regard the Caucasian visitor as a normal person or an equal in any sense. This of course made it difficult to get on with the man-in-the-street but fortunately there were many sophisticated Japanese who had travelled abroad, spoke English and did not hold these prejudices.

*   *   *

We had a wooden Japanese-style house on Lake Chuzenji in the mountains north of Tokyo where we took the children to ski in the winter and to breathe the cool air when Tokyo became stiflingly hot in July and August and later we had a tiny Japanese beach house on Tokyo Bay. The Chuzenji house had a fairly primitive bath which was really only a huge metal bowl in which one sat or crouched while a log fire beneath almost boiled the water in which one was sitting. There were floor boards to prevent direct contact with the metal bottom of the bath which was licked by flames on the other side.

*   *   *

There are many jokes about the Japanese being unable to distinguish between the 'l' and the 'r' when speaking English. It is true that they cannot easily do so. When I first arrived in Tokyo I attended a luncheon party given by the Minister, Bill Harpham, to speed the journey to London of the Japanese Vice-Minister of Foreign Affairs, Mr Ohno, who had been appointed Ambassador to the Court of St James. Mr Ohno rose at the end of lunch to reply to Bill's good wishes. 'I shall never forget, Mr Harpham,' he said, 'those happy days last summer when we copulated so successfully together while you were Chargé d'Affaires.' I stifled a guffaw but looking round the table all the other faces were dead pan: they accepted that 'copulate' was a normal Japanese version of 'cooperate'.

*   *   *

We were remarkably lucky to find in Japan an old friend, Ivan Morris, living in Tokyo. Ivan spoke fluent Japanese and had married Ayako Ogawa, a tall and beautiful Japanese girl who was dancing in the Sadler's Wells ballet when he originally met her in London. The Morrises loved sightseeing and so did we, so that, once we were firmly ensconced in the prison-like embassy compound where the children could be abandoned for the weekend under the watchful eyes of a dozen neighbouring mums on the staff, we were able to make numerous journeys to different parts of the country. Ayako, as a good Japanese wife, would go into the Japanese inns and if they were up to Ivan's exacting standards would book us two double rooms. At one hotel in Shikoku the proprietor said to her: 'I know that you students have to take round these foreign barbarians [*gaijin*] because you can do with the money, but there is really no need for you to sleep with them as well.' Yaki was so furious that she broke into a torrent of ungrammatical English, shouting: 'I not student. I wife of this *gaijin*.' Her English was actually very good though sometimes eccentric. Some years after we had left Japan, the Morrises were in England and had been staying with our friends and neighbours in the country, Violet and Anthony Powell. The Powells have a fascinating eighteenth-century grotto in the grounds of their house which interested Yaki very much. In her bread-and-butter letter to Violet she said how much they had enjoyed their stay and that she had been particularly interested in their 'private ghetto'.

IVAN MORRIS was an outstanding scholar and his books about Japan include one of the best ever written about Heian Japan – *The World of the Shining Prince*. His translation of Sei Shonagon's *Makura no Soshi* ('Pillow Book') is unique. I first met Yaki Morris in London before she married Ivan when she was a student protégée of Otome Daniels (see 'Otome and Frank Daniels' by Ronald Dore in *Biographical Portraits*, Vol. I, published for the Japan Society by Japan Library in 1994). Ivan and Yaki were divorced soon after the Mayalls left Japan.

NICHOLAS BARRINGTON (Sir Nicholas Barrington) described himself as not a Japanese specialist, but an admirer:-

●

There was only one time in my diplomatic career that I had a clear choice of next posting, and I chose Tokyo. I had done an unusually long stint as No.2 in the Secretary of State's private office, and personnel were as helpful as they could be. I had said at the beginning of my service, when asked to state preferences, that I would hope to go to places where the work was interesting, the people agreeable and hot countries rather than cold. Head of Chancery in the big Tokyo mission, in a country beginning to emerge as an economic superpower, would certainly be interesting; and the fact that the dynamic Fred Warner was shortly going there as ambassador was also an attraction.

I had been intrigued by Japanese culture from a distance, an interest reinforced when I had accompanied Michael Stewart as Secretary of State on an official visit to Japan two years before and managed to get away from my duties to see *kabuki* (and visit the bars of Shinjuku!). I had known and admired Carmen Blacker for many years and I had a

Japanese actor friend; both promised to introduce me to their friends and contacts.

In addition to the usual Foreign Office briefing I had time to read up on Japanese history and culture, including absorbing Mishima, Tanizaki and other writers, in translation. Later, I got great pleasure from *The Tale of Genji* and *The Pillow Book of Sei Shonagon*. In those days one could acclimatize on the journey to Tokyo: I flew to Singapore and then took a berth on a freighter which arrived in Tokyo harbour via Hong Kong and Manila. This was at the beginning of 1972. I was thirty-eight years old.

Eventually, I served under three ambassadors. I was privileged to coincide with the last months of Sir John Pilcher, a legendary Japanese expert who had served in the area before the Second World War. He was primarily a representative, rather than an operational ambassador: he left daily reporting and export promotion etc. to his staff, but when the British Ambassador arrived at any sort of function the buzz went round and he became the centre of attention. I was told he spoke a rather antiquated form of Japanese, but he spoke it fluently and wittily; he was deeply knowledgeable about the country, with great feeling for the Arts, and his enthusiasm for things Japanese was infectious; some of it rubbed off on to me. Beneath the panache he was a perceptive political and social observer. Lady Pilcher was a contrasting down-to-earth tower of strength – looking formidable but actually very kind. I remember that they took me along to an elaborate tea ceremony dinner given by a 'Master' for them as a farewell. I was fascinated by the aesthetics and the conversation (though I found the food rather disagreeable). I noted that Delia Pilcher plumped herself down by a window where she could stretch her legs even though it was not the high protocol place she should have occupied.

Coordinating the work of the large embassy establishment as a first secretary, with many counsellors in charge of sections, was demanding (I was promoted to counsellor halfway through my posting, after a short spell when they took me away to be chargé d'affaires in Hanoi). Some toes were sensitive. But with the backing of successive heads of post I was able to see that everything worked smoothly, especially for the visits of numerous prominent people from home, who were all anxious to learn about the Japanese phenomenon. Mr Heath was the first British Prime Minister to visit Japan, and the Japanese were pleased that this was a special bilateral visit coming all the way from Britain just to Japan, i.e. not just tacking the visit on to an Asian tour. He got on well with Prime Minister Tanaka, a kindred spirit who had also risen to lead a right-of-centre party from a modest background. It helped that Tanaka's Gaimusho private secretary had become a close friend, as had other Foreign Office officials in Tokyo. I remember successive visits by Geoffrey Howe, Tony Benn (in his white heat of technology phase), Anthony

Crosland, Selwyn Lloyd as Speaker, and many others, including top industrialists who were staggered by the automation and efficiency in Japanese factories.

I acquired some experience on Japanese management theory (cf Chie
Nakane and how the ethos of education and collective consent was so
suited to a modern industrial society). There was a very good visit by
the Duke of Kent, with his trade promotion hat, and the culmination
of my work on visits was the Queen's State visit in 1975, in every detail
of which I was closely involved. On the day of her arrival the Queen, after
she had reviewed an honour parade and met members of the Imperial
family and a long line up of VIPS, had presented to her by Fred Warner a
few senior members of the embassy. When she heard my name, she said,
'Oh, you're the man who writes all the letters!' She had bothered to notice
and I felt like rolling on my back and putting my paws in the air!

The Imperial Household was not easy to deal with, being even more
officious in that respect, in those days, than the Lord Chamberlain's Office, in London. I could not get *yabusame* (archery from horseback) in the
programme – 'not sophisticated enough sport for Royals' – and they insisted that the principal Kabuki performer should be not someone lively
like Koshiro or Shoroku, but the aged Utaemon. But we did get a short
drive in an open car; we got all the great Ikebana (flower arrangement)
Masters to display alongside each other; and visits to Kyoto and Ise/
Mikimoto, with helpful Gaimusho escorts, were very enjoyable. What I
was most proud of was the Queen's main speech at the emperor's banquet. Hardly a word of my draft was changed, either by my ambassador,
the Foreign Office or the Palace. I included a quote from the introduction to the English translation of Kaempfer (an original copy of which I
had bought in London) and set out the many things that the British and
Japanese have in common. Not least of these, of course, a generally respected and ancient monarchy. Cassettes of that speech were sold widely
in the markets, partly as an aid to English-speaking, on which so many
Japanese were very keen.

I was lucky to meet at an early stage, probably through Peter Wakefield,
the Economic and Commercial Counsellor and his wife Felicity, who
have remained good friends over the years, some of the more sophisticated Japanese who had been traditional friends of Britain. I remember
being roped in to go to a Cherry Blossom Ball (and being taken aback at
the price of my ticket!). There I met Kazuko Aso, for whom I came to
have great admiration and affection, with her amazing capacity to be
both very Japanese with Japanese and very British with British. Under
her charming exterior was a toughness born of experience as the hostess
for her father the great Shigeru Yoshida, but the atmosphere in her large
attractive family was friendly and relaxed. One of her charming daughters later married Prince Tomohito, the emperor's nephew, whom I met at

the Aso house and for whom I had been designated by John Pilcher as unofficial tutor – primarily a means of keeping informal contact with the prince, who had been educated at Oxford.

I met the Yasudas, the Mikimotos, the Hattoris and also Akio Morita, but in that sophisticated group the most outstanding was another great lady, Mrs Chako Hatakeyama, married to Seiji, an upright rather shy samurai of the old school, Chairman of Ebara pumps, who between them taught me much about how to behave in Japan (including exactly what to do at a tea ceremony). The family had a famous collection-house of tea-ceremony items and beautiful houses in Tokyo, Atagawa, Zushi and Hokkaido in most of which I stayed, with groups of friends.

We also explored *onsen* together, particularly *rotemburo*, the open-air hot spring baths which for me were one of the great pleasures of Japan. I visited these places all over the country, from Hokkaido to Kyushu, but my favourite was Takaragawa in Gumma prefecture, where we used to go, by train and bus, in winter, with branches heavy with snow. The old *ryokan* was by a stream, with two great natural-looking open-air pools of hot water. We would book one room for men and one for women in groups of about twelve, including both married and single people, Japanese and *gaijin*, diplomats and others. Long walks, prodigious meals, excellent companionship. Actually, I helped introduce quite a few Japanese to the pleasures of mixed bathing in open-air hot spring baths!

I still say, only half joking, that the things I liked about Japan were *rotemburo, zazen*, Sumo and Kabuki. Visiting the baths was only one element in extensive travels which I managed to organize, sometimes alone, around the country. I learned enough Japanese to get around. I did not try to compete with the proper Japanese speakers in the embassy, of which we had about fifteen, who had all done over two years' full-time study. In Kyushu I loved Kagoshima and the Ibusuki Kanko Hotel with its huge 'jungle bath'. I was in Kagoshima when the volcano Sakurajima erupted in front of me: an unforgettable sight. I went to Beppu, and stayed in the extensive traditional Aso house in Fukuoka. I visited Matsue, Niigata and Sado on the Japan Sea side, Hokkaido and Sendai, Izu and Wakayama (where there was a fine *onsen* in a cave overlooking the sea). Festivals were always great fun, often with marvellous drumming, since the Japanese enjoy dressing up just as much as the British do – the most spectacular festival I attended was the *Hadaka matsuri* in Okayama with the steam rising from hundreds of bodies as the sacred sticks were thrown, hidden and passed around.

I managed to get to Kyoto at least twice a year, each time extending the range of temples and gardens visited. Just before the State Visit I produced my own cyclostyled guide to Kyoto, which was apparently useful to many. I was particularly fascinated by the great complexes at Daitokuji, Myoshinji, Nanzenji and Tofukuji, where with persistence and courtesy, one can visit many beautiful temples and gardens not normally open to the public. My favourite garden of all was Sambo-in at Daigo-ji. I also loved the statues in otherwise dull Koryuji, especially the magical Miro-ku-Bosatsu. It was coming out of one of the Tofukuji subtemples one day that I met a young Japanese family who had been learning English by radio and with whom I became good friends. They were simple people, but hospitable and open-minded and never attempted to take advantage of the relationship. When my parents visited they gave us *sushi* in their tiny apartment.

But for me the most important person in Kyoto was a monk at Daito-kuji called the Rev. Sohaku Kobori, sadly now dead, who was one of the most remarkable and impressive men I have met in my life. John Pilcher, who knew him well, was kind enough to pass him on to me as a contact; Kobori-san always received me with simple formality in different parts of his subtemple and garden. Once I was there when numerous precious scrolls were hanging up all over the place, to be aired. Kobori-san could talk about anything: politics, art, social problems etc. with wisdom and often humour, as well as about Zen Buddhism and religion in general. He emanated a sort of positive goodness and harmony which one felt in his presence. I learnt much from him and from Zen: for example, to concentrate on what you are doing in the present, and to do it well. I visited Nikko, of course, Nara and Koya-san and temples and shrines in other parts of the country.

Sumo was another great passion. I still regularly read a Sumo magazine and follow the fortunes of the *yokozuna* and *ozeki*. Mizuno-san, the embassy receptionist, used to get tickets for me to see the wrestling live. I loved the elegant ceremony, interspersed with violent bouts of action. Behind all the immaculate courtesy there was drama; the position of *Yokozuna*, grand champion, was being passed from Kitanofuji and Kotozakura to young heroes Wajima and Takanohana (the latter never quite made it, though his two sons have done). And there were up-and-coming champions whom I can claim to have spotted early, like Kitanoumi and, best of all, Chiyonofuji.

That leaves *kabuki*. My long-standing actor friend, Yoshi Oida, who has worked with Peter Brook in Paris for many years, and written two good books on Japanese and Western acting techniques, introduced me to some of his mentors, including the liberal-minded playwright Tadasu Izawa, and through Izawa-sensei I met a number of people involved with the theatre in Japan, notably the effervescent TV star and actress Tetsuko Kuroyanagi, who became a firm friend. Through them, and through the splendid Duke family (British Council) I met several Kabuki actors, and on occasion was privileged to watch them being made up, dressed and be-wigged, with great deference from acolytes in the theatre. I loved the spectacle of Kabuki and the intensity of the acting. The names, which changed as younger stars inherited their fathers' titles, were confusing and I produced a rare chart of the main families which helped. I enjoyed all Japanese theatre from productions of Shakespeare by companies such as *Bungaku-za* (remember a marvellous Troilus and Cressida) with new lively translations by Professor Odajima, to the experimental 'underground'. I can claim to be an early fan of Hijikata, the founder of *Butoh*-style of acting and presentation. *Noh* I found more difficult to take, though I met some of the principal families. Love of the theatre in all its forms is one of the things that the Japanese share with the British.

With all these cultural and social interests, which greatly enhanced my enjoyment of life, I did not, I hope, neglect my political and coordination responsibilities as head of Chancery. Britain and Japan were becoming closer on a range of foreign policy issues. We watched internal political developments closely (though there were limits to my own contacts here, not speaking Japanese). And we gave maximum support to British export efforts and those to attract Japanese investment to the UK.

Speaking generally, what I found difficult to understand, and in some ways I still do, was the contrast between the friendly demonstrative Japanese people I knew and Japanese behaviour in the last war, in prison camps etc. I can only put it down to their intense nationalism or rather consciousness of their own identity, which made them react overseas in ways which we find unacceptable. Although the Japanese have the reputation of being stiff and difficult to get to know, I think this is really another trait we share with them: a slowness to make friends, but, once friends, great emotional loyalty. I know that many friends I made in Japan, by breaking down political barriers, will be friends for life. This is one of the many reasons why my period of service in Tokyo, although I was not a Japanese expert, will always be one of the most important in my life.

37

An Eccentric Diplomat

VERE REDMAN

VERE REDMAN (Sir Vere Redman) was the subject of one of my biographical portraits, which appeared in *Biographical Portraits* Vol. II, published for the Japan Society by Japan Library in 1997. In this I quoted some of his writings about Japan. As I explained, he was a notable eccentric, but devoted to the improvement of Anglo-Japanese relations. He addressed the Japan Society a number of times, for example, on the subject of the Japan-British Society (in Tokyo) on 7 October 1952; but his most interesting and relevant lecture for our purposes was probably that which he gave to the Society on 16 September 1958 on 'Things I have learned in and from Japan'.

A book on post-war Japan through British eyes without any piece by Vere Redman would lack a significant element. Despite the fact that it is not confined solely to experiences of post-war Japan and refers back to Vere Redman's experiences before and during the war, I am including extracts from the text of his 1958 lecture. It is all the more interesting because it bridges pre- and post-war Japan:-

•

I have been in Japan, on and off, for just over thirty-one years. It is really most of my adult life, for I went there soon after graduation from the university. Japan, then, has naturally had a great effect on me. . .

I would start my list of things learned with something at the sensory, not to say sensual, level, the conception of the bath as an instrument of pleasure rather than convenience. I suppose we in the West enjoy our baths up to a point, although I am sometimes inclined to doubt it in view of the increase in the number of showers as replacements for baths in private houses, which is a characteristic modern development. In any case, I feel that we do not enjoy the bath as the Japanese enjoy it. For the test, of course, is the domestic bath.

. . . the enjoyment of ordinary hot water in the tub at home or in the public bath house, where groups gather to gossip in the steam, is something peculiarly Japanese at least in its intensity. In this connection, I always recall my experience when I was in Sugamo prison. We prisoners were taken to the bath usually once in anything from seven to ten days. All of us regarded this as the one great break in the drabness and suffering of our lives. I remember, too, that, when I was being interrogated, the prospect of a hot bath was often placed before me as an inducement to answer in the manner required, which is an indication of how my *kempeitai* friends regarded it. The hot bath was the great luxury, the great enjoyment. As such, it is a frequent literary theme. As such, it finds its place among the hedonistic pleasures. And so I have learned to regard it. I use a foreign bath; I *enjoy* a Japanese one. It is an enjoyment I have learned from Japan.

. . . I have also learned a good many aesthetic enjoyments in Japan. I think I should put first among these the conception of the importance of space in domestic architecture. I went to Japan from a small home in the suburbs of London. The rooms in our house were not large and they always seemed crowded. My youthful memories are of a multiplicity of things about the place either to knock over or fall over. When my wife and I went to Tokyo, we rented a small Japanese house for which, incidentally, we paid 60 yen a month. The rooms there were not, indeed, larger than those in my mother's house; they were probably even smaller. But they seemed much larger because there was so much less in them in the way of furniture and knick-knacks. I found that I liked that sense of extra space. I discovered later, of course, that it was a deliberate and part of a carefully developed scheme of Japanese aesthetics, to concentrate the line of vision on a single focal point, the *tokonoma* in a room, or the most distant tree, plant or stone in a garden, and never to break that line of vision. . . The basic lesson that I have got from Japan in this matter is that space in the house is more soothing than clutter. I now find that, when I go home in England, my first impulse, on entering my flat, is to put a few things away.

I would put next among the things I have learned from Japan the conception that human relationships are in accordance with a system of reciprocal obligation, which is economic up to a point but much more social and personal. We learn this, first, like so much else in Japan, in our homes from our servants. I had no experience of personal service before I went to Japan but I have seen something of it in the West since. It is now there, I think, increasingly a purely economic relationship; . . . nowhere in the West is there the sort of identification of the two which is still so common in Japan. The Japanese servant is responsible to his master; the Japanese master is responsible to and for his servant. And that is a personal and intimate responsibility. It covers virtually every aspect of human activity and interest. . .

. . . When I first went to Japan, I was a teacher in what was then known as the Tokyo University of Commerce and is now called Hitotsubashi University. Young teachers were recognized as the specific disciples of older teachers. I was recognized as the disciple of the specific teacher who had arranged in London for my engagement by the University... once the association was established and recognized, then came the series of reciprocal obligations as that between master and servant.

This system of association worked in the practical business of the university in much the same way, I suppose, as would associations imposed by friendship and similarity of tastes at home. And yet there was something, if not more formal, then more binding, about the obligation for protector and disciple to vote together in faculty meetings, back-scratch each other in public and private by both the written and the spoken word, for protector to promote the interests of disciple, for disciple to defend the interests of protector; for disciple to collect research material for protector, for protector to see that he is suitably 'helped' for so doing, and so on...

The protector-disciple relationship was not on the faculty alone. It existed just the same as between students and teachers and even, to some extent, among the students themselves. The students attach themselves to one or more particular teacher; the teachers begin to feel responsibility for the students and thus a firm relationship of reciprocal responsibility is welded which goes on through the years. I must say that, in practical ways, I have seen both sides of the medal of this relationship. In postwar days, former students whose fortunes had not been all that good came along and naturally expected me to help them: others, who had been luckier were eminent and powerful and took it for granted that they must help me with anything they could, contacts, information, entertainment, etc. It works both ways...

I do not want to exaggerate the importance of this *oyabun-kobun* relationship, as it is called, or stress unduly its peculiar character... it has its advantages: it promotes a limited form of social solidarity, it softens the crudities of the straight economic relationships of employer and employed. It has its disadvantages: it creates cliques, limited loyalties which tend to obscure a general community sense. But there it is, an important factor in Japanese life, a possible factor in any kind of life...

I should put next among the things I have learned from Japan the conception of what I would call agreement by emotional attunement. Generally speaking, agreements are reached among occidentals by alignment of arguments on this side or that in a particular case. It often happens that, in the process of such alignment, many of the differences of point of view are seen to disappear or even not in fact to have had much reality. Or again, it may emerge that a certain minimum of difference of view may remain but the overall advantages of agreement are deemed so great as to justify a certain measure of concession on either side in order to produce what is called a compromise. Or yet again, there are circumstances in which agreement, or at least decision, is essential with regard to the matter in hand, as, for example, the form of government in a given country, or the policy of a government in relation to some other country, in which case it is felt that the best way of reaching the necessary decision is by majority vote.

In Japan the process is not the same. The initial alignment of arguments is similar and, in so far as exposition removes misunderstanding and thus reduces the area of disagreement, the process is again more or less parallel to that of the West. The next stage, however, is definitely different. The Japanese do not like a clearly defined and worked-out compromise. 'Face' is lost by evident concession and also by the acceptance thereof. Similarly, majority ruling has the same disadvantage, for in such cases the majority 'wins' or 'imposes' decision, while the minority 'loses' and accepts the decision of others, all of which conceptions are face-spoilers and should not be applied if essential harmony is to be preserved. Anybody who has attended a Japanese committee meeting or board meeting or anything of the kind knows that when affairs have reached the stage where divergence of view is clear what is essential is not more argument on the relevant points but more tea, more desultory discussion of this and that, more calm concentrated effort on the attainment of what I have called emotional attunement.

Now what happens? Well, I have not much more than an inkling of the process itself and while I have occasionally found it working for me and even in me I have had, of course, much more experience of its being worked on me. I can, however, tell you that what emerges after a bit is a unanimous decision. The relationship this decision bears to the conflicting views hitherto expressed varies. What never varies is that the form of words used to express that decision bears no relationship at all to anything that has been said before. In the word form, then, nobody has won. In actual form, to some extent, obviously somebody has. But such analyses as I have attempted of decisions reached in this way, undertaken by the most rigidly cartesian methods, would seem to correspond roughly to what we should have reached by a compromise. But they are not compromises: they are unanimous decisions reached by the process of emotional attunement. . .

Before leaving this concept I would seek to relate it to another, that of sincerity. Most occidentals in my time have had difficulty with that, and I imagine many more will in the future. Most of my experience as a newspaperman was gained in the ten-year period between 1929 and 1939 when the tide of Japanese militarism which finally swept the nation into war was rising at first gradually and then with ever increasing force. We used to hear a lot then about Japan's sincerity and the insincerity of her victims and opponents. I find now in a diary written in 1937 the following: 'The Japanese motto would seem to be: 'He only is sincere who also agrees with me'.' It was the bitter reflection of a young man and, like most bitterness, I suppose, it not altogether justified and arose, in part, from misunderstanding. The Japanese conception of sincerity begins like ours with wholeheartedness. A man is sincere who believes absolutely in the cause he serves, in the absolute righteousness of the act he is performing. Here we are on common ground. But that absolute belief must be more than an intellectual conviction. It must be such a spiritual dedication as to blot out any other consideration as, for example, that of the sanctity of human life, one's own or anybody else's. Hence, the man who, for certain political beliefs would kill a prime minister or a banker in the certain knowledge that he would lose his own life as a result was held to be sincere. No doubt, we should call him sincere too, although we should certainly feel that his sincerity was misguided. But that willingness, even eagerness, to sacrifice his life would be the supreme qualification among the Japanese. . .

The Japanese conception of sincerity has another element and one more difficult to define. It is willingness and/or capacity to enter into the process of emotional attunement with other sincerities, to reach that terribly subjective, but nonetheless real – to the Japanese – conception of truth, unanimously accepted.

Sincerity, therefore, for the Japanese is a combination of wholeheartedness and desire and capacity to find with those equally wholehearted an emotional attunement from which truth will emerge. Now, in the pre-war years, the Japanese believed that their enemies possessed neither of these characteristics and, therefore, that they were insincere. They tend in modern times to come to the same conclusions about many of us occidentals for the same reasons.

Now, quite frankly, I am inclined to think that, as an ethic of conception, this is all nonsense, but, the older I get, the more convinced I become that to understand the important nonsense about humans is the first step towards understanding them. I feel, then, that I have learned much about men in general from these conceptions of emotional attunement and sincerity with which I have become familiar in Japan.

And that brings me naturally to the last and most important thing that I have learned in Japan, namely, that the only way to get on with people is really to like them. The Japanese, almost terrifyingly, like to be liked. They came into the world community late and have never been sure of their welcome. They know that world standards are at once exigent and complex, that we despise the weak, are morally minatory of the strong, unless the strong be ourselves, and actually approve most of those who are strong enough to inspire our respect without threatening our comfort or complacency. Yes, it is hard to be liked in the modern world and the Japanese have always felt intensely how hard it is and, just because it is so hard, they want it all the more. And they want to be liked as a nation; in fact I sometimes feel that they are more eager to be liked as Japanese than as their individual selves. . .

Another aspect of this appeal for affection is the almost instinctive showmanship of the Japanese. They want to impress; they are always putting on an act, as artists, scholars, warriors, or high-powered businessmen, or a combination of all four. Not only do they want to impress; they also want to absorb, another natural consequence of their late arrival in the modern world. They want the latest and they worship the latest. One nuclear scientist is greater, for the time being, than ten ordinary industrial technicians and a host of moral philosophers, and two nuclear scientists are very near to God. The latest fellow of any kind is sure of a great welcome among the Japanese because, like the Athenians of old, they are eager to learn of 'any new thing'. But still, most of all they want to be liked, and anybody who can give them that liking can count on getting on with them in a human relationship as satisfying as that to be experienced anywhere. On this liking business, no deception is possible. You cannot successfully pretend to like the Japanese. . . If you like them, they know it. If you don't, they know it too. And if you don't, well – there does not seem to be much sense in being in Japan any longer than you must.

38

The British Ambassadors

THE POST-WAR British Ambassadors to Japan:

1946 Sir Alvary GASCOIGNE, GBE, KCMG. (1893-1970) as head of
the United Kingdom Liaison Mission (UKLM) to SCAP.

1951 Sir Esler DENING, GCMG, OBE. (1897-1977) first as head of the
UKLM and from April 1952 as Ambassador to Japan

1957 Sir William David (Dan) LASCELLES, KCMG. (1902-67)

1959 Sir Oscar MORLAND, GBE, KCMG. (1904-80)

1963 Sir Francis (Tony) RUNDALL, GCMG, OBE. (1908-87)

1967 Sir John PILCHER, GCMG. (1912-90)

1972 Sir Fred WARNER, GCVO, KCMG. (1918-95)

1975 Michael (later Sir Michael) WILFORD, GCMG. (1922-)

1980 Sir Hugh CORTAZZI, GCMG. (1924-)

1984 Sir Sydney GIFFARD, KCMG. (1926-)

1986 Sir John WHITEHEAD, GCMG, CVO. (1932-)

1992 Sir John BOYD, KCMG. (1936-)

1996 Sir David WRIGHT, KCMG, LVO. (1944-)

1999 Sir Stephen GOMERSALL, CMG. (1948-)

Of the fourteen ambassadors since the war six have not been Japanese specialists. These were Alvary Gascoigne, Dan Lascelles, Tony Rundall, Fred Warner, Michael Wilford and John Boyd. Three, namely Bill Dening, Oscar Morland and John Pilcher, were former members of the Japan Consular Service. Between 1946 and 1980 the proportion of Japanese specialists to generalists was one to three. Since 1980 the proportion has been six to one.

Why was the proportion so low in the first thirty years after the war? Was there still in some parts of the Foreign Office a snobbish prejudice against former members of the specialist consular services? On the whole I do not think that this was the case. Was it because other former members of the Japan Consular Service were not regarded as sufficiently high fliers to qualify for Tokyo? This also seems unlikely. Sir F. S. (Tommy) Tomlinson became a deputy undersecretary and Sir Arthur de la Mare held three ambassadorial posts ending as ambassador in Thailand. Henry Hainworth was ambassador to Indonesia. Perhaps they were just unfortunate in not being in the right place at the right time.

The service now seems to have recognized that if you put considerable resources into training officers in hard languages and do not use them properly
you are wasting the taxpayers' money. Moreover, if you persuade/require officers to do two years' full-time study of a difficult language and do not give
them the opportunity to rise to the top you are at least damaging morale. I
do not wish to criticize the non-Japanese specialists who were appointed to
Tokyo, but I think that all would have agreed that if they had known Japan
when they were younger and been able to communicate freely in Japanese this
would have added an important dimension to their ability to do a good job. I
hope that the powers that be in the FCO, and ministers, will bear this in mind
in making future appointments to Tokyo.

SIR ALVARY GASCOIGNE seems never to have been a member of the
Japan Society or addressed its members.

SIR ESLER DENING became Chairman of the Japan Society after General Piggott and was a firm supporter of the Society. Roger Buckley contributed an essay about him 'In Proper Perspective: Sir Esler Dening (1897-1977)'
to *Britain and Japan 1859-1991: Themes and Personalities*, edited by Sir Hugh Cortazzi and Gordon Daniels, published by Routledge for the Japan Society in 1991.
Dening's lectures to the Society on such topics as 'Reminiscences of the Meiji
and Taisho Eras', June 1969 (Bulletin No. 58) are not relevant to the subject of
this book. Dening's despatches, including his final despatch, are now in the
public domain under the thirty-year rule. No doubt further studies of his role
in Anglo-Japanese relations will be made by scholars. My own encounters
with him as my first head of mission in Japan are briefly recounted in my
memoir *Japan and Back and Places Elsewhere*, published by Global Oriental in
1998. I do not intend to repeat them here. Suffice it to say that Bill Dening
who was born of missionary parents in Japan remained a bachelor throughout
his life. He was a remote but dominating figure of considerable ability. He
never forgot what Japan was like before the war and he was accordingly sceptical about Japanese adherence to democratic principles. He loved music and
played the piano well.

SIR DAN LASCELLES was a misfit and it is hard to understand what the
board responsible for senior appointments were thinking about when they
selected him for the job. His service in Ethiopia and his knowledge of Amharic were hardly relevant. But he was known to be a good linguist and taught
himself some Japanese before he arrived in Tokyo. Perhaps the board concentrated on the fact that like Bill Dening he was a bachelor and said to themselves,
'Of course, Japan is a man's country where wives hardly count'. If they did so
they made a grave error. Or did they say to themselves, 'We really must find a
good last post for old Dan who has served in a lot of difficult places and anyway
at this point in time Japan is not really important'? Again, if that was their
thinking they were seriously underestimating Japan. Or did the appointment
go through on the nod in face of a recommendation from the Chief Clerk who
wanted to find a solution to what to do with Dan?

The following paragraphs from the memoirs of Sir Lees Mayall (*Fireflies in
Amber*, published by Michael Russell in 1989), who was his head of Chancery

for part of his short time in Tokyo, help to explain why his posting to Japan was such a mistake:-

•

Dan Lascelles, our Ambassador when we first arrived in Tokyo, was a man of great charm, great intelligence and strong prejudices. He had numerous foibles, one of which was never to answer an invitation to dinner though he was punctilious in other social matters. As a result his unfortunate hostesses never knew whether he was coming to dine or not. Occasionally they would telephone to me in desperation to ask me to find out for them but when I approached Dan he regarded my enquiries as a gross invasion of his personal privacy and would give me an ambiguous or evasive answer. On one occasion he told me that he was taking two weeks' holiday but would not be leaving Japan. As the Minister was away on leave in England this meant that I would be in charge of the Embassy but since the Ambassador would still be in the country he would still be responsible for it and I would not be Chargé d'Affaires. So I asked if I might have his address while he was away so that I could get in touch with him if necessary. He clearly regarded this request as impertinent but reluctantly gave me the name of a hotel near Osaka where he would be staying.

A few days after his departure I thought I should consult him on some minor matter and telephoned to the hotel. They said that Dan had spent the night there four days ago but had left the next morning on a hired bicycle and had given instructions that if he did not return in a fortnight they were to send his luggage back to Tokyo. When he did reappear after two weeks he did not say where he had been and I did not feel like asking. I used to see him in his office every morning at ten o'clock to discuss the day's work and anything that had happened in the last twenty-four hours.

One morning shortly before he left Tokyo on retirement he asked me I if I would shake his hand. We stood up, shook hands across his desk and sat down again. 'Did you notice anything?' he enquired. 'Nothing at all,' I replied. 'My hand did not feel scaly or otherwise unpleasant?' 'Certainly not.' 'Thank you. You see I am having a farewell luncheon with the Emperor and Empress today' - the Emperor entertained all retiring Ambassadors to lunch when they left Tokyo - 'and it occurred to me that I would probably have to shake hands with them and that I might have some sort of rash on my hand which would be unpleasant for them to touch.' I assured him that he could only have imagined a rash.

When he returned in the afternoon, he sent for me again and I asked him how things had gone at the Imperial Palace. He said that from his point of view the whole thing had been a complete disaster. He had been placed at lunch on the right hand of the Empress with an elderly lady-in-waiting sitting behind his left shoulder to interpret. Owing to their inability to distinguish between the English 'l' and 'r', Lascelles was usually known to the Japanese as 'Ambassador Russell'. Dan had therefore adopted as his personal emblem a fox and had had a representation of the animal carved on a little marble seal such as many Japanese carried: Dan Russell the Fox, so called in Chaucer's *The Nun's Priest's Tale*, presumably because of the fox's red colour. The story was long and, for a Japanese to understand, appallingly complicated, but Dan had considered it suitable to relate to the Empress, including the play on the words of Chaucer and his name and the pronunciation difficulties of the Japanese. The elderly lady-in-waiting had a major problem in understanding what he was talking about let alone translating it and passing it on to the wondering Empress. (Dan understood Japanese well and suffered as much as she did while listening to her efforts.)

There were two other Ambassadors there with their wives who were also leaving the country. The drill was that after lunch the guests would stand while the Imperial couple would walk round to each in turn and have a few words before retiring behind a curtain. Dan was the last to be addressed but somehow managed to walk backwards through the curtain with the Emperor and Empress. The curtain was drawn as soon as they were through but Dan found himself, not in another room but alone in a very small alcove with his hosts who had apparently intended to wait behind the curtain until the guests had gone and the field was clear for them to come out. Dan at once realized what had happened but could not find any opening in the curtain and had to be rescued ignominiously by a courtier. He was in a wretched state by the time he got back home. In the end he only got out of the Embassy twenty-four hours before his successor, Oscar Morland, arrived.

AS LEES MAYALL explained OSCAR MORLAND was quite different:-

•

O scar was just as shy as Dan had been but much easier to get on with. He had served in Japan or Japanese-occupied China throughout almost his whole career (which began in the old Japan Consular Service) and he of course read, wrote and spoke Japanese and knew the people very well and the way their minds worked. On one occasion he had written a long despatch on Japanese internal affairs when things had been going particularly badly and he ended it with the gloomy conclusion that the Japanese political scene would probably revert to the bad old days when riots, demonstrations, xenophobia and political assassinations must be expected. He gave me the draft to read and asked for my comments. I said that I fully agreed with him but suggested that to predict political assassinations in the new post-war and less barbaric Japan might be a little exaggerated. He smiled apologetically and crossed out the words 'political assassinations'. I went on leave a day or two later to England and had not been there long when I read in the newspapers that the Socialist Party Chairman, Inejiro Asanuma, had been stabbed to death with a bayonet at a political meeting by a student who had mounted the platform from which Asanuma was speaking; the whole incident had been witnessed and televised by Japanese and American television journalists. A few days later it was reported that the Liberal Democrat Prime Minister Kishi had been stabbed, but not fatally, outside the Diet building. I wrote a grovelling letter to Oscar and made a mental note not to dissent from the prophecies of experts in future.

OSCAR MORLAND spoke to the Japan Society in February 1964 (Bulletin No. 43, June 1964) on the theme 'A Foreigner's Life in Japan'. After an historical introduction Oscar Morland gave his own views which are worth quoting:-

•

The quotations I have given are I think typical of what foreign visitors felt in the past about Japan and I believe they are fully representative now. I have tried to compile a list of my own superficial impressions from thirty years ago. As time went on some of them were modified but I do not think substantially changed. My own feelings of being a foreigner also gradually disappeared – not because I did not remain in a world separate in many respects from the ordinary flow of Japanese daily life, but because I became so conditioned to the limitations, and the pleasures of living in Japan that I more or less forgot them. I must have been a very typical foreign resident, since the things that struck me most seem to have been the same things that have been related in countless books by foreigners about life in Japan.

In the first place, the natural beauty of the countryside and appreciation of that beauty by the Japanese people; together with what seemed to be a very high degree of distinctive good taste displayed in building, decoration and arrangement which combine simplicity with appropriateness to its environment. Tokyo thirty years ago was a more beautiful city than it is now, but even now this instinctive good taste shows itself wherever an opportunity is left. Within a stone's throw of the British Embassy, in the heart of the city, are little lanes and corners where the love of beauty and effective arrangement can take one's breath away – and some of them show that traditional Japanese elegance and simplicity can be blended successfully with modern architecture and materials – and what is even more significant – that the occupation of these modern media has not killed the instinct to put things in the right place and to combine them beautifully.

Secondly – what Kaempfer described as the Japanese love of 'civilitie and good manners'. Wherever I went, in the city or the country, I found a strong anxiety to give me help of every kind – to guide me on my way or to provide me with information. It is more than formal politeness and springs from a strong desire to be of real service to the stranger. Many Japanese have told me that this kind of help tends to be more readily given to a foreigner than to another Japanese and that it derives, partly at any rate, from the wish to produce in the foreigner's mind, a favourable impression of Japan and Japanese courtesy. The foreigner cannot judge to what extent that may be true; my guess is that in many instances this is an element in the helpfulness, but not the main one.

Other first impressions formed by foreign visitors and residents usually include some bewilderment at the alleged Japanese inscrutability and apparent reluctance to speak, or explain things, directly. In so far as this exists (and I always wonder whether the Japanese are in fact any more inscrutable to the European than the European is to the Japanese) it certainly derives partly from the dissimilarity between Japanese and European ways of thinking and scales of value, and from the consequent difference between modes of expression, even when both parties are speaking the same language. And it is also increased by the historical circumstances which I have mentioned earlier: isolation from the outside world in the past, and even now comparatively rare contacts with foreigners.

Other first impressions often gained is that of, to the foreigner, excessive diffidence and self-depreciation on the part of the Japanese to their country, their civilisation and culture, their families, their belongings and their own abilities. Here I believe that it is to a great extent a purely linguistic misunderstanding: age long convention and forms of speech in Japanese oblige the possessor or giver of anything to speak of it in a deprecating manner, and he would be horrified if this mode of expression were interpreted as a true expression of his feelings. We do the same thing here of course, but in a rather different way. I say I am afraid the entertainment I am offering is inadequate, or the lecture I am giving is dull, but not only do I not expect hearty agreement, but I usually hope for a denial which I can take as a compliment.

Finally, I was impressed when I first went to Japan and am still impressed today, by the tireless energy of the Japanese people, and the way in which everybody, from Cabinet Ministers to roadmenders, keep on the job. Hours of work then were probably too long (I remember shop boys asleep on their feet in the Tokyo trams late in the evening) and holidays too few. Even now a five-day week is practically unknown in Japan. I used to try to put it across to my friends in the Government service that the freshness gained by a Tokyo commuter from two days' complete change of occupation would more than make up for the four or five hours lost at his desk on Saturday morning. But I had no success. Nor does the capacity and urge to stay on the job mean the lack of outside interests: though there are no country houses and private yachts and few foreign tours and weekend cottages, almost everyone has his own hobbies – whether new ones like golf, photography, western music and bridge, or the traditional ones like poetry, calligraphy, gardens, flower arrangement or Go.

*   *   *

To sum up – this is the kind of balance sheet one might draw up for an Englishman living now in Japan.

On the debit side, he is a long way from home and he will get out of touch with his family and friends in England and with the constantly changing atmosphere at home. He will be living a more artificial life in some ways than he would in England, particularly if he were in the country and not in a city in England; he won't be able to drop into a pub in the evening to watch English television or go occasionally to an English theatre. He will have to buy the English books he needs since he will not be able to borrow them from a library. Except for golf (and that is expensive) and perhaps tennis he may not be able to play games. Language difficulties will always make it something of an effort to communicate with his neighbours and to go though the ordinary routine of daily life. He will probably feel a little conspicuous and isolated and he may sometimes yearn to be – as he would be at home – indistinguishable in a crowd. He may get tired of always being polite and always receiving courtesies and of receiving rather formal entertainment. He is unlikely to find really good bread to eat, good sausages and bacon or a steak and kidney pudding, or English beer or cheese. And in most parts of Japan he will be too hot in the summer. Finally he is liable to complain of the traffic and the litter in the streets and in the countryside.

On the other side of the balance sheet he will in the first place be living in one of the most beautiful countries in the world, in a climate not very unlike his own. He will be living in an energetic, vital and extremely cheerful atmosphere with something going on all the time. In the country, though now alas not much in the cities, he will be surrounded by natural beauty and by artistic and beautiful works of man. He can indulge his liking for skiing, mountaineering, walking, sailing and swimming. He can hear first class western music. He can travel easily by train and if he knows little Japanese he will find a hundred would-be English speakers at hand to help him over any difficulty. And he will be very unlucky if he ever meets with anything but courtesy and kindness. If he is interested in Japanese history or art or any of the traditional games and sports he will find a multitude of enthusiastic Japanese to guide him and instruct him and all the time he will have the fascinating spectacle of a culture and institutions in a state of what might described as a constructive flux – new things coming in and old things going out, or more likely – developing in new ways. The same changes are of course going on in England, but the speed and variety of the change in Japan is still much greater than it is here. To move from a Yorkshire village to London is an enormous change, and things go on, and customs and habits persist, in the Yorkshire village which would astonish the untravelled Londoner. But the contrast between Tokyo and a farming, fishing or mountain village a hundred miles away is still greater: electric light, television and a washing machine can it seems be superimposed upon a Japanese village community without – so far – any great change in the social life, habits or conventions.

TONY RUNDALL who arrived late in 1963 was a very conscientious Ambassador who tried very hard, but as he explained in a lecture to the Japan Society on 18 April 1968 (Bulletin No. 56 of October 1968) he did not find it easy. While there may be a case for *kokusiki romazi*, as used in Dunn and Yanada's introduction to Japanese, it certainly does not make learning easy for someone coming to the language at a mature age especially when all dictionaries use the Hepburn system of romanization:-

•

The basic task of an Ambassador is to interpret, without fear or favour, the policies of his home Government to the Government of the country to which he is accredited, and to report to his own Government enough of the views and policies of the Government and people amongst whom he lives to help them form their own policies.

To do this properly an Ambassador must have contacts. First, and most important, he must get to know the people of the country – members of the Government, its politicians, bankers, businessmen and labour leaders. He must travel widely – because it is true, I think, in all states, that the capital is not very representative of the country as a whole. He must meet prefectural Governors and mayors; he must visit factories, farms, universities and shipyards. He must have ordinary friends, amongst whom he can relax and have free discussion. He must cultivate his diplomatic colleagues, who will always be more knowledgeable and better informed than he is when he first arrives. He must get to know his own community, whom he represents, and learn about any difficulties and problems they may have. He must look out for and help any visiting businessmen from his country, because the promotion of trade is one of his most important responsibilities.

*   *   *

My wife and I arrived in Yokohama with all this before us, on Christmas Eve, 1963. We had been at sea feverishly trying to learn some Japanese. Had we known it, we were wasting our time, because the book we were using was in some queer system of phonetics, so that Mount Fuji was written Fuzi. This we *knew* was wrong, but we found out that most of the rest we had learned was pronounced quite differently. Anyhow, the Japanese language defeated me. I took lessons intensively for two months and then decided that I was too old and too busy to make any worthwhile progress. Some did seep in over the years, and I found that in the end I could understand quite a bit, but I never learned to speak or read.

I turned instead to the study of Igorish, which I found much more useful. Very many Japanese have a good knowledge of English, but because they lack practice in hearing and speaking it, some never entirely lose their Igorish accent. So Igorish repays study, because when someone is talking to you in your own language it is very 'imporite' not to understand him, and unless you know some Igorish you may get confused.

But I am getting ahead of myself. One never forgets one's first day in a new country, and the impact of Tokyo on a new arrival is rather breathtaking. It is not a beautiful city at first sight. One is, rather, bewildered by its size, its noise, and its traffic. Only later does one find beauty – its shrines and temples, the parks and gardens and the few, fairylike days when the cherry blossom casts a white mist of loveliness over its streets. Certainly the old road from Yokohama to Tokyo is not the best of introductions, but we were greatly comforted when we saw the Embassy compound, which is the best by far in Tokyo.

I have one more recollection of that confusing day. We had met our staff, inspected our house and made our first contact with our household. (They became such friends, and looked after us so well, that it is hard to remember those beginnings.) Anyhow, we were worn out by the end of it and decided to sleep for a little after dinner before going to the midnight Church Service. My wife, I remember, was asleep, when suddenly the whole room started to shake and sway about. My wife woke with start and said 'Goodness, what's happening?' I said: 'Darling, that's your first earthquake!' It was, I think, the worst one we had during our time – we never got quite used to them.

Well, that was the start – and it hardly ever stopped for 3^1/2 years. Our first few days were quiet, except for a party we gave on Boxing Day for 130 of the staff, but after I had presented my credentials to His Majesty the Emperor we were officially *en poste* and started calling on officials and upon our colleagues. They in turn began to invite us out. I see from my diary that we went to 27 parties in the first 30 days, and 37 in the next 28. That is the pace of Tokyo, the most social city in the world.

Our calls took some time. Besides officials, one must call upon every Head of Mission, and there were between 70 and 80 of them. Further-more, all the roads in Tokyo were at that time being dug up in preparation for the Olympic Games, so that my chauffeur, who had been driving in the city for over 30 years, used to get lost in the back streets when the main roads were closed. Some of the smaller streets, as most of you know, are very narrow – we once got the car stuck between two telegraph poles, one on each side of the road.

*   *   *

We made one unforgettable trip through the Inland Sea, from Nagasaki to Yokohama, with HIH Princess Chichibu after a ship launching, during which we got shipwrecked. Perhaps shipwrecked is putting it a bit strongly, because the *ship* was all right – but we couldn't get back on board because a storm came up whilst we were visiting a small island. We spent the whole day shuttling between Honshu and Shikoku, and various islands in between, trying to catch up. It was a startling day in many ways, because we had originally landed on our island to go for a walk, in the belief that no one lived there. In this we were quite wrong, because it turned out to be the site of a large, new Buddhist temple, and we were met by several hundred people on the dock, led by the Chief Priest and the Governor of the Prefecture. Princess Chichibu was dressed for a country walk and not for the ceremonies that followed, but she per-formed them with her usual charm and grace and we were regaled after-wards with ceremonial green sweets and some tomato soup which the Chief Steward of our ship had thoughtfully brought ashore. We were glad of it, because we got nothing more till the late evening. No, that is not quite correct, because the Chief Priest had presented Her Highness with a purple knitted woollen poodle containing a bottle of Black Label whis-ky. The Princess was kind enough to entrust the bottle to the weaker male members of the party, and it sustained us most adequately. I have the poodle at home now; the souvenir of a very happy day.

The Rundalls hired a little seaside cottage at Akiya and also made use of the Embassy's villa at Lake Chuzenji:

Akiya showed us a side of Japanese life which had changed little for centuries. The patient men in small boats just off shore, leaning over the side with their heads in glass-bottomed buckets collecting seaweed from the rocks, and the fishermen coming back to shore in the evenings to a welcoming party of the *Oba-san*, the wife and the children, waiting to haul the boat ashore and carry in the catch.

Chuzenji was more spectacular and beautiful – but somehow never quite so close to my heart as Akiya. Yet the view from our verandah out over the lake, with the light changing all the time as the clouds moved on the mountains opposite, was a constant fascination. We learned to catch the Chuzenji fish – silver outside and pink inside and very good eating – but I never succeeded in catching any of the very big trout which one sometimes saw cruising around the lake in the evening.

The great day of the summer was the *O-bon* festival at the end of July; the night when the spirits of the ancestors come down from the mountains and put to sea on the lake in thousands of little floats, each with its lighted candle in a paper lantern. All through the night these tiny lights flicker across the surface of the lake, whilst at the temple the villagers dance in preparation for climbing Nantai San, the sacred mountain which towers to 7,000 feet above the lake. The dance went on without stopping for several hours, and I always wondered how the dancers would find strength enough to climb to the top before dawn. For sheer beauty, I have seen few places in the world that compare with Lake Chuzenji. In the spring the wild azalea and mountain cherry gleam through the woods; in the autumn the scarlet and gold maples and sumac light up the hills like a page from an illuminated manuscript. Even the thunderstorms – and there are many in summer – are more spectacular than elsewhere.

JOHN PILCHER who took over in 1967 cannot be mentioned without a reference to Delia! I have attempted to write a biographical portrait of Sir John Pilcher which appeared in *Biographical Portraits*, Volume III, published for the Japan Society by Japan Library in 1999. He is also referred to elsewhere in this collection especially in Ben Thorne's piece which forms Chapter 20. I quoted some of what he wrote in my biographical portrait. Sadly, John Pilcher never wrote a memoir and no text has been preserved of the lecture which he gave to the Society on his retirement from Japan. He was certainly a memorable figure.

FRED WARNER who succeeded John Pilcher in 1972 does not seem to have given a lecture to the Society on his retirement. His widow SIMONE (Lady Warner) has sent me the following account of their time in Tokyo, concentrating on the Queen's visit which is also covered by Nicholas Barrington (see Chapter 36):-

•

In 1972, after eight months of SOAS and the Department of Japanese Studies at Sheffield University, trying to grasp some fundamentals of the language, history and culture of Japan, Dr Martin Collick gave me some blunt, parting advice: 'You're going to a country which is unlike any other in the developed world. You know the complexity of it by trying to understand the language. The only thing you can absolutely rely on is your capacity to remain yourself. That is something the Japanese will recognize and appreciate – it will relieve them of the responsibility of feeling they have to take care of you.' These were words that came back to me frequently and proved invaluable as I settled into my life in Japan. Superficially, the Japanese came to meet and greet us but our individual style of being spontaneous and curious seemed to be the linch-pin on which many of our friendships hinged.

It was particularly important during the first few months of settling into embassy life. I was a novice, newly married to an ambassador with a seven-year-old daughter and an infant son, living in a country I had long dreamed of visiting but with only a smattering of the language. It was a steep learning curve which sometimes seemed like ascending a cliff face.

We arrived in Japan when their industries were making rapid incursions into positions long held by the British (and other Europeans); it was a period of great change and competition. The strangeness of the Japanese style of doing things was quite at odds with our own individualistic culture, both commercially and socially. It was hard to penetrate and understand a society which had such ingrained customs, so at odds with our own. The notion of group activity and group decision-making was particularly hard to grasp with any subtlety.

Fortunately, I became close friends with Kazuko Aso (former prime minister Yoshida's daughter) and Hiroshi Hayakawa of the Hayakawa publishing house, both of whom had lived long enough away from Japan to be able to comprehend my difficulties. They were also brave enough, as only deep patriots can be, to risk the seeming disloyalty of being uncompromising in their explanations of what, to the outsider, looked like archaic behaviour and trusting enough to believe that I could understand it. I had to recognize that 85% of Japanese lived crowded together on the southern coastline of a country that had been recently destroyed by earthquake and fire, and that this had been a major factor in the Japanese emphasis on conformity and living together as a group.

During a year of intensive activity, in which we had the prime minister and many other cabinet ministers making visits to Japan, as well as a busy social programme I developed a number of cultural interests and began to find a way of 'being' in Japan. We had an increasing number of good and interesting friends and, as we began to feel safer, those friendships proved deeply rewarding. Contrary to general belief, we found friends, both men and women, who were unusually forthright, sometimes extremely indiscreet. We had many dinners which went on late into the night with intense exchanges over politics, the future of language, the importance of design, freedom, immigration, city planning, justice, peace; the ideas flowed and flowed and it was exciting to be amongst a group of people who could express themselves so coherently and vividly. I learnt to be a better listener. I was impressed by the detail which any Japanese seemed to have at his fingertips. Although I suppose their ideas could not always have been correct, they were usually accompanied by a thoughtfulness that I have continued to find unique. Perhaps it was timing, or the juxtaposition of two very different cultures meeting freely and exchanging passionate points of view which left me with an impression that has not changed in twenty-eight years. Every time I visit Japan I am reminded of their sharp attention to detail and how this compares with the comparative slackness of others.

By 1974 we were in full swing. We had produced another son and the embassy domestic staff, the most wonderful group of supporters, enthusiastically coped with the extra nursery meals and teaching the children to play cards and sing Japanese songs, whilst never stinting on a punishing schedule of lunches and dinners. Sometimes there were enormous numbers if there was a visiting British business group, a trade union, an orchestra, the RSC or a group of artists visiting Tokyo.

In the autumn of 1974, it was officially announced that the Queen, accompanied by Prince Philip, had accepted an invitation from the Emperor to visit Japan for six days the following June. We were both very pleased but, as Fred had never had a royal visit in any of his other postings, neither of us quite understood how much it would involve. Nor did we anticipate what surprises would emerge from the most unlikely sources.

My first duty, which was a great pleasure to perform, was to visit Buckingham Palace and choose the gold plate for the banquet that the Queen would give for the Emperor in the embassy. All the beautiful (and not so beautiful) things belonging to the Queen and to the State are laid out in a series of enormous underground vaults beneath the Palace. There was a charming and well-informed man (who, judging from his complexion, rarely saw the light of day) to show us around and help me choose from the two vast collections clearly separated from one another. I had been given an hour's appointment but managed to spin it out to three hours. My companion seemed happy to have someone to whom he could show the collections. I chose with care and was flattered to have been given such a free rein. This assembly of vast épergnes, dishes, salts and pepperpots and candelabra of amazing beauty quite simply staggered the eighty guests at the resulting banquet. They could not believe that the Queen could have taken so much trouble to fly it out to Japan with her for one dinner – albeit for their monarch.

After that the year passed swiftly, with all the usual merriment and duties but with an enormous added weight on Fred's schedule. The Queen's private office was very efficient and very modest. Whereas the preparation for Gerald Ford's two-day trip to Japan necessitated a visit of some three hundred personnel on a special plane to ensure a smooth visit (a shame they did not also check his tailor), the royal household sent only two people: one of the Queen's senior Private Secretaries and a most sympathetic but sharp-eyed private detective. The Kunaicho (Imperial Household Agency), the stern group of civil servants who have run (one might almost say 'ruled') the imperial household for centuries, were amazed. Was this some sort of trick or lack of respect for the emperor's invitation? They scratched their heads perplexedly, quite unsure of how to treat this group, who along with my husband and his private secretary Robert Cooper, seemed too modest a bunch to represent the only other monarchy the Japanese take seriously.

They were in for some surprises. Everyone on the British side was well briefed and the five days of meetings went very smoothly with one exception. The Queen had told Fred that she would like to do an open car drive through the centre of Tokyo – something that she always tried to do on state visits as it gave a great number of people an opportunity to see her. This could not be resolved during the first round of meetings and a couple of weeks later Fred had to tell the Queen that the emperor would prefer that this plan was not insisted on. The Queen did insist. It was what she definitely wished to do. All this discussion had to be couched in tactful diplomatic language hedging around the central question of what a guest can insist on doing in the host's country.

The Imperial family in those days was rarely seen out at all in Tokyo, or anywhere else. The emperor had had divine status only thirty years previously; in his presence, even in a passing car, the people lowered their eyes. It was hardly surprising, therefore, how *outré* this suggestion of the Queen being driven at eight mph through the crowded streets of Tokyo would seem to both the Emperor and his fearsomely old-fashioned chamberlains. We had reached a stalemate and it seemed as though the whole visit might even be in jeopardy.

I abandoned my lists and menus, amused by the seriousness of the royal games, mildly disappointed that I would possibly not, after all, spend six days in the Queen's company, but pleased to be able to assume my family life and diplomatic duties which had become surprisingly dislocated by the extra meetings that had to be slotted into my already busy programme. Then back came a belated message from the Kunaicho. The Queen could do a drive through the middle of Tokyo but at forty mph in a bullet-proof car. Fred responded by saying that Her Majesty would not be *able* to stand up at that speed and the bullet-proof glass would largely obscure her; it had to be an open car. This farcical discussion dragged on for weeks. Finally, Fred walked into the Residence one day and said 'It's going to be all right – the only thing they could think of saying at the meeting today was that if she insisted on going so slowly the outriders would fall off their motorbikes.' We all laughed.

On both the Japanese and British side everyone seemed very excited at the prospect of the visit. Princess Chichibu, whom by this time I had come to know quite well and whom I visited for tea regularly, began to get quite frisky. There had never been a royal visit by a reigning monarch and her enthusiasm for it, as well as her passion for Britain, where her beloved late husband had been at Oxford University, led her to become very animated and politically incorrect at our tea parties. She had deeply held views about peace and the unsatisfactory effects of the last war on our two nations. She regaled me with wonderful stories of her time as a travelling princess with a humorous and modern approach to life, which, however, in no way compromised her innate dignity.

I began to get a much clearer picture of the extent to which the Imperial family had been protected and isolated from the public eye and how little that had changed for them since the war. One afternoon, the princess asked me if I knew how to do the Gay Gordons. Yes, I did. 'Maybe Her Majesty might wish to do it at the embassy ball after the banquet?' I said I doubted it but she decided we would have a practice anyway with me playing the male partner. When I pointed out that this would be considerably harder for her in a kimono than in the silk dress she was wearing, we were giggling like children. Even her very correct lady-in-waiting was enjoying the fun. Then the princess described a hilarious scene when Prince Chichibu was preparing for a visit to England in the 1920s where he would be attending a ball at Buckingham Palace. Not having the first notion of what European dancing was like, a young equerry (who, I think, may have been to Europe with the Japanese navy) was detailed to come and teach the prince to dance. I can imagine the horrified embarrassment of the poor young lieutenant playing the girl's role, attempting to teach the prince how to lead him in a waltz and foxtrot while he, keen to do an honourable job, negotiated his way backwards in the unfamiliar and overwhelming surrounds of the Imperial Palace. Princess Chichibu wept with laughter as she recounted this tale. Apparently, the prince did take to the floor in Britain but it is not recorded what happened to the hapless equerry.

Things hotted up as the arrival date drew nearer. The programme for the visit was packed with events, each one having to be minutely planned. An example of this was the preparations for the bullet train ride to Kyoto on the fourth day. Her Majesty is a disciplined and conscientious worker. She spends hours at her desk every day, keeping up with what is happening at home, meticulously reading and signing state papers. Whenever the Queen goes on an extended trip she takes the equivalent of a large office with her, packed into special trunks. Much of the contents are confidential and need to be secure at all times. The bullet train waits for no man or woman, whoever they may be: only an earthquake disrupts its schedule. This meant that all two hundred of the Queen's cases would have to be offloaded in the three minutes the train stopped in Kyoto. It was clear that it would not be possible to unload them from the four doors of the Queen's special carriages fast enough to keep to the schedule. Finally, it was decided to spread them through-out the train with two guards to each door to get them out when the time came. This brought home a perplexing contradiction in the Japanese si-tuation which was a frequently encountered tripwire in the preparations. Whilst Japan has a deep respect for order, ritual and monarchy, it has also, I believe, a profoundly democratic ethic. There can be no setting aside the rights of the group for the benefit or convenience of one.

* * *

After so many months of exhaustive planning, we were at last ready to greet the Queen knowing that we had covered everything that could be reasonably anticipated. The Queen's Private Office had been easy to work with but we had local glitches and problems which could only be solved at the Tokyo end. The grand finale was to be a ball in the embassy which would follow on immediately after the banquet. The Queen had made it clear that she wanted a good mix of guests. Captains of industry, politi-cians, figures from the world of business, the professions, academia and the arts. The emphasis was to be largely focused on the Japanese. We were also firm in our belief it should be as much fun as possible but we realized that royalty often induces anxiety in many people. We sought to assemble as good a mix of guests as possible to produce a merry atmosphere. We discussed with no one outside Fred's private office the lists that we had to choose from or the selection process, but nevertheless there was much jostling for invitations. On one occasion, there was an attempt to bribe me. Coming home one night I found a package containing a beautiful long string of large pearls on a diamond clasp and a note from the wife of a very senior industrialist saying how sad she was not to have seen me for so long. The pearls went back the next day and, coincidentally, it was the very day that all the invitations were finally posted with theirs included. I regretted that I could not remove them from their place on the list – and keep the necklace!

After a couple of days it was clear that the visit was going very well. The Japanese crowds were delighted by the dignity and the warmth of the Queen's responses. Whatever private thoughts she may have had, there was an absolute professionalism and courtesy in every aspect of her tour. There was great diversity in the programme, but from the very formal Imperial household events, to watching the pearl fishers or talking to the members of Elizabeth Kai her curiosity was maintained. The impeccable way she had been briefed was noted. There were no muffed lines or wrong names. This must have involved many hours of preparation and memorising information. Both Fred and I were very impressed and proud.

The open car drive down the Ginza was an overwhelming success.

People had travelled miles from the country – many of them with step-ladders to ensure a good view – and they waited several hours for her to pass by. Seated in a car a couple behind the Queen and Prince Philip, both Fred and I were profoundly moved by the warmth and enthusiasm of the crowd's response. It was both physically animated and vocal. It was as if there was a sense of the Japanese nation wishing for reconciliation and a return to the relationship we had had in the Meiji period when the British had played a seminal and practical part in Japan's emergence from its isolation and provided a sort of avuncular social and industrial role model for its modernization. There was a palpable wish that the Queen's visit would bring our 'two island countries' back together again and cement this relationship. Despite some mild initial cynicism on my part (during the preparations), being present with the Queen and Prince Philip on a daily basis, I felt that I witnessed a real breakdown of barriers. It was astonishing to witness this – something magical in the presence of an icon that can actually provoke people to open their hearts.

When the day came to say goodbye, we found that the Queen had, without telling us, slotted into her early morning programme an hour for thanking individually all the senior Japanese staff in the residence, and others working in the chancery, who had done so much extra work to make things run so smoothly. They were both surprised and thrilled at this unexpected bonus.

Everyone, both Japanese and British, proclaimed the visit a great success. There had been a surprising show of emotion on all sides when the Queen departed which confirmed this. Within five days, there was a large hardback picture book of the visit on sale all over Tokyo. The first printing of 500,000 sold out within a couple of days. It was reprinted in large quantities several times. Fred and I became like diplomatic pop stars. Strangers would walk up to us in the street and greet us, often shaking our hands, unusual for Japanese and ask for autographs. The visit seemed to release a great flow of goodwill. There was a wholehearted show of a new curiosity which I feel sure enhanced both our political and commercial relations, and made dialogue easier, and even smoothed the path for future development.

When we finally left Japan ourselves a few months later, I felt I was not only leaving behind a group of good friends, but losing that peculiar sense of safety that Japan provides. Not just a physical safety but one which comes from a society where respect for order and hierarchy is not thought to be undemocratic. It is something I still miss.

MICHAEL WILFORD (Sir Michael Wilford) was British Ambassador to Japan from 1975 to 1980. He has commented as follows on his years in Japan:-

•

I had had no previous experience of Japan except for short business visits. I had, however, served in Peking where I had acquired some knowledge of Chinese characters although I did not learn how they were read in Japanese. I had a degree in engineering and a golf handicap of 5. My wife Joan had never set foot in Japan.

I was given the impression before I set out for Japan that few Japanese could really make themselves understood in English, however much they had studied the language at school. This was, of course, to encourage both my wife and myself to make a real effort from the start to learn the language. For my part during my first two years in Japan I had lessons two afternoons a week whenever possible. I do not regard myself as a good linguist and at the end of two years I felt that I had learned all that I was likely ever to assimilate. I could deal with normal social situations, could find my way round and deal with shopping etc, but I would never have tried to conduct a business discussion in Japanese. I delivered one speech annually in Japanese – at the *Bonenkai* (end-of-year party).

My wife, however, was faced with a more difficult situation in the house. While she had both an English and a Japanese secretary – and the butler's English was pretty good – none of the cooks or gardeners spoke any English. She set to with a will and in the end I am sure that she spoke more Japanese than I did and more often – even if my little may have been a bit more grammatical.

So much for our own efforts. I must say, however, that I thought the Japanese performance was considerably better than I had been led to believe not only in Ministries outside the Ministry of Foreign Affairs (Gaimusho), but elsewhere in the country generally. A mixture of our Japanese plus their English almost always made a conversation possible.

We had been told especially that few Japanese ladies would be able to hold their own in conversation. My wife, while accepting that some lunches and dinners had to be men only, disapproved of the idea and we, therefore, did our very best to make social occasions male and female. We were amazed to find how well Japanese ladies did in such circumstances. It made the whole occasion more fun; they clearly enjoyed themselves and so did we. Moreover, the fact that we were always able to ensure that they had at least one Japanese speaker beside them thanks to the many embassy staff who did speak Japanese was a tremendous help.

We soon discovered the need for aids to conversation on social occasions. We found several useful ones. For example, I had on display in the drawing-room autographed photographs of both the Emperor and Empress given to me when I was the Assistant Under Secretary dealing with Asia at the time of the Emperor's State Visit to London. It was not the photographs which caused interest; it was the Emperor's handwriting which many of the visitors said that they had never seen before. The embassy's silver was also a source of interest. Since it had only become an embassy at the beginning of the twentieth century when Edward VII was on the throne it bore hallmarks of his reign and also that of the Edinburgh Assay office rather than the more usual London one. Our dogs – Lhasa Apsos – were always of much interest not least when towards the end of an evening they would appear in a crocodile behind their 'nanny' Kikue-san (who had been a maid in the residence for many years) and walk through the drawing-room into the garden to spend their pennies. Finally, we had a wonderful book of old photographs of Japan belonging to the embassy. It was successful if all else failed.

*   *   *

Since we knew nothing of Japan outside Tokyo we travelled whenever we could. We tried to get away for at least two week-long visits each year to see different parts of the country. On each trip there were not only the obligatory calls on governors of prefectures and mayors of cities as well as meals with them, but we always tried to include a visit to an educational establishment (school or university) and a factory, especially of an engineering nature for me. Thus, we visited Komatsu's factory where all sorts of mechanical equipment is made, shipyards, steelworks and, perhaps most amusing of all, NSK's ball-bearing works at Kawasaki. We arrived to find a lot of glum faces and were told that the annual wage struggle (*shunto*) was on. I asked if they would rather we came back another day. They were embarrassed because while working normally the workers would be wearing arm bands indicating that they were on strike. It was a bit different from a British strike!

Travelling on the *shinkansen* (the broad gauge new railway) was always fun and on one occasion having entertained leaders of the Railway Trades Union I was invited to travel with the driver up front. It showed how little the driver had to do except to obey the instruments which instructed him as to speed. Once we were involved in an emergency due to an earthquake when all trains were halted for a short space. My wife was not allowed to join me in the driver's cab for some reason, nor, more strangely would they allow her to enter the Seikan tunnel being built between Honshu and Hokkaido. There at least there was an explanation for Joan's exclusion as in Japan tunnels are female and they are jealous of other women. To me the tunnel building was of particular interest and the hole through had just been completed, the tunnel being both much longer and deeper than the Channel Tunnel though the water gap was much the same.

In five years we succeeded in visiting all but three of Japan's prefectures. We got to Okinawa very early because there was a UN Expo 'The

Sea we want to see' to which Anthony Crosland, then Environment Secretary, was coming. He came again to Japan as Foreign Secretary. We
were not winter sports enthusiasts. So we never got to Yamagata; the
other two prefectures we did not visit were Mie (so we never got to the
Imperial Shrines at Ise) and Tottori. We usually took the Rolls to wherever
we were going even if we travelled there by air or train. It was so much
more comfortable with our own transport to go round the chosen area. It
also enabled us to take our 'return' presents for governors and so on and
we filled it up with those we received which were invariably larger. Sometimes the police escort used to help, in which case at prefectural boundaries our 'loot' had to be transferred from one police car to another!

*   *   *

Workwise the most important thing which happened in our time was the
arrival of so many merchant bankers and other financial representatives
from Britain. Fortunately, thanks to the foresight of Gordon Richardson
when he was Governor of the Bank of England, we had a Bank of England representative on the staff. The Treasury had withdrawn their man
years earlier and were unwilling to pay the cost of a resident representative. The Bank's money was well spent and we had splendid representatives whose value to our increasing financial community was immense.
They formed a sizeable part of the whole British community by the time
we left. I always found it difficult, as is sometimes the case elsewhere, to
say that the community was the sphere of interest of the consul or consul
general and not of the ambassador. We felt we both had a substantial role
to play with them through the Royal British Legion, St George's and St
Andrew's Societies and, of course, the Japan-British Society. I think it
was well worth it. Joan set up something of a record by being President
of the Japan Branch of the Fleet Air Arm Officers' Association having
ended her wartime career as Squadron Staff Officer of the Deck Landing
School at Easthaven in Scotland.

    And so to golf. I was told that no Ambassador since Sir Robert Craigie
before the war had ever played golf. So I was given a great welcome by the
Japanese who are so keen on the game. Ambassadors are honorary members of five of the best golf courses around Tokyo. One of our Japanese-
speaking staff, usually a service attaché, was given the task of coordinating all the ambassador's activities and he, too, got these privileges. I
found that often instead of calling at offices on the heads of Japanese
banks and companies I received invitations to meet them at one of the
best golf clubs where I had the greater part of the day with them and got
to know them really well. One is often asked, 'Did you get to know Japanese people?' The answer is yes. We often went to stay for weekends at
their country houses at Hakone or elsewhere in the mountains, like Nasu,

to play golf. Sometimes, it was me to the mountains for golf, while Joan went with their wives to the seaside.

Perhaps the golf relationship can best be described thus. When Masayoshi Ohira was Prime Minister I used to be telephoned by his private secretary at the Gaimusho to ask if Rod Miller, the New Zealand Ambassador, and I would take the Prime Minister out for a day's golf to get him clear of work! Needless to say we were delighted and if in five hours or so on the course or in the clubhouse you could not find the time to ask him pertinent questions one was in the wrong business. How many ambassadors got only twenty minutes or half an hour!

I (HUGH CORTAZZI) succeeded Michael Wilford in 1980. I have said more than enough in my memoir *Japan and Back and Places Elsewhere*, and there is no need to repeat any of the book here.

In 1984 I was succeeded by SYDNEY GIFFARD (Sir Sydney). He has contributed a piece about his early days in the Kansai (see Chapter 29).

Next came JOHN WHITEHEAD (Sir John) whose memoirs of his early time in Japan are contained in Chapter 32. It seems appropriate, however, to include here what he has termed 'Development and Middle Game':-

•

Japan 2001 will be the third Japanese cultural manifestation in the United Kingdom in the past twenty years. The first such development was the Great Japan Exhibition of 1981/2 at the Royal Academy. The second was the Japan Festival in the United Kingdom in 1991 which marked the 100th anniversary of the Japan Society.

The third event, lasting upwards of twelve months, was in concept a nationwide, grass-roots occasion with planned focal points such as Kabuki and so on. These cultural festivals have been mirrored in part by UK90 and the more recent UK98. I remember that in 1990 one could write, without too much fear of contradiction, that UK90 was one of our biggest cultural festivals ever held overseas, with nearly a hundred and forty events – exhibitions, concerts, theatrical performances and the like – in a period of three months in many parts of Japan. Mr Gaishi Hiraiwa, Chairman of Tokyo Electric Power Company, was the honorary chairman of the festival. He did much to give the occasion a high profile in Japan and he and his company did a great deal then and at other times and in other ways, including the endowment of a chair of Japanese at Cambridge University and subsequently a fellowship at Oxford, to strengthen academic and cultural links between Japan and the UK. We were fortunate as a country to have been the recipients of such benefactions and cultural activity at a time in the 1980s when the Japanese economy was at one of its peaks.

But despite this we noted, at the beginning of 1994, at two conferences, one of the UK-Japan 2000 Group in South Wales and the other embracing a much wider participation in the Queen Elizabeth Conference Centre on 'Britain and Japan: A New Era' that, despite the undoubted progress of recent years, we still had not achieved a critical mass – of knowledge, of exchanges, of enthusiasm – to achieve 'take-off', a self-sustaining coming and going in these fields between Britain and Japan. It is not clear how long it may take to achieve it. It probably does not matter how long, provided there is a will to maintain and broaden the interest and keep up the momentum. Many different organizations and individuals are working heroically to do just that: greatly expanded JET programmes, English language teaching, festivals, scientific exchanges, the broadly-based and highly important work of the British Council and its concentration not only on the more purely cultural and straight educational exchanges work but on its efforts to put culture and education firmly into the social context – the 'how we live now in Britain and Japan' elements; all of these are highly important developments, as is the work of our Japanese counterparts.

This is important work. Culture in the broadest sense and the role of the media are essential ways of influencing favourably a wide section of the population and of underpinning relationships which otherwise are run in large part by group professionals. Interests which can move sizeable sections of the population, 'mass culture', underpin and sustain a professional relationship; they underwrite its credibility and legitimacy. They can add weight to a relationship which could otherwise become top-heavy and hence unnecessarily vulnerable to squalls.

And then there is the need to combat plain straight ignorance about each other's countries on the part of many. In the mid-1990s a British taxi driver commented: 'Oh you live in Japan do you? How is that going to affect your life when it reverts to China?' which was mirrored by a Japanese taxi driver; who enquired: 'Ah, you come from England do you? What language do they speak there, then?'

The British Council was well represented in Japan back in 1956. That its work has now changed almost out of recognition is indicative of a far more complex, involved and mature relationship across the board between Britain and Japan. During the 1950s and 60s the embassy for the most part looked for work rather than, as now, being bombarded with it. Much of this increase has occurred as an inevitable consequence of Japan's rise to economic pre-eminence with a GDP second only to the United States and a long way ahead of No.3. This was a rise over a period of thirty years (roughly the 1960s, 70s and 80s), of which twenty-five years were spent protecting the economy behind dense thickets of rules and regulations.

Hugh Cortazzi, and particularly David Wright and I, spent much of the three years at the end of the 1960s and in the early 70s trying to crack the Japanese bureaucratic system of import controls. At the end of that time we understood a great deal of how the system worked – semi-secret lists of those Japanese companies who were granted import licences and quotas and all the rest. But we were scarcely able to chip away at it because of widely drawn regulations or guidance and the interpretation of that guidance by Japanese administrators on a case-by-case basis designed essentially to protect all sectors of the Japanese economy (at least until they were demonstrably of world class) and to thwart the foreigner, particularly those who sought to export to Japan.

Myriads of customs officials, import clerks, type-approval testers and the like were dedicated to the proposition that imports were bad and exports were good. But in the 1980s the officials were told to stand on their heads, sometimes towards the end of their careers; a difficult proposition. Everyone knew that now Japan was a world beater, imports were good and exports had to be moderated. The period of almost total frustration on the part of foreigners was receding. MITI, the bogeyman of the 1960s and much of the 70s, was in the van of the new-look Japan of the 1980s.

Throughout that period one used to categorize the relations between Japan and Britain as 'good'. And so, in a sense, they were. The Japanese import regime in the 1960a and 70s and the growing trade imbalance were troubling. But there were no serious issues of dispute between us, for the good reason that for most of the time Japanese preoccupations and British preoccupations did not overlap. It was like a piece of machinery with two separate wheels whirring around but not in any way touching: there was no friction, but equally there was little or no synergy.

This started to change in the early 1980s as Japan became concerned about the possible emergence of a fortress Europe and decided as a result progressively to invest in European countries in order to protect her markets there. Hugh Cortazzi was one of the first to recognize the potential of this development, and it was of course a major political as well as economic plus for Britain which was eagerly grasped by senior British politicians. When Mrs Thatcher visited Japan for the first time as Prime Minister in 1982 she sat down in the ambassador's residence for dinner with the heads of all twenty-two Japanese companies that had invested in Britain by that stage. It was a love-in: the Japanese welcomed a Prime Minister who was galvanizing the British economy at last and hence adding powerfully to all the national advantages which Britain had as a destination for Japanese investment – the English language, good communications, an across-the-board welcome for that investment; Mrs Thatcher was anxious to give a powerful push to these inward investment trends on the part of those who were dining with her.

As moves towards a Single European Market gathered pace and in Britain trade union reform was carried through against a background of a favourable period in the economic cycle, so the flow of Japanese investment became a torrent. By the time I returned to Japan as ambassador in late 1986 (after four years as minister between 1980 and 1984) there were over forty investments by companies such as Sony, NEC and Nissan. When I left in mid-1992 there were nearly two hundred, including Toyota, Fujitsu and Honda. Britain was receiving about 40% of total Japanese investment in the European Community. The embassy was fortunate in having two outstanding economic counsellors in the 1980s – David Wright in the earlier years, Stephen Gomersall in the latter, both of whom went on in fairly quick time to become British Ambassadors to Japan. The scene was set for a major change of gear in relations in all fields between Britain and Japan. All that was needed were the right circumstances and senior political follow-through.

The occasion arose in 1987 as a result, perhaps inevitably, of trade disputes, focusing essentially on British access to Japan – investment in the international aspects of Japanese telecommunications, the granting of a suitable number of seats on the rapidly developing Tokyo Stock Exchange, and the long outstanding problem of liquor tax harmonization (tax on Scotch whisky was forty times as high as tax on Japanese *shochu*). The three issues came to a head almost simultaneously, and against a background of a further deterioration in the trade balance. I saw them as test cases: on the one hand of Japanese willingness to open up to a worthwhile extent to British investment in fields where we clearly had much to offer but were not threatening the Japaneseness of certain peaks in the Japanese economy (telecommunications and financial services) and of their willingness also to abide by longstanding GATT rulings over liquor tax; and on the other of British Ministers' preparedness to concentrate over an extended period on relations with Japan – first to clear away the disputes and then to set in motion a programme designed virtually to revolutionize relations and place them on a markedly higher plane.

Inevitably, it took an enormous amount of effort to deal with both parts (Japanese and British) of this equation. The sequence of events could not have got off to a better start. Some judicious briefing ensured that Mrs Thatcher's interest was captured and in little time a then junior minister (Parliamentary Under-Secretary) in the Department of Trade and Industry, Michael Howard, was despatched to Tokyo to remonstrate with the Japanese. As a QC he was naturally quick to pick up a brief and the ensuing series of meetings with Japanese ministers and officials constituted a brilliant bravura performance (on the part of some of the Japanese particularly Koji Watanabe, then a deputy under-secretary in the *Gaimusho* and subsequently ambassador in Moscow, as well as by Michael Howard). Progress was made in subsequent weeks on all three issues – some seats on the Tokyo Stock Exchange for British firms earlier than

had originally been planned; reduction in the disparity in liquor tax between whisky and *shochu* from 40:1 to 10:1; and, after one of those almost
unbelievable meetings between the Minister of Posts and Telecommunications and me in an anonymous central Tokyo hotel ostensibly so that his
officials could not intervene, a deal agreed over tea and cream cakes
which provided for Cable and Wireless and British Telecom to acquire a
little over 17% of the shares in two separate international communications consortia to compete with KDD (prior to this the Japanese had
sought to prevent any foreign investment and subsequently shifted to a
proposal to approve 3%).

This was the breakthrough we had been seeking. British ministers saw
clearly that provided we were persistent and consistent some movement
would be forthcoming from the Japanese; deals could be done. It was
then clear that these issues could not be the sum total of our relations
with a country with the economic power and potential international
clout of Japan. In January 1988 Geoffrey Howe, then Foreign Secretary,
visited Japan (his fifth visit and by his own account by far the most important and interesting of the five) at the end of which a new era of relations between Britain and Japan was ushered in – designated by Geoffrey
Howe as 'a dynamic, plain-speaking partnership'. The intensity and
warmth of political and other visits and exchanges was visibly enhanced
and became a model for other European countries including Germany
where Genscher, not to be outdone, suggested that there should be
twice-yearly meetings at foreign minister level, only to be told by the
Japanese that this might be a good idea but that on that basis he had
missed the last fourteen meetings! The Howe visit did much, I think,
to deepen his interest in Japan. A visit to Oita Prefecture in Kyushu where
his host was Governor Hiramatsu, a very experienced official but also
adept politician whose slogan *'isson ippin'* – 'one village one product' –
did much to galvanize the people and the economy of his not over-en-
dowed prefecture, was a genuine success. And a side trip to Yufuin in the
mountains gave him first-hand experience of a Japanese hot-spring
resort.

In May of the same year he was followed by David Young, Secretary of
State for Trade and Industry. This also was a crucial visit, which announced the start of the 'Opportunity Japan' campaign, with Michael
Perry of Unilever as its private sector head – an ideal, no-nonsense, thoroughly enthusiastic senior businessman, able to enthuse or cajole many of
his peers in the business world. We had sought on a number of occasions
with only very limited success to persuade business leaders not to write
off Japan as an impossible market. The Japanese had often said we were
'not trying hard enough'. 'Opportunity Japan', with its strong political
endorsement, solid business involvement and, let it be said, cooperation
from the Japanese side, provided just the combination we had been look-

ing for. Our message was that business should look seriously at the Japanese market. If after careful research they decided that it was too difficult, too competitive, too expensive, too distant or for some other reason was not easily absorbable as part of their strategic plan, so be it; but at least they would have looked and considered. We tried initially to interest 1,750 companies this way; 650 to a greater or lesser degree took the plunge. As a result our exports shot ahead in the following three years and the follow-on programme, 'Priority Japan', was launched. It was an exhilarating period. And the coping stone was put in the arch with the second visit of Mrs Thatcher as Prime Minister in 1989 in which she called for the maximum cooperation between Britain and Japan in all fields.

JOHN BOYD (Sir John) succeeded John Whitehead as British Ambassador to Japan in 1992. John and his wife Julia provided the following recollections:-

•

We were the inexpert ones. But how we enjoyed Japan!

Piccadilly Circus saw our first assault on the language. After class Julia used to put questions to the tourists outside Buckingham Palace but had trouble with the answers. On the plane out, in early July, we rehearsed '*Mushi-atsui, desu-ne*'. We were greeted naturally as experts on arrival. A first lesson in Japanese courtesy. Later, driven on by Omura-san, I risked a week on the *tatami* at Kamakura. The school was wonderful but local police having spotted the Rolls on the pavement were concerned about my personal safety.

The next lesson was the personal bond. The embassy has been hugely fortunate, always, in its Japanese staff. We were superbly cared for at Number One House: on a visit to London in 1994 Adachi-san showed the same meticulous care in examining the carpets in the refurbished FCO. When we asked our girls, at a country fair, who would look after the fluffy rabbits they yearned for, they chorused 'Sugawara-san'. Our drivers could have competed on any global track. When we were pulled over on the highway to Nikko, on a super busy Saturday, a policeman commented dryly that it was unusual to see an ambassador going to a meeting of the utmost importance without a tie.

Right through the embassy there was brilliant support for the work required to service a burgeoning bilateral relationship, expressed not only professionally but by participation in British activities ranging from cricket to Scottish piping to the *Pirates of Penzance*. Picking up an old tradition, John expanded the embassy choir and raised its ambitions. It brought a truly bicultural flavour to Handel, Sullivan and Parry. At our departure we did the *Magnificat* in the ballroom, with string band and a clutch of Tokyo trumpeters, most of the audience being forced out into the hall.

The third lesson was the pleasure that young Brits get from their association with Japan, inside or outside the embassy. There was a pretty seamless robe uniting our young diplomats with young British business folk, Daiwa scholars and the rest. John's private secretary and others would go without sleep to get seats at some provincial *basho* (*sumo* tournament). They were correspondingly expert in entertaining, say, the Oxford and Cambridge Light Rowing Crews or the Barbarians. Visitors like Bobby Charlton or Andrew Lloyd Webber were icons. There was fine support from the Chamber, and British business generally, for culture, sport and charity work, Ian de Stains's Christmas readings setting the tone.

Next point, personal friendships. One is rigorously tested in Japan for this. If you pass you are bound in. The friendships that come out of our time in Japan are permanent, from the upper end of Tokyo society through bonds formed in temples, say on the Chichibu round, or fishing for *ayu*, to those developed by Julia in Kumamoto, to the man we met in a provincial bar who invited us to bed down in the straw with the temple horse. Julia once prevailed, through sheer personality, on a station-master to hold up a Japanese train (we had been drinking to restore circulation after the twenty-year ceremony at Ise). In a northern coastal village, our elderly hostess sent her husband out on a turbulent evening sea to catch fresh fish for our dinner.

Particular points for us. The landscape. Still ravishing to the seeing eye. But you have to look through billions of wires and acres of poles first. Nevertheless, it is still there and magical. Leaving aside the many visits to Kyushu, special moments were the Noto *Hanto* (peninsula), Sadogashima, with all the lilies out, and of course Hiraizumi (that was where we were spotted by the *Sunday Telegraph* in a remote inn on grounds of our green wellies outside the door). We always stayed in the same B&B in Kyoto where the hospitality gene is strong and where we incidentally met the man who determined the true cause of stomach ulcers. Mrs Uemura took the best possible care of us. But we have known some rugged times. In Nara, for something like 6,000 yen a night we had to dash periodically from our freezing room across an icy if ravishing courtyard to revive ourselves on the heated loo seat. (Japanese hi-tech plumbing is always a fruitful theme.) In Yakushima John was left at base camp with a monstrously sprained ankle while Julia did the cedars and the summit.

Northern and northmost Japan were also rewarding. The British Council, there as elsewhere wonderfully imaginative and effective under Mike Barrett, decided to show the flag in Hokkaido. Julia and I met a bevy of distinguished British stallions doing their stuff for the Japanese blood stock, rightly encouraged by keen young British stable hands. Similarly, right round the compass, one met JETs and other English teachers from the UK deeply dug into Japanese society, not all uncritical by any means but invested with understanding. Wherever we went in Japan we discovered more about Britain. In off-shore islands there were links with Kew (Yakushima) or British astrophysics (the Tanegashima space launch). Nearer home, at British Hills, heroic efforts were being made to secure from and restore an abandoned Father Willis organ in North London. The spiritual authorities, however, deemed that the Ambassador's pleadings 'lacked merit'. British cultural troupes made a great impact. We remember a Japanese Prime Minister, detained by duty, arriving a little late for *Don Giovanni* by Pavilion Opera, becoming a little entangled in a pitch black armed confrontation between the Don and the Commendatore.

Which brings me to the *onsen*. Par for the course for old Japan hands but a big discovery for us. We were regulars at a particular one at Yumoto above Chuzenji. A vigorous walk, the hottest of baths, *soba* and saké. A good recipe for what ails you. We tried to introduce visiting British ministers through Chuzenji to a wider view of Japan. The villa itself always worked its magic, as it did on embassy staff. Those old bulgy chairs, the *shoji*, the early morning light. Dragonflies. The puttering of the motorized fishing fleet on the water. Nicholas Barrington's cyclostyled notes on Nikko. Hamada-san's thoughtful care (which included in John's case endless, fruitless, fishing expeditions). Chuzenji also saw bilateral consultations at PUS (permanent under-secretary) level, with John Coles and Vice-Minister Hayashi striding off across the moors.

But a particularly treasured memory is Douglas and Judy Hurd's stay, with the Foreign Secretary inveigled into the *onsen*, furnished with saké (over which we discussed losses in the trenches in the First War) and persuaded to play competitive quizzes with guards, drivers and secretaries. Ministerial visits ranged ever wider as the bilateral agenda developed and as the two societies got to know each other better. The embassy was particularly energetic in its promotion of whisky. On the five hundredth anniversary of the discovery of the Scotch variety the ambassador was presented with a particularly delicious bottle by the Captain of the QE2. Unfortunately, Gary Lineker, also supporting us, prevailed on John to draw the cork then and there rather than wait for Cambridge.

Our own albums are full of Chuzenji – walks whether in sun or snow, among upland flowers or towering trees. Also figures of children jumping into freezing water. Also charades or bridge at the villa. Also friends, including the former editor of the *Far Eastern Economic Review* savaging British policy in Asia and Asa Briggs reflecting on the fate of empire as the local wildlife, sitting on the bonnet of the Rolls, shredded the Union flag. Not only ambassadors lost time or place at Chuzenji. We also lost the then chief clerk. John and his administration counsellor tramped despondently many miles in pursuit, hissed at and bombarded by monkeys from the treetops as night fell. It was also possible on still winter nights up at Chuzenji (and we spent our last Christmas there, with snow edging between the boards of the house) to hear the deer bark mysteriously.

Two final points. Julia's book. This was written at the suggestion of the Japanese. Julia was not keen at first, but the project as it proceeded took wing, opening a window for us not only on Kumamoto – and the support from down there was a given – but also on missionary records back in the UK and then on a wider part of the late-nineteenth century relationship. Julia discovered herself befriended – continuity being the point – by the grandchildren of those who had backed the original Kumamoto leprosy hospital. John kept hands well off but the project was educative for him too, and it certainly helped to raise the British profile. We owe a particular debt to Jerry Matsumura for his encouragement and support.

Second, and powerfully, we saw Japan in affliction. Our last year in Tokyo was the year of the fiftieth anniversary, of *Aum Shinrikyo*, of the Kobe earthquake. Japan did not cope particularly well with these events, part of a difficult continuing passage. We were torn for her and for all the victims. Our own children were out on the underground on the day of the poison gas attack, though mercifully elsewhere on the network. Our immediate post-earthquake visit to Kobe confronted us with up-ended traditional houses, fruitless searches, shoes torn from victims' feet. David Cockerham's reports from the heart of the disaster were deeply human, horribly vivid. As I write, or so the papers say, not all Kobe victims have been re-housed. Yet Japanese friends walked many miles at the time to check that my brother Stephen (whose house had been completely destroyed) had food and water. Supporting Japan as she handles difficult events remains an important part of the British agenda. Supporting bilateral science and education is now part of my own. The friendships continue.

DAVID WRIGHT (Sir David) took over from John Boyd as Ambassador in 1996. He had served in Japan as a language student, as a junior secretary in the Commercial Department in the late 1960s and as Economic Counsellor in the 1980s. Before his appointment to Tokyo he had served as Ambassador to Korea. David Wright sent me the following piece which concentrates on relations with the bureaucracy:-

●

My early dealings with Kasumigaseki (the Japanese equivalent of Whitehall) marked my entire diplomatic career. They provided me with the best possible training which I could have had – a sort of reverse engineered school in Japanese management. Dealing daily with the Japanese bureaucracy not only guided me in how to handle them better but also gave me the benefit of learning how to use Japanese techniques in handling others.

In 1969, as newly graduated language officer, I joined what was then a distinct part of the commercial section dealing with what would now be described as trade, economic and financial relations in a new post as third secretary. John Whitehead was first secretary on his return to Tokyo for his second posting there. The commercial counsellor, responsible for trade and economic relations in the absence of an economic counsellor, was Hugh Cortazzi.

Although John Whitehead and I made up the new economic relations section, we were fully integrated into the commercial section. Later, I found myself joined as third secretary by someone who had been studying history with me at Cambridge and had joined the Home Civil Service when I joined the Foreign Service. And since that loan to the embassy from the then Board of Trade, Tom Harris and I have had careers in London and Seoul which have crossed and recrossed.

This close juxtaposition of those of us who promoted trade and tried to remove barriers to trade was of huge importance. There was close integration between problems in one area fed directly into the work of the other. The direct needs of the exporters dealing with promotion were immediately communicated to those of us whose role was to try to facilitate the ability of British companies to exploit opportunities in the Japanese market.

I recall the director general for international trade in MITI, Harada, with whom Hugh Cortazzi and visitors from London used to spar regularly over market opening. The bespectacled, cerebral Namiki ran the MITI division which dealt with the UK; my daily dealings were with the friendly, if indecisive, Endo. Subsequently, the division head became Fumitake Yoshida who progressed to becoming one of Japan's toughest trade negotiators and is now Vice President of Tokyo Gas.

Two particular issues with which we dealt in those days and also in my second period as economic counsellor are worth reflection – mainly for what they say about how our perspectives have so entirely changed over thirty-five years.

First, John Whitehead and I were especially preoccupied with the restraints on the ability of British companies to secure access to the Japanese market for their goods. This takes us back to the dark world of quantitative quotas on the entry of goods. My recollection is that at the end of 1968, there were around 120 import items on specific quantitative control. That is to exclude certain items which were entirely prohibited imports. These were largely in the agricultural sector.

This means that a host of items of interest to British producers, from cars and tractors, through confectionery and biscuits, to Scotch whisky could only be imported into Japan up to pre-specified limits each year.

This meant annual negotiations about the precise numbers, down to the numbers of cases of whisky which could enter the Japanese market in a single year. To make the system not only punitive for the Japanese consumers and the foreign suppliers, importers could only bring those goods in if they 'held a quota'. In other words, the quotas themselves were parcelled out to various importers allowing them to import a specific amount and no more. Punitive for free trade it might have been, but it was a paradise for the bureaucrats who administered the system and allocated the quotas, and also for the quota holders themselves who had a licence to print money either from the sales they made or, from time to time, from trading the quotas themselves.

I was thrown into all this as my first baptism of diplomatic activity and Japanese bureaucracy as part of the preparations for the 1969 British Week [see Chapter 22]. Many consumer products were subject to quota controls. The promotions would never have succeeded if the department stores had been limited in their potential sales to the goods they could offer through the regular quotas for imports. Hence we were involved in the then totally unprecedented process of trying to ensure that the British government was allocated increases in the fixed quotas for imports of restricted categories of goods to allow them to be on show for sale at the department store promotions. John Whitehead and I not only had the department stores and the UK suppliers breathing down our necks to secure meaningful increases but also Hugh Cortazzi, who was determined to ensure that the major national promotion would make an impact on the Japanese market, and Ben Thorne, who had come from the DTI to run this event.

Perhaps the strangest aspect of dealing with the Japanese bureaucracy then, and little changed even now, was the ease – indeed the total freedom – with which one was permitted to move around government buildings. Together with this went the unchecked ability to park one's car in the forecourt of the ministry. Now, the most restrictive arrangement (apart from the Prime Minister's Office) is in the Ministry of Foreign Affairs where a visiting diplomat is obliged to check in with a receptionist who confirms that he has an appointment. Then he is free to go off to that appointment – without escort. That is highly permissive by UK standards. It is even more so in other government departments where the only obstacle to access to the rooms on the ministerial floor is provided by a guard who in his demeanour seems more like a janitor. Elsewhere, one can wander freely – though now the Ministry of Posts and Telecommunications is more restrictive, perhaps because they know that they are the ministry at the cutting edge of the new technologies.

Compared with those days, the Ministry of Foreign Affairs is larger but little changed. The Ministry of Finance (MOF or *Okurasho*) continues to squat brooding and uninviting across the road. (Curious for me to find its twin in the same position in Seoul across the road from the embassy. The Seoul City Hall was planned and designed to match the MoF in Tokyo.) The Ministry of Agriculture is also there little changed, though modernized. The jewel in the architectural crown of the Japanese tradition of government buildings is the Ministry of Education which continues to sit at the corner of Toranomon. I know that there are plans to demolish it. It should be preserved. For those who have spent much of their working life stepping in and out of government buildings the world over, the Japanese tradition is unique and worthy of high regard. It demonstrates that the psychology of how a government works is reflected in the way in which it organizes itself.

Though, in the same way as the MoF broods over Kasumigaseki, the real *aficionados* of Japanese government buildings most profoundly regret the passing of the old Ministry of Trade and Industry (MITI) building which used to sit at the corner of Kasumigaseki facing both the Ministries of Finance and Foreign Affairs. A building less self-indulgent of personal comfort, more indicative of the pain of industrial reconstruction and of pride at the vicissitudes which Japan had experienced at the end of the Second World War, it would be difficult to have found. It is no more. I have seen no photographs. It remains in the memory only. But my almost daily journeys there at the end of the 1960s will never be forgotten for what the buildings said about the capacity of Japan and its bureaucrats to endure privation and simplicity in the interests of building prosperity and success.

*   *   *

Fifteen or so years after those daily journeys to MITI, I found myself on a very different and now wholly unacceptable daily visiting pattern to the new MITI building. For those were the days in the early 1980s of complex and time-consuming negotiations over the euphemistically labelled 'Voluntary Restraint Agreements' (VRAs designed to give certain British industries time to reorganize themselves and not be overwhelmed by the tidal wave of imports from Japan.) Those were the days of what is now labelled and reviled as 'managed trade', the process by which bureaucrats in cahoots with industrialists decided on what level of imports the local industry could sustain and settle those with the relevant industrial association of the exporting country. It is now illegal.

There is no need to go into detail about the precise issues and results. But it is worth reflecting on how the handling of these VRAs worked with the grain of Japanese bureaucracy.

The UK industrial association used to arrive over the weekend. We dined with them on the Sunday evening to build up personal ties. Monday, we spent the morning understanding their objectives and setting out a plan for holding the negotiations between them and their Japanese counterparts. These normally began on the Monday afternoon and carried on for one or two days depending on the difficulty of the industrial sector we were seeking to handle. But the negotiations were initiated on the basis of positions agreed in advance with us in the embassy. After the first and subsequent parts of the negotiations, both industrial sides would break from negotiations to discuss future moves with their respective official sides, the embassy, and probably DTI officials in the case of the UK side, and MITI officials in the case of the Japanese. What, of course, were also being pursued simultaneously were talks between the two official sides to narrow the area of what were in effect four-sided negotiations, before agreement could be reached.

What made all this the easier was the ease with which we were able to move around and talk to officials from MITI. Many, if not all, of these talks were the result of extensive preambles at official level. In Tokyo, we used to spend many hours camped in the offices of the MITI division responsible in order to probe the Japanese negotiating position in advance and establish where there were points of agreement with our own. Often these talks would consider the actual numbers of units of machinery and products which would be exported to the UK in the coming year. These were very much talks about talks. They made progress and were successful because of the measure of mutual trust which existed between the two sides through hours of contact at official level. In meeting the needs of the time and alleviating the pressures on the bilateral relationship by excessive imports from Japan the process delivered the necessary results. But that time is now past.

DAVID WRIGHT adds the following postscript about the problems of running an ambassadorial hostel:-

•

Intermittently, ambassadors reflect on their role as manager of a country house hotel and boutique travel agency. British diplomatic tradition is unique. It is deemed customary for Heads of Missions to accommodate visiting members of the royal family, ministers and their immediate entourage. Though occasionally a strain (often as the whiskies-and-soda stretch into the early hours), this quaint tradition brings sparks of humour to the life of an ambassadorial residence.

On the odd occasion, ministers decline to stay at the residence. A former Minister of State for Defence once declined to stay. His Private Secretary revealed that he 'liked a little nibble in the night'. The implications were entirely lost on this writer until the minister's well-publicized diaries emerged.

A Minister for Trade once asked me why he had not been invited to stay. As a long-standing personal friend, he thought it surprising. So did I. But in the tradition of private secretarial autonomy, his Private Secretary had already declined the invitation. Source for a pungent triangular exchange!

Ministers can also not be averse to saving the odd penny. Arriving without any local currency is a familiar lament. Blame the Private Secretary and then look helpless.

The wife of a Cabinet Minister let out her bath water without knowing that the waste pipe had been disconnected: calamity in the kitchen below preparing for their welcoming reception. The technical mysteries of mixer taps in Tokyo often proved too much for high-level visitors. And from time to time the private bar in the bedroom proved too much for members of a visiting entourage.

One visiting couple will be fondly remembered for everything going wrong that possibly could. Drama began on arrival with the realization that Japan suffered from earthquakes. Surprisingly this had not been expected. The Private Secretary took the stick for poor briefing. The newly arrived wardrobes proved a challenge: two shelves dropped onto the visitor while clothing was being unpacked and stowed. The chapter of incidents continued unabated until respite arrived with their departure for the UK.

Little to our knowledge, their return flight to London was diverted over Siberia and returned to Tokyo because of the presence of an unruly passenger – not our guest or his wife. But we slept in blissful peace that night in ignorance that one of Her Majesty's ministers was sitting in the departure lounge at Narita awaiting a return flight to Europe, having instructed his Private Secretary not to call the embassy for assistance. So private secretaries do have their use after all!

Postscript

CANTERBURY

AN ADDRESS BY JOHN WHITEHEAD

In February 1995 I received a letter from Rear Admiral David Macey, the Receiver General at Canterbury Cathedral, which stated in part: 'On Sunday 20 August 1995 at 5 pm a service will be held in Canterbury Cathedral to mark the 50th Anniversary of VJ Day. A similar service will be held in St Paul's Cathedral at which the Archbishop will preach. The Dean and Chapter here asked me to invite you to give the Address at Canterbury. The service will be held in the Nave which will undoubtedly be packed – some 1,200 people. The Duke and Duchess of Kent and the Lord Lieutenant, Lord Kingsdown (formerly Governor of the Bank of England), will be present as will the High Sheriff, the Lord Mayor and other local dignitaries. The local representatives of the British Legion will parade their banners and I am sure members of the Burma Star Organization will be there.

'You will realize that these occasions require careful handling by the preacher imposing a need both to acknowledge the sacrifice of those who fought and died and to look to reconciliation now and in the future. The Chapter feel that with your experience of Japan and knowledge of the British viewpoint you would be ideally equipped to give the Address.'

A few days later, after some careful thought, I replied that I felt honoured and flattered to have been invited and was delighted to accept. I added that I was 'indeed fully aware of the sensitivities associated with this occasion'; it was 'something of a challenge as well as an opportunity'.

After a highly agreeable visit to Canterbury in the early summer to meet the Dean, the Very Reverend John Simpson, to 'walk the course' and some discussion by letter of the length and final shape of the address, I found myself, with some trepidation, processing with the Bishops (including Archbishop Runcie the immediate past Archbishop of Canterbury) and clergy on that warm August evening and in due course climbing up into the pulpit of the central and best-known cathedral of the Anglican church to deliver the following address:

'We have come here today, as one congregation, for three 'shuns'. No, they are not attention, although we look forward to the beating of the retreat after this service; nor fashion, although there are not many things better than a special service in this magnificent cathedral to produce a feast of ladies' fashion to delight the eyes; nor even relaxation, no nodding off at the back of the nave no matter how hot the afternoon.

Rather we are here for celebration, for commemoration and for reconciliation. There may be some of you who have qualifications in your mind about certain aspects of those 'shuns': 'no triumphalism' has been the theme of some; 'no forgiveness' has been the cry of others. But my starting point is that we are here not only as individuals but also as a group, as a congregation. We have come to share in a *special* service to mark the 50th Anniversary of VJ Day – a half century, short in the history of this cathedral, but long in the course of one person's life.

For those of us who were alive at the time the war made a major impact, whether directly or indirectly. What was it all about? and what exactly is our reason for celebration today? No triumphalism, certainly; but the cause of legitimate celebration was, and is, the end of a global war in which our country had been totally committed for nearly six years in one theatre or another, in which we had fought against the forces of fascism, militarism and those who sought to overthrow our country, our systems and our legitimate interests, and at the end of which we emerged as a nation – with our allies – victorious. Of course as a country and as a people we were drained and exhausted. Of course there were innumerable problems facing us once the war was over. But the supreme matter in hand at that time was the winning of the war. Without that the world would have been a very different place.

In that war all the pieces interlocked, whether we are talking about the campaigns in Burma, the relief operations in Southern China, the battles on Pacific islands or the final air attacks on the Japanese mainland. And these in turn were part of the fight for survival and part of the endurance of people involved in so many ways to ensure ultimate success – in north west Europe, in Italy, in North Africa, in the Middle East or in the Atlantic. All contributed, as did those who maintained morale in prisoner-of-war and civilian camps.

We also fought the war in order to ensure that the Japanese military machine, which had been built up over the previous sixty years, was utterly crushed and that it would not be rebuilt for as far ahead as one could see. That purpose was achieved. We have now had fifty years of peace with Japan, virtually two generations; and Japan has become one of the most pacifist countries in the world. 'The military led us astray and we must never ever let that situation arise again' was a familiar theme on the part of very many Japanese during my tours of duty in that country.

And what was achieved in the aftermath of that victory?

First, a renunciation by Japan forever of the use of force as a means of solving international disputes. It took until the 1990s for the party to which the present prime minister [Mr Murayama] belongs to recognize the constitutionality of the Japanese Self-Defense Forces and it also took until the 1990s for any Japanese government to agree that those Self Defense Forces should wear blue berets, and even then they are only to be committed to a peace-keeping, not peace-making, role.

Second, putting Japan on a far more democratic path through the introduction of a new education system, land reform and an imperial system in which the emperor is merely the symbol of the unity of the Japanese people.

Third, a conscious trade-off between ensuring that the Japanese, surrounded as they were by a hostile Soviet Union, North Korea and China, should not fall prey as a result of utter deprivation to Communist ideology. This was not a free ride for the Japanese — it was reconstructing Japanese industry while keeping Japan as a fundamentally non-military power out of strategic Western self-interest.

All of this has substantially stood the test of time — truly a cause for celebration.

But all war is terrible, as we have learnt from experiences in the twentieth century: a mixture of extended boredom, extreme discomfort, fear, and for many, excruciating pain and death. Wars can also be determining periods in a country's history. It is right that on an occasion such as this we should commemorate what was done by so many for us who effectively came afterwards, whether it was bravery in battle or endurance elsewhere. We should think first of those who made the ultimate sacrifice by dying for their country. They had no future, but their sacrifice should be and is commemorated. They may not have seen the fruits of their sacrifice; but they are there.

And then there are those who survived but whose bodies or minds were damaged, sometimes irreparably, by the war. They are a living reminder to us of how much we owe to them. And there are those whose lives were changed, deeply even if almost invisibly, by the loss of relatives, loved ones and friends. Others simply lost a period of years in their lives.

There are yet others who had 'a good war' in the sense of heroism, of leadership, of brilliant strategic or tactical planning. Their exploits and example are rightly remembered as are those of the units to which they belonged. The banners in this cathedral this afternoon carry on them in many cases references to campaigns and battles which have become rightly a part of their history. We should, and do, salute you all with thanks and with humility. And it is right that here in Kent we should commemorate particularly the crucial role played by The Buffs (The Royal East Kent Regiment) and The Queen's Own Royal West Kent Regiment in Burma whether this was in 1943 in the Arakan sector or at Kohima when the Japanese were at the gates of India; or in the spring of 1945 at the crossing of the Shweli river in the push to Mong Mit, or at Tiddim and the Sittang River which forced the Japanese out of Rangoon and marked the virtual reconquest of Burma.

And what of reconciliation? It is not my purpose on this of all days and from this privileged vantage point to ignore or belittle the views of my fellow countrymen, particularly those who fought and suffered, often grievously, for our country. But to echo my point at the beginning: we are here as one congregation and we are part of a nationwide series of services. As such, particularly in this cathedral, we should not give vent to those easy visceral feelings. Legitimate pride, yes; but prejudice, particularly racial prejudice based in most cases now on ignorance, resoundingly no. Those who as prisoners of war suffered at Japanese hands those fifty and more years ago had a particular experience in which fortunately none of the rest of us have shared. But more of those in Britain who have feelings of antipathy towards Japan have not been within several thousand miles of that country. Theirs is an unproductive set of received views. The grievance of some should be seen as one element in a much broader picture of our present relations with Japan – a new Japan from which we have had much to learn in recent years, from whom we have benefited not least by the number of people who are now employed in Britain by Japanese manufacturing concerns here and from whom we may have much to learn in the future.

A large majority of those in this cathedral today, and an even larger majority in the country as a whole, were too young to remember any aspect of the Second World War. How fortunate, for them and for our country. How good. And should we not, with that thought in mind, leave this cathedral with a greater conviction than before that one of our overriding purposes in life should be to do all we can to ensure that there are no more global wars of the sort that we experienced in the 1940s. We cannot know the long-term future; but another fifty years of peace with those who we fought and defeated fifty years go would be an excellent start.

Addendum

Tokyo Medical and Surgical Clinic

GREN WEDDERBURN

JUST AS I HAD almost completed reading through the proofs of *Japan Experiences* and was preparing the index my attention was drawn to a book published in Hong Kong in 1979 entitled *No Lotus Garden: A Scottish Surgeon in China and Japan* by Gren Wedderburn who was one of the first two doctors at the Tokyo Medical and Surgical Clinic set up by Tokyo Tower in 1951 as the Occupation was coming to an end. There cannot have been many expatriates at least in the 1950s and 60s who did not, from time to time, call on the services of the clinic and it would have left a hole in this book if nothing were said about it and its members except for the odd reference in other chapters. So I was delighted when I was lent a copy of this memoir which has a foreword by Michael Sandberg, former Chairman of the Hongkong and Shanghai Banking Corporation. I decided that the late Gren Wedderburn's reminiscences deserved a place in this collection even if for reasons of space I had to summarize most of what he had written.

Gren Wedderburn was the son of Scottish missionaries in China. He graduated from Edinburgh University in 1938 and served as a medical officer in the RAF during the second World War during which he was posted to India and Burma. After the war he took up surgery and in 1947 became an FRCS (Edinburgh). He worked as a doctor and surgeon in Shanghai. During his time there he was called on to help with the wounded from HMS *Amethyst* and HMS *Consort* in the famous 1949 incident. Following the establishment of the Chinese Communist regime in Shanghai he found himself without a job and moved to Hong Kong.

Up to late 1950 during the Occupation of Japan American and other foreign civilians had the right to use US Army clinics and hospitals. But the Occupation was drawing to a close and when the facilities were withdrawn the American and British Chambers of Commerce agreed to 'sponsor some doctors to set up a clinic'. The American Chamber selected an American doctor, Tom Gentry. Gren Wedderburn was chosen by the British Chamber to be Gentry's partner.

Wedderburn and his family (wife and two daughters) together with the few possessions they had been able to salvage from China made his way by freighter from Hong Kong to Japan. Such little money as he had saved had been largely used to fund their passages to Japan. When his ship called at Kobe, however, he did not have enough money to pay for his and his family's train fares to Tokyo. Happily, Robin White, the head of Jardine Matheson's office in Kobe, came to his rescue. He bought the tickets for Wedderburn and lent him 20,000 yen, saying: 'It is an unauthorized expense, Gren. Try to pay it back through the Tokyo Office in the next six months!'

At Tokyo they were met by John Besford, a British dentist who had first suggested to Wedderburn that he should go to Japan. Besford after giving them breakfast took the Wedderburns to a house on the Tamagawa, handed him 30,000 yen and promised that a car would be delivered to him the next day.

Wedderburn and Gentry found consulting rooms in the Suikosha building near what was to become the site of Tokyo Tower, but before they could start to practise they had to qualify by passing the Japanese medical examinations. Until the entry into force of the Peace Treaty in 1952 foreign doctors were able to take the examination in English (after 1952 the examinations were conducted in the Japanese language). The examinations covered 'the whole of a student's career'. Wedderburn passed with an overall mark of ninety-four per cent although he only scored five per cent in dermatology as he was 'ignorant of the classification of the forms of fungus which are parasitic to the human body'. They could now start treating patients. While waiting for the necessary authority his expenses and debts had been mounting.

Wedderburn records that at this time his 'chief nightmare was anaesthesia. We relied completely on open ether – ether dropped on a mask. A Japanese anaesthetist could only be cajoled into giving a sufficient dose by a combination of patience and encouragement.' A slim Japanese needed much less than 'a robust hard-drinking Dutchman' of almost twice the weight.

He also encountered problems in getting proper suture material. 'The Japanese used plain sewing thread for all ordinary purposes, and small stitch abscesses were the order of the day.' 'To have a parcel delivered by the Post Office was to try to pass a camel through the eye of a needle.' So he had to bring suture material in as part of his baggage when he went on trips to Hong Kong or the USA.

'Another feature of the practice of medicine in Japan which was reprehensible was the reluctance of doctors to get a second opinion.' Wedderburn discovered this first when he was treating a patient in the Bluff Hospital at Yokohama and found that his patient had been transferred to the Japanese gynaecologist without consulting him. The superintendent at the Bluff Hospital was an American, Dr Milton Morton, who had been attached to the medical administration of the occupation. (Some years later Morton joined the Tokyo clinic as a partner.) Dr Morton had to 'exercise great tact with the doctor before we ended up doing the operation together'.

The clinic prospered and Wedderburn assumed that they would soon be able to pay off their debts. Suddenly, Gentry and his wife left for the USA never to return. Wedderburn discovered that there were no account books and he was faced with shouldering a huge debt to the American Chamber of Commerce.

The latter, however, generously forgave a large part of the debt.

Wedderburn who at this stage was left on his own to run the clinic asked Dr Bernard Rosenberg, a German Jewish heart specialist to join him as a partner. He 'was one of the finest men I have ever met and the best partner I have had'. They needed someone to look after the accounts. Duncan Fraser (see p. 352 to 362) who was a friend of Wedderburn had just married Mary 'Miss BOAC of 1950/51' in Tokyo. Duncan Fraser, Bernard Rosenberg and Wedderburn decided that Mary was ideally qualified for the job of looking after the accounts. 'Mary Fraser was not consulted, but just told to turn up for work. Mary has a very strong character. . . The accounts system was born and grew up with Mary. To be elected Miss BOAC was a tribute not only to her good looks but also to her character and personality. Delinquents in the matter of payments were greeted with charm or withering contempt as best fitted the occasion.' Wedderburn also had help from an Irish accountant, Paul Donelly, who took it on himself to arrange Wedderburn's tax affairs. These were complicated by the fact that some payments were in US dollars and some in Yen. He obviously knew his way around the notoriously bureaucratic Japanese tax authorities in those days as in the first year Wedderburn and Rosenberg only had to pay 9,000 yen each in tax.

Rosenberg and Wedderburn soon recruited Derek Fair, a New Zealand paediatrician, who had been working for United Nations Relief and Rehabilitation in Korea. He, too, was 'more interested in his medicine than in money' and was always turning up some rare type of case. Both Bernard and Derek were, in Wedderburn's words, 'men of utter integrity'. However, 'We both had to curb Derek a bit. Derek was a perfectionist'. He always bought the latest model of camera and 'liked equipment for equipment's sake'. 'Both Bernard and Derek were men of deep culture with well stocked libraries. . . and fond of music with big record collections.' Gren Wedderburn and John Besford had rather different interests.

John Besford 'was a man of tremendous enthusiasms. He had been in Britain's team at the Berlin Olympics in 1936 as a backstroke swimmer. He held the 600 metres backstroke world record for nineteen years. For recreation he would go swimming for several hours covering long distances. One weekend, while engaged in this pursuit he came across an inlet at Aburatsubo on the Miura peninsula. There was a long narrow arm of the sea, sheltered and inaccessible where the hillsides descended steeply to the edge of the sea.' Here he managed to buy a strip of the foreshore and build a small Japanese-style cottage. He then took up scuba diving and made friends with the local fishermen whom he helped by diving to salvage their nets when they became fouled on the bottom of the sea. In return he was allowed to catch one or two prime fish from the 'larder' in their nets. The Wedderburns spent many weekends with John and Mary Besford and their daughter. When the two men went down to Aburatsubo on their own in winter and played scrabble (John Besford was an expert) there was a considerable consumption of Scotch which John had bought up when the British Commonwealth Forces camp at Ebisu closed down.

Wedderburn recounts how having operated on John Besford for a hernia John left hospital after three days and went off swimming at Aburatsubo. Fortunately, no harm resulted from this escapade.

John Besford had strong views about the dangers from and uselessness of wisdom teeth. He managed to extract two of Wedderburn's. (I am glad to say that I refused to allow him to extract mine!)

Some British subjects had remained in Japan during the war. Many fell on hard times after the war and it fell to the British Consul to try to alleviate their plight. Wedderburn was called in from time to time to help. The British Consul in Tokyo was then Leo Pickles, a Yorkshireman, who had studied Japanese as a consular service language student before the war. He was a good linguist, kind and warm-hearted, but slow. (If any file seemed to be missing we always checked Leo's papers first as he might well be sitting on it!) But he was a most conscientious Consul as the following episode related by Gren Wedderburn which deserves to be quoted in full shows:-

•

Leo Pickles was typical of the best of our consuls. A British consul, if he is worth his salt, and most of them are, goes into action almost automatically in support of one of his nationals, right or wrong. One day, he came into my office, sat down and started on the story of one such unfortunate British subject. He was surprised by my lack of resistance to the plea for help, but Pickles was not one who asked often or without good cause. His honesty was apparent, and his very diffidence commanded respect.

Mrs Nakayama was such a case. She was a Japanese national but ethnically English. She had married a Japanese before the war, was in Japan during the war, and was now a widow. She was destitute and subsisted on the little money that her son, who had a very poorly paid job in Tokyo, managed to give her. The son had approached the embassy as his mother had been English. Pickles explained that this presented a peculiar problem as there were no funds or official channels to deal with such a person who was technically a Japanese. Nevertheless, he hoped to help her and, though it was not my line of country as she was mentally abnormal, a case for repatriation might be made out for her if a medical report was pitched in strong enough terms. She lived in the country and the best part of a day would be needed for a visit for which my only reward would be his thanks.

It was a cold dark morning when an Embassy car called for me. The driver set off through the incredibly drab northern section of Tokyo and out into the Kanto plain. The small villages we passed were depressing. The country, broken up into small fields, was bleak in the February morning. The roads were of gravel and narrow and seemed to intersect aimlessly. Progress was slow and far from comfortable. At times, the car pulled half off the road, close to ditches full of evil-looking water, to allow other vehicles to pass. Flurries of sleet beat on the windows of the car. As we cleared the town the driver handed me a note from Pickles. Presumably he had been told to hold on to it until the signs of civilization had fallen behind and I could not change my mind.

I opened it and read.

'Dear Dr Wedderburn

When you meet Mrs Nakayama it would be better not to mention that you are a doctor or a Scot. Avoid the subject of politics. Perhaps it would be best if you said you were a member of the Embassy.

She is troubled by a witch.

Regards,
L. Pickles'

I looked for a second page in explanation of these cryptic warnings but there was nothing else in the envelope. By now it had started snowing in earnest. A cup of coffee in some congenial inn would have made a welcome halt but nothing that looked remotely like a suitable place came into view. In the late morning we drew up at a small Japanese house, one of four forming a small hamlet at a crossroads. The driver indicated that we were at our destination.

Squelching through some mud I pulled aside the *shoji* door, took my shoes off and entered, immediately realizing that the temperature inside was no warmer than out, and that my thin socks were not going to preserve my feet in any degree of comfort. Mrs Nakayama greeted me in Japanese but soon got the hang of the fact that English was my preferred medium. She was tallish, gaunt, and with long dark grey unkempt hair. Sombre eyes stared at me. Her dress was black and hung in uneven folds. She was not quite one of the witches in Macbeth but going on that way.

We crouched cross-legged on the *tatami* floor at a low table with nothing to support our backs. I kept my overcoat and gloves on but my toes were already icy. A small bowl of tepid Japanese tea did not match my thoughts of hot coffee.

We chatted away for a quarter of an hour about where she came from in England, her son in Tokyo, the countryside, the weather and so on. She seemed normal enough and even rose in my estimation for a few seconds when she asked me what position I held in the Embassy.

This caught me short for a moment before I vouchsafed that I was Head of Chancery. It was the first idea which occurred to me and seemed a likely enough post. There was some justification for this assumption as a short while previously I had extracted half the stomach and the first part of the duodenum from the Head of the Chancery; this action for his duodenal ulcer gave me some ephemeral rights for such a claim, I felt.

'Oh,' said Mrs Nakayama, disappointed. 'I thought you were the Ambassador!'

Seldom has a simple surgeon set off in the morning as a plain citizen, been accepted into the Diplomatic Corps by late breakfast time, promoted afterwards to Head of the Chancery, to become obvious ambassadorial material by coffee-break time.

As all feeling had now long since gone from my feet and the frost-bite was about mid-calf level, I decided to hurry things along. I was well aware that a psychiatrist would have approached the problem in an oblique fashion. Mrs Nakayama's childhood, relations with her mother and father, relations with her boyfriends, dreams, feelings, psyche and conscious elements would have been established as a base before the present was tactfully introduced. Aware of my lack of knowledge on these matters, I adopted as an alternative the plain brusque direct surgical approach.

'I understand, Mrs. Nakayama,' I said, that you are troubled by a witch.'

The floodgates were opened. It was long and complicated but in essence this was the story.

There was, she said, a Scots doctor who practised in Harley Street in London. The doctor had a witch at his disposal, and a very degenerate and willing tool the witch was. From time to time the prime minister would visit the doctor and ask him to despatch the witch to Japan to trouble Mrs Nakayama. The Scots doctor, a really rotten type, was only too happy to oblige the prime minister and off the witch went without delay. That was bad enough, but the Scots doctor took a malicious pleasure in this activity and, working entirely on his own initiative, would send off the witch unknown to either the prime minister, the Foreign Office, the Secret Service or any other government agency. The prime minister had a lot of problems on his hands. This action was a sort of mental aberration on his part, not to be condoned of course, but politicians were, after all, politicians. The prime minister requested the doctor to provide this service about once a year but the doctor took it upon himself to make this a monthly occurrence. There was only one slight saving grace: the prime minister might want the witch for other nefarious tasks, so that about four days was as long as he could be absent without the Scots doctor having to answer embarrassing questions.

The warnings in Pickles' note were now amply clear. Having kept quiet about being Scots and a doctor, I hastened to assure Mrs Nakayama that it was my impression that the diplomatic corps were not allowed to vote politically, and secondly, that I had never been in Britain during an election, had never voted and, furthermore, had never lost a wink of sleep at being deprived of the privilege. I was glad to be able to make three truthful statements in a row.

The witch, it transpired, was not of the female sex. He was a very nasty little man standing four feet high. He wore a long dark green cloak to keep him warm, pretty sensible it would seem in view of the heating problem in the Nakayama household. When he travelled he spread this cloak as wings, no broom or other aid to aviation forming part of his equipment. He made the journey London-Tokyo in four hours flat.

'What does the witch do that upsets you?' I asked Mrs Nakayama.

It was his presence, rather than anything else, that upset her, she answered. He was always in the room with her, and it was very embarrassing when she wanted to undress and go to bed. He bothered her. She was shocked when my enquiries indicated that the witch might have taken liberties. As an amateur psychiatrist I felt that Freud and sexual questions should somehow be brought into the matter. No, there was no question of that sort of thing. She was not frightened, just bothered. The witch dossed down in the corner of the bedroom and she would finally go off to sleep, only to wake and find him still there. He never spoke and suddenly, after a few days, he would go without farewell or salutation.

'When was he last here?' I asked.

'Over three weeks ago.'

'You mean he may be back any time?'

'Yes.'

I took a quick peek over my shoulder just in case he had arrived ahead of schedule. I felt the facts were marshalled and it was time I was gone.

I only saw Mrs Nakayama once more after that, when my nurse came with me to the Embassy to give Mrs Nakayama her cholera and smallpox inoculation immediately prior to her departure. When Pickles asked me why it was necessary for the nurse to be there I enjoyed watching his eyebrows shoot up half an inch on being told that Mrs Nakayama would think it strange to have the Head of Chancery sticking needles into her.

Appendix
to Chapter 15
Shell in Japan
by Neville Fakes

To understand the post-war development of oil in Japan, a brief survey of the industry from its early days of the nineteenth century is needed. We must also note the major role taken by Britain in assisting Japan to industrialize, to modernize and thereby to gain international recognition. Those early days in Japan are inextricably bound up with the origins of the now vast Shell Petroleum Group.

In 1859, oil had been struck in Pennsylvania but this was not the first discovery of this substance. In around 200 BC oil was first produced in China using bamboo poles and brass attachments. In 1272 Marco Polo passed through Baku on the shores of the Caspian Sea and noted that the people were using oil lamps.

In 1859, the ports of Yokohama, Nagasaki and Hakodate were opened to foreign trade. Among the earliest foreign traders to establish themselves in Yokohama was the trading firm of Samuel, Samuel & Co., set up in 1878 by Marcus Samuel, son of the owner of a London-based business that had prospered in the 1860s by trading with a network of agents in Japan. During those early years the company exported Formosan camphor (Formosa was then under Japanese rule), fish oil, manganese, cereals, china and lacquer ware, copper wares, hides etc. and imported textiles, sugar, iron and steel, machinery etc.

In addition, and importantly for Japan, Samuel, Samuel & Co. were able to provide the channel by which British capital was made available for many large projects e.g. the Kyoto-Kobe railway in 1874, the 1902 design and construction of a potable water system for Yokohama, supervised by a British engineer, H.S. Palmer, the 1902 design and construction of the harbour/port works at Osaka, the 1906 development of the Kansai railway system, the 1907 issue of £317,000 for port construction at Yokohama etc.

The foreigners who in the 1880s were taking up residence in Yokohama were looking for 'illuminating oil' (kerosene or paraffin) to light the lamps they had brought with them and with which the Japanese were much taken. Some kerosene had in fact, been brought in to Kobe by Chinese merchants as early as 1868 from a source in China, but it was of poor quality and supplies were unreliable.

After the Meiji restoration, the government endeavoured to promote the nation's industry with emphasis on military and export industries. As a result, from around 1887 the number of factories equipped with generative power began to increase. Also, so did the demand for oil.

In 1888, another trading firm, Jardine Matheson & Co, brought the first cases (67,525 of them) of Russian oil (kerosene) into Japan by a British ship from Baku. Noting the success of this shipment, the Samuel group began importing their own Russian oil also in wooden cases each containing two tins of four gallons capacity. (These tins were considered valuable for fashioning household utensils and as light storage containers for water.)

Because the freight and packing costs of Baku kerosene in cases were high, and in order to compete with the US Standard Oil's export of better quality kerosene to China and the Far East, the Samuels began to concentrate on oil in bulk. A 4,000-ton tanker, the *Murex* was built for them by William Grey & Sons of West Hartlepool and in 1892, with a full cargo of oil from the Baku fields via the Baltic, the vessel passed on her maiden voyage through the Suez Canal to China, the first time an oil-carrying ship had been allowed through the Canal.

The Samuel group built receiving tanks in both Kobe and Yokohama (against considerable local opposition) and in 1893 received a bulk oil shipment into the latter port from Baku. Customers who brought their own containers were sold 'Shell' kerosene, so-named after the sea-shells that were then being taken by Samuel ships from Indonesia and the Philippines for sale to Victorian England.

The business prospered to such an extent that in 1897 it was decided to make Samuel's Petroleum Division independent of the Group's other activities. This new company was named the Shell Transport & Trading Company.

The Samuels had been seeking reliable oil sources closer to the Far East and had noted that in 1896 the Royal Dutch Petroleum Company was extracting a small quantity of oil from Sumatra and Balikpapan in Indonesian Borneo. Shell Transport & Trading developed its own oil sources near Balikpapan, transporting it to Britain and Japan. In Yokohama the company was given a more Japanese identity in 1900 and named the Rising Sun Petroleum Co. with head office in that city; oil supplies were then switched entirely from Baku to Balikpapan.

In 1900, the company with the aid of an Italian geologist, investigated the possibilities of an oil field in Niigata prefecture where a type of illuminating oil had been produced for the local market. However, the survey showed that the geology of the area was unfavourable for development and no investment was made.

As industry developed in Japan, accelerated by the Russo-Japanese War (1904-05) which completely stopped any oil imports from Russia, there was an increasing demand for kerosene, fuel oil and machine oil. Candles, too, at that time, were a staple of the Rising Sun's trade.

In Balikpapan, the increasing shared interests of producing and transporting oil brought about the 1907 historic alliance of the Royal Dutch Petroleum Company and the Shell Transport & Trading Company, each becoming a parent company of the Royal Dutch/Shell Group of Companies on a 60/40 basis.

Before this alliance, the world's oil industry had been dominated by John D. Rockefeller's Standard Oil of Ohio but by 1910 the efforts and strategies of the Royal Dutch/Shell Group had successfully reduced Standard's lead.

In 1908 the Rising Sun had begun construction of a small refinery at Fukuoka to provide oil supplies more economically to southern Japan. The construction work was marred by tragedy when a tank exploded while under test, but despite this setback the plant came on stream the following year and continued to operate until 1915 on Borneo and Sumatran crude.

The record of subsequent years has been one of steady development despite increasing competition. In the great earthquake of 1923 the company's head office in Yokohama was destroyed and many of its local and expatriate staff killed. A new office was built on the former site in 1929 but the post-war growth of the company necessitated the establishment of its head office in Tokyo.

However, Japan was a difficult market for oil companies in the 1930s. The 1936 Petroleum Law was designed to extract from the oil trading community what amounted to '. . . a very substantial contribution towards the defence measures which are considered advisable by the government'. In 1948 the Rising Sun oil company was able to resume a business that had been interrupted by the war and was renamed Shell Sekiyu KK.

During the occupation of Japan, it was realized that whilst the development of the local coal industry (mainly from Kyushu and Hokkaido) could supply some of the fuel that was urgently needed to revitalize the economic health of the nation, the major source of increased energy would have to come from oil.

Though refined products could be bought from foreign oil sources as an interim measure, even a medium-term solution involved the securement of reliable crude oil supplies, the provision of tanker transport, the building of modern refineries and the setting up of distribution facilities throughout the country.

Shell Sekiyu KK was among the first major companies to emerge as a post-war supplier. At an early stage it was backed by Shell. The company was able to rely on the loyalty of many of its early dealers who, during the war had not only hidden records of the company for safe-keeping but also in some instances had preserved distribution machinery and other facilities.

The Japanese government insisted that each foreign oil company must seek or be allocated a Japanese refining partner if it were to participate in supplying the local market. Considerable foreign investment was made in the construction of such facilities alongside the setting up of marketing-dealer arrangements.

As crude oil sources were procured, the Japanese oil industry began to lurch forward while technicians and refinery operators were trained. Some such refining partnerships prospered while others stumbled as contrary policies emerged. These were usually based on a narrow local attitude of 'Japan is a special case needing special treatment'.

Huge sums were spent by the international oil majors in training Japanese personnel abroad, in providing the latest technology on a freely given basis, in sending foreign personnel to advise on the building and setting up of the whole gamut of the oil business. Local suspicion and recalcitrance gradually faded and chief executives on both sides progressively merged their objectives. At the same time, the situation gradually improved as the Japanese government diminished its earlier intractable attitude towards foreign intervention, realizing no doubt that the vast experience of the international oil majors coupled with their technical, human and financial resources was the only practical answer to the rapid rehabilitation of energy supply.

Japan's crude oil sources were still based on Indonesia but, as industry began to develop and rapidly broaden its perspective, the market needed a wider spectrum of crude oil types so that refinery output could better match offtake requirements. Such heavier crude oils came mainly from the Middle East which meant that more tankers of increasing capacity had to be designed and built by the international majors or other interested shipowners.

It was in this special activity that Japan's own shipyards organized to meet a great part of the demand and in a relatively short time made a major contribution to success by achieving astounding records for quality and speed of delivery of oil tankers up to 200,000 tons capacity.

A very well run and tightly organized Japanese family company, Uyeno Unyu Shokai, offshoot of the Rising Sun, set up as a major local coastal and inland distributor of Shell's refined products, and later entered the crude oil supply business with its own ocean-going tankers.

LIQUIFIED NATURAL GAS

As crude oil imports increased, so also did coal with Australia as an emerging regional source. However, at this time (early 1960s), a new petroleum fraction began to create considerable interest, viz: methane (CH_4) or natural gas. As oil reserves were broadened and the exploitation of fields escalated to supply increasing world demand, the availability of natural gas also advanced to the point where it became a marketable fuel. Its calorific value was high, it was clean burning and therefore environmentally friendly. But there was a difficulty. How to transport it from one country to another?

In the USA and many European countries, natural gas pipeline networks supplied industries and homes with clean gaseous fuel over long distances from local oilfields. There was no great problem on land but how to carry natural gas across the oceans?

The answer was to liquify the gas under conditions of high pressure and low temperature at the well-head, a process developed by the majors, particularly Shell, and which reduced an enormous quantity of gas to a relatively small volume of liquid. The liquified natural gas or LNG as it came to be called was pumped under pressure to spherical, insulated containers in specially developed tankers that were provided with refrigeration and compression machinery to maintain liquidity during transport. Some tankers even bled a little of their LNG load to fuel such machinery while on the high seas.

The question arose – could the import of LNG be of interest to Japan's burgeoning industrial activity which was then developing at a rate surprising to the rest of the world? In the mid 1960s Japan, in fact, had held talks with Russia about the possible supply of natural gas from Sakhalin by undersea pipeline. However, the idea languished. Perhaps the political issue of the Kurile islands was at least partly responsible for this lack of action.

Early in 1968, Shell was able to approach MITI with the assurance that because natural gas was becoming available from the Sarawak/Brunei Shell oilfields in Borneo if satisfactory negotiations could be finalized without delay, LNG could be delivered by Shell to Japan in less than three years' time.

MITI at first looked askance at this rather bold assertion but finally agreed to receive a firm proposal from Shell and its chosen partner Mitsubishi which, meanwhile, had secured considerable interest from several of the large electricity-generating companies in Honshu.

Negotiations began in earnest and with a background of valuable experience in handling and transporting LNG around Europe in special tankers built in France, Shell was well qualified to achieve positive and rapid progress. With agreement in view, six tankers were put on order with French yards to carry LNG from Brunei/Sarawak to Japan. Construction also began on supply and receiving facilities at each end.

Finally, in 1971, well ahead of schedule, a world-first for the long distance ocean transport of LNG, the maiden shipment arrived safely in Japan and was unloaded into the Shore Terminal. Others followed on a regular basis by a well coordinated supply route that continues today with well over 100 million tons of LNG delivered without major problems. This £650 million investment has been of outstanding benefit to Japan's economic growth and with Australia augmenting supply from the NW Shelf the dependable supply of this form of energy to Japan's industry is likely to continue for years to come.

THE SEARCH FOR INDIGENOUS CRUDE OIL

Against the background of the country's progressive extensions of hydrocarbon energy supplies, the fundamental question remained. Was Japan endowed with its own indigenous source of crude oil? This uncertainty became increasingly urgent. Again, Shell took the initiative.

Japan's land mass was largely of igneous origin and therefore did not offer any geological encouragement for the formation and accumulation of crude oil deposits. Whilst this prospect was valid for land deposits, was it possible that offshore subsurface formations could be interesting?

The sea-bed to the immediate east of Japan is known to be formed of a narrow continental shelf before a precipitous drop-off to a deep trench, an abyssal canyon far beyond the reach of even modern drilling techniques. However, the Sea of Japan to the west was fairly shallow (300 to 500 feet) at least in the vicinity of Japan's Tsushima island and the Korea Strait. This area might possibly be worth prospecting. With the government's blessing, Shell and Mitsubishi formed the Nishi Nihon Oil Search Co. on a 50/50 basis, with Shell as the operator.

However, there arose the immediate and difficult problem of international hydrospace. Did Japan's jurisdiction extend beyond the normally accepted limit of its continental shelf? If so, what then was the agreed international boundary between Japan and its immediate neighbour, South Korea?

Further, if initial seismic surveys trended north-westerly towards the Yellow Sea, where did Chinese interests commence? To these basic and many other questions, there were no answers – not a reassuring basis on which a company could commit considerable investment and effort.

However, in a spirit of cooperation and to give some degree of responsible information to the understandably eager Japanese government, the paperwork seeking continental shelf offshore oil leases and the conditions under which they would be investigated was begun.

An early complication was the lack of Japanese legislation for oil search. Japan's mining legislation applied to coal and minerals where leases are small and on land. Offshore oil leases, however, are considerably larger quite apart from the added difficulty of international hydrospace.

To await legislation being formulated and passed by the Japanese government on offshore oil search leases was impracticable and would no doubt lead to considerable delay. A quick solution had to be found so a decision was made to apply for such oil leases on the basis of coal and mineral legislation. This involved the production of thousands of pieces of paper, drawn up by an assemblage of draftsmen, each sheet to the maximum area permitted under the coal legislation. The vast majority of such sheets showed nothing more than co-ordinates outlining the boundaries because, apart from the few that indicated the position of islands, reefs etc there was nothing but sea.

Because each sheet had to be presented in triplicate as required by law, vast quantities of paper were produced, labelled, identified, bundled and loaded into two trucks for transport to Nagoya where examination and processing by the relevant authorities would take place. It is droll to contemplate the fate of this enormous load of paper but the problem was solved and face saved by all. Nishi Nihon (see above) soon received permission to proceed with the search for oil on the continental shelf in the vicinity of Tsushima.

Early aerial seismic surveys were not encouraging but several sub-surface areas were identified as being of sufficient interest to Shell to arrange for their newly-designed floating drill platform to be towed to Japan from its Brunei/Sarawak fields, together with operating personnel. Such a drilling platform is stabilized in position by a series of thrusters that automatically limit the lurch of the drill stem at sea level to within a metre radius.

In the busy waterway of the Japan Sea, the relevant maritime authorities were kept advised of the drilling platform's location as it was moved from one area to another during the search programme. The slightest degree of oil pollution of the sea is a particularly sensitive issue in Japanese waters where fishing activity is extensive and the growing of seaweed a flourishing industry. However by virtue of its many years of ocean oil search, the Shell Group was able to reassure the authorities that such fears, if indeed oil was found, were minimal and that any untoward incident would be immediately controlled.

After more than a year of diligent search and the consequent expenditure of considerable sums of money, all exploration wells drilled were dry and therefore abandoned after sealing. This was a great disappointment for all concerned. Perhaps the search could have been extended to waters further north closer to South Korea and perhaps even to parts of the China Sea but until these nations agree on a clear legal regime concerning international boundaries, any extension beyond the safe limits of the Japanese continental shelf would be dangerous. Nishi Nihon was not prepared to proceed further without the safeguards of such a regime.

So the import of crude oil, LNG and coal (mainly from Australia) to Japan had to continue to supply the vast bulk of its energy requirements. In the 1960s, the concept of nuclear energy was understandably a sensitive issue.

Index

(Personal names of individuals referred to in the text. Titles have been generally omitted, unless essential for identification. Spouses are only listed where they have contributed to the text. Given names are only listed where these appear in the text.)